The Enjoyment of
Music

TENTH EDITION/SHORTER

TENTH EDITION/SHORTER

W · W · NORTON & COMPANY · NEW YORK · LONDON

The Enjoyment of
MUSIC

AN INTRODUCTION TO PERCEPTIVE LISTENING

Kristine Forney
PROFESSOR OF MUSIC, CALIFORNIA STATE UNIVERSITY, LONG BEACH

Joseph Machlis
LATE PROFESSOR EMERITUS, QUEENS COLLEGE OF THE CITY OF NEW YORK

W. W. Norton & Company has been independent since its founding in 1923, when William Warder Norton and Margaret D. Herter Norton first published lectures delivered at the People's Institute, the adult education division of New York City's Cooper Union. The Nortons soon expanded their program beyond the Institute, publishing books by celebrated academics from America and abroad. By mid-century, the two major pillars of Norton's publishing program—trade books and college texts—were firmly established. In the 1950s, the Norton family transferred control of the company to its employees, and today—with a staff of 400 and a comparable number of trade, college, and professional titles published each year—W. W. Norton & Company stands as the largest and oldest publishing house owned wholly by its employees.

for Earle Fenton Palmer

Editor: Maribeth Payne
Developmental and Copy Editor: Kathryn Talalay
Project Editor: Kathryn Talalay
Managing Editor: Marian Johnson
Electronic Media Editor: Steve Hoge
Photograph Editor: Neil Ryder Hoos
Associate Editor: Allison Courtney Fitch
Editorial Assistant: Graham Norwood
Design Director: Antonina Krass
Senior Production Manager: JoAnn Simony
Music Typesetter: David Budmen
Page Layout: Carole Desnoes, GGS Book Services
Indexer: Marilyn Bliss
Composition by GGS Book Services

Library of Congress Cataloging-in-Publication Data
Forney, Kristine.
   The enjoyment of music : an introduction to perceptive listening /
Kristine Forney, Joseph Machlis. —10th shorter ed.
      p. cm.
   Includes index.
   ISBN-13: 978-0-393-92888-4 (pbk.)
   ISBN-10 : 0-393-92888-8 (pbk.)
   1. Music appreciation.   I. Machlis, Joseph, 1906–1998.   II. Title.
MT90.M23 2007b
780—dc22   2006102254

W. W. Norton & Company, Inc., 500 Fifth Avenue, New York, NY 10110
www.norton.com

W. W. Norton & Company Ltd., Castle House, 75/76 Wells Street, London W1T 3QT
2 3 4 5 6 7 8 9 0

Contents

PART 1   The Materials of Music

UNIT 1   The Elements of Music   2

PART 2   Medieval and Renaissance Music

TIMELINE: MEDIEVAL/RENAISSANCE ERA

PART 3 | More Materials of Music

UNIT V   The Organization of Musical Sounds   108

PART 5 More Materials of Form

PART 6 Eighteenth-Century Classicism

TIMELINE: CLASSICAL ERA

PART 7   The Nineteenth Century

TIMELINE: ROMANTIC ERA

UNIT XX Choral and Dramatic Music in the Nineteenth Century   291

PART 8 The Twentieth Century and Beyond

TIMELINE: POST-ROMANTICISM, IMPRESSIONISM, AND EARLY TWENTIETH CENTURY

Listening Guides

Cultural Perspectives

iMusic Examples (alphabetical listing) on Student Resource Disc

Amazing Grace (traditional hymn, United Kingdom)
America (traditional, patriotic song)
Avaz of Bayate Esfahan (Iran)

Bach, J. S.: *Brandenburg Concerto* No. 1, I
Bach, J. S.: Contrapunctus I, from *The Art of Fugue*
Bach, J. S.: *The Art of Fugue*, theme (original)
Bach, J. S.: *The Art of Fugue*, theme (inversion)
Bach, J. S.: *The Art of Fugue*, theme (retrograde)
Bach, J. S.: *The Art of Fugue*, theme (retrograde inversion)
Bach, J. S.: *The Art of Fugue*, theme (augmentation)
Bach, J. S.: *The Art of Fugue*, theme (diminution)
Bach, J. S.: *Jesu, Joy of Man's Desiring*
Bach, J. S.: Sarabande, from Cello Suite No. 2
Bach, J. S.: Toccata in D minor
Battle Hymn of the Republic (traditional, Civil War song)
Beethoven: *Für Elise*
Beethoven: *Moonlight* Sonata, Adagio
Beethoven: *Ode to Joy*, from Symphony No. 9, IV
Beethoven: Symphony No. 5, I
Bernstein: *Tonight*, from *West Side Story*
Bhimpalási (North India, Ravi Shankar)
Bizet: *Toreador Song*, from *Carmen*
Brahms: *Lullaby*

Catán: Interlude, from *Rappaccini's Daughter*
El Cihualteco (Mexico, mariachi song)

Dougla Dance (Trinidad)

Foster: *Camptown Races*
Foster: *Oh, Susannah!*

Gota (Ghana, West Africa)
Greensleeves (traditional folk song, United Kingdom)

Handel: Alla hornpipe, from *Water Music*
Handel: "Hallelujah Chorus," from *Messiah*
Haydn: *Emperor* Quartet, Op. 76, No. 3, II
Haydn: *Military* Symphony No. 100, II
Haydn: *Surprise* Symphony No. 94, II
Hildegard of Bingen: Kyrie

If I Had a Hammer (Pete Seeger)
In a Mountain Path (China)

Los Jilicatas (Peru)
Joplin: *Pine Apple Rag*
Josquin: *El grillo*
Joy to the World (Christmas carol)

La Marseillaise (French national anthem)
Mbira (Zimbabwe)
Mendelssohn: *Spring Song*, Op. 62, No. 6
Minuet in D minor (*Anna Magdalena Notebook*)
Mouret: Rondeau, from *Suite de symphonies*
Mozart: *Ah! vous dirai-je, maman* (*Twinkle, Twinkle, Little Star*)
Mozart: Clarinet Concerto, II
Mozart: *Eine kleine Nachtmusik*, I
Mozart: *Eine kleine Nachtmusik*, III
Mozart: Symphony No. 40, III
My Bonnie Lies over the Ocean (traditional folk song, America)

O Canada (Canadian national anthem)
Osain (Cuba, Santería)

Pachelbel: Canon in D
Pop Goes the Weasel (traditional, United Kingdom)
Purcell: Rondeau

Reicha: Woodwind Quintet, Op. 88, No. 2
Rossini: *William Tell* Overture
Row, Row, Row Your Boat (traditional, America)

Schumann: "In the lovely month of May"
Simple Gifts (traditional, Shaker hymn)
Skye Crofters (bagpipe, Scottish dance music)

Sleep Song (Hopi lullaby, Native America)
Sousa: *Stars and Stripes Forever*
The Star-Spangled Banner (U.S. national anthem)
Swing Low, Sweet Chariot (African-American spiritual)

Tabuh Kenilu Sawik (Sumatra, Indonesia)
Tchaikovsky: *March*, from *The Nutcracker*

Wagner: *Ride of the Valkyries*
When the Saints Go Marching In (traditional, America)

Preface: *The Enjoyment of Music* Package

You have just purchased perhaps the most comprehensive package of materials available for the study of music appreciation and literature. This book is a classic—it's been around for more than half a century—but its contents and pedagogical approach are very much up-to-date, featuring appealing musical repertory, the latest scholarship, an eye-catching design, and an unparalleled package of electronic ancillaries. This preface introduces you to some of the important pedagogical features in your text, on the CDs, and on the Web. Knowing how to use and integrate these resources will enhance your music listening and study skills and ultimately your performance in class.

Using the Book

The Enjoyment of Music is designed for maximum readability. The narrative is accompanied by many useful and instructive features that will help you in your study of music. These features are described below.

- A **varied repertory** broadly represents classical masters, including women composers and living composers, as well as American music and non-Western musical styles.
- **Key Points**, at the beginning of each chapter, provide a brief summary of the terms and main ideas in each chapter.
- **Marginal icons**, placed throughout the book, direct you to the relevant Web and CD-ROM resources.
- **Marginal sideheads** identify key terms defined in the text and focus attention on important concepts.

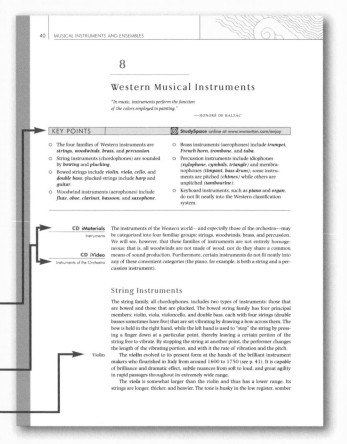

- **Cultural Perspectives** expand on issues discussed in the text and allow you to view music within a larger cultural and interdisciplinary framework. Relevant links for more information are found on StudySpace.
- **Full-color photographs** and illustrations bring to life the figures and events discussed in the text.
- **Listening Guides** for each piece on the CDs enhance your understanding of the music with moment-by-moment descriptions of the work. (See **About the Listening Guides** and also read about the **eLGs** on the **Student Resource Disc.**)
- **What to Listen For boxes,** featured in each Listening Guide, offer helpful suggestions for what to focus on while hearing the music.
- **In His/Her Own Words,** placed throughout all chapters, offer informative and relevant quotes from composers and important historical figures.
- **Timelines,** placed at the beginnings of each Part or era, provide a chronological orientation for world events as well as for principal literary and artistic figures and composers.
- **Maps** placed throughout the book reinforce the locations and names of composers associated with the major musical centers.

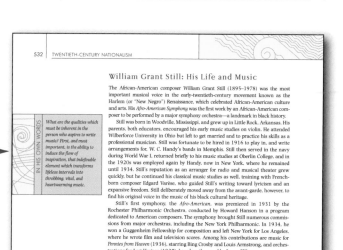

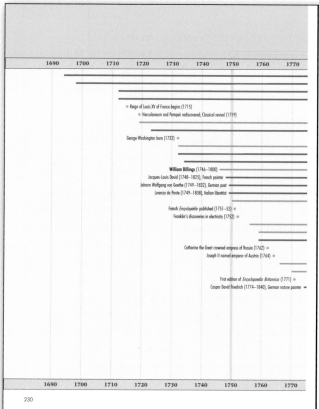

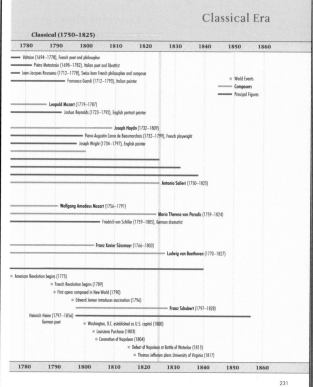

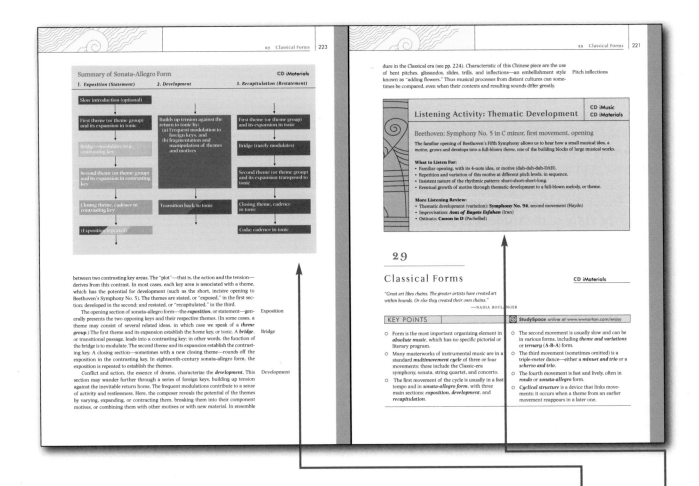

- **Colorful charts** visually reinforce concepts presented in the text.
- **Listening Activities,** bulleted points at the end of each Materials of Music chapter, provide suggested listening exercises for reviewing the building blocks of music.
- **Era introductions** provide overviews of major artistic and intellectual trends in each historical period.
- **Highlighted Materials of Music** chapters are visible (with a 1/4-inch colored strip) when the book is closed, for quick reference to important concepts and terms.

Some other useful reference tools are provided in the text to help in your studying.
- **Glossary** (Appendix II) offers clear, concise definitions of all musical terms.
- **Musical Notation** section (Appendix I) gives explanations of musical symbols used for pitch and rhythm to assist in understanding musical examples.
- **Table of Listening Guides and Recordings** (inside the front and back covers) provides quick reference for locating Listening Guides in the book, as well as pieces on the recording packages.
- All **iMusic examples** are listed in the front of the book for easy reference.
- **World map** (at the back of the book) offers a quick view of continents, countries, and major cities. Inserts provide detail on Europe, the United States, Canada, and Mexico.
- **World music examples** from iMusic and main repertory are indexed on a **world map** (see p. xxvii).
- **Index** (at the back of the book) gives the page number in boldface for definitions, and in italics for illustrations.

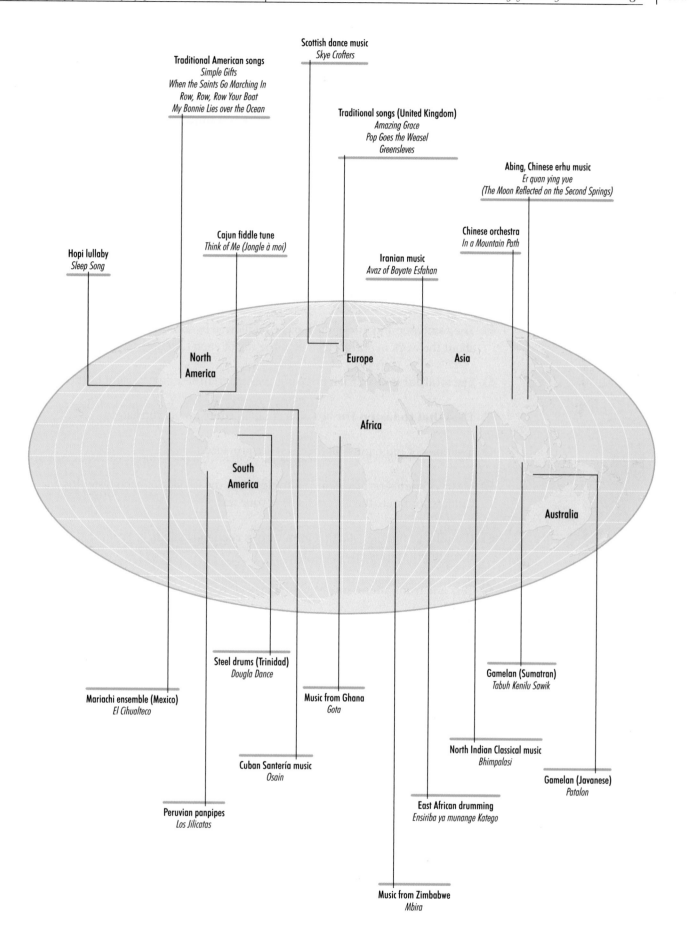

Scottish dance music
Skye Crofters

Traditional American songs
Simple Gifts
When the Saints Go Marching In
Row, Row, Row Your Boat
My Bonnie Lies over the Ocean

Traditional songs (United Kingdom)
Amazing Grace
Pop Goes the Weasel
Greensleves

Abing, Chinese erhu music
Er quan ying yue
(The Moon Reflected on the Second Springs)

Cajun fiddle tune
Think of Me (Jongle à moi)

Chinese orchestra
In a Mountain Path

Iranian music
Avaz of Bayate Esfahan

Hopi lullaby
Sleep Song

North
America

Europe

Asia

Africa

South
America

Australia

Steel drums (Trinidad)
Dougla Dance

Gamelan (Sumatran)
Tabuh Kenilu Sawik

Mariachi ensemble (Mexico)
El Cihualteco

Music from Ghana
Gota

Cuban Santería music
Osain

North Indian Classical music
Bhimpalasi

Gamelan (Javanese)
Patalon

Peruvian panpipes
Los Jilicatas

East African drumming
Ensiriba ya munange Katego

Music from Zimbabwe
Mbira

About the Listening Guides

The **Listening Guides** are an important feature of your textbook; you should use them while listening to the CDs. The guides are easy to follow and will enhance your knowledge and appreciation of each piece. Refer to the sample **Listening Guide** and numbers on the facing page as you read through the following points:

❶ The CD locator, boxed in the upper-right-hand corner of each Listening Guide, provides CD and inclusive track numbers for both the 4-CD set (to accompany the Shorter version) on top, and the 8-CD set (to accompany *The Enjoyment of Music*) beneath.

❷ There is also an interactive electronic Listening Guide (**eLG**) for each work. Once you download the eLG software from the Student Resource Disc, you can use your CD set to study the musical selections on your computer.

❸ The composer and title of each piece is followed by some basic information about the work in outline format at the top of each Listening Guide.

❹ The total duration of each piece is given in parentheses to the right of the title.

❺ The **What to Listen For** box offers helpful study tips as you listen.

❻ Examples of main musical theme(s) are provided.

❼ CD track numbers, boxed and running down the left side of each Listening Guide, coordinate the CD tracks with your text.

❽ Cumulative timings, starting from zero in each movement, are provided throughout the Listening Guide.

❾ Text and translations are given for all vocal works.

❿ A moment-by-moment description of events helps you follow the musical selection throughout.

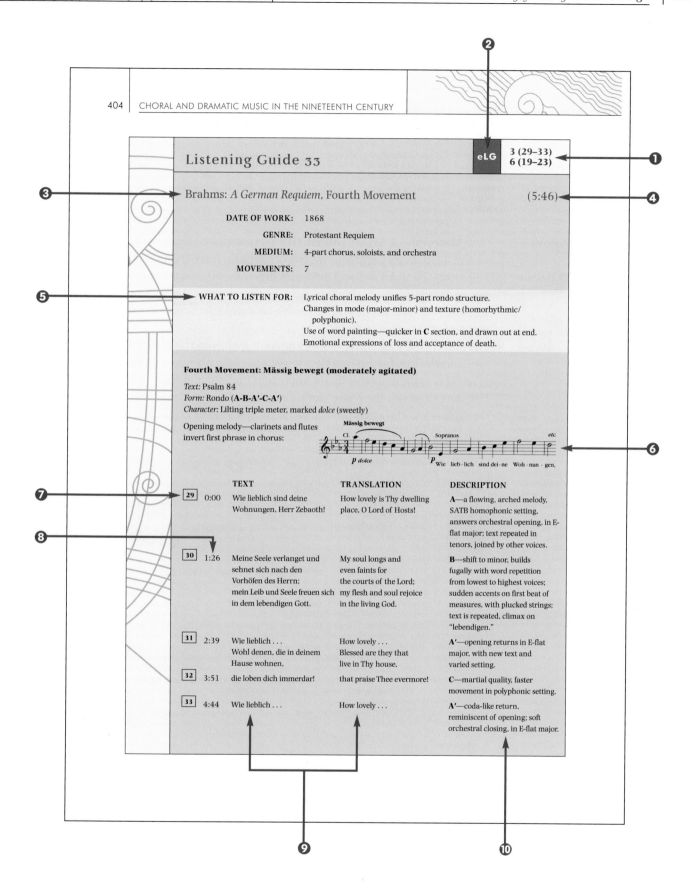

404   CHORAL AND DRAMATIC MUSIC IN THE NINETEENTH CENTURY

Listening Guide 33

eLG   3 (29–33)
6 (19–23)

Brahms: *A German Requiem*, Fourth Movement   (5:46)

DATE OF WORK:	1868
GENRE:	Protestant Requiem
MEDIUM:	4-part chorus, soloists, and orchestra
MOVEMENTS:	7

WHAT TO LISTEN FOR: Lyrical choral melody unifies 5-part rondo structure.
Changes in mode (major-minor) and texture (homorhythmic/
polyphonic).
Use of word painting—quicker in **C** section, and drawn out at end.
Emotional expressions of loss and acceptance of death.

Fourth Movement: Mässig bewegt (moderately agitated)

Text: Psalm 84
Form: Rondo (**A-B-A'-C-A'**)
Character: Lilting triple meter, marked *dolce* (sweetly)

Opening melody—clarinets and flutes
invert first phrase in chorus:

	TEXT	**TRANSLATION**	**DESCRIPTION**
29 0:00	Wie lieblich sind deine Wohnungen, Herr Zebaoth!	How lovely is Thy dwelling place, O Lord of Hosts!	**A**—a flowing, arched melody, SATB homophonic setting, answers orchestral opening, in E-flat major; text repeated in tenors, joined by other voices.
30 1:26	Meine Seele verlanget und sehnet sich nach den Vorhöfen des Herrn; mein Leib und Seele freuen sich in dem lebendigen Gott.	My soul longs and even faints for the courts of the Lord; my flesh and soul rejoice in the living God.	**B**—shift to minor, builds fugally with word repetition from lowest to highest voices; sudden accents on first beat of measures, with plucked strings; text is repeated, climax on "lebendigen."
31 2:39	Wie lieblich . . . Wohl denen, die in deinem Hause wohnen,	How lovely . . . Blessed are they that live in Thy house,	**A'**—opening returns in E-flat major, with new text and varied setting.
32 3:51	die loben dich immerdar!	that praise Thee evermore!	**C**—martial quality, faster movement in polyphonic setting.
33 4:44	Wie lieblich . . .	How lovely . . .	**A'**—coda-like return, reminiscent of opening; soft orchestral closing, in E-flat major.

Using the Electronic Resources

The Enjoyment of Music is coordinated with several electronic resources that will enhance your learning; these are available on the Student Resource Disc and the online StudySpace.

Resource CD   ABOUT THE STUDENT RESOURCE DISC

This disc, in DVD format, has many useful study resources coordinated with the book:

CD iMaterials
- New **Materials of Music Interactive** exercises allow you to manipulate music on-screen; all main concepts are covered, drawing on more than 70 **iMusic** examples.

CD iMusic
- More than 70 short musical examples illustrate the elements, or materials, of music (**iMusic**)—featuring familiar traditional songs, a diverse array of world and folk music excerpts, and accessible classical selections. Seven complete movements are also included.

eLG
- The **electronic Listening Guides** interact with both the 4- and 8-CD sets. Each musical selection has an overview (composer, title, date, genre, context), translation when appropriate, sound clips of important musical moments, and an interactive Listening Guide for the entire work. Once the software is installed, you listen from the audio CDs. The **eLGs** provide moment-by-moment explanations, synchronized with the music. In addition, all the terms are linked to an electronic glossary.

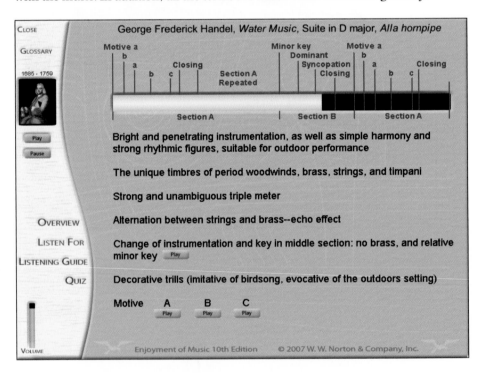

CD iVideo
- **Instruments of the Orchestra** video, produced at the Eastman School of Music, in Rochester, New York, helps you learn the sights and sounds of different instruments.
- **Britten's *Young Person's Guide to the Orchestra*** is now available in a new performance, accompanied by an **eLG** (see LG 1 in text, p. 56). You can listen to the recording on your computer, accompanied by the digital listening guides.

ABOUT THE ONLINE LISTENING LAB

Available at www.wwnorton.com/web/listenonline, this low-cost alternative to audio CDs includes many of the core works on the *Norton Recordings* CD sets in near-CD-quality streaming. Students can link directly to the Lab from StudySpace for a modest fee. Resources include Listening Guides and enhanced composer biographies. The Online Listening Lab also provides access to the Naxos Music Library, an archive of thousands of pieces, for an additional subscription upgrade.

ABOUT STUDYSPACE

Available at www.wwnorton.com/enjoy, this Web site integrates excellent online material within an assignment-driven pedagogy. Each chapter has a homepage with the following structure:

- **Organize**
  - StudyPlan, including a sequenced progression of assignments
  - Chapter Outline, in printer-friendly format
  - Progress Report: a checklist for students to monitor their work

- **Learn**
  - Listen: an index page with each chapter's listening selections, linked to audio CDs, iMusic examples, Online Listening Lab, and other online music resources
  - Flashcards for all boldfaced terms, which cross-reference with the book's glossary
  - Quizzes on terms, concepts, and listening that are computer-graded and linked to the instructor and student gradebooks

- **Connect**
  - Composers: biographies, with illustrations, audio examples, and links to online resources
  - Resources, including
    - Transitions between historical eras, with comparative charts and audio examples
    - Listening to music: essays on musical style enhanced with listening examples
    - Timelines from the text that help with chronological orientation of key figures and events
    - Baroque-era orchestra video, featuring three video segments from Telemann's *Tafelmusik*—performed by the Los Angeles Baroque Orchestra on period instruments.

Other features of StudySpace:
- Materials of Music drills, with musical examples
- *Today in Music History*: daily news feeds about music
- Music video and audio podcasts
- Glossary from text in alphabetical listing

To the Instructor

The Enjoyment of Music, Tenth Edition, presents a comprehensive teaching and learning package that integrates innovative technological resources with the traditional book and audio CDs. If you have not already done so, please review the previous section (pp. xxiv–xxxi) and be sure to have your students read this as well. We encourage you and your students to take full advantage of the features we have developed. *The Enjoyment of Music* text is also available in a **Complete** version; both versions take a chronological approach. An Essentials edition, which is briefer than the Shorter, is planned for 2008.

We have addressed many pedagogical issues in this new Tenth Edition, with a goal of providing innovative teaching and learning resources; these include the following (boldface text designates a new selection or recording):

- Increased computer and Web resources for classroom and individual use
- More Materials of Music resources for students
- Improved balance of genres
- Updated content, including film music, popular and traditional music, jazz, and music by living composers
- Accessible and highly "teachable" repertory
- Excellent quality recordings, including more period-instrument performances of early music
- "Front-loading" of information in each chapter (*Key Points*)
- Clear guidelines for listening (*What to Listen For*)
- Integration of women musicians (as composers, performers, and patrons) in each era
- Focus on comparative cultures (Western vs. non-Western/traditional musics)
- Increased emphasis on traditional and art music of the Americas
- New, colorful design that reinforces learning

ABOUT THE REPERTORY AND LISTENING GUIDES

The Tenth Edition is accompanied by two CD sets: a shorter 4-CD set, with 60 works, and an 8-CD version, which has 100 works. Every work on the CDs is supported by both an in-text Listening Guide and an electronic Listening Guide (**eLGs** on the **Student Resource Disc**).

The electronic Listening Guides have been redesigned to meet the needs of today's students and faculty. These interactive guides are ideal for use in lectures and for individual study; they help students follow the music closely while focusing on key structural and stylistic features.

Highlights of the repertory are provided below (boldface text designates a new selection or recording).

Repertory

60 works with Listening Guides in the **Shorter** version of the book:
- 20 of these are new to the Tenth Edition.
- All are recorded on the 4-CD set.

100 works with Listening Guides in the **Complete** book:
- 28 of these are new to the Tenth Edition.
- All are recorded on the 8-CD set.

17 continuing works from past editions are featured with new and improved recordings.

World/traditional music examples set against Western pieces influenced by the style:
- **Javanese gamelan work**, following **Cage, *Sonatas and Interludes***
- Chinese traditional music, following **Bright Sheng, *China Dreams: Prelude***

Traditional and art music of the Americas:
- Cajun dance tune (*Think of Me*), performed by BeauSoleil
- Symphonic work by Mexican composer Silvestre Revueltas (*Homenaje a Federico García Lorca*)
- **Mariachi selection**, following Revueltas, *Homanaje a Federico García Lorca*

Chapter on film music, with one listening example:
- **John Williams, *Raiders of the Lost Ark***

Excellent coverage of music by women composers (spanning the full chronological range) and of women performers:
- Hildegard of Bingen chant: *Alleluia, O virga mediatrix*
- Barbara Strozzi Italian cantata: *Begli occhi*
- **Clara Schumann piano work: Nocturne**
- **Fanny Mendelssohn choral work: *Under the Greenwood Tree***
- Billie Holiday piece: *Billie's Blues*
- **Libby Larsen song cycle: *Sonnets from the Portuguese***

Well-known women performers in the package include:
- Jeanne Lamon, director of Tafelmusik
- Midori, violin; Ingrid Seifert, Baroque violin
- Cecile Licad and Yoshiko Iwai, piano
- Guillaumette Laurents, Karen Clift, Miriam Gaudi, Lucy Shelton, Jan deGaetani, Arleen Auger, and Billie Holiday, voice

Major coverage of jazz (including its influence on art music):
- Ragtime—Joplin: *Maple Leaf Rag*
- Blues—Holiday: *Billie's Blues*
- Bebop—Gillespie/Parker: *A Night in Tunisia*
- Merger of classical and jazz styles:
  Bernstein: *Mambo*, from *West Side Story*

New, accessible, and highly teachable selections include:
- **Mouret: Rondeau (*Masterpiece Theatre* theme)**
- **Beethoven: Piano Sonata, Op. 27, No. 2 (*Moonlight*)**
- **Stravinksy: *Rite of Spring*, Part I**
- **Schumann: "In the lovely month of May," from *A Poet's Love***
- **John Williams: *Raiders March*, from *Raiders of the Lost Ark***

Improved early music examples (with excellent recordings):
- **New examples,** including a medieval troubadour dance song; Renaissance dances (Susato) and Italian madrigal (Monteverdi); and French Baroque music (Mouret)
- Continuing works (by Machaut, Josquin, Palestrina, Farmer, Strozzi, and Purcell) representing all major genres (Mass, motet, chansons, madrigals, instrumental music, early opera, Italian cantata)

Excellent coverage of period-instrument performances—many new to this edition—representing wide-ranging eras:
- Medieval and Renaissance dance; Baroque opera, oratorio, concerto, and suite; and Classical orchestral music
- Exceptional performances by the Lionhart, Oxford Camerata, The Sixteen, Delitiae Musicae, Convivium Musicum, Philharmonia Baroque, Tafelmusik, English Baroque, Boston Baroque, Los Angeles Baroque, Hanover Band, La Grande Ecurie et la Chambre du Roy, Orchestra of the 18th Century, Academy of Ancient Music, as well as a solo performance by Anthony Newman

Five new contemporary pieces by major composers:
- **Adams: *Tromba lontana* (1986)**
- **Larsen: *Sonnets from the Portuguese* (1993)**
- **Sheng: *China Dreams: Prelude* (1995)**
- **Pärt: *Cantate Domino canticum novum* (1977; rev. 1996)**
- **Machover: *Begin Again Again . . .* (1991; rev. 2004)**

Outstanding Ancillaries for Students and Instructors

In addition to the Student Resource Disc, StudySpace, and two CD sets with eLGs—all described above—Norton offers a pedagogically rich array of ancillary materials unique to this text.

The Norton Scores

This two-volume anthology includes scores for nearly all the works on both 8- and 4-CD sets. A unique highlighting system—long a hallmark of this collection—assists students in following full orchestral scores, as well as stylistic commentary for each piece. These scores are essential for instructor use in the classroom and for the preparation of lectures.

Study Guide

This workbook assists students with reviewing and listening exercises as well as cultural explorations. It also includes projects for groups and individuals and for concert report outlines.

Music Example Bank

This unique and highly useful ancillary consists of four fully indexed audio CDs that illustrate—with examples from classical, folk, and popular music—the musical concepts discussed in the text.

Norton Media Library DVD

This resource features PowerPoint slides for every chapter of the text; 140 musical excerpts from the Music Example Bank illustrating key concepts in the text; a PDF of in-text listening guides; PowerPoint-ready Instruments of the Orchestra videos; and StudySpace questions formatted in PowerPoint for use with classroom response systems.

Instructor's Resource Manual

Available in paper and PDF formats, this resource includes an overview of ancillaries to accompany *The Enjoyment of Music;* suggested approaches to teaching, a sample course syllabus, and exam schedule; lecture notes to accompany PowerPoint slides (see above, Norton Media Library CD- ROM); resources (books, videos, recordings) for enhancing key concepts; and answers to the student Study Guide questions.

Test Bank and Computerized Test-Item File in ExamView® Format

Featuring over 2,000 multiple-choice, true/false, and essay questions, the Test Bank is available in print and in ExamView® formats that enable the instructor to edit questions and add new ones.

WebCT e-packs and BlackBoard Coursepacks

These ready-to-use coursepacks offer assignment sequences and questions from StudySpace for each chapter, all StudySpace quizzes, the Instructor's Resource Manual PowerPoint lecture slides, and Electronic Transparency PDFs of Listening Guides.

Britten, The Young Person's Guide to the Orchestra DVD (49 minutes)

This popular item is now available on DVD. It also allows the instructor to take PowerPoint-ready audio and video files from the DVD.

Instruments of the Orchestra DVD

Recorded at the Eastman School of Music, this DVD shows all the instruments of the orchestra—45 of them, including 11 percussion instruments—in action. Ideal for classroom use, this easily manageable, high-quality, full-screen DVD allows instructors to select video clips by instrument family and includes complete descriptions of each instrument.

Videos

This collection of music, opera, and dance videos offers instructors an exceptional library of video resources. Consult the Instructor's Resource Manual for a list of specific works and performances distributed by W. W. Norton.

So what's new in the Tenth Edition? The answer is a lot—more technology, more pedagogical resources, more diversity, and more visual and aural stimulation—within the same dependable package of teaching materials. You will find a greater breadth of musical styles than ever before, and music repertory that speaks to today's student in this diverse, multicultural society. Although this edition continues to focus on Western art music, it addresses issues and events in the contemporary world around us. The Tenth Edition of *The Enjoyment of Music* combines an authoritative text, a stimulating new design that integrates text, pedagogy, and emedia, and unparalleled print and online ancillaries. The result is an exceptional teaching—and learning—package.

Any project of this size is dependent on the expertise and assistance of many individuals to make it a success. First, we wish to acknowledge the many loyal users of *The Enjoyment of Music* who have taken the time to comment on the text and ancillary package. As always, their suggestions help us shape each new edition. We also wish to thank those instructors who participated in focus groups held at the University of California, Santa Barbara, and at California State University, Long Beach. These forums encouraged a free exchange of ideas on teaching methods, repertory, and the instructional use of technology.

The list of specialists who offered their expertise to this text continues to grow. In addition to those acknowledged in the last several editions, whose insights have helped shape the book, we wish to thank Roger Hickman (California State University, Long Beach), for updating the chapter on film music in this edition and for his transcription of the Cajun dance song; Revell Carr (University of California, Santa Barbara), for updating the rock chapter and for his analysis of the Javanese gamelan work; Dolores Hsu (University of California, Santa Barbara), for her advice on the Chinese erhu work; Bahram Osqueezadeh (University of California, Santa Barbara), for his transcription of an Iranian santur piece and for his image included in the text; Junko Ueno Garrett, for her help with transcribing the Japanese kouta music and text; Mark Scatterday (Eastman School of Music), for producing the video clips of the *Instruments of the Orchestra*; the Eastman School of Music students who performed in the instrument videos, and especially Julie Barnes (harp), Hae Sung Choe (flute), Isrea Butler (trombone), and Melanie Sehman (percussion), whose images appear in the text; Gregory Maldonado (California State University, Long Beach), for providing audio and video segments performed by the Los Angeles Baroque Orchestra, which he directs; the Americus Brass Band (many members of which are CSU Long Beach alumni; Richard Birkemeier, director), for commissioned recording of five iMusic examples; the CSU Long Beach Opera, Choral, Woodwind, Brass, and Percussion programs (David Anglin, Richard Rintoul, Jonathan Talberg, John Barcellona, Robert Frear, Michael Carney, directors), for recording many iMusic examples; David Garrett (Los Angeles Philharmonic), for licensing his performance of the Sarabande to Bach's Second Cello Suite; Allan Bevan (University of Calgary), for licensing his arrangement of *O Canada*; and David Düsing, for a specially commissioned arrangement of *Simple Gifts*.

The team assembled to prepare the ancillary materials accompanying this edition is unparalleled: it includes our Webmaster Russell Murray (University of Delaware); Irene Girton (Occidental College), author of the electronic Listening Guides; John Husser (Virginia Technological Institute and State University), who designed and programmed the emedia; James Forney (St. Lawrence University) and Tom Laskey and Jeff Zaraya (Sony Special Products), who assembled, licensed, and mastered the recording package; Roger Hickman (California State University, Long Beach), who prepared the commentary for the Norton Scores, assisted with recording selection and coordination with the scores, and who updated and edited the Test Bank File; Alicia Doyle (California State University, Long Beach), who created the Materials of Music Interactive module and who prepared the new Instructor's Resource Manual and PowerPoint slides for classroom presentation; Peter Hesterman (Eastern Illinois University) and John Miller (North Dakota State University), for their creative software design for the Materials of Music Interactive module; David Brown (Brigham Young University), for his contributions to the PowerPoint lectures in the Norton Media Library; Gregory Maldonado (California State University, Long Beach), who highlighted the new scores for this edition; and research assistants Denise Odello and Sarah Gerk.

This new edition would not have been realized without the capable assistance of the W. W. Norton team. We owe profound thanks to Maribeth Payne, music editor at W. W. Norton, for her dedication and counsel to the whole project; to Kathy Talalay, for her expert copyediting and project management, as well as her patience, encouragement, and advice; to electronic media editor Steve Hoge, for creating and coordinating our outstanding emedia package; to Courtney Fitch, for her able editing of *The Norton Scores* and her coordination of many of the ancillaries; to Graham Norwood, for overseeing innumerable details of the package; to Antonina Krass, for her inviting and elegant design; to Neil Ryder Hoos, for his excellent illustration research; to Carole Desnoes, for her artistic layout; to JoAnn Simony, for her expert oversight of the production for the entire *Enjoyment* package; and to Peter Lesser and Dan Jost, for their insightful marketing strategies. I would also like to thank Marilyn Bliss, for her thorough index; Maura Burnett, for her expert proofreading; David Budmen, for his skilled music typesetting; and John McAusland, for his attractive maps.

We wish finally to express our deep appreciation to three former music editors at Norton—Michael Ochs, Claire Brook, and David Hamilton—who over the years have guided and inspired *The Enjoyment of Music* to its continued success.

Kristine Forney
Joseph Machlis

The Enjoyment of
Music

TENTH EDITION/SHORTER

Marc Chagall (1887–1985), *La musicienne.*

PART ONE

The Materials of Music

The Elements of Music

Prelude

Listening to Music Today

"Ah, Music . . . a magic beyond all we do here!"
—ALBUS DUMBLEDORE, HEADMASTER,
HOGWARTS SCHOOL OF WITCHCRAFT AND WIZARDRY

With increased personalization and portability, technology like the iPod has transformed the way we listen to music.

Our lives are constantly changing, with new avenues of the supertechnology highway opening every day. This technological revolution has a strong impact on our work and our leisure activities. It also conditions how, when, and where we listen to music. From the moment we are awakened by our clock radios or cell phone ring tones, our days unfold against a musical background. We listen to music—in our cars, on the move with our iPods and mp3 players in hand, and at home for relaxation. We can hardly avoid it in grocery and department stores, in restaurants and elevators, at the dentist's office, or at work. We also experience music at live concerts—outdoor festivals, rock concerts, jazz clubs, symphony halls, opera stages—and we hear it on television, at the movies, and on the Internet. Since the advent of MTV in 1981 and music video downloads, our means for "listening" to popular music has become an multimedia experience. This increased use of our eyes makes our ears work less actively, a trend we will attempt to counteract in this book.

Composers have welcomed the technological revolution; the basic tools of music composition—formerly, a pen, music paper, and a piano—now include a computer, a laser printer, and a synthesizer. Modern technology has provided us with a wider diversity of music of every historical period, with every kind of instrument, and from every corner of the globe than has ever been available before.

Given this diversity, we must choose our path of study. In this book, we will focus on the classics of Western music while also paying special attention to the important influences that traditional, popular, and non-Western musics have had on the European and American heritage. Our purpose is to expand the listening experience through a heightened awareness of many styles of music, including those representing various subcultures of the American population. We

These girls share music and earbuds on an iPod.

will hear the uniquely American forms of ragtime, blues, jazz, and musical theater, as well as rock and contemporary world music. The book seeks to place music, whether art, traditional, or popular, within its cultural context, and to highlight the relationships between different styles. It also helps you make connections in your broad range of studies. To this end, the **Cultural Perspectives** (informative boxed texts placed throughout the book) open windows onto the music of other cultures and the interrelationship among music and other fields of study, including science, philosophy, religion, literature, economics, political science, sociology, and the fine arts. You can also explore these topics further on the *Enjoyment* online **StudySpace** (www.wwnorton.com/enjoy), which provides links to related sites of interest.

Cultural Perspectives

The language of music cannot be translated into the language of words. You cannot deduce the actual sound of a piece from anything written about it; as the great violinist Yehudi Menuhin notes below, the ultimate meaning lies in the sounds themselves and in the ears of the listener. While certain styles are immediately accessible without any explanation, the world of music often brings us into contact with sounds and concepts that we need some time to digest. What, you might wonder, can prepare the nonmusician to understand and appreciate an eighteenth-century symphony, a contemporary opera, or an example of African drumming? A great deal. We will discuss the social and historical context in which a work was born. We will explore the characteristic features of the various styles throughout the history of music so that we can relate a particular piece or style to parallel developments in other disciplines. We will read about the lives of the composers who left us so rich a heritage, and take note of what they said about their art. We will acquaint ourselves with the elements, or building blocks, out of which music is made, and discover how composers combine these into a work. And we will come to understand music as an art form, as a means of expression that is created by the composer, interpreted by the performer, and processed by the listener. All this knowledge can be interrelated, enabling us to develop a total picture of a work, one that will clarify the character and meaning of a composition.

Some Practical Suggestions for Listening

Like any new endeavor, it takes practice to become an experienced listener. We often "listen" to music as a background to another activity—perhaps studying or for relaxation. In either case, we are probably not concentrating on the music. But with

IN HIS OWN WORDS

There is no such thing as music divorced from the listener. Music as such is unfulfilled until it has penetrated our ears.
—*YEHUDI MENUHIN*

A fireworks display ends a packed concert at the Hollywood Bowl in Los Angeles.

practice, you will develop listening skills and expand your musical memory. To do this, you should listen to the examples several times, focusing solely on what you are hearing. As you listen to the music, follow along with the **Listening Guides** in this book or use the electronic guides on your **Resource CD**. Not everyone learns the same way, so be sure to read about *The Enjoyment of Music* Package" (pp. xxiv–xxxi) that provides an overview of all the study tools available to you. The short music examples in the Listening Guides may be useful if you can follow the general line of the music (see **Appendix I, "Musical Notation"**). But don't worry if you can't read music; the verbal descriptions of each piece and its sections will tell you what to listen for. An explanation of the format for the Listening Guides is found on pages xxviii–xxix.

It is also important to hear music in live performance. Why not try something new and unfamiliar? There are many possibilities. Read the upcoming section, "Attending Concerts," to learn some of the conventions of the concert hall. The goal is to open up a new world of musical experiences that you can enjoy for the rest of your life.

You will notice that each historical era begins with a general discussion of the culture, its arts, and its ideas. This introduction, along with the Cultural Perspectives, should help you integrate the knowledge you have gained from other disciplines into the world of music and help you understand that developments in music are closely related to those in art, literature, philosophy, religion, politics, and even science.

You may be surprised at how many new terms are presented here. Studying music is not easier than studying other subjects, but it can be more fun. Make use of the **Glossary** in **Appendix II**, and note that the most important terms, when introduced in the book, are highlighted in boldface and italics. Many music terms—such as the directions for musical expression, tempo, and dynamics—come from foreign languages. We will begin building this vocabulary in the first chapters by breaking music into its basic elements. Your Resource CD will be helpful: it contains familiar examples of folk and classical music you have probably heard previously. These examples support and illustrate the terms you are learning. There are also **Listening Activities** at the end of each chapter that help you review concepts with music on your CDs. We will consider how a composer shapes a melody, how that melody is fitted with accompanying harmony, how music is organized in time, and how it becomes a form we can perceive easily. These basic principles apply to all styles of music (popular and classical, Western and non-Western), to music from all eras and countries, and beyond that, to the other arts as well. Our goal is perceptive listening, which is the one sure road to the enjoyment of music.

Resource CD

IN HIS OWN WORDS

Music must never offend the ear, but must please the listener, or, in other words, must never cease to be music.

—W. A. MOZART

Attending Concerts

Nothing can equal the excitement of a live concert. The crowded hall, the visual and aural stimulation of a performance, and even the element of unpredictability—of what might happen on a particular night—all contribute to the unique communicative powers of people making music. There are, however, certain traditions surrounding concerts and concertgoing: these include the way performers dress, the appropriate moments to applaud, and even the location of the most desirable seats. These aspects of performance differ between art music and popular music concerts. Understanding the differing traditions—and knowing what to expect—will contribute to your enjoyment of the musical event.

CHOOSING CONCERTS, TICKETS, AND SEATS

You probably have a rich choice of musical events available regardless of where you live. These might be visiting groups sponsored by your campus and performed by your school's Music Department, or they might be civic events, held at a local performing arts center. To explore concerts in your area, check with the Music Department for on-campus concerts, read local and college newspapers for a calendar of upcoming events in the area, consult Web sites for nearby concert venues and calendars, or scan bulletin boards at your local university or college and in public buildings for concert announcements.

Ticket prices vary, depending on the event. For university events, including both popular and classical music, tickets are usually reasonable (under $20 and often much less). For a performance in a major concert hall, you will probably pay more, generally $35 to over $100, depending on the location of your seat. Orchestra section seats—those closest to the stage—are usually the most expensive; balcony seats are more economical and the sound is as good or sometimes better than seats on the main floor, depending on the hall. It is also sometimes easier to see the performers from the balcony. Today, most new concert halls are constructed so that virtually all the seats are satisfactory (see Cultural Perspective 1, p. 8, on the new Disney Concert Hall in Los Angeles). Where you choose your seats depends on the type of the event. For small chamber groups, front orchestra seats, close to the performers, are best. For large ensembles—orchestras and operas, or even popular concerts—the best places are probably near the middle of the hall or in the balcony, where you also have a good view. For some concerts,

Patrons awaiting a performance at the Kravis Center for the Performing Arts, West Palm Beach, Florida.

you may need to purchase tickets in advance, either by phone or online, paying with a credit card. Be sure to ask for student discounts when appropriate.

PREPARING FOR THE CONCERT

Researching the concert Before you attend a concert, you may want to prepare by doing some reading. First, find out what works (or at least which composers) will be performed at the upcoming concert. Then check your textbook and the StudySpace for information about the composers, works, genres, or styles. You can also look for information about the music in your campus library and on the Internet, or you can ask your instructor. There are excellent reference books available that contain program notes for standard concert music and opera plots. It is especially important to read about an opera before the performance because it may be sung in the original language (e.g., Italian, German, or French).

What you chose to wear to a concert should depend on the degree of formality and the location of the event. For an evening performance at a large concert hall or for the opening of an opera, people will generally be very dressed up. But more often, attire is less formal, especially for university concerts. Whatever the occasion, you should be neatly attired out of respect for the performers. If you are attending a jazz or pops concert, however, or an outdoor event, very casual dress is appropriate.

ARRIVING AT THE CONCERT

Plan to arrive at least twenty minutes before a concert starts, and even earlier if it is open seating or if you have ordered your tickets by phone or online and must pick them up at the box office. People often mingle with friends or enjoy a beverage at the lobby bar before an event. Be sure to pick up a concert program—they are usually

Summary: Attending Concerts

o Consult your local and college newspapers, the Music Department, Web sites, and bulletin boards on campus to learn about upcoming concerts in your area.

o Determine if it is necessary to purchase your tickets in advance or if you can acquire them at the door.

o Read about the works in advance in your textbook, at your library, or on the Internet.

o Consider what to wear; the degree of formality in your attire should suit the occasion.

o Arrive early to purchase or pick up your ticket and to get a good seat.

o Review the program before the concert starts to learn what you can about the music and the performers.

o Be respectful to the performers and those sitting near you by not making noise during the concert (turn off cell phones and pagers).

o Follow the program carefully so that you know when to applaud (after complete works or sets of pieces).

o Be aware of and respectful of concert hall traditions.

o Above all, enjoy the event!

free—from the usher and read about the music and the performers before the event begins. You will enjoy the event more if you can follow the selections. Translations into English of vocal texts are generally provided as well. If you arrive late, after the concert has begun, you will not be able to enter the hall until after the first piece is finished or an appropriate break in the music occurs. Be respectful of the performers and those around you by not talking and not leaving your seat except at intermission (the break that usually occurs about halfway through the performance).

THE CONCERT PROGRAM

One key aspect of attending a concert is understanding the program. Below is a sample program for an orchestra concert, such as you might find at your college or in your community.

Concert program

A glance at the program confirms that three works will be performed. The concert will open, as is often the case, with an overture. The title of this particular work might be familiar because it is based on Shakespeare's well-known play *A Midsummer Night's Dream*. We will see later that some works have a literary basis that helps us interpret the composer's ideas. The dates for this composer, Felix Mendelssohn, establish him as an early Romantic master. (We will review style periods of music in Chapter 10. You could also read more about this composer in later chapters of this book and at the online StudySpace.)

The concert will continue with a symphony by Mozart, a composer whose name you have undoubtedly heard. We can deduce by the title that Mozart wrote many symphonies; what we would not know without reading about him is that this one (No. 41) is his last. The symphony is in four sections, or movements, with contrasting tempo indications for each movement. The tempo pattern is a traditional one:

PROGRAM

Overture to *A Midsummer Night's Dream*	Felix Mendelssohn (1809–1847)
Symphony No. 41 in C major, K. 551 (*Jupiter*) I. Allegro vivace II. Andante cantabile III. Menuetto (Allegretto) & Trio IV. Finale: Molto allegro	W. A. Mozart (1756–1791)

Intermission

Concerto No. 1 for Piano and Orchestra in B-flat minor, Op. 23
  I.   Allegro non troppo e molto maestoso;
      Allegro con spirito
 II. Andantino simplice; Prestissimo; Tempo I
III. Allegro con fuoco
	P. I. Tchaikovsky (1840–1893)

Barbara Allen, piano

The University Symphony Orchestra
Eugene Castillo, conductor

Music and Sound

What is the difference between sound and music? A *sound* is produced by a vibrating object—actually, it is the air particles surrounding the object that move to and fro, producing a sound wave that moves away from the source. Some sounds are not periodic (or regular) in the movement of the particles and therefore do not produce a definable sound, or steady pitch. *Pitch* is the highness or lowness of a sound, described by *frequency* (the number of vibrations per second, measured in *Hertz*). We might consider sounds without a distinct pitch to be *noise*. A *musical sound*, or *tone*, on the other hand, has a perceivable pitch and a measurable frequency, which depends on the vibrating object. The pitch is determined by the length or size of the vibrating object. A short string or column of air on an instrument vibrates faster than a longer one and thus produces a higher pitch. This is why a piccolo or a violin sounds higher than a trombone or a cello.

We represent a musical sound in a symbol called a *note*, which indicates not only its pitch but its *duration* as well—that is, the length of time the vibration can be heard. We also perceive the *amplitude* of a musical sound—that is, its *volume*, or loudness. Volume is measured in *decibels*, a term derived from a larger measurement, the bell—both named after the Scottish inventor Alexander Graham Bell, who is popularly credited with the invention of the telephone. (Imagine what our lives would be like today without his research into telecommunications technology.)

We hear musical sounds when the waves travel through our outer ears and are converted in our inner ears to neural impulses, which are then interpreted by various parts of our brain. Listening to and producing music is fascinating because it involves nearly every cognitive function of the brain. You may have heard of the recent research suggesting that listening to music makes you "smarter." We will discuss one of these theories—the so-called Mozart effect—in a later Cultural Perspective. If this is true, that music can boost the brain's functions, just think what a whole term of music listening can do for you!

Because music affects the listener emotionally, it has often been associated with far-reaching, sometimes magical, powers. The Greeks and Romans viewed music not only as the force that unified the human body and soul but also as an all-pervading force in the universe, whose arithmetical ratios kept the planets in their orbits. Modern scientists continue to study the "music of the spheres," investigating the sounds produced by black holes in the universe and by the earth—both emit tones that are inaudible to the human ear but can be measured with scientific equipment. The earth's constant hum, probably generated by atmospheric pressure and oceanic forces, is detected with seismographs (devices that measures earthquakes).

Although we appreciate the modern technological advances that bring us high-quality digital music reproduction, scientists continue to explore and master the forces of nature, offering us superb sound quality in the concert hall as well. Unlike venues for digitally engineered music (as in some popular music concerts), where amplified sound needs a relatively dead, nonreverberant space, concert halls for *acoustic music* (nonamplified) require exact engineering for optimum sound reflection. A pioneer in the field of architectural acoustics was Harvard University physicist Wallace Sabine (1868–1919), who designed Boston's Symphony Hall (1900), still considered one of the finest concert halls in the world. The new Disney Hall in Los Angeles, which opened in 2003, is a recent synthesis of

An image from a computer-generated representation of voice patterns.

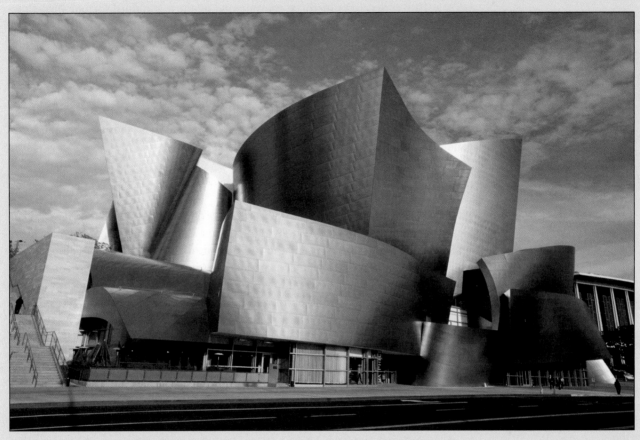

The new Walt Disney Concert Hall in Los Angeles, designed by architect **Frank Gehry**, is noted for its superb acoustics.

acoustics and architecture. Designed by the well-known Canadian architect Frank Gehry and the brilliant Japanese acoustician Yasuhisa Toyota, the building's exterior features dramatically curved stainless steel panels that resemble a ship sailing at full mast while the curved interior walls wrap around the audience, who in turn surround the stage. The magical sound of Disney Hall is both warm and exceptionally clear—in short, an acoustical triumph. Such successful projects make live music an experience that cannot be rivaled by any means of reproduction, and help keep our esteemed musical performance ensembles a vibrant part of our culture. Visit a concert hall near you and hear the difference.

Terms to Note

sound	pitch	note	frequency
vibration	Hertz	duration	noise
amplitude	decibel (bell)	volume	acoustic music

---

fast (Allegro vivace), slow (Andante cantabile), a moderate dance (Menuetto & Trio), and fast (Molto allegro). (You can read more about the tempo terms in Chapter 6 and the multimovement instrumental cycle and the forms of individual movements in Chapter 29.)

After the intermission, the second half of the concert will be devoted to a single work—a piano concerto by the late-nineteenth-century Russian composer Tchaikovsky. This concerto is in three movements, again a standard format (fast-slow-fast). The tempo markings are, however, much more descriptive than those for the Mozart symphony, using words like *maestoso* (majestic), *con spirito* (with spirit), and *con fuoco* (with fire). This is typical of the Romantic era, as is the work's somber minor key. In the concerto, your interest will be drawn sometimes to the soloist, performing virtuoso passages, and at other times to the orchestra.

In addition to the works being performed, the printed program may include short notes about each composition and biographical sketches about the soloist and conductor.

DURING THE PERFORMANCE

Concert etiquette There are certain concert conventions and rules of etiquette of which you should be aware. The house lights are usually dimmed just before the concert begins. Out of consideration for the performers and those around you, be sure your cell phone or pager is turned off and that you do not make noise with candy wrappers or shuffling papers if you are taking notes. It is customary to applaud at the entrances of performers, soloists, and conductors. In an orchestra concert, the concertmaster (the first violinist) will make an entrance and then tune the orchestra by asking the oboe player to play a pitch, to which all the instruments tune in turn. When the orchestra falls silent, the conductor enters, and, after another round of applause, the performance begins.

Knowing when to applaud during a concert is part of the necessary etiquette. Generally, the audience claps after complete works such as a symphony, a concerto, a sonata, or a song cycle, rather than between movements of a multimovement work. Sometimes, short works are grouped together on the program, suggesting that they are a set. In this case, applause is generally suitable at the close of the group. If you are unsure, follow the lead of others in the audience. At the opera the conventions are a little different; the audience might interrupt with applause after a particularly fine delivery of an aria or an ensemble number.

THE PERFORMERS

Onstage decorum You might be surprised at the formality of the performers' dress. It is traditional for ensemble players to wear black—long dresses or black pants and tops for the women, tuxedos or tails for the men—to minimize visual distraction. Soloists, however, often dress more colorfully.

Other formal traditions prevail for concerts. For example, the entire orchestra may stand at the entrance of the conductor, who shakes the hand of the first violinist before beginning. A small group, such as a string quartet, will often bow to the audience in unison. The conductor or solo performer often does not speak to the audience until the close of the program—although this tradition is changing—and then only if an additional piece or two is demanded by the extended applause. In this case, the *encore* (French for "again," and used for an added piece) is generally announced.

Some musicians—especially pianists, singers, and instrumental soloists—perform

IN HER OWN WORDS

Applause is the fulfillment . . . . Once you get on the stage, everything is right. I feel the most beautiful, complete, fulfilled.

—LEONTYNE PRICE

Martha Argerich performs a piano concerto with the Houston Symphony Orchestra at the Lucerne Concert Hall in Switzerland.

long, complex works from memory. To perform without music requires intense concentration and many arduous hours of study and practice before the concert.

Even if you are familiar with some of the above observations, you will sense an aura of suspense surrounding concerts. You should try to take full advantage of the opportunities available—try something completely unfamiliar, perhaps the opera or the symphony, and continue enjoying concerts of whatever music you already like.

For more information about concertgoing and for sample concert reports visit the StudySpace at www.wwnorton.com/enjoy.

I

Melody: Musical Line

CD iMaterials

"It is the melody which is the charm of music, and it is that which is most difficult to produce. The invention of a fine melody is a work of genius."

—JOSEPH HAYDN

| KEY POINTS | (S) StudySpace online at www.wwnorton.com/enjoy |

- A *melody* is the line, or tune, in music, a concept that is shared by most cultures.
- Each melody is unique in its *contour* (how it moves up and down) and in its *range*, or span of pitches.
- An *interval* is the distance between any two pitches in a melody. A melody that moves in small,

connected intervals is considered *conjunct*, while one that moves by leaps is called *disjunct*.

- The units that make up a melody are *phrases*.
- Phrases end in resting places called *cadences*.
- A melody may be accompanied by a secondary melody, or a *countermelody*.

The skyline of the majestic Grand Teton mountains in Wyoming resembles the rise and fall of melodic lines.

Melody is the element in music that appeals most directly to the listener. It is what we remember, what we whistle and hum. We know a good melody when we hear one, and we recognize its power to move us. We will see that melody is a universal concept shared by most musical cultures of the world.

Defining Melody

A **melody** is a succession of single pitches that we perceive as a recognizable whole. We relate to the pitches of a melody in the same way we hear the words of a sentence—not singly but as an entire cohesive thought. Each melody has its own distinct character based on its range, contour, and movement. A melody goes up and down, with one pitch being higher or lower than another; its **range** is the distance between the lowest and highest notes. This span can be very narrow, as in a children's song that is easy to sing, or very wide, as in some melodies played on an instrument. Although this distance can be measured in numbers of notes, we will describe range in approximate terms—narrow, medium, or wide.

Range

The **contour** of a melody is its overall shape as it turns upward, downward, or remains static. We can visualize a melody in a simple line graph, resulting in an ascending or descending line, an arch, or a wave (see Melodic Examples on facing page).

Contour

The distance between any two pitches of a melody is called an **interval**. Melodies that move principally by small intervals in a joined, connected manner are called **conjunct**, while those that move in larger, disconnected intervals are described as **disjunct**. The movement of a melody does not necessarily remain the same throughout: it may, for example, begin with a small range and conjunct motion and, as it develops, expand its range and become more disjunct.

Interval

Conjunct and disjunct movement

The Structure of Melody

The component units of a melody are like parts of a sentence. A **phrase** in music, as in language, is a unit of meaning within a larger structure. The phrase ends in a resting place, or **cadence**, which punctuates the music in the same way that a comma or period punctuates a sentence. The cadence may be inconclusive, leaving the listener with the impression that more is to come, or it may sound final, giving the listener the sense that the melody has reached the end. The cadence is where a singer or instrumentalist pauses to draw a breath.

Phrase

Cadence

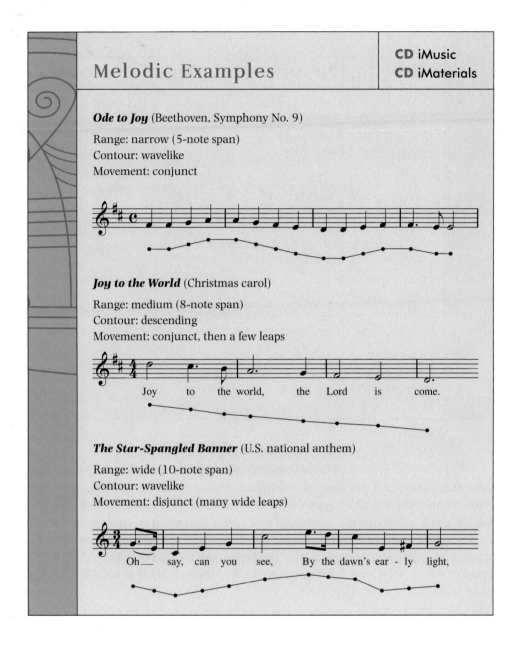

Melodic Examples

CD iMusic
CD iMaterials

Ode to Joy (Beethoven, Symphony No. 9)

Range: narrow (5-note span)
Contour: wavelike
Movement: conjunct

Joy to the World (Christmas carol)

Range: medium (8-note span)
Contour: descending
Movement: conjunct, then a few leaps

Joy   to   the world,   the   Lord   is   come.

The Star-Spangled Banner (U.S. national anthem)

Range: wide (10-note span)
Contour: wavelike
Movement: disjunct (many wide leaps)

Oh— say, can you   see,   By the dawn's ear - ly   light,

If the melody has words, the text lines and the musical phrases will generally coincide. Let's consider the well-known hymn *Amazing Grace* (see p. 14). Its four phrases, both the text and the music, are of equal length, and the rhyme scheme of the text is *a-b-a-b*. (The **rhyme scheme** of a poem describes the similarity in sound of the last syllables in each line—here they are "sound," "me," "found," and "see.") The first three cadences (at the end of each of the first three phrases) are inconclusive, or incomplete; notice the upward inflection like a question at the end of the second phrase. The fourth phrase, with its final downward motion, provides the answer; it gives the listener a sense of closure.

Rhyme scheme

A world of variety is possible when it comes to forming melodies. In order to maintain the listener's interest, a melody must be shaped carefully, either by the composer who plans it out in advance or by the performer who invents it on the spot. What makes a striking effect is the **climax,** the high point in a melodic line, which usually represents a peak in intensity as well as in range. Sing through, or listen to, *The Star-Spangled Banner* and note its climax in the last stirring phrase, when the line rises to the words "O'er the land of the free."

Climax

Melodic Phrases and Cadences

CD iMusic
CD iMaterials

Amazing Grace (traditional hymn):
4 text phrases = 4 musical phrases
Final cadence = end of verse

A · maz · ing grace, how sweet the sound
Phrase 1

That saved a wretch like me!
Phrase 2

I once was lost, but now am found,
Phrase 3

Was blind, but now I see.
Phrase 4

More complex music can feature several simultaneous melodies. Sometimes the relative importance of one melody over the other is clear, and the added tune is called a ***countermelody*** (literally, "against a melody"). In other styles, each melodic line is of seemingly equal importance, as we will note in our discussion of musical texture.

Countermelody

For much of the music we will study, melody is the most basic element of communication between the composer or performer and the listener. As the twentieth-century composer Aaron Copland aptly put it, "The melody is generally what the piece is about."

Line is as important in art as in music. Notice how the eye is drawn to the disjunct movement implied in the mobile sculpture from 1955, by **Alexander Calder** (1898–1976).

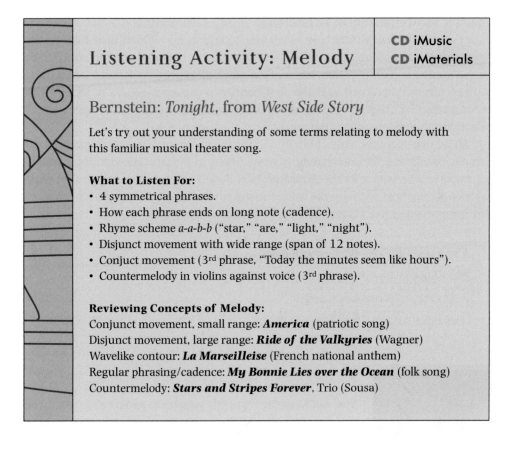

Listening Activity: Melody

CD iMusic
CD iMaterials

Bernstein: *Tonight,* from *West Side Story*

Let's try out your understanding of some terms relating to melody with this familiar musical theater song.

What to Listen For:
- 4 symmetrical phrases.
- How each phrase ends on long note (cadence).
- Rhyme scheme *a-a-b-b* ("star," "are," "light," "night").
- Disjunct movement with wide range (span of 12 notes).
- Conjuct movement (3rd phrase, "Today the minutes seem like hours").
- Countermelody in violins against voice (3rd phrase).

Reviewing Concepts of Melody:
Conjunct movement, small range: *America* (patriotic song)
Disjunct movement, large range: *Ride of the Valkyries* (Wagner)
Wavelike contour: *La Marseilleise* (French national anthem)
Regular phrasing/cadence: *My Bonnie Lies over the Ocean* (folk song)
Countermelody: *Stars and Stripes Forever*, Trio (Sousa)

2

Rhythm and Meter: Musical Time
CD iMaterials

"I got rhythm, I got music. . ."

—IRA GERSHWIN

KEY POINTS	Ⓢ **StudySpace** online at www.wwnorton.com/enjoy

- ○ *Rhythm* is what moves music forward in time.
- ○ *Meter*, marked off in *measures*, organizes the *beats* in music.
- ○ Measures often begin with a strong *downbeat*.
- ○ *Simple meters*—duple, triple, and quadruple—are the most common.

- ○ *Compound meters* subdivide each beat into three, rather than two, subbeats.
- ○ Rhythmic complexities occur with *upbeats, offbeats, syncopation*, and *polyrhythm*.
- ○ *Additive meters* are used in some world musics.
- ○ Some music is *nonmetric* or has an obscured pulse.

Music is propelled forward by *rhythm*, the movement of music in time. Each individual note has a length, or duration—some long and some short. The *beat* is the basic unit of rhythm—it is a regular pulse that divides time into equal segments. Some beats are stronger than others—we perceive these as *accented*, or strong, beats. In

Beat

much of the Western music we hear, these strong beats occur at regular intervals—every other beat, every third beat, every fourth, and so on—and thus we hear groupings of two, three, four, or so on. These organizing patterns of rhythmic pulses are called **meters** and, in notation, are marked off in **measures.** Each measure contains a fixed number of beats, and the first beat in a measure generally receives the strongest accent. Measures are marked off by **measure lines**, regular vertical lines through the staff (on which the music is notated; see p. A-4).

Meter organizes the flow of rhythm in music. In Western music, its patterns are simple, paralleling the alternating accents heard in poetry. Consider, for example, this well-known stanza by the American poet Robert Frost. It has a meter that alternates a strong beat with a weak one. A metrical reading of the poem will bring out the regular pattern of accented (´) and unaccented (‾) syllables:

The woods are love-ly, dark and deep.
But I have prom-is-es to keep,
And miles to go be-fore I sleep,
And miles to go be-fore I sleep.

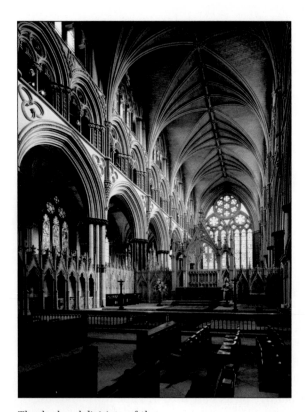

The duple subdivisions of the bays above the vaulted arches in Lincoln Cathedral (c. 1282) in England can be compared to simple meters in music.

Metrical Patterns

You will hear the regularly recurring patterns of two, three, or four beats in much of the music we will study. As in poetry, these patterns, or meters, depend on the regular recurrence of an accent. In music, the first accented beat of each pattern is known as a **downbeat**, referring to the downward stroke of a conductor's hand (see conducting patterns on p. 55). The most basic pattern, known as **duple meter**, alternates a strong downbeat with a weak beat: ONE-two, ONE-two, or, in marching, LEFT-right, LEFT-right.

Triple meter, another basic pattern, has three beats to a measure—one strong beat and two weak ones (ONE-two-three). This meter is traditionally associated with dances such as the waltz and the minuet.

Quadruple meter contains four beats to the measure, with a primary accent on the first beat and a secondary accent on the third. Although it is sometimes difficult to distinguish duple and quadruple meter, quadruple meter usually has a broader feeling.

Meters in which the beat has duple subdivisions are called **simple meters.** However, in some patterns, the beat is divided into three; these are known as **compound meters.** The most common compound meter is **sextuple meter,** which has six beats to the measure, with accents on beats one and four (ONE-two-three, FOUR-five-six). Marked by a gently flowing effect, this pattern is often found in lullabies and nursery rhymes:

Lit – tle Boy Blue, come blow your horn, the
sheep's in the meadow, the cow's in the corn.

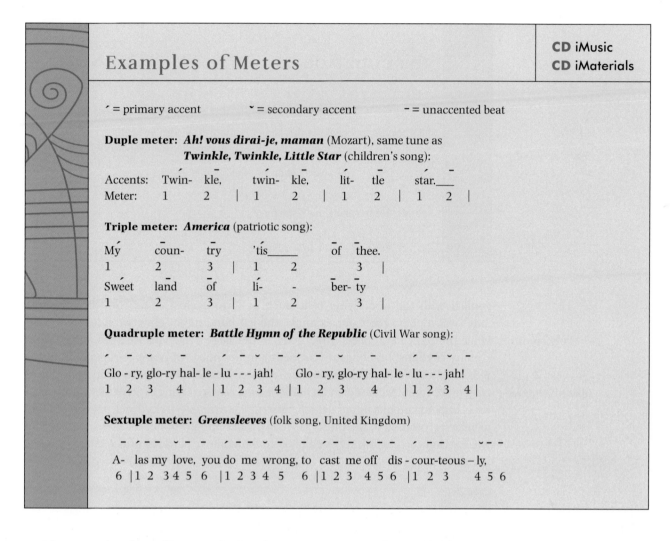

Examples of Meters

CD iMusic
CD iMaterials

´ = primary accent   ˘ = secondary accent   ‾ = unaccented beat

Duple meter: *Ah! vous dirai-je, maman* (Mozart), same tune as
**   *Twinkle, Twinkle, Little Star*** (children's song):

Accents:	Twin-	kle,	twin-	kle,	lit-	tle	star.___	
Meter:	1	2	1	2	1	2	1	2

Triple meter: *America* (patriotic song):

My	coun-	try	'tis____		of	thee.
1	2	3	1	2		3
Sweet	land	of	li-	-	ber-	ty
1	2	3	1	2		3

Quadruple meter: *Battle Hymn of the Republic* (Civil War song):

Glo - ry, glo-ry hal- le - lu - - - jah!   Glo - ry, glo-ry hal- le - lu - - - jah!
1   2   3   4 |1 2 3 4 |1   2   3   4 | 1 2 3 4 |

Sextuple meter: *Greensleeves* (folk song, United Kingdom)

A- las my love, you do me wrong, to cast me off dis - cour-teous – ly,
6 |1 2 34 5 6 |1 2 3 4 5   6 |1 2 3 4 5 6 |1 2 3   4 5 6

The examples above illustrate the four basic patterns. Not all pieces begin on a downbeat (or beat one). For example, *Greensleeves* is in sextuple meter and begins with an **upbeat**, that is, the last beat of the measure. (Notice that the Frost poem given earlier is in duple meter and begins with an upbeat on "the.")

Composers have devised a number of ways to keep the recurrent accent from becoming monotonous. The most common technique is **syncopation**, a deliberate upsetting of the normal pattern of accentuation. Instead of falling on the strong beat of the measure, the accent is shifted to a weak beat or to an **offbeat** (in between the stronger beats). Syncopation is a device used in the music of all centuries and is particularly characteristic of the African-American dance rhythms out of which jazz developed. The example on page 18 illustrates the technique.

Syncopation is only one technique that throws off the regular patterns. A composition may change meters during its course. Indeed, certain twentieth-century pieces shift meters nearly every measure. Another technique is the simultaneous use of rhythmic patterns that

Like meter in music, basic repeated patterns provide the interest in this painting by artist **Robert Delaunay** (1885–1941). *Rhythm No. 1*, 1937.

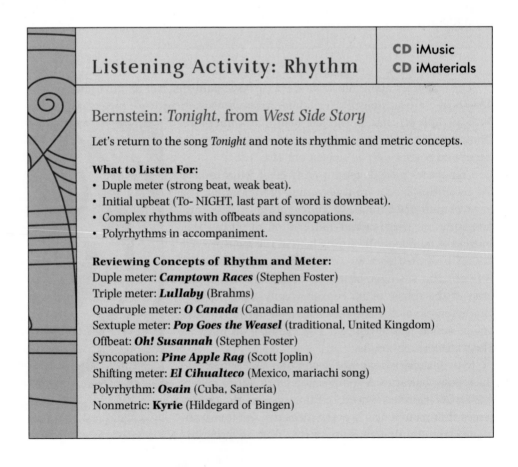

Syncopation

CD iMusic
CD iMaterials

Swing Low, Sweet Chariot (African-American spiritual):

Try singing or speaking this song in time with a regular beat.
(Note that the words in the first measure come between the beats.)

Swing low,_____ sweet char   i- ot,_____
1   2 | 1   2 |

comin' for to car-ry me   home   _____
1   2 | 1   2 |

conflict with the underlying beat, such as "two against three" or "three against four"—in a piano piece, for example, the left hand might play two notes to a beat, while the right hand plays three notes to the same beat. This is called ***polyrhythm*** ("many rhythms") and occurs frequently in the music of many African cultures as well as in jazz and rock. In some non-Western musics, the rhythmic organization is even more complex, based on an ***additive meter***, or grouping of irregular numbers of beats that add up to a larger overall pattern. For example, a rhythmic pattern of fourteen beats common in the music of India divides into groupings of $2 + 4 + 4 + 4$. We will see that certain folk styles employ similar additive patterns of accents.

Polyrhythm

Additive meter

Listening Activity: Rhythm

CD iMusic
CD iMaterials

Bernstein: *Tonight*, from *West Side Story*

Let's return to the song *Tonight* and note its rhythmic and metric concepts.

What to Listen For:
- Duple meter (strong beat, weak beat).
- Initial upbeat (To- NIGHT, last part of word is downbeat).
- Complex rhythms with offbeats and syncopations.
- Polyrhythms in accompaniment.

Reviewing Concepts of Rhythm and Meter:
Duple meter: ***Camptown Races*** (Stephen Foster)
Triple meter: ***Lullaby*** (Brahms)
Quadruple meter: ***O Canada*** (Canadian national anthem)
Sextuple meter: ***Pop Goes the Weasel*** (traditional, United Kingdom)
Offbeat: ***Oh! Susannah*** (Stephen Foster)
Syncopation: ***Pine Apple Rag*** (Scott Joplin)
Shifting meter: ***El Cihualteco*** (Mexico, mariachi song)
Polyrhythm: ***Osain*** (Cuba, Santería)
Nonmetric: ***Kyrie*** (Hildegard of Bingen)

Some music moves without any strong sense of beat or meter. We might say that such a work is *nonmetric* (this is the case in the chants of the early Christian church) or that the pulse is veiled or weak, with the music moving in a floating rhythm that typifies certain non-Western styles.

Nonmetric

Time is a crucial dimension in music, and music's first law is rhythm. This is the element that binds together the parts within the whole: the notes within the measure and the measure within the phrase. It is thereby the most fundamental element of music.

3

Harmony: Musical Space

CD iMaterials

"We have learned to express the more delicate nuances of feeling by penetrating more deeply into the mysteries of harmony."
　　　　　　　　　　　　—ROBERT SCHUMANN

| KEY POINTS | Ⓢ **StudySpace** online at www.wwnorton.com/enjoy |

- *Harmony* describes the simultaneous events in music.
- A *chord* is the simultaneous sounding of three or more pitches; chords are built from a particular *scale*, or sequence of pitches.
- The most common chord in Western music is a *triad*, which has three notes built on alternate pitches of a scale.
- Most Western music is based on *major* or *minor scales*, from which melody and harmony are derived.

- The *tonic* is the central tone around which a melody and its harmonies are built; this principle of organization is called *tonality*.
- *Dissonance* is created by an unstable, or discordant, harmony, while *consonance* occurs with the resolution of dissonance, producing a concordant sound.
- In music of some cultures, a single sustained tone, or *drone*, constitutes the harmony.

To the linear movement of the melody, harmony adds another dimension: depth, which results from simultaneous events in music. Harmony can be compared to the concept of perspective in painting (see illustration, p. 20)—it introduces the impression of musical space. Not all musics of the world rely on harmony for interest, but it is central to most Western styles.

We know that an *interval* is the distance between any two tones. Intervals can occur successively—that is, when one note follows another—or simultaneously. When three or more tones are sounded together, a *chord* is produced. *Harmony* describes the simultaneous sounding of notes to form chords and the progression from one chord to the next. We hear chords in terms of their relationships to each other. Harmony therefore implies movement and progression. It is the progression of harmony in a musical work that creates a feeling of order and unity.

Chord and harmony

Let us consider first how simple chords are formed. The intervals from which

Scale and octave chords and melodies are built are chosen from a particular collection of pitches arranged in ascending or descending order known as a *scale*. To the tones of the scale we assign syllables, *do-re-mi-fa-sol-la-ti-do*, or numbers, 1–2–3–4–5–6–7–8. An interval of eight notes is called an *octave*.

Do	re	mi	fa	sol	la	ti	do
1	2	3	4	5	6	7	8

Octave

Triad The most common chord in Western music is a particular combination of three tones known as a *triad*. Such a chord may be built on any note of the scale by combining every other note. For example, a triad built on the first tone of a scale consists of the first, third, and fifth pitches of the scale *(do-mi-sol);* on the second degree, steps 2–4–6 *(re-fa-la);* and so on. The triad is a basic formation in our music. In the example on p. 21, the melody of *Camptown Races* is harmonized with triads. We can see at a glance how melody is the horizontal aspect of music, while harmony, comprising blocks of tones (the chords), constitutes the vertical. Melody and harmony do not function independently of one another. On the contrary, the melody suggests the harmony that goes with it, and each constantly influences the other.

The Organization of Harmony

Tonic In all music, regardless of the style, certain tones assume greater importance than others. In Western music, the first note of the scale, *do,* is considered the **tonic** and serves as a home base around which the others revolve and to which they ultimately gravitate. We observed this principle at work earlier with the tune *Amazing Grace* (p. 14), noting that it does not have a final cadence until its last phrase. It is this sense

Harmony lends a sense of depth to music, as perspective does in this photograph, by **Fernand Ivaldi**, of a view down a tree-lined canal in France.

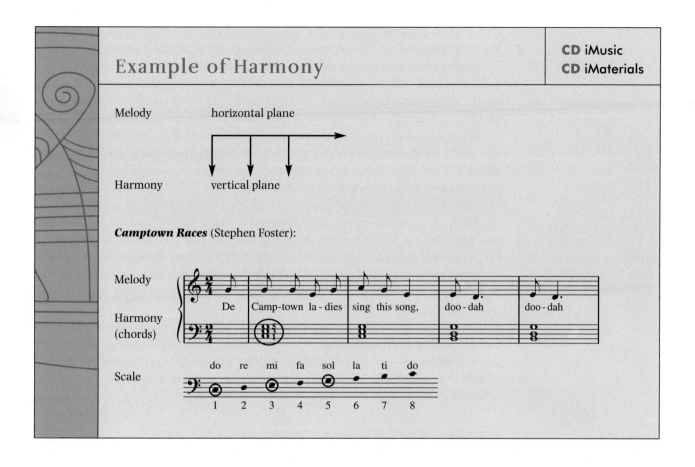

Example of Harmony

CD iMusic
CD iMaterials

Melody — horizontal plane

Harmony — vertical plane

Camptown Races (Stephen Foster):

Melody / Harmony (chords) / Scale

De | Camp-town la-dies | sing this song, | doo-dah | doo-dah

do re mi fa sol la ti do
1 2 3 4 5 6 7 8

of a home base that helps us recognize when a piece of music ends.

The principle of organization around a central tone, the tonic, is called ***tonality.*** The scale chosen as the basis of a piece determines the identity of the tonic and the tonality. Two different types of scales predominate in Western music written between about 1650 and 1900: major and minor. Each scale has a distinct sound because of its unique combination of intervals. (We will learn more about the formulation of scales later, in Chapter 17.) For the moment, we should note the difference in character or mood between scales: music in major is usually thought of as bright or cheerful, while minor often sounds more subdued and sometimes sad. A composer would not be likely to choose a minor tonality for a triumphal march, nor a major tonality for a lament.

Consonance and Dissonance

The movement of harmony toward resolution is the dynamic force in Western music. It shapes the forward movement, providing focus and direction. As music moves in time, we feel moments of tension and release. The tension is a perceived instability that results from ***dissonance***, a combination of tones

Just as dissonance provides tension in music, the discord and conflict in life is underscored by this juxtaposition of a slum in São Paulo, Brazil, against modern, high-rise apartments in the background.

Dissonance

Consonance

that sounds discordant, in need of resolution. Dissonance introduces conflict into music in the same way that suspense creates tension in drama. Dissonance resolves in *consonance*, a concordant, or agreeable, combination of musical tones that provides a sense of relaxation and fulfillment. At their extremes, dissonance can sound harsh, while consonance is more pleasing to the ear. Each complements the other, and each is a necessary part of the artistic whole.

In general, music has grown more dissonant through the ages. You may wonder why this is so. A combination of tones that sound extremely harsh when first introduced will seem less dissonant as the sound becomes increasingly familiar through frequent exposure to it. As a result, each later generation of composers uses ever more dissonant harmonies in order to maintain a high level of excitement and tension.

Harmony appeared much later historically than melody and its development took place largely in Western music. In many Asian cultures, harmony is relatively simple, consisting of a single sustained tone, called a *drone*, against which melodic and rhythmic complexities unfold. This harmonic principle also occurs in some types of European folk music, where, for example, a bagpipe might play one or more accompanying drones to a lively dance tune.

Our system of harmony has advanced steadily over the past millennium (harmony was first introduced around the year 900), continually responding to new needs. Composers have tested the rules as they have experimented with innovative sounds and procedures. Yet their goal remains the same: to impose order on sound, organizing the pitches so that we perceive a unified idea.

IN HIS OWN WORDS

Do you know that our soul is composed of harmony?
—LEONARDO DA VINCI

Listening Activity: Harmony

CD iMusic
CD iMaterials

Haydn: Symphony No. 94 in G major (*Surprise*), second movement

This symphonic work will help us recognize elements of harmony.

What to Listen For:
- Simple, folklike melody with accompaniment (chords).
- Melody and chords built on a major scale (sounds cheery and bright).
- Melody revolving around a central tone, or tonic.
- "Surprise" as a loud, crashing chord, or block of harmony.
- Changes to minor tonality, becoming louder, more dramatic, and emotional.
- Return to original melody and chords, built on major scale.
- Predominate consonant harmonies.

Reviewing Concepts of Harmony:
Chord: *If I Had a Hammer* (Pete Seeger)
Tonic: *Greensleeves* (folk song, United Kingdom)
Major scale and tonality: *Joy to the World* (Christmas carol)
Minor scale and tonality: *Moonlight* Sonata (Beethoven)
Consonance: *America* (patriotic song)
Dissonance: "In the lovely month of May" (Schumann)
Drone: *Skye Crofters* (bagpipe, Scottish dance music)

4

Musical Texture

CD iMaterials

"The composer . . . joins Heaven and Earth with threads of sound."
—ALAN HOVHANESS

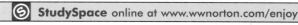

KEY POINTS	**StudySpace** online at www.wwnorton.com/enjoy

- ○ *Texture* refers to the interweaving of the melodic lines with harmony in music.
- ○ The simplest texture is *monophony,* or single-voiced music without accompaniment.
- ○ *Heterophony* refers to multiple voices elaborating the same melody at the same time.
- ○ *Polyphony* describes a many-voiced texture based on *counterpoint*—one line set against another.

- ○ *Homophony* occurs when one melodic voice is prominent over the accompanying lines, or voices; *homorhythmic texture* is a subcategory of homophony in which all the voices move in the same rhythm.
- ○ *Imitation*—when a melodic idea is presented in one voice, then restated in another—is a common unifying technique in polyphony; *canons* and *rounds* are two types of strictly imitative works.

Types of Texture

Melodic lines may be thought of as the various threads that make up the musical fabric, or the *texture*. The simplest texture is *monophony*, or single-voiced. ("Voice" refers to an individual part or line, even when we are talking about instrumental music.) Here, the melody is heard without any harmonic accompaniment or other melodic lines. It may be accompanied by rhythm and percussion instruments that embellish it, but interest is focused on the single melodic line rather than on any harmony. Until about a thousand years ago, the Western music we know about was monophonic, as some music of the Far and Middle East still is today.

One type of texture widely found outside the tradition of Western art music is based on two or more voices (lines) simultaneously elaborating the same melody, usually in an improvised performance. Called *heterophony*, this technique usually results in a melody combined with an ornamented version of itself. It can be heard too in some folk musics as well as in jazz and spirituals, where *improvisation* (in which some of the music is created on the spot) is central to performance.

Distinct from heterophony is *polyphony* ("many-voiced" texture), in which two or more different melodic lines are combined, thus distributing melodic interest among all the parts. Polyphonic texture is based on *counterpoint*. This term comes from the Latin *punctus contra punctum*, "point against point" or "note against note"—that is, one musical line set against another. Counterpoint is the art of combining two or more simultaneous melodic lines, usually with rules defined in a particular era.

Line and texture are the subject of **Paul Klee**'s (1879–1940) painting *Neighborhood of the Florentine Villas* (1926).

Homophony   In another commonly heard texture, **_homophony_**, a single voice takes over the melodic interest, while the accompanying lines take a subordinate role. Normally, they become blocks of harmony, the chords that support, color, and enhance the principal line. Here, the listener's interest is directed to a single melodic line, but this is conceived in relation to harmony. Homophonic texture is heard when a pianist plays a melody in the right hand while the left sounds the chords, or when a singer or violinist carries the

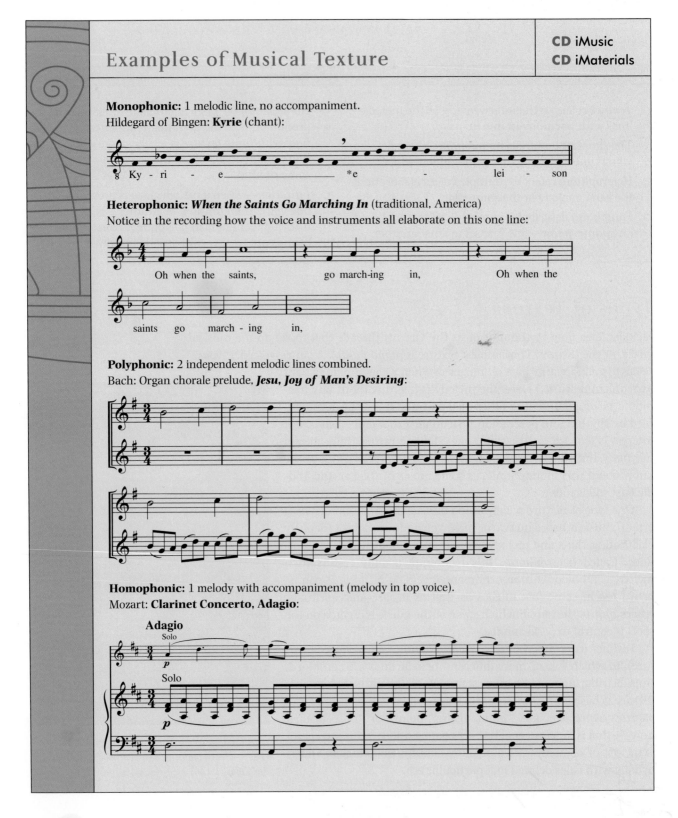

Examples of Musical Texture

CD iMusic
CD iMaterials

Monophonic: 1 melodic line, no accompaniment.
Hildegard of Bingen: **Kyrie** (chant):

Ky - ri - e⸻ *e - lei - son

Heterophonic: ***When the Saints Go Marching In*** (traditional, America)
Notice in the recording how the voice and instruments all elaborate on this one line:

Oh when the   saints,   go march-ing   in,   Oh when the

saints   go   march - ing   in,

Polyphonic: 2 independent melodic lines combined.
Bach: Organ chorale prelude, ***Jesu, Joy of Man's Desiring***:

Homophonic: 1 melody with accompaniment (melody in top voice).
Mozart: **Clarinet Concerto, Adagio**:

Adagio
Solo
Solo

Homorhythmic: a type of homophonic texture with all voices moving together. Handel: **"Hallelujah Chorus,"** opening, from ***Messiah***:

tune against a harmonic accompaniment on the piano. Homophonic texture, then, is based on harmony, just as polyphonic texture is based on counterpoint.

Finally, there is ***homorhythm***, a kind of homophony where all the voices, or lines, move together in the same rhythm. When there is text, all words are clearly sounded together. Like homophonic structure, it is based on harmony moving in synchronization with a melody.

Homorhythm

A composition need not use one texture exclusively throughout. For example, a large-scale work may begin by presenting a melody with accompanying lines (homophony), after which the interaction of the parts becomes increasingly complex as more independent melodies enter (creating polyphony).

We have noted that melody is the horizontal aspect of music, while harmony is the vertical. Comparing musical texture to the cross weave of a fabric makes the interplay of the parts clear. The horizontal threads, the melodies, are held together by the vertical threads, the harmonies. Out of their interaction comes a texture that may be light or heavy, coarse or fine.

Contrapuntal Devices

When several independent lines are combined (in polyphony), one method that composers use to give unity and shape to the texture is ***imitation***, in which a melodic idea is presented in one voice and then restated in another. While the imitating voice restates the melody, the first voice continues with new material. Thus, in addition to the vertical and horizontal threads in musical texture, a third, diagonal line results from imitation (see the example on p. 26).

Imitation

The duration of the imitation may be brief or it may last the entire work. A strictly imitative work is known as a ***canon***. (The name comes from the Greek word for "law" or "order.") The simplest and most familiar form of canon is a ***round***, in which each voice enters in succession with the same melody, that can be repeated endlessly. Well-known examples include *Row, Row, Row Your Boat* and *Frère Jacques* (*Are You Sleeping?*). In the example on page 26, the round begins with one voice singing "Row, row, row your boat," then another voice joins it in imitation, followed by a third voice and finally a fourth, creating a four-part polyphonic texture.

Canon and round

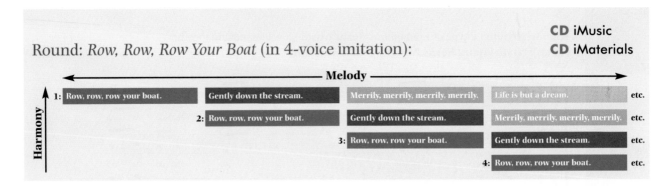

Round: *Row, Row, Row Your Boat* (in 4-voice imitation):

CD iMusic
CD iMaterials

Musical Texture and the Listener

Different textures require different kinds of listening. Monophonic music has only one focus—the single line of melody unfolding in real time. In homophonic music, the primary focus is on the main melody with subordinate harmonies as accompaniment. Indeed, much of the music we have heard since childhood—including many traditional and popular styles—consists of melody and accompanying chords. Homorhythmic texture is easily recognizable as well, in its simple, vertical conception and hymnlike movement. Here, the melody is still the most obvious line. Polyphonic music, with several independent melodies woven together, requires more experienced listening. The simplest polyphonic texture is the round. With practice, we can hear the roles of individual voices and determine how they relate to each other, providing texture throughout a musical work.

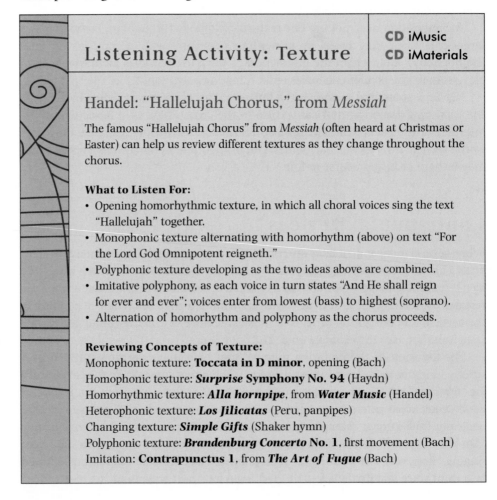

Listening Activity: Texture

CD iMusic
CD iMaterials

Handel: "Hallelujah Chorus," from *Messiah*

The famous "Hallelujah Chorus" from *Messiah* (often heard at Christmas or Easter) can help us review different textures as they change throughout the chorus.

What to Listen For:
- Opening homorhythmic texture, in which all choral voices sing the text "Hallelujah" together.
- Monophonic texture alternating with homorhythm (above) on text "For the Lord God Omnipotent reigneth."
- Polyphonic texture developing as the two ideas above are combined.
- Imitative polyphony, as each voice in turn states "And He shall reign for ever and ever"; voices enter from lowest (bass) to highest (soprano).
- Alternation of homorhythm and polyphony as the chorus proceeds.

Reviewing Concepts of Texture:
Monophonic texture: **Toccata in D minor**, opening (Bach)
Homophonic texture: ***Surprise* Symphony No. 94** (Haydn)
Homorhythmic texture: ***Alla hornpipe***, from ***Water Music*** (Handel)
Heterophonic texture: ***Los Jilicatas*** (Peru, panpipes)
Changing texture: ***Simple Gifts*** (Shaker hymn)
Polyphonic texture: ***Brandenburg Concerto* No. 1**, first movement (Bach)
Imitation: **Contrapunctus 1**, from ***The Art of Fugue*** (Bach)

5

Musical Form

"The principal function of form is to advance our understanding. It is the organization of a piece that helps the listener to keep the idea in mind, to follow its development, its growth, its elaboration, its fate."

—ARNOLD SCHOENBERG

KEY POINTS

 StudySpace online at www.wwnorton.com/enjoy

- ○ *Form* is the organizing principle in music; its basic elements are repetition, contrast, and variation.
- ○ *Strophic form*, common in songs, features repeated music for each stanza of text.
- ○ Some music is created spontaneously in performance, through *improvisation*.
- ○ *Binary form* (**A-B**) and *ternary form* (**A-B-A**) are basic structures in music.
- ○ A *theme* is a melodic idea used as a building block in a large-scale work and can be broken into small,

- component fragments known as *motives*. A *sequence* results when a motive is repeated at a different pitch.
- ○ Many cultures use *call-and-response* (or *responsorial*) music, a repetitive style involving a soloist and a group.
- ○ An *ostinato* is the repetition of a short musical melodic, rhythmic, or harmonic pattern.
- ○ Large-scale compositions, such as symphonies and sonatas, are divided into sections, or *movements*.

Form refers to a work's structure or shape, the way the elements of a composition have been combined, or balanced, by the composer to make it understandable to the listener. In all the arts, a balance is required between unity and variety, symmetry and asymmetry, activity and repose. Nature too has embodied this balance in the forms of plant and animal life and in what is perhaps the supreme achievement—the human form.

Structure and Design in Music

Music of all cultures mirrors life in its basic structural elements of *repetition* and *contrast*—the familiar and the new. Repetition fixes the material in our minds and satisfies our need for the familiar, while contrast stimulates our interest and feeds our desire for change. The contours of musical form come from the interaction between the repeated elements and the contrasting ones. Every kind of musical work, from a nursery rhyme to a symphony, has a conscious structure. One of the most common in vocal music, both popular and classical, is *strophic form*, in which the same melody is repeated with each stanza of the text. In this structure, while the music of one stanza offers contrast, the repetition binds the song together.

Repetition and contrast

Strophic form

One principle of form that falls between repetition and contrast is *variation*, where some aspects of the music are altered but the original is still recognizable. We hear this formal technique when we listen to a new arrangement of a well-known popular song: the tune is recognizable, but many features of the version we know may be changed. All musical structures are based in one way or another on

Variation

The Gates in Central Park (2005), by artists **Christo** and **Jeanne-Claude**, show the reliance of art on the basic element of repetition. This massive public art installation included 7,500 orange gates extending over 23 miles of footpaths in New York's Central Park.

repetition and contrast. The forms, however, are not fixed molds into which composers pour their material. What makes each piece of music unique is the way the composer adapts a general plan to create a wholly individual combination. We will see that no two symphonies of Haydn or Mozart, no two sonatas of Beethoven, are exactly alike. Each work presents a fresh and distinctive solution to the problem of fashioning musical material into a logical and coherent form.

Performers sometimes participate in shaping a composition. In works based primarily on *improvisation* (pieces created spontaneously in performance—typical of jazz, rock, and in certain non-Western styles), all the elements described above—repetition, contrast, and variation—play a role. Thus, even when a piece is created on the spot, a balance of these structural principles is present.

Two-Part and Three-Part Form

Binary and ternary form

Two of the most basic structural patterns found in art and in music are two-part, or *binary* form, based on a statement and a departure, without a return to the complete opening section; and three-part, or *ternary*, form, which extends the idea of statement and departure by bringing back the first section. Formal patterns are generally outlined with letters: binary form as **A-B** and ternary form as **A-B-A** (illustrated in the chart on the facing page).

Both two-part and three-part forms are common in short pieces such as songs and dances. Ternary form, with its logical symmetry and its balance of the outer sections against the contrasting middle one, constitutes a clear-cut formation that is favored by architects and painters as well as musicians.

The Building Blocks of Form

Theme

When a melodic idea is used as a building block in the construction of a larger musical work, we call it a *theme*. The introduction of a theme and its spinning out, sometimes weaving and reweaving its lines, is the essence of musical thinking. This

Binary and Ternary Form

Binary form: *Greensleeves* (traditional, United Kingdom)

Statement **A** (repeated with varied final cadences):

Departure **B** (with different cadences):

Ternary Form: *Simple Gifts* (Shaker hymn)

Statement **A** (repeated):

'Tis the gift to be sim-ple, 'tis the gift to be free, 'Tis the gift to come down where we ought to be, And when we find our-selves_ in the

Departure **B** (ending resembles **A** with new text):

When true sim-pli-ci-ty is gained, To bow and to bend we will not be a-shamed. To turn,_ to_ turn,_ will_ be our de-light, And by

Repeated Statement **A**:

'Tis the gift to be sim-ple, 'tis the gift to be free,

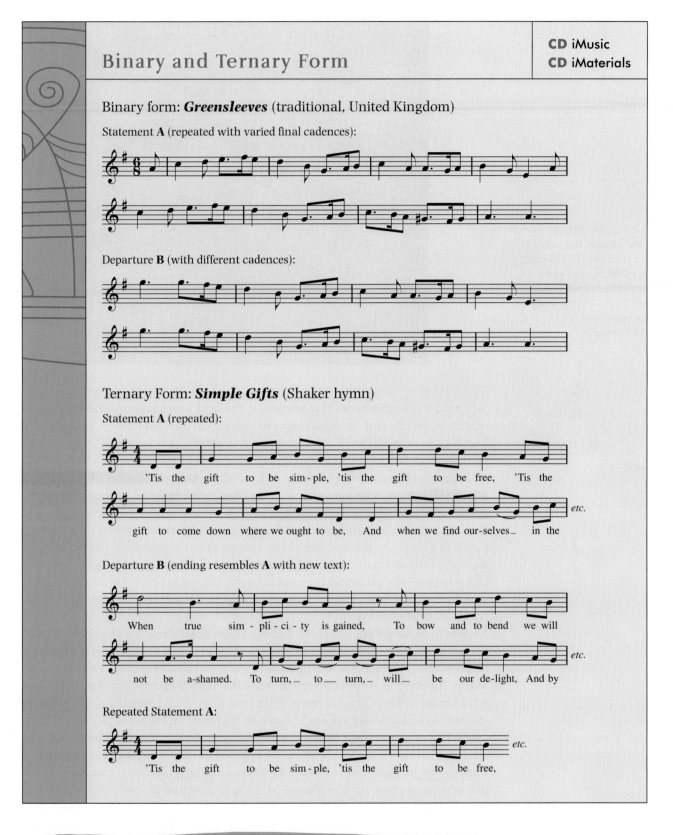

process of growth has its parallel in writing, where an idea—a topic sentence—is stated at the beginning of a paragraph and enlarged upon and developed by the author. Just as each sentence leads logically from one to the next, every phrase in a musical work takes up where the one before left off and continues convincingly to the next.

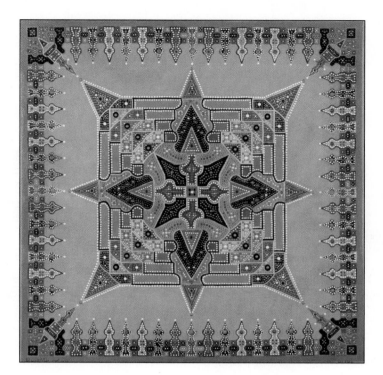

Some artists explore symmetrical patterns that relate to the compositional building blocks of motives and sequences in music. *Rosace* (1941), by **Fleury-Joseph Crépin** (1875–1948), is a good example.

Sequence and motive

Certain procedures aid the process of musical development. The simplest is repetition, which may be either exact or varied. Or the idea may be restated at a higher or lower pitch level; this restatement is known as a *sequence*. A melody, or theme, can be broken up into its component parts, or motives. A *motive* is the smallest fragment of a theme that forms a melodic-rhythmic unit. Motives are the cells of musical growth, which, when repeated, varied, and combined into new patterns, impart the qualities of evolution and expansion. These musical building blocks can be seen even in simple songs, such as the popular national tune *America* (see facing page). In this piece, the opening three-note motive ("My country") is repeated in sequence (at a different pitch level) on the words "Sweet land of." A longer melodic idea is treated sequentially in the second line of the work, where the musical phrase "Land where my fathers died" is repeated one note lower beginning on the words "Land of the pilgrim's pride."

Whatever the length or style of a composition, it will show the principles of repetition and contrast, of unity and variety. One formal practice based on repetition and

Call-and-response

heard in music throughout much of the world is *call-and-response*, or *responsorial music*. This style of performance, predominant in early Western church music, is also common in music of African, Native American, and African-American cultures, and involves a singing leader who is imitated by a chorus of followers. Another widely

Ostinato

used structural procedure linked to the principle of repetition is *ostinato*, a short musical pattern—melodic, rhythmic, or harmonic—that is repeated throughout a work or a major section of a composition. This unifying technique is especially prevalent in popular styles such as blues, jazz, rock, and rap, which rely on repeated harmonies that provide a scaffolding for musical development.

Movement

Music composition is an organic form in which the individual tones are bound together within a phrase, the phrases within a section, the sections within a *movement* (a complete, comparatively independent division of a large-scale work), and the movements within the work as a whole—just as a novel binds together the individual words, phrases, sentences, paragraphs, chapters, and parts.

Motive and Sequences

CD iMusic
CD iMaterials

America (also *God Save the Queen*):

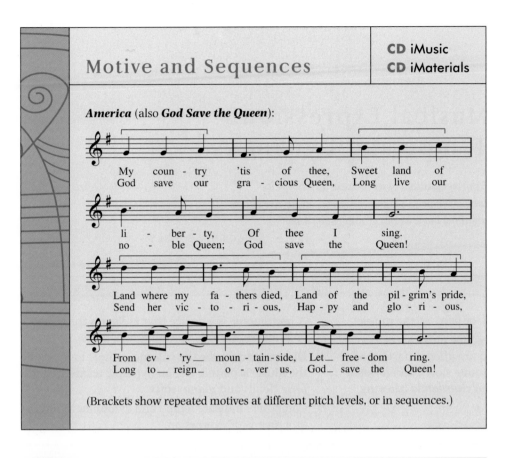

My coun - try 'tis of thee, Sweet land of
God save our gra - cious Queen, Long live our

li - ber - ty, Of thee I sing.
no - ble Queen; God save the Queen!

Land where my fa - thers died, Land of the pil - grim's pride,
Send her vic - to - ri - ous, Hap - py and glo - ri - ous,

From ev - 'ry__ moun - tain - side, Let__ free - dom ring.
Long to__ reign__ o - ver us, God__ save the Queen!

(Brackets show repeated motives at different pitch levels, or in sequences.)

Listening Activity: Musical Form

CD iMusic
CD iMaterials

Tchaikovsky: *March,* from *The Nutcracker*

The march from the popular ballet *The Nutcracker* helps us test our musical memory in listening for form, or structure, of a composition.

What to Listen For:
- Catchy, accented march tune set in 3-part form (ternary, **A-B-A**).
- Opening melody (**A**) played by brass, answered by strings, then repeated.
- Short middle section (**B**), with rushing downward lines; heard first in woodwinds, then in strings.
- Return of opening music (**A**), with variation in accompaniment.
- Use of basic formal components: repetition, contrast, variation.

Reviewing Concepts of Form:
Variation: ***Pop Goes the Weasel*** (traditional, United Kingdom)
Improvisation: ***Amazing Grace*** (traditional hymn)
Strophic form: ***Lullaby*** (Brahms)
Binary form: **Minuet in D** (*Anna Magdelena Notebook*)
Ternary form: ***March,*** from ***The Nutcracker*** (Tchaikovsky)
Motive and sequence: **Symphony No. 5** (Beethoven)
Responsorial: ***If I Had a Hammer*** (Pete Seeger)

6

CD iMaterials

Musical Expression: Tempo and Dynamics

"Any composition must necessarily possess its unique tempo. . . . A piece of mine can survive almost anything but a wrong or uncertain tempo."

—IGOR STRAVINSKY

KEY POINTS	**StudySpace** online at www.wwnorton.com/enjoy

- O **Tempo** is the rate of speed, or pace, of the music.
- O We use Italian terms to describe musical tempo: some of the most common are **allegro** (fast), **moderato** (moderate), **adagio** (quite slow), **accelerando** (speeding up the pace), and **ritardando** (slowing the pace).
- O A **metronome** is a device that indicates the tempo, or beats per minute, by sounding a pulse.
- O **Dynamics** describe the volume, or how loud or soft the music is played; Italian dynamic terms include **forte** (loud) and **piano** (soft).
- O Composers indicate tempo and dynamics in music as a means of expression.

The Pace of Music

We know that most Western music has steady beats underlying the movement; whether these occur slowly or rapidly determines the **tempo**, or rate of speed, of the music. Consequently, the flow of music in time involves meter patterns, governing the groupings and relative emphasis of the beats, and tempo.

Tempo carries emotional implications. We hurry our speech in moments of agitation or eagerness. Vigor and gaiety are associated with a brisk speed, just as despair usually demands a slow one. Music is a temporal art (one that moves in time), therefore its pace is of prime importance, drawing from listeners responses that are both physical and psychological.

Because of the close connection between tempo and mood, tempo markings indicate the character of the music as well as the pace. The markings, along with other indications of expression, are traditionally given in Italian. This practice reflects the domination of Italian music in Europe during the period from around 1600 to 1750, when performance directions were established. Here are some of the most common tempo markings:

Italian Futurist painter **Giacomo Balla** (1871–1958) creates a pictorial depiction of speed and movement in *Girl Running on a Balcony* (1912).

grave	solemn (very, very slow)
largo	broad (very slow)
adagio	quite slow
andante	a walking pace
moderato	moderate
allegro	fast (cheerful)
vivace	lively
presto	very fast

IN HIS OWN WORDS

Voices, instruments, and all possible sounds—even silence itself—must tend toward one goal, which is expression.

—C. W. GLUCK

Frequently, we also encounter modifiers such as *molto* (very), *meno* (less), *poco* (a little), and *non troppo* (not too much). Also important are terms indicating a change of tempo, among them *accelerando* (getting faster), *ritardando* (holding back, getting slower), and *a tempo* (in time, or returning to the original pace).

Loudness and Softness

Dynamics denote the volume (degree of loudness or softness) at which music is played. Like tempo, dynamics can affect our emotional response. The main dynamic indications, listed below, are based on the Italian words for soft *(piano)* and loud *(forte)*.

pianissimo (**pp**)	very soft
piano (**p**)	soft
mezzo piano (**mp**)	moderately soft
mezzo forte (**mf**)	moderately loud
forte (**f**)	loud
fortissimo (**ff**)	very loud

Directions to change the dynamics, either suddenly or gradually, are also indicated by words or signs. Here are some of the most common ones:

crescendo	($\diagup$): growing louder
decrescendo or	
diminuendo	($\diagdown$): growing softer
sforzando (**sf**)	"forcing": accent on a single note or chord; also shown by an accent (>)

Tempo and Dynamics as Elements of Musical Expression

The composer adds markings for tempo and dynamics to help shape the expressive content of a work. We will see that these expression marks increased in number during the late eighteenth and nineteenth centuries, when composers tried to make their intentions known ever more precisely, until in the early twentieth century when few decisions were left to the performer.

If tempo and dynamics are the domain of the composer, what is the role of performers and conductors in interpreting a musical work? Performance directions can be somewhat imprecise—what is loud or fast to one performer may be

Dynamic contrasts in music may be compared to light and shade in painting. *The Concert* (1626), by **Hendrik Terbruggen** (1588–1629).

Metronome

moderate in volume and tempo to another. Even when composers give precise tempo markings in their scores (using a device known as a ***metronome***, which measures the exact number of beats per minute), performers have the final say in choosing a tempo that best delivers the message of the music. And for the many styles of music—non-Western, folk, and popular, among others—that do not rely on composer directions or even printed music, the performer takes full responsibility for interpreting the music.

Tempo and Dynamics in a Musical Score

CD iMusic

Beethoven: **Symphony No. 5**, opening:

Allegro con brio

Tempo: Fast (*Allegro*) with vigor (*con brio*)
Dynamics: Very loud (*fortissimo*), then soft (*piano*), growing louder (*crescendo*) to loud (*forte*)

Listening Activity: Tempo and Dynamics

CD iMusic
CD iMaterials

Haydn: Symphony No. 94 in G major (*Surprise*), second movement

Let's return to the slow movement of Haydn's *Surprise* Symphony to consider how he treats elements of expression in the music:

What to Listen For:
- How tempo (pace) and dynamics (volume) affect the listener's response.
- Moderate tempo (*Andante*), a walking pace.
- Soft opening (marked *piano*), then repeated even softer (*pianissimo*).
- Jarring, loud chord played *fortissimo*, which abruptly changes the mood.
- Alternation between soft (*piano*) and loud (*forte*) sections.
- New character in middle section, set in minor key and very loud (*fortissimo*).

Reviewing Concepts of Tempo and Dynamics:

Tempos:
Adagio: **Clarinet Concerto** (Mozart)
Andante: ***Lullaby*** (Brahms)
Moderato: ***Für Elise*** (Beethoven)
Allegro: **Symphony No. 5** (Beethoven)
Presto: ***William Tell* Overture** (Rossini)

Dynamics:
Pianissimo: ***Moonlight* Sonata** (Beethoven)
Piano: **Clarinet Concerto** (Mozart)
Forte: ***Eine kleine Nachtmusik***, minuet (Mozart)
Fortissimo: ***Ode to Joy*** (Beethoven)
Crescendo: ***William Tell* Overture** (Rossini)
Changing dynamics: ***Toreador Song***, from ***Carmen*** (Bizet)

Musical Instruments and Ensembles

7

Voices and Musical Instrument Families

"It was my idea to make my voice work in the same way as a trombone or violin—not sounding like them but 'playing' the voice like those instruments."

—FRANK SINATRA

| KEY POINTS | (S) **StudySpace** online at www.wwnorton.com/enjoy |

○ Properties of sound include pitch, duration, volume, and *timbre*, or tone color.

○ An *instrument* generates vibrations and transmits them into the air.

○ The human voice can be categorized into various ranges, including *soprano* and *alto* for female voices, and *tenor* and *bass* for male voices.

○ The world instrument classification system divides into *aerophones* (such as flutes or horns), *chordophones* (such as violins or guitars), *idiophones* (such as bells or cymbals) and *membranophones* (drums).

CD iMaterials

Timbre

Musical Timbre

We know that musical tone has pitch, duration, and volume. A fourth property of sound—known as tone color, or *timbre*—accounts for the striking differences in the sound quality of instruments. It is what makes a trumpet sound altogether different from a guitar or a drum. Timbre is influenced by a number of factors, such as the size, shape, and proportions of the instrument, the material from which it is made, and the manner in which the vibration is produced. A string, for example, may be bowed, plucked, or struck.

People produce music vocally (by singing or chanting) or by playing a musical instrument. An **instrument** is a mechanism that generates musical vibrations and launches them into the air. Each voice type and instrument has a limited melodic range (the distance from the lowest to the highest tone) and dynamic range (the degree of softness or loudness beyond which the voice or instrument cannot go). We describe a specific area in the range of an instrument or voice, such as low, middle, or high, as its **register**.

Instrument

Register

The Voice as Instrument

The human voice is the most natural of all musical instruments; it is also one of the most widely used—all cultures have some form of vocal music. Each person's voice has a particular quality, or character, and range. Our standard designations for vocal ranges, from highest to lowest, are **soprano**, **mezzo-soprano**, and **alto** (short for **contralto**) for female voices, and **tenor**, **baritone**, and **bass** for male voices.

Vocal ranges

In earlier eras, Western social and religious customs severely restricted women's participation in public musical events. Thus young boys, and occasionally adult males with soprano- or alto-range voices, sang female roles in church music and on the stage. In the sixteenth century, women singers came into prominence in secular (nonreligious) music. Tenors were most often featured as soloists in early opera; the lower male voices, baritone and bass, became popular soloists in the eighteenth century. In other cultures, the sound of women's voices has always been preferred for certain styles of music; for example, in certain Muslim cultures of northern Africa, wedding songs are traditionally performed by professional women singers, and in many cultures, lullabies are the domain of women (see CP 2, p. 60).

Throughout the ages, the human voice has served as a model for instrument

IN HIS OWN WORDS
If you can walk you can dance. If you can talk you can sing.
—ZIMBABWE PROVERB

(Left): Angela Gheorghiu and tenor Roberto Alagna are two of the most talented young opera singers today.

(Right): A European bagpipe aerophone, often used in folk music, sounds a drone under the melodic line.

(Left): A native woman strums a ukulele, a traditional chordophone from the Hawaiian islands.

(Right): A Chinese band, with children playing cymbals (idiophones).

builders and players who have sought to duplicate its lyric beauty, expressiveness, and ability to produce *vibrato* (a throbbing effect) on their instruments.

The World of Musical Instruments

The diversity of musical instruments played around the world defies description. Since every conceivable method of sound production is used, and every possible raw material employed, it would be impossible to list them all here. However, specialists have devised a method of classifying instruments that is based solely on the way their sound is generated. Called the Sachs-Hornbostel System (after its inventors Curt Sachs and Erich von Hornbostel), the system uses four basic categories.

A drum (membranophone) ensemble from Burundi in Central Africa.

Aerophones produce sound by using air. Common instruments in this grouping are flutes, whistles, accordions, bagpipes, and horns—in short, nearly any wind instrument. *Chordophones* are instruments that produce sound from a vibrating string stretched between two points. The string may be set in motion by bowing, plucking, or striking, so the instruments are as disparate as the violin, harp, guitar, Japanese koto, Chinese hammered dulcimer (yangqin), and Indian sitar.

Idiophones produce sound from the substance of the instrument itself. They may be struck, shaken, scraped, or rubbed. Examples of idiophones are bells, rattles, xylophones, and cymbals—in other words, a wide variety of percussion instruments. *Membranophones* are drum-type instruments that are sounded from tightly stretched membranes. These instruments can be struck, plucked, rubbed, or even sung into, thus setting the skin in vibration (see illustrations on p. 38).

In the next chapter we will review, the instruments used most frequently in Western music. Throughout the book, however, you will learn about other instruments associated with popular and art music cultures around the world that have influenced the Western tradition.

Aerophones

Chordophones

Idiophones

Membranophones

Listening Activity: Voices

CD iMusic
CD iMaterials

Row, Row, Row Your Boat

Let us investigate the character and range of the standard voice designations in this round, which allows us to hear four of the vocal ranges, first in succession and then singing together.

What to Listen For:
- Voices that differ in timbre (tone color) and range.
- Standard voice ranges (soprano, alto, tenor, bass).
- Each choral voice sings the tune individually.
- Performance of round has voices entering from highest to lowest.

Reviewing Concepts of Timbre:

Voices:
Soprano: **Lullaby** (Brahms)
Mezzo-soprano: **Amazing Grace** (traditional hymn)
Tenor: **Tonight**, from **West Side Story** (Bernstein)
Baritone: **Toreador Song**, from **Carmen** (Bizet)
Vocal quartet (soprano, alto, tenor, bass): **Row, Row, Row Your Boat**

Instruments:
Aerophones: **Los Jilicatas** (panpipes, Peru)
 Skye Crofters (bagpipe, Scotland)
Idiophones: **Dougla Dance** (steel drums, Trinidad)
 Tabuh Kenilu Sawik (gongs, Indonesia)
Chordophones: **Avaz of Bayate Esfahan** (santur or hammer dulcimer, Iran)
 In a Mountain Path (bowed erhu, China)
Membranophones: **Gota** (drums, Ghana, West Africa)
 Bhimpalási (tabla drum, North India)

8

Western Musical Instruments

"In music, instruments perform the function of the colors employed in painting."

—HONORÉ DE BALZAC

KEY POINTS

StudySpace online at www.wwnorton.com/enjoy

- The four families of Western instruments are *strings*, *woodwinds*, *brass*, and *percussion*.
- String instruments (chordophones) are sounded by *bowing* and *plucking*.
- Bowed strings include *violin*, *viola*, *cello*, and *double bass*; plucked strings include *harp* and *guitar*.
- Woodwind instruments (aerophones) include *flute*, *oboe*, *clarinet*, *bassoon*, and *saxophone*.

- Brass instruments (aerophones) include *trumpet*, *French horn*, *trombone*, and *tuba*.
- Percussion instruments include idiophones (*xylophone*, *cymbals*, *triangle*) and membranophones (*timpani*, *bass drum*); some instruments are pitched (*chimes*) while others are unpitched (*tambourine*).
- Keyboard instruments, such as *piano* and *organ*, do not fit neatly into the Western classification system.

CD iMaterials

Instruments

CD iVideo

Instruments of the Orchestra

The instruments of the Western world—and especially those of the orchestra—may be categorized into four familiar groups: strings, woodwinds, brass, and percussion. We will see, however, that these families of instruments are not entirely homogeneous; that is, all woodwinds are not made of wood, nor do they share a common means of sound production. Furthermore, certain instruments do not fit neatly into any of these convenient categories (the piano, for example, is both a string and a percussion instrument).

String Instruments

The string family, all chordophones, includes two types of instruments: those that are bowed and those that are plucked. The bowed string family has four principal members: violin, viola, violoncello, and double bass, each with four strings (double basses sometimes have five) that are set vibrating by drawing a bow across them. The bow is held in the right hand, while the left hand is used to "stop" the string by pressing a finger down at a particular point, thereby leaving a certain portion of the string free to vibrate. By stopping the string at another point, the performer changes the length of the vibrating portion, and with it the rate of vibration and the pitch.

Violin   The *violin* evolved to its present form at the hands of the brilliant instrument makers who flourished in Italy from around 1600 to 1750 (see p. 41). It is capable of brilliance and dramatic effect, subtle nuances from soft to loud, and great agility in rapid passages throughout its extremely wide range.

The *viola* is somewhat larger than the violin and thus has a lower range. Its strings are longer, thicker, and heavier. The tone is husky in the low register, somber

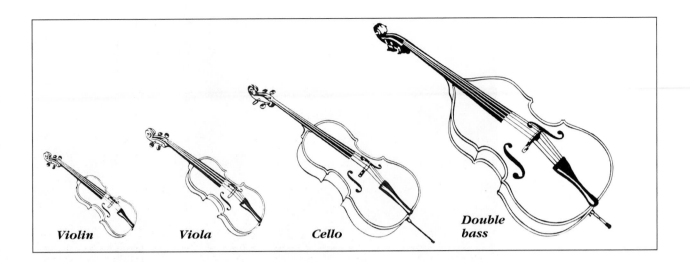

Violin   **Viola**   **Cello**   **Double bass**

and penetrating in the high. It often fills in the harmony, or it often may double another part. One instrument is said to *double* (reinforce) another when it plays the same notes an octave higher or lower.

The *violoncello*, popularly known as *cello*, is lower in range than the viola and is notable for its singing quality and its dark resonance in the low register. Cellos often play the melody and they enrich the sound with their full timbre.

Violoncello

The *double bass*, known also as a *contrabass* or *bass viol*, is the lowest of the string instruments of the orchestra. Accordingly, it plays the bass part—that is, the foundation of the harmony. Its deep tones support the cello part an octave lower.

Double bass

These four string instruments constitute the core or "heart of the orchestra," a designation that indicates the section's versatility and importance.

Orchestral string instruments can be played in many styles and can produce many special effects. They excel at playing *legato* (smoothly, connecting the notes) as well as the opposite, *staccato* (with notes short and detached). A special effect, *pizzicato* (plucked), is created when a performer plucks the string with a finger instead of using the bow. *Vibrato*, a throbbing effect, is achieved by a rapid

Special effects

(Left): Violinist Hilary Hahn.

(Right): The virtuoso cellist Yo-Yo Ma.

(Left): Julie Barnes playing harp.

(Right): Milt Hinton playing the double bass.

wrist-and-finger movement on the string that slightly alters the pitch. For a *glissando*, a finger of the left hand slides along the string while the right hand draws the bow, thereby sounding all the pitches under the left-hand finger, in one swooping sound. *Tremolo*, the rapid repetition of a tone through a quick up-and-down movement of the bow, is associated with suspense and excitement. No less important is the *trill*, a rapid alternation between a tone and one adjacent to it.

String instruments are capable of playing several tones simultaneously, thereby producing harmony: *double-stopping* means playing two strings at once; playing three or four strings together is called *triple-* or *quadruple-stopping*. Another effect is created by the *mute*, a small attachment that fits over the bridge, muffling the sound. *Harmonics* are crystalline tones in a very high register that are produced by lightly touching the string at certain points while the bow is drawn across the string.

Guitarist Carlos Santana, during his 2005 *Embrace the Light* tour.

Two popular plucked string instruments are the harp and the guitar. The *harp* is one of the oldest of musical instruments, with a home in many cultures outside Europe. Its plucked strings, whose pitches are changed by means of pedals, produce an ethereal tone. Chords on the harp are frequently played in broken form—that is, the tones are sounded one after another instead of simultaneously. From this technique comes the term *arpeggio*, which means a broken chord (*arpa* is Italian for "harp"). Arpeggios can be created in a variety of ways on many instruments.

The *guitar*, another old instrument, dating back at least to the Middle Ages, probably originated in the Middle East. A favorite solo instrument, it is associated today with folk and popular music as well as classical styles. The standard *acoustic* (as opposed to electric) *guitar* is made of wood and has a fretted fingerboard and six nylon strings, which are plucked with the fingers of the right hand or with a pick. The *electric guitar*, an electronically amplified instrument capable of many specialized techniques, comes in two main types: the hollow-bodied (or electro-acoustic), favored by jazz and popular musi-

Banjo player Béla Fleck and the Flecktones.

cians, and the solid-bodied, used more often by rock musicians. Related to the guitar are such traditional instruments as the **banjo** (see illustration above) and **mandolin**.

Woodwind Instruments

Woodwind instruments (aerophones) produce sound with a column of air vibrating within a pipe that has fingerholes along its length. When one or another of these holes is opened or closed, the length of the vibrating air column within the pipe is changed. Woodwind players are capable of remarkable agility on their instruments by means of an intricate mechanism of keys arranged to suit the natural position of the fingers.

This group is less homogeneous than the strings. Nowadays woodwinds are not necessarily made of wood, and they employ several different methods of setting up vibration: blowing across a mouth hole (flute family), blowing into a mouthpiece that has a single reed (clarinet and saxophone families), or blowing into a mouthpiece fitted with a double reed (oboe and bassoon families). They do, however, have one important feature in common: the holes in their pipes. In addition, their timbres are such that composers think of them and write for them as a group.

The **flute** is the soprano voice of the woodwind family. Its tone is cool and velvety in the expressive low register, and often brilliant in the upper part of its range. The present-day flute, made of a silver alloy rather than wood, is a cylindrical tube, closed at one end, that is held horizontally. The player blows across a mouth hole cut in the side of the pipe near the closed end. The flute is used frequently as a melody instrument—its timbre stands out against the orchestra—and offers the performer great versatility in playing rapid repeated notes, scales, and trills. The **piccolo** (from the Italian *flauto piccolo*, "little flute") is actually the highest pitched instrument in the orchestra. In its upper register, it takes on a shrillness that is easily heard even when the orchestra is playing *fortissimo*.

Flutist Hae Sung Choe.

Oboe players in an orchestra.

Oboe

The *oboe* continues to be made of wood. The player blows directly into a double reed, which consists of two thin strips of cane bound together with a narrow passage for air. The oboe's timbre, generally described as nasal and reedy, is often associated with pastoral effects and nostalgic moods. The oboe traditionally sounds the tuning note for the other instruments of the orchestra. The *English horn* is an alto oboe. Its wooden tube is wider and longer than that of the oboe and ends in a pear-shaped opening called a *bell*, which largely accounts for its soft, expressive timbre.

The *clarinet* has a single reed, a small thin piece of cane fastened against its chisel-shaped mouthpiece. The instrument possesses a smooth, liquid tone, as well as a remarkably wide range in pitch and volume. It too has an easy command of rapid scales, trills, and repeated notes. The *bass clarinet*, one octave lower in range than the clarinet, has a rich dark tone and a wide dynamic range.

(Above): Richard Stolzman playing the clarinet in Carnegie Hall.

(Right): Jaroslaw Augustyniak playing bassoon.

The **bassoon**, another double-reed instrument, possesses a tone that is weighty in the low register and reedy and intense in the upper. Capable of a hollow-sounding staccato and wide leaps that can sound humorous, it is at the same time a highly expressive instrument. The **contrabassoon** produces the lowest tone of the woodwinds. Its function in the woodwind section of supplying a foundation for the harmony may be compared with that of the double bass among the strings.

The **saxophone**, invented by the Belgian Adolphe Sax in 1840, is the most recent of the woodwind instruments. It was created by combining the features of several other instruments—the single reed of the clarinet along with a conical bore and the metal body of the brass instruments. There are various sizes of saxophone: the most common are soprano, alto, tenor, and baritone. By the 1920s, the saxophone had become the characteristic instrument of the jazz band, and it has remained a favorite sound in popular music today.

Brass Instruments

The main instruments of the brass family (also aerophones) are the trumpet, French horn (or horn), trombone, and tuba. All these instruments have cup shaped mouthpieces attached to a length of metal tubing that flares at the end into a bell. The column of air within the tube is set vibrating by the tightly stretched lips of the player, which are buzzed together. Going from one pitch to another involves not only mechanical means, such as a slide or valves, but also muscular control to vary the pressure of the lips and breath. Brass and woodwind instrument players often speak about their **embouchure**, referring to the entire oral mechanism of lips, lower facial muscles, and jaw.

Trumpets and horns were widely used in the ancient world. At first, they were fashioned from animal horns and tusks and were used chiefly for religious ceremonies and military signals. Their tone could be terrifying—remember that in the biblical account, the walls of Jericho came tumbling down to the sound of trumpets.

Joshua Redman playing tenor saxophone.

(Above): The French horn section of the orchestra.

(Left): World-famous trumpet player Wynton Marsalis.

(Top): Trombonist Isrea Butler.

(Bottom): Carol Jantsch recently won the tuba position in the Philadelphia Orchestra.

The *trumpet*, highest in pitch of the brass family, possesses a brilliant, clear timbre. It is often associated with ceremonial display. The trumpet can also be muted, using a pear-shaped, metal or cardboard device that is inserted in the bell to achieve a muffled, buzzy sound.

The *French horn* is descended from the ancient hunting horn. Its mellow resonance can be mysteriously remote in soft passages and sonorous in loud ones. The muted horn has a distant sound. The horn is played with the right hand inserted in the bell and is sometimes "stopped" by plugging the bell with the hand, producing an eerie and rasping quality. The timbre of the horn blends well with woodwinds, brasses, and strings.

The *trombone*—the Italian word means "large trumpet"—has a full and rich sound in the tenor range. In place of valves, it features a movable U-shaped slide that alters the length of the vibrating air column in the tube.

The *tuba* is the bass instrument of the brass family. Like the string bass and contrabassoon, it furnishes the foundation for the harmony. The tuba adds depth to the orchestral tone, and a dark resonance ranging from velvety softness to a rumbling growl.

Other brass instruments are used in concert and brass bands as well as marching bands. Among these is the *cornet*. In the early twentieth century, the cornet was very popular in concert bands. The *bugle*, which evolved from the military (or field) trumpet of early times, has a powerful tone that carries well in the open air. Since it has no valves, it is able to sound only certain tones of the scale, which accounts for the familiar pattern of duty calls in the army. The *fluegelhorn*, used in jazz and brass bands, is really a valved bugle with a wide bell. The *euphonium* is a tenor-range instrument whose shape resembles the tuba. And the *sousaphone*, an adaptation of the tuba designed by the American bandmaster John Philip Sousa, features a forward bell and is coiled to rest over the shoulder of the marching player.

Percussion Instruments

The percussion section of the orchestra is sometimes referred to as "the battery." The instruments are used to accentuate the rhythm, generate excitement at the climaxes, and inject splashes of color into the orchestral sound.

The percussion family (encompassing a vast array of idiophones and membranophones) is divided into two categories: instruments capable of producing definite pitches, and those that produce an indefinite pitch. In the former group are the *tim-pani*, or *kettledrums*, which are generally played in sets of two or four. The timpani has a hemispheric copper shell across which is stretched a "head" of plastic or calf-

Timpani

skin held in place by a metal ring. A pedal mechanism enables the player to change the tension of the head, and with it the pitch. The instrument is played with two padded sticks. Its dynamic range extends from a mysterious rumble to a thunderous roll. The timpani first arrived in western Europe from the Middle East, where Turks on horseback used them in combination with trumpets (see CP 9).

Also among the pitched percussion instruments are several members of the *xylophone* family; instruments of this general type are used in Africa, Southeast Asia, and throughout the Americas. The xylophone consists of tuned blocks of wood or metal laid out in the shape of a keyboard. Struck with mallets with hard heads, the instrument produces a dry, crisp sound. The *marimba* is a more mellow xylophone of African origin. The *vibraphone*, used in jazz, combines the principle of the xylophone with resonators, each containing revolving disks operated by electric motors that produce an exaggerated vibrato.

The *glockenspiel* (German for "set of bells") consists of a series of horizontal tuned steel bars of various sizes, which when struck produce a bright, metallic, bell-like sound. The *celesta*, a kind of glockenspiel that is operated by means of a keyboard, resembles a miniature upright piano. The steel plates are struck by small hammers to produce a sound like a music box. *Chimes*, or *tubular bells*, a set of tuned metal tubes of various lengths suspended from a frame and struck with a hammer, are frequently called on to simulate church bells.

The percussion instruments that do not produce a definite pitch include the *snare drum* (or *side drum*), a small cylindrical drum with two heads (top and bottom) stretched over a shell of metal and played with two drumsticks. This instrument owes its brilliant tone to the vibrations of the lower head against taut snares (strings). The *tenor drum*, larger in size, has a wooden shell and no snares. The *bass drum* is played with a large soft-headed stick and produces a low, heavy sound. The *tom-tom* is a colloquial name given to Native American or African drums of indefinite pitch. The *tambourine* is a round, hand-held drum with "jingles"—little metal plates—inserted in its rim. The player can strike the drum with the fingers or elbow, shake it, or pass a hand over the jingles. Of Middle Eastern origin, it is particularly associated with music of Spain, as are *castanets*, little wooden clappers moved by the player's thumb and forefinger.

The *triangle* is a slender rod of steel bent into a three-cornered shape; when struck with a steel beater, it gives off a bright, tinkling sound. *Cymbals* came to the West from central Asia during the Middle Ages. They consist of two large circular brass plates of equal size, which when struck against each other produce a shattering sound. The *gong*, or *tam-tam*, is a broad circular disk of metal, suspended in a frame so as to hang freely. When struck with a heavy drumstick, it produces a deep roar. The gong has found its widest use in the Far East and Southeast Asia, where it is central to the ensemble known as the *gamelan* (see pp. 431–33).

(Top): Evelyn Glennie, who is profoundly deaf, is percussionist with the Los Angeles Philharmonic.

(Bottom): Melanie Sehman plays xylophone.

Indefinite pitch instruments

Piano virtuoso Cecile Licad.

Keyboard Instruments

The *piano* was originally known as the *pianoforte*, Italian for "soft-loud," which suggests its wide dynamic range and capacity for nuance. Its strings are struck with hammers controlled by a keyboard mechanism. The piano cannot sustain tone as well as the string and wind instruments, but in the hands of a fine performer, it is capable of producing a singing melody.

The piano has a notable capacity for brilliant scales, arpeggios, trills, rapid passages, and octaves, as well as chords. Its range from lowest to highest pitch spans more than seven octaves, or eighty-eight semitones. It has several pedals that govern the length of time a string vibrates as well as its volume.

The *organ* is a type of wind instrument. The air flow to each of its many pipes is controlled by the organist from a console containing two or more keyboards and a pedal keyboard played by the feet. The organ's multicolored sonority can easily fill a huge space. Electronic keyboards, or synthesizers, capable of imitating pipe organs and other timbres, have become commonplace. (On early organ types and their music, see pp. 98, 146, and 157–58.)

Listening Activity: Western Instruments
Resource CD

Britten: *The Young Person's Guide to the Orchestra*

Britten's *The Young Person's Guide to the Orchestra* introduces the listener first to the entire orchestra, then to each of its instrument families. The work passes the principal melody through each instrument individually, proceeding from the highest-ranged instrument to the lowest.

What to Listen For:
- Entire orchestra playing together, then the 4 groups of instruments: *woodwinds, brass, strings, percussion.*
- Individual instruments in each family, playing in order from highest to lowest (see Listening Guide 1 on pp. 56–57).

CD iMusic
CD iMaterials

Reviewing Instruments and Families:
Strings: **Canon in D** (Pachelbel)
Woodwinds: **Woodwind Quintet Op. 88, No. 2** (Reicha)
Brass: **Contrapunctus I**, from **The Art of Fugue** (Bach)
Percussion (bass drum, cymbals, glockenspiel): **Stars and Stripes Forever** (Sousa)
Cornet: **Oh! Susannah** (Stephen Foster)
Guitar: **Greensleeves** (traditional, United Kingdom)
Piano: **Spring Song** (Mendelssohn)
Organ: **Toccata in D minor** (Bach)
Harpsichord: **Minuet in D minor** (*Anna Magdelena Notebook*)

Another early keyboard instrument, much used in the Baroque era, is the **harp-sichord**. Its sound is produced by quills that pluck its metal strings (see p. 146). The instruments described in this and the previous chapter form a vivid and diversified group, which can be heard and viewed through the iVideo module of your Resource CD. To composers, performers, and listeners alike, they offer an endless variety of colors and shades of expression.

Harpsichord

9

Musical Ensembles

CD iMaterials

○ Choral groups often feature *a cappella singing*, with no accompaniment.

○ *Chamber music* is ensemble music for small groups, with one player per part.

○ Standard chamber ensembles include *string quartets* as well as *woodwind quintets* and *brass quintets*.

○ The modern *orchestra* features eighty to one hundred players.

○ Large ensembles generally use a *conductor* who beats patterns with a *baton* to help the performers keep the same tempo.

The great variety in musical instruments is matched by a wide assortment of ensembles, or performance groups. Some are homogeneous—for example, choral groups using only voices or perhaps only men's voices. Others are more heterogeneous—for example, the orchestra, which features instruments from the different families. Across the world, nearly any combination is possible.

Choral Groups

Choral music is sung around the world, both for religious purposes (sacred music) and for non-spiritual (secular) occasions. Loosely defined, a **chorus** is a fairly large body of singers who perform together; their music is usually sung in several voice parts. Many groups include both men and women, but choruses can also be restricted to women's or men's voices only. A **choir** is traditionally a smaller group, often connected with a church or with the performance of sacred music. The standard voice parts in both chorus and choir correspond to the voice ranges described earlier: soprano, alto, tenor, and bass (abbreviated as SATB). In early times,

Elektra Women's Choir, from Vancouver, British Columbia.

The Jupiter String Quartet performing in Banff, Alberta (Canada).

choral music was often performed without accompaniment, a style of singing known as *a cappella* (meaning "in the chapel").

Smaller, specialized vocal ensembles include the **madrigal choir** and **chamber choir**. The madrigal choir might perform *a cappella* secular works, known as **part songs**. The designation "chamber choir" refers to a small group of up to twenty-four singers, performing either *a cappella* or with piano accompaniment.

A cappella singing

Instrumental Chamber Ensembles

Chamber music is ensemble music for a group of two to about a dozen players, with one player to a part—as distinct from orchestral music, in which a single instrumental part may be performed by as many as eighteen players or more. The essential trait of chamber music is its intimacy.

Many of the standard chamber music ensembles consist of string players. One well-known combination is the **string quartet**, made up of two violins, viola, and cello. Other popular combinations are the **duo sonata** (soloist with piano); the **piano trio**, **quartet**, and **quintet**, each made up of a piano and string instruments; the **string quintet**; as well as larger groups—the **sextet**, **septet**, and **octet**. Winds too form

String quartet

Sitarist Ravi Shankar and his daughter Anoushka perform in a charity concert in Kuala Lampur. The traditional Indian ensemble also includes *tabla*, a hand drum (not shown).

standard combinations, especially **woodwind** and **brass quintets**. Some of these ensembles are listed below.

We will see that contemporary composers have experimented with new groupings that combine the voice with small groups of instruments and electronic elements with live performers. In some cultures, chamber groups mix what might seem to be unlikely timbres to the Western listener—in India, plucked strings and percussion are standard (see opposite), and in some styles of Chinese music, plucked and bowed strings are combined with flutes.

The Orchestra

In its most general sense, the term "orchestra" may be applied to any performing body of diverse instruments—this would include the Japanese ensemble used for court entertainments (called **gagaku**) or the **gamelan** orchestras of Bali and Java, made up largely of gongs, xylophone-like instruments, and drums (see illustration on p. 336). In the West, the term is now synonymous with **symphony orchestra**, an ensemble of strings coupled with an assortment of woodwinds, brass, and percussion instruments.

IN HIS OWN WORDS

You listen to four sensible persons conversing, you profit from their discourse, and you get to know the peculiar properties of their instruments.

—JOHANN WOLFGANG VON GOETHE (ABOUT QUARTETS)

Standard Chamber Ensembles

DUOS

Solo instrument
Piano

TRIOS

String trio
Violin 1
Viola or Violin 2
Cello

Piano trio
Piano
Violin
Cello

QUARTETS

String quartet
Violin 1
Violin 2
Viola
Cello

Piano quartet
Piano
Violin
Viola
Cello

QUINTETS

String quintet
Violin 1
Violin 2
Viola 1
Viola 2
Cello

Piano quintet
Piano
String quartet
(Violin 1, Violin 2, Viola, Cello)

Woodwind quintet
Flute
Oboe
Clarinet
Bassoon
French horn (a brass instrument)

Brass quintet
Trumpet 1
Trumpet 2
French horn
Trombone
Tuba

Cincinnati Symphony Orchestra, Paavo Järvi, Music Director, 2005.

The Orchestra's seating plan.

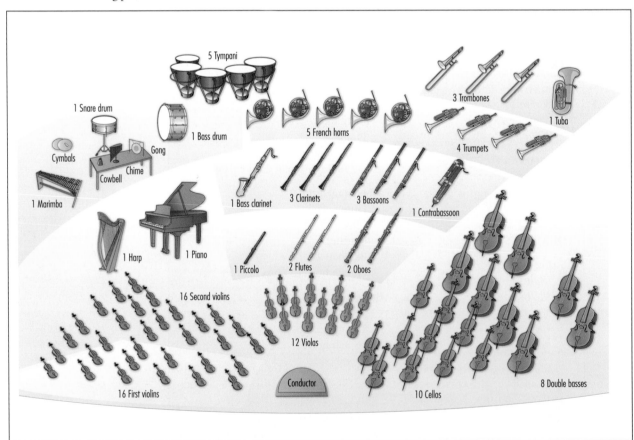

Typical Distribution of Orchestral Instruments

STRINGS	18	first violins
	15	second violins
	12	violas
	12	cellos
	9	double basses
	1–2	harps, when needed
WOODWINDS	3	flutes, 1 piccolo
	3	oboes, 1 English horn
	3	clarinets, 1 bass clarinet
	3	bassoons, 1 double bassoon
BRASS	4–6	French horns
	4	trumpets
	3	trombones
	1	tuba
PERCUSSION	3–5	players
	1	timpani player (2–4 timpani)
	2–4	on the other instruments

The symphony orchestra has varied in size and makeup throughout its history but has always featured string instruments as its core. From its origins as a small group of twenty or so members, the orchestra has grown into an ensemble of more than a hundred musicians, approximately two-thirds of whom are string players. The list above shows the distribution of instruments typical of a large orchestra today.

The instruments of the orchestra are arranged to achieve the best balance of tone. Thus, most of the strings are near the front, as are the gentle woodwinds. The louder brass and percussion are at the back. A characteristic seating plan for the Cincinnati Symphony Orchestra is shown opposite; this arrangement varies somewhat from one orchestra to another.

Concert, Jazz, and Rock Bands

"Band" is a generic name applied to a variety of ensembles, most of which feature winds and percussion at their core. The band is a much-loved American institution, whether it is a concert, marching, or military band or a jazz or rock ensemble. The earliest wind and percussion groups (including Turkish "Janissary" bands—see p. 214) were used for military purposes: musicians accompanied soldiers to war, playing their brass and percussion instruments from horseback and their fifes and drums from among the ranks of the foot soldiers to spur the troops on into battle. Concert wind groups originated in the Middle Ages. In northern Europe, a wind band of three to five musicians played each evening, often from the high tower of a local church or city hall. From these traditions grew the military bands of the French

IN HIS OWN WORDS

The string-band and the wind-band are among the brightest constellations in the melodic heavens. The former may be likened to a woman, the latter to a man, for like maid and man, brought together in divine harmony, they can breathe into life the soulful, the sentimental, the heroic and the sublime.

—JOHN PHILIP SOUSA

The Indiana University marching band in formation at a football game.

Revolution and American Civil War. One American bandmaster, John Philip Sousa (1854–1932), achieved worldwide fame with his concert band and the repertory of marches he wrote for it.

Concert band

In the United States today, the ***concert band*** (sometimes called a ***wind ensemble***) ranges in size from forty to eighty or so players; it is an established institution in most secondary schools, colleges, and universities, and in many communities as well. Modern composers like to write for this ensemble, since it is usually willing to play new compositions. The ***marching band***, well known today in the United States and Canada, commonly entertains at sports events and parades. Besides its core of winds and percussion, this group often features remnants from its military origins, including a display of drum majors (or majorettes), flags, and rifles.

Marching band

The precise instrumentation of ***jazz bands*** depends on the particular music being played but generally includes a reed section made up of saxophones of various sizes and an occasional clarinet, a brass section of trumpets and trombones, and a rhythm section of percussion, piano, double bass, and electric guitar. ***Rock bands*** typically feature amplified guitars, percussion, and synthesizers. We will discuss jazz and rock bands in later chapters.

The Role of the Conductor

American conductor Leonard Bernstein.

Large ensembles, such as an orchestra, concert band, or chorus, generally need a conductor, who serves as the group's leader. Conductors beat time in standard metric patterns to help the performers keep the same tempo; many conductors use a thin stick known as a ***baton***, which is easy to see. These conducting patterns, shown in the diagrams on page 55, further emphasize the strong and weak beats of the measure. Beat 1, the strongest in any meter, is always given a downbeat, or a downward motion of the hand; a secondary accent is shown by a change of direction; and the last beat of each measure, a weak beat, is always an upbeat or upward motion, thereby leaving the hand ready for the downbeat of the next measure.

Equally as important is the conductor's role in interpreting the music for the group. This includes deciding the precise tempo—how fast or

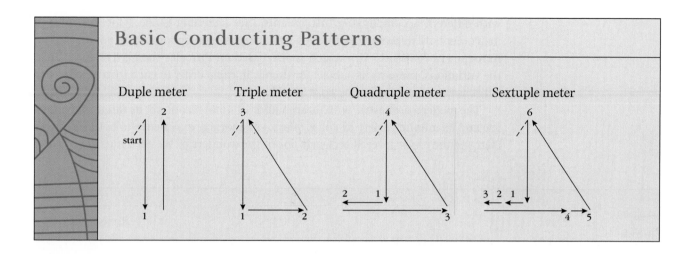

Basic Conducting Patterns

Duple meter   Triple meter   Quadruple meter   Sextuple meter

slow—and the dynamics—how soft or loud—for each section of the piece. In most cases, the composer's markings are relative (how loud is *forte?*) and thus open to interpretive differences. Conductors also rehearse ensembles in practice sessions, helping the musicians to learn and interpret their individual parts. String players depend on the conductor, or sometimes the ***concertmaster*** (the first-chair violinist), to standardize their bowing strokes so that the musical emphasis, and therefore the interpretation, is uniform.

Below is the process that a musical work undergoes before you hear it.

Concertmaster

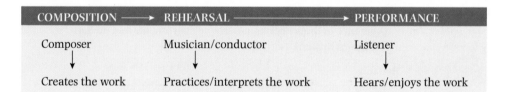

COMPOSITION →	REHEARSAL	→ PERFORMANCE
Composer	Musician/conductor	Listener
↓	↓	↓
Creates the work	Practices/interprets the work	Hears/enjoys the work

The Orchestra in Action

A helpful introduction to the modern orchestra is Benjamin Britten's *Young Person's Guide to the Orchestra,* which was written expressly to illustrate the timbre of each instrument. The work, composed in 1946 and subtitled *Variations and Fugue on a Theme of Purcell,* is based on a dance tune by Henry Purcell (1659–1695), a great seventeenth-century English composer. You can listen to Purcell's original dance tune—a rondeau in a broad triple meter, set in a minor key—included in the iMusic examples; the work is played here by the Los Angeles Baroque Orchestra, using Baroque-period string instruments (with gut rather than metal strings) and harpsichord. You will note that Britten uses only the first section of the dance as the basis for his composition. Compare the soft, sweet sound of the Baroque string instruments with the louder and richer sonorities of the modern orchestral strings.

In Britten's *Young Person's Guide,* the composer introduces the sound of the entire orchestra playing together, then the sonorities of each instrumental family as a group—woodwinds, brasses, strings, percussion—and finally repeats the statement by the full orchestra. Once the listener has the theme, or principal melody, well in mind, every instrument is featured in order from highest to lowest within each family. Next we encounter variations of the theme, each played by a new instrument

CD iMusic

Purcell: Rondeau

with different accompanying instruments. (See Listening Guide 1 for the order of instruments.) The work closes with a grand fugue, a polyphonic form popular in the Baroque era (1600–1750), which is also based on Purcell's theme. The fugue, like the variations, presents its subject, or theme, in rapid order in each instrument. (For a discussion of the fugue, see pp. 158–59.)

The modern orchestra, with its amplitude of tonal resources, its range of dynamics, and its infinite variety of color, offers a memorable experience to both the musician and the music lover. It is clearly one of the wonders of Western musical culture.

Listening Guide 1   Resource CD

Britten: *The Young Person's Guide to the Orchestra*
(Variations and Fugue on a Theme of Purcell)   (Total time: 17:14)

DATE OF WORK:	1946
THEME:	Based on a dance (rondeau) from Henry Purcell's incidental music to the play *Abdelazar (The Moor's Revenge)*; theme played by the Los Angeles Baroque Orchestra
MUSICAL FORM:	Theme and variations, followed by a fugue

WHAT TO LISTEN FOR: **Purcell**   **CD iMusic**
Original dance tune played on Baroque-period string instruments.
Difference in timbre between Baroque instruments and modern strings (in Britten).

Britten
Stately dance theme, played first by the full orchestra.
Different timbres of each of the 4 instrument families.
Sounds of individual instruments, played in turn by each instrument family (highest to lowest).
Imaginative variations of the original theme.
Special orchestral effects *(pizzicato, glissando, trill)*.
Change from major to minor tonality; changing meters (duple, triple, compound).
Complex fugue at end, with overlapping statements of the theme.

1   0:00   **I. Theme:** 8 measures in D minor, stated 6 times to illustrate the orchestral families:
1. Entire orchestra
2. Woodwinds
3. Brass
4. Strings
5. Percussion
6. Entire orchestra

II. Variations: 13 short variations, each illustrating a different instrument.

		VARIATION	FAMILY	SOLO INSTRUMENT	ACCOMPANYING INSTRUMENTS
2	2:03	1	Woodwinds:	flutes, piccolo	violins, harp, and triangle
		2		oboes	strings and timpani
		3		clarinets	strings and tuba
		4		bassoons	strings and snare drum
3	4:55	5	Strings:	violins	brass and bass drum
		6		violas	woodwinds and brass
		7		cellos	clarinets, violas, and harp
		8		double basses	woodwinds and tambourine
		9		harp	strings, gong, and cymbal
4	9:36	10	Brass:	French horns	strings, harp, and timpani
		11		trumpets	strings and snare drum
		12		trombones, tuba	woodwinds and high brass
5	12:14	13	Percussion:	various	strings

(Order of introduction: timpani, bass drum, and cymbals; timpani, tambourine, and triangle; timpani, snare drum, and wood block; timpani, castanets, and gong; timpani and whip; whole percussion section)

6 14:13 **III. Fugue:** Subject based on a fragment of the Purcell theme, played in imitation by each instrument of the orchestra in same order as variations:

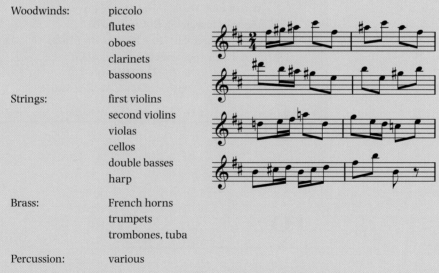

Woodwinds:	piccolo
	flutes
	oboes
	clarinets
	bassoons
Strings:	first violins
	second violins
	violas
	cellos
	double basses
	harp
Brass:	French horns
	trumpets
	trombones, tuba
Percussion:	various

7 16:22 Full orchestra at the end with Purcell's theme heard over the fugue.

Listening Activity: Reviewing Ensembles

CD iMusic
CD iMaterials

Choral Groups:
Chamber choir: *Simple Gifts* (Shaker hymn)
Chorus: *America* (patriotic song)
Men's chorus: *El grillo* (Josquin)

Chamber Groups:
String quartet: *Emperor* **Quartet, Op. 76, No. 3** (Haydn)
Brass quartet: **Contrapunctus I**, from *The Art of Fugue* (Bach)
Woodwind quintet: **Quintet, Op. 88, No. 2** (Reicha)

Orchestra:
Baroque orchestra: *Alla hornpipe*, from *Water Music* (Handel)
Classical orchestra: *Surprise* **Symphony No. 94** (Haydn)
Romantic orchestra: *Ride of the Valkyries* (Wagner)
Late Romantic orchestra: *March*, from *The Nutcracker* (Tchaikovsky)
Comtemporary orchestra: *Interlude*, from *Rappaccini's Daughter* (Catán)
Music theater orchestra: *Tonight*, from *West Side Story* (Bernstein)

Other Western Ensembles:
Concert band: *Stars and Stripes Forever* (Sousa)
Brass band: *Battle Hymn of the Republic* (Civil War song)
Jazz band: *When the Saints Go Marching In* (traditional, America)

World and Traditional Music Ensembles:
Mexican mariachi: *El Cihualteco*
Chinese ensemble: *In a Mountain Place*
North Indian ensemble: *Bhimpalási*
Peruvian ensemble: *Los Jilicatas*
Indonesian gamelan: *Tabuh Kenilu Sawik*

10

Style and Function of Music in Society

"A real musical culture should not be a museum culture based on music of past ages. . . . It should be the active embodiment in sound of the life of a community—of the everyday demands of people's work and play and of their deepest spiritual needs."

—WILFRID MELLERS

O   Music provides different functions—for religion, work, entertainment—in societies around the world.

O   Most cultures have *sacred music*, for religious functions, and *secular music*, for nonreligious activities.

O   There are many *genres*, or categories, of music; some works *cross over* categories, borrowing elements of one style for use in another.

O   The *medium* is the specific group (e.g., orchestra, chorus) that performs a piece.

O   Some music is not written down, but is known through *oral transmission*.

O   The distinctive features of any artwork make up its *style*.

O   A musical style is created through individual treatment of the elements (melody, rhythm, harmony, texture, form, dynamics, tempo).

O   We organize styles of artworks into *historical periods*, each with its own characteristics.

In every culture, music is intricately interwoven with the lives and beliefs of its people. This is especially true of many non-Western societies where, just as in the West, the "classical" exists alongside the "popular" and both are nourished from the rich store of traditional music that is closely allied with daily living. Music serves different functions in different societies, though some basic roles are universal. It accompanies religious and civic ceremonies, it helps workers establish a uniform rhythm to get the job done more efficiently, and it provides entertainment through song and dance. The social organization of any particular culture has much to do with its musical types and styles. In some cultures, such as in the Western classical tradition, only a few people are involved with the actual performance of music; in others, such as that of the African Pygmies, cooperative work is so much a part of society that the people sing as a group, with each person contributing a separate part to build a complex whole.

There is music for every conceivable occasion, but the specific occasions celebrated vary from one culture to another. Thus musical *genres*, or categories of repertory, do not necessarily transfer from one society to the next, though they may be similar. For example, Japanese *Noh* drama and Peking opera serve essentially the

Genres

same social role as opera does in the Western world. And we can distinguish in most cultures between *sacred music*, for religious or spiritual functions, and *functions of secular music*, for and about everyday people outside a religious context.

It is important to differentiate between genre and form: a *genre* is a more general term that suggests something of the overall character of the work as well as its function. For example, the term *symphony* is a genre designation for a standard format—usually a four-movement orchestral work. As we will see later, each movement has a specific internal *form*, or structure. "Symphony" also implies the *medium*, or the specific group that performs the piece—in this case, an orchestra.

Actors performing in a Noh play (a Japanese theatrical genre of music and dance).

The Roles of Music around the World

Music enhances many of our activities, including work, worship, and even warfare. As we noted earlier, music can help synchronize group tasks; such songs tend to be rhythmic, and both the melody and words fit the activity. Work songs are most often responsorial, or sung call-and-response—a leader improvises lyrics and the group responds rhythmically ("Michael rowed the boat ashore, Hallelujah"). Blues and spirituals, for example, grew out of the field hollers of slaves brought to the United States from West Africa. Frederick Douglass, a former slave, wrote in his autobiography *My Bondage and My Freedom* (1855) that "Slaves are generally expected to sing as well as to work." With emancipation, the tradition of singing at work continued on projects such as the building of the transcontinental railroad ("John Henry was a steel-driving man").

Most lullabies are sung in the vernacular—that is, the language of the people—and many such songs use vocables, or nonsense syllables, and speak to the child in diminutive or endearing terms. For example, a native American Hopi lullaby compares the child to a "small beetle riding on top of another." Lullabies from around the world share some other common musical traits: they are often repetitive, slowly paced, with a gentle rhythmic motion. In Western tradition, many cradle songs are set in triple or sextuple meter to simulate a rocking motion ("Rock-a-bye baby, on the tree top"). One famous example, Brahms's *Lullaby* ("Lullaby and good night"), was written by the Romantic composer Johannes Brahms as an art song for voice and piano (entitled *Wiegenlied*); however, it has entered the realm of traditional music because it is so widely known, having been passed down through oral transmission.

Music for worship can take many forms, but whether it is sung, played, or danced, it helps shape rituals, or ceremonial acts. African-American spirituals, such as *Swing Low, Sweet Chariot,* were sung at revival meetings in the nineteenth century, and these continue to be popular today. Modern music for worship in America can be as diverse as a traditional Protestant hymn, such as *A Mighty Fortress Is Our God,* or a gospel rendition of *Amazing Grace.*

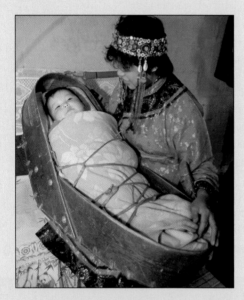

A woman in Shibazhan, China, sings a lullaby to her child, who is secured in a traditional wooden cradle.

Titles for musical compositions occasionally indicate the genre and key, such as Symphony No. 94 in G major, by Joseph Haydn. Another way works are identified is through a cataloguing system, often described by **opus number** (*opus* is Latin for "work"; an example is Nocturne, Opus 48, a piano work by Chopin). Other titles are more descriptive, such as *The Nutcracker* (a ballet by the Russian composer Tchaikovsky), *The Trout* (a song by Schubert, an Austrian composer), and *The Moon Reflected on the Second Springs* (by the Chinese musician Abing).

The Americus Brass Band, a Civil War reenactment group that plays authentic Civil War–era brass and percussion intruments. The group has been featured in numerous movies and TV series and is included in our iMusic recordings.

Since ancient times, horns (later trumpets) and drums have been associated with warfare. Music serves military campaigns as a means to signal and give orders, to mark the military day (*Reveille* is the wake-up call), and to excite troops in battle. The idea of a military band accompanying soldiers seems to have originated in India or the Middle East. The bagpipe, a popular folk instrument in various world cultures, spurred Scottish and Irish troops to battle from at least the sixteenth century; and in America, fife-

and-drum corps, and later brass bands, accompanied Revolutionary and Civil War soldiers on the march. (A fife is a small wooden transverse flute with fewer holes than a piccolo.)

Much of the music we will hear is intended as entertainment. In addition to the symphonies and art songs heard in our concert halls, we will explore great jazz and blues performances more typically enjoyed in nightclubs; the ceremonial drum ensemble of Uganda, who performed within the royal compound of the king; and a Japanese song traditionally sung in teahouses by geisha—a class of professional women entertainers.

Terms to Note

work song	oral transmission
call-and-response	bagpipe
vocable	fife
vernacular	brass band
spiritual	gospel

Suggested Listening   CD iMusic

Amazing Grace (traditional hymn, United Kingdom)
Battle Hymn of the Republic (Civil War song)
Gota (healing song from Ghana, West Africa)
Lullaby (Brahms)
Skye Crofters (bagpipe, Scottish dance music)
Sleep Song (Hopi lullaby, Native America)
Swing Low, Sweet Chariot (African-American spiritual)

Just as the context for music—when, why, and by whom a piece is performed— varies from culture to culture, so do aesthetic judgments of what is beautiful and what is appropriate. For example, the Chinese consider a thin, tense vocal tone desirable in their operas, while the Italians prefer a full-throated, robust sound in theirs. Likewise, certain performers and styles gain or lose popularity as cultural preferences change.

Not all music is written down. Music of most cultures of the world, including

Reviewing Terms   CD iMusic

Title: Symphony No. 5 in C minor, Op. 67 (Op. = Opus = work number)
Composer: Ludwig van Beethoven
Genre: Symphony
Form: 4-movement work for orchestra
Medium: Symphony orchestra

Title: *Wiegenlied*, Op. 49, No. 4 *(Lullaby)*
Composer: Johannes Brahms
Genre: Romantic song (in German, *Lied*)
Form: Strophic (2 stanzas sung to same music)
Medium: Solo voice and piano

Oral transmission

some styles of Western popular and traditional music, is transmitted by example (through a master-apprentice relationship) or by imitation and is performed from memory. The preservation of music without the aid of written notation is referred to as *oral transmission*.

We will focus much of our study on Western art music—that is, the notated music of a cultivated and largely urban society. We often label art music as "classical," or serious, for lack of better terms. However, the lines that distinguish art music from other kinds are often blurred. Popular and traditional musics are art forms in their own right: performers of these styles may be as talented as those that present classical music; and both jazz and rock are considered by many to be new art forms, having already stood the test of time. To confuse these categories further, some composers and performing artists *crossover* from one type of music to another—from jazz to rock, from rock to Western classical—or simply borrow elements of one style

French Roccoco artist **Jean Siméon Chardin** (1699–1779) is known for his beautifully textured still life paintings that focus on the objects themselves. *Musical Instruments and a Basket of Fruit* (1730–34).

Early-twentieth-century artist **Pablo Picasso** (1881–1973) explores similar subject matter—musical instruments and fruit—in this very stylized Cubist painting *Still Life with Guitar* (1924).

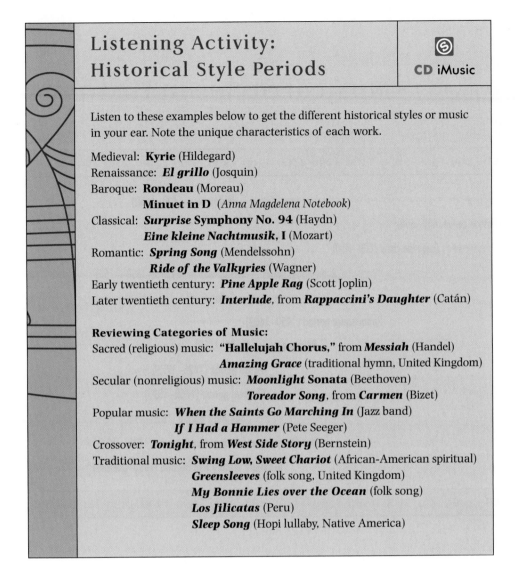

Listening Activity: Historical Style Periods

CD iMusic

Listen to these examples below to get the different historical styles or music in your ear. Note the unique characteristics of each work.

Medieval: **Kyrie** (Hildegard)
Renaissance: ***El grillo*** (Josquin)
Baroque: **Rondeau** (Moreau)
      Minuet in D (*Anna Magdelena Notebook*)
Classical: ***Surprise* Symphony No. 94** (Haydn)
      ***Eine kleine Nachtmusik*, I** (Mozart)
Romantic: ***Spring Song*** (Mendelssohn)
      Ride of the Valkyries (Wagner)
Early twentieth century: ***Pine Apple Rag*** (Scott Joplin)
Later twentieth century: ***Interlude***, from ***Rappaccini's Daughter*** (Catán)

Reviewing Categories of Music:
Sacred (religious) music: **"Hallelujah Chorus,"** from ***Messiah*** (Handel)
      Amazing Grace (traditional hymn, United Kingdom)
Secular (nonreligious) music: ***Moonlight* Sonata** (Beethoven)
      Toreador Song, from ***Carmen*** (Bizet)
Popular music: ***When the Saints Go Marching In*** (Jazz band)
      If I Had a Hammer (Pete Seeger)
Crossover: ***Tonight***, from ***West Side Story*** (Bernstein)
Traditional music: ***Swing Low, Sweet Chariot*** (African-American spiritual)
      Greensleeves (folk song, United Kingdom)
      My Bonnie Lies over the Ocean (folk song)
      Los Jilicatas (Peru)
      Sleep Song (Hopi lullaby, Native America)

to use in another, drawing these styles ever closer. Later we will hear elements of Latin-American dance music in the musical theater work *West Side Story* (Chapter 73) and some references to Mexican mariachi music in an orchestral work by Silvestre Revueltas (Chapter 70).

The Concept of Style

Style may be defined as the characteristic way an artwork is presented. The word may also indicate the creator's personal manner of expression—the distinctive flavor that sets one artist apart from all others. Thus we speak of the literary style of Dickens or Shakespeare, the painting style of Picasso or Rembrandt, or the musical style of Bach or Mozart. We often identify style with nationality, as when we refer to French, Italian, or German style; or with an entire culture, as when we contrast a Western musical style with one of Africa or East Asia.

What makes one musical work sound similar to or different from another? It is the individualized treatment of the elements of music. We have seen that Western

Musical Styles in History

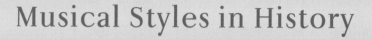

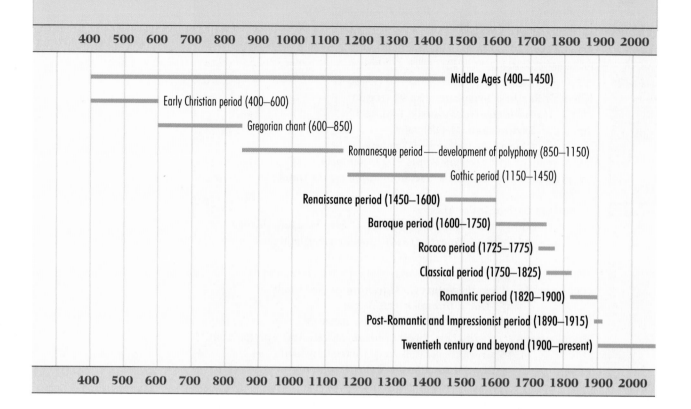

Middle Ages (400–1450)

Early Christian period (400–600)

Gregorian chant (600–850)

Romanesque period—development of polyphony (850–1150)

Gothic period (1150–1450)

Renaissance period (1450–1600)

Baroque period (1600–1750)

Rococo period (1725–1775)

Classical period (1750–1825)

Romantic period (1820–1900)

Post-Romantic and Impressionist period (1890–1915)

Twentieth century and beyond (1900–present)

music is largely a melody-oriented art based on a particular musical system from which the underlying harmonies are also built. Musics of other cultures may sound foreign to Western ears, because they are based on entirely different musical systems, and many do not involve harmony to any great extent. One important factor in these differing languages of music is the way in which the octave is divided and scales are produced, an area we will explore in more detail in Chapter 17. Complex rhythmic procedures and textures set some world musics apart from Western styles, while basic formal considerations—such as repetition, contrast, and variation—bring musics of disparate cultures closer. In short, a style is made up of pitch, time, timbre, and expression, creating a sound that each culture recognizes as its own.

Musical Styles in History

The arts change from one age to the next, and each historical period has its own stylistic characteristics. Although the artists, writers, and composers of a particular era may vary in personality and outlook, when seen in the perspective of time, they turn out to have certain qualities in common. Because of this, we can tell at once that a work of art—whether music, poetry, painting, sculpture, or architecture—dates from the Middle Ages or the Renaissance, from the eighteenth century or the nineteenth. The style of a period, then, is the total language of all its artists as they react to the artistic, political, economic, religious, and philosophical forces that shape their environment. We will find that a knowledge of historical styles will help us place a musical work within the context (time and place) in which it was created.

Scholars will always disagree as to precisely when one style period ends and the next begins. Each period leads by imperceptible degrees into the following one, dates and labels being merely convenient signposts. The timeline on the facing page shows the generally accepted style periods in the history of Western music. Each represents a conception of form and technique, an ideal of beauty, a manner of expression and performance attuned to the cultural climate of the period—in a word, a style!

Historical periods

Mary, Queen of Heaven, by the Master of the St. Lucy
Legend, c. 1485.

PART TWO

Medieval and Renaissance Music

Middle Ages (476–1450)

500	600	700	800	900	1000	1100	1200	1300	1400	1410	1420	1430	1440	1450

Fall of Roman Empire (476 C.E.)

Charlemagne crowned first Holy Roman Emperor (800)

Hildegard of Bingen (1098–1179)

Chanson de Roland, French epic

Notre Dame composers (Léonin, Pérotin)

Raimbaut de Vaqueiras (c. 1155–1207)

Kublai Khan (1214–1294), emperor of China

Adam de la Halle (c. 1237–c. 1287)

Last crusade to the Holy Land (1270)

Marco Polo to China (1271)

Guillaume Machaut (c. 1300–1377)

Francesco Petrarch (1304–1374), Italian poet, scholar

Dante Alighieri, Italian poet, *Divine Comedy* (1307)

Black Death begins (1347)

Ambrogio Lorenzetti (c. 1290–1348), Italian painter

Geoffrey Chaucer, English poet, *Canterbury Tales* (1386)

Guillaume Du Fay (c. 1397–1474)

Joan of Arc executed (1431)

Sandro Botticelli (1444–1510)

Fall of Constantinople (1453)

500	600	700	800	900	1000	1100	1200	1300	1400	1410	1420	1430	1440	1450

Renaissance Era (1450–1600)

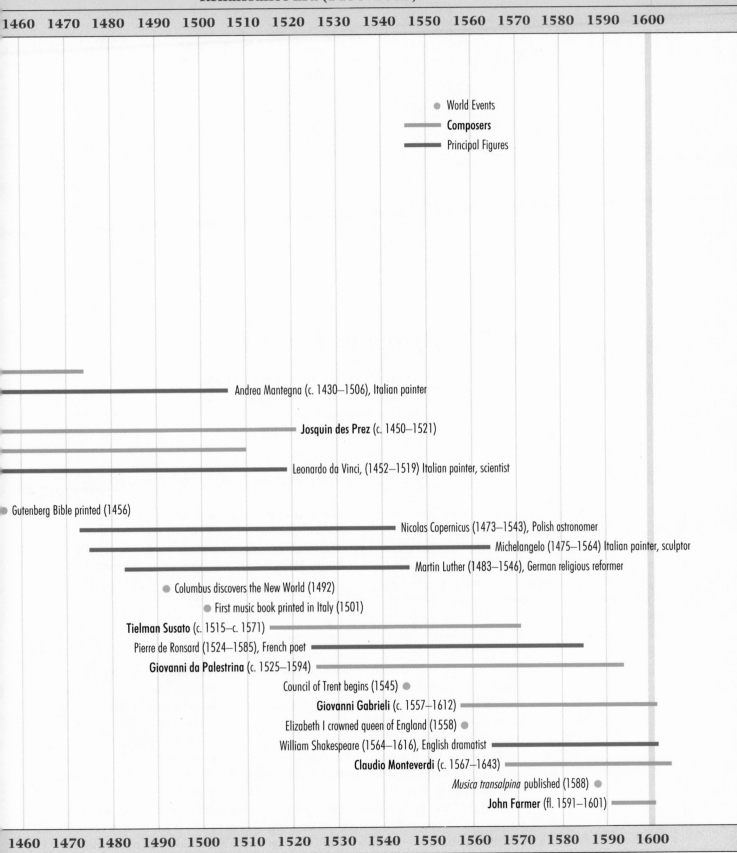

Legend	
●	World Events
▬	**Composers**
▬	Principal Figures

Andrea Mantegna (c. 1430–1506), Italian painter

Josquin des Prez (c. 1450–1521)

Leonardo da Vinci, (1452–1519) Italian painter, scientist

● Gutenberg Bible printed (1456)

Nicolas Copernicus (1473–1543), Polish astronomer

Michelangelo (1475–1564) Italian painter, sculptor

Martin Luther (1483–1546), German religious reformer

● Columbus discovers the New World (1492)

● First music book printed in Italy (1501)

Tielman Susato (c. 1515–c. 1571)

Pierre de Ronsard (1524–1585), French poet

Giovanni da Palestrina (c. 1525–1594)

Council of Trent begins (1545) ●

Giovanni Gabrieli (c. 1557–1612)

Elizabeth I crowned queen of England (1558) ●

William Shakespeare (1564–1616), English dramatist

Claudio Monteverdi (c. 1567–1643)

Musica transalpina published (1588) ●

John Farmer (fl. 1591–1601)

| 1460 | 1470 | 1480 | 1490 | 1500 | 1510 | 1520 | 1530 | 1540 | 1550 | 1560 | 1570 | 1580 | 1590 | 1600 |

The Middle Ages

II

The Culture of the Middle Ages

"Nothing exists without music, for the universe itself is said to have been framed by a kind of harmony of sounds, and the heaven itself revolves under the tone of that harmony."

—ISIDORE OF SEVILLE

KEY POINTS		Ⓢ **StudySpace** online at www.wwnorton.com/enjoy

- The Middle Ages span nearly one thousand years (c. 476–1450).
- The early Christian church and the state were the centers of powers during this time.
- Much of the surviving music from the Middle Ages is religious, or sacred, because of the sponsorship (*patronage*) of the church.

- The later Middle Ages saw the rise of cities, cathedrals, and great works of art and literature.
- The ideals of knighthood and the devotion to the Virgin Mary helped raise the status of women.

While we believe that many ancient civilizations enjoyed flourishing musical cultures, only a few fragments of their music survive today. We cannot know what sounds echoed through the Greek amphitheatre or the Roman coliseum, but we do know that the ancient Mediterranean culture provided the foundation on which music of later ages was based. It is a fundamental part of the Western heritage.

Early Middle Ages   The fall of the Roman Empire, commonly set in the year 476 C.E., marked the beginning of a one-thousand-year period known as the Middle Ages. The first half of this millennium, from around 500 to around 1000 and formerly referred to as the "Dark Ages," was not a period of decline but rather of ascent and development. During this era, all power flowed from the king, with the approval of the Roman Catholic Church and its bishops. The two centers of power, church and state, were bound to clash, and the struggle between them shaped the next chapter of European history. The modern concept of a strong, centralized government as the guardian of law and order is generally credited to Charlemagne (742–814), the legendary emperor of the Franks. A progressive monarch, who regretted until his dying day that he did not know how to write (he regarded writing as an inborn talent he simply did not possess), Charlemagne encouraged education and left behind him a magnificent library as well as a system of social justice that illuminated the perceived "darkness" of the early medieval world.

The culture of this period was shaped largely by the rise of monasteries. It was the members of these religious communities who preserved the learning of the ancient world and transmitted it, through their manuscripts, to later European scholars. Because music was an effective enhancement in the church service, the members of these religious communities supported it extensively, and because of their *patronage*, the art music of the Middle Ages was predominantly religious. Women as well as men played a role in preserving knowledge and cultivating music for the church, as nuns figured prominently in church society. One woman who stands out is Hildegard of Bingen, head of a monastery in a small town in western Germany. She is remembered today for her writings on natural history and medicine as well as for her poetry and music for special church services. We will study a religious chant by Hildegard in Chapter 12.

The late Middle Ages, from around 1000 to 1450, witnessed the construction of the great cathedrals and the founding of universities throughout Europe. Cities emerged as centers of art and culture, and within them the townspeople played an ever-expanding role in civic life.

Trade flourished in the later Middle Ages when a merchant class arose outside of feudal society. Although travel was perilous—the roads plagued by robbers and the seas by pirates—each region of Europe exchanged its natural resources for those they lacked: the plentiful timber and furs of Scandinavia were traded for English wool and cloth manufactured in Flanders; England wanted German silver, and above all, French and Italian wine; and European goods of all kinds flowed through the seaport of Venice to Constantinople in exchange for Eastern luxuries. This growing economic strength allowed medieval merchants a measure of freedom from

The coronation of Charlemagne, crowned emperor on Christmas night in 800 C.E. Stained-glass window from Strasbourg Cathedral (c. 1200), now in Musée de l'Oeuvre Notre Dame, Strasbourg.

Music is a part of civic life, as shown in a detail of **Ambrogio Lorenzetti's** (d. 1348?) fresco *Good Government in the City*.

Roland blows his horn to summon the army of Charlemagne. From 13th-century manuscript of the *Chanson de Roland*.

local feudal landlords—a freedom that soon turned to a form of self-government through the growth of organized trade guilds.

Developing national literatures helped shape languages throughout Europe. Literary landmarks, such as the *Chanson de Roland* (c. 1100) in France, Dante's *Divine Comedy* (1307) in Italy, and Chaucer's *Canterbury Tales* (1386) in England, find their counterparts in painting—for example, Lorenzetti's frescoes in Siena's Town Hall (1338–40, see p. 67).

In an era of violence brought on by deep-set religious beliefs, knights embarked on holy—and bloody—Crusades to capture the Holy Land from the Muslims. Although feudal society was male-dominated and idealized the figure of the fearless warrior, the status of women was raised by the universal cult of Mary, mother of Christ, and by the concepts of chivalry that arose among the knights. In the songs of the court minstrels, women were adored with a fervor that laid the foundation for our concept of romantic love. This poetic attitude found its perfect symbol in the faithful knight who worshipped his lady from afar and was inspired by her to deeds of great daring and self-sacrifice.

The Middle Ages, in brief, encompassed a period of enormous turmoil and change. Out of this turbulent age emerged a profile of what we know today as Western civilization.

12

Sacred Music in the Middle Ages

*"When God saw that many men were lazy, and gave
themselves only with difficulty to spiritual reading,
He wished to make it easy for them, and added the melody
to the Prophet's words, that all being rejoiced by the charm
of the music, should sing hymns to Him with gladness."*

—ST. JOHN CHRYSOSTOM

KEY POINTS

StudySpace online at www.wwnorton.com/enjoy

- Many world cultures use a kind of chant, a *mono-phonic* (single-line) melody, in their worship (CP 3).

- The music of the early Christian church, called *Gregorian chant*, features monophonic, nonmetric melodies set in one of the church *modes*, or scales.

- Chant melodies fall into three categories (*syllabic, neumatic, melismatic*) based on how many notes are set to each syllable of text.

- The most solemn ritual of the Catholic Church is the *Mass*, a daily service with two categories of prayers: the *Proper* (texts that vary according to

the day) and the *Ordinary* (texts that remain the same for every Mass).

- Some chants are sung alternating a soloist and chorus in a *responsorial* performance.

- The Paris Cathedral of Notre Dame was a center for *organum*, the earliest type of *polyphony*, with two-, three-, or four-voice parts sung in fixed rhythmic patterns (*rhythmic modes*).

- Preexisting chants formed the basis for early polyphony, including organum and the *motet*; the latter features multiple texts (*polytextual*).

The early music of the Christian church was shaped in part by Greek, Hebrew, and Syrian influences. In time, it became necessary to assemble the ever-growing body of music into an organized liturgy. The *liturgy* refers to the set order of church services and to the structure of each service. The task extended over several generations, though tradition credits Pope Gregory the Great (r. 590–604) with codifying these melodies, known today as Gregorian chant.

Gregorian chant (also known as *plainchant* or *plainsong*) consists of a single-line melody; it is monophonic in texture and lacking harmony and counterpoint. Its freely flowing vocal line subtly follows the inflections of the Latin text and is generally free from regular accent.

The Gregorian melodies, numbering more than three thousand, form an immense body of music, nearly all of it anonymous. Gregorian chant avoids wide leaps, allowing its gentle contours to create a kind of musical speech. Free from regular phrase structure, the continuous, undulating vocal line is the musical counterpart to the lacy ornamentation typical of medieval art and architecture (see the Paris Cathedral of Notre Dame, p. 74).

Chant melodies fall into three main classes, according to the way they are set to the text: *syllabic*, with one note sung to each syllable of text; *neumatic*, generally with small groups of up to five or six notes sung to a syllable; and *melismatic*, with long groups of notes set to a single syllable of text. The melismatic style, which descended from the elaborate improvisations heard in Middle Eastern music, became an expressive feature of Gregorian chant and exerted a strong influence on subsequent Western music.

At first the chants were handed down through oral tradition from one generation to the next. But as the number of chants increased, singers needed help remembering the general shapes of the different melodies. Thus *neumes*, little ascending and descending symbols, were written above the words to suggest the

Manuscript illumination of Pope Gregory the Great dictating to his scribe Peter. The dove, representing the Holy Spirit, is on his shoulder.

Text settings

Neumes

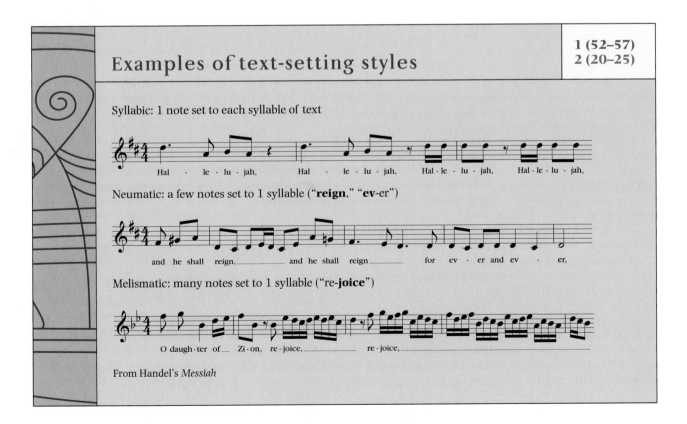

Examples of text-setting styles

1 (52–57)
2 (20–25)

Syllabic: 1 note set to each syllable of text

Hal - le - lu - jah,   Hal - le - lu - jah,   Hal - le - lu - jah,   Hal - le - lu - jah,

Neumatic: a few notes set to 1 syllable ("**reign**," "**ev**-er")

and he shall   reign,_____ and he shall   reign_____   for   ev - er and ev - er,

Melismatic: many notes set to 1 syllable ("re-**joice**")

O daugh - ter of ___ Zi - on,   re - joice,_____   re - joice,_____

From Handel's *Messiah*

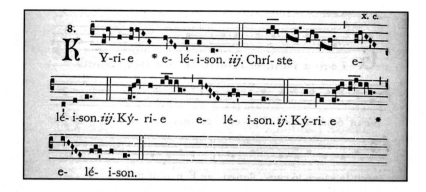

The opening of the Kyrie chant in Gregorian notation, from the *Liber usualis*.

contours of the melody. Neumes eventually developed into a musical notation consisting of square notes on a four-line staff (see above).

Modes   From Gregorian chant through Renaissance polyphony, Western music used a variety of scale patterns, or *modes*. These preceded major and minor modes, which possess a strong pull toward a tonic note; the earlier modes lacked this sense of attraction. The modes served as the basis for European art music for a thousand years. With the development of polyphony—music for several independent lines—a harmonic system evolved based on these scale patterns. The adjective *modal* thus refers to various melodic and harmonic types that prevailed in the medieval and early Renaissance eras.

The Mass

Offices   The services of the Roman Catholic Church can be divided into two categories: the daily *Offices*—a series of services celebrated at various hours of the day in monasteries and convents—and the Mass. A reenactment of the sacrifice of Christ, the *Mass* is the most solemn ritual of the Catholic Church, and the one generally attended by public worshippers. Its name is derived from the Latin words *ite, missa est* (go, the Mass is ended), recited at the end of the service by the priest. (The Mass texts are in **Latin**, the language of the ancient Romans and the language of learning throughout the Middle Ages and Renaissance.) The collection of prayers that makes **Proper and Ordinary**   up the Mass (its liturgy) falls into two categories: the *Proper*, texts that vary from day to day throughout the church year, depending on the feast being celebrated; and the *Ordinary*, texts that remain the same in every Mass. (A chart showing the organization of the Mass with the individual movements of the Proper and Ordinary appears in Chapter 15, p. 94.) There are Gregorian melodies for each section of the ceremony; a Kyrie melody, from the Mass Ordinary, is shown above. In this way, Gregorian chant has been central to the celebration of the Mass, which was and remains the primary service in the Catholic Church.

Life in the Medieval Cloister

One vocation available to men and women in the Middle Ages revolved around the Catholic Church. Life in a cloister (a place for religious seclusion) allowed people to withdraw from secular society into the shelter of monasteries and convents, where they devoted themselves to prayer, scholarship, preaching, charity, or healing the sick, depending on the religious order they joined.

A life devoted to the church was not an easy one. Some religious orders, such as the Franciscans, required vows of poverty; each new member discarded all worldly possessions upon joining. The discipline was arduous. A typical day began at 2:00 or 3:00 a.m. with the celebration of the first of the daily services (the Offices), the reading of lessons, and the singing of psalms. Each day in the church calendar had its own ritual and its own order of prayers. The members of the community interspersed their religious duties with work in the fields, in the library, or in the workshop. Some produced items that could be sold—wine, beer, or cheese, for example—thus bringing in revenue to the order.

Despite the grueling schedule, many men and women in religious life dedicated themselves to writing and preserving knowledge from earlier times. Such a person was Hildegard of Bingen, one of the most remarkable women of the Middle Ages, who was renowned in her day as a poet and prophet and who is popular today for her serenely beautiful music.

The Music of Hildegard of Bingen

"The words of the musical performance stand for the body, and the musical performance itself stands for the spirit.

Hildegard of Bingen (1098–1179) was the tenth child of a noble couple who promised her to the service of the church as a tithe. Raised by a religious recluse, she lived in a stone cell with a single window and took her vows at the age of fourteen. From childhood, Hildegard experienced visions, which intensified in later life. She was reportedly able to foretell the future.

With the death of her teacher, Hildegard became head of the community, and around the year 1150 founded her own convent in Rupertsberg, Germany, on the Rhine River near Bingen. Her reported miracles and prophecies made her famous throughout Europe; popes, kings, and priests sought her advice on political and religious issues. She was also known for her scientific and medical writings. Although never officially canonized, Hildegard is regarded as a saint by the church.

Moved to record her visions and prophecies, Hildegard completed three collections in manuscript entitled *Scivias*. After a vision she had in 1141, when "the heavens were opened and a blinding light of exceptional brilliance flowed through my flame," she claimed to understand fully the meaning of the Scriptures.

Hildegard also wrote religious poetry with music, which she collected in a volume entitled *Symphony of the Harmony of Celestial Revelations*. These works form a liturgical cycle appropriate for singing at different religious feasts throughout the year. Hildegard's musical style is highly original; it resembles Gregorian chant, but unlike most music of the time, it does not draw on the existing repertory.

A CHANT TO THE VIRGIN BY HILDEGARD

Hildegard wrote many of the texts she set to music; her poetry is characterized by brilliant imagery and creative language. Many of her songs praise the Virgin Mary, comparing her to a blossoming flower or branch and celebrating her purity. Our example is an Alleluia (Listening Guide 2, p. 73), a movement from the Mass Proper, to be sung on a feast day for the Virgin. The performance here is ***responsorial***, alternating between a soloist and a chorus. The chant is three-part, with the choral *Alleluia* framing the solo verse in an **A-B-A** structure. It is sung monophonically to a conjunct, or connected, melody with few leaps and with a free nonmetric rhythm. One of Hildegard's musical signatures can be heard here: an occasional upward leap of a fifth that gives the line a soaring feeling. It is the text that shapes the line, reaching its highest peaks on evocative words such as "holy womb," "flower," and "chastity." The setting alternates between neumatic, with small groups of notes per syllable, and melismatic, especially on the last syllables of *Alleluia* and in the last text line, describing the Virgin's purity or chastity.

The priest Volmar records Hildegard of Bingen's visions. The image, a miniature, is from her poetry collection *Scivias* (1141–51).

CD iMusic

Hildegard of Bingen: Kyrie

IN HER OWN WORDS

The words I speak come from no human mouth; I saw and heard them in visions sent to me. . . . I have no confidence in my own capacities—I reach out my hand to God that He may carry me along as a feather borne weightlessly by the wind.

Alleluia

Chant as Music for Worship

Many cultures employ music when worshipping or performing certain rituals. These sacred songs take various forms, including chant, a simple, monophonic melody sung or recited to a text. The chants and practices of the early Christian church owe much to Judaism, the religion from which Christianity sprang. In particular, the two religions are linked by the singing of the 150 texts from the Old Testament Book of Psalms. Some of these psalms celebrate singing (we will hear a contemporary setting of "Sing unto the Lord a new song" later in the book). In the Judaic tradition, the psalm texts are sung responsorially, by the cantor (soloist and singing leader) and the congregation. In the Roman Catholic Church, the recitation of the psalms, a style more like speaking than singing, became the core of many religious services; here, too, performances are often responsorial. The practice of singing psalms was adopted in the services of the Protestant churches during the Reformation and after (see CP 6 on music and religion in the Americas).

As we move further east to the Islamic world, the texts of the Koran (the sacred text of Islam) are also recited rhythmically in a kind of chant. The practice of chanting the Koran is governed by established oral traditions that specify the vocal timbre, rhythmic treatment of texts, pronunciation, and the use of a special vibrato (a wavering fluctuation of the pitch). One of the most familiar sounds in Islamic cultures is the call to prayer, which is sounded publicly five times per day from a minaret (a tower on a mosque, the Muslim house of worship) and helps regulate Muslim daily life.

On the other side of the world, the Afro-Cuban religion of Santería is practiced in many Caribbean cultures. Santería has its roots in the ancient religions of West Africa, but in the New World, beliefs are mingled with Catholicism. Santería is a magical religion in which humans communicate with an orisha, or saint, through song and trance. Unlike Gregorian chant, the music of Santería is highly rhythmic and dancelike, and is often accompanied by drums and various idiophones, including cowbells and güiros (hollow gourds scraped with a stick). The call-and-response singing is heard over a complex polyrhythmic pattern, producing a kind of "conversation" with the deity.

The ethereal sounds of chant—Western and Eastern alike—have drawn many listeners to this soothing, meditative music. Some performers have even popularized religious chant by creating "New Age" arrangements, launching, for example, the music of Hildegard of Bingen to the top of the classical charts.

Illuminated initial from Psalm 114 (in Hebrew) depicting the exodus from Egypt, in which Moses led the Israelites from bondage. (From the Kaufmann Haggadah)

Terms to Note

Book of Psalms	mosque
cantor	minaret
responsorial	Santería
Gregorian chant	orisha
Islam	idiophone
Koran	güiro

Suggested Listening

Buddhist throat singing
Islamic call to prayer
Jewish cantorial chant
CD iMusic *Osain*, Santería chant
CD iMusic Plainchant, Hildegard: Kyrie

Hildegard of Bingen: *Alleluia, O virga mediatrix*
(Alleluia, O mediating branch)

(3:30)

GENRE:	Plainchant
CHANT TYPE:	Alleluia, from the Mass Proper
TEXT:	In praise of the Virgin Mary (poet, Hildegard of Bingen)
OCCASION:	For feasts of the Virgin Mary
PERFORMANCE:	Responsorial (solo and chorus; sung chorus-solo verse-chorus)
STYLE:	Opening melismatic, then neumatic

WHAT TO LISTEN FOR:
Alternation between solo and chorus (responsorial).
Monophonic texture (unaccompanied) and free rhythm (nonmetric).
Text setting shifts between melismatic (many notes to a syllable) and
   neumatic (small groups of notes to a syllable).
Conjunct movement with a few leaps.
Range of 9 notes (just over an octave).
Climaxes (highest range) on words "holy flesh," "beautiful flower,"
   "chastity."
Repeat of opening Alleluia at close.

	TEXT	**TRANSLATION**	**PERFORMANCE**
1 0:00	Alleluia.	Alleluia.	Solo intonation, then choral resonse; very melismatic.
2 0:45	O virga mediatrix	O mediating branch	Solo verse, with several melismas.
	sancta viscera tua mortem superaverunt,	Your holy flesh has overcome death,	Higher range, neumatic text setting.
	et venter tuus omnes creaturas illuminavit	And your womb has illuminated all creatures	
	in pulchro flore de suavissima integritate	Through the beautiful flower of your tender purity	
	clausi pudoris tui orto.	That sprang from your chastity.	Melismatic at end.
3 2:56	Alleluia.	Alleluia.	Chorus; return to opening.

Opening of solo chant, with melismatic setting on *Alleluia*:

Rising fifth and melisma on word "mortem" (death):

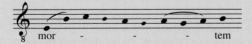

Higher range on "sancta viscera" (holy flesh), in neumatic setting:

The Rise of Polyphony

Façade of Cathedral of Notre Dame, Paris (1163–1235). In both architecture and music, the Gothic period saw great advances in construction.

Polyphony, or the combination of two or more simultaneous melodic lines, is the single most important development in the history of Western music. This style began to emerge toward the end of the Romanesque era (c. 850–1150). Polyphony helped bring about the use of regular meters, which was necessary if the different voices were to keep together. Because this music had to be written down in a way that would indicate precise rhythm and pitch, a more exact notational system developed, not unlike the one in use today. (For an explanation of our modern notational system, see Appendix I, "Musical Notation," p. A-1.)

With the development of a more exact notation, music progressed from an art of improvisation and oral tradition to one that was carefully planned and preserved. During the Gothic era (c. 1150–1450), which saw the rise of cathedrals with their choirs and organs, the period of anonymous creation drew to a close, and the individual composer came to be recognized. Learned musicians, mostly clerics in religious communities, mastered the art of writing extended musical works in varied textures and forms.

Organum

The earliest polyphonic music, called *organum*, grew out of the custom of adding a second voice to a Gregorian melody at the interval of a fifth or fourth. In the forefront of this evolution were the composers centered at the Cathedral of Notre Dame in Paris during the twelfth and thirteenth centuries. Their leader, Léonin (fl. 1150–c. 1201), is the first composer of polyphonic music whose name is known to us. He compiled the *Great Book of Organum* (*Magnus liber organi*), music for the entire church year, in this new musical style. His successor, Pérotin (fl. c. 1200), expanded the dimensions of organum by increasing the number of voice parts, first to three and then to four.

 Léonin and Pérotin

To the medieval mind, the new had to be founded on the old. Therefore composers of organum based their pieces on preexisting Gregorian chants. While the lower voice sang the fixed melody in extremely long notes, the upper voice sang a freely composed part that moved rapidly above it.

Rhythmic mode

Tenor

In the organum *Gaude Maria virgo* (Listening Guide 3), the opening polyphonic section features two voices singing in a *rhythmic mode*—a fixed pattern of long and short notes that is repeated or varied—over a sustained bottom voice, the *Tenor* (from *tenere*, "to hold"), that is drawn from the chant of the same name. The setting, in the style of Pérotin (and possibly by him), is highly melismatic, with many notes sung to each syllable of text. The form of this organum is typical in that it alternates polyphony, sung by soloists, and monophonic chant, sung by the choir. This early polyphonic style featured open, hollow-sounding harmonies built on intervals of fifths and octaves. The text, a responsory (from the Offices rather than the Mass), is in praise of the Virgin Mary and thus appropriate for feasts of the Blessed Virgin.

Motet

Polytextual

One of the most important developments in medieval polyphony was the *motet* (from the French word *mot*, for "word"), which came about with the addition of new texts to highly melismatic organum. Sometimes two different texts—in Latin or French—were added to the same piece, making it *polytextual* (more than one text). While built on a Gregorian chant hidden among the voices, much like organum, the motet's texts could be quite secular, even racy. With this development, secular polyphony was born.

Listening Guide 3

eLG 1 (4–5) 1 (7–8)

Notre Dame School Organum: *Gaude Maria virgo*
(Rejoice Mary, virgin)

(1:26)

GENRE:	Organum, in 3 voices
CHANT TYPE:	Responsory for one of the Offices
COMPOSER:	From the Notre Dame School, in the style of Pérotin (13th century)
TEXT:	In praise of the Virgin Mary
OCCASION:	For feasts of the Blessed Virgin Mary (especially Purification)

WHAT TO LISTEN FOR:
2 upper voices singing rhythmically over sustained bottom voice.
2 upper parts exchanging melodic ideas.
Long-short rhythm repeated, then faster, even notes.
Highly melismatic (only 2 words in organum).
Open, hollow chords at cadences.
Shifts from organum to chant (sung monophonically).
Chant is melismatic (many notes) on "virgo," then neumatic
   (a few notes per syllable).

		TEXT	TRANSLATION	PERFORMANCE
4	0:00	Gaude Maria	Rejoice Mary,	Organum style: upper 2 voices moving rhythmically over sustained third voice.
5	1:07	virgo cunctas hereses sola interemisti.	O virgin, you alone have destroyed all heresies.	Monophonic chant, melismatic, then continuing in neumatic setting.

Opening of organum, with 2 rhythmic upper voices over long chant note:

13

Secular Music in the Middle Ages

"A verse without music is a mill without water."

—ANONYMOUS TROUBADOUR

KEY POINTS | StudySpace online at www.wwnorton.com/enjoy

- Secular music arose in courts, performed by aristocratic **troubadours** and **trouvères** in France and by **Minnesingers** in Germany, and in cities, performed by wandering minstrels (**jongleurs**).

- Secular song texts focused on idealized love and the values of chivalry (code of behavior).

- Secular songs and dances were sung monophonically, with improvised instrumental accompaniment.

- Guillaume de Machaut was a poet-composer of the French **Ars nova** (new art) who wrote sacred

- music and polyphonic **chansons** (secular songs) set to fixed text forms (**rondeau, ballade, virelai**).

- Instrumental music was generally improvised, performed by ensembles of soft (**bas**) or loud (**haut**) instruments, categorized by their use.

- The religious wars (Crusades) and medieval explorations enabled the exchange of musical instruments as well as theoretical ideas about music with Middle Eastern and Far Eastern cultures (CP 4).

The Minnesinger Heinrich von Meissen, called "Frauenlob" (champion of ladies), is exalted by musicians playing drum, flute, shawm, fiddles, psaltery, and bagpipe.

Alongside the learned (or art) music of the cathedrals and choir schools grew a popular repertory of songs and dances that reflected every aspect of medieval life. Minstrels emerged as a class of musicians who wandered among the courts and towns. Some were versatile entertainers who played instruments, sang and danced, juggled, presented tricks and animal acts, and performed plays. In an age that had no newspapers, they regaled their audience with gossip and news. These itinerant actor-singers—called **jongleurs** (male) and **jongleuresses** (female)—lived on the fringes of society.

On a different social level were the poet-musicians who flourished at the various courts of Europe. Those who lived in the southern region of France known as Provence were called **troubadours** (women were also called **trobairitz**), those living in northern France were called **trouvères**. Some troubadours and trouvères were members of the aristocracy and some were even royalty. They either sang their music and poetry themselves or entrusted its performance to other musicians. In Germany, they were known as **Minnesingers**, or singers of courtly love.

Secular music was integral to medieval court life, supplying the necessary accompaniment for dancing, dinner, tournaments, and processions. Military music supported campaigns, inspired warriors departing on the Crusades, and welcomed them on their return.

The poems of the troubadour and trouvère repertory ranged from simple ballads to love songs, political and moral ditties, war songs, chronicles of the Crusades, laments, and dance songs. They praised the virtues of the age of chivalry: valor, honor, nobility of character, devotion to an ideal, and the quest for perfect love. Like so many of our popular songs today, many of the medieval lyrics dealt with the subject of unrequited—or unconsummated—passion. The object of the poet's desire was generally unattainable, either because of rank or because the beloved was already wed to another. This poetry dealt with love in its most idealized form. The subjects of poems by women ranged from the sorrow of being rejected by a lover to the joy of true love. The songs in praise of the Virgin Mary were cast in the same style and language, and sometimes even set to the same melodies, as those that expressed a more worldly kind of love.

The 13th-century troubadour Raimbaut de Vaqueiras, armed for battle, from a manuscript. Paris, Bibl. nat. ms. fr. 12473

Raimbaut de Vaqueiras and the Troubadour Tradition

Raimbaut de Vaqueiras (c.1155–1207) typifies the tradition of the courtly troubadour. He was of humble origin, the son of a "poor knight" from Provence, in southern France, and as a young man he entered the service of the marquis of Montferrat, whose court was in northwestern Italy. Raimbaut was later knighted for saving the life of his patron in battle. When Boniface of Montferrat set off in 1202 on the Fourth Crusade to the Holy Land (see CP 4, p. 82), Raimbaut did not go at first but later joined the forces in Constantinople, where he wrote a famous epic describing the colorful events. It is likely that Raimbaut was killed in 1207 on the battlefield, alongside his patron.

Raimbaut's most famous work is *Kalenda maya* (*The First of May*), a love song addressed to a noble lady—specifically, Beatrice, marquise of Montferrat—whose husband the poet wished to make jealous. The text celebrates, on one level, the return of spring but also confirms the poet's pledge of honor, love, and service to the lady (see Listening Guide 4).

Kalenda maya

This work is an *estampie*, a sung dance-form common in late medieval France. As the poem's stanzas unfold, we learn more about the lady to whom the text is addressed; the poet compares his devotion to well-known lovers (Eric and Enide) in an ancient epic poem, and at the end, identifies the work as an estampie (estampida). The melody is heard in three sections, each of which is repeated. The overall musical form is *strophic*, meaning the same melody is repeated with every stanza of the poem. Notice how the tune is balanced by phrases rising upward at the beginning, then closing with a repeated downward line.

Estampie

In our recording, we hear the dance version first, performed with a *rebec* (an early version of the violin) playing the tune, accompanied by a *pipe* (a three-holed, end-blown flute), *guitarra moresca* (a strummed string instrument introduced into Spain by the Moors), and small hand drums known as *nakers*. Not only the instruments but also the improvisational style and structure of *Kalenda maya* echo the sounds of Middle Eastern music, which Raimbaut certainly heard on his brave quest to the East.

IN HIS OWN WORDS

I have served you . . . with a glad heart; I have wooed ladies with you; and I have ridden at your side at war. . . . All good usage rules in your court: munificence and courting, elegant clothing and handsome armor, trumpets and games and viols and songs.

Raimbaut de Vaqueiras: *Kalenda maya* (*The First of May*) (2:26)

DATE OF WORK:	Late 12th century
GENRE:	Estampie (troubadour dance song)
TEXT:	Strophic poem (6 stanzas of irregular lines; only 4 stanzas sung on recording)
MUSICAL FORM:	**A-A-B-B-C-C** (3 short sections, each repeated), for each stanza

WHAT TO LISTEN FOR: Nasal tone of rebec.
Improvisational quality of instrumentalists (guitar and nakers).
Gentle rise and fall of melodic line.
Repetition of individual phrases and strophic reiteration of melody.
Triple-meter, dancelike character .

Opening melody with solo rebec, in upward-rising phrases:

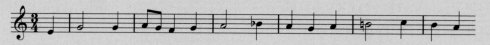

Instrumental dance: Entire melody played once (A-A-B-B-C-C)

6 0:00 Solo rebec (phrase **A**).

0:10 Accompaniment with strummed guitar (on repeat of **A**).

0:16 Hand drum (nakers) accompaniment enters (on new phrase, **B**).
Melody continues through phrase **C**, with more complex rhythms in accompaniment; flutelike pipe enters at end with ostinato figure.

Stanza 1, with voice

7 0:32

Kalenda maya,	**A**
ni fueills de faia	
ni chans d'auzell ni flors de glaia	
non es qe.m plaia,	**A**
pros dona gaia	
tro q'un i snell mes sagier aia	
del vostre bell cors, qi.m retraia	**B**
plazer novell q'amors m'atraia	**B**
e jaia e.m traia vas vos	**C**
dona veraia,	
e chaia de plaia .lgelos,	**C**
anz qe.m n'estraia.	

Neither May Day nor the beech tree's leaves nor the song of birds nor gladiolus flowers are pleasing to me, noble and vivacious lady, until I receive a swift messenger from your fair person to tell me of some new pleasure that love brings me; and may I be joined to you and drawn toward you, perfect lady; and may the jealous fall stricken before I must leave you.

Stanza 2

8 0:59

Mabell' amia,	**A**
per Dieu non sia
qe ja.l gelos de mon danria,

qe car vendria,	A
sa gelozia	
si aitals dos amantz partia,	
q'ieu ja joios mais non seria,	B
ni jois ses vos pro no.m tenria;	B
tal via faria q'oms ja	C
mais no.m veiria;	
cell dia moria donna pros,	C
q'ie.us perdria.	

My sweet beloved, for the sake of God, may the jealous one never laugh at my pain, for his jealousy would be very costly if it were to separate two such lovers; for I would never be joyful again, nor would joy be of any benefit to me without you; I would set out on such a road that no one would ever see me again; on that day would I die, worthy lady, that I lost you.

Stanza 3

9 1:27

Con er perduda,	A
ni m'er renduda	
donna, s'enanz non l'ai aguda?	
Qe drutz ni druda	A
non es per cuda,	
mas qant amantz en drut si muda,	
l'onors es granz qe.l n'es creguda,	B
e.l bels semblanz fai far tal bruda;	B
qe nuda enguda no.us ai,	C
ni d'als vencuda,	
vol guda, cresuda vos ai	C
ses autr' ajuda.	

How shall my lady be lost, or restored to me, if she has not yet been mine? For a man or woman is not a lover just by thinking so. But when a suitor is accepted as a lover, the reputation that he gains is greatly enhanced, and the attractive appearance causes much stir; but I have not held you naked nor conquered you in any other sense; I have only desired you and believed in you, without any further encouragement.

[stanzas 4 and 5 omitted on recording]

Stanza 6

10 1:57

Dona grazida,	A
qecs lauz'e crida	
vostra valor q'es 'abelli da,	
e qi.us oblida,	A
pauc li val vida,	
per q'ieus azor, don'eissernida	
gar per gençor vos ai chauzida	B
e per meilhor de prez complida,	B
blandida, servida genses	C
q'Erecs Enida.	
Bastida, finida, n'Engles,	C
ai l'estampida.	

Worthy lady, everyone praises and proclaims your merit which is so pleasing; and whoever would forget you places little value on life; therefore I worship you, distinguished lady, for I have singled you out as the most pleasing and the best, accomplished in worth, and I have courted you and served you better than Eric did Enide. Lord Engles [Boniface, marquis of Montferrat], I have constructed and completed the estampida.

Guillaume de Machaut and the French *Ars nova*

"Music is a science that would have us laugh, sing, and dance."

Ars nova

Ars antiqua

The breakup of the feudal social structure inspired new concepts of life, art, and beauty. These changes were reflected in the musical style known as **Ars nova** (new art), which appeared at the beginning of the fourteenth century in France, and soon thereafter in Italy. The music of the French Ars nova is more refined and complex than music of the **Ars antiqua** (old art), which it displaced. Writers such as Petrarch, Boccaccio, and Chaucer were turning to human subjects; painters soon discovered the beauty of nature and the attractiveness of the human form. Similarly, composers turned increasingly from religious to secular themes. The *Ars nova* ushered in developments in rhythm, meter, harmony, and counterpoint that transformed the art of music.

Guillaume de Machaut (c. 1300–1377) was the foremost composer-poet of the *Ars nova* style. He took holy orders at an early age, became secretary to John of Luxembourg, king of Bohemia, and was active at the court of Charles, duke of Normandy, who subsequently became king of France. Machaut spent his old age as a canon at the Cathedral of Rheims, admired as the greatest musician of the time.

Chansons

Machaut's double career as cleric and courtier inspired him to write both religious and secular music. His output includes more than twenty motets, many secular **chansons** (French for "songs" and referring to a French secular polyphonic work), and an important polyphonic setting of the complete Ordinary of the Mass. His own poetry embraces the ideals of medieval chivalry. One of his writings, a long autobiographical poem of more than nine thousand lines in rhymed couplets, tells the platonic love story of the aging Machaut and a young girl named Peronne. The two exchanged poems and letters, some of which the composer set to music.

A polyphonic chanson is performed with voice and lute in this miniature representing the Garden of Love, from a Flemish manuscript of *Le Roman de la Rose* (c. 1500).

THE CHANSON *PUIS QU'EN OUBLI*

Machaut's music introduced a new freedom of rhythm characterized by gentle syncopations and the interplay of duple and triple meters. Machaut favored the chanson, which was generally set to courtly love poems written in one of several fixed text forms. These poetic forms—the **rondeau**, **ballade**, and **virelai**—established the musical repetition scheme of the chansons. We will study his love song *Puis qu'en oubli*, a rondeau for three voices with a refrain echoing the pain of unrequited love ("Since I am forgotten by you, sweet friend, I bid farewell to a life of love and joy"; see Listening Guide 5). In Machaut's elegant chanson, whose low melodic range makes it appropriate for three men's voices or a solo male voice accompanied by instruments, the two musical sections alternate in a pattern dictated by the poetry. The influence of this last great poet-composer was far-reaching, his music and poetry admired long after his death.

Listening Guide 5

eLG 1 (11–15) 1 (16–20)

Machaut: *Puis qu'en oubli (Since I am forgotten)* (1:46)

DATE OF WORK:	Mid-14th century
GENRE:	Polyphonic chanson, 3 voices
POEM:	Rondeau by the composer (with 2-line refrain)
MUSICAL FORM:	2 short musical sections, **A** and **B**, repeated as follows: **A-B-a-A-a-b-A-B** (capital letters indicate refrain text)

WHAT TO LISTEN FOR: Low range—all 3 parts for men's voices.
2 short sections of music (**A-B**), repeated in set scheme (rondeau).
Opening refrain text (2 lines of poetry) repeated in middle and at end.
Slow triple meter, with subtle rhythmic movement and syncopations.
Open, hollow cadences at ends of phrases.
3-part polyphonic texture.

Top-line melody of **A** section, with refrain text:

Puis qu'en ou - bli sui de vous, dous a - mis,

Top-line melody of **B** section, with refrain text:

Vie a - mou - reu - se et joie a Dieu com - mant.

			TEXT	MUSICAL FORM	TRANSLATION
11	0:00	Refrain	Puis qu'en oubli sui de vous, dous amis,	**A**	Since I am forgotten by you, sweet friend, I bid farewell to a life of love and joy.
			Vie amoureuse et joie a Dieu commant.	**B**	
12	0:25	Verse	Mar vi le jour que m'amour en vous mis;	**a**	Unlucky was the day I placed my love in you;
13	0:38	Partial refrain	Puis qu'en oubli sui de vous, dous amis.	**A**	Since I am forgotten by you, sweet friend.
14	0:52	Verse	Mais ce tenray que je vous ay promis:	**a**	But what was promised you I will sustain: That I shall never have any other love.
			C'est que jamais n'aray nul autre amant.	**b**	
15	1:17	Refrain	Puis qu'en oubli sui de vous, dous amis,	**A**	Since I am forgotten by you, sweet friend, I bid farewell to a life of love and joy.
			Vie amoureuse et joie a Dieu commant.	**B**	

Opening Doors to the East

The Middle Ages was an era of religious wars and exploration, both of which opened doors to the East. Between
1096 and 1221, there were five organized Crusades,
military expeditions undertaken by European Christians
in an attempt to capture the Holy Land of Palestine from
the Muslims. Along the way, crusaders massacred local
people, plundered their riches, and destroyed their artwork. Yet out of these violent episodes came a significant meeting of cultures. The crusading knights learned
from the expert military skills and weapons of the Turkish and Moorish warriors. The advanced medical and
scientific knowledge of the Arab world was imported to
Europe, and the Arab number system was adopted in
Western commerce and banking. (Until then, Euro-

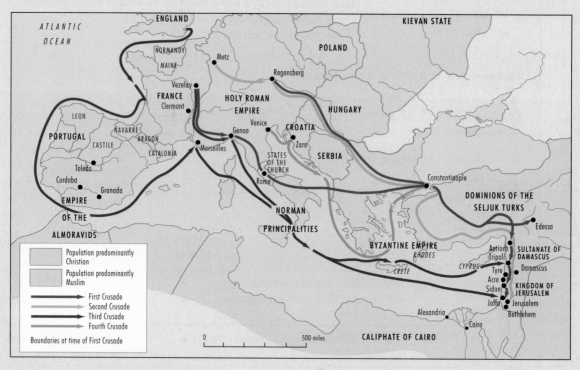

Boundaries at the time of the First Crusade.

Early Instrumental Music

The fourteenth century witnessed a steady growth in the scope and importance of
instrumental music. Though the central role in art music was still reserved for
vocal works, instruments played a supporting role in vocal music, doubling or
accompanying the singers. Instrumental arrangements of vocal works grew
increasingly popular. And instruments found their earliest prominence in dance
music, where rhythm was the prime consideration.

peans had used Roman numerals—I, II, III, IV, V; today, we primarily use Arabic numerals—1, 2, 3, 4, 5.)

What of the musical interaction of these cultures? Musicians often accompanied their noble lords to war: we have heard of one troubadour, Raimbaut de Vaqueiras, who left a colorful description of his adventures and who died in battle alongside his patron while on a crusade. These traveling minstrels brought music, theoretical ideas, and instruments of all types back to Western Europe. For example, the medieval rebec, a small, violinlike instrument, was derived from the Arab rabab (see illustration above right), and the loud, double-reed shawm used for outdoor events was closely related to the Turkish zurna. We will see later that more Turkish instruments—especially percussion—found their way into Western ensembles in the eighteenth century. Crusaders heard the sounds of the Saracen military trumpets and drums and soon adopted these as their call to battle. The foundations of our Western system of modes (or scale forms) also felt the influence of Eastern theoretical systems.

In this miniature from the *Prayer Book* of Alfonso the Wise, King David is playing a rebec on his lap, in the manner of the Middle Eastern rabab.

In 1271, the Venetian merchant and explorer Marco Polo (1254–1324) made a historic journey to China. Polo was welcomed by the great Kublai Khan, a Mongol ruler who had conquered northern China and further modernized the already highly sophisticated civilization there.

The information Marco Polo recorded throughout his travels helped open routes for the exchange of goods (especially silks and spices), arts, and ideas from East to West. Although these early encounters were isolated, in the centuries that followed they helped immeasurably to encourage communication between different nations and cultures.

Terms to Note

rebec	rabab
shawm	zurna
mode	troubadour

Suggested Listening

CD iMusic Iranian (Persian) music (*Avaz of Bayate Esfahan*)
Medieval dance with rebec (*Kalenda maya*)
    CD 1 (6–10); CD 1 (11–15)
CD iMusic Modern Chinese orchestra (*In a Mountain Path*)
Turkish music (Janissary ensemble; see p. 214)

We have already heard one medieval dance, *Kalenda maya*, which is also a song, and we have noted that much of what was played was improvised rather than written down. We can therefore only estimate the extent and variety of instrumental repertory during the Middle Ages. But our speculation is guided by an ever-growing body of knowledge from painting, historical documents, and surviving instruments. We can group medieval instruments into the same general families as modern ones— strings, woodwinds, brass, percussion, and keyboard—but they were also divided into soft (***bas***), or indoor, and loud (***haut***), or outdoor, categories according to their use.

Improvised music

Soft instruments   Among the most commonly used soft instruments were the *recorder*, an end-blown flute with a breathy tone, and its smaller cousin, the three-holed *pipe*; the *lute*, a plucked string instrument with a rounded back (of Middle Eastern origin); the *harp* and *psaltery*, plucked string instruments of biblical fame; the *hammered dulcimer* (derived from the santur of Persia); and the *rebec* (we heard this on *Kalenda maya*) and *vielle*, the two principal bowed string instruments of the Middle Ages.

Loud instruments   The loud category of instruments, used mainly for outdoor occasions such as tournaments and processions, included the *shawm*, an ancestor of the oboe, with a loud, nasal tone; and the slide trumpet, which developed into the early trombone known as the *sackbut*. Two other wind instruments became popular toward the end of the medieval era. The *crumhorn* (crooked horn) is a woodwind instrument shaped like the letter ⌡ with a cap over its double reed. The *cornetto* was made of wood and had a cup-shaped mouthpiece like a brass instrument's, with fingerholes like a woodwind's. We will hear some of these in our study of Renaissance dance music. Percussion instruments of the time included a large cylindrical drum called the *tabor* and small drums known as *nakers*, usually played in pairs. Several of these instruments had their origins in the Middle East, and nakers are mentioned in Marco Polo's account of his travels in Asia.

Organs   Several types and sizes of organ were already in use in the Middle Ages. There were large ones, used in churches, requiring a team of men to pump their giant bellows and often several more men to manipulate the cumbersome slider mechanisms that opened and closed the pipes. At the other extreme were *portative* and *positive organs*—smaller instruments with keyboards and a few ranks of pipes.

Performance practice   The revival of early music has grown in recent decades, as scholars and performers have worked to reconstruct some of the conditions under which the music was originally performed. Most of the ensembles that now specialize in this repertory boast players who have mastered the old instruments. Their concerts and recordings have made the public aware of the sound of these instruments to a degree that was undreamed of fifty years ago.

Three shawms and a trombone accompany dancers in this detail from the Adimari wedding chest, c. 1450.

The Renaissance

14

The Renaissance Spirit

"I am not pleased with the Courtier if he be not also a musician, and besides his understanding and cunning [in singing] upon the book, have skill in like manner on sundry instruments."

—BALDASSARE CASTIGLIONE

| KEY POINTS | ⑤ **StudySpace** online at www.wwnorton.com/enjoy |

- The Renaissance was an era of exploration, scientific inquiry, and artistic awakening and secularization.
- Artists and writers found inspiration in the cultures of ancient Greece and Rome (CP 5).
- Renaissance musicians were employed in churches, cities, and courts or in the trades of instrument building and music printing.

- The Renaissance is known as the golden age of *a cappella* singing (unaccompanied vocal music).
- Renaissance music features a fuller, more consonant sound (with thirds and sixths) than medieval music.
- Some Renaissance pieces are built on a fixed, pre-existing melody (*cantus firmus*); others closely reflect the text in music (*word painting*).

The Renaissance (c. 1450–1600) is one of the most beautiful but misleading names in the history of culture: beautiful because it implies an awakening of intellectual awareness, and misleading because it suggests a sudden rebirth of learning and art after the presumed stagnation of the Middle Ages. We now understand that history moves continuously rather than by leaps and bounds. The Renaissance was the next phase in a cultural process that, under the leadership of the church, universities, and princely courts, had long been under way.

The Arts in the Renaissance

Humanism

The Renaissance marks the passing of European society from a predominately religious orientation to a more secular one, and from an age of unquestioning faith and mysticism to one of reason and scientific inquiry. The focus was on human fulfillment on earth rather than on the hereafter, and a new way of thinking centered on human issues and the individual. This awakening—called humanism—was inspired by the ancient cultures of Greece and Rome (see CP 5), its writers, philosophers, and artworks.

New World

A series of momentous circumstances helped to set off the new era from the old. The development of the compass made possible the voyages of discovery that opened up new worlds and demolished old superstitions. While the great European explorers of this age—Christopher Columbus, Amerigo Vespucci, and Ponce de León, among others—were in search of a new trade route to the riches of China and the Indies, they stumbled on North and South America. During the course of the sixteenth and seventeenth centuries, these new lands became increasingly important to European treasuries and society.

The revival of ancient writings mentioned earlier, spurred by the introduction of printing (c. 1455)—a development generally credited to the German goldsmith and inventor Johannes Gutenberg—had its counterpart in architecture, painting, and sculpture. Instead of the Gothic cathedrals and fortified castles of the medieval world, lavish Renaissance palaces and spacious villas were built according to the harmonious proportions of the classical style. (The term "classical," in this context, refers to the art of the ancient Greeks and Romans, which exemplified the ideals of order and balanced proportions.) The strangely elongated saints and martyrs of medieval painting were replaced by the realism of Michelangelo's famous statue and the gentle smiling Madonnas of Leonardo da Vinci. The nude human form, denied or covered for centuries, was revealed as a thing of beauty and used as an object of anatomical study. Nature entered painting as did a preoccupation with the laws of perspective and composition.

Medieval painting had presented life through symbolism; the Renaissance preferred realism. Medieval painters posed their figures impersonally, facing frontally; Renaissance artists developed portraiture and humanized their subjects. Medieval painting dealt in stylized portraits while the Renaissance was concerned with individuals. Space in medieval painting was organized in a succession of planes that the eye perceived as a series of episodes, but Renaissance painters made it possible to see the whole simultaneously. They discovered the landscape, created the illusion of distance, and focused on the physical loveliness of the world.

The Renaissance first came to flower in Italy, the nation that stood closest to the classical Roman culture. As a result, the great names we associate with its painting and sculpture are predominantly Italian: they include Botticelli (1444–1510), Leonardo da Vinci (1452–1519), and Michelangelo (1475–1564).

The colorful tapestry of Renaissance life presents a galaxy of great names, including the German religious reformer Martin Luther (1483–1546), the Italian

The Renaissance painter preferred realism to allegory and psychological characterizations to unnatural, stylized poses. *Mona Lisa*, by **Leonardo da Vinci** (1452–1519).

statesman Machiavelli (1469–1527), and his compatriot the scientist Galileo (1564–1642). This was an age of great writers as well: among them were Cervantes (1547–1616) in Spain and, of course, Shakespeare (1564–1616) in England.

The Renaissance marks the birth of the modern European spirit and of Western society as we have come to know it. That turbulent time shaped the moral and cultural climate we live in today.

Musicians in Renaissance Society

Musicians of the fifteenth and sixteenth centuries were supported by the chief institutions of their society—the church, city, and state, as well as aristocratic courts. Musicians found employment as choirmasters, singers, organists, instrumentalists, copyists, composers, teachers, instrument builders, and music printers. There was a corresponding growth in supporting musical institutions: church choirs and schools, music publishing houses, and civic wind bands. A few women can be identified as professional musicians in this era, earning their living as court instrumentalists and singers. (In Chapter 16, we will learn more about a famous ensemble of vocalists known as the Concerto delle donne, or the Singing Ladies of Ferrara.)

The rise of the merchant class brought with it a new group of music patrons. This development was paralleled by the emergence, among the cultivated middle and upper classes, of the amateur musician. When the system for printing from movable type was successfully adapted to music in the early sixteenth century, printed music books became available and affordable, making possible the rise of great publishing houses in Venice, Paris, and Antwerp. As a result, musical literacy spread dramatically.

The human form, denied for centuries, was revealed in the Renaissance as an object of beauty. *David*, by **Michelangelo** (1475–1564).

Renaissance Musical Style

The vocal forms of Renaissance music were marked by smoothly gliding melodies conceived especially for the voice. In fact, the sixteenth century has come to be regarded as the golden age of the *a cappella* style (the term refers to a vocal work without instrumental accompaniment). Polyphony in such works was based on the principle of *imitation*. In this procedure, the musical ideas are exchanged between vocal lines, the voices imitating one another so that the same phrase is heard in different registers. The result is a close-knit musical fabric capable of subtle and varied effects. (See Listening Guide 6 for examples.)

Most church music was written for *a cappella* performance. Secular music, on the other hand, was divided between purely vocal works and those in which the singers were supported by instruments. The Renaissance also saw the growth of solo instrumental music, especially for lute and for keyboard instruments. In the matter of harmony, composers of the Renaissance leaned toward fuller chords. They turned away from the open fifths and octaves preferred in medieval times to the more "pleasing" thirds and sixths. The expressive device of *word painting*—that is, making the music reflect the meaning of the words—was much favored in secular music. An unexpected, harsh dissonance might coincide with the word "death," or an ascending line might lead up to the word "heavens" or "stars."

A cappella **music**

Imitation

Harmony

Word painting

Mythology in Music and Art

The rich mythology of ancient Greece and Rome—with its legendary gods, heroes, and otherworldly creatures—inspired many works of art, music, and literature. Renaissance composers frequently invoked figures such as Fortuna, Roman goddess of luck; Amor (better known as Cupid), god of love; and lesser spirits, such as nymphs, in their songs.

The Italian artist, Andrea Mantegna, depicted Venus, goddess of love, in a setting rich with musical symbolism. He was commissioned by his wealthy patroness Isabella d'Este to paint Mars and Venus on Mount Parnassus (see opposite). In the foreground we see the nine Muses gaily participating in a round dance and singing to a lyre played by Apollo, god of light and reason. (Some have identified this figure as Orpheus, who was renowned for his musical abilities.) Each of the Muses—daughters of Zeus (father of the gods)—presided over an art (poetry, dance, music). One legend tells that the song of the Muses caused volcanic eruptions (note the mountain on the left) which could only be stopped by the horse-god, Pegasus. Above them all stands Mars, the god of war, and his lover Venus; just to the left, Cupid aims at the jealous god Vulcan, who is forging metal strings, perhaps for Apollo's instrument. This work was painted for Isabella's private chambers at court in Mantua (in northern Italy), and the central figures undoubtedly represent Isabella herself and her husband Francesco, as embodiments of beauty and strength. All the musical imagery was in Isabella's honor as well, since she was an accomplished singer and lute player.

Another ancient musical god was Pan, who watched over shepherds and their flocks and who invented the syrinx, or pan pipe. Legend tells how Pan, who is half man, half goat, pursued a lovely nymph named Syrinx through the fields. Terrified by Pan's appearance, the nymph threw herself into a river and was transformed into a bed of reeds. The despairing Pan heard the mournful sound as the wind blew across the swaying reeds, and cut and bound some together to create a musical instrument. The Greek name for this instrument remains syrinx. Pan was so proud of his sweet-sounding music that he challenged Apollo to a musical contest. Pan played first, music so enchanting that the creatures of the forest gathered around to listen; but Apollo's touch on his golden lyre produced such ethereal music that the world was briefly silenced. After this, Apollo became the acknowledged god of music.

A statue of Pan playing pipes.

Cantus firmus Polyphonic writing offered the composer many possibilities, such as the use of a *cantus firmus* (fixed melody) as the basis for elaborate ornamentation in the other voices. As we have seen, triple meter had been especially attractive to the medieval mind because it symbolized the perfection of the Trinity. The new era, much less preoccupied with religious symbolism, showed a greater interest in duple meter.

The panpipe is one of the oldest and most widespread instruments—amazingly, a form of it developed on every continent across the globe. This simple shepherd's pipe can have from three to thirteen tubes, but seven is the most common number. It is still heard as a South American folk instrument—and panpipe ensembles, some even amplified, are frequently heard in city squares and streets today. The haunting breathy tone of this instrument reminds us of a thwarted love from early times.

Andrea Mantegna (1431–1506), *Mars and Venus*, or *Parnassus* (1497).

Terms to Note

panpipe (syrinx)	quadrivium
lyre	Orpheus
Muses	

Suggested Listening

Horner: soundtrack for *Troy*
Lerner and Lowe: *My Fair Lady*
CD iMusic Peruvian panpipes: *Los Jilicatas*

The preeminent composers of the early Renaissance (1450–1520) were from northern Europe, and in particular from present-day Belgium and northern France. Paramount among them was Josquin, who created some of the masterworks of the epoch. In the later Renaissance (1520–1600), Italian composers such as Palestrina and Monteverdi rose to prominence in both the realms of sacred and secular music.

15

Renaissance Sacred Music

*"We know by experience that song has great force and vigor
to move and inflame the hearts of men to invoke and
praise God with a more vehement and ardent zeal."*

—JOHN CALVIN

KEY POINTS   **StudySpace** online at www.wwnorton.com/enjoy

○ Renaissance composers set texts from the Ordinary of the Mass (Kyrie, Gloria, Credo, Sanctus, Agnus Dei) for their polyphonic Masses.

○ Important composers of sacred music (Masses, motets, hymns) include Josquin des Prez and Giovanni Pierluigi da Palestrina.

○ Composers used chant, and sometimes popular songs, as a **cantus firmus** (fixed song) in their masses.

○ *Ave Maria . . . virgo serena*, by Josquin des Prez, is a motet to the Virgin Mary set in varied textural styles (**imitative**, **homorhythmic**).

○ Palestrina's *Pope Marcellus* Mass met the musical demands made by the Council of Trent for *a cappella* singing with clearly declaimed text.

Music played a prominent role in the ritual of the church during the Renaissance. In addition to the monophonic Gregorian chant, music for church services included polyphonic settings of the Mass, motets, and hymns. These were normally multi-voiced and, especially in the early sixteenth century, based on preexisting music. Such works were sung by professional singers trained from childhood in the various cathedral choir schools.

The Motet in the Renaissance

In the Renaissance, the motet became a sacred form with a single Latin text, for use in the Mass and other religious services. Motets in praise of the Virgin Mary were extremely popular because of the many religious groups all over Europe devoted to her worship. These works, written for three, four, or more voices, were sometimes based on a chant or other cantus firmus.

One of the greatest masters of the Renaissance motet was the northern French composer Josquin des Prez (c. 1450–1521) who completes the transition from the anonymous composers of the Middle Ages and the shadowy figures of the late Gothic to the highly individual artists of the Renaissance.

Josquin des Prez and the Motet

*"He is the master of the notes. They have to do as he bids them;
other composers have to do as the notes will."*

—MARTIN LUTHER

Josquin (as he is known) exerted a powerful influence on generations of composers to follow. After spending his youth in the north, his varied career led him to Italy, where he served at several courts. Toward the end of his life, Josquin returned to his

IOSQVINVS PRATENSIS.

Josquin des Prez

native France, where he served as a provost at the collegiate church of Condé. He was buried in the choir of the church.

Josquin appeared at a time when the humanizing influences of the Renaissance were being felt throughout Europe. He was able to craft his work to the highest end: the expression of emotion. His music is rich in feeling, characterized by serenely beautiful melodies and expressive harmony. Josquin composed more than one hundred motets, at least seventeen Masses, and numerous secular pieces (including his delightful Italian song *El grillo*), making use of a variety of techniques. Some works were based on pre-existent monophonic or polyphonic models, others were original throughout.

CD iMusic

El grillo

Ave Maria . . . virgo serena is a prime example of how Josquin used the motet to experiment with varied combinations of voices and textures (see Listening Guide 6). In this four-voice composition, which sets a rhymed poem to the Virgin Mary, high voices engage in a dialogue with low ones and imitative textures alternate with **homorhythmic** settings (a texture in which all voices move together rhythmically). Josquin opens the piece with a musical reference to a chant for the Virgin but soon drops this melody in favor of a freely composed form that is highly sensitive to the text. The final couplet (two lines of text), a personal plea to the Virgin ("O Mother of God, remember me"), is set in a simple texture that emphasizes the words, proclaiming the emotional and humanistic spirit of a new age.

Homorhythmic

Listening Guide 6

eLG   **1 (16–22)**   **1 (25–31)**

Josquin: *Ave Maria . . . virgo serena* (*Hail Mary . . . gentle virgin*)   (4:38)

DATE OF WORK:	1480s?
GENRE:	4-voice motet
BASIS:	Chant to Virgin Mary (opening only)
TEXT:	Rhymed poem (a couplet, 5 quatrains, and a closing couplet)

WHAT TO LISTEN FOR: Rhymed strophic poem to the Virgin Mary, each verse beginning *Ave* (Hail).

4 voices (SATB) in varied settings, including imitative polyphony, dialogue (high vs. low voices), and homorhythm (all voices moving together).

A cappella performance (choral, without accompaniment).

Expressive final text (*O Mater Dei*) set homorhythmically, in personal plea from composer; closing hollow cadence.

Meter change, from duple to triple and back.

		TEXT	TRANSLATION	DESCRIPTION
16	0:00	Ave Maria, gratia plena,	Hail Mary, full of grace,	4 voices in imitation (SATB);
		Dominus tecum, virgo serena.	The Lord is with you, gentle Virgin.	chant used; duple meter.
17	0:45	Ave cujus conceptio	Hail, whose conception,	2 and 3 voices, later 4 voices;
		Solemni plena gaudio	Full of solemn joy,	more homorhythmic texture.
		Caelestia, terrestria,	Fills the heaven, the earth,	
		Nova replet laetitia.	With new rejoicing.	

Listening Guide continues

		TEXT	TRANSLATION	DESCRIPTION
18	1:21	Ave cujus nativitas Nostra fuit solemnitas,	Hail, whose birth Was our festival,	Voice pairs (SA/TB) in close imitation, then 4 voices in imitation.
		Ut lucifer lux oriens, Verum solem praeveniens.	As our luminous rising light Coming before the true sun.	
19	1:59	Ave pia humilitas, Sine viro fecunditas, Cujus annuntiatio, Nostra fuit salvatio.	Hail, pious humility, Fertility without a man, Whose annunciation Was our salvation.	Voice pairs (SA/TB); a more homorhythmic texture.
20	2:27	Ave vera virginitas, Immaculata castitas, Cujus purificatio Nostra fuit purgatio.	Hail, true virginity, Unspotted chastity, Whose purification Was our cleansing.	Triple meter; clear text declamation; homorhythmic texture.
21	3:04	Ave praeclara omnibus Angelicis virtutibus, Cujus fuit assumptio Nostra glorificatio.	Hail, famous with all Angelic virtues, Whose assumption was Our glorification.	Imitative voice pairs; return to duple meter.
22	3:59	O Mater Dei, Memento mei. Amen.	O Mother of God, Remember me. Amen.	Completely homorhythmic; text declamation in long notes, separated by simultaneous rests.

Opening of motet with imitative voice entries at regular intervals:

Imitation with paired voices (top 2 voices answered by bottom 2):

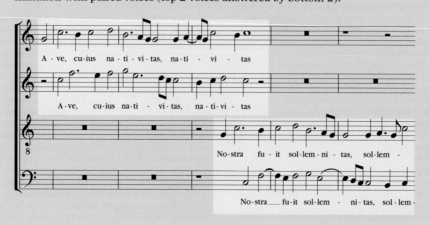

The Renaissance Mass

With the rise of Renaissance polyphony, composers concentrated their musical settings on the Ordinary, the fixed portion of the Mass that was sung daily. Its five movements are the Kyrie, Gloria, Credo, Sanctus, and Agnus Dei. (Today, these sections of the Mass are recited or sung in the *vernacular*, that is, the language of the country, rather than in Latin.) The first section, the Kyrie, is a prayer for mercy that dates from the early centuries of Christianity, as its Greek text attests. The Kyrie has an **A-B-A** form that consists of nine invocations: three of "Kyrie eleison" (Lord, have mercy), three of "Christe eleison" (Christ, have mercy), and again three of "Kyrie eleison." This movement is followed by the Gloria ("Glory be to God on high"), a joyful hymn of praise.

The third movement, the Credo ("I believe in one God, the Father Almighty"), is the confession of faith and the longest of the Mass texts. Fourth is the Sanctus ("Holy, holy, holy"), a song of praise, which concludes with the "Hosanna" ("Hosanna in the highest"). The fifth and last part of the Ordinary, the Agnus Dei ("Lamb of God, Who takes away the sins of the world"), is sung three times. Twice it concludes with "miserere nobis" (have mercy on us), and the third time with the prayer "dona nobis pacem" (grant us peace). A summary of the order of the Mass, with its Proper and Ordinary movements, may be found on p. 94. (Remember that we studied an Alleluia from the Proper of the Mass in Chapter 12.)

Early polyphonic settings of the Mass were usually based on a fragment of Gregorian chant (and sometimes on a popular song), which became the *cantus firmus* (fixed melody). The cantus firmus thus served as the foundation of the work, supporting the florid patterns that the other voices wove around it. It provided composers with a fixed element that they could embellish, using all the resources of their artistry, and when set in all the movements, it helped unify the Mass.

The *Requiem*, or Mass for the Dead, sung at funerals and memorial services, is the most important of the Masses for special services. Its name comes from the opening verse, "Requiem aeternam dona eis, Domine" (Grant them eternal rest, O Lord). Among the solemn prayers for the occasion is the "Dies irae" (Day of Wrath), an awesome evocation of the Last Judgment.

Ordinary of the Mass

Vernacular

Cantus firmus

Requiem

The Late Renaissance Mass

At the time of Josquin's death in 1521, major religious reforms were spreading across Northern Europe. After the Reformation—the Protestant revolt led by Martin Luther (1483–1546)—the Catholic Church responded with its own reform movement focused on a return to true Christian piety. Known as the Counter-Reformation, this movement by the church strove to recapture the loyalty of its people. The Counter-Reformation, which extended from the 1530s to the end of the sixteenth century, witnessed sweeping changes because of the deliberations of the Council of Trent, which extended, with some interruptions, from 1545 to 1563.

In its desire to regulate every aspect of religious discipline, the Council of Trent took up the matter of church music. The attending cardinals noted the corruption of traditional chants by the singers, who added extravagant embellishments to the Gregorian melodies. The council members objected to the use of certain instruments in religious services, to the practice of incorporating popular songs in Masses, to the secular spirit that had invaded sacred music, and to the generally irreverent attitude

Counter-Reformation

Council of Trent

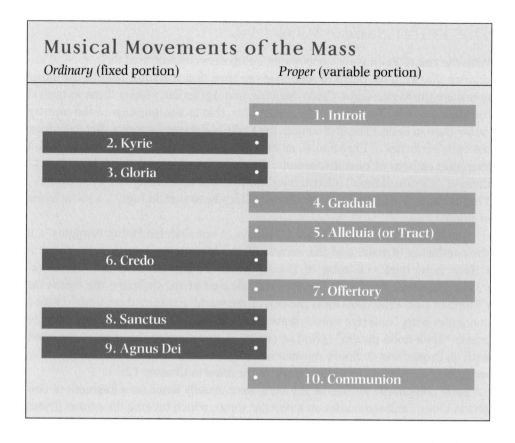

Musical Movements of the Mass

Ordinary (fixed portion)	*Proper* (variable portion)
	• 1. Introit
2. Kyrie •	
3. Gloria •	
	• 4. Gradual
	• 5. Alleluia (or Tract)
6. Credo •	
	• 7. Offertory
8. Sanctus •	
9. Agnus Dei •	
	• 10. Communion

of church musicians. In polyphonic settings of the Mass, the cardinals claimed, the sacred text was made unintelligible by the elaborate texture.

The committee assigned to deal with the problem issued only general recommendations in favor of a pure vocal style that would respect the integrity of the sacred texts, avoid virtuosity, and encourage piety. One composer who answered the demands for a reformed church music was Giovanni Pierluigi da Palestrina.

A choir and instruments participate in the celebration of Mass in this engraving by **Philip Galle**, after **J. Stradanus**, from *Encomium musices* of 1595.

Palestrina and the *Pope Marcellus* Mass 🅢

"I have held nothing more desirable than what is sung throughout the year, according to the season, should be more agreeable to the ear by virtue of its vocal beauty."

Giovanni Pierluigi da Palestrina (c. 1525–1594), called Palestrina after his birthplace, worked as an organist and choirmaster at various churches, including St. Peter's in Rome. His patron, Pope Julius III (r. 1550–55), appointed him to the Sistine Chapel Choir even though, as a married man, he was ineligible for the post. He was dismissed by a later pope but ultimately returned to direct another choir at St. Peter's, where he spent the last twenty-three years of his life.

Palestrina wrote over a hundred Masses, including his famous *Pope Marcellus* Mass (Marcellus was successor to Julius III). Since the papal choir at the time sang without instrumental accompaniment, the *Pope Marcellus* Mass was probably performed *a cappella*. It was written for six voice parts—soprano, alto, two tenors, and two basses, a typical setting for the all-male church choirs of the era. The highest voice was sung by boy sopranos or male falsettists (singing in falsetto, or head voice), the alto part by male altos, or countertenors (tenors with very high voices), and the lower parts were distributed among the normal ranges of the male voice.

Palestrina presents his earliest printed work to Pope Julius III, in this 16th-century engraving.

Listening Guide 7	eLG	1 (23–24) 1 (32–33)

Palestrina: *Pope Marcellus* Mass, Gloria (5:50)

DATE OF WORK:	Published 1567
GENRE:	Mass; Gloria, from a setting of the Ordinary
VOICES:	6 (SATTBB)
CHARACTERISTICS:	Frequent textural changes, reduction of voices

WHAT TO LISTEN FOR: Monophonic chant opening (*Gloria in excelsis Deo*).
Changes of density and texture set in various registers (high vs. low voices).
A cappella performance (choral, with no accompaniment).
Clearly audible text set syllabically.
Alternation of homorhythmic and polyphonic textures.
Full, consonant harmony.

First phase of Gloria, sung monophonically, shown in chant notation:

G Ló- ri- a in ex-cél-sis De- o.

Listening Guide continues

Second phase of Gloria, in 6 voice parts (4 singing at one time), with clear word declamation:

		TEXT	NO. OF VOICES	TRANSLATION
23	0:00	Gloria in excelsis Deo	1	Glory be to God on high,
		et in terra pax hominibus	4	and on earth peace to men
		bonae voluntatis.	4	of good will.
		Laudamus te. Benedicimus te.	4	We praise Thee. We bless Thee.
		Adoramus te.	3	We adore Thee.
		Glorificamus te.	4	We glorify Thee.
		Gratias agimus tibi propter	5/4	We give Thee thanks for
		magnam gloriam tuam.	3/4	Thy great glory.
		Domine Deus, Rex caelestis,	4	Lord God, heavenly King,
		Deus Pater omnipotens.	3	God, the Father Almighty.
		Domine Fili	4	O Lord, the only-begotten Son,
		unigenite, Jesu Christe.	6/5	Jesus Christ.
		Domine Deus, Agnus Dei,	3/4	Lord God, Lamb of God,
		Filius Patris.	6	Son of the Father.
24	2:44	Qui tollis peccata mundi,	4	Thou that takest away the sins of the world,
		miserere nobis.	4	have mercy on us.
		Qui tollis peccata mundi,	4/5	Thou that takest away the sins of the world,
		suscipe deprecationem nostram.	6/4	receive our prayer.
		Qui sedes ad dexteram Patris,	3	Thou that sittest at the right hand of the Father,
		miserere nobis.	3	have mercy on us.
		Quoniam tu solus sanctus.	4	For Thou alone art holy.
		Tu solus Dominus.	4	Thou only art the Lord.
		Tu solus Altissimus.	4	Thou alone art most high.
		Jesu Christe, cum Sancto Spiritu	6/3/4	Jesus Christ, along with the Holy Spirit
		in gloria Dei Patris.	4/5	in the glory of God the Father.
		Amen.	6	Amen.

The Gloria from the *Pope Marcellus* Mass exhibits Palestrina's hallmark style. The work begins with a monophonic intonation of the opening line, "Gloria in excelsis Deo" (Glory be to God on high), which, according to church practice, is chanted by the officiating priest. Palestrina constructed a polyphonic setting for the remaining text, balancing the harmonic and polyphonic elements so that the words are clear and audible, an effect desired by the Council of Trent. Changes in register (setting high voices vs. lower ones) and in the number of voices singing at any one time vary the musical texture throughout. (See Listening Guide 7 for the text and analysis.) Palestrina's music is representative of the pure *a cappella* style of vocal polyphony. This was his ideal sound—restrained, serene, and celestial.

> **IN HIS OWN WORDS**
>
> *Our wisest mortals have decided that music should give zest to divine worship. If people take great pains to compose beautiful music for profane [secular] songs, they should devote at least as much thought to sacred song, nay, even more than to mere worldly matters.*

16

Renaissance Secular Music

"Come sing to me a bawdy song, make me merry."
—FALSTAFF, IN WILLIAM SHAKESPEARE'S *HENRY IV, PART 1*

| KEY POINTS | **StudySpace** online at www.wwnorton.com/enjoy |

- The Renaissance saw a rise in amateur music-making and in secular music (French *chansons* and the Italian and English *madrigals*).
- Instrumental *dance music* was played by professional and amateur musicians; *embellishments* (melodic decoration) were often improvised.

- The *madrigal* originated in Italy as a form of aristocratic entertainment.
- Monteverdi was a master of the Italian madrigal and of expressive devices such as *word painting*.
- The *English madrigal* was often simpler and lighter in style than its Italian counterpart.

Music in Court and City Life

In the Renaissance, both professionals and amateurs took part in music-making. Professionals entertained noble guests at court and civic festivities, and with the rise of the merchant class, music-making in the home became increasingly popular. Most prosperous homes had a lute (see p. 98) or a keyboard instrument, and the study of music was considered part of the proper upbringing for a young girl or, to a lesser degree, boy. Women began to have prominent roles in the performance of music both in the home and at court. During the later sixteenth century in Italy, a number of professional women singers achieved great fame (see p. 101). From the union of poetry and music arose two important secular genres: the *chanson* and the *madrigal*.

The Chanson

In the fifteenth century, the chanson was the favored genre at the courts of the Burgundian dukes and the kings of France, all great patrons of the arts. Chansons

Musicians perform a polyphonic chanson with voice, flute, and lute. *The Prodigal Son among the Courtesans* (16th century, artist unknown).

were usually written for three or four voices and set to the courtly love verses of French Renaissance poets. We saw in the case of a Machaut chanson that the text, in a fixed form (rondeau), established the type of setting and musical repetition scheme. By the early sixteenth century, poetic structures were freer, without set repetition patterns.

The Renaissance chanson continued to be a favorite secular form throughout the sixteenth century. As the era progressed, the texts covered a wider range of emotions, from amorous to lusting to religious.

Instrumental Dance Music

With the advent of music printing, books of instrumental dance music became readily available for solo instruments as well as for small ensembles. The dances were often fashioned from vocal works such as madrigals and chansons, which were published in simplified versions that were played instead of sung.

These dance arrangements did not specify which instruments to use. As in medieval performances, they were determined by the particular occasion. Outdoor performances called for loud instruments such as the shawm and sackbut (medieval oboe and trombone); for intimate settings, soft instruments such as recorders and bowed strings were preferred. Although percussion parts were not written out in Renaissance music, evidence suggests that they were improvised.

One of the most popular dance collections of the century was published in Antwerp (in modern-day Belgium) in 1551 by Tielman Susato (c. 1515–c. 1571), a well-known printer, composer, and instrumentalist. Our selection is a set of three *rondes*. (A ronde is a lively round dance, usually performed outdoors.) Our recording features the loud (haut) wind band, which includes double reeds (*shawms* of various sizes), brass (*sackbut* and *cornetto*—a hybrid brass/woodwind instrument) and percussion (*tabor* and *tambourine*). (See Listening Guide 8.)

Loud winds accompany an aristocratic group dancing a *ronde*. From a 15th-century French manuscript.

Listening Guide 8

eLG 1 (25–28) 1 (38–41)

Susato: Three Dances   (2:29)

DATE:	1551 (published in *Danserye* collection)
DANCE TYPE:	Ronde (a round dance), in duple meter, arranged for 4-part ensemble
MUSICAL FORM:	Binary form (2 sections, each repeated, **A-A-B-B**)
ENSEMBLE:	Loud (*haut*) wind band (shawm, cornetto, sackbut, tabor, tambourine)

WHAT TO LISTEN FOR: Lively, quick-paced dance tunes.
Each dance in binary form, with 2 repeated sections.
Regular phrases of 4 or 8 measures.
Prominence of melody, played by various loud solo instruments.
Occasional embellishments on the melody.
Transition between second and third dance to change key.
Final repeat of first dance and chord for dancers' bow.

Ronde 1

		SECTION	INSTRUMENTS
25	0:00	**A**	Solo shawm playing melody alone (4 measures).
	0:06	**A**	Shawm with tabor.
	0:11	**B**	Loud ensemble (shawm, trombones, tabor), 8 measures.
	0:22	**B**	Repeat of **B**.

Opening phrase (**A**) of Ronde 1:

Ronde 2

26	0:33	**C**	Softer solo instrument (cornetto), with trombones, shawm, and tambourine, 4 measures; modal harmony.
	0:38	**C**	Repeat of **C**.
	0:44	**D**	New section, more contrapuntal, 8 measures.
	0:55	**D**	Repeat of **D**, with embellishments.

Opening phrase (**C**) of Ronde 2:

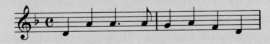

Transition (added link to modulate to next dance).

1:12	**A**	Based on Ronde 1 opening, heard 4 times, each with melody played by a different instrument.

Listening Guide continues

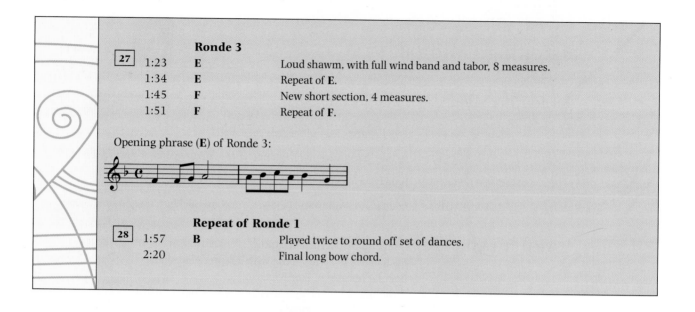

Ronde 3

27	1:23	E	Loud shawm, with full wind band and tabor, 8 measures.
	1:34	E	Repeat of **E**.
	1:45	F	New short section, 4 measures.
	1:51	F	Repeat of **F**.

Opening phrase (**E**) of Ronde 3:

Repeat of Ronde 1

| 28 | 1:57 | B | Played twice to round off set of dances. |
| | 2:20 | | Final long bow chord. |

Embellishments

Each dance is in two repeated sections (**A-A-B-B**) in a structure known as *binary form* (see p. 28). On the repeats, the musicians devise *embellishments*, or melodic decorations, and the sound is deepened and enriched by adding instruments. The second ronde in our set provides contrast through the softer sound of the cornetto and the modal quality of the harmony. The third dance, which features a noisy shawm, sounds raucous in comparison.

The dances unfold in regular four- or eight-measure phrases. The set closes with a brief return to the first tune, rounding out and unifying the form. A final chord provides a cue for the dancers to make a sweeping bow. One can just imagine the merriment of the crowd performing these circle dances at a street fair, a wedding, or even a courtly feast!

The Italian Madrigal

"By shallow rivers to whose falls
melodious birds sing madrigals."

—CHRISTOPHER MARLOWE

Poetry

The sixteenth-century *madrigal*—perhaps the most important secular genre of the era—was an aristocratic form of poetry and music that flourished at the Italian courts. The text consisted of a short poem of lyric or reflective character, often including emotional words for weeping, sighing, trembling, and dying, which the Italian madrigalists set with a wealth of expression. Love and unsatisfied desire were popular topics, but by no means the only ones. Humor and satire, political themes, and scenes and incidents of city and country life were also portrayed; the Italian madrigal literature of the sixteenth century therefore presents a vivid panorama of Renaissance thought and feeling.

Instruments participated in the performance of madrigals, duplicating or even substituting for the voices. Sometimes only the top part was sung while the other lines were played on instruments. During the first period of the Renaissance madrigal (c. 1525–50) the composer's chief concern was to give pleasure to the perform-

ers, often amateurs, without much thought to virtuosic display. In the middle phase (c. 1550–80), the
madrigal became an art form in which words and
music were clearly linked.

The final phase of the Italian madrigal (1580–
1620) extended beyond the late Renaissance into the
world of the Baroque. The form became the direct
expression of the composer's musical personality and
feelings. Certain traits were carried to an extreme: rich
chromatic harmony, dramatic declamation, vocal virtuosity, and vivid depiction of emotional words in
music.

A stylized 16th-century painting of four singers performing
from music part books. The
couple in back are beating
time. *Concert in the Open Air*,
Anonymous (Italian School).

Monteverdi and the Madrigal

The late Renaissance madrigal came to full flower in the music of Claudio Monteverdi (1567–1643), who between 1587 and 1643 published eight books of madrigals that span the transition from Renaissance to Baroque styles (his ninth book was
published after his death).

Monteverdi's five-voice *Ecco mormorar l'onde* (*Hear, now, the waves murmur*) is
one of his most attractive madrigals and one frequently performed by choirs today.
The courtly text—an idealized nature study—by Torquato Tasso inspired Monteverdi toward rich musical pictorialization of the imagery, a technique referred to
as **word painting**. Listen for the murmuring of the gentle waves ("ecco mormorar
l'onde") as they rise and fall; the rustling of the leaves ("tremolar le fronde") in
quicker notes; the melismatic song of the birds ("vaghi augelli cantar soavemente"), and the delicate melodic turns depicting the calm morning breeze
("l'aura matutina"). The five voices function in groups of two or three, tossing the
ideas back and forth, until the last line; here the image of the "heavy hearts" is
magnified by the drawn-out, overlapping chords (see Listening Guide 9).

Word painting

By the time of his second madrigal publication in 1590, in which *Ecco mormorar
l'onde* appeared, Monteverdi had already traveled to the city of Ferrara, where he
heard a new style of singing that featured a famous ensemble of professional women
singers known as the Concerto delle donne (Ensemble of the Ladies). One court
visitor described their brilliant florid singing:

> The ladies vied with each other . . . in the design of exquisite passages. . . . They mod-
> erated their voices, loud or soft, heavy or light, according to the demands of the piece
> they were singing; now slow, breaking off sometimes with a gentle sigh, now singing
> long passages legato or detached, now turns, now leaps, now with long trills, now
> short, or again with sweet running passages sung softly to which one sometimes
> heard an echo answer unexpectedly. They accompanied the music and the sentiment
> with appropriate facial expressions, glances, and gesture. . . . They made the words
> clear in such a way that one could hear even the last syllable of every word.

Monteverdi, one of many composers who wrote music for these famous singers,
created a unique style that intermingled their high voices in sweet dissonance and
elaborate ornamentation, accompanied by a bass instrument and a harpsichord or
lute. Although *Ecco mormorar l'onde* was written for five singers, we already hear the
contrast of high and low voices that sounded the beginnings of the new Baroque
style.

 Claudio Monteverdi

Listening Guide 9

eLG 1 (29–31)
1 (42–44)

Monteverdi: *Ecco mormorar l'onde (Here, now, the waves murmur)*

DATE OF WORK: Published 1590, Second Book of Madrigals

GENRE: Italian madrigal, 5 voices (SSATB)

TEXT: 14 lines, rhyming *a-a-b-b-c-c-d-d-e-e-f-f-g-g* by Torquato Tasso

WHAT TO LISTEN FOR: Careful musical pictorialization of each image of nature (waves, rustling leaves, birds' song, breeze).
Alternation of voice groups, from low to high, in playful exchange.
Clear text declamation and repeated phrases.
Somber mood and slower pace in closing line, to portray "heavy heart."

		TEXT	TRANSLATION
29	0:00	Ecco mormorar l'onde	Here, now, the waves murmur
		e tremolar le fronde	And the leaves and young poplars tremble
		a l'aura matutina e gli arborscelli,	In the morning breeze
		[Ecco mormorar . . .]	[Here, now, the waves murmur . . .]
	1:04	e sovra i verdi rami i vaghi augelli	And upon the green branches the enchanting birds
		cantar soavemente,	Sing sweetly,
		e rider l'oriente.	And the East smiles.
30	1:31	Ecco già l'alba appare	Here, now, the dawn breaks
		e si specchia nel mare,	And is mirrored in the sea,
		e rasserena il cielo,	And calms the sky,
		e imperla il dolce gielo,	And adorns the light frost with pearls,
		e gli alti monti indora.	And gilds the towering mountains.
		Oh, bella e vag'aurora,	O lovely, gentle dawn,
31	2:30	l'aura è tua messaggiera, e tu de l'aura	The breeze is your messenger, and you of the breeze
		ch'ogni arso cor ristaura!	That restores every heavy heart.

—Translation by William F. Prizer

Examples of word painting:

Rustling of leaves ("tremolar le fronde"), in wavelike pattern:

Morning breeze ("a l'aura matutina"), with flowing melisma:

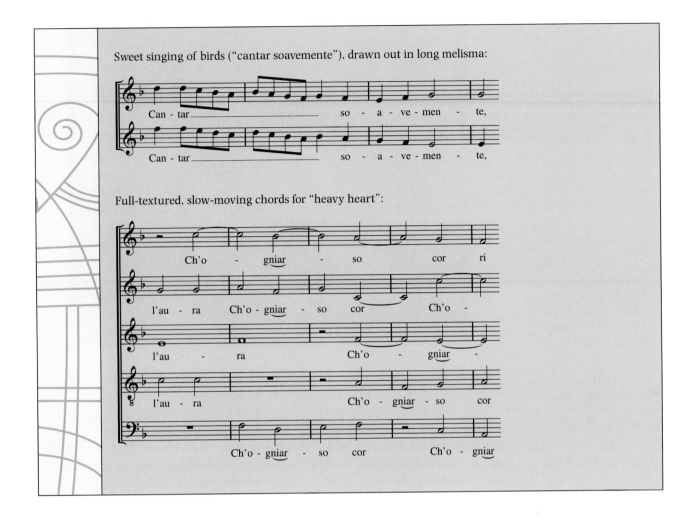

Sweet singing of birds ("cantar soavemente"), drawn out in long melisma:

Full-textured, slow-moving chords for "heavy heart":

The English Madrigal

"Since singing is so good a thing,
I wish that all men would learne to sing."

—WILLIAM BYRD

Just as Shakespeare adapted the Italian sonnet, so the English composers developed the Italian madrigal into a native art form. The brilliance of the Elizabethan age is reflected in the school of madrigalists who flourished in the late sixteenth century, during the reigns of Elizabeth I (1558–1603) and James I (1603–25). Important figures include Thomas Morley and John Farmer, whom we will study.

In the first collection of Italian madrigals published in England, titled *Musica transalpina* (*Music from beyond the Alps*, 1588), the songs were "Englished"—that is, the texts were translated. In their own madrigals, the English composers preferred simpler texts. New, humorous madrigal types were cultivated, some with refrain syllables such as "fa la la."

JOHN FARMER'S *FAIR PHYLLIS*

Born around 1570, John Farmer (fl. 1591–1601) was active in the 1590s in Dublin, Ireland, where he was organist and master of the choirboys at Christ Church. In

A shepherd and shepherdess frolicking in the field, painting by **Abraham Bloemart** (1564–1651).

1599, he moved to London and published his only collection of four-part madrigals. One of these, *Fair Phyllis*, is particularly popular today.

The pastoral text and cheerful mood of *Fair Phyllis* make it a typical English madrigal. Also characteristic are the sectional repetitions, the fragments of imitation that overlap and obscure the underlying meter, the changes from homorhythmic to polyphonic texture, and the cadences on the weaker pulse of the measure. The last line of the poem is set to homorhythmic chords, with a change to triple meter.

The English composers also adopted the Italian practice of word painting. For example, the opening line, "Fair Phyllis I saw sitting all alone," is sung by a single voice (see Listening Guide 10 for the text). Note too that the statement that Phyllis's lover wandered "up and down" is pictured musically by the shape of the line; on the repeat of this section, one might imagine the lovers at play.

The Renaissance madrigal inspired composers to develop new techniques of combining music and poetry. In doing so, it prepared the way for one of the most influential forms of Western music—opera, which blossomed in the earliest years of the Baroque era.

Listening Guide 10

eLG **1 (32–33)**
1 (45–46)

Farmer: *Fair Phyllis* (1:21)

DATE OF WORK:	Published 1599
GENRE:	English madrigal, 4 voices
TEXT:	6 lines (*a-b-a-b-c-c*), 10 or 11 syllables each
MUSICAL STYLE:	Polyphonic, with varied textures

WHAT TO LISTEN FOR: Lighthearted, pastoral English text.

4 voices (SATB), in varied textures (monophonic at opening, later polyphonic, then homorhythmic).

Change from duple or triple meter ("oh, then they fell a-kissing").

Obvious word painting as expressive device.

TEXT

| 32 | 0:00 | Fair Phyllis I saw sitting all alone, |

Feeding her flock near to the mountain side.
The shepherds knew not whither she was gone,
But after her [her] lover Amyntas hied.

| 33 | 0:23 | Up and down he wandered, whilst she was missing; |

When he found her, oh, then they fell a-kissing.

0:48   Up and down . . .

Examples of word painting:

"Fair Phyllis I saw sitting all alone"—sung by soprano alone:

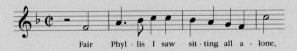

"Up and down"—descending line, repeated in all parts imitatively; shown in soprano and alto (overlapping in same register):

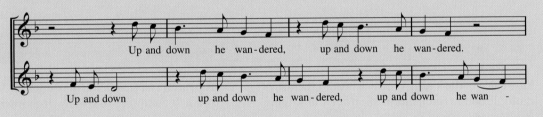

From Renaissance to Baroque

"The [Venetian] church of St. Mark was . . . so full of people that one could not move a step . . . a new platform was built for the singers, adjoining . . . there was a portable organ, in addition to the two famous organs of the church, and the other instruments made the most excellent music, in which the best singers and players that can be found in this region took part."

—FRANCESCO SANSOVINO

| KEY POINTS | Ⓢ **StudySpace** online at www.wwnorton.com/enjoy |

- Music at St. Mark's, in Venice, featured the use of multiple choirs (*polychoral singing*) and singing in alternation (*antiphonal*).

- Giovanni Gabrieli, choirmaster at St. Mark's, was the first composer to specify instruments and dynamics in music.

Polychoral Music in Venice

Polychoral singing

Giovanni Gabrieli

The highly polyphonic style of the late Renaissance did not die away suddenly but rather progressed to a new aesthetic of sound. In Venice, famous for its magnificent Basilica of St. Mark's (see p. 107) and its impressive line of choirmasters and organists who worked there, a new grandiose style evolved. The chief characteristic of the Venetian school was **polychoral singing**, involving the use of two or three choirs that either answered each other antiphonally, making possible all types of echo effects, or sang together. (*Antiphonal* performance suggests groups singing in alternation and then together.) This Venetian tradition reached its high point in the works of Giovanni Gabrieli (c. 1557–1612), who fully exploited the possibilities of multiple choirs, often accompanied by organ, strings, and wind instruments. (Gabrieli was the first composer to specify which instruments should play, and also to mark dynamics in the music.) The use of such large forces drew him away from

A COMPARISON OF RENAISSANCE AND BAROQUE STYLES

	RENAISSANCE (1450–1600)	BAROQUE (1600–1750)
COMPOSERS	Du Fay, Josquin, Susato, Palestrina, Farmer Monteverdi (early works)	Monteverdi (late works), Strozzi, Purcell, Mouret, Vivaldi, Handel, Bach
HARMONY	Modal harmony	Major and minor tonality
TEXTURE	Imitative polyphony	New monodic or solo style; polyphony in late Baroque
MEDIUM	*A cappella* vocal music	Concerted music (voices and instruments)
SACRED VOCAL GENRES	Mass and motet dominant	Oratorio, Lutheran cantata
SECULAR VOCAL GENRES	Chanson, madrigal	Opera, cantata
INSTRUMENTAL GENRES	Derived from vocal forms: dance music (instruments not specified)	Sonata, concerto grosso, sinfonia, suite (instruments specified)
USE OF PREEXISTENT WORKS	Some works built on cantus firmus	Works are freely composed
PERFORMANCE SITES	Church and court	Public theaters

the complexities of the older contrapuntal tradition to a broad, homophonic style in which the words were completely understandable. These traits look toward the dawning of a new era—the opulent and dramatic Baroque.

Venetian painters captured the splendid pageantry of their city. Singers and instrumentalists take part in a religious ceremony. **Gentile Bellini** (c. 1429–1507), *Procession in Piazza San Marco.*

Hans Hofman (1880–1966), *Rising Moon* (1965).

PART THREE

More Materials of Music

The Organization of Musical Sounds

17

CD iMaterials Musical Systems

"Composing is like driving down a foggy road toward a house.
Slowly you see more details of the house, the color and
slates and bricks, the shape of the windows.
The notes are the bricks and mortar of the house."

—BENJAMIN BRITTEN

| KEY POINTS | StudySpace online at www.wwnorton.com/enjoy |

○ An *octave* is the interval spanning eight notes of the scale.

○ In Western music, the octave is divided into twelve *half steps*, the smallest interval used; two half steps make a *whole step*.

○ The *chromatic scale* is made up of these twelve half steps, while a *diatonic scale* is built on patterns of seven whole and half steps that form *major* and *minor scales*.

○ A *sharp* (♯) is a symbol that raises a pitch by a half step; a *flat* (♭) lowers a tone by a half step.

○ Other scale types used around the world include *tritonic* (three-note patterns), *pentatonic* (five-note patterns), and *heptatonic* (seven-note patterns other than major or minor).

○ Some world cultures use *microtones*, which are intervals smaller than half steps; scales from other cultures—for example, Indian *ragas*—have extra-musical associations.

We have seen how the various elements of music form the building blocks of musical compositions. Now we can consider how these elements—in particular melody and harmony—function to construct a musical system, both in the West and elsewhere.

Pitch names for notes are the first seven letters of the alphabet (A through G), **Octave** which repeat when we reach an octave. An *octave* is an interval spanning eight notes of the scale. When we hear any two notes an octave apart sounding together, we recognize a very strong similarity between the two tones. Indeed, if we were not listening carefully, we might think we are hearing a single tone. (We give these two notes the same pitch name: for example, C and C an octave higher.) To understand why this is so, we need to review some basic principles of physics. A string that is set in motion vibrates at a certain rate per second and produces a certain pitch. Given the same conditions, a string half as long will vibrate twice as fast and sound an octave higher. A string twice as long will vibrate half as fast and sound an octave lower. This "miracle of the octave" was observed thousands of years ago in many musical cultures, with the result that the octave became the basic interval in music.

One important variable in the different languages of music around the world is the way the octave is divided. In Western music, it is divided into twelve equal semitones, or **half steps**; from these are built the major and minor scales (each with a different combination of seven notes), which have constituted the basis of this musical language for nearly four hundred years.

Half steps

> ## IN HIS OWN WORDS
>
> *There are only twelve tones. You must treat them carefully.*
>
> —PAUL HINDEMITH

The Formation of Major and Minor Scales

It is helpful to visualize a piano keyboard to understand how scales are formed. The twelve semitones that make up the octave constitute what is known as the ***chromatic scale***. You can see these twelve half steps on the keyboard (see p. 110), counting all the white and black keys from C to the C above it. Virtually all Western music, no matter how intricate, is made up of the same twelve tones and their duplications in higher and lower octaves.

You will notice that the black keys on the piano are named in relation to their white-key neighbors. The black key between C and D can be called C sharp (♯) or D flat (♭), depending on the context of the music. This plan applies to all the black keys. Thus a ***sharp*** raises a tone by a half step, and a ***flat*** lowers a tone a half step. Note that the distance between C and D is two half steps, or one ***whole step*** (the sum of two half steps).

Sharp and flat
Whole step

We introduced the notion earlier that certain tones in music assume greater importance than others; in Western music, the first tone of the scale, the ***tonic***, is the home base around which the music gravitates. Two main scale types—major and minor—function within this organizational system known as ***tonality***. When we listen to a composition in the ***key*** of C major, we hear a piece built around the central tone C, using the harmonies formed from the C-major scale. (Note that the term key here applies to the group of related tones.) Tonality is the basic harmonic principle at work in most Western music written from around 1600 to 1900.

Tonic

Tonality
Key

THE MAJOR SCALE

The major scale is the most familiar sequence of pitches. You can produce a C-major scale (*do-re-mi-fa-sol-la-ti-do*) by playing only the white keys on the piano from one pitch C to the next C. Looking at the keyboard you will notice that there is no black key between E and F (*mi-fa*) or between B and C (*ti-do*). These tones, therefore, are a half step apart, while the other white keys are a whole step apart. Consequently, a major scale is created by a specific pattern of whole (W) and half (H) steps—(W-W-H-W-W-W-H)—and can be built with this pattern starting on any pitch.

Within each major scale are certain relationships based on tension and resolution. One of the most important is the thrust of the seventh tone to the eighth

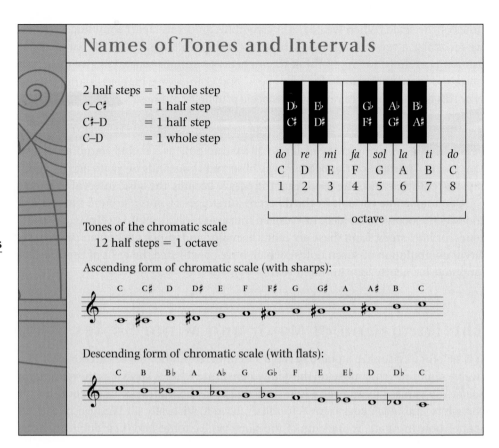

Names of Tones and Intervals

2 half steps = 1 whole step
C–C♯ = 1 half step
C♯–D = 1 half step
C–D = 1 whole step

Tones of the chromatic scale
12 half steps = 1 octave

Ascending form of chromatic scale (with sharps):

Descending form of chromatic scale (with flats):

CD iMaterials

(*ti* resolving to *do*). Similarly, if we sing *do-re,* we are left with a sense of incompleteness that is resolved when *re* moves back to *do; fa* gravitates to *mi;* and *la* descends to *sol.* We can hear some of these relationships at work in the beginning to the well-known carol *Joy to the World.* It starts on the tonic (*Joy*), then descends and pauses on the dominant (*World*), after which it continues downward, feeling a strong pull to the final *do* (on the word *come;* see melody on p. 13). Most important of all, the major scale defines two poles of traditional harmony: the tonic (*do*), the point of ultimate rest; and the fifth note, the dominant (*sol*), which represents the active harmony. Tonic going to dominant and returning to tonic is a basic progression of harmony in Western music.

THE MINOR SCALE

The minor scale provides a contrast to the major. One difference is that the minor scale has a lowered third degree. Therefore, in the scale of C minor, there is an E flat rather than the E natural (white key E) of the major scale; the interval C to E flat is smaller than the interval C to E in the major. The minor scale is very different from the major in mood and coloring. The pattern of the minor scale (W-H-W-W-H-W-W) may begin on any of the twelve tones of the octave. (See table on facing page for patterns of major and minor scales.)

Pattern of Major and Minor Scales

CD iMaterials

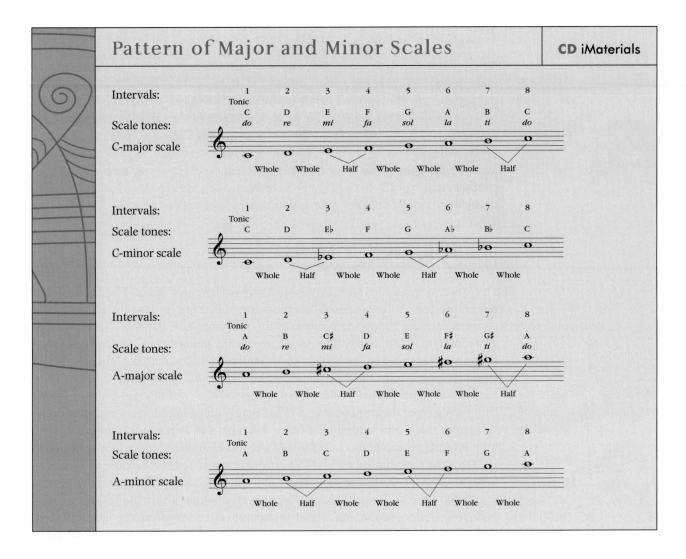

You can compare the sounds of the major and minor scales while listening to two versions of a tune from Haydn's Symphony No. 94 (see example below and the Listening Activity in Chapter 18). The work starts in C major with a folklike tune and then later shifts to the more dramatic key of C minor.

Haydn's Symphony No. 94, II, in Major and Minor Keys

CD iMusic
CD iMaterials

Original melody, in C major (with E natural, at the beginning):

Variation 2, in C minor (with E flat), at 1:58:

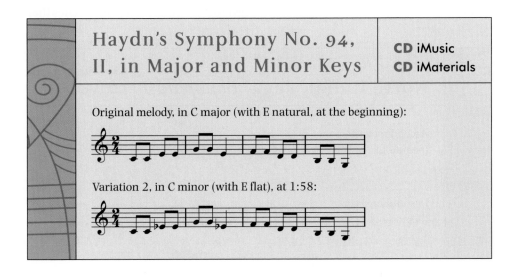

Diatonic and Chromatic Scales

Diatonic

Chromatic

Music that is clearly in a major or minor key uses the seven tones of the respective scale (primarily) and is therefore considered *diatonic*. In diatonic music, both the melody and the harmony are firmly rooted in the key. Some compositions introduce other tones that are foreign to the scale, drawing from the full gamut of the twelve half-steps that span the octave. These works are considered *chromatic* (from the Greek word *chroma* for color). Romantic-era composers such as Liszt and Wagner explored the possibilities of chromaticism to charge their music with emotion. In contrast, music of the Baroque and Classical eras tended to be largely diatonic, centering more closely on a key note and its related harmonies.

Other Scale Types

Pentatonic scale

Tritonic and heptatonic scales

Microtones

Inflection

Ragas

The Western musical system is only one way to structure music. The musical languages of other cultures often divide the octave differently, producing different scale patterns. Among the most common is the *pentatonic*, or five-note, scale, used in some African, Asian, and Native American musics. Pentatonic scales can be formed in a number of patterns, each with its own unique quality of sound. Thus the scales heard in Japan and China, although both pentatonic, sound quite different from each other. (Later we will hear a pentatonic scale in a traditional Chinese work.) Other scale types include *tritonic*, a three-note pattern found in the music of some African cultures, and a number of other seven-note, or *heptatonic*, scales fashioned from interval combinations other than those found in major and minor scales.

Some scales are not easily playable on Western instruments because they employ intervals smaller than our half step. Such intervals, known as *microtones*, may sound "off-key" to Western ears. One way of producing microtonal music is by *inflecting* a pitch, or making a brief microtonal dip or rise from the original pitch; this technique, similar to that of the "blue note" in jazz (see Chapter 71), makes possible a host of subtle pitch changes. Microtonal inflections can be sung and played on a wide variety of string and wind instruments. We will hear inflected pitches played and sung in such diverse styles as jazz, Cajun dance, and traditional Chinese music.

In some cultures, the ascending and descending orders of a scale may differ from each other, and even melodic formulas can be built into scales. In some music of India, for example, the scale formations—called *ragas*—contain certain pitches that

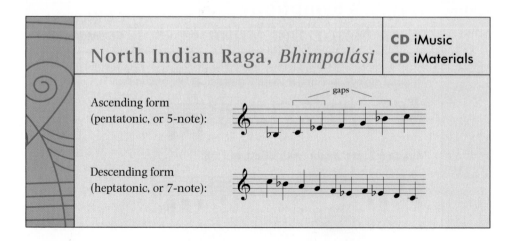

are heard in only one direction (see example opposite). These "scales" also have extra-musical associations connected with certain emotions, colors, seasons, times of day, or magical properties. The example opposite, entitled *Bhimpálasi*, is penta-tonic (B♭-C-E♭-F-G) when it ascends (with gaps between its notes) and heptatonic (seven-note) when it descends—its downward pattern also turns back up for one note. This raga, performed in the afternoon, is meant to evoke a mood of tenderness and longing in the listener.

Thus it is the musical system and the tones chosen in that system that determine the sound and character of each work, whether classical, popular, or traditional. They are what make Western music sound familiar to us and why sometimes the music of other cultures may sound foreign to us.

18

The Major-Minor System

CD iMaterials

"All music is nothing more than a succession of impulses that converge towards a definite point of repose."

—IGOR STRAVINSKY

KEY POINTS	**StudySpace** online at www.wwnorton.com/enjoy

- The **tonic chord**, built on the first scale tone, is the home base to which **active chords** (**dominant**, on V; **subdominant**, on IV) need to resolve.

- Composers can shift the pitch level of an entire work (**transposition**), or change the center, or key, during a work (**modulation**).

- Composers change the **key**, or modulate, during a piece to create tension and drama.

Active and Rest Chords

Just as melodies have inherent active and rest notes, so do the harmonies supporting them. The three-note chord, or **triad**, built on the first scale tone is known as the I chord, or the **tonic**, and serves as a point of rest. But rest has meaning only in re-lation to activity. The rest chord is counterposed against other chords, which are active. The active chords in turn seek to be completed, or resolved, in the rest chord. This striving for resolution is the dynamic force in Western music, providing a forward direction and goal.

Triad
Tonic

The fifth scale step (*sol*), the **dominant**, forms the chief active chord, which has a feeling of restlessness and seeks to resolve to the tonic. The triad built on the fourth scale step (*fa*) is known as the **subdominant**. The movement from the subdominant to the tonic (IV to I) is familiar from the chords accompanying the "Amen" sung at the close of many hymns.

Dominant

Subdominant

These three triads, the basic ones of our system, are enough to harmonize many simple tunes. The Civil War song *Battle Hymn of the Republic* (also known as *John Brown's Body*) is a good example (see p. 114).

Glory,	glory!	Hallelujah!	Glory,	glory!	Halle-lujah!
I			IV		I

Glory,	glory!	Hallelujah!	His truth	is	marching	on.
I			IV		V	I

The Key as a Form-Building Element

The three main chords of a musical work—tonic (I), dominant (V), and subdominant (IV)—are the focal points over which melodies and harmonic progressions unfold. Thus the key becomes a prime factor for musical unity.

At the same time, the contrast between keys adds welcome variety. Composers can pit one key against another, thereby achieving dramatic opposition between them. They begin by establishing the home key, then change to a related key, perhaps **Modulation** the dominant, through a process known as ***modulation***. In so doing, they create tension, because the dominant key is unstable compared to the tonic. This tension requires resolution, which is provided by the return to the home key.

The progression, or movement, from home key to contrasting key and back outlines the basic musical pattern of statement-departure-return. The home key is the anchor, the safe harbor; the foreign key represents adventure. The home key provides unity; the foreign key ensures variety and contrast.

The twelve major and twelve minor keys may be compared to rooms in a house, with the modulations equivalent to corridors leading from one to the other. (See illustration on p. 122 of the terraced levels in the Residenz, home of the prince-bishop of Würzburg.) We will see that modulation was a common practice of the Baroque period and was refined as a formal procedure in the Classical era. The eighteenth-century composer established the home key, shaped the passage of modulation—the "corridor"—in a clear-cut manner, and usually passed to a key area that was not too far away from the starting point. These procedures resulted in a spaciousness of structure that can be thought of as the musical counterpart to the balanced facades of eighteenth-century architecture.

Nineteenth-century Romanticism, on the other hand, demanded a whipping-up of emotions, an intensifying of all musical processes. In the Romantic era, modulations were more frequent and abrupt, leading to an emotion-charged music that wandered restlessly from key to key and fulfilled the Romantic artist's need for excitement.

Another concept in our musical system allows composers to take an entire work and set it, or transpose it, in a new key. This is convenient when a song's original key is too high or low to sing or play easily. You could begin on a different

Sophie Taeuber-Arp (1889–1943), *Composition in Circles and Overlapping Angles* (1930). The overlapping and repeated shapes in this artwork can be compared, in music, to new pitch levels or to modulations to another key.

pitch and shift all the tones a uniform distance to a different level through the process known as *transposition*. In this way, the same song can be sung in various keys by differing voice ranges (soprano, alto, tenor, or bass).

Transposition

Why does a composer choose one key rather than another? There are some historical reasons: for example, up to about the year 1815, brass instruments were not able to change keys as readily as they are now, since they had no valves. In writing for string instruments, composers considered the fact that certain effects, such as playing on the open strings, could be achieved in one key but not in another. Composers have even associated an emotional atmosphere or a color with certain keys, a concept not too far removed from the extra-musical meanings found in the ragas of India.

Although we are not always conscious of key centers and chord progressions while we are listening to music, these basic principles are deeply ingrained in our responses. We perceive and react to the tension and resolution provided by the movement of harmony, and we can sense how composers have used the harmonic system to give a coherent shape and meaning to their works.

Listening Activity: Musical Key

CD iMusic
CD iMaterials

Haydn: Symphony No. 94 in G major (*Surprise*), second movement

Let's return to Haydn's Symphony No. 94 to enrich your understanding of the musical principles of tonality. Sing the opening melody, using the scale syllables shown below:

What to Listen For:
- Opening key of C major, with melody and chords centered on the pitch C.
- First chord—the tonic (I), on C (*do*)—recurs often as a place of rest.
- Other important chords—the dominant (V), on G (*sol*), and the subdominant (IV), on F (*fa*)—are active chords that need resolution to the tonic, on C.
- Each part of the melody suggests a chord: first the tonic (I), then subdominant (IV), then dominant (V), then tonic (I) again, followed by a new chord on II, then dominant (V). At this point, *sol* (V) needs resolution to tonic.
- Try to keep the pitch C, the tonic, in mind.
- The key change (*modulation*) from C major to C minor (in 2nd variation; 2:20 into work).

Reviewing Concepts of Scale and Tonality:
- Major scale and tonality: ***Eine kleine Nachtmusik***, first movement (Mozart)
- Minor scale and tonality: **Toccata in D minor** (Bach)
- Pentatonic scale: ***In a Mountain Path*** (China)
- Pentatonic/heptatonic scale: ***Bhimpálasi*** (North India)
- Chromaticism: **"In the lovely month of May"** (Schumann)
- Modulation: ***Eine kleine Nachtmusik*** (Mozart), first movement (during first minute, modulates from G major to D major)

Do do mi mi sol sol mi	*fa fa re re*	*ti ti sol*
I (tonic)	**IV (subdom.)**	**V (dom.)**

do do mi mi sol sol mi	*do do fa(#) fa(#)*	*sol*
I (tonic)	**II^7 (new)**	**V (dom.)**

Jan Vermeer (1632–1675). *Lady Seated at a Virginal.*

PART FOUR

The Baroque Era

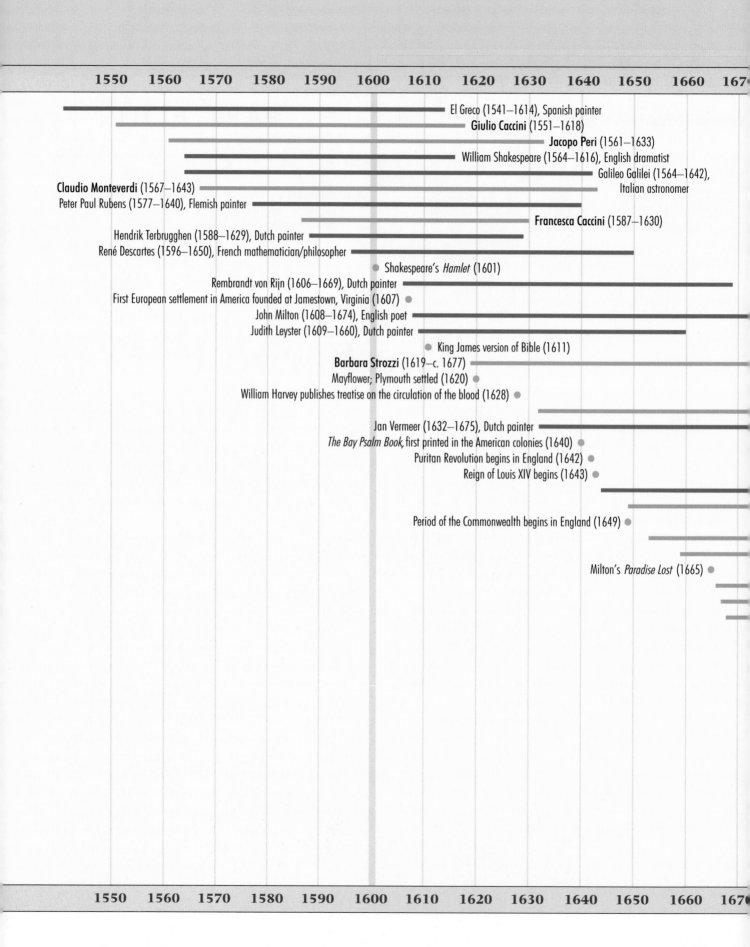

| 1550 | 1560 | 1570 | 1580 | 1590 | 1600 | 1610 | 1620 | 1630 | 1640 | 1650 | 1660 | 1670 |

El Greco (1541–1614), Spanish painter

Giulio Caccini (1551–1618)

Jacopo Peri (1561–1633)

William Shakespeare (1564–1616), English dramatist

Galileo Galilei (1564–1642), Italian astronomer

Claudio Monteverdi (1567–1643)

Peter Paul Rubens (1577–1640), Flemish painter

Francesca Caccini (1587–1630)

Hendrik Terbrugghen (1588–1629), Dutch painter

René Descartes (1596–1650), French mathematician/philosopher

Shakespeare's *Hamlet* (1601)

Rembrandt von Rijn (1606–1669), Dutch painter

First European settlement in America founded at Jamestown, Virginia (1607)

John Milton (1608–1674), English poet

Judith Leyster (1609–1660), Dutch painter

King James version of Bible (1611)

Barbara Strozzi (1619–c. 1677)

Mayflower; Plymouth settled (1620)

William Harvey publishes treatise on the circulation of the blood (1628)

Jan Vermeer (1632–1675), Dutch painter

The Bay Psalm Book, first printed in the American colonies (1640)

Puritan Revolution begins in England (1642)

Reign of Louis XIV begins (1643)

Period of the Commonwealth begins in England (1649)

Milton's *Paradise Lost* (1665)

| 1550 | 1560 | 1570 | 1580 | 1590 | 1600 | 1610 | 1620 | 1630 | 1640 | 1650 | 1660 | 1670 |

Baroque (1600–1750)

680	1690	1700	1710	1720	1730	1740	1750	1760	1770	1780	1790	1800

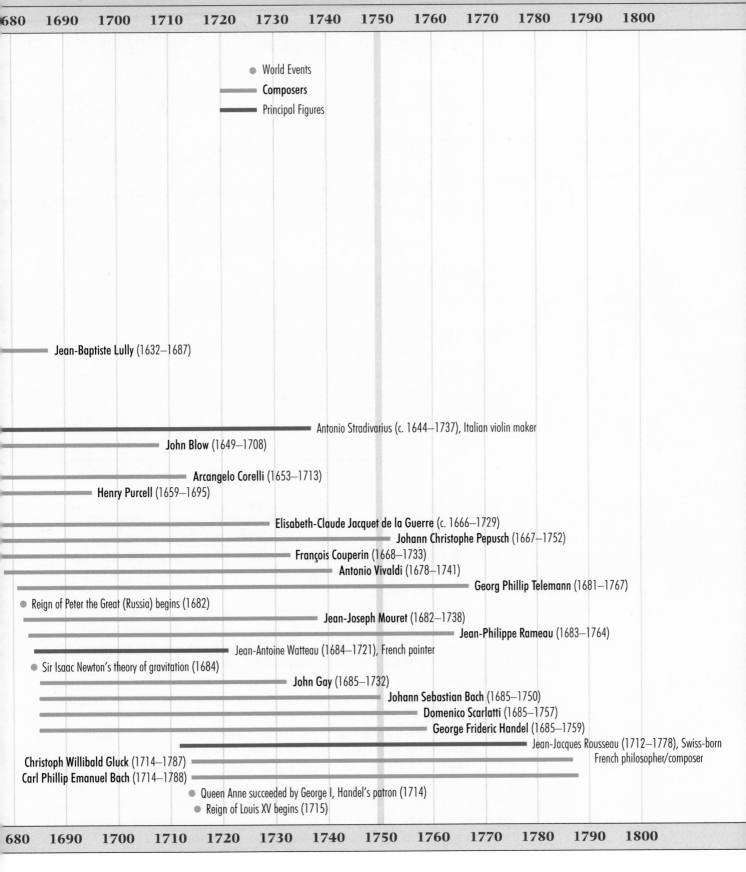

● World Events
— Composers
— Principal Figures

Jean-Baptiste Lully (1632–1687)

Antonio Stradivarius (c. 1644–1737), Italian violin maker

John Blow (1649–1708)

Arcangelo Corelli (1653–1713)

Henry Purcell (1659–1695)

Elisabeth-Claude Jacquet de la Guerre (c. 1666–1729)

Johann Christophe Pepusch (1667–1752)

François Couperin (1668–1733)

Antonio Vivaldi (1678–1741)

Georg Phillip Telemann (1681–1767)

● Reign of Peter the Great (Russia) begins (1682)

Jean-Joseph Mouret (1682–1738)

Jean-Philippe Rameau (1683–1764)

Jean-Antoine Watteau (1684–1721), French painter

● Sir Isaac Newton's theory of gravitation (1684)

John Gay (1685–1732)

Johann Sebastian Bach (1685–1750)

Domenico Scarlatti (1685–1757)

George Frideric Handel (1685–1759)

Jean-Jacques Rousseau (1712–1778), Swiss-born French philosopher/composer

Christoph Willibald Gluck (1714–1787)

Carl Phillip Emanuel Bach (1714–1788)

● Queen Anne succeeded by George I, Handel's patron (1714)

● Reign of Louis XV begins (1715)

680	1690	1700	1710	1720	1730	1740	1750	1760	1770	1780	1790	1800

The Baroque and the Arts

19

The Baroque Spirit

*"I do not know what I may appear to the world; but to myself I seem
to have been only like a boy playing on the seashore . . . whilst the
great ocean of truth lay all undiscovered before me."*

—SIR ISAAC NEWTON

| KEY POINTS | **StudySpace** online at www.wwnorton.com/enjoy |

- The Baroque era (1600–1750) was a time of turbulent change in politics, science, and the arts.
- It was also a time of religious wars (Protestants vs. Catholics) and of exploration and colonization of the New World.
- The era saw the rise of middle-class culture, with music-making centered in the home, church, and at the universities (in a group called the *collegium musicum*); art portrayed scenes of bourgeois life.
- In the New World, music served religion through the singing of psalms, important to both Protestants and Catholics (CP 6).

The Baroque period stretched across a stormy century and a half of European history. It began shortly before the year 1600 (a convenient date that need not be taken too literally) and came to a close with the death of Bach in 1750. The term "baroque" was probably derived from the Portuguese word *barroco*, an irregular-shaped pearl much used in jewelry of the time.

The years between 1600 and 1750 represent a period of change and adventure. The conquest of the New World stirred the imagination and filled the treasuries of Western Europe. The middle classes acquired wealth and power in their struggle against the aristocracy. Empires clashed for control of the globe. The era was characterized by appalling poverty and wasteful luxury, magnificent idealism and savage oppression. Against contradictions such as these evolved the pomp and splendor of Baroque art, in all its vigor, elaborate decoration, and grandeur.

The transition from the classically minded Renaissance to the Baroque was foreshadowed in the art of Michelangelo (1475–1564). His turbulent figures, their bodies twisted in struggle, reflect the Baroque love of the dramatic. In like fashion, the Venetian school of painters and northern masters such as Rubens studied and adopted their techniques, capturing the dynamic spirit of the new age and producing canvases ablaze in color and movement (see p. 118).

The Baroque was an era of absolute monarchy. Rulers throughout Europe modeled their courts on Versailles, a great palace on the outskirts of Paris built by Louis XIV. Courts large and small maintained elaborate musical establishments, including opera troupes, chapel choirs, and orchestras. Baroque opera, the favorite diversion of the aristocracy, told stories of gods and heroes of antiquity, in whom the nobility and courtiers saw flattering likenesses of themselves.

The middle classes created a culture of their own. Their music-making took place in the home, the church, and the university group known as *collegium musicum* (which still functions on many campuses today). It was for the middle classes that the comic opera and the prose novel, both genres filled with keen and witty observations on life, came into being. For them, painting abandoned its grandiose themes and turned to intimate scenes of bourgeois life. The Dutch School, embodying the vitality of a new middle-class art, reached its high point with Rembrandt (1606–1669) and Vermeer (1632–1675).

Under the leadership of wealthy merchants and financiers, the culture of the city came to rival that of the palace. These new art lovers embraced the beauty of brocade and velvet, marble and jewels. This aspect of the Baroque finds expression in the painting of Peter Paul Rubens (1577–1640), whose canvases exude a driving energy and a celebration of life. His voluptuous nudes established the seventeenth-century ideal of feminine beauty.

The Baroque was an age of discovery. The ideas of Kepler, Galileo, and Copernicus in physics and astronomy, of Descartes in mathematics and Spinoza in philosophy, were milestones in the intellectual history of Europe. The English physician

The bold and vigorous Baroque style was foreshadowed in this dramatic drawing by **Michelangelo** (1474–1564), *Studies for the Libyan Sibyl.*

Scientific frontiers

The Concert, by the Dutch painter **Judith Leyster** (1609–1660), presents a bourgeois, or middle-class, music scene.

The Flemish painter **Peter Paul Rubens** (1577–1640) instills his tribute to the pleasures of life with energy and drama. *The Garden of Love.*

William Harvey explained the circulation of the blood, and Sir Isaac Newton formulated the theory of gravity.

The Baroque was also an intensely devout period, with religion a rallying cry on some of the bloodiest battlefields in history. Protestants were centered in England, Scandinavia, Holland, and northern Germany, all strongholds of the rising middle class. On the Catholic side were two powerful dynasties: the French Bourbons and the Austrian-Spanish Hapsburgs, who fought one another as fiercely as they did their Protestant foes. Religion was an equally important part of life in the New World as well. Settled largely by Protestant refugees who emigrated from northern Europe during the seventeenth century, the American colonies founded their new society on religious principle, which some zealots carried to an extreme. The Spanish colonists of New Spain (Mexico, Central America, and the U.S. southwest) brought a fervent Catholicism to this region (see CP 6).

England's John Milton (1608–1674) produced the poetic epic of Protestantism (*Paradise Lost*), just as Dante had expressed the Catholic point of view in *The Divine Comedy* three and a half centuries earlier. The Catholic world answered Martin Luther's call for reforms with the Counter-Reformation, whose rapturous mysticism found expression in the canvases of El Greco

The rapturous mysticism of the Counter-Reformation found expression in this eerie landscape of **El Greco** (1541–1614), *View of Toledo.*

(1541–1614). These paintings were the creations of a visionary mind that distorted the real in its search for a reality beyond.

Creative artists played a variety of roles in Baroque society. Peter Paul Rubens and Anthony Van Dyck were not only famous painters but also ambassadors and friends of princes. The composer Antonio Vivaldi was also a priest, and George Frideric Handel an opera impresario. Artists usually functioned under royal or princely patronage, or, like Johann Sebastian Bach, they might be employed by a church or city administration. In all cases, artists were in direct contact with their public. Many musical works were created for specific occasions—an opera for a royal wedding, a dance suite for a court festivity, a cantata for a religious service—and for immediate use.

Role of the artist

20

Main Currents in Baroque Music

"The end of all good music is to affect the soul."
—CLAUDIO MONTEVERDI

KEY POINTS	**StudySpace** online at www.wwnorton.com/enjoy

- ○ The Baroque era marks the introduction of a new style—*monody*, featuring solo song with instrumental accompaniment.
- ○ Monody was developed by groups of writers and musicians (such as the Florentine Camerata) to recreate the musical-dramatic art of ancient Greece.
- ○ Harmony was notated with *figured bass*, a shorthand that allowed the performer to supply the chords through **improvisation**. The bass part, or *basso continuo*, was often played by two instruments (harpsichord and cello, for example).

- ○ The *major-minor tonality* system was established in the Baroque era, as was the *equal temperament* tuning system.
- ○ While early Baroque music moved more freely, later Baroque style is characterized by regular rhythms and continuous melodic expansion.
- ○ As musical instruments developed technically, the level of virtuosity and playing techniques rose.
- ○ The union of text and music was expressed in the Baroque *doctrine of the affections*.
- ○ Women musicians figured among the professional singers and instrumentalists of the Baroque era.

Origins of Monody

The transition from Renaissance to Baroque brought with it a great musical change: interest shifted from a texture of several independent parts (polyphony) to one in which a single melody stood out. The new style, which originated in vocal music around the year 1600, was named **monody**. Literally "one song," monody is solo song with instrumental accompaniment (not to be confused with monophony, which is a single unaccompanied line; see p. 23).

Monody (in right margin)

Monody was first cultivated by a group of Florentine writers, artists, and musicians known as the Camerata, a name derived from the Italian word for "salon." The members of the Camerata were aristocratic humanists who aimed to resurrect the musical-dramatic art of ancient Greece. Although little was known of ancient music, the Camerata deduced that music must heighten the emotional power of the text. Thus the monodic style came into being, consisting of a melody that moved freely over a foundation of simple chords.

The Camerata (in right margin)

The Camerata's members engaged in excited discussions about *le nuove musiche*, "the new music," which they proudly named "the expressive style." The group soon realized that this style could be applied not only to a short poem but also to an entire drama. With this realization, they fostered the single most important achievement of Baroque music: the invention of opera.

Origins of opera (in right margin)

New Harmonic Structures

The melody and chords of the new music were far removed from the complex interweaving of voices in the older Renaissance style, and a new kind of notation

Music and the Religious Spirit in the New World

Throughout history, music has helped people express and disseminate their beliefs. European settlers in the New World brought their faiths with them and, with the aid of music, converted some of the indigenous population. As a result, many people of modern-day Mexico (colonized by the Spanish) and of northeastern Canada (settled by the French) are Roman Catholics.

Some of the most elaborate compositions written in the New World during this era were composed in Mexico. From the onset of the Spanish conquest in 1519, missionaries used music as "an indispensable aid in the process of conversion" to Catholicism, according to the first bishop of Mexico. A polyphonic style arose that infused the rich musical tradition of Spain with native elements in their Masses, hymns, psalm settings, and in a secular (and sometimes devotional) genre known as the villancico.

In comparison, the music of the early Protestant settlers on the Eastern Seaboard of the United States and parts of coastal Canada was considerably simpler; their religious and social lives centered around the singing of psalms from the Old Testament. Although psalm books became increasingly available—imported from Europe and eventually published in the colonies—not everyone had one, nor were all colonists even literate. Hence, a singing style known as lining out came into practice, characterized by a slow, drawn-out tempo, with a leader chanting the text line by line before it was sung by the congregation. Some people embellished the tune, thus creating dissonant heterophony—two or more decorated versions of the melody sung simultaneously—a practice typical of many music cultures around the world.

Folklike devotional music was cultivated throughout the New World, in Mexico as noted above, and by African Americans and whites alike in the nineteenth and twentieth centuries in the form of dance tunes, spirituals, and gospel hymns (religious songs such as *Amazing Grace* sung at revivals and prayer meetings). One of the most famous examples is the so-called Shaker hymn, a dance song entitled *Simple Gifts* ("'Tis the gift to be simple"), written in 1848 by a church elder of the nearly defunct Shaker religious sect.

Today, gospel—an eclectic style of Protestant African-American hymns popular in worship and entertainment—and Contemporary Christian music—a type of sacred country rock—have supplanted these traditional songs and expressions of faith with new sounds that appeal to the hearts and ears of modern listeners.

Gospel singer Cece Winans performs at the 8th Annual Soul Train Lady of Soul Awards, on August 24, 2002.

Hernándo Cortés meets Aztec emperor Moctezuma, in 19th-century lithograph of *The Entrance of Cortez into Mexico*.

Terms to Note

villancico
heterophony
lining out

spiritual
gospel music

Suggested Listening

CD iMusic Gospel hymn (*Amazing Grace*)
CD iMusic Shaker hymn (*Simple Gifts*)
Spiritual (African American or white)

accommodated these changes. Since musicians were familiar with the basic harmonies, the composer put a numeral above or below the bass note, indicating the chord required (this kind of notation was called *figured bass*), and the performer filled in the necessary harmony. This system, known as **basso continuo**, often employed two instrumentalists for the accompaniment. One played the bass line on a cello or bassoon, and another filled in the harmonies on a chordal instrument (generally harpsichord, organ, or lute), thereby providing a foundation over which a vocal or instrumental melody could unfold.

Figured bass
Basso continuo

This shift to a simpler style based on a single-line melody and less complex harmonies lead to one of the most significant changes in all music history: the establishment of **major-minor tonality**. With this development, the thrust to the keynote, or tonic, became the most powerful force in music. Each chord could assume its function in relation to the key center, and the movement between keys, governed by tonality, helped shape musical structure. With this system, composers developed forms of instrumental music larger than had ever before been known.

Major-minor tonality

This transition to major-minor tonality was marked by a significant technical advance: the establishment of a new tuning system that allowed instruments to play in any key. Called **equal temperament**, this tuning adjusted (or tempered) the mathematically "pure" intervals within the octave to equalize the distance between adjacent tones, making it possible to play in every major and minor key without experiencing unpleasant sounds. This development greatly increased the range of harmonic possibilities available to the composer.

Equal temperament

Johann Sebastian Bach demonstrated that he could write in every one of the twelve major and twelve minor keys. His *Well-Tempered Clavier* is a two-volume keyboard collection, each containing twenty-four preludes and fugues, or one in every possible key. Today, our ears are conditioned to the equal tempered system, since this is how pianos are now tuned.

The Well-Tempered Clavier

Baroque Musical Style

*"If there is nothing new to be found in melody
then we must seek novelty in harmony."*

—GEORG PHILIP TELEMANN

During the Baroque era, the rhythmic freedom of the monodic style eventually gave way to a vigorous rhythm based on regular accent and carried by a moving bass part. Rhythm helped capture the drive and movement of this dynamic age. The elaborate scrollwork of Baroque architecture found its musical equivalent in the principle of continuous expansion of melody. A movement might start with a striking musical figure that spins out ceaselessly. In vocal music, wide leaps and chromatic tones helped create melodies that were highly expressive of the text.

Rhythm and melody

Baroque musicians used dissonant chords more freely, for emotional intensity and color. In setting poetry, for example, a composer might use a dissonance to heighten the impact of a particularly expressive word.

Dissonance

The dynamic contrasts achieved in Renaissance music through varied imitative voicings gave way to a more nuanced treatment in the Baroque. While few dynamic markings occur in seventeenth-century music, subtle dynamic shadings were very much a feature of Baroque performance and contributed to the expression of emotions, especially of the text. Baroque keyboard instruments, such as harpsichord and organ, inherently produced a kind of graduated, or terraced, dynamics by the use of different registers and timbres, and *forte/piano* contrasts and echo effects were also

Dynamics

The grand staircase of the Residenz, home of the prince-bishop of Würzburg, is a superb example of Baroque interior design, with its sculptural ornaments and elaborate decorations.

typical of the era. By comparison with later eras, Baroque composers were sparing in their use of expression marks, leaving these interpretive decisions to performers.

The Doctrine of the Affections

The Baroque inherited from the Renaissance an impressive technique of text painting, in which the music vividly mirrored the words. It was generally accepted that music ought to arouse the emotions, or affections—for example, joy, anger, love, fear, or exaltation. By the late seventeenth century, an entire piece or movement was normally built on a single affection, applying what was known as the *doctrine of the affections*. The opening musical idea established the mood of the piece, which prevailed until the work's end. This procedure differs markedly from the practice of later eras, when music was based on two or more contrasting emotions.

The Rise of the Virtuoso Musician

As the great musical instrument builders in Italy and Germany improved and refined their instruments, Baroque performers responded with more virtuosic playing. Composers in turn wrote works demanding even more advanced playing techniques. Out of these developments came the virtuosic violin works of Antonio Vivaldi (see p. 148), among others.

The emergence of instrumental virtuosity had its counterpart in the vocal sphere. The rise of opera saw the development of a phenomenal vocal technique, exemplified in the early eighteenth century by the *castrato*, a male singer who was castrated during boyhood in order to preserve the soprano or alto register of his voice for the rest of his life. What resulted, after years of training, was an incredibly agile voice of enormous range, powered by breath control unrivaled by most singers today. The castrato's voice combined the lung power of the male with the brilliance of the female upper register. When castrato roles are performed today, they are usually sung in lower register by a tenor or baritone, or in the original register by a countertenor, or a woman singer in male costume.

Improvisation | Improvisation played a significant role in Baroque music. In addition to realizing the abbreviations of the figured bass, musicians added their own embellishments to what was written down (a custom found today in jazz and pop music). The practice was so widespread that Baroque music sounded quite different in performance from what was notated on the page.

Castrato

Women in Baroque Music

Women continued to play an active and expanded role in the music of the Baroque. Barbara Strozzi (1619–1677), a prolific Italian composer of secular and sacred vocal music, is remembered as a singer and as a participant in the famous literary academies of early-seventeenth-century Venice. We will consider one of her vocal compositions in Chapter 22.

With the establishment of opera houses throughout Europe (the first was in Venice in 1637), the opportunity for women to enter the ranks of professional musicians greatly increased. Some reached the level of superstars, such as the Italian sopranos Faustina Bordoni and Francesca Cuzzoni, who engaged in a bitter, notorious rivalry. One French musician who enjoyed the patronage of King Louis XIV was Elisabeth-Claude Jacquet de la Guerre (c. 1666–1729), renowned for her harpsichord music and her biblical cantatas. Women also continued their important role as patrons of the arts and as hostesses at the salons where music was actively cultivated.

The Baroque was a culturally international period in which national styles existed—but without nationalism. Jean-Baptiste Lully, an Italian, created the French lyric tragedy. Handel, a German, wrote Italian operas for English audiences and gave England the oratorio. There was free interchange among national cultures. The sensuous beauty of Italian melody, the pointed precision of French dance rhythm, the luxuriance of German polyphony, the freshness of English choral song—these nourished an all-European art that absorbed the best of each national style.

The Baroque era also saw great voyages of exploration open up unknown regions of the globe, sparking a vivid interest among Europeans in remote cultures and far-off locales. As a result, exoticism became a discernible element of Baroque music. A number of operas looked to faraway lands for their settings—Persia, India, Turkey, the Near East, Peru, and the Americas. These operas offered picturesque scenes, interesting local color, and dances that may not have been authentic but that delighted audiences through their appeal to the imagination. Thus an international spirit combined with an interest in the exotic to produce music that flowed easily across national boundaries.

Portrait of French composer Elisabeth-Claude Jacquet de la Guerre (c. 1666–1729), by **François de Troy** (1645–1730).

Exoticism

A performance at the Teatro Argentina in Rome, 1729, as portrayed by **Giovanni Paolo Pannini** (1697–1765).

Vocal Music of the Baroque

21

Baroque Opera

"Opera is the delight of Princes."

—MARCO DA GAGLIANO

KEY POINTS ⑤ **StudySpace** online at www.wwnorton.com/enjoy

○ The most important new genre of the Baroque era was *opera*, a large-scale music drama that combines poetry, acting, scenery, and costumes with singing and instrumental music.

○ The principal components of opera include the orchestral *overture*, solo *arias* (lyrical songs) and *recitatives* (speechlike declamations of the text), and ensemble numbers, including *choruses*. The *librettist* writes the text of the opera.

○ The early Baroque master Claudio Monteverdi wrote operas based on mythology and Roman history, and he helped establish the love duet as a central component of opera.

○ The English composer Henry Purcell wrote *Dido and Aeneas*, based on *The Aeneid*, a Roman epic by Virgil.

The Components of Opera

An *opera* is a large-scale drama that is sung. It combines the resources of vocal and instrumental music—soloists, ensembles, chorus, orchestra, and sometimes ballet—with poetry and drama, acting and pantomime, scenery and costumes. To unify diverse elements is a challenge that has attracted some of the most creative minds in the history of music.

Recitative   In opera, the plot and action are generally advanced through a kind of musical declamation, or speech, known as *recitative*. This vocal style, which grew out of the earliest monodies of the Florentine Camerata, imitates the natural inflections of

124

speech; its movement is shaped to the rhythm of the language. Rarely presenting a purely musical line, recitative is often characterized by a patter and "talky" repetition of the same note, as well as rapid question-and-answer dialogue that builds tension. In time, two styles of recitative became standard: *secco* (Italian for "dry"), which is accompanied only by continuo instruments and moves with great freedom, and *accompagnato*, which is accompanied by the orchestra and thus moves more evenly.

Recitative gives way at lyric moments to the *aria* (Italian for "air"), which **Aria** releases through melody the emotional tension accumulated in the course of the action. The aria is a song, usually of a highly emotional nature. It is what audiences wait for, what they cheer, what they remember. An aria, because of its tunefulness, can be effective even when sung out of context—for example, in a concert or on a CD. Indeed, many arias are familiar to people who have never heard the operas from which they are excerpted. One formal convention that developed early in the genre's history is the *da capo aria*, a ternary, or **A-B-A**, form that brings back the first sec- **Da capo aria** tion with embellishments improvised by the soloist.

An opera may contain ensemble numbers—duets, trios, quartets, and so on—in **Ensemble** which the characters pour out their respective feelings. The chorus may be used to back up the solo voices or may function independently. Sometimes it comments and reflects on the action, as in the chorus of a Greek tragedy, or is integrated into the action.

The orchestra supports the action of the opera as well, setting the appropriate mood for the different scenes. The orchestra also performs the *overture*, an instru- **Overture** mental number heard at the beginning of most operas, which may introduce melodies from the arias. Each act of the opera normally opens with an orchestral introduction, and between scenes we may find interludes, or *sinfonias*, as they were called in Baroque opera.

The opera composer works with a *librettist*, who writes the text of the work, using dramatic insight to create characters and the storyline, with its main threads and subplots. The *libretto*, the text or script of the opera, must be devised to give the **Libretto** composer an opportunity to write music for the diverse numbers—recitatives and arias, ensembles, choruses, interludes—that have become the traditional features of this art form.

Early Opera in Italy

An outgrowth of Renaissance theatrical traditions and the musical experiments of the Florentine Camerata, early opera lent itself to the lavish spectacles and scenic displays that graced royal weddings and similar ceremonial occasions. Two such operas, *Orfeo* (1607) and *Arianna* (1608), were composed by the first great master of the new genre, Claudio Monteverdi (1567–1643). In Monteverdi's operas, the **Claudio Monteverdi** innovations of the Florentine Camerata reached artistic maturity, and the dramatic spirit of the Baroque found its true representative.

Although his earliest operas derived their plots from Greek mythology, for *The Coronation of Poppea* (1642), a late work from his Venetian period, Monteverdi turned to history. By this time, the first public opera houses had opened in Venice; opera was moving out of the palace and becoming a popular entertainment. In his early court operas, Monteverdi used an orchestra of diverse instruments. But in writing *Poppea* (his last opera) for a theater that would include works by other composers, he developed a more standardized ensemble with strings at its core.

Arioso style

Monteverdi's late operas have powerful emotions that find expression in recitatives, arias, choruses, and passages in ***arioso style*** (between aria and recitative). With Monteverdi, Italian opera took on the basic shape it would maintain for the next several hundred years. The love duet, established in *The Coronation of Poppea*, became an essential operatic feature, and his powerful musical portrayal of human passions is echoed in the soaring melodies of Giuseppe Verdi's Romantic masterworks, as we will see later.

Opera in France

Tragédie lyrique

Jean-Baptiste Lully

By the turn of the eighteenth century, Italian opera had gained wide popularity in the rest of Western Europe. Only in France was the Italian genre rejected; here composers set out to fashion a French national style, drawn from their strong traditions of court ballet and classical tragedy. The result was the ***tragédie lyrique***, which combined colorful, sumptuous dance scenes and spectacular choruses in tales of courtly love and heroic adventure. The most important composer of the tragédie lyrique was Jean-Baptiste Lully (1632–1687), whose operas won him favor with the French royal court under King Louis XIV. Lully was the first to succeed in adapting recitative to the inflections of the French language. In a later chapter, we will hear a famous dance movement that typifies the splendor of the French royal court and its grand entertainments under King Louis XV.

Opera in England

Masque

During the early seventeenth century, the English ***masque***, a type of entertainment that combined vocal and instrumental music with poetry and dance, became popular among the aristocracy. Many masques were presented privately in the homes of the nobility.

In this richly colored painting, *The Death of Dido* by **Giovanni Barbieri**, called **Guercino** (1591–1666), Dido has stabbed herself with Aeneas's sword and thrown herself on the funeral pyre. Her sister and handmaidens look on in horror; in the background, Aeneas's ships leave the harbor.

In the period of the Commonwealth at midcentury (1649–60), stage plays were forbidden because the Puritans regarded the theater as an invention of the devil. A play set to music, though, could be passed off as a "concert." The "semi-operas" that flourished were essentially plays with a liberal mixture of solo songs, ensembles, and choral numbers interspersed with instrumental pieces. Although the dramatic tradition in England was much stronger than the operatic, John Blow (1649–1708) took an important step toward opera with his *Venus and Adonis*, which was sung throughout; this work paved the way for the first great English opera, *Dido and Aeneas*, by Blow's pupil Henry Purcell.

John Blow

Henry Purcell: His Life and Music

"As Poetry is the harmony of Words, so Musick is that of Notes;
and as Poetry is a Rise above Prose and Oratory, so is
Musick the exaltation of Poetry."

It was the composer Henry Purcell (1659–1695) who won England a leading position in the world of music. Purcell's brief career began at the court of Charles II (r. 1660–85) and extended through the turbulent reign of James II (r. 1685–88) and into the period of William and Mary (r. 1689–1702). At these courts, he held various posts as singer, organist, and composer.

Purcell was truly an international figure: he assimilated the achievements of the Continent—the dynamic instrumental style, the movement toward major-minor tonality, the recitative and aria of Italian opera, and the accentuated rhythms of the French—and acclimated these to his native land.

Purcell's court odes and religious anthems are solemn and ceremonial, with great breadth and power. His instrumental music ranks among the finest achievements of the middle Baroque. His songs display the charm of his lyricism as well as his gift for setting the English language. And in the domain of the theater, Purcell produced much incidental music for plays, including *Abdelazar* (*The Moor's Revenge*, 1695), from which Britten borrowed a dance as the basis for his *Young Person's Guide*. He also composed *Dido and Aeneas*, one of the gems of English opera.

Henry Purcell

CD iMusic

Purcell: Rondeau

Dido and Aeneas

First presented in 1689 "at Mr. Josias Priest's boarding school at Chelsy by young Gentlewomen . . . to a select audience of their parents and friends," *Dido and Aeneas* achieved a then unprecedented level of musical expression in English vocal works. Purcell's genius adapted to the obvious limitations in size and scope of a school production. Each character in the opera is projected in a few telling strokes. Likewise, the mood of each scene is established with the utmost economy (the opera takes only an hour to perform), with only a few main characters but ample choral singing and dancing.

Dido and Aeneas is based on an episode in Virgil's *Aeneid*, the ancient Roman epic that traces the adventures of the hero Aeneas after the fall of Troy. Since Baroque audiences knew this Virgil classic, librettist Nahum Tate could compress the plot and suggest rather than fill in the details. Aeneas and his men are shipwrecked at Carthage on the northern shore of Africa. Dido, the Carthaginian queen, falls in love with him, and he returns her affection. But Aeneas cannot forget that the gods have commanded him to continue his journey until he reaches Italy, as he is

IN HIS OWN WORDS

Poetry and painting have arrived to their perfection in our own country: music is yet but in its nonage [immaturity], a forward Child, which gives hope of what it may be hereafter in England, when the masters of it shall find more Encouragement.

destined to be the founder of Rome. Much as he hates to hurt the queen, he knows that he must depart.

In her grief, Dido decides her fate—death—in the moving recitative "Thy hand, Belinda," and the heartrending lament that is the culminating point of the opera, "When I am laid in earth." (For the text, see Listening Guide 11.) In Virgil's poem, Dido mounts the funeral pyre, whose flames light the way for Aeneas's ships as they sail out of the harbor. Dido's Lament unfolds over a five-measure *ground bass*, or *ostinato* (a repeated idea), that descends along the chromatic scale, always symbolic of grief in Baroque music. The opera closes with an emotional chorus mourning Dido's fate.

Ground bass

Handel and Late Baroque Opera

Opera in the late Baroque was dominated by George Frideric Handel (1685–1759), who worked in London during the first decades of the eighteenth century. A German by birth, Handel was in every sense an international figure. His music united the beautiful vocal melody of the Italian style with the stately gestures of French music and the contrapuntal genius of the Germans. To these elements he added the majestic choral tradition of the English. The result was perfectly suited to the London scene.

Opera seria

Handel's dramatic works were in the vein of *opera seria*, or serious Italian opera, which projected heroic or tragic subjects. His operas about the First Crusade (*Rinaldo*, 1711) and about Julius Caesar (*Giulio Cesare*, 1724) are among his finest. When opera seria declined in popularity, Handel turned his talents toward the *oratorio*, a music drama based on a religious subject, producing his famous masterwork *Messiah* in 1742. (Handel's life and works are discussed in Chapter 24.)

Listening Guide 11

eLG 1 (34–36)
1 (52–55)

Purcell: *Dido and Aeneas*, Act III, Dido's Lament   (4:00)

DATE OF WORK:	1689
GENRE:	Opera, English
BASIS:	Roman epic *The Aeneid*, by Virgil
CHARACTERS:	Dido, queen of Carthage (soprano)
	Aeneas, adventuring hero (baritone)
	Belinda, Dido's serving maid (soprano)
	Sorceress, Spirit, Witches

WHAT TO LISTEN FOR:	Free-flowing recitative ("Thy hand, Belinda"), with much chromaticism and half-step movement (sigh motive).
	Descending chromatic line as a repeated ground bass in triple meter, heard before aria begins and throughout aria (11 statements).
	Emotional, slow-moving aria in 2 sections, each repeated (**A-A-B-B**); **B** section begins "Remember me."
	Silvery, transparent sounds of Baroque-period string instruments.

Recitative: "Thy hand, Belinda," sung by Dido   (0:57)

Introduces lament aria; accompanied by continuo only

TEXT

34 0:00   Thy hand, Belinda; darkness shades me.
           On thy bosom let me rest;
           More I would, but Death invades me;
           Death is now a welcome guest.

Aria: "When I am laid in earth," Dido's Lament   (3:03)

Basis: Ground bass, 5-measure pattern in slow triple meter, descending chromatic scale, repeated 11 times

Opening of aria, with 2 statements of the ground bass (first statement shaded):

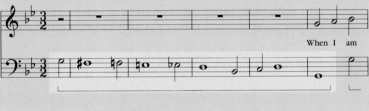

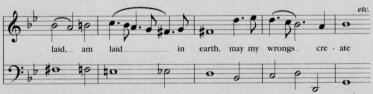

		TEXT	GROUND BASS STATEMENT NO.
35	0:00	Instrumental introduction	1
	0:12	When I am laid in earth, may my wrongs create	2
		no trouble in thy breast.	3
		When I am laid . . .	4
		no trouble . . .	5
36	1:19	Remember me, remember me, but ah, forget	6
		my fate, remember me, but ah, forget my fate.	7
		Remember me . . .	8
		forget my fate . . .	9
		Instrumental closing	10
		Instrumental closing	11

22

Barbara Strozzi and the Italian Secular Cantata

"Had she been born in another era she would certainly have usurped or enlarged the place of the muses."

—G. F. LOREDANO, OF BARBARA STROZZI

KEY POINTS

 StudySpace online at www.wwnorton.com/enjoy

○ The Italian *cantata* was a vocal genre for solo singers and instrumental accompaniment based on *lyric*, *dramatic*, or *narrative poetry*.

○ Barbara Strozzi was a noted singer and composer of cantatas, madrigals, and solo motets in the virtuosic new style *(monody)*.

We have seen that the Baroque inherited the great vocal polyphony of the sixteenth century, while, at the same time, composers pursued a new interest in monody—solo song in dramatic declamation accompanied by instruments. Out of the fusion of these styles came opera as well as another new Baroque form, the cantata.

Cantata   The *cantata* (from the Italian *cantare*, "to sing") is a work for one or more solo vocalists with instrumental accompaniment (chorus was later added to the genre) based on one of three poetic genres: *lyric*, which expresses personal emotion and allows the music to dominate the story; *dramatic*, which is written for performance in a play (a comedy or tragedy, for example); or *narrative*, which tells a story, following characters through a plot.

The earliest cantatas were short and intimate, and usually based on a secular text; they generally consisted of several sections set as recitatives and arias. Among the important proponents of this genre is the composer and singer Barbara Strozzi.

Barbara Strozzi: Her Life and Music

○ **Barbara Strozzi**

Barbara Strozzi (1619–1677) is a unique figure in the early Baroque era. She was the adopted (and probably illegitimate) daughter of the Venetian poet and playwright Giulio Strozzi; her mother, Isabella Garzoni, was his servant. Giulio oversaw Barbara's education and introduction to the intellectual elite of Venice through an academy (not unlike the Florentine Camerata) that he founded. The records of the Accademia degli Unisoni demonstrate her activity as a singer, as a participant in debates, and as a hostess or mistress of ceremonies—all highly unusual, since the meetings of such academies were generally open to men only.

It has been suggested that Barbara Strozzi was a courtesan, and while it is true she possessed the artistic skills of this profession—singing, playing the lute, and writing poetry—this remains a theory. The provocative portrait (by Bernardo Strozzi, see left) is generally believed to be of Barbara. Her musical talents were praised by her contemporaries, one noting her "bold and graceful singing," and another comparing her voice to the harmonies of the spheres.

Although Barbara did not hold any official musical posts at court, in churches, or at the theater, she did publish many of her compositions. In 1644, she issued a volume of madrigals on texts by her father; this collection was dedicated to a prominent noblewoman, Vittoria della Rovere, grand duchess of Tuscany. In the dedication, Strozzi modestly wrote: "I must reverently consecrate this first work, which as a woman I publish all too boldly, to the most august name of your highness so that, under an oak of gold, it may rest secure against the lightning bolts of slander prepared for it." (Here, she makes a pun on the name of her patron—"rovere" is Italian for oak.) Apparently, Barbara had been the subject of slander and was having difficulty finding a patron to sponsor her music. At this time, women were often discouraged from taking part in theatrical or public musical activities, a view that Strozzi clearly challenged.

A prolific composer of high-quality music, Strozzi wrote seven secular collections, including madrigals, arias, and cantatas, as well as one book of sacred motets for solo voice. Her works show mastery of the new virtuosic solo style, for which Strozzi wrote out the desired ornamentation, and of **stile concitato** (agitated style), first introduced by Monteverdi. Our selection is *Begli occhi (Beautiful Eyes*, Listening Guide 12), a short cantata on a lyric poem for two sopranos and continuo from her 1654 collection. This work is characterized by many shifts between unmeasured and measured rhythms, and abrupt tempo and mood changes. The sinuous dialogue between the two voices tells of the bitterness of unrequited love, which we hear through poignant dissonances and expressive half-step movement, in alternation with lighter, dancelike sections.

Begli occhi

> IN HER OWN WORDS
>
> *These harmonic notes are the language of the soul and the instruments of the heart.*

Listening Guide 12

eLG 1 (37–42)
1 (62–67)

Strozzi: *Begli occhi (Beautiful Eyes)*   (4:36)

DATE OF WORK:	Published in 1654 collection (Opus 3)
GENRE:	Italian secular cantata
MEDIUM:	Vocal duet (soprano and mezzo-soprano) and basso continuo
TEXT:	Love poem (lines of 7 or 11 syllables)
RHYME SCHEME:	*a-b-b-c-c-d-d-c-c-e-e*

WHAT TO LISTEN FOR:	Shifts between unmeasured, slow sections and fast, dancelike sections. Expressive chromaticism and dissonance. Word painting (dissonance and half steps) on "langue" (languishing), and "mordaci" (biting). Sighing motive on "oh." Long melisma on "aspetta" (awaits) stretches out final idea. Accompaniment by harpsichord (early keyboard instrument) and bass lute.

Listening Guide continues

		TEXT	TRANSLATION	DESCRIPTION
37	0:00	Mi ferite oh begli occhi.	You wound me, oh beautiful eyes.	Slow, free opening, then short imitative exchanges.
38	0:32	Pensate che farebbono quei baci si cocenti e mordaci.	Imagine what these kisses could do so burning and biting.	Quicker, dancelike compound meter; imitation between voices.
39	0:59	Langue l'anima e il cor vien meno ahi ch'io vi moro in seno!	My soul languishes and my heart faints: Oh that I die there in my breast!	Slower; chromatic and dissonant; movement by half steps.
40	1:57	Pensate che farebbono gli strali; si pungente e mortali.	Imagine what arrows could do; So sharp and deadly.	Return to quick, dancelike music, then fanfare-like motive.
41	2:23	Langue l'anima e il cor vien meno ahi ch'io vi moro in seno!	My soul languishes and my heart faints; Oh that I die there in my breast!	Repeated text and music; chromatic and dissonant.
42	3:19	Ma forse non morrò senza vendetta; ch'al fin chi morte da, la morte aspetta!	But perhaps I will not die without revenge; For he who deals death, awaits it in the end!	Fast, triple meter, in imitation; then the voices coming together; long melisma on "aspetta" (awaits).

Examples of word painting:

Descending "sigh" motive on "oh," alternating between 2 voices:

Chromaticism and half-step movement on "Langue l'anima" (my soul languishes):

Melisma at end to signify the long wait ("aspetta") for death :

23

Bach and the Sacred Cantata

"I wish to make German psalms for the people, that is to say sacred hymns, so that the word of God may dwell among the people also by means of song." —MARTIN LUTHER

KEY POINTS

 StudySpace online at www.wwnorton.com/enjoy

- The *sacred cantatas* of north German composer Johann Sebastian Bach were mostly written for the Lutheran church service; they are multimovement works with solo arias, recitatives, and choruses, all with orchestral accompaniment.
- Lutheran cantatas are generally unified by a *chorale*, or hymn tune, sung in four-part harmony.
- J. S. Bach was better known in his lifetime as a virtuoso organist than as a composer.

- In addition to his many cantatas and one Mass, Bach wrote orchestral suites, concertos, and much keyboard music for organ and harpsichord.
- The cantata, *A Mighty Fortress Is Our God*, is an eight-movement work based on a familiar Protestant chorale tune, probably written by Martin Luther. The opening movement is an elaborate choral *fugue* (a form based on imitation).

Baroque cantatas could be based on either secular or sacred themes. The late-Baroque master J. S. Bach wrote both types, but it is his sacred Lutheran cantatas that are his enduring legacy. In the Lutheran tradition, to which Bach belonged, the sacred cantata was an integral part of the church service, related, along with the sermon and prayers that followed it, to the Gospel for the day. Most Sundays of the church year required their own cantata. Extra works for holidays and special occasions brought the annual cycle to about sixty cantatas. Bach composed four or five such cycles, from which only two hundred works survive.

Lutheran service

By the second quarter of the eighteenth century, the German cantata had absorbed the recitative, aria, and duet of the opera, the pomp of the French operatic overture, and the dynamic instrumental style of the Italians. These elements were unified by the anchoring presence of the Lutheran chorale.

The Lutheran Chorale

A *chorale* is a hymn tune specifically associated with German Protestantism. The chorales served as battle hymns of the Reformation. For one of his reforms, Martin Luther required that the congregation participate in the service. To this end, he inaugurated services in German rather than Latin, and allotted an important role to congregational singing.

Chorale

Martin Luther

Luther and his fellow reformers created the first chorales by adapting melodies from Gregorian chant, secular art music, and even popular tunes. Originally sung in unison, these hymns soon were written in four-part harmony and sung by the choir. The melody was put in the soprano, where all could hear it and join in the singing. In this way, the chorales greatly strengthened the trend toward clear-cut melody supported by chords (homophonic texture).

Polyphonic settings

In the elaborate cantatas that were sung in the Protestant church service, the chorale served as a unifying thread. When at the close of an extended work the chorale sounded in simple four-part harmony, its strength reflected the faith of a nation. The chorale nourished centuries of German music and came to full flower in the art of Bach.

Johann Sebastian Bach

"The aim and final reason of all music should be nothing else but the Glory of God and the refreshment of the spirit."

Johann Sebastian Bach (1685–1750) was heir to the polyphonic art of the past. He is the culminating figure of the Baroque style and one of the giants in the history of music.

HIS LIFE

Johann Sebastian Bach

Bach was born at Eisenach, Germany, in a family that had supplied musicians to the churches and town bands of the region for several generations. Left an orphan at the age of ten, he was raised by an older brother, who prepared him for the family vocation of organist. From the first, Bach displayed inexhaustible curiosity concerning every aspect of his art. "I had to work hard," he reported in later years, adding with unfounded optimism "Anyone who works as hard will get just as far."

Weimar period

At the age of twenty-three, Bach was appointed to his first important position: court organist and chamber musician to the duke of Weimar. The Weimar period (1708–17) saw the rise of his fame as an organ virtuoso and the composition of many of his most important works for that instrument. His first six children were born in this period. Bach's two marriages produced at least nineteen offspring, many

Cöthen period

of whom did not survive infancy. Four of his sons became leading composers of the next generation.

Disappointed because the duke of Weimar had failed to promote him, Bach accepted an offer from the prince of Anhalt-Cöthen, who happened to be partial to chamber music. In his five years at Cöthen (1717–23), Bach produced suites, concertos, sonatas for various instruments, and a wealth of keyboard music; he also wrote the six concerti grossi dedicated to the margrave of Brandenburg. During this period, Bach's wife died, and in late 1721, he married Anna Magdalena Wilcke, a young singer at court.

Bach was thirty-eight when he was appointed to one of the most important music positions in Germany, that of cantor at St. Thomas's Church in Leipzig. His duties at St. Thomas's were formidable. He supervised the music for the city's four main churches, selected and trained their choristers, and wrote music for the church services as well as for special occasions such as weddings and funerals. In

An 18th-century engraving of St. Thomas's Church in Leipzig, where Bach worked from 1723 until he died, in 1750.

1729, he was appointed to an additional post in Leipzig: director of the *collegium musicum*, a group of university students and musicians that gave regular concerts. In the midst of all this activity, Bach managed to produce truly magnificent works during his twenty-seven years in Leipzig (1723–50).

The routine of his life was enlivened by frequent professional journeys, when he was asked to test and inaugurate new organs. His last expedition, in 1747, was to the court of Frederick the Great at Potsdam, where Bach's son Carl Philipp Emanuel served as accompanist to the flute-playing monarch. Frederick announced to his courtiers with some excitement, "Gentlemen, old Bach has arrived," then led the composer through the palace, showing him the new pianos that were beginning to replace harpsichords as the preferred keyboard instruments. At Bach's invitation, the king suggested a theme, on which the composer improvised one of his astonishing fugues. After his return to Leipzig, Bach further elaborated on the royal theme, added a trio sonata based on the same theme, and dispatched the *Musical Offering* to Frederick.

The labors of a lifetime took their toll; after an apoplectic stroke and several operations for cataracts, Bach was stricken with blindness. Nevertheless, he persisted in his final task, the revising of eighteen chorale preludes for the organ. The dying master dictated to a son-in-law the last of these, *Before Thy Throne, My God, I Stand.*

HIS MUSIC

Bach was one of the greatest religious artists in history. He believed that music must serve "the glory of God." The prime medium for Bach's talents was the organ, and during his life he was known primarily as a virtuoso organist. Since he was a devout Lutheran, the **chorale prelude** (a short organ piece based on the embellishment of a chorale tune) was central to his output.

Bach's most important keyboard work is *The Well-Tempered Clavier.* The forty-eight preludes and fugues in these two volumes have been called the pianist's Old Testament (the New Testament being Beethoven's thirty-two piano sonatas). Of the sonatas for various instruments, the six for unaccompanied violin are central to the repertory. In these, Bach created an intricate polyphonic structure, drawing unheard-of forms and textures from the instrument. The often-performed six *Brandenburg Concertos* present various unique instrumental combinations pitted against one another, and the lyricism of the four orchestral suites has made them immensely popular as well.

The two hundred or so church cantatas that have reached us form the centerpiece of Bach's religious music. They constitute a personal document of spirituality, projecting the composer's vision of life and death. The monumental Mass in B minor, which occupied Bach for a good part of the Leipzig period, was inappropriate for the Catholic service because of its length, but it found its eventual home in the concert hall.

Bach's last works reveal the composer at the height of his contrapuntal wizardry; these include the *Musical Offering* and *The Art of Fugue,* which was left unfinished at his death. In Chapter 27, we will consider one of his most famous fugues, the masterwork that forms the basis for *The Art of Fugue* collection.

Bach's position in history is that of one who raised existing forms to the highest level rather than one who originated new forms. His sheer mastery of contrapuntal composition has never been equaled.

CANTATA NO. 80:
A MIGHTY FORTRESS IS OUR GOD

Bach's cantatas typically have five to eight movements, of which the first, last, and usually one middle movement are choral numbers—normally fashioned from a chorale tune—ranging from simple hymnlike settings to intricate choral fugues. Interspersed with the choruses are solo arias and recitatives, some of which may also be based on a chorale melody or its text.

IN HIS OWN WORDS

Whereas the Honorable and Most Wise Council of this Town of Leipzig have engaged me as Cantor of the St. Thomas School . . . I shall set the boys a shining example. . . , serve the school industriously, . . . bring the music in both the principal churches of this town into good estate, . . . faithfully instruct the boys not only in vocal but also in instrumental music . . . arrange the music so that it shall not last too long, and shall . . . not make an operatic impression, but rather incite the listeners to devotion . . . treat the boys in a friendly manner and with caution, but, in case they do not wish to obey, chastise them with moderation or report them to the proper place.

Keyboard and chamber music

Cantatas

CD iMusic

Contrapunctus I, from *The Art of Fugue,*

Brandenburg Concerto No. 1, I

Jesu, Joy of Man's Desiring

Sarabande, from *Cello Suite No. 2*

Toccata in D minor

In *The Flute Concert*, by the 19th-century painter **Adolf von Menzel,** Frederick the Great performs with J. S. Bach's son Carl Philipp Emanuel at the harpsichord.

In the cantata *A Mighty Fortress Is Our God,* Bach set Martin Luther's chorale of that name, for which Luther probably composed the music as well as the words. Luther's words and chorale melody are used in the first, second, fifth, and last movements of this cantata; the rest of the text is by Bach's favorite librettist, Salomo Franck.

Bach could take it for granted that the devout congregation of St. Thomas's knew Luther's chorale by heart. A majestic and inspiring melody, it is today a familiar Protestant hymn tune. Except for an occasional leap, the melody moves stepwise along the scale and is presented in nine phrases that parallel the nine lines of each stanza of Luther's poem (the first two phrases are repeated for lines three and four of the poem; see Listening Guide 13).

The cantata opens with an extended choral movement in D major, in which each line of text receives its own fugal treatment. (A *fugue* is a polyphonic composition based on imitation; the form will be discussed in detail in Chapter 27.) In this movement, each musical phrase is announced by one voice part of the choir, then imitated in turn by the other three. Each phrase is an embellished version of the original chorale tune. The trumpets and drums we hear in this movement were added after Bach's death by his son Wilhelm Friedemann, who strove to enhance the pomp and splendor of the sound.

The middle movements of the cantata feature freely composed recitatives and arias grouped around an energetic chorus based on Luther's chorale. In each movement, Bach captures a single affection (see p. 122), a practice typical of the era.

The final movement rounds off the cantata, with the chorale sounded by full chorus and orchestra. We can now easily recognize Luther's melody in a hymnlike, four-part harmonization, with each vocal line doubled by instruments. In this homorhythmic texture, the great melody of the chorale is sounded in all its simplicity and grandeur.

A German cantata performance with orchestra and organ, as depicted in **J. G. Walther's** *Dictionary* (1732).

Listening Guide 13

eLG 1 (43–51)
2 (1–7, 12–13)

Bach: Cantata No. 80, *A Mighty Fortress Is Our God* (*Ein feste Burg ist unser Gott*), Nos. 1 and 8

(6:11)

DATE OF WORK:	1715/c. 1744; for the Feast of the Reformation (October 31)
FORM:	8 movements, for chorus, soloists, and orchestra
BASIS:	Chorale (hymn) tune (probably by Martin Luther)

OVERALL STRUCTURE:

Movement	Medium	Use of chorale tune
1. Choral fugue	Chorus and orchestra	Embellished fugal chorale
2. Aria, duet	Soprano and bass solo	Soprano line only
3. Recitative/arioso	Bass solo	
4. Aria	Soprano solo	
5. Chorus	Chorus and orchestra	Unison chorale
6. Recitative/arioso	Tenor solo	
7. Aria, duet	Alto and tenor solo	
8. Chorale	Chorus and orchestra	4-part chorale

Original chorale tune:

Ein fe·ste Burg_ ist   un·ser Gott, ein' gu·te Wehr und_ Waf·fen;
er   hilft uns frei_ aus al·ler Not, die uns jetzt hat be·trof·fen.

Der al·te bö·se Feind, mit Ernst er's jetzt meint, gross Macht und viel

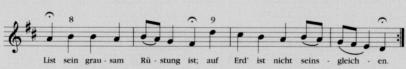

List sein grau·sam Rü·stung ist; auf Erd' ist nicht seins·gleich·en.

1. Choral fugue (chorus and orchestra), 4/4 meter, D major (4:51)

WHAT TO LISTEN FOR:	Elaborate, imitative treatment of the familiar tune in all voice parts and in the trumpets.
	Dense polyphonic texture created between chorus and orchestra for each line of text.
	Canon (in strict imitation) on chorale tune heard in the instruments (trumpets and oboes vs. cellos), played in augmentation (long note-values).

Listening Guide continues

		TEXT	TRANSLATION	FIRST SUNG BY
43	0:00	Ein feste Burg ist unser Gott,	A mighty fortress is our God,	Tenors
		ein' gute Wehr und Waffen;	a good defense and weapon;	Sopranos
44	1:15	er hilft uns frei aus aller Not,	He helps free us from all the troubles	Tenors
		die uns jetzt hat betroffen.	that have now befallen us.	Sopranos
45	2:29	Der alte böse Feind,	Our ever evil foe,	Basses
46	2:59	mit Ernst er's jetzt meint,	in earnest plots against us,	Altos
47	3:24	gross Macht und viel List	with great strength and cunning	Tenors
48	3:45	sein grausam Rüstung ist;	he prepares his dreadful plans.	Sopranos
49	4:09	auf Erd' ist nicht seinsgleichen.	Earth holds none like him.	Tenors

Opening fugal melody in tenors (notes of chorale marked with x):

Instrumental canon, based on chorale tune in augmentation:

8. Chorale, for full chorus (with orchestra), 4/4 meter, D major   (1:20)

WHAT TO LISTEN FOR: 4-part hymn setting with the tune clearly heard in the top voice.
All voices moving together (in homorhythmic texture).

50	0:00	Das Wort sie sollen lassen stahn	Now let the Word of God abide
		und kein Dank dazu haben.	without further thought.
		Er ist bei uns wohl auf dem Plan	He is firmly on our side
		mit seinem Geist und Gaben.	with His spirit and strength.
51	0:35	Nehmen sie uns den Leib,	Though they deprive us of life,
		Gut, Ehr', Kind, und Weib,	wealth, honor, child, and wife,
		lass fahren dahin,	we will not complain,
		sie haben's kein Gewinn;	it will avail them nothing;
		das Reich muss uns doch bleiben.	for God's kingdom must prevail.

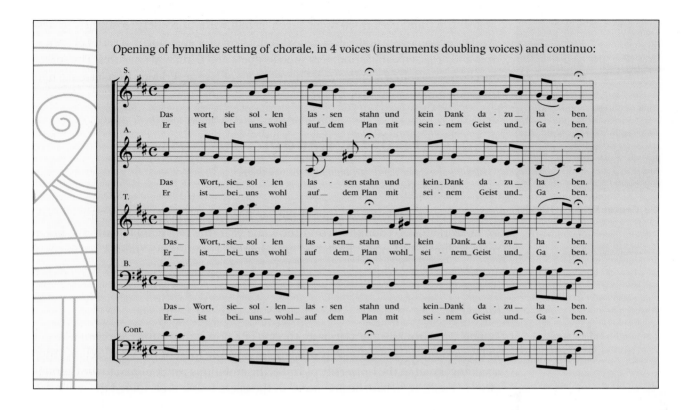

Opening of hymnlike setting of chorale, in 4 voices (instruments doubling voices) and continuo:

24

Handel and the Oratorio

*"What the English like is something they can beat time to,
something that hits them straight on the drum of the ear."*

KEY POINTS

StudySpace online at www.wwnorton.com/enjoy

- The *oratorio* is a large-scale dramatic genre with a religious or biblical text performed by solo voices, chorus, and orchestra; it is not staged or costumed.

- George Frideric Handel was known for his Italian operas and, later in life, his English-texted oratorios (including *Messiah*).

- *Messiah* is an oratorio in three parts: it opens with a **French overture** and features recitatives (*secco* and *accompagnato*), lyrical arias, and majestic choruses, including the famous "Hallelujah Chorus."

- The text for *Messiah* is drawn from a compilation of Old and New Testament verses.

The Oratorio

The *oratorio*, one of the great Baroque vocal forms, descended from the religious play-with-music of the Counter-Reformation. Although the first oratorios were sacred operas, toward the middle of the seventeenth century the genre shed the trappings of the stage and developed its own characteristics as a large-scale musical work for solo voices, chorus, and orchestra. An oratorio was generally based on a biblical story and performed in a church or hall without scenery, costumes, or acting. The action was usually depicted with the help of a narrator, in a series of recitatives and arias, ensemble numbers such as duets and trios, and choruses. The role of the chorus was often emphasized. The oratorios of George Frideric Handel make him the consummate master of this vocal form.

George Frideric Handel

George Frideric Handel

"Milord, I should be sorry if I only entertained them.
I wished to make them better."

If Bach represents the spirituality of the late Baroque, Handel (1685–1759) embodies its worldliness. Though born in the same year, the two giants of the age never met. As cantor of Leipzig, Bach had little point of contact with Handel, a composer who was destined for an international career.

HIS LIFE

Handel was born in Halle, Germany, the son of a prosperous barber-surgeon who did not regard music as a suitable profession for a young man of the middle class. After spending a year at the University of Halle, the ambitious youth moved to the German city of Hamburg, where he gravitated to the opera house and entered the orchestra as a second violinist. Handel absorbed the Italian operatic style popular in Hamburg,

Early operas

then spent the next three years in Italy, where his operas were received just as enthusiastically.

At the age of twenty-five, Handel was appointed conductor to the elector of Hanover; in this position, he received the equivalent of fifteen hundred dollars a year (Bach at Weimar was being paid only eighty). A visit to London in the autumn of 1710 brought him to the city that was to be his home for nearly fifty years.

His great opportunity came in 1720 with the founding of the Royal Academy of Music, launched for the purpose of presenting Italian opera. Handel was appointed one of the musical directors and, at age thirty-five, found himself occupying a key position in the artistic life of England. For the next eight years, he was active in producing and directing his operas as well as writing them. His pace was feverish; he worked in bursts of inspiration, turning out a new opera in two to three weeks. To this period belongs *Rinaldo*, his first opera for London audiences, and *Julius Caesar*,

Opera seria

perhaps his most famous ***opera seria*** (serious Italian opera).

Despite Handel's productivity, the Royal Academy failed. The final blow came in 1728 with the sensational success of John Gay's *The Beggar's Opera*. Sung in English and with tunes familiar to the audience, this humorous ***ballad***, or ***dialogue***, ***opera*** was the answer of middle-class England to the gods and heroes of the aristocratic *opera seria*.

Oratorio

Rather than accept failure, Handel turned from opera to oratorio, quickly realizing the advantages offered by a type of entertainment that dispensed with costly foreign singers and lavish scenery. Among his greatest achievements in this new genre were *Israel in Egypt, Messiah, Judas Maccabaeus*, and *Jephtha*. The British public could not help but respond to the imagery of the Old Testament as set forth in Handel's heroic music.

Handel suffered the same affliction as Bach—loss of eyesight from cataracts. Like Bach and the English poet John Milton, he dictated his last works, which were mainly revisions of earlier ones. But he continued to appear in public, conducting his oratorios and performing on the organ.

In 1759, shortly after his seventy-fourth birthday, Handel began his usual oratorio season, conducting ten major works in little over a month to packed houses. His most famous oratorio, *Messiah*, closed the series. He collapsed in the theater at the end of the performance and died some days later. The nation he had served for half a century accorded him its highest honor, as a London paper recounted: "Last night about Eight O'clock the remains of the late great Mr. Handel were deposited . . . in Westminster Abbey. . . . There was almost the greatest Concourse of People of all Ranks ever seen upon such, or indeed upon any other Occasion."

HIS MUSIC

Handel's rhythm has the powerful drive of the late Baroque. Unlike Bach, who favored chromatic harmony, Handel leaned toward the diatonic. His melodies, rich in expression, rise and fall in great majestic arches. His works are based on massive pillars of sound (a choral basis) within which the voices interweave. And with his roots in the world of the theater, Handel knew how to use tone color for atmosphere and dramatic expression.

A performance of Handel's *Messiah* in 1784, from an 18th-century engraving.

Handel's more than forty operas tell stories of heroes and adventurers, in ingenious musical settings that not only appealed to the London public but enjoyed popularity in Germany and Italy as well. His arias run the gamut from brilliant virtuosic displays to poignant love songs.

The oratorios are choral dramas that embody the splendor of the Baroque, with their soaring arias, dramatic recitatives, grandiose fugues, and majestic choruses.

Handel made the oratorio chorus—the people—the center of the drama. Freed from the rapid pace imposed by stage action, he expanded the chorus's role in each scene. The chorus at times touches off the action and at other times reflects on it. As in Greek tragedy, it serves as both protagonist and spectator.

CD iMusic

Alla hornpipe, from *Water Music*

"Hallelujah Chorus," from *Messiah*

Handel was prolific as well in composing instrumental music; his most important works are his concertos and his two memorable orchestral suites, the *Water Music* (1717) and *Music for the Royal Fireworks* (1749). (We will consider a movement from the *Water Music* in Chapter 26.)

MESSIAH

In the spring of 1742, the city of Dublin witnessed the premiere of one of the world's best-loved works, Handel's *Messiah*. Writing down the oratorio in only twenty-four days, the composer worked as if possessed. His servant found him, after the completion of the "Hallelujah Chorus," with tears in his eyes. "I did think I did see all Heaven before me, and the Great God Himself!" Handel said.

The libretto is a compilation of biblical verses from the Old and New Testaments, set in three parts. The first part (the Christmas section) relates the prophecy of the coming of Christ and his birth; the second (the Easter section), his suffering, death, and the spread of his doctrine; and the third, the redemption of the world through faith. With its impressive choruses, moving recitatives, and broadly flowing arias, the work represents the pinnacle of the Handelian oratorio.

IN HIS OWN WORDS

Whether I was in my body or out of my body as I wrote it [the "Hallelujah Chorus"], I know not. God knows.

Handel's orchestration of *Messiah* was modest and clear in texture. He wrote mainly for strings and continuo; oboes and bassoons were employed to strengthen the choral parts. Trumpets and drums were reserved for special numbers.

The work opens with a ***French overture***, which consists of two sections: a slow, somber introduction with dotted rhythms, followed by an Allegro in imitative style. (The two-part French overture had been developed a century earlier by the master of

French overture

Baroque opera in France, Jean-Baptiste Lully.) The first part of the oratorio proceeds with a series of arias, recitatives, and choruses, including the jubilant "Glory to God," which illustrates well the pomp and majesty of Handel's music.

The soprano aria "Rejoice greatly, O daughter of Zion" is in three-part, or **A-B-A′**, form. In this type of aria, the composer usually did not write out the third part, since it duplicated the first. Instead we find the words *da capo* at the end of the second section, indicating that the performer was to repeat the first section, freely elaborating it with ornamentation. (*Da capo* is Italian for "from the head," that is, from the beginning.) This

Da capo aria   kind of structure therefore came to be known as a ***da capo aria***. For "Rejoice greatly," Handel did write out the last section, varying it considerably from the first.

At the beginning of this aria, violins introduce an energetic figure that will soon be taken up by the voice. Notable are the melismatic passages on the word "rejoice." Throughout, the instruments exchange motives with the voice and help provide an element of unity with the ritornellos, or instrumental refrains, that brings back certain passages.

Chorus   The climax of *Messiah* comes at the close of the second part, the Easter section, with the familiar "Hallelujah Chorus." In this movement, we hear shifting textures that alternate between overlapping imitative entries of the voice parts and homorhythmic sections in which all the voices clearly declaim the text together. The musical emphasis given the key word "Hallelujah" is one of those strokes of genius that resound through the ages.

Listening Guide 14

eLG 1 (52–57)
       2 (20–25)

Handel: *Messiah*, Nos. 18 and 44   (7:48)

DATE OF WORK:	1742
GENRE:	Oratorio, in 3 parts
PARTS:	I—Christmas section
	II—Easter section
	III—Redemption section

WHAT TO LISTEN FOR:	Lyrical soprano aria ("Rejoice greatly"), with long melismas on "re-**joice**"; set in 3-part form (**A-B-A′**), with shortened last section. Famous chorus ("Hallelujah"), set in contrasting textures with interjections of "Hallelujah."

18. Soprano aria (A-B-A′)   (4:15)

52 0:00   Instrumental ritornello, vocal theme presented in violins in B♭ major.

A
Rejoice greatly,   Disjunct rising line, melismas on "rejoice";
O daughter of Zion   melody exchanged between soprano and
shout, O daughter of Jerusalem,   violin.
behold, thy King cometh unto thee.   Syncopated, choppy melody, ends in F major.
                                          Instrumental ritornello.

		B	
53	1:30	He is the righteous Saviour and he shall speak peace unto the heathen.	Begins in G minor, slower and lyrical; modulates to B♭ major.
		A'	
54	2:33	Rejoice greatly . . .	Abridged instrumental ritornello; new melodic elaborations; longer melismas on "rejoice."

Extended melisma on "rejoice" from last section:

PART II: EASTER SECTION

44. Chorus   (3:33)

		TEXT	**DESCRIPTION**
55	0:00		Short instrumental introduction.
		Hallelujah!	4 voices, homorhythmic at opening.
56	0:24	For the Lord God omnipotent reigneth.	Textural reductions, leading to imitation and overlapping of text, builds in complexity, imitative entries.
	1:12	The kingdom of this world is become the Kingdom of our Lord and of His Christ;	Homorhythmic treatment, simple accompaniment.
57	1:29	and He shall reign for ever and ever.	Imitative polyphony, voices build from lowest to highest.
	1:51	King of Kings and Lord of Lords. Hallelujah!	Women's voices introduce the text, punctuated by "Hallelujah"; closes in homorhythmic setting with trumpets and timpani.

Opening of chorus, in homorhythmic style:

Instrumental Music of the Baroque

25

The Baroque Sonata and Concerto

"If music be the food of love, play on."
—WILLIAM SHAKESPEARE, *TWELFTH NIGHT*

KEY POINTS	ⓢ **StudySpace** online at www.wwnorton.com/enjoy

○ In the Baroque, instruments were perfected, and new large-scale instrumental forms (***sonata, concerto***) emerged.

○ The ***trio sonata*** was the favorite form of instrumental chamber music in the Baroque. Sonatas were also written for solo instruments.

○ Two types of ***concertos*** were popular during the Baroque: the ***solo concerto***, with one instrument

set against the orchestra; and the ***concerto grosso***, with a small group of soloists and orchestra.

○ Antonio Vivaldi, a virtuoso violinist, composed *The Four Seasons*, a well-known set of solo violin concertos representing ***program music***.

○ J. S. Bach's 6 *Brandenburg Concertos* are excellent examples of the concerto grosso.

The Rise of Instrumental Music

During the Baroque era, instrumental music became as important as vocal music for the first time in history. New instruments were developed while old ones were perfected. Great virtuosos such as Bach and Handel at the organ, Vivaldi on the violin, and Scarlatti on the harpsichord raised the technique of playing to new heights.

On the whole, composers still thought in terms of line rather than instrumental color, which meant that the same line of music might be played on a string, a woodwind, or a brass instrument. (In the Classical and Romantic periods, instrumental color was changed frequently.) But the late Baroque composers began to choose specific instruments according to their timbre, and they wrote more idiomatically for particular instruments, asking them to do what they could do best. As instrument designations became more precise, the art of orchestration was born.

Timbre

Baroque Instruments

The seventeenth century saw a dramatic improvement in the construction of string instruments. Some of the finest violins ever built came from the workshops of Stradivarius, Guarneri, and Amati. The best of these now fetch sums unimagined even a generation ago.

The strings of Baroque instruments were made of gut rather than the steel used today. Gut, produced from animal intestines, yielded a softer yet more penetrating sound. In general, the string instruments of the Baroque resemble their modern descendants except for certain details of construction. Playing techniques, though, have changed somewhat, especially bowing.

Strings

In the late Baroque, composers used woodwind instruments increasingly for color. The penetrating timbres of the recorder, flute, and oboe, all made of wood at the time, were especially effective in suggesting pastoral scenes, while the bassoon cast a somber tone. Great improvements in the fingering mechanisms of these instruments making them more reliable and easier to play were still to come.

Woodwinds

The trumpet developed from an instrument used for military signals to one with a solo role in the orchestra. It was still a "natural instrument"—that is, without the valves that would enable it to play in all keys—demanding real virtuosity on the part of the player. Trumpets contributed a bright sonority to the orchestral palette, to which the French horns, also natural instruments, added their mellow, huntlike sound. Timpani were occasionally added to the orchestra, furnishing a bass to the trumpets.

Brass

The Los Angeles Baroque Orchestra, led from the first violin stand by founder/director Gregory Maldonado, is one of a growing number of period-instrument ensembles. The Baroque bows the players use are shorter and lighter than their modern counterparts and produce crisp, articulate strokes on gut strings.

An evening outdoor concert in 1744 by the Collegium Musicum of Jena, Germany, featuring an orchestra of strings, woodwinds, trumpets, and drums gathered around a harpsichord.

Keyboard instruments

The three important keyboard instruments of the Baroque were the organ, the harpsichord, and the clavichord. In ensemble music, these provided the continuo (continuous bass), and they were used extensively for solo performance as well. The Baroque *organ*, used both in church (see p. 158) and in the home, had a pure, transparent timbre. The colors produced by the various sets of pipes contrasted sharply, so that the ear could pick out the separate lines of counterpoint. And the use of multiple keyboards made it possible to achieve terraced levels of soft and loud.

The *harpsichord* differed from the modern piano in two important ways. First, its strings were plucked by quills rather than struck with hammers, and its tone could not be sustained like that of the piano, a product of the early Classical era. Second, the pressure of the fingers on the keys varied the tone only slightly, producing subtle dynamic nuances but not the piano's extremes of loud and soft. Rather, in order to obtain different sonorities and levels of sound on the harpsichord, makers often added another set or two of strings, usually with a second keyboard.

The *clavichord* was a favorite instrument for the home. Its very soft, gentle tone was produced by the action of a metal tangent, or lever, that exerted pressure on the string, allowing for some delicate effects not available on the harpsichord. By the end of the eighteenth century, both the harpsichord and the clavichord had been supplanted by the piano.

In recent years, a new drive for authenticity has made the sounds of eighteenth-century instruments familiar to us. Recorders and wooden flutes, restored violins with gut strings, and mellow-toned, valveless brass instruments are being played again, so that the Baroque orchestra has recovered not only its smaller scale but also its transparent tone quality. Our recordings of the instrumental selections that follow feature the silvery sound of period string instruments, supported by the colorful timbre of historical woodwinds and the bright sonority of early trumpets and horns.

A French-style, two-manual harpsichord made in 1769.

Sonata Types

The sonata was the most widely cultivated form of chamber music in the Baroque. In its early stages, the sonata consisted of either a movement in several sections or several movements that contrasted in tempo and texture. A distinction was drawn between the *sonata da camera*, or *chamber sonata*, which was usually a group of stylized dances, and the *sonata da chiesa*, or *church sonata*, which was more serious in tone and more contrapuntal in texture, its four movements arranged in the sequence slow-fast-slow-fast. Many church sonatas ended with one or more dancelike movements, while many chamber sonatas opened with an impressive introductory movement in the church-sonata style.

Chamber sonata
Church sonata

Sonatas were written for one to six or even eight instruments. The favorite ensemble combination in the Baroque was two violins and continuo. Because of the three printed staves in the music, such compositions were called *trio sonatas*; yet the title is misleading, because it refers to the number of parts rather than to the number of players. In addition to the two violins, the basso continuo often employed two performers—a cellist (or bassoonist) to play the bass line and a harpsichordist or organist to realize the harmonies indicated by the figures.

Trio sonata

Some Baroque composers wrote sonatas for unaccompanied instruments. Notable among these is Bach, whose sonatas for unaccompanied violin and cello are centerpieces of the repertory. Domenico Scarlatti (1685–1757) is remembered for his some 550 sonatas for solo harpsichord, characterized by brilliant passagework, hand crossing, and other virtuoso techniques that helped lay the foundation for modern piano technique. Set in one-movement binary form, Scarlatti's works bear the seed that was to develop into the Classical sonata.

Solo sonata

Concerto Types

Contrast was as basic an element of Baroque music as unity. This twofold principle found expression in the *concerto*, an instrumental form based on the opposition between two dissimilar bodies of sound. (The Latin verb *concertare* means "to contend with," or "to vie with.")

Baroque composers produced two types: the *solo concerto* and the *concerto grosso*. The first type, a concerto for solo instrument and an accompanying instrumental group, lent itself to experiments in sonority and virtuoso playing, especially in the hands of the Italian master Antonio Vivaldi. The violin was the instrument featured most frequently in the solo concerto, which usually consisted of three movements, in the sequence Allegro–Adagio–Allegro. This flexible form prepared the way for the solo concerto of the Classical and Romantic periods.

Solo concerto

The *concerto grosso* was based on the opposition between a small group of instruments, the *concertino*, and a larger group, the *tutti*, or *ripieno* (Italian for "full"). Bach captured the spirit of the concerto grosso in his six *Brandenburg Concertos*, written for presentation to the Margrave Christian of Brandenburg. Each features a unique instrumentation in the solo group. Concerto No. 2 of this set has long been a favorite because of its brilliant trumpet part.

Concerto grosso

The concerto embodied what one writer of the time called "the fire and fury of the Italian style." This Italian style spread all over Europe and strongly influenced the German masters Bach and Handel, among others. Of the many Italian concerto composers, Vivaldi was the most famous and the most prolific.

Antonio Vivaldi: His Life and Music

"Above all, he was possessed by music."

—MARC PINCHERLE

Antonio Vivaldi

Antonio Vivaldi (1678–1741), the son of a violinist, grew up in his native Venice. He was ordained in the church while in his twenties and became known as "the red priest," a reference to the color of his hair. For the greater part of his career, Vivaldi was *maestro de' concerti*, or music master, at the most important of the four music schools for which Venice was famous, the Conservatorio dell'Ospedale della Pietà. These schools were attached to charitable institutions established for the upbringing of orphaned children—mostly girls—and played a vital role in the musical life of Venetians. Much of Vivaldi's output was written for concerts at the school, which attracted visitors from all over Europe. One visitor, a French diplomat, recorded his impressions of Vivaldi's all-girl orchestra in 1739:

> The girls are educated at the expense of the state, and they are trained exclusively with the purpose of excelling in music. Thus, they sing like angels and play violin, flute, organ, oboe, cello, and bassoon; in short, no instrument, regardless of its size, frightens them. They live like nuns in a convent. All they do is perform concerts, generally in groups of about forty girls. I swear that there is nothing as pleasant as seeing a young and pretty nun, dressed all in white, with a flower over her ear, conducting the orchestra with all the gracefulness and precision imaginable.

While maintaining his position in Venice, Vivaldi traveled widely, composing operas for other cities and building his reputation as a virtuoso performer. His life came to a mysterious end: a contemporary Venetian account notes that the composer, who had once earned 50,000 ducats in his day (about 4 million dollars today), died in poverty as a result of his extravagance.

Musical works   Vivaldi is remembered for his more than 500 concertos—some 230 of which are for solo violin. Many of these have descriptive titles, such as *The Four Seasons*, a group of violin concertos that we will study. One of the most prolific composers of his era, he also wrote much chamber music and numerous operas, as well as cantatas, an oratorio, and an extended setting of the Gloria, which is today one of his most-performed works.

Vivaldi was active during a period that was crucially important to the exploration of a new style in which instruments were liberated from their earlier dependence on vocal music. His novel use of rapid scale passages, extended arpeggios, and contrasting registers contributed decisively to the development of violin style and technique. And he played a leading part in the history of the concerto, effectively exploiting the contrast in sonority between large and small groups of players.

THE FOUR SEASONS

Vivaldi's best-known work is *The Four Seasons*, a group of four violin concertos. We have observed the fondness for word painting in Baroque vocal works, where the music is meant to portray the action and emotion described by the words. In *The Four Seasons*, Vivaldi applies this principle to instrumental music. Each concerto is accompanied by a poem, describing the joys of that particular season. Each line of the poem is printed above a certain passage in the score; the music at that point mirrors graphically the **Program music**   action described; this literary link is called ***program music***.

In *Concert in a Girls' School,* **Francesco Guardi** (1712–1793) depicts a Venetian concert by an orchestra of young women (upper left) similar to the one directed by Vivaldi.

In *Spring (La primavera),* the mood and atmosphere of the poem are literally evoked. The poem is a sonnet whose first two quatrains (making eight lines of text) are distributed throughout the first movement, an Allegro in E major. (See Listening Guide 15 for the text.) The solo violin is accompanied by an orchestra consisting of strings—first and second violins, violas, and cellos—with the basso continuo realized (improvised from the figured bass) on harpsichord or organ.

First movement

Both poem and music evoke the birds' joyous welcome to spring and the gentle murmur of streams, followed by thunder and lightning. The image of birdcalls takes shape in staccato notes, trills, and running scales; the storm is portrayed by agitated repeated notes answered by quickly ascending minor-key scales. Throughout, an orchestral **ritornello,** or refrain, returns again and again (representing the general mood of spring) in alternation with the episodes, which often feature the solo violin. Ultimately, "the little birds take up again their melodious song" as we return to the home key. A florid passage for the soloist leads to the final ritornello.

Ritornello form

In the second movement, a Largo in 3/4, Vivaldi evokes an image from the poem of the goatherd who sleeps "in a pleasant, flowery meadow" with his faithful dog by his side. Over the bass line played by the violas, which sound an ostinato rhythm, he wrote, "The dog who barks." This dog clearly has a sense of rhythm. The solo violin unfolds a tender, melancholy melody in the most lyrical Baroque style. In the finale, an Allegro marked "Rustic Dance," we can visualize nymphs and shepherds cavorting in the fields as the music suggests the drone of bagpipes. Ritornellos and solo passages alternate in bringing the work to a happy conclusion.

Second and third movements

Like Bach, Vivaldi was renowned in his day as a performer rather than a composer. Today, he is recognized both as the "father of the concerto," having established ritornello form as its basic procedure, and as a herald of musical Romanticism in his use of pictorial imagery.

Listening Guide 15

eLG   1 (62–67)
2 (35–40)

Vivaldi: *Spring*, from *The Four Seasons* (*La primavera*, from *Le quattro stagioni*), Op. 8, No. 1, First Movement   (3:33)

DATE OF WORK: Published 1725

GENRE: Programmatic concerto for solo violin, Op. 8 (*The Contest Between Harmony and Inspiration*), Nos. 1–4, each based on an Italian sonnet, with 3 movements each:

No. 1: *Spring (La primavera)*	No. 3: *Autumn (L'autunno)*
No. 2: *Summer (L'estate)*	No. 4: *Winter (L'inverno)*

I. Allegro

Joyful spring has arrived,
the birds greet it with their cheerful song,
and the brooks in the gentle breezes
flow with a sweet murmur.

The sky is covered with a black mantle,
and thunder and lightning announce a storm.
When they fall silent, the little birds
take up again their melodious song.

II. Largo

And in the pleasant, flowery meadow,
to the gentle murmur of bushes and trees,
the goatherd sleeps, his faithful dog at his side.

III. Allegro
(*Rustic Dance*)

To the festive sounds of a rustic bagpipe
nymphs and shepherds dance in their favorite spot
when spring appears in its brilliance.

First Movement: Allegro; in ritornello form, E major   (3:33)

WHAT TO LISTEN FOR: Distinctive timbre of Baroque-period string instruments.
Musical pictorialization of images of spring, based on the poem (birds, babbling brooks, gentle breezes, thunder and lightning).
Virtuosity of solo violin part, with fast-running scales and trills.
Recurring theme (ritornello, representing spring) that unifies the movement.

Ritornello theme:

		DESCRIPTION	PROGRAM
62	0:00	Ritornello 1, in E major.	Spring
	0:32	Episode 1; solo violin with birdlike trills and high running scales, accompanied by violins	Birds
63	1:07	Ritornello 2.	Spring
64	1:15	Episode 2; whispering figures like water flowing, played by orchestra.	Murmuring brooks
	1:39	Ritornello 3.	Spring
65	1:47	Episode 3 modulates; solo violin with repeated notes, fast ascending minor-key scales, accompanied by orchestra.	Thunder, lightning
	2:15	Ritornello 4, in relative minor (C-sharp).	Spring
66	2:24	Episode 4; trills and repeated notes in solo violin.	Birds
	2:43	Ritornello 5, returns to E major; brief solo passage interrupts.	
67	3:12	Closing tutti.	

26

The Baroque Suite

KEY POINTS

 StudySpace online at www.wwnorton.com/enjoy

○ The Baroque *suite* is a group of dances, usually in the same key, with each piece in binary form (**A-A-B-B**) or ternary form (**A-B-A**). The standard dances in the suite are the *allemande, courante, sarabande*, and *gigue*.

○ Handel's best-known orchestral suites are the *Water Music* and *Music for the Royal Fireworks*.

○ The French love for dancing and spectacular staged entertainments contributed to the development of the orchestra.

○ The ensemble suites by Jean-Joseph Mouret were probably meant for an outdoor festival at the French Royal Court.

The suite of the Baroque era was a natural outgrowth of earlier traditions that paired dances of contrasting tempos and character. The suite presented an international galaxy of dance types, all in the same key: the German *allemande*, in quadruple meter at a moderate tempo; the French *courante*, in triple meter at a moderate tempo; the Spanish *sarabande*, a stately dance in triple meter; and the English *jig* (*gigue*), in a lively 6/8 or 6/4. These began as popular dances but by the late Baroque

Dance types

CD iMaterials
CD iMusic

Minuet in D minor (*Anna Magdalena Notebook*)

Handel: Alla hornpipe, from *Water Music*

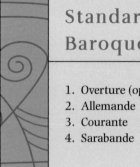

Standard Order of the Baroque Dance Suite

1. Overture (optional)
2. Allemande
3. Courante
4. Sarabande
5. Other dances (optional, e.g., hornpipe, minuet)
6. Gigue (jig)

had left the ballroom far behind and become abstract types of art music. Between the slow sarabande and fast gigue, composers could insert a variety of optional dances—the **minuet**, the **gavotte**, the lively **bourrée**, the **passepied**, the jaunty **hornpipe**; some were of peasant origin and thus introduced a refreshing earthiness to their more formal surroundings. The suite sometimes opened with an **overture**, and might include other brief pieces with descriptive titles.

Binary and ternary structure

Each piece in the Baroque suite was set either in binary structure, consisting of two sections of approximately equal length, each rounded off by a cadence and each repeated (**A-A-B-B**), or in ternary form (**A-B-A**), which we will hear in a movement from Handel's *Water Music.* In both structures, the **A** part usually moves from the home key (tonic) to a contrasting key (dominant), while the **B** part makes the corresponding move back. The two sections often use closely related melodic material. The form is easy to hear because of the modulation and the full stop at the end of each part.

Keyboard suites

The principle of combining dances into a suite could be applied to chamber, orchestral, and solo instrumental music as well. Bach's French and English suites for harpsichord are splendid examples of solo keyboard suites, as are those of French composers François Couperin (1668–1733) and Elisabeth-Claude Jacquet de la Guerre (c. 1666–1729), an extraordinary harpsichordist and composer at the French Royal Court.

Orchestral suites

French composers, such as Jean-Baptiste Lully and Jean-Joseph Mouret, were central to the development of the orchestral suite; the four orchestral suites of J. S. Bach are indebted to seventeenth-century French ballet music. Bach's contemporary Georg Philipp Telemann (1681–1767) was amazingly prolific in this genre, contributing over 125 orchestral suites to the repertory, thereby establishing the French-style orchestral suite in Germany. Telemann's suites from his *Tafelmusik* collection (Table or Dinner Music, 1733) begin with a French overture—a work with a slow and stately introduction followed by a quick, fugal section—and follow with a series of contrasting dances that include both binary and ternary forms. These dances often bear fanciful or descriptive titles but have the character of one of the standard dances (for example, *Flaterie*, or flattery, is a sarabande in typical binary structure).

 Tafelmusik

Handel and the Orchestral Suite

The two orchestral suites by Handel, the *Water Music* and *Music for the Royal Fireworks,* are memorable contributions to the genre. The *Water Music* was surely played (although probably not first composed) for a royal party on the Thames River in London on July 17, 1717. Two days later, the *Daily Courant* reported:

> On Wednesday Evening, at about 8, the King took Water at Whitehall in an open Barge, . . . and went up the River towards Chelsea. Many other Barges with Persons of Quality attended, and so great a Number of Boats, that the whole River in a manner was cover'd; a City Company's Barge was employ'd for the Musick, wherein were 50 Instruments of all sorts, who play'd all the Way from Lambeth (while the Barges drove with the Tide without Rowing, as far as Chelsea) the finest Symphonies, compos'd express for this Occasion, by Mr. Handel; which his Majesty liked so well, that he caus'd it to be plaid over three times in going and returning.

WATER MUSIC

The twenty-two numbers of the *Water Music* were performed without continuo instruments, since it was not possible to bring a harpsichord aboard the barge. The conditions of an outdoor performance, in which the music would have to contend with the breeze on the river, birdcalls, and similar noises, prompted Handel to create music that was marked by lively rhythms and catchy melodies.

The *Water Music* opens with a French overture (see p. 141) and includes a variety of dance numbers (not in the standard order of the suite), among them minuets in graceful 3/4 time, bourrées in fast 4/4, and hornpipes (an English country dance) in lively triple meter.

The Suite in D major opens with a majestic three-part Allegro that sounds a fanfare in the trumpets, answered by the French horns and strings. One of the most recognized dances from the *Water Music* is the hornpipe from the Suite. Its catchy opening theme features decorative trills in the strings and woodwinds, answered by

CD iMusic

Handel: Alla hornpipe, from *Water Music*

A royal sortie on the Thames River in London, as depicted by **Giovanni Antonio Canaletto** (1697–1768).

majestic brass and timpani; this is followed by a more reflective **B** section set in a minor key. The return of **A** completes the ternary form that is typical of many Baroque dances. (See Listening Guide 16.)

More than two and a half centuries after it was written, Handel's *Water Music* is still a favorite with the public, indoors or out. We need to hear only a few measures of the work to understand why.

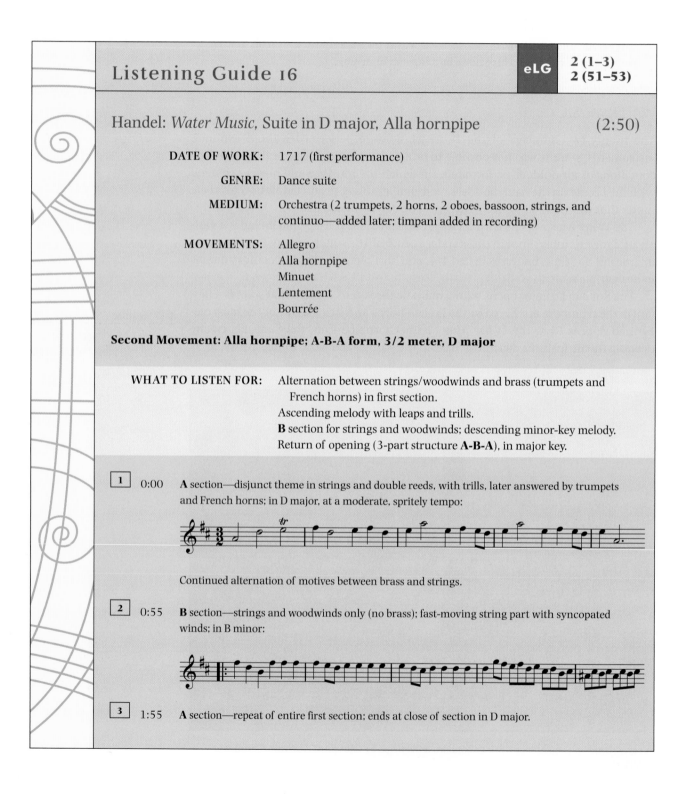

Listening Guide 16

eLG 2 (1–3)
2 (51–53)

Handel: *Water Music*, Suite in D major, Alla hornpipe   (2:50)

DATE OF WORK:	1717 (first performance)
GENRE:	Dance suite
MEDIUM:	Orchestra (2 trumpets, 2 horns, 2 oboes, bassoon, strings, and continuo—added later; timpani added in recording)
MOVEMENTS:	Allegro
	Alla hornpipe
	Minuet
	Lentement
	Bourrée

Second Movement: Alla hornpipe; A-B-A form, 3/2 meter, D major

WHAT TO LISTEN FOR:	Alternation between strings/woodwinds and brass (trumpets and French horns) in first section.
	Ascending melody with leaps and trills.
	B section for strings and woodwinds; descending minor-key melody.
	Return of opening (3-part structure **A-B-A**), in major key.

1 0:00 **A** section—disjunct theme in strings and double reeds, with trills, later answered by trumpets and French horns; in D major, at a moderate, spritely tempo:

Continued alternation of motives between brass and strings.

2 0:55 **B** section—strings and woodwinds only (no brass); fast-moving string part with syncopated winds; in B minor:

3 1:55 **A** section—repeat of entire first section; ends at close of section in D major.

Music at the French Royal Court

*"To enjoy the effects of music fully, we must
completely lose ourselves in it."*

—JEAN-PHILIPPE RAMEAU

Few cultural centers could equal the splendor of the courts of the French kings Louis XIV (r. 1643–1715) and Louis XV (1715–1774). The opulence of the palace of Versailles, just outside Paris, was echoed in the grand entertainments celebrated at court. Jean-Baptiste Lully, court composer to Louis XIV, was central to the development of French stage works, including comedy-ballets and tragic operas. He also served as director of the instrumental groups at court, including the famous 24 Violons du Roy; this string ensemble was an important precursor to the modern orchestra.

Among the musicians who worked in this rich cultural milieu was Jean-Joseph Mouret (1682–1738). A native of Avignon, in southern France, Mouret came to Paris to serve the duke of Maine, a son of Louis XIV. His first opera, *Les fêtes ou le triomphe de Thalia*, is notable for its use of comedy. Besides his stage works, including grand **divertissements** (entertainments), he wrote several instrumental suites for large ensembles. We will hear a movement from a collection entitled *Suite de symphonies*, written in 1729. Scored for trumpets, oboes, bassoons, timpani, and strings, this suite was most likely intended for an outdoor festival. You may recognize our selection: it is the theme for *Masterpiece Theatre*, a PBS program that has been coming into our homes since 1971.

Mouret's familiar fanfare is a **rondeau,** a French form that led directly to the **rondo** (the words are cognates), frequently employed by later eighteenth-century composers. The rondeau here has a five-part structure (**A-B-A-C-A**); its opening material serves as a refrain (**A**, usually in the tonic key) between contrasting sections. (You may recall that the term *rondeau* also describes a medieval vocal genre

Divertissements

CD iMaterials
CD iMusic

Rondeau

The architectural plan of Chambord, a French castle in the Loire Valley, evokes a seven-part form related to a rondo (**A-B-A-C-A-B-A**).

with a refrain.) The main theme is a majestic one, stated twice by the full orchestra. The trumpets and timpani drop out for the short **B** section, but return for a restatement of the opening. The contrasting **C** section is the longest, and meanders through various key centers before the brilliant refrain returns to close off the movement. (See Listening Guide 17.) This music conjures up the grandeur of the sumptuous banquets, elegant ballets, and spectacular pageants that dominated life at the French Royal Court.

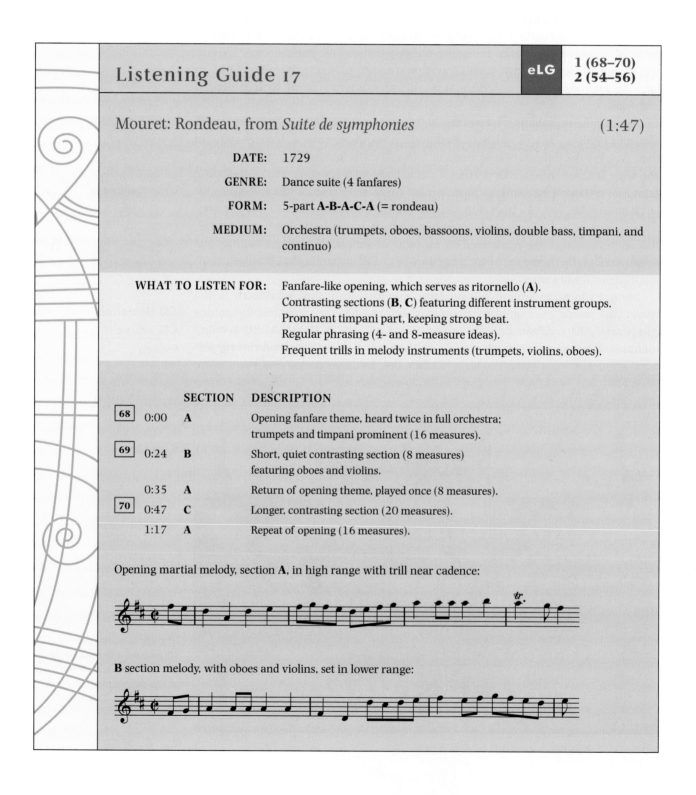

Listening Guide 17

eLG 1 (68–70)
2 (54–56)

Mouret: Rondeau, from *Suite de symphonies* (1:47)

DATE:	1729
GENRE:	Dance suite (4 fanfares)
FORM:	5-part **A-B-A-C-A** (= rondeau)
MEDIUM:	Orchestra (trumpets, oboes, bassoons, violins, double bass, timpani, and continuo)

WHAT TO LISTEN FOR: Fanfare-like opening, which serves as ritornello (**A**).
Contrasting sections (**B**, **C**) featuring different instrument groups.
Prominent timpani part, keeping strong beat.
Regular phrasing (4- and 8-measure ideas).
Frequent trills in melody instruments (trumpets, violins, oboes).

		SECTION	DESCRIPTION
68	0:00	A	Opening fanfare theme, heard twice in full orchestra; trumpets and timpani prominent (16 measures).
69	0:24	B	Short, quiet contrasting section (8 measures) featuring oboes and violins.
	0:35	A	Return of opening theme, played once (8 measures).
70	0:47	C	Longer, contrasting section (20 measures).
	1:17	A	Repeat of opening (16 measures).

Opening martial melody, section **A**, in high range with trill near cadence:

B section melody, with oboes and violins, set in lower range:

27

Other Baroque Instrumental Forms

"He, who possessed the most profound knowledge of all the contrapuntal arts, understood how to make art subservient to beauty."
—C. P. E. BACH, ABOUT HIS FATHER, J. S. BACH

KEY POINTS **StudySpace** online at www.wwnorton.com/enjoy

- Baroque instrumental music was often set in one of several forms built on a repeating bass line (*ground bass*).
- Two main types of overture were the *French overture* (slow-fast) and the *Italian overture* (fast-slow-fast).
- J. S. Bach's keyboard music includes *chorale preludes* (short organ works elaborating on a chorale

melody) and *preludes and fugues* (a free-form piece followed by a strict imitative piece).
- Bach's *Well-Tempered Clavier* is his most famous collection of preludes and fugues, and *The Art of Fugue* is his last and most comprehensive example of contrapuntal writing.
- The French Rococo and the German "sentimental" styles ushered in the new Classical era.

Throughout the seventeenth century, Baroque composers explored a variety of techniques and formal procedures to give their works both variety and coherence. One such technique derived from a repeating bass line or *ground bass*. (We heard a similar procedure earlier in Dido's Lament from Purcell's *Dido and Aeneas*.) These structures exemplify the Baroque urge toward abundant variation and embellishment of a musical idea, and that desire to make "much out of little" which is the essence of the creative act. One of the most famous examples of a ground ostinatio is Johann Pachelbel's Canon in D. Its mesmerizing elaborations unfold over a relentless ostinato, making us unaware of the strict *canon* (an imitative genre like a round) that engages the three violins.

Another important orchestral genre is the operatic overture, of which two types were popular during this period. The *French overture* generally followed the pattern slow-fast, its fast section in a loosely fugal style known as *fugato*. The *Italian overture* consisted of three short, simple sections: fast-slow-fast, with a vivacious, dancelike finale. This pattern, expanded into three separate movements, was later adopted by the concerto grosso and the solo concerto. In addition the opera overture of the Baroque was one of the ancestors of the symphony of later eras.

Ground bass

CD iMaterials
CD iMusic

Pachelbel: Canon in D

Overtures: French and Italian

Keyboard Forms

The keyboard forms of the Baroque fall into two categories: free forms based on harmony, with a strong element of improvisation, such as the prelude and chorale prelude; and stricter forms based on counterpoint, such as the fugue. Bach's keyboard music shows mastery of both types.

A spectacular Baroque organ (1738) in St. Bavo's Cathedral, Haarlem, The Netherlands.

A *prelude* is a short piece based on the continuous expansion of a melodic or rhythmic figure. It originated in improvisations performed on the lute and keyboard instruments. In the late Baroque, the prelude was used to introduce a group of dance pieces or a fugue. Since its texture was mostly homophonic, it made an effective contrast with the contrapuntal texture of the fugue that followed. The *toccata* was another such free, often highly virtuosic, form—you may know Bach's famous Toccata and Fugue in D Minor (**CD iMusic**), which was the opening music for Disney's *Fantasia* and has been used in many films since.

Church organists, in introducing the chorale to be sung by the congregation, adopted the practice of embellishing the traditional melodies. A body of instrumental works—*chorale preludes* and *chorale variations*—was developed in which organ virtuosity of the highest level was combined with inspired improvisation. In his capacity as a church organist, Bach wrote more than 140 organ chorales. Some were short, with the tune stated in its original form. Others presented a longer elaboration of the tune, giving free rein to the imagination. You might recognize the famous chorale known as *Jesu, Joy of Man's Desiring* (**CD iMusic**).

The Fugue and Its Devices

From the art and science of counterpoint came one of the most exciting forms of Baroque music, the fugue. The name is derived from *fuga*, the Latin word for "flight," implying a flight of fancy, or possibly the flight of the theme from one voice to the other. A *fugue* is a contrapuntal composition in which a single theme pervades the entire fabric, entering in one voice and then in another. The fugue, then, is based on the principle of imitation. Its main theme, the *subject*, constitutes the unifying idea, the focal point of interest in the contrapuntal web.

We have already encountered the fugue or fugal style in a number of works: at the beginning of the book, in Britten's *Young Person's Guide to the Orchestra (Variations and Fugue on a Theme of Purcell)*; in Handel's "Hallelujah Chorus" from *Messiah*; and in the opening movement of Bach's cantata *A Mighty Fortress Is Our God.* Thus a fugue may be written for a group of instruments, for a full chorus, or, as we shall see, for a solo instrument. Whether the fugue is vocal or instrumental, its several lines are **Fugal voices** called *voices*. In vocal and orchestral fugues, each voice is sounded by a different performer or group of performers. In fugues for keyboard instruments, the ten fingers—and the feet, on the organ, playing the pedals—manage the complex interweaving of the voices.

Subject The *subject*, or main theme of the fugue, is stated alone at the beginning in one of the voices—referred to by the range in which it sounds: soprano, alto, tenor, or **Answer** bass. It is then imitated in another voice—this is the *answer*—while the first often **Countersubject** continues with a *countersubject*, or countertheme. Depending on the number of voices in the fugue, the subject then appears in a third voice and is answered in the fourth (if any), while the other voices weave a free contrapuntal texture against these.

Exposition When the theme has been presented in each voice once, the first section of the fugue, the *exposition*, is at an end. From then on, the fugue alternates between sec-

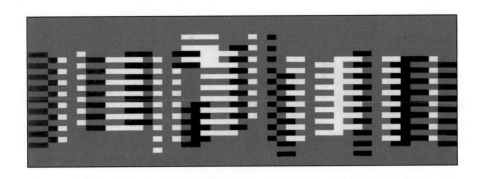

In **Josef Alber**'s (1888–1976) *Fugue* (1925), the interlocking and parallel lines resemble the polyphonic textures of the fugue.

tions that feature entrances of the subject and *episodes*—interludes that serve as areas of relaxation—until it reaches its home key.

Episodes

The subject of the fugue is stated in the home key, the tonic. The answer is given in a related key, the dominant, which lies five tones above the tonic. There may be modulation to foreign keys in the course of the fugue, which builds up tension before the return home. The Baroque fugue thus embodies the opposition between home and contrasting keys, which was one of the basic principles of the new major-minor system.

Contrapuntal writing is marked by a number of devices used since the earliest days of polyphony. A melody can be presented in longer time values, often twice as slow as the original, using *augmentation,* or in shorter time values that go by faster, called *diminution*. The pitches can be stated backwards (starting from the last note and preceding to the first), in *retrograde,* or turned upside down (in mirror image), moving by the same intervals but in the opposite direction, a technique called *inversion*. (See "Examples of Contrapuntal Devices," p. 160) We will observe the use of *stretto* as well, in which the theme is imitated by different voices in close succession. The effect is one of voices crowding upon each other, creating a heightening of tension that brings the fugue to its climax.

Contrapuntal devices

The Baroque fugue, then, was a form based on imitative counterpoint that combined the composer's technical skill with imagination, feeling, and exuberant ornamentation to produce one of the supreme achievements of the era.

Bach's Keyboard Fugues

Bach is undisputedly the greatest master of fugal writing. His *Well-Tempered Clavier,* a collection of preludes and fugues issued in two volumes and demonstrating the new system of equal temperament for tuning keyboard instruments, is a testament to his skill. The first volume of the collection, completed in 1722 during the years Bach worked in Cöthen, contains a prelude and fugue in each of the twelve major and twelve minor keys. The second volume, also containing twenty-four preludes and fugues, appeared twenty years later. The whole collection is thus made up of forty-eight preludes and fugues.

Well-Tempered Clavier

Bach's last demonstration of contrapuntal mastery was *The Art of Fugue*, a collection of fourteen fugues and four canons that systematically explores all the wizardry of fugal devices. Scholars have argued over the intent of this highly technical work: was it meant as a theoretical exercise or for performance? And if performed, by what instruments? Because of the intricacies of the lines, the four voices are written on separate staves rather than in keyboard notation (on two staves); this has prompted widely diversified recordings by orchestras, chamber ensembles and even brass groups—among them the well-known Canadian Brass.

The Art of Fugue

The collection is generally accepted today as keyboard music, probably meant for organ or harpsichord.

BACH'S CONTRAPUNCTUS I, FROM *THE ART OF FUGUE*

We will consider the opening fugue, called Contrapunctus I. Its four voices introduce the subject successively in the order alto-soprano-bass-tenor. This constitutes the

Exposition

exposition. (The soprano and tenor have the answer form of the subject, set in the key of the dominant; see Listening Guide 18.) At this point, the first ***episode*** distracts

Episode

our attention from the subject, and for the extended middle section of the fugue, we wait with anticipation for other statements of the now-familiar tune that alternate with episodes. Bach tricks the ear with several false entries that anticipate a full statement of the theme, and in one case, he overlaps the subjects, beginning one before the previous statement is completed (in stretto). The tonic (D minor) is reestablished by a bold statement in the bass, heard on the organ pedals, and we feel solidly in the home key with the sustained pedal note on D. The final chord—a major triad—jolts us from the contemplative minor-key setting.

Although this fugue does not exploit all the compositional devices described, nor does it even have a real countersubject that recurs, Bach increases the complexity of

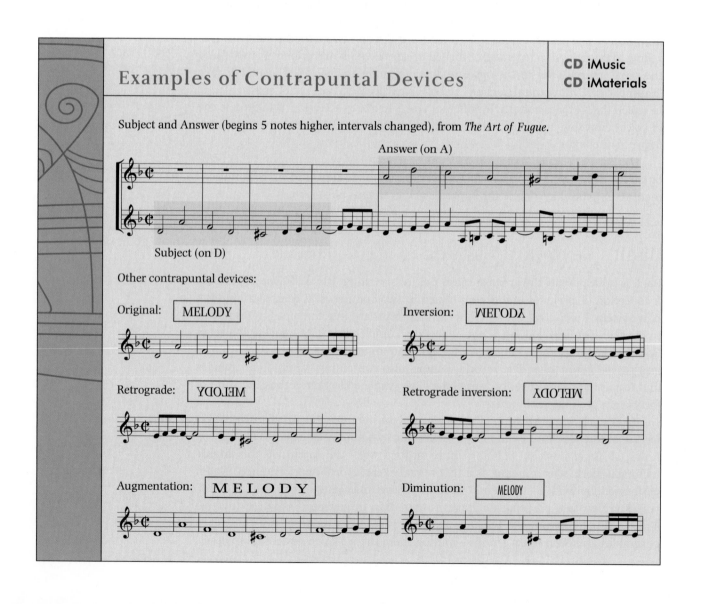

Examples of Contrapuntal Devices

CD iMusic
CD iMaterials

Subject and Answer (begins 5 notes higher, intervals changed), from *The Art of Fugue*.

Answer (on A)

Subject (on D)

Other contrapuntal devices:

Original: MELODY

Inversion: ΜΕΓΟDΧ

Retrograde: ΥDOΛƎΜ

Retrograde inversion: ΧDOΊƎΜ

Augmentation: MELODY

Diminution: MELODY

the counterpoint with each fugue in this collection, trying his hand at using multiple subjects, mirror techniques, and even symbolism (he incorporates his name as a countersubject—B♭-A-C-H; in German, the letter H refers to the pitch B natural). There is no question this collection was the climax of Bach's keyboard art.

Listening Guide 18

eLG   **1 (58–61)**
       2 (31–34)

Bach: Contrapunctus 1, from *The Art of Fugue*   3:12

DATE:	Completed 1749; published posthumously 1751
MEDIUM:	Keyboard (organ or harpsichord)
FORM:	Fugue (4 voices)

WHAT TO LISTEN FOR: Repeated entries of main theme (*subject* on D, *answer* on A), in different registers (see "Examples of Contrapuntal Devices," p. 160, for themes).
Opening *exposition* has 4 voice entries without gaps.
Alternation of subject (and answer) with connecting sections (*episodes*).
Anticipation of subject statements and overlapping of subject (*stretto*).
Final statement over sustained pedal note.
Overall minor harmony but closing major chord.

EXPOSITION

`58`

4 entries of subject (answer) in alternation:

0:00	alto (subject)
0:10	soprano (answer)
0:19	bass (subject)
0:28	tenor (answer)

`59` 0:38 Episode 1 (6 measures)—ends exposition.

MIDDLE ENTRIES

`60`

Subject stated 2 times:

0:52	alto
1:05	soprano (transposed to A)
1:12	Answer in bass (overlaps soprano in stretto).
1:21	Episode 2 (4 measures).
1:30	Answer in tenor.
1:40	Episode 3 (5 measures).
1:52	Answer heard; anticipated in alto, then full statement in soprano.

CLOSING SECTION

`61`

2:10	Subject in bass (but anticipated in soprano).
2:19	Episode 4.
2:26	Pedal point in bass.
2:44	Rhetorical pauses.
2:52	Answer—final statement over sustained pedal on tonic.
	Ends with major chord.

To the Age of Enlightenment

*"A musician cannot move others unless he too is moved. He must
feel all the emotions that he hopes to arouse in his audience."*

—C. P. E. BACH

 StudySpace online at www.wwnorton.com/enjoy

○ Two pre-Classical styles prevailed in the early eighteenth century: the decorative *Rococo*, in France, and the sensitive style (*Empfindsamkeit*), in Germany.

○ Several pre-Classical musicians wrote important music treatises and instruction manuals.

○ Taste in opera changed radically during this era; preferred styles were Italian comic opera and *ballad opera* (such as *The Beggar's Opera*), with familiar songs and spoken text.

○ Christoph Willibald Gluck's lyric drama brought about new operatic reforms in the later eighteenth century.

The Rococo and the Age of Sensibility

In the reigns of the French kings Louis XIV and Louis XV, the old regime was waning. By the mid-eighteenth century, the privileged minority at the top of the social pyramid had exchanged their games of power for games of frivolity. Art had moved from the monumentality of the Baroque to the caprice and intimacy of the Rococo.

The word derives from the French *rocaille*, "a shell," suggesting the decorative scroll- and shellwork characteristic of the style. The Rococo took shape as a reaction against the grandiose gesture of the Baroque. Out of the disintegrating world of the Baroque came a miniature, ornate art aimed at the enchantment of the senses and asserting a doctrine whose first law was "enjoy yourself."

Artists   The greatest painter of the French Rococo was Jean-Antoine Watteau (1684–1721). To the dream world of love and gallantry that furnished the themes of his art, Watteau brought the techniques of the Dutch school of Rubens.

Watteau's intimate, pastoral scenes reflected the shift in French society.

The musical counterpart to Watteau was François Couperin (1668–1733), the greatest composer of the French keyboard school. Couperin came from a family of distinguished musicians. His works, along with those of Elisabeth-Claude Jacquet de la Guerre, crystallized the miniature world of the Rococo. Their goal was to charm, to delight, to entertain.

The coming era, known as the Age of Enlightenment, was characterized by the desire to systematize all knowledge, and this impulse also made itself felt on the musical scene. Jean-Philippe Rameau (1683–1764), the foremost French composer of the era, tried to establish a rational foundation for the harmonic practice of

his time. His *Treatise on Harmony* (1722) set forth concepts that served as the point of departure for modern music theory.

The Rococo witnessed as profound a change in taste as any that has ever occurred in the history of music. In turning to a sophisticated music for entertainment, composers adopted a new ideal of beauty. Elaborate polyphonic textures yielded to a single melody line with a simple chordal accompaniment (homophony), in much the same way that the contrapuntal complexities of late Renaissance music gave way to the early Baroque ideal of monody. This era desired its music to be, above all, simple and to express natural feelings. Thus was born the "sensitive," or "sentimental," style of the ***Empfindsamkeit***, as well as the Age of Sensibility—an age that saw the first stirrings of a direct and natural expression that flowered fully with Romanticism.

The new style reached its apex in Germany in the mid–eighteenth century when Bach's four composer sons—Wilhelm Friedemann, Carl Philipp Emanuel, Johann Christoph, and Johann Christian—were active. Along with their contemporaries, the Bach sons oversaw a revolution in taste that resulted in neglect of their father's music after his death. In this musical revolution, the sonata and the concerto were expanded, and symphonic styles were enriched with elements drawn from the operatic aria and overture and with the tunes and rhythms of Italian comic opera. From these developments was born something new—the Classical multimovement cycle, which will be described in Chapter 29 and examples of which we will hear in forthcoming chapters. This new art form was the collective achievement of several generations of musicians who were active in Italy, France, and Germany throughout the pre-Classical period (c. 1725–75).

Jean-Antoine Watteau (1684–1721), with his dream world of love and gallantry, was the artistic counterpart of François Couperin. *La gamme d'amour (The Gamut of Love)*.

Empfindsamkeit

Bach's sons

The Changing Opera

The vast social changes taking shape in the eighteenth century were bound to be reflected in the lyric theater. Grandiose Baroque opera, geared to an era of absolute monarchy, had no place in the shifting societal structure. Increasingly its pretensions were satirized all over Europe.

In 1728, *The Beggar's Opera*, by John Gay (1685–1732), a satirical play with folk songs and popular tunes arranged by Johann Christoph Pepusch (1667–1752),

The Beggar's Opera

sounded the death knell of opera seria in England, and ushered in a vogue of racy pieces with popular songs and dances.

In 1752, a troupe of Italian singers in Paris brought about a similar revolution with a performance of Giovanni Battista Pergolesi's comedy with music *La serva padrona* (*The Maid as Mistress*). The so-called War of the Buffoons ensued, between those who favored the traditional French court opera and those who saw in the rising Italian comic opera, called **opera buffa**, a new, realistic art. In the larger sense, the War of the Buffoons was a contest between the rising bourgeois music and a dying aristocratic art.

Opera buffa

Gluck and Opera Reform

It fell to a German-born composer trained in Italy to liberate serious opera from some of its outmoded conventions. Christoph Willibald Gluck (1714–1787) developed a style that met the new need for dramatic truth and expressiveness; his ideas epitomized the aesthetic of the new age: "Simplicity, truth, and naturalness are the great principles of beauty in all forms of art."

Gluck's convictions shaped the works he wrote for the Imperial Court Theater at Vienna, notably *Orpheus and Eurydice* (1762) and *Alceste* (1767). In these works, Gluck successfully fused a number of elements: the monumental choral scenes and dances that had always been a feature of French lyric tragedy, the animated ensembles of comic opera, the vigor of the new instrumental style in Italy and Germany, and the broadly arching vocal line that was part of Europe's operatic heritage. The result was a music drama whose truth and expressiveness profoundly affected the course of operatic history.

IN HIS OWN WORDS

There is no musical rule I have not willingly sacrificed to dramatic effect.

In *The Sacrifice of Iphigenia* by **Giuseppe Angeli** (1712–1798), the goddess Artemis is about to spare the life of Iphigenia from the blade of the High Priest and will substitute the sacred stag in her place. This version of the Greek legend was used by Gluck in his opera.

A COMPARISON OF BAROQUE AND CLASSICAL STYLES

	BAROQUE (C. 1600–1750)	CLASSICAL (C. 1750–1825)
COMPOSERS	Monteverdi, Purcell, Barbara Strozzi, Corelli, Vivaldi, Handel, Mouret, Bach	Haydn, Mozart, Beethoven, Schubert
MELODY	Continuous melody with wide leaps, chromatic tones for emotional effect	Symmetrical melody in balanced phrases and cadences; tuneful, diatonic, with narrow leaps
RHYTHM	Single rhythm predominant; steady, energetic pulse; freer in vocal music	Dance rhythms favored; regularly recurring accents
HARMONY	Chromatic harmony for expressive effect; major-minor system established with brief excursions to other keys	Diatonic harmony favored; tonic-dominant relationship expanded, becomes basis for large-scale form
TEXTURE	Monodic texture (early Baroque); polyphonic texture (late Baroque); linear-horizontal dimension	Homophonic texture; chordal-vertical dimension
INSTRUMENTAL GENRES	Trio sonata, concerto grosso, suite, prelude, fugue, chaconne, passacaglia	Symphony, solo concerto, solo sonata, string quartet, other chamber music genres
VOCAL GENRES	Opera, Mass, oratorio, cantata	Opera, Mass, oratorio
FORM	Binary and ternary forms predominant	Larger forms, including sonata-allegro form, developed
DYNAMICS	Subtle dynamic nuances; *forte/piano* contrasts; echo effects	Continuously changing dynamics through *crescendo* and *decrescendo*
TIMBRE	Continuous tone color throughout one movement	Changing tone colors between sections of works
PERFORMING FORCES	String orchestra, with added woodwinds; organ and harpsichord in use	Orchestra standardized into four families; introduction of clarinet, trombone; rise of piano to prominence
IMPROVISATION	Improvisation expected; harmonies realized from figured bass	Improvisation largely limited to cadenzas in concertos
EMOTION	Single affection; emotional exuberance and theatricality	Emotional balance and restraint

Wassily Kandinsky (1866–1944), *Contrasting Sounds* (1924).

PART FIVE

More Materials of Form

Expanded Elements of Form

28

CD iMaterials ## The Development of Musical Ideas

*"I alter some things, eliminate and try again until I am satisfied.
Then begins the mental working out of this material in
its breadth, its narrowness, its height and depth."*

—LUDWIG VAN BEETHOVEN

KEY POINTS	Ⓢ **StudySpace** online at www.wwnorton.com/enjoy

- Melodic ideas, or *themes*, are used as building blocks in a composition; these melodies are made up of short melodic or rhythmic fragments known as *motives*.

- Themes can be expanded by varying the melody, rhythm, or harmony through *thematic development*; this usually happens in large-scale works.

- Development and variation are processes found in all styles of music.

- Repeated short patterns, or *ostinatos*, can also be used to build compositions.

Thinking, whether in words or music, demands continuity. Every thought should flow from the one before and lead logically into the next, thereby creating steady progress toward a goal. Uniting the first phrase of one melody and the second phrase of a different one would not make any more sense than joining the beginning of one sentence to the end of another.

Theme
An impression of cause and effect, a natural flow, is essential to any musical work and is achieved in a variety of ways, depending on the musical style of a work. In Western music, a musical idea that is used as a building block in the construction of a composition is called a *theme*. The expansion of a theme, achieved by varying its melodic outline, rhythm, or harmony, is considered *thematic development*. This is one of the most important techniques in musical composition and requires both imagination and craft on the part of the creator. In addition to its capacity for

British optical artist **Bridget Riley** (b. 1931) explores the large-scale development of a motive through subtle variations in size, shape, and position. *Evoë 3* (2003).

growth, a theme can be fragmented by dividing it into its constituent motives, a *motive* being its smallest melodic or rhythmic unit. A motive can grow into an expansive melody, or it can be treated in *sequence*, that is, repeated at a higher or lower level. A short, repeated musical pattern—called an *ostinato*—can also be an important organizing feature of a work. One well-known work that uses this technique is the Pachelbel Canon in D, in which rich string lines unfold very gradually over an ever-present bass pattern.

We have already considered the form of a fugue, and seen that it is based on a single theme (the subject) that is manipulated in various ways— through imitation, transposition to another pitch level (the answer is on the dominant), inversion (turning it upside down), retrograde (playing it backward), and a combination of retrograde and inversion. A fugue's subject is, then, not developed so much through expansion as by the exploitation of these contrapuntal devices (see p. 160).

The use of thematic development is generally too complex for short pieces, where a simple contrast between sections and modest expansion of material usually supply the necessary continuity. But thematic development is necessary in larger forms of music, where it provides clarity, coherence, and logic.

The development of thematic material—through extension, contraction, and repetition—occurs in music from all corners of the world. We have already seen that some music is improvised, or created spontaneously, by performers. Although it might seem that structure and logic would be alien to this process, this is rarely the case. In jazz, for example, musicians organize their improvised melodies within a highly structured, pre-established harmonic pattern, time frame, and melodic outline that is understood by all the performers. In many parts of Asia, improvisation is a refined and classical art, where the seemingly free and rhapsodic spinning out of the music is tied to a prescribed musical process that results in a lacework of variations.

Let's compare the way themes are developed in music from two very different cultures. The first example, from the opening of Beethoven's Symphony No. 5, which we will study later, illustrates the thematic development of a short, four-note motive that is repeated in sequence one step lower and then grows into a theme. Here the composer has developed and expanded his short idea to realize all its possibilities.

The second example comes from *The Moon Reflected on the Second Springs*, a traditional Chinese work we will study in detail later in the book. Played on an *erhu* (a bowed two-string fiddle) and accompanied by a *yangqin* (a hammered dulcimer; see p. 438), this piece evolves gradually from a short melodic phrase (shown in the chart on p. 168) through a kind of variation process that continuously spins out new ideas with changing pitches and rhythms. Here, instead of sequence and repetition, there is a metamorphosis of the melody, much like we might hear in a jazz improvisation; but

CD iMaterials
CD iMusic

Pachelbel: Canon in D
Bach: *The Art of Fugue*

Thematic development

Variation process in Chinese music

also like jazz, the tune is always recognizable and comes back at established intervals that make its appearance feel comfortable to the listener. We have already observed the variation process in Britten's *Variations and Fugue on the Theme by Purcell (Young Person's Guide to the Orchestra)*, and we will study it shortly as a major structural proce-

Beethoven: Symphony No. 5 in C minor **CD iMusic**

Opening of first movement:

Allegro con brio

Theme based on repetitions of motive:

Theme based on extension of motive:

The Moon Reflected on the Second Springs, Chinese traditional piece **4 (93–95) 8 (63–65)**

Original melody:

3 transformations of the melodic idea:

dure in the Classical era (see p. 172). Characteristic of this Chinese piece are the use of bent pitches, glissandos, slides, trills, and inflections—an embellishment style known as "adding flowers." Thus musical processes from distant cultures can sometimes be compared, even when their contexts and resulting sounds differ greatly.

Pitch inflections

Listening Activity: Thematic Development

CD iMusic
CD iMaterials

Beethoven: Symphony No. 5 in C minor, first movement, opening

The familiar opening of Beethoven's Fifth Symphony allows us to hear how a small musical idea, a *motive*, grows and develops into a full-blown *theme*, one of the building blocks of large musical works.

What to Listen For:
- Familiar opening, with its 4-note idea, or motive (dah-dah-dah-DAH).
- Repetition and variation of this motive at different pitch levels, in sequence.
- Insistent nature of the rhythmic pattern: short-short-short-long.
- Eventual growth of motive through thematic development to a full-blown melody, or theme.

More Listening Review:
- Thematic development (variation): **Symphony No. 94**, second movement (Haydn)
- Improvisation: *Avaz of Bayate Esfahan* (Iran)
- Ostinato: **Canon in D** (Pachelbel)

29

Classical Forms

CD iMaterials

"Great art likes chains. The greater artists have created art within bounds. Or else they created their own chains."
—NADIA BOULANGER

KEY POINTS

StudySpace online at www.wwnorton.com/enjoy

- Form is the most important organizing element in *absolute music*, which has no specific pictorial or literary program.

- Many masterworks of instrumental music are in a standard *multimovement cycle* of three or four movements; these include the Classic-era symphony, sonata, string quartet, and concerto.

- The first movement of the cycle is usually in a fast tempo and in *sonata-allegro form*, with three main sections: *exposition*, *development*, and *recapitulation*.

- The second movement is usually slow and can be in various forms, including *theme and variations* or *ternary* (**A-B-A**) form.

- The third movement (sometimes omitted) is a triple-meter dance—either a *minuet and trio* or a *scherzo and trio*.

- The fourth movement is fast and lively, often in *rondo* or *sonata-allegro* form.

- *Cyclical structure* is a device that links movements; it occurs when a theme from an earlier movement reappears in a later one.

In *Convex and Concave* (1955), Dutch graphic artist **M. C. Escher** (1898–1972) stimulates the brain to recognize patterns and to perceive a centrality in the image by funneling the action toward the center, much like the pull of the tonic in a large-scale musical form.

Every musical work has a form; it is sometimes simple, other times complex. In some cases, the form is dictated by considerations outside the music, such as a text or an accompanying program, as we observed in Vivaldi's *The Four Seasons*.

Absolute music

In *absolute music*, however, form is especially important, because there is no prescribed story or text to hold the music together. The story is the music itself, so its shape is of primary concern for the composer, the performer, and the listener. Large-scale works have an overall form that determines the relationships between the movements and their tempos. In addition, each movement has an internal form that binds its different sections into one artistic whole. We have already learned two of the simplest forms: two-part, or binary (**A-B**), and three-part, or ternary (**A-B-A**).

Multimovement cycle

Now let's examine an important structural procedure in Western instrumental music—the standard *multimovement cycle* that was used from around 1750 through the Romantic era. This cycle generally consists of three or four movements in prescribed forms and tempos and is employed in various genres, including the symphony, the sonata, the string quartet (and many other chamber works as well), and the concerto.

The First Movement

Sonata-allegro form

The most highly organized, and often the longest movement in this cycle is the opening one, which is usually in a fast tempo such as Allegro and is written in *sonata-allegro form* (also known as *sonata form*). A movement in sonata-allegro form establishes a home key, then moves or modulates to another key, and ultimately returns to the home key. We may therefore regard sonata-allegro form as a drama

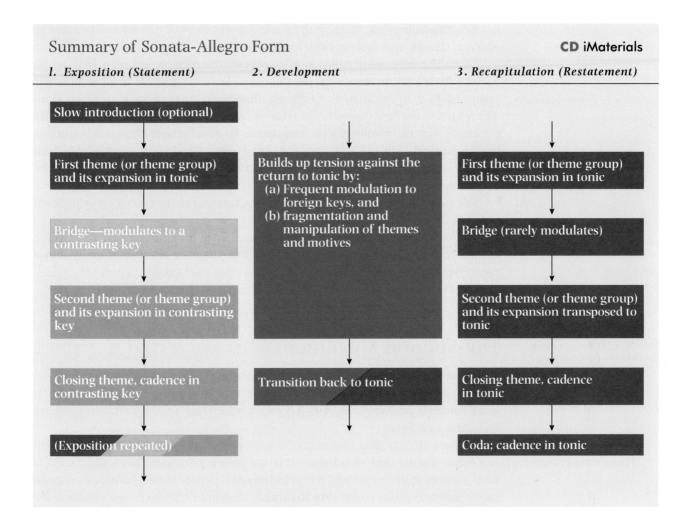

Summary of Sonata-Allegro Form — **CD iMaterials**

1. Exposition (Statement) | **2. Development** | **3. Recapitulation (Restatement)**

- Slow introduction (optional)
- First theme (or theme group) and its expansion in tonic
- Bridge—modulates to a contrasting key
- Second theme (or theme group) and its expansion in contrasting key
- Closing theme, cadence in contrasting key
- (Exposition repeated)

Builds up tension against the return to tonic by:
(a) Frequent modulation to foreign keys, and
(b) fragmentation and manipulation of themes and motives
- Transition back to tonic

- First theme (or theme group) and its expansion in tonic
- Bridge (rarely modulates)
- Second theme (or theme group) and its expansion transposed to tonic
- Closing theme, cadence in tonic
- Coda; cadence in tonic

---

between two contrasting key areas. The "plot"—that is, the action and the tension—derives from this contrast. In most cases, each key area is associated with a theme, which has the potential for development (such as the short, incisive opening to Beethoven's Symphony No. 5). The themes are stated, or "exposed," in the first section; developed in the second; and restated, or "recapitulated," in the third.

The opening section of sonata-allegro form—the ***exposition***, or statement—generally presents the two opposing keys and their respective themes. (In some cases, a theme may consist of several related ideas, in which case we speak of a ***theme group***.) The first theme and its expansion establish the home key, or tonic. A ***bridge***, or transitional passage, leads into a contrasting key; in other words, the function of the bridge is to modulate. The second theme and its expansion establish the contrasting key. A closing section—sometimes with a new closing theme—rounds off the exposition in the contrasting key. In eighteenth-century sonata-allegro form, the exposition is repeated to establish the themes.

Conflict and action, the essence of drama, characterize the ***development***. This section may wander further through a series of foreign keys, building up tension against the inevitable return home. The frequent modulations contribute to a sense of activity and restlessness. Here, the composer reveals the potential of the themes by varying, expanding, or contracting them, breaking them into their component motives, or combining them with other motives or with new material. In ensemble

Exposition

Bridge

Development

works, a fragment of the theme may be presented by one instrument and imitated by another, thereby changing register and timbre.

When the development has run its course, the tension lets up and a bridge passage leads back to the key of the tonic. The beginning of the third section, the *recapitulation*, or restatement, is the psychological climax of sonata-allegro form. The return of the first theme in the tonic satisfies the listener's need for unity. Like the exposition, the recapitulation restates the first and second themes more or less in their original form, but with new and varied twists. One important difference from the exposition is that the recapitulation remains in the tonic, thereby asserting the dominance of the home key.

The movement often ends with a *coda*, an extension of the closing idea that leads us to the final cadence in the home key.

The features of sonata-allegro form, summed up in the chart on page 171 (which is color-coded to show keys), are present in one shape or another in many movements, yet no two pieces are exactly alike. Thus what might at first appear to be a fixed plan provides a supple framework for infinite variety in the hands of the composer.

The Second Movement

The second is usually the slow movement of the cycle, offering a contrast to the Allegro that preceded it, and characterized by lyrical, songful melodies. Typically, it is an Andante or Adagio in **A-B-A** form, a shortened sonata form, or a theme-and-variations forms.

We have already seen that variation is an important procedure in music, but in one form—*theme and variations*—it is the ruling principle. There, the theme is clearly stated at the outset and serves as the point of departure. The melody may be newly invented or borrowed (like the theme in Britten's *Young Person's Guide to the Orchestra*). The theme is likely to be a small two- or three-part idea, simple in character to allow room for elaboration. The statement of the theme is followed by a series of structured variations in which certain features of the original idea are retained while others are altered. Each variation sets forth the idea with some new modification—one might say in a new disguise—through which the listener glimpses something of the original theme.

Any musical element may be developed in the variation process. The melody may be varied by adding or omitting notes or by shifting the theme to another key. *Melodic variation* is a favorite procedure in jazz, where the solo player embellishes a popular tune with a series of decorative flourishes. In *harmonic variation*, the

Recapitulation

Coda

Theme and variations

Melodic variation
Harmonic variation

Minuet and Trio		
Minuet (**A**)	Trio (**B**)	Minuet (**A**)
‖ : **a** : ‖ : **b-a** : ‖	‖ : **c** : ‖ : **d-c** : ‖	**a-b-a**
or	or	or
‖ : **a** : ‖ : **b** : ‖	‖ : **c** : ‖ : **d** : ‖	**a-b**

chords that accompany a melody are replaced by others, perhaps shifting from major to minor mode. The shape of the accompaniment may be changed, or the melody may be shifted to a lower register with new harmonies sounding above it. Note lengths, meter, or tempo can also be changed through *rhythmic variation*, and the texture may be enriched by interweaving the melody with new themes or countermelodies. By combining these methods with changes in dynamics and tone color, composers can also alter the expressive content of the theme; this type of character variation was especially favored in the nineteenth century.

Rhythmic variation

The Third Movement

In the Classical symphony, the third movement is almost invariably a *minuet and trio*. The minuet was originally a Baroque court dance whose stately triple (3/4) meter embodied the ideal of an aristocratic age. But in the eighteenth century, it served as the third movement of some large-scale instrumental works. (Note that this dance movement does not figure in all multimovement instrumental cycles.)

Minuet and trio

Since dance music lends itself to symmetrical construction, we often find in a minuet a clear-cut structure based on phrases of four and eight measures. In tempo, the minuet ranges from stately to lively and whimsical. Indeed, certain of Haydn's minuets are closer in spirit to folk dance than to the palace ballroom.

It was customary to present two dances as a group, the first repeated at the end of the second (resulting in **A-B-A**). The dance in the middle was originally arranged for only three instruments, hence the name "trio," which persisted even after the customary setting for three had long been abandoned. The trio as a rule is thinner in texture and more subdued in mood. At the end of the trio, we find the words *da capo* ("from the beginning"), signifying that the first section is to be played over again (as it was in the Baroque aria; see p. 125).

Da capo

Minuet-trio-minuet is a symmetrical three-part structure in which each part in turn subdivides into two-part, or binary, form (**a-a-b-b**). The second (**b**) section of the minuet or trio may bring back the opening theme, making a *rounded binary form*. (See chart on p. 172.) The composer indicates the repetition of the subsections within repeat signs (‖ : : ‖). However, when the minuet returns after the trio, it is customarily played straight through, without repeats.

Rounded binary form

In the nineteenth century, the minuet was replaced by the *scherzo*, a quick-paced dance in triple meter with the same overall three-part structure (scherzo-trio-scherzo). The scherzo—Italian for "jest"—is marked by abrupt changes of mood, from the humorous or the whimsical to the mysterious and even demonic. In Beethoven's hands, the scherzo became a movement of great rhythmic drive.

Scherzo

The Fourth Movement

The Classical sonata and symphony often ended with a spirited *rondo*. This form is based on the recurrence of a musical idea—the rondo theme, or refrain—in alternation with contrasting episodes, much like the ritornello procedure of the Baroque era. Its symmetrical sections create a balanced architecture that is satisfying aesthetically and easy to hear. In its simplest form, **A-B-A-C-A**, the rondo is an extension of three-part form. We saw a version of this form in the French rondeau by Mouret (see p. 155). As developed by the Classical masters, the rondo was more

Rondo

MULTIMOVEMENT CYCLE: GENERAL SCHEME

CD iMaterials

MOVEMENT	CHARACTER	FORM	TEMPO
FIRST	Long and dramatic	Sonata-allegro	Allegro
SECOND	Slow and lyrical	Theme and variations, sonata form, **A-B-A**, or rondo	Andante, Adagio, Largo
THIRD (optional)	Dancelike Minuet (18th century) Scherzo (19th century)	Minuet and trio Scherzo and trio	Allegretto Allegro
FOURTH	Lively, "happy ending" (18th century) Epic-dramatic with triumphal ending (19th century)	Sonata-allegro Sonata-rondo Theme and variations	Allegro, Vivace, Presto

ambitious in scope, often taking a longer, arched form (**A-B-A-C-A-B-A**; see illustration on p. 155). As the last movement, it featured a catchy, dancelike theme that lent itself to being heard over and over again.

The Multimovement Cycle as a Whole

The multimovement cycle of the Classical masters, as found in their symphonies, sonatas, string quartets, concertos, and other types of chamber music, became the vehicle for their most important instrumental music. The outline above sums up the common practice of the Classical-Romantic era. The outline will be helpful provided you remember that it is no more than a general scheme.

Eighteenth-century composers thought of the movements of the cycle as self-contained entities connected by key. First, third, and fourth movements were in the home key, the second movement in a contrasting key. Nineteenth-century composers sought a more obvious connection between movements—a thematic link. **Cyclical structure** This need was met by a *cyclical structure*, in which a theme from earlier movements reappears in the later ones as a kind of motto or unifying thread. We will see that Beethoven's famous Fifth Symphony displays elements of cyclical structure, with each movement making reference to the famous opening idea, and his magnificent Ninth Symphony (which includes the *Ode to Joy*) epitomizes this structure.

This large-scale structure satisfied composers' need for an extended instrumental work of an abstract nature, and showcased the contrasts of key and mode inherent in the major-minor system. With its fusion of emotional and intellectual elements, its intermingling of lyricism and action, the multimovement cycle may justly claim to be one of the most ingenious art forms ever devised.

Listening Activity: Hearing Larger Forms

CD iMusic
CD iMaterials

Mozart: *Eine kleine Nachtmusik*, first movement

This delightful opening movement to this 4-movement serenade by Mozart allows us to hear the juxta-position of two key centers and themes that is typical of sonata-allegro form.

What to Listen For:
• Overall 3-part structure: Exposition—Development—Recapitulation.
• Strongly rhythmic, ascending 1st theme vs. gentle, falling 2nd theme.
• Change of key; 1st theme = tonic; 2nd theme = dominant.
• Very short developmental section.
• Return of both themes in tonic, in final section.

Mozart: *Eine kleine Nachtmusik*, third movement

The triple-meter dance, a *minuet and trio,* from Mozart's *Eine kleine Nachtmusik,* will help us practice hear-ing on two levels: the big picture of its overall structure, and the detailed view of smaller sections. This is the third, or dance, movement of the standard multimovement cycle.

What to Listen For:
• Overall 3-part structure of the movement: minuet-trio-minuet.
• Rhythmic and strongly accented minuet.
• More lyrical and flowing trio.
• Minuet: 2 short sections, each repeated (**a-a-b-b**).
• Trio: 2 short sections, each repeated (**c-c-d-d**).
• Return of minuet music, this time without repeats (**a-b**).

More Listening Review:
• Theme and variations: **Symphony No. 94**, second movement (Haydn)
• Rondo (**A-B-A-C-A**): Rondeau, from **Suite de symphonies** (Mouret)

Jacques-Louis David (1748–1825), Detail from *The Consecration of the Emperor Napoleon I and Coronation of the Empress Josephine in the Cathedral of Notre-Dame de Paris, 2 December 1804* (1806–7).

PART SIX

Eighteenth-Century Classicism

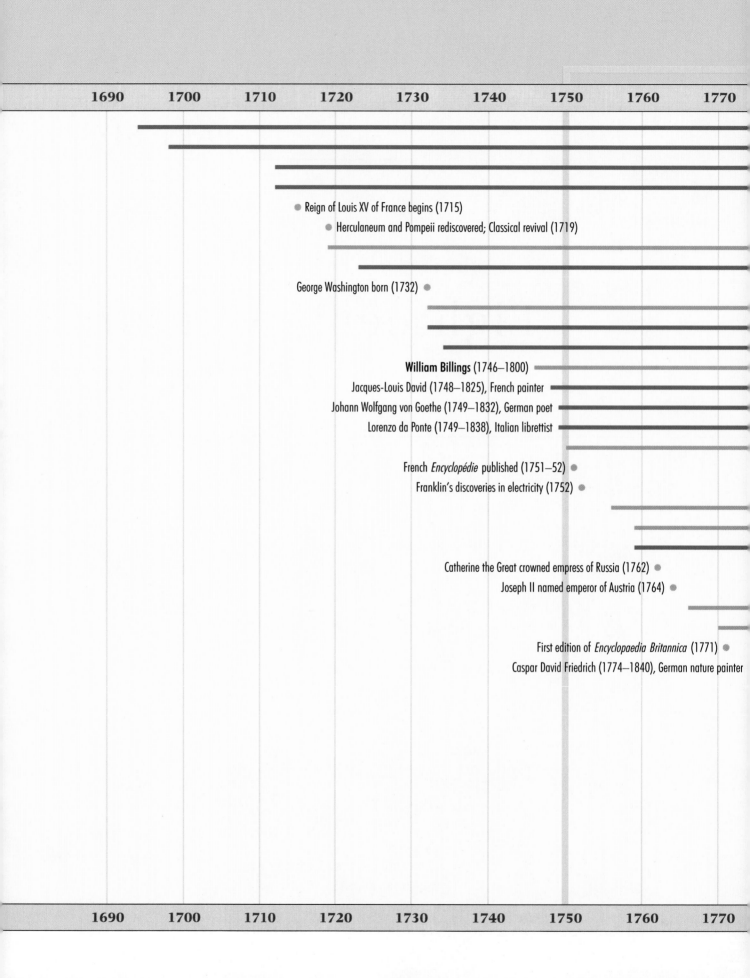

Reign of Louis XV of France begins (1715)

Herculaneum and Pompeii rediscovered; Classical revival (1719)

George Washington born (1732)

William Billings (1746–1800)

Jacques-Louis David (1748–1825), French painter

Johann Wolfgang von Goethe (1749–1832), German poet

Lorenzo da Ponte (1749–1838), Italian librettist

French *Encyclopédie* published (1751–52)

Franklin's discoveries in electricity (1752)

Catherine the Great crowned empress of Russia (1762)

Joseph II named emperor of Austria (1764)

First edition of *Encyclopaedia Britannica* (1771)

Caspar David Friedrich (1774–1840), German nature painter

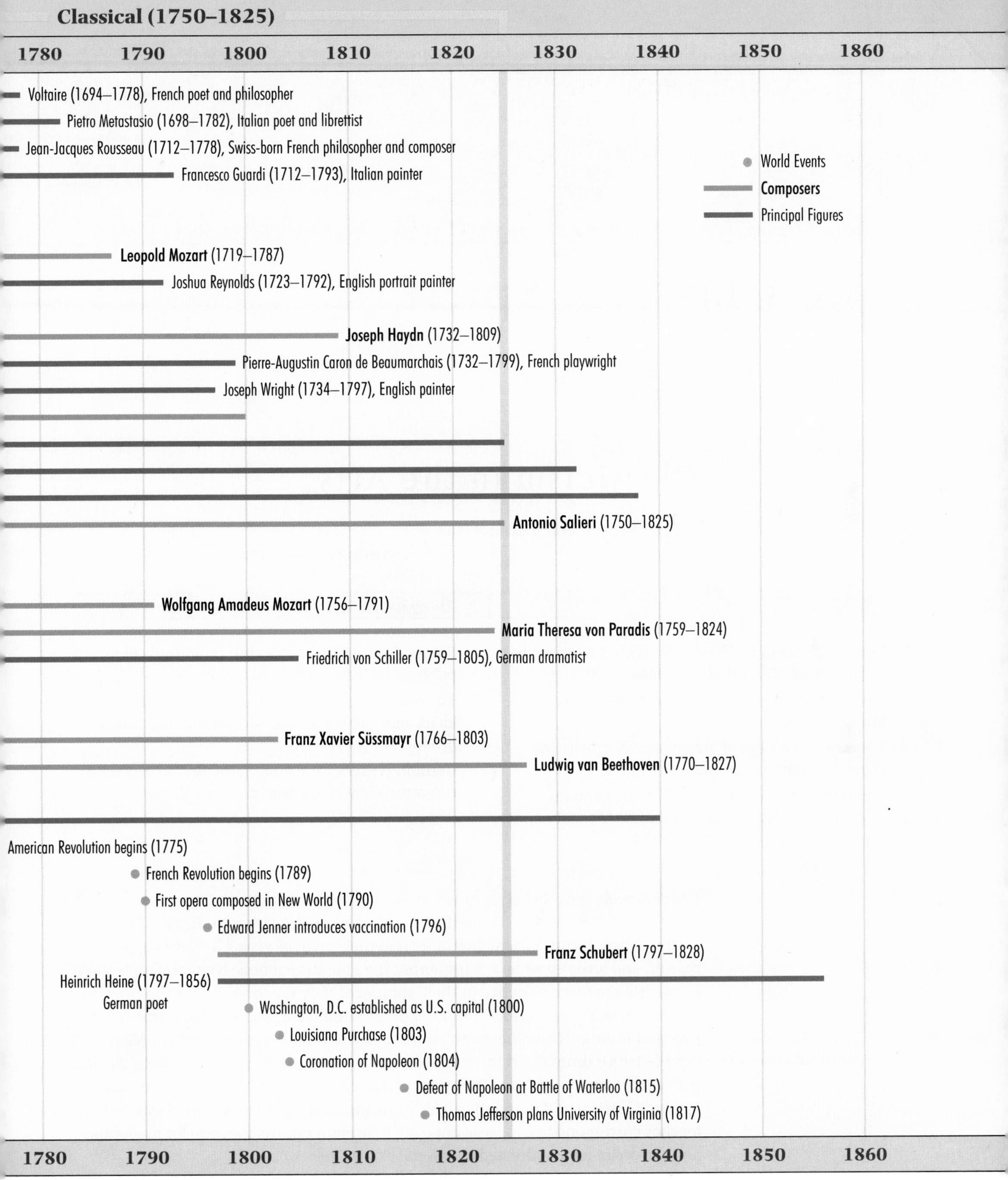

Classical (1750–1825)

1780	1790	1800	1810	1820	1830	1840	1850	1860

Voltaire (1694–1778), French poet and philosopher

Pietro Metastasio (1698–1782), Italian poet and librettist

Jean-Jacques Rousseau (1712–1778), Swiss-born French philosopher and composer

Francesco Guardi (1712–1793), Italian painter

● World Events

Composers

Principal Figures

Leopold Mozart (1719–1787)

Joshua Reynolds (1723–1792), English portrait painter

Joseph Haydn (1732–1809)

Pierre-Augustin Caron de Beaumarchais (1732–1799), French playwright

Joseph Wright (1734–1797), English painter

Antonio Salieri (1750–1825)

Wolfgang Amadeus Mozart (1756–1791)

Maria Theresa von Paradis (1759–1824)

Friedrich von Schiller (1759–1805), German dramatist

Franz Xavier Süssmayr (1766–1803)

Ludwig van Beethoven (1770–1827)

American Revolution begins (1775)

● French Revolution begins (1789)

● First opera composed in New World (1790)

● Edward Jenner introduces vaccination (1796)

Franz Schubert (1797–1828)

Heinrich Heine (1797–1856)
German poet

● Washington, D.C. established as U.S. capital (1800)

● Louisiana Purchase (1803)

● Coronation of Napoleon (1804)

● Defeat of Napoleon at Battle of Waterloo (1815)

● Thomas Jefferson plans University of Virginia (1817)

1780	1790	1800	1810	1820	1830	1840	1850	1860

The Classical Spirit

30

Classicism in the Arts

"Music [is] the favorite passion of my soul."

—THOMAS JEFFERSON

| KEY POINTS | StudySpace online at www.wwnorton.com/enjoy |

- The Classical era (1750–1825) is characterized by order, objectivity, and harmonious proportion.
- Classicists emulated the art and architecture of ancient Greece and Rome.
- This era was an age of strong aristocratic sovereigns throughout Europe.
- The American Revolution (1775–83) and the French Revolution (1789–99) profoundly changed political systems and social order.
- The era saw significant advances in science and ideas, and the Industrial Revolution made mass production possible.
- German writers were among the first to express a romantic view of the world.

Apollo and Dionysus   Historians observe that style in art moves between two extremes, the classical and the romantic. Both the classicist and the romanticist strive to express emotions within artistic forms. Where they differ is in their point of view. Classicists seek order, reason, and serenity while the romantics long for strangeness, wonder, and ecstasy. Classicists are more objective in their approach; they try to view life rationally and "to see it whole." Romanticists, on the other hand, view the world in terms of their personal feelings. The nineteenth-century German philosopher Friedrich Nietzsche (1844–1900) dramatized this contrast using two Greek deities as symbols: Apollo, god of light and reason, and Dionysus, god of passion and intoxication. Throughout history, Classical and Romantic ideals have alternated and even existed side by side, for they correspond to two basic impulses in human nature: the need for moderation and the desire for uninhibited emotional expression.

The "Classical" and "Romantic" labels are also attached to two important stylistic periods in European art. We will deal with the Classical era first; it encompasses the last half of the eighteenth century and the early decades of the nineteenth, when literature and art of the ancient Greeks and Romans were considered models of excellence to be emulated. We have come to associate the qualities of order, stability, and harmonious proportion with the Classical style.

Spacious palaces and formal gardens—with their balanced proportions and finely wrought detail—formed the setting for the era's great courts. In the middle of the century, Louis XV presided over extravagant celebrations in Versailles, and Frederick the Great ruled in Prussia, Maria Theresa in Austria, and Catherine the Great in Russia. In such societies, the ruling class enjoyed its power through hereditary right. The past was revered and tradition was prized, no matter what the cost.

Near the end of the eighteenth century, Europe was convulsed by the French Revolution (1789–99). The Classical era therefore witnessed both the twilight of the old regime and the dawn of a new political-economic alignment in Europe—specifically, the transfer of power from the aristocracy to the middle class, whose wealth was based on a rapidly expanding capitalism. Such a drastic shift was made possible by the Industrial Revolution, which gathered momentum in the mid–eighteenth century through a series of important inventions, from James Watt's steam engine and James Hargreaves's spinning jenny in the 1760s to Eli Whitney's cotton gin in the 1790s.

These decades saw significant advances in science as well. Benjamin Franklin harnessed electricity, Joseph Priestley discovered oxygen, and Edward Jenner perfected vaccination. There were important events in intellectual life too, such as the publication of the French *Encyclopédie* (1751–52) and the first edition of the *Encyclopaedia Britannica* (1771), a source you undoubtedly know and use today.

The Parthenon, Athens (448–432 B.C.E.). The architecture of ancient Greece embodied the ideals of order and harmonious proportions.

Thomas Jefferson's design for the Rotunda of the University of Virginia at Charlottesville reflects his admiration for classical architecture.

Sir Joshua Reynolds (1723–1792) captured the era's idealization of antiquity in his portrait *Mrs. Siddons as the Tragic Muse.*

The American Revolution (1775–83) broke out more than fourteen years before the French. Its immediate cause was the anger of the colonists at the economic injustices imposed on them by English king George III. Beyond that, however, was the larger issue of human equality and freedom; this vision impelled Thomas Jefferson, principal author of the Declaration of Independence, to incorporate into that document the idea that all people have the right to life, liberty, and the pursuit of happiness. These words remain fundamental to the principles of democracy.

The intellectual climate of the Classical era, then, was nourished by two opposing streams. While Classical art captured the exquisite refinement of a way of life that was drawing to a close, it also caught the first wave of a new social structure. The eighteenth century has been called the Age of Reason and the Enlightenment. Philosophers such as Voltaire and Rousseau, among other intellectuals, considered social and political issues with reason and science, but they were also advocates for the rising middle class. They therefore became prophets of the approaching social upheaval.

Just as eighteenth-century thinkers idealized the civilization of the Greeks and Romans, artists revered the unity and proportions of ancient architecture and fine arts. Accordingly, the foremost painter of revolutionary France, Jacques-Louis David, filled his canvases with symbols of Greek and Roman democracy. Strangely enough, a favorite subject was the French general Napoleon Bonaparte, whose military compaign was, he claimed, to liberate the peoples of Europe. In this spirit too, Thomas Jefferson patterned the nation's Capitol, the University of Virginia (see p. 177), and his home at Monticello after Greek and Roman temples. His example spurred on a classical revival in the United States, which made Ionic, Doric, and Corinthian columns indispensable features of public buildings well into the twentieth century.

By the 1760s, though, a romantic point of view was emerging in literature. The French philosopher Jean-Jacques Rousseau (1712–1778), sometimes called the "father of Romanticism," produced some of his most significant writings during this time. His celebrated declaration "Man is born free, and everywhere he is in chains" epitomizes the temper of the time. The first manifestation of the Romantic spirit in Germany was a literary movement known as *Sturm und Drang* (storm and stress). Two characteristic works appeared in the 1770s by the era's most significant young writers: the *Sorrows of Young Werther*, by Johann Wolfgang von Goethe, and *The Robbers*, by Friedrich von Schiller. The famous *Ode to Joy*, a hymn set by Beethoven in his Ninth Symphony, was Schiller's proclamation of universal brotherhood; and as we will see, Goethe became the favorite lyric poet of the Romantic composers. By the end of the century, the atmosphere had completely changed. The old world of the aristocracy had given way to a new society of the people and to an era that produced some of the greatest artworks of Western culture.

IN HIS OWN WORDS

I closed the gulf of anarchy and brought order out of chaos. I rewarded merit regardless of birth or wealth, wherever I found it. I abolished feudalism and restored equality to all regardless of religion and before the law. I fought the decrepit monarchies of the Old Regime because the alternative was the destruction of all this. I purified the Revolution.

—NAPOLEON BONAPARTE

31

Classicism in Music

*"Passions, whether violent or not, must never be expressed in such
a way as to disgust, and [music] must never offend the ear."*

—W. A. MOZART

○ The masters of the Classical musical style (Haydn, Mozart, Beethoven, Schubert—all members of the Viennese school), composed large-scale musical forms (symphony, concerto, sonata).

○ Classical music is characterized by a singable, lyrical melody; diatonic harmony; regular rhythms and meters; homophonic texture; and frequent use of folk elements.

○ Music-making centered around the court, with composers (especially Haydn) employed under the patronage system. Women also held court positions as musicians and as teachers.

The Classical period in music (c. 1750–1825) is characterized best by the masters of the so-called Viennese School—Haydn, Mozart, Beethoven, and their successor Franz Schubert. These composers worked in an age of great musical experimentation and discovery, when musicians took on new challenges: first, to explore fully the possibilities offered by the major-minor system; and second, to perfect a large-scale form of instrumental music that exploited those possibilities to the fullest degree. Having found this ideal structure, composers then developed it into the solo and duo sonata, the trio and quartet (especially the string quartet), the concerto, and the symphony.

The Viennese School

"Classicism" did not imply a strict adherence to traditional forms; as we will see, the composers of the Viennese School experimented boldly and ceaselessly with the materials at their disposal. And it should not surprise us to find that Romantic elements appear as well in the music of Haydn, Mozart, and Beethoven, especially their late works. These composers dealt with musical challenges so brilliantly that their symphonies and concertos, piano sonatas, duo sonatas, trios, string quartets, and similar works have remained unsurpassable models for all who followed.

Elements of Classical Style

The music of the Viennese masters is notable for its elegant, lyrical melodies. Classical melodies "sing," even those intended for instruments. These melodies are usually based on symmetrical four-bar phrases marked by clear-cut cadences, and they often move stepwise or by small leaps within a narrow range. Clarity is further provided by repetition and the frequent use of sequence (the repetition of a pattern at a higher or lower pitch). These devices make for balanced structures that are readily accessible to the listener. (In CP 7, on The "Mozart Effect," we will consider how the brain hears and processes such patterns.)

Lyrical melody

Map of Europe, 1763–1789, showing major musical centers.

Diatonic structure

The harmonies that sustain these melodies are equally clear. The chords are built from the seven tones of the major or minor scale (meaning they are *diatonic*) and therefore are firmly rooted in the key. The chords underline the balanced symmetry of phrases and cadences, and they form vertical columns of sound over which the melody unfolds freely and easily, generally in a *homophonic* texture (a melody with accompanying harmony). Note that this is somewhat different from the *homorhythmic* textures we heard in earlier eras, in which all voices moved together.

Homophonic texture

Rhythmic regularity

Melody and harmony are powered by strong rhythms that move at a steady tempo. Much of the music is in one of the four basic meters—2/4, 3/4, 4/4, or 6/8. If a piece or movement begins in a certain meter, it is apt to stay there until the end. Classical rhythm works closely with melody and harmony to make clear the symmetrical phrase-and-cadence structure of the piece. Clearly shaped sections establish the home key, move to contrasting but closely related keys, and return to the home key. The result is the beautifully molded architectural forms of the Classical style, fulfilling the listener's need for both unity and variety.

Despite its aristocratic elegance, music of the Classical era absorbed a variety of folk and popular elements. This influence made itself felt not only in the German dances and waltzes of the Viennese masters but also in their songs, symphonies, concertos, string quartets, and sonatas.

The Patronage System

The culture of the eighteenth century thrived under the patronage, or sponsorship, of an aristocracy that viewed the arts as a necessary adornment of life. Music was part of the elaborate lifestyle of the nobility, and the center of musical life was the palace.

IN HIS OWN WORDS

The master of music, Mr. Haydn, is reminded to apply himself more assiduously to composition than he has done so far . . . and, to show his zeal, he will hand in the first piece of every composition in a clean, tidy copy.

—PRINCE ESTERHÁZY

The social events at court created a steady demand for new works from composers, who had to supply whatever their patrons wanted. The patronage system gave musicians economic security and provided a social framework within which they could function. It offered important advantages to the great masters who successfully adjusted to its requirements, as the career of Haydn clearly shows. On the other hand, Mozart's tragic end illustrates how heavy the penalty could be for those unable to make that adjustment.

Women too found a place as musicians under the patronage system. In Italy and France, professional female singers achieved prominence in opera and in court ballets. Others found a place within aristocratic circles as court instrumentalists and music teachers, offering private lessons to members of the nobility. As we will see, a number of women pianists and violinists also made their mark as solo performers. And as more amateurs participated in music-making, women of the middle as well as upper classes found an outlet for their talents.

At this time, musical performances were beginning to move from the palace to the concert hall. The rise of the public concert gave composers a new venue (site) in which to perform their works. Haydn and Beethoven conducted their own symphonies at concerts, and Mozart and Beethoven played their own piano concertos. The public flocked to hear the latest works—unlike modern concertgoers who are interested mainly in the music of the past. The eagerness of eighteenth-century audiences for new music surely stimulated composers to greater productivity.

A private performance by a chamber music ensemble. Engraving by **Daniel Nikolaus Chodowiecki**, 1769.

Public concerts

An aristocratic concert. Oil and wood panel, attributed to **Jean-Honoré Fragonard** (1732–1806).

Classical Chamber Music

32

Eighteenth-Century Chamber Music Style

*"The free arts and the beautiful science of composition will not
tolerate technical chains. The mind and soul must be free."*

—JOSEPH HAYDN

KEY POINTS   StudySpace online at www.wwnorton.com/enjoy

- The Classical era is considered the golden age of
  chamber music (ensemble music for two to about
  ten performers, with one player per part).

- The ***string quartet*** (made up of 2 violins, viola,
  and cello) was the most important chamber music
  genre of the era; duos, trios, quintets, serenades,
  and divertimentos were also cultivated.

- The form of a string quartet generally follows a
  standard four-movement structure of fast-slow-
  moderate dance-fast.

- Haydn's string quartets, characterized by dense
  textures and the use of folk elements, are central
  to the literature for this ensemble.

Chamber music, as we have seen, is music for a small ensemble—two to about ten
players—with one player to a part. In this intimate genre, each instrument is
expected to assert itself fully, but the style of playing differs from that of the solo virtuoso. Virtuosos are encouraged to display their own personalities; chamber music
players function as part of a team.

The Classical era was the golden age of chamber music. Haydn and Mozart,
Beethoven and Schubert established the true chamber music style, a friendly conversation among equals. The central position in Classical chamber music was held by
String quartet   the ***string quartet***, which consists of two violins (a first and a second), a viola, and a
cello. Other favored combinations were the ***duo sonata***—violin and piano, or cello

and piano; the trio—violin, cello, and piano; and the *quintet*, usually a combination of string or wind instruments, or a string quartet and solo instrument such as the piano or clarinet. (See chart on p. 51.) Composers of the era also produced some memorable examples of chamber music for larger groups, including sextets, septets, and octets.

Some types of compositions stood midway between chamber music and the symphony, their chief purpose being entertainment. Most popular among these were the *divertimento* and the *serenade*. Both are lighter genres that were performed in the evening or at social functions.

IN HIS OWN WORDS

You listen to four sensible persons conversing, you profit from their discourse, and you get to know their several instruments.
—JOHANN WOLFGANG VON GOETHE, WRITING ABOUT QUARTETS

The String Quartet

The string quartet soon became the most influential chamber music genre of the Classical period. Although composers found its four-line texture ideal, its focused string timbre posed a special challenge to both composer and listener. In its general structure, the string quartet follows the four-movement scheme of the standard multimovement cycle described in Chapter 29.

The musical texture is woven out of the movements' themes and motives, which the composer distributes among the four instruments. Haydn favored a dense musical texture based on the continual expansion and development of motives, while Mozart was more lyrical and melodic. Beethoven and Schubert further expanded the architecture of the quartet, the former through motivic development and the latter through song, which was his special gift. Folk elements abound in Haydn's quartets, while Mozart's exude the elegance of court dances. Beethoven's rousing scherzos replaced the graceful minuet movement.

Style traits

Because the string quartet was intended as salon music, to be enjoyed by a small group of cultivated music lovers, composers did not need expansive gestures here. They could present their most private thoughts, and indeed, the final string quartets of Haydn, Mozart, and Beethoven contain some of their most profound expressions.

This watercolor depicts a performance of a string quartet, the most influential chamber music genre of the era.

33

Mozart and Chamber Music

"People make a mistake who think that my art has come easily to me. Nobody has devoted so much time and thought to composition as I. There is not a famous master whose music I have not studied over and over."

KEY POINTS

 StudySpace online at www.wwnorton.com/enjoy

- The Austrian composer Wolfgang Amadeus Mozart was a child prodigy who started to write music before the age of five.
- Although he lived only thirty-five years, Mozart made significant contributions to nearly all musical genres, including the symphony, sonata, concerto, chamber music, sacred music, and various

types of opera (*buffa*, or comic; *seria*, or serious; and *Singspiel*, or with spoken dialogue).
- Mozart's music is notable for its lyrical melodies, colorful orchestration, and dramatic content.
- One of Mozart's best-known works is *Eine kleine Nachtmusik* (*A Little Night Music*), a serenade for strings.

Something of the miraculous hovers about the music of Mozart. His masterful melodic writing, his elegance of style, and his rich instrumental colors sound effortless. This deceptive simplicity is the secret of his art.

His Life

Wolfgang Amadeus Mozart (1756–1791) was born in Salzburg, Austria, the son of Leopold Mozart, an esteemed composer-violinist at the court of the Archbishop of Salzburg. Wolfgang began his career as the most extraordinarily gifted child in the history of music. He first started to compose before he was five, and, with his talented sister Nannerl, performed at the court of Empress Maria Theresa at the age of six. The following year, his ambitious father organized a concert tour that included Paris, London, and Munich. By the time he was thirteen, the boy had written sonatas, concertos, symphonies, religious works, and several operas. By adulthood, Mozart had mastered all musical forms.

The high-spirited young artist rebelled against the social restrictions imposed by the patronage system, and relations with his patron, the Archbishop of Salzburg, were strained. Mozart was finally dismissed after quarreling with the archbishop and at twenty-five established himself in Vienna as a freelance musician. His remaining ten years were spent in a struggle to achieve financial security.

In 1782, he married Constanze Weber, against his father's wishes. The union signaled Mozart's liberation from the very close ties that had bound him to his father, a domineering man who strove to ensure his son's success.

With the opera *The Marriage of Figaro*, written in 1786 on a libretto by Lorenzo da Ponte, Mozart reached the peak of his career. The following year, he was commissioned to compose another work for the Prague Opera; the result was *Don Giovanni*, a favorite with audiences today. A success in Prague, this opera baffled the Viennese public.

 Wolfgang Amadeus Mozart

Though his final years were spent in poor health, in the last year of his life he still managed to produce the Clarinet Concerto and, for the Viennese theater, *The Magic Flute*. With a kind of fevered desperation, he then turned to the Requiem Mass, which had been commissioned by a music-loving count.

Mozart was cheered in his last days by the growing popularity of his opera, *The Magic Flute*. One afternoon, singers from the theater visited the gravely ill composer to sing through a completed movement of his Requiem. He died that same night, December 4, 1791, shortly before his thirty-sixth birthday.

The cause of Mozart's death has spurred many scientific theories over the years, including rheumatic fever, heart disease, and even trichinosis from eating undercooked pork. None can be proven definitively, for, unlike the case of Beethoven (see p. 198), no remains of the composer are extant for modern testing.

Leopold Mozart with his two young children, Nannerl and Wolfgang, performing in Paris (1763–64), after a watercolor by **Louis de Carmontelle** (1717–1806).

His Music

Mozart is preeminent among composers for the inexhaustible wealth of his elegant and songful melodies. In all his instrumental music, Mozart infused a sense of drama, with contrasts of mood ranging from lively and playful to solemn and tragic. His orchestration is richly colorful, his part writing notable for its careful interweaving of the lines and imitative procedures, and his development sections full of moderately chromatic harmonies.

He wrote a large quantity of social music—divertimentos and serenades of great variety, the most famous of which is *Eine kleine Nachtmusik* (1787), the work we will study. In chamber music, Mozart, like Haydn, favored the string quartet. His last ten quartets are some of the finest in the literature, among them the set of six dedicated to Haydn, his "most celebrated and very dear friend." His string quintets (for two violins, two violas, and cello) and the enchanting Quintet for Clarinet and Strings are favorites with today's audiences. Mozart was one of the first composers to write for the clarinet—a new instrument in his day. In addition to his Quintet, he used the clarinet in many symphonies and composed one of the earliest concertos for it.

One of the outstanding pianists of his time, Mozart wrote many works for his own instrument. The Fantasia in C minor, K. 475, and the Sonata in C minor, K. 457, are among his finest solo piano works. (The K followed by a number refers to the catalogue of Mozart's works by Ludwig Köchel, who numbered them chronologically.) And his twenty-seven concertos for piano and orchestra elevated this genre to one of the most prime importance in the Classical era.

Mozart's symphonies are characterized by a richness of orchestration, a freedom in part writing, and a remarkable depth of emotion. The exact number of them is difficult to determine. Although four of the forty-one numbered symphonies are probably not by Mozart, newly discovered and reworked compositions still bring the number to over fifty. His symphonic masterpieces are the six written in the final decade of his life; with these works, the symphony achieved its position as the most significant form of abstract music in this period.

But the genre most central to Mozart's art was opera. He wrote in the three dramatic styles of his day: **opera buffa**, or Italian comic opera (including *The Marriage of Figaro* and *Don Giovanni); **opera seria**, or Italian serious opera (including *Idomeneo*); and **Singspiel**, a lighter form of German opera with spoken dialogue (*The Magic Flute*). No one has ever surpassed his power to delineate character in music or his lyric gift, so carefully molded to the human voice.

CD iMusic

Ah! vous dirai-je, maman
Clarinet Concerto, II
Eine kleine Nachtmusik, I, III
Symphony No. 40, III

Symphonies

Operas

A Classical orchestra, with the leader at a large rectangular harpsichord while the string players and singers are distributed on both sides of the garden. *Open-Air Orchestra*, c. 1790. Engraving by **Giuseppe Servellini**.

EINE KLEINE NACHTMUSIK

Mozartean elegance is embodied in *Eine kleine Nachtmusik*, a serenade for strings whose title means literally *A Little Night Music*. The work was most likely written for a string quartet supported by a bass and was meant for public entertainment, in outdoor performance. The four movements of the version we know (originally there were five) are compact, intimate, and beautifully proportioned.

The first movement, a sonata-allegro form in 4/4 time in G major, is marchlike at the opening. The first theme ascends rapidly to its peak (this is sometimes called a **rocket theme**), then turns downward at the same rate. The second theme, with the downward curve of its opening measure, presents a graceful contrast to the upward-leaping character of the first. An insistent closing theme then rounds off the exposition. As befits the character of a serenade, which is shorter and less serious than a symphony or a concerto, the development section is brief. The recapitulation follows the course of the exposition but expands the closing theme into a vigorous coda. (See Listening Guide 19 for themes and an analysis of all four movements.)

First movement

The second movement is the Romanza, an eighteenth-century Andante that maintains the balance between lyricism and restraint. In this movement, symmetrical sections are arranged in a rondo-like structure.

Third movement

The minuet and trio is an Allegretto in G major, marked by regular four-bar phrases set in rounded binary form. The minuet opens brightly and decisively. The trio, with its polished soaring melody, presents a lyrical contrast. The opening music then returns, satisfying the Classical desire for balance and symmetry.

The last movement, a sprightly Allegro in the home key of G, alternates with an idea in the key of the dominant, D major. We have here a prime example of the Classical sonata-rondo finale—bright, jovial, and stamped with an aristocratic refinement.

Listening Guide 19	**eLG**	1 (71–78) 3 (1–5, 12–14)

Mozart: *Eine kleine Nachtmusik (A Little Night Music)*, K. 525, I and III (7:39)

DATE OF WORK:	1787
MEDIUM:	String quartet with double bass, or chamber orchestra
MOVEMENTS:	I. Allegro; sonata-allegro form, G major
	II. Romanza, Andante; sectional rondo form, C major
	III. Allegretto; minuet and trio, G major
	IV. Allegro; sonata-rondo form, G major

First Movement: Allegro; sonata-allegro form, 4/4 meter, G major   (5:30)

WHAT TO LISTEN FOR:	Intimate string chamber music style.
	Quick-paced movement with 3 themes, sonata-allegro form.
	Overall homophonic texture.
	First theme is disjunct, marchlike, and ascends quickly (rocket theme); second theme graceful and conjunct.

EXPOSITION

71   0:00   Theme 1—aggressive, ascending "rocket" theme, symmetrical phrasing, in G major:

Transitional passage, modulating.

72   0:46   Theme 2—graceful, contrasting theme, less hurried, in key of dominant, D major:

0:58   Closing theme—insistent, repetitive, ends in D major:

Repeat of exposition.

DEVELOPMENT

73   3:07   Short, begins in D major, manipulates theme 1 and closing theme; modulates, and prepares for recapitulation in G major.

RECAPITULATION

74   3:40   Theme 1—in G major.

75   4:22   Theme 2—in G major.

4:34   Closing theme—in G major.

5:05   Coda—extends closing, in G major.

Third Movement: Allegretto; minuet and trio form, 3/4 meter, G major   **(2:09)**

WHAT TO LISTEN FOR: Strongly rhythmic dance, in triple meter.
Lyrical, expressive trio.
Regular 4-measure phrases.
Marked contrast between minuet and trio.
Balanced, regular form (minuet returns at end).
Homophonic texture.

76   0:00   Minuet theme—in accented triple meter, decisive character, in 2 sections (8 measures each), both repeated:

77   0:44   Trio theme—more lyrical and connected, in 2 sections (8 + 12 measures), both repeated:

78   1:41   Minuet returns, without repeats.

The "Mozart Effect"

Can listening to Mozart make you smarter? Does music have healing qualities?

You may have heard of the "Mozart effect," a phenomenon that has been widely discussed in both the scientific community and the general media. It is based on the observation that participants in several studies improved their scores on spatial-temporal tests after listening to one of Mozart's piano sonatas. Spatial-temporal reasoning is rather like thinking in pictures and is an important guide to one's aptitude for solving math problems.

The results of early studies have prompted further interest in the relationship between music, intelligence, and learning. Experiments carried out at the MIND (Music Intelligence Neural Development) Institute at Irvine, California, are examining how we hear and process music. There, a team established by physicist Dr. Gordon Shaw (1933–2005)—co-founder of the Mozart effect— is working with musicians, mathematicians, and psychiatrists to discover how the brain processes music and how listening to certain styles affects our thinking skills. From a scientific point of view, the columns of neurons in the brain's cortex produce patterns that become a common language; the brain is then able to search out and recognize similar symmetries in operations it performs. Listening to music, doing math problems, and playing chess are all high-level brain functions that involve spatial-temporal reasoning and that draw on this language of symmetrical patterns. The Institute's research has shown that cognitive musical abilities and reasoning are present even in infants and that music is a kind of "pre-language" that produces firing patterns which enhance the brain's reasoning ability for other tasks.

In a study with college students, the research team demonstrated that listening to the first ten minutes of the Mozart Sonata for Two Pianos in D Major (K. 448) can produce at least a short-term enhancement of spatial-temporal reasoning. (You might try this before doing your math homework.) A later study with preschoolers was even more striking—it showed that keyboard training over a six-month period produced enhanced reasoning skills that lasted for days.

Clinical researchers hope to demonstrate a positive correlation between listening to music and reducing

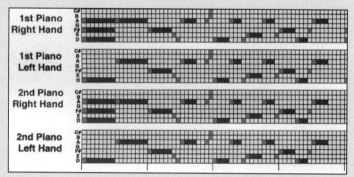

A graph of how the brain comprehends the organized repetition patterns while listening to the opening of Mozart's Sonata for Two Pianos in D major, K. 448, interpreted by scientists at the MIND Institute.

seizures among epileptics. They also already see positive results in drawing autistic children out of their silent worlds. According to Shaw, "Music will not only help us understand how we think, reason, and create, but will enable us to learn how to bring each child's potential to its highest level." As research continues, we can expect to hear much more about this fascinating phenomenon of how music can enhance our abilities to think, reason, and even create. And perhaps we will understand how Mozart came to be a composer and capable pianist at the tender age of four!

Resources

www.mindinstitute.net
Gordon Shaw, *Keeping Mozart in Mind*, 2nd ed.

Suggested Listening

CD iMusic Mozart: *Ah! vous dirai-je, maman* (*Twinkle, Twinkle, Little Star*)
Mozart: Sonata for Two Pianos in D major, K. 448

The Classical Symphony

34

The Nature of the Symphony

*"I frequently compare a symphony with a novel in which the themes
are characters. After we have made their acquaintance, we follow
their evolution, the unfolding of their psychology."*

—ARTHUR HONEGGER

KEY POINTS	StudySpace online at www.wwnorton.com/enjoy

○ The symphony was one of the principal instrumental forms of the Classical era.

○ Several techniques became standard in the symphony, including quickly ascending *rocket themes* and *steamroller effects* (drawn-out crescendos).

○ The heart of the Classical orchestra (about thirty to forty players) was the strings, assisted by woodwinds, brass, and percussion.

○ The Classical symphony was generally set in the standard four-movement structure: I) fast, II) slow, III) moderate dance, and IV) fast.

Historical Background

The symphony, which held the central place in Classical instrumental music, grew in dimension and significance throughout the era. With the final works of Mozart and Haydn, it became the most important type of absolute music.

The symphony had its roots in the Italian opera overture of the early eighteenth century, an orchestral piece in three sections: fast-slow-fast. First played to introduce an opera, these sections eventually became separate movements, to which the early German symphonists added a number of effects that were later taken over by Haydn and Mozart. One innovation was the use of a quick, aggressively rhythmic theme rising from low to high register with such speed that it became known as a

Mannheim School

Natural horns (without valves) and woodwinds are clearly visible in this painting of a small Classical orchestra performing in a Venetian palace (18th century, artist unknown).

rocket theme (as in the opening of Mozart's *Eine kleine Nachtmusik*). Equally important was the use of drawn-out *crescendos* (sometimes referred to as a **steamroller effect**) slowly gathering force as they rose to a climax. With the addition of the minuet and trio, the symphony paralleled the string quartet in following the four-movement multimovement cycle.

The Classical Orchestra

The Classical masters established the orchestra as we know it today: as an ensemble of the four instrumental families. The heart of the orchestra was the string choir. Woodwinds provided varying colors and ably assisted the strings, often doubling them. The brass sustained the harmonies and contributed body to the sound mass, while the timpani supplied rhythmic life and vitality. The eighteenth-century orchestra numbered from thirty to forty players (see opposite); thus the volume of sound was still more appropriate for the salon than the concert hall. (We will hear a movement from Haydn's Symphony No. 94 played on eighteenth-century period instruments.) It was only near the end of the Classical period that musical life began its move toward the public concert.

Haydn and Mozart created a dynamic style of orchestral writing in which all the instruments participated actively and each timbre could be heard. The interchange and imitation of themes among the various instrumental groups assumed the excitement of a witty conversation. The Classical orchestra also brought effects to absolute music that had long been familiar in the opera house, such as abrupt alternations of soft and loud, sudden accents, dramatic pauses, and the use of tremolo and pizzicato, all of which added drama and tension.

The Movements of the Symphony

First movement

The first movement of a Classical symphony is an Allegro in sonata-allegro form, sometimes preceded by a slow introduction. Sonata-allegro form, as we saw in Chap-

IN HIS OWN WORDS

The rudimentary instruments . . . that have helped constitute an orchestra may be considered to have undergone a natural evolution. . . . The orchestra has always existed; it merely had to be discovered. It represents not so much an invention as a human conquest.

—GIAN FRANCESCO MALIPIERO

The Classical Orchestra (30–40 players)

	HAYDN'S ORCHESTRA *(Symphony No. 94, 1792)*	BEETHOVEN'S ORCHESTRA *(Symphony No. 5, 1807–08)*
STRINGS	Violins 1 Violins 2 Violas Cellos and Double basses	Violins 1 Violins 2 Violas Cellos Double basses
WOODWINDS	2 Flutes 2 Flutes 2 Oboes	1 Piccolo (4th movement only) 2 Flutes 2 Oboes 2 Clarinets 2 Bassoons 1 Contrabassoon (4th movement only)
BRASS	2 French horns 2 Trumpets	2 French horns 2 Trumpets 3 Trombones (4th movement only)
PERCUSSION	Timpani	Timpani

ter 29, is based on the opposition of two keys, made clearly audible by the contrast between two themes. Haydn, however, sometimes based a sonata-allegro movement on a single theme, which was first heard in the tonic key and then in the contrasting key. Such a movement is referred to as *monothematic.* Mozart, on the other hand, preferred two themes with maximum contrast, which he frequently achieved through varied instrumentation; for example, the first theme might be played by the strings and the lyrical second theme by the woodwinds.

The slow movement of a symphony is often a three-part form (**A-B-A**)—a theme and variations, or a *modified sonata-allegro* (without a development section). Generally a Largo, Adagio, or Andante, this movement is in a key other than the tonic, with colorful orchestration that often emphasizes the woodwinds. The mood is essentially lyrical, and there is less development of themes here than in the opening movement.

Second and third movements

Third is the minuet and trio in triple meter, a graceful **A-B-A** form in the tonic key; as in the string quartet, its tempo is moderate. The trio is gentler in mood, with a moderately flowing melody and a prominent wind timbre. Beethoven's scherzo (a replacement for the minuet and trio), also in 3/4 time, is taken at a swifter pace, as we will hear in his famous Fifth Symphony.

CD iMusic

Mozart: Symphony No. 40, III

The fourth movement (the finale), normally a vivacious Allegro molto or Presto in rondo or sonata-allegro form, is not only faster but also lighter than the first movement and brings the cycle to a spirited ending. The finale often features themes with a folk-dance character, especially in Haydn's works. We will see that with Beethoven's Fifth Symphony, however, the fourth movement was transformed into a triumphant finale in sonata-allegro form.

Fourth movement

35

Haydn and the Symphony

*"Can you see the notes behave like waves? Up and down they go!
Look, you can also see the mountains. You have to amuse yourself
sometimes after being serious so long."*

KEY POINTS

 StudySpace online at www.wwnorton.com/enjoy

○ The Austrian composer Joseph Haydn worked under the patronage of the Eszterházy court.

○ Haydn is remembered for his contributions to the development of Classical instrumental music, especially the symphony and the string quartet.

○ One of Haydn's best-known symphonies, No. 94, the *Surprise*, was part of a set of twelve commissioned for a London concert series.

Ⓢ **Joseph Haydn**

Haydn's long career spanned from the decades when the Classical style was first emerging until the dawn of the Romantic era. The contribution he made to his art—especially to the symphony and string quartet—was second to none.

His Life

Joseph Haydn (1732–1809) was born in Rohrau, a village in lower Austria, and was the son of a wheelwright. Folk song and dance were his natural heritage. The beauty of his voice secured him a place as a choirboy at St. Stephen's Cathedral in Vienna, where he remained until he was sixteen and his voice had broken (the natural change that occurs at puberty in an adolescent boy's voice). Haydn then settled in Vienna, where he made his living by teaching and accompanying.

Before long, Haydn attracted the notice of the music-loving aristocracy of Vienna. In 1761, when he was twenty-nine, he entered the service of the Esterházys, a family of enormously wealthy Hungarian princes famous for their patronage of the arts. He remained with this family for almost thirty years, the greater part of his creative career. The family palace of Eszterháza was one of the most splendid in Europe, and music played a central part in the constant round of festivities there—the court even boasted its own opera house. His life exemplifies the patronage system at its best.

By the time Haydn reached middle age, his music had brought him much fame. After the prince's death, he made two visits to England (1791–92 and 1794–95), where he conducted his works with phenomenal success. He died in 1809, revered by his countrymen and acknowledged throughout Europe as the premier musician of his time.

His Music

It was Haydn's historic role to help perfect the new instrumental music of the late eighteenth century. His concise, angular themes lent themselves readily to motivic development. Significant too was his expansion of the orchestra's size and resources

A modern-day photograph
of the Eszterháza Palace in
Fertöd, Hungary.

in his late symphonies through greater emphasis on the brass, clarinets (new to the orchestra), and percussion (for more on the new percussion instruments, see CP 9). His expressive harmony, structural logic, and endlessly varied moods expressed the mature Classical style.

String quartets

The string quartet occupied a central position in Haydn's output; his works in that genre are among the best loved and most frequently performed in the repertory today. Like the quartets, the symphonies—over a hundred in number—extend across Haydn's entire career. Among the most popular are the twelve written in the 1790s for his appearances in England. Known as the *London* Symphonies, they abound in effects generally associated with later composers: syncopation, sudden *crescendos* and accents, dramatic contrasts of soft and loud, daring modulations, and an imaginative plan in which each choir of instruments plays its own part. Haydn's symphonies, like his quartets, are the spiritual birthplace of Beethoven's style.

Symphonies

Haydn was also a prolific composer of church music; he completed fourteen Masses as well as many motets. His two oratorios, *The Creation* (1798) and *The Seasons* (1801), follow the grand tradition of Handel.

CD iMusic

Emperor Quartet, Op. 76, No. 3, II

Military Symphony No. 100, II

Surprise Symphony No. 94, II

SYMPHONY NO. 94 (*SURPRISE*)

The best-known of Haydn's symphonies, the *Surprise*, in G major, is one of the twelve works composed for his concerts in London. The orchestra that presented these compositions to the world consisted of about forty members: a full string section; two each of flutes, oboes, bassoons, French horns, and trumpets; and harpsichord and timpani (see p. 191). The work is subtitled *Surprise* because of a sudden *fortissimo* crashing chord in the slow movement, intended to startle a dozing audience.

The work opens with a slow, reflective introduction, followed by a forceful Vivace assai (very fast) in sonata-allegro form. The abrupt changes from *piano* to *forte* impart a dramatic quality to the movement and look ahead to Beethoven's emotion-charged style.

IN HIS OWN WORDS

My Prince was always satisfied with my works. I not only had the encouragement of constant approval but as conductor of an orchestra I could make experiments, observe what produced an effect and what weakened it, and . . . improve, alter, make additions, or omissions, and be as bold as I pleased.

The hall in the Eszterháza Palace where Haydn presented his symphonies.

Second movement

The second movement, a great favorite with audiences, presents a theme and four variations. (See Listening Guide 20.) This memorable theme, with all the allure of a folk song, is set in two repeated sections of eight measures each (a binary structure). The opening melody, in C major, is announced by the violins playing *staccato* (short, detached notes); the phrase is repeated *pianissimo* and ends abruptly in a loud crash—the "surprise" chord of the work's nickname. The end of the **B** section of the tune refers back to the opening phrase; the section is then repeated with flute and oboe accompanying the melody.

Variations

The variations that follow display Haydn's workmanship and wit. The first variation opens at a *forte* level, then retreats to *piano*, with violin arabesques and flutes entering in dialogue with the tune. The second variation, with its dramatic shift to C minor, is played *fortissimo* by all the woodwinds and strings. A solo violin leads into the third variation, which presents the melody in quick, repeated sixteenth notes. In the **B** section of this variation, the theme is heard beneath countermelodies woven by the solo flute and oboe. The final variation is marked by changes in dynamics (now at *fortissimo*); in register (a shift to high range); in orchestration (woodwinds, brass, and timpani take the melody); and in Haydn's employment of a new triplet rhythm in the first violins, heard against offbeat chords in the other strings. The **B** section introduces a new version of the melody based on an uneven, dotted rhythm. The coda brings a return to the opening theme with new harmonies below, quietly summing up the movement.

Third and fourth movements

The third movement, a minuet in G major, is a rollicking Allegro molto that leaves the elegant, courtly dance far behind in favor of a high-spirited, folklike romp. The finale, an energetic Allegro molto in sonata-allegro form, captures for its aristocratic listeners all the charm and humor of a traditional peasant dance. This work radiates the precise qualities that made the London symphonies so successful—innocent, appealing melodies within a masterful treatment of forms.

Listening Guide 20

eLG 1 (79–85)
3 (26–32)

Haydn: Symphony No. 94 in G major (*Surprise*), Second Movement

(6:11)

DATE OF WORK:	First performed 1792
MEDIUM:	Orchestra, with pairs of flutes, oboes, bassoons, French horns, and trumpets, along with strings and timpani
MOVEMENTS:	I. Adagio cantabile; Vivace assai; sonata-allegro form, G major
	II. Andante; theme and variations form, C major
	III. Menuetto: Allegro molto; minuet and trio form, G major
	IV. Allegro molto; sonata-allegro form, G major

WHAT TO LISTEN FOR:	Folklike theme in 2 regular phrases, each repeated (***binary structure***). Loud, crashing chord (the "surprise") at the end of the first theme. 4 variations on the theme: changes in dynamics and texture (Var. 1); shift in key center, from major to minor (Var. 2); quick-paced rhythms treatment (Var. 3); and varied orchestration and dynamics (Var. 4). Eighteenth-century period string, wind, and percussion instruments.

Second Movement: Andante; theme and variations form, 2/4 meter, C major

79 0:00 Theme—folklike melody; in 2 parts, each repeated (binary).

A section—melody outlines triad, played staccato in strings; 8 measures:

A section repeated, pianissimo, followed by fortissimo chord.

80 0:33 B section—disjunct theme, ending in style of **A**, 8 measures:

B section repeated, with flutes and oboes.

Listening Guide continues

81 1:05   Variation 1—**A** section begins with loud chord, has violin countermelody:

       A repeated.

1:38   **B**, with decorated violin line.

       B repeated.

82 2:09   Variation 2—**A** heard *fortissimo*, in C minor (later shifts to major):

2:42   **A** repeated.

       Development of **A**, with fast passages in strings, remains in minor.

       Solo violins lead into Variation 3.

83 3:17   Variation 3—**A** in fast rhythm, heard in oboes:

       A repeated in violins, with woodwind countermelody; low strings drop out.

3:49   **B** continues with violins and woodwinds alone.

       B repeated.

84 4:22   Variation 4—**A** heard in full orchestra, loud statement, accents on offbeats:

       A heard in violins in uneven, dotted rhythm, with accompaniment playing offbeats.

4:55   **B** continues in uneven rhythms in strings.

       B repeated in loud statement by full orchestra.

5:26   Bridge to coda; staccato pattern, followed by sustained chord.

85 5:40   Coda returns to **A** melody, with varied harmony underneath; ends quietly in C major.

36

Beethoven and the Symphony in Transition

"Freedom above all!"

KEY POINTS

 StudySpace online at www.wwnorton.com/enjoy

○ The Viennese master Ludwig van Beethoven was a transitional figure whose music straddles the Classical and Romantic eras.

○ Beethoven's nine symphonies are monumental works intended for the concert hall; the Fifth Symphony, his best-known composition, is built on a famous four-note motive that permeates all four movements.

○ Beethoven expressed his political views through his music that included Symphonies Nos. 5 and 9 and his battle piece, *Wellington's Victory* (CP 8).

Beethoven belonged to the generation that felt the full impact of the French Revolution. He created the music of a heroic age and, in sounds never to be forgotten, proclaimed a faith in the power of people to shape their own destinies.

His Life

Ludwig van Beethoven (1770–1827) was born in Bonn, Germany, where his father and grandfather were singers at the court of the local prince, the elector Max Friedrich. The family situation was unhappy; his father was an alcoholic, and Ludwig at an early age was forced to support his mother and two younger brothers. At eleven and a half, he was assistant organist in the court chapel, and a year later he became harpsichordist in the court orchestra. At seventeen, during a visit to Vienna, he played for Mozart; the youth improvised so brilliantly on a theme given to him that Mozart remarked to his friends, "Keep an eye on him—he will make a noise in the world some day."

 Ludwig van Beethoven

Beethoven's talents as a pianist took the music-loving aristocracy by storm. He functioned under a modified form of the patronage system. Though he was not attached to the court of a prince, the music-loving aristocrats of Vienna helped him in various ways—by paying him handsomely for lessons or presenting him with gifts. He was also aided by the emergence of a middle-class public and the growth of concert life and music publishing. A youthful exuberance pervades the first decade of his career, an almost arrogant consciousness of his strength.

Then fate struck in a vulnerable spot: Beethoven began to lose his hearing. His helplessness in the face of this affliction dealt a shattering blow to his pride: "Ah, how could I possibly admit an infirmity in the one sense that should have been more perfect in me than in others. A sense I once possessed in highest perfection. Oh, I

Onset of deafness

Beethoven walking the streets of Vienna; drawing by **Joseph Daniel Böhm** (1794–1865).

cannot do it!" As deafness closed in on him—the first symptoms appeared when he was in his late twenties—it brought a sense of isolation from the world. On the advice of his doctors, he retired in 1802 to a summer resort outside Vienna called Heiligenstadt. There he was torn between the destructive forces in his soul and his desire to live and create: "But little more and, I would have put an end to my life. Only art . . . withheld me."

Beethoven realized that art must give him the happiness that life withheld. The will to struggle reasserted itself; he fought his way back to health, although he never regained his hearing. The remainder of his career was spent in ceaseless effort to achieve his artistic goals. Biographers and painters have made familiar the image of the squat, sturdy figure (he was five foot four, the same height as that other conqueror of the age, Napoleon) walking through Vienna, stopping to jot down an idea in his sketchbook—an idea that, because he could not hear its sonorous beauty, he envisioned all the more vividly in his mind. A ride in an open carriage during severe weather brought on an attack of edema that proved fatal. Beethoven died at age fifty-seven, famous and revered.

Modern science has offered a theory on Beethoven's deafness and the internal disorders he suffered later in life. DNA analysis of a lock of the composer's hair, cut off at his death and preserved through the years, has revealed a massive lead content, possibly from his china, pots, or the wine he drank—all potential sources of lead. We now know that lead toxicity can cause serious health problems, many of which matched Beethoven's symptoms. A fascinating book, *Beethoven's Hair*, by Russell Martin (2000), traces the history of this remarkable relic.

His Music

Beethoven is the supreme architect in music. His genius found expression in the structural type of thinking required in large-scale forms like the sonata and the symphony. The sketchbooks in which he worked out his ideas show how his pieces gradually reached their final shape.

First and middle periods

Beethoven's compositional activity fell into three periods. The first reflected the Classical elements he inherited from Haydn and Mozart. The middle period saw the appearance of characteristics more closely associated with the nineteenth century: strong dynamic contrasts, explosive accents, and longer movements. Beethoven expanded the dimensions of the first movement, especially the coda, and he made the development section the dynamic center of sonata-allegro form. In his hands, the slow movement acquired a hymnlike character, the essence of Beethovenian pathos. (We will hear a famous example of this from his *Moonlight* Sonata.) The scherzo became a movement of rhythmic energy spanning many moods; his goal here was powerful expression rather than elegance. And he enlarged the finale into a movement comparable in size and scope to the first, ending the symphony on a triumphant note.

CD iMusic

Für Elise

Moonlight Sonata, Adagio

Ode to Joy, from Symphony No. 9

Symphony No. 5, I

In his third period—the years of his final piano sonatas and string quartets as well as his Ninth Symphony—Beethoven used more chromatic harmonies and developed a skeletal language from which all nonessentials were rigidly pared away. It was a language that transcended his time.

Beethoven's nine symphonies are conceived on a scale too large for the aristocratic salon; they demand the concert hall. The first two symphonies are closest in style to the two Classical masters who preceded him, but with his Third Symphony, the *Eroica*, Beethoven achieved his own mature approach. The Fifth Symphony is popularly viewed as the model of the genre, and the Seventh rivals it in universal appeal. The finale of the Ninth, or *Choral* Symphony, in which vocal soloists and chorus join the orchestra, is a setting of Schiller's *Ode to Joy*, a ringing prophecy of the time when "all people will be brothers."

The concerto offered Beethoven an ideal form in which to combine virtuosity with symphonic structure. His Violin Concerto displays the technical abilities of the soloist within a much enlarged form, and his five piano concertos both coincided with and encouraged the rising popularity of the instrument. The piano itself occupied a central position in Beethoven's art. His thirty-two sonatas form an indispensable part of its literature. They range from the highly expressive *Pathétique*, an early work, to the dramatic *Appassionata* and the powerful *Hammerklavier* of his later years. The sonatas are often considered the pianist's New Testament (the Old being Bach's *Well-Tempered Clavier*).

Concertos and piano sonatas

Beethoven wrote a great deal of chamber music, the string quartet lying closest to his heart. His supreme achievements in this genre are the last five quartets, which, together with the Grand Fugue, Op. 133, occupied the final years of his life. In these works, as in the last five piano sonatas, the master employs a searching, introspective style, far from the exuberance of his youth.

String quartets

Beethoven also made significant contributions to vocal music. His one opera, *Fidelio*, centers on wifely devotion, human freedom, and the defeat of those who would destroy that freedom. The *Missa solemnis* (Solemn Mass), which transcends the limits of any specific creed or faith, ranks in importance with the Ninth Symphony and the final quartets. In his manuscript for the Kyrie of the Mass, the composer wrote a sentence that applies to the whole of his music: "From the heart . . . may it find its way to the heart."

Vocal music

THE FIFTH SYMPHONY

Perhaps the best-known of all symphonies, Beethoven's Symphony No. 5 in C minor, Op. 67, is also the most concentrated expression of his art. The first movement, in a sonata-allegro form marked Allegro con brio (lively, with vigor), springs out of the rhythmic idea of "three shorts and a long" that dominates the entire symphony. This idea, perhaps the most commanding gesture in the whole symphonic literature, is pursued with an almost terrifying single-mindedness in this dramatic movement. In an extended coda, the basic rhythm reveals yet a new fount of explosive energy. (See Listening Guide 21.)

First movement

The second movement is a serene theme and variations, with two melodic ideas. In the course of the movement, Beethoven exploits his two themes with all the procedures of variation—changes in melodic outline, harmony, rhythm, tempo, dynamics, register, key, mode, and timbre. The familiar three-note rhythm (short-short-short-long) is sounded in the second theme, providing unity to the symphony.

Second movement

Third in the cycle of movements is the scherzo, which opens with a rocket theme introduced by cellos and double basses. After the gruff, humorous trio in C major, the

Third movement

IN HIS OWN WORDS

I carry my thoughts about with me for a long time . . . before writing them down. . . . once I have grasped a theme, I shall not forget it even years later. I change many things, discard others, and try again and again until I am satisfied; then, in my head . . . [the work] rises, it grows, I hear and see the image in front of me from every angle . . . and only the labor of writing it down remains.

Beethoven and the Politics of Music

Composers have produced some of their most powerful music in response to the political climate in which they lived. This is especially true of Ludwig van Beethoven, who was born in Germany but adopted Austria as his homeland during a time of great tumult and change.

An advocate for democracy and the underprivileged, Beethoven watched the French general Napoleon Bonaparte rise to power after the French Revolution (1789–99). At first, he greatly admired Napoleon, idealizing him in his only opera, *Fidelio*. The composer's Third Symphony (*Eroica*) was to have celebrated Napoleon as well (he originally called it *Bonaparte*), but when the ruler declared himself emperor in 1804, Beethoven tore up the title page bearing the dedication. "So he too is nothing more than an ordinary man," Beethoven wrote.

The composer had great affection for the peace-loving Austrians and the British, whose democratic parliamentary system he much admired. These heartfelt nationalistic sentiments found expression in his *Battle Symphony* (1813), also known as *Wellington's Victory*, a patriotic work celebrating the British victory at the Battle of Vittoria (1813), when the Allied Forces, led by the British duke of Wellington, demolished the Napoleonic army's advance in Spain. Beethoven scored a version of the work for orchestra, which included a large battery of percussion replete with muskets and cannons. Not strictly a symphony, *Wellington's Victory* is programmatic in its vivid retelling of the battle through fanfares and patriotic tunes associated with both the French and the British. (Program music is instrumental music with literary or pictorial associations.) Today, this work is heard most frequently at Fourth of July celebrations in the United States to accompany fireworks and ceremonial pageantry.

The title page of Beethoven's *Wellington's Victory*, arranged for the piano by the composer.

scherzo returns in a modified version, followed by a transitional passage to the final movement in which the memorable four-note motive returns, sounded by the timpani.

Fourth movement   The monumental fourth movement bursts forward from this transition, once again bringing back the unifying rhythmic motive. This unification makes the symphony an early example of *cyclical form* (in which a theme or musical idea from one

To the strains of *Ode to Joy*, student protestors erected a statue of the Goddess of Democracy in Beijing's Tiananmen Square as part of their pro-democracy demonstrations in 1989.

One of Beethoven's most famous works is the last movement of his Symphony No. 9, which includes *Ode to Joy*, a poem by Friedrich von Schiller. The text is an expression of universal brotherhood inspired by the powerful social forces behind the French Revolution. This great symphony, written between 1822 and 1824, has become a rallying cry for widely divergent philosophies ever since. The German dictator Adolf Hitler demanded that Beethoven's work be played for his birthday in 1941; it was then the most performed symphony in Germany. The hymn is now played on official occasions of both the Council of Europe and the European Union; and in 1989, it was selected to celebrate the fall of the Berlin Wall. The ideology behind this work is valued outside of Western culture as well: in 1971, it was named the national anthem of Rhodesia (now Zimbabwe) in Africa; in 1989, student protestors at China's Tiananmen Square revolt chose the *Ode to Joy* as their freedom statement; and each year, the work is performed in Japan with a colossal choir to ring in the New Year.

Today, Beethoven's music continues to be a force that brings distant people together. Perhaps through his great masterworks, we can better understand the composer as a person who held strong yet progressive and influential political views.

Suggested Listening

CD iMusic *America* (*God Save the King*) (see p. 31)
Beethoven:
   CD iMusic *Ode to Joy*, from Symphony No. 9, Op. 91
   Symphony No. 3, Op. 55 (*Eroica*)
   Wellington's Victory (or *Battle Symphony*)

movement returns in a later movement). This last movement is in sonata-allegro form with an extended coda, which closes with the tonic chord proclaimed triumphantly by the orchestra again and again.

Beethoven's career bridged the transition from the old society to the new. His commanding musical voice and an all-conquering will forged a link to the coming Romantic age.

Listening Guide 21

eLG 2 (4–28)
3 (33–57)

Beethoven: Symphony No. 5 in C minor, Op. 67   (31:34)

DATE OF WORK:	1807–8
MOVEMENTS:	I. Allegro con brio; sonata-allegro form, C minor
	II. Andante con moto; theme and variations form (2 themes), A-flat major
	III. Allegro; scherzo and trio form, C minor
	IV. Allegro; sonata-allegro form, C major

First Movement: Allegro con brio; sonata-allegro form, 2/4 meter, C minor   **(7:31)**

WHAT TO LISTEN FOR:	Famous motive (short-short-short-long) is basis for entire movement; heard in sequence, extended beyond 4 notes, and turned upside down. Sonata-allegro form, with fiery opening theme and sweet 2nd theme. Dramatic tonal shifts between major and minor.

EXPOSITION

4 0:00   Theme 1—based on famous 4-note motive, in C minor:

0:06   Motive treated sequentially:

0:43   Expansion from 4-note motive; horns modulate to key of second theme:

5 0:46   Theme 2—more lyrical, in woodwinds, in E-flat major; heard against rhythm of 4-note motive:

1:07   Closing theme—descending staccato passage, then 4-note motive.

1:26   Repeat of exposition.

DEVELOPMENT

6 2:54   Beginning of development, announced by horns.

3:05   Manipulation of 4-note motive through a descending sequence:

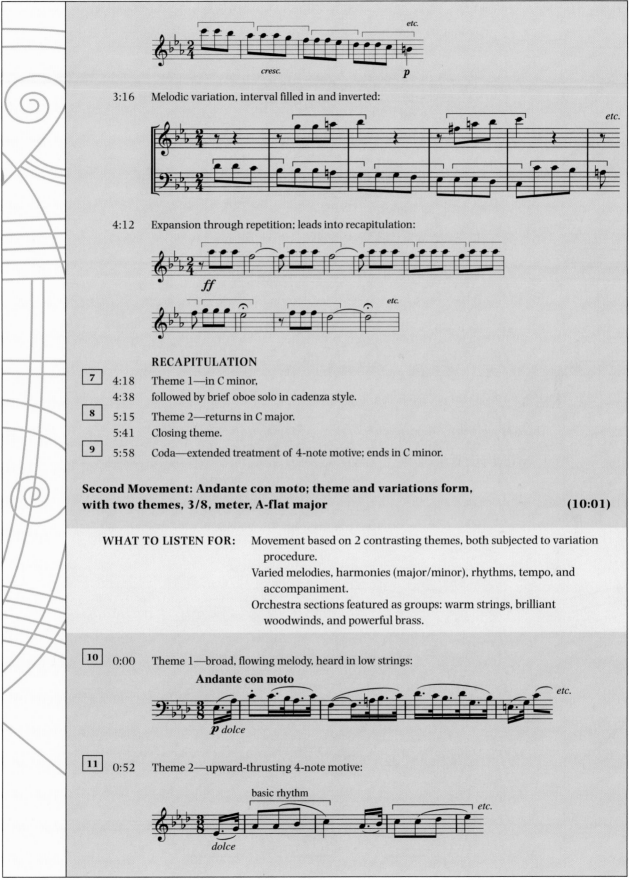

3:16   Melodic variation, interval filled in and inverted:

4:12   Expansion through repetition; leads into recapitulation:

RECAPITULATION

7   4:18   Theme 1—in C minor,
       4:38   followed by brief oboe solo in cadenza style.
8   5:15   Theme 2—returns in C major.
       5:41   Closing theme.
9   5:58   Coda—extended treatment of 4-note motive; ends in C minor.

**Second Movement: Andante con moto; theme and variations form,
with two themes, 3/8, meter, A-flat major**   **(10:01)**

WHAT TO LISTEN FOR: Movement based on 2 contrasting themes, both subjected to variation
procedure.
Varied melodies, harmonies (major/minor), rhythms, tempo, and
accompaniment.
Orchestra sections featured as groups: warm strings, brilliant
woodwinds, and powerful brass.

10   0:00   Theme 1—broad, flowing melody, heard in low strings:

Andante con moto

11   0:52   Theme 2—upward-thrusting 4-note motive:

Listening Guide continues

Examples of variations on theme 1

12   1:57   Embellished with running sixteenth notes:

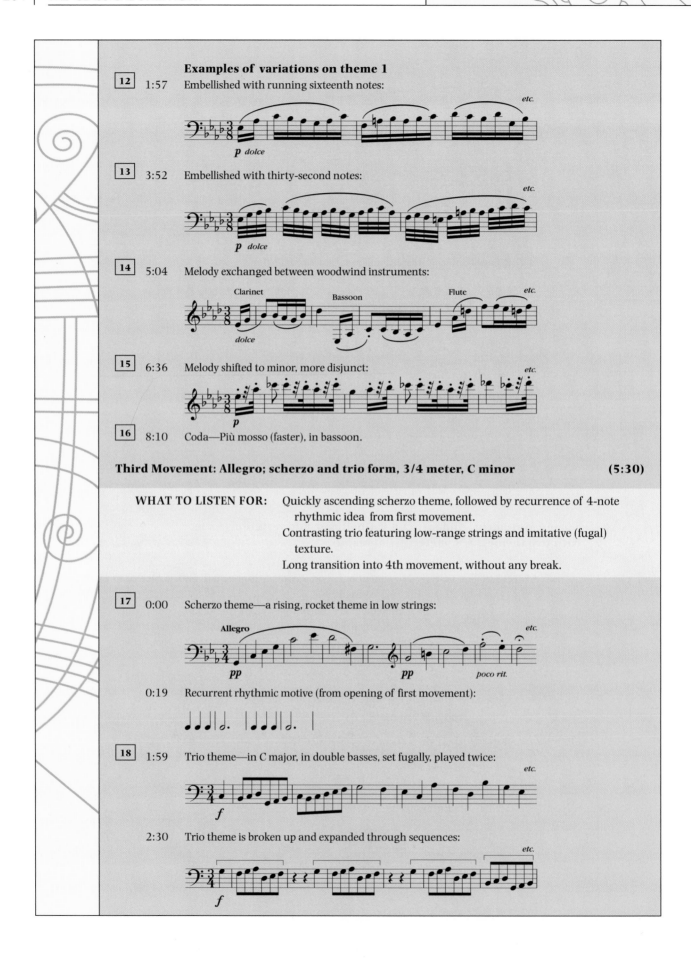

13   3:52   Embellished with thirty-second notes:

14   5:04   Melody exchanged between woodwind instruments:

15   6:36   Melody shifted to minor, more disjunct:

16   8:10   Coda—Più mosso (faster), in bassoon.

Third Movement: Allegro; scherzo and trio form, 3/4 meter, C minor   **(5:30)**

WHAT TO LISTEN FOR: Quickly ascending scherzo theme, followed by recurrence of 4-note rhythmic idea from first movement.

Contrasting trio featuring low-range strings and imitative (fugal) texture.

Long transition into 4th movement, without any break.

17   0:00   Scherzo theme—a rising, rocket theme in low strings:

    0:19   Recurrent rhythmic motive (from opening of first movement):

18   1:59   Trio theme—in C major, in double basses, set fugally, played twice:

    2:30   Trio theme is broken up and expanded through sequences:

19 3:29 Scherzo returns, with varied orchestration, including pizzicato strings

20 4:46 Transition to next movement with timpani rhythm from opening 4-note motive:

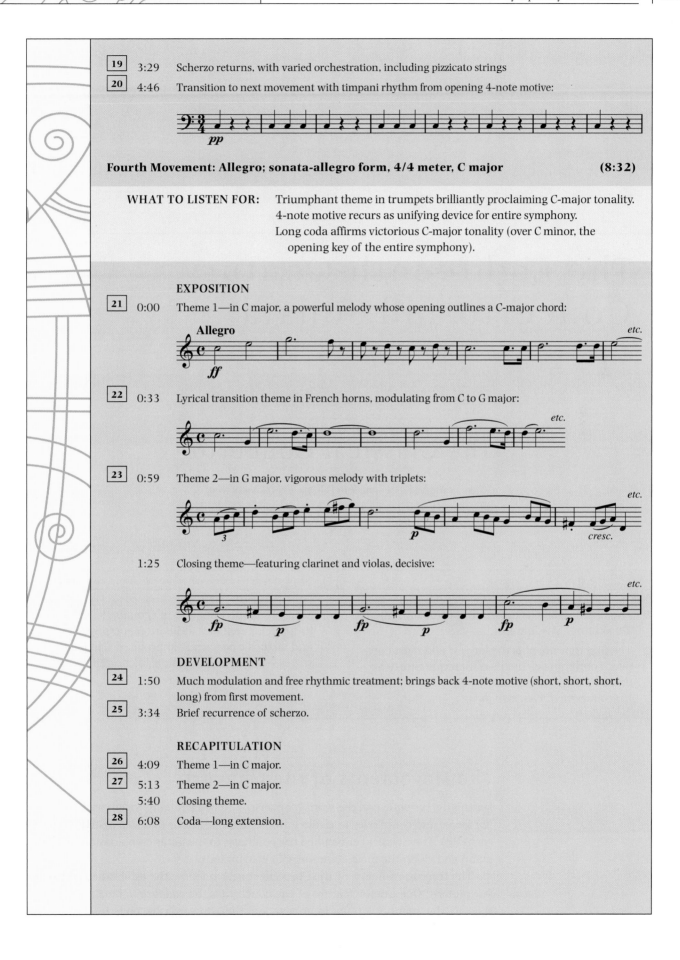

Fourth Movement: Allegro; sonata-allegro form, 4/4 meter, C major (8:32)

WHAT TO LISTEN FOR: Triumphant theme in trumpets brilliantly proclaiming C-major tonality.
4-note motive recurs as unifying device for entire symphony.
Long coda affirms victorious C-major tonality (over C minor, the
opening key of the entire symphony).

EXPOSITION

21 0:00 Theme 1—in C major, a powerful melody whose opening outlines a C-major chord:

22 0:33 Lyrical transition theme in French horns, modulating from C to G major:

23 0:59 Theme 2—in G major, vigorous melody with triplets:

1:25 Closing theme—featuring clarinet and violas, decisive:

DEVELOPMENT

24 1:50 Much modulation and free rhythmic treatment; brings back 4-note motive (short, short, short, long) from first movement.

25 3:34 Brief recurrence of scherzo.

RECAPITULATION

26 4:09 Theme 1—in C major.

27 5:13 Theme 2—in C major.

5:40 Closing theme.

28 6:08 Coda—long extension.

The Eighteenth-Century Concerto and Sonata

37

The Classical Concerto

"Give me the best instrument in Europe, but listeners who understand nothing or do not wish to understand and who do not feel with me in what I am playing, and all my pleasure is spoilt."

—W. A. MOZART

KEY POINTS	Ⓢ **StudySpace** online at www.wwnorton.com/enjoy

○ The Classical concerto form has three movements, alternating fast-slow-fast.

○ The first movement is the longest and most complex, combining elements of Baroque ritornello procedure and *sonata-allegro form*, resulting in *first-movement concerto form*.

○ Mozart's Piano Concerto in G major, K. 453—with its graceful melodies, brilliant piano passagework, and virtuosic *cadenzas* (improvised solo passages)—is a notable example of the genre.

The Movements of the Concerto

During the Baroque era, the word "concerto" implied a mixing together of contrasting forces and could refer to a solo group and orchestra or to a solo instrument and orchestra. The Classical era shifted the emphasis to the latter combination, with the piano and violin the most common solo instruments.

Cadenza   The three movements of the Classical concerto follow the established fast-slow-fast pattern. One unique feature of the concerto is the *cadenza*, a fanciful solo passage in the manner of an improvisation that, toward the end, interrupts the movement. The cadenza evolved from a time when improvisation was an important element in art music, as it still is in jazz and in many styles of world music. In the solo concerto, the cadenza has a dramatic effect: the orchestra falls silent, and the soloist launches into a free play of fantasy on one or more themes of the movement.

The Classical concerto begins with a first-movement form that adapts the principles of the Baroque concerto's ritornello procedure (based on a recurring theme) to those of sonata-allegro form. *First-movement concerto form* is sometimes described as a sonata-allegro form with a double exposition. The movement usually opens with an orchestral exposition, or ritornello, in the tonic key, often presenting several themes. A second exposition, for the solo instrument and orchestra, then makes the necessary key change to the dominant (or to the relative major). The soloist plays elaborated versions of the themes first heard in the orchestra, and often has new material as well. The development section offers ample opportunity for solo virtuosic display, in dialogue with the orchestra. In the recapitulation, the soloist and orchestra bring back the themes in the tonic. The solo cadenza, a brilliant improvisation, appears near the end of the movement, and a coda brings the movement to a close with a strong affirmation of the home key.

Mozart's fortepiano, now in the Mozarteum in Salzburg. Notice how the colors of the white and black keys are the reverse of today's piano.

The slow and lyrical second movement, generally an Andante, Adagio, or Largo, features songlike melodies. This movement is often composed in a key closely related to the home key. Thus, if the first movement is in C major, the second might be in F major (the subdominant), four steps above.

A typical finale is an Allegro molto or Presto (very fast) that is shorter than the first movement and in rondo form, which could be modified to adopt some developmental features of sonata-allegro form. This movement may contain its own cadenza that calls for virtuoso playing and brings the piece to an exciting end.

MOZART'S PIANO CONCERTO IN G MAJOR, K. 453

Mozart played a crucial role in the development of the piano concerto. His concertos, written primarily as display pieces for his own public performances, abound in the brilliant flourishes and elegant gestures characteristic of eighteenth-century music.

First movement

The first movement of this G-major concerto, marked Allegro, opens with an orchestral ritornello; the piano then ushers in its own exposition, which includes a new theme. An orchestral tutti leads to the development section, and the ritornello is heard again in the recapitulation. This concerto, notable for its graceful writing for piano and woodwinds, is usually performed today with a cadenza that Mozart wrote for this work. (For analysis, see Listening Guide 22.)

Second and third movements

The lyrical slow movement features a kind of double exposition format that is more typical of concerto first movements. The closing movement, an Allegretto in 2/2, or cut time, is in theme and variations form. The theme is a graceful, dancelike tune made up of two short phrases, each of which is repeated. The five variations that follow set the piano and orchestra in a dialogue of melodic, rhythmic, and harmonic elaborations on the memorable theme. (Mozart was so fond of this tune that he taught it to his pet starling, who consistently missed one note and got the rhythm wrong.)

Listening Guide 22

eLG 2 (29–39)
4 (1–11)

Mozart: Piano Concerto in G major, K. 453, I   (11:42)

DATE OF WORK: 1784

MOVEMENTS: I. Allegro; first-movement concerto form, G major
II. Andante; first-movement concerto form, C major
III. Allegretto, Presto; theme and variations form, G major

First Movement: Allegro; first-movement concerto form, 4/4 meter, G major   (11:29)

WHAT TO LISTEN FOR: Opening orchestral ritornello, or exposition, contrasts with solo piano exposition that follows (double exposition).
Elegant melodies and colorful harmonies.
First-movement concerto form featuring 4 themes, including one introduced in piano exposition.
Solo cadenza in improvisational style develops out of earlier melodic ideas.

ORCHESTRAL RITORNELLO (EXPOSITION), in G major

29 0:00   Theme 1—refined theme in violins, with woodwind figurations:

0:27   Transitional theme—forceful, in full orchestra.

30 1:01   Theme 2—gently undulating theme in violins, answered in woodwinds:

1:40   Closing theme—stated quietly in orchestra.

SOLO EXPOSITION

31 2:10   Theme 1—piano enters with sweep into main theme, decorated, in G major; woodwind accompaniment; scales and arpeggio figurations in piano.

2:45   Transitional theme—orchestral ritornello; piano with decorative part; modulates to key of dominant.

32 3:11   Piano theme—introduced by piano alone in D major, then presented in woodwinds:

33 4:01   Theme 2—in piano, with string accompaniment.
4:55   Closing—decisive, in D major.

		DEVELOPMENT
34	5:16	Virtuosic piano part, references to piano theme, runs and arpeggios against woodwinds; various modulations, leading back to tonic.
		RECAPITULATION
35	6:34	Theme 1—returns in strings, with woodwind accompaniment; piano joins in with decorated version of theme.
	7:01	Transition theme—forceful, in full orchestra.
36	7:32	Piano theme, solo, in G major, more decorated, with light orchestral accompaniment.
37	8:23	Theme 2—in piano, then in woodwinds, now in G major.
38	9:28	Cadenza—solo piano, variations on earlier themes; ends on dominant.
39	10:44	Closing—final ritornello, in G major.

Famous Women Virtuosos of the Eighteenth Century

Because eighteenth-century society deemed it proper for noble and upper-middle-class women to study music, many became highly skilled amateurs. Some women were able to make a living as music teachers, and a few became professional performers. Three women in particular—all associated with Mozart—stand out as impressive keyboard players of the late eighteenth century. Maria Anna Mozart (1751–1829), known as Nannerl, was an accomplished pianist who as a child toured extensively with her brother Wolfgang, performing concertos and four-hand piano works. Her father noted that Nannerl, at age twelve, was "one of the most skillful players in Europe," able to perform the most difficult works with "incredible precision," and that she played "so beautifully that everyone is talking about her and admiring her execution." Later, when she had retired from professional life to raise a family, her brother wrote several works for her and sent his piano cadenzas for her to try out.

The career of the blind musician Maria Theresa von Paradis (1759–1824) parallels that of her friend Mozart. An excellent pianist and organist, she was renowned for her remarkable musical memory, which was able to retain some sixty different concertos that she prepared for an extended European tour (1783–86). Paradis was a composer herself, but many of her works, including two concertos, a piano trio, and a number of sonatas, have been lost.

Engraving of a concerto performance (1777), with woman soloist, by **Johann Rudolf Holzhalb**.

The blind pianist Maria Theresa von Paradis. Etching by **Faustine Parmantié** (1784).

The third gifted pianist was Barbara von Ployer, a young student of Mozart's for whom he wrote two concertos, including the G-major work we just studied. Mozart was so proud of his talented student that he invited the composer Giovanni Paisiello (1740–1816) to the premiere of the concerto. He wrote to his father, "I am fetching Paisiello in my carriage, as I want him to hear both my pupil and my compositions."

The public prominence achieved by these women performers was unusual for the era. However, the many engravings and paintings of the time illustrating music-making scenes make it clear that women participated frequently in performances at home, in aristocratic salons, and at court. (See pp. 181, 209, and below.)

38

The Classical Sonata

"The sonatas of Mozart are unique; they are too easy for children, and too difficult for artists."

—ARTUR SCHNABEL

| KEY POINTS | Ⓢ StudySpace online at www.wwnorton.com/enjoy |

- ○ Classical sonatas were set either for one solo instrument (the *fortepiano*, an early piano) or for duos (violin and piano, for example).
- ○ Haydn, Mozart, and Beethoven all wrote music influenced by the Turkish *Janissary*, or military, band (CP 9).

- ○ The *Moonlight* Sonata, Beethoven's best-known piano work, evokes the new Romantic style.

An 18th-century engraving dated 1773 and showing a typical violin-piano duo.

The Movements of the Sonata

We saw in an earlier chapter that Haydn, Mozart, and their successors understood the term "sonata" as an instrumental work for one or two instruments, consisting of three or four contrasting movements. The movements followed the basic multimovement cycle described earlier in the discussions of string quartet, symphony, and concerto.

In the Classical era, the sonata—for piano solo or for two instruments—became an important genre for amateurs in the home, as well as for composers performing their own music at concerts. In duo sonatas for violin or cello and piano, the piano initially took the leading role, with the string instrument acting as accompaniment. Mozart and Beethoven, however, began to treat the two instruments as equal partners.

It is the piano sonatas of Beethoven that are the most significant in the solo literature for that instrument. They truly epitomize the genre in the Classical era.

BEETHOVEN'S *MOONLIGHT* SONATA

Shortly after Beethoven's death, the *Moonlight* Sonata was given its title by the poet Ludwig Rellstab, who likened the work to the moonlit scenery along Lake Lucerne in Switzerland. When Beethoven composed the sonata in 1801 (at the end of his first style period), he was already enamored of his young pupil, Countess Giuletta Guicciardi. The sonata is dedicated to her, but since this dedication seems to have been a last-minute decision, the work is probably not a programmatic statement of his love. This sonata, one of a set from Op. 27, breaks the formal molds we have considered—he called it a fantasy sonata (sonata *quasi una fantasia*), although he retains the typical three-movement format. In the dreamy first movement, perhaps the most famous of any of his works, Beethoven makes the piano sing; the melody spins out continuously, moving through various keys and registers. A short contrasting idea intervenes between two statements of the melody. While the form of this movement has elements of development and recapitulation, it does not present the opposition of themes nor keys typical of a first movement. Instead it looks ahead to the modified strophic song forms favored by Romantic composers (see Listening Guide 23).

Countess Giuletta Guicciardi, the dedicatee of the *Moonlight* Sonata.

The second movement is a gentle scherzo and trio form that sounds a little off balance because of its frequent syncopations. Set in a major key, the *Allegretto* provides necessary psychological relief between the emotionally charged opening movement and the stormy finale. Unlike most multimovement works we have studied, the full force of Beethoven's dramatic writing is reserved for this closing movement, which he finally sets in a full-blown sonata-allegro form. The movement is marked *Presto agitato*, and in performance the pianist's hands seem to fly over the keyboard. There are contrasting themes, but each seems to give way to restless motion. Only for a moment in the coda does the motion slow to a free cadenza-like passage, leading to a forceful close. Although Beethoven was not particularly won over by this sonata—he argued, "Surely I have written better things"—it was an immediate success with audiences and remains one of the most beloved works in the Classical repertory.

Beethoven's study in Schwarzspanierhaus, where he lived during the last year and a half of his life.

Listening Guide 23

eLG 2 (40–48)
4 (38–46)

Beethoven: Piano Sonata in C-sharp minor, Op. 27, No 2 (*Moonlight*), I and II

(15:02)

DATE OF WORK:	1801
MOVEMENTS:	I. Adagio sostenuto; modified song form, 2/2, C-sharp minor
	II. Allegretto; scherzo and trio, 3/4, D-flat major
	III. Presto agitato; sonata-allegro form, 4/4, C-sharp minor

First Movement: Adagio sostenuto; modified song form, 2/2, C-sharp minor   (5:45)

WHAT TO LISTEN FOR:	Delicate character of melody, played very softly.
	Singing quality of the piano.
	Continuous melody and arpeggios (outlining harmony).
	Strophic return of melody after middle section.
	No pause before second movement (*attaca*).

INTRODUCTION

40 0:00   Four-measure arpeggiated chords.

STROPHE 1

0:23   Melody in right hand, with dotted figure on repeated note accompanied by left-hand arpeggios, C-sharp minor; 4-measure phrases:

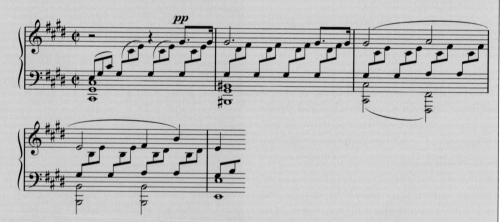

0:48   Melody in new key, expands and modulates.

1:12   New 3-note idea in dialogue between two hands:

1:51   Melody returns set in higher range.

MIDDLE SECTION

41 2:14 Motivic development of dialogue, exchanged between hands.
Pedal on dominant (G sharp) under arpeggiated chords.

STROPHE 2

42 3:20 Returns to opening melody and key center (C-sharp minor), followed by short dialogue idea.

CODA

43 4:52 Closes with melody stated in bass on repeated pitch (left hand).
Resolution on tonic cadence with arpeggios and chords.

Second Movement: Allegretto; scherzo and trio form, 3/4, D-flat major (2:10)

WHAT TO LISTEN FOR: Syncopations in triple meter give asymmetrical feeling.
Characteristic rhythmic pattern (♩ ♩ ♩ ♩).
Short, repeated sections (except first); overall **A-B-A** structure.

SCHERZO (A-A′-B-B)

44 0:00 **A** section—scherzo theme, 8 measures, lilting triple meter, in short 4-note ideas (bracketed):

A′ section—with more connected rhythm.

45 0:14 **B** section—more lyrical, closing with return of **A**; 20 measures.
0:33 **B** section—repeated.

TRIO (C-C-D-D)

46 0:53 **C** section—trio theme, with emphasis on third beat of measure alternating with accented bass chord on downbeat; 8 bars:

1:00 **C** section—repeated.
47 1:08 **D** section—hands alternate chords, 16 measures.
1:23 **D** section—repeated.

SCHERZO (A-A′-B)

48 1:39 **A** section—repeated, followed by repeat of **A′**.
1:52 **B** section—leads to gentle closing.

East Meets West: Turkish Influences on the Viennese Classics

We are all fascinated by the new and the mysterious. For the men and women of eighteenth-century Vienna, it was the East that satisfied their appetite for the unusual. Over the centuries, there had been ample opportunities, most of them military, for cultural interaction between the Austrian Hapsburg Empire and the large and powerful Ottoman Empire, which included Turkey. When the dust from their hostile skirmishes had settled, more civil relations were established. Viennese cuisine smacked increasingly of Eastern spices, fashions hinted at an Eastern look, and the city's music took on a distinctly martial sound, derived from the Turkish Janissary, or military, bands.

The Janissary band originated in Turkey in the fourteenth century as an elite corps of mounted musicians composed of shawm and bass drum players. (We have already noted in CP 4 the introduction of these instruments into Western Europe as a result of the Crusades and the establishment of early trade routes.) In the seventeenth century, the trumpet, small kettledrums, cymbals, and bell trees were added to this ceremonial ensemble, thereby producing a loud and highly percussive effect. The Turkish sound captured the imagination of the Viennese masters, who attempted to re-create it in their orchestral and theatrical works. Haydn wrote three "military" symphonies, Beethoven composed three orchestral works with Turkish percussion (including his monumental Symphony No. 9, which has a Turkish march in the last movement), and Mozart and Haydn, among others, used this military sound in their operas. Mozart noted that "Music must never offend the ear, but must please the listener, or in other words must never cease to be music. . . . The Janissary chorus [from *Die Entführung*] . . . is all that can be desired, that is, short, lively, and written to please the Viennese." The influence was felt even in piano music—notably in Mozart's appealing *Rondo alla turca* from his Sonata in A major, which we will hear. So popular was this style that some nineteenth-century pianos featured a "Janissary pedal" to add percussive effects.

Although the fascination with Turkish music proved to be a passing fancy, it nevertheless affected the makeup of the Western orchestra by establishing percussion instruments of Turkish origin (bass drum, cymbals, bells, triangle) as permanent members of the ensemble. It's hard to imagine an orchestra today without them! The Turkish Janissary ensemble also influenced the military band in the West; these same instruments now form the heart of every marching and concert band.

A Turkish Janissary band featuring mounted players of trumpets *(boru)*, cymbals *(zil)*, cylindrical drums *(davul)*, and kettledrums *(kös)*. Miniature from *The Festival Book of Vehbi*, written and illuminated for Ahmed III (r. 1703–30).

Whirling dervishes dancing, from the Mevlevi sect ceremony in Konya, Turkey.

Beethoven was fascinated by another Turkish musical tradition—this one a mystical religious ceremony to which he alluded in his incidental music for the stage work *The Ruins of Athens* (1811). The ceremony derives from one of the sects of Islam, that of the Mevlevis, who were famous for their whirling dance ritual: dancing in a circle with a slow, controlled spinning motion as a part of their religious experience. This ceremony was sung to the accompaniment of flute, lute, and percussion, including kettledrum and cymbals. Beethoven's *Chorus of Whirling Dervishes*, a pale imitation of the original, is an example of exoticism filtered through Western culture.

Both the Janissary band and the whirling dervish ceremony are obsolete in modern-day Turkey, except as tourist attractions. The term "whirling dervish"—implying one who twists and turns, like a restless child—has, however, endured in the West.

Terms to Note

Janissary band
whirling dervish

Suggested Listening

CD iMusic Beethoven: *Ode to Joy*, from Symphony No. 9
Beethoven: *The Ruins of Athens*, "Turkish March"
CD iMusic Haydn: *Military* Symphony No. 100, Second Movement
Mozart: *Rondo alla turca*, from Piano Sonata in A major, K. 331
Mozart: *The Abduction from the Seraglio*, Overture
CD iMusic Sousa: *Stars and Stripes Forever*
Turkish music (Janissary ensemble)

Choral Music and Opera in the Classical Era

39

Sacred Choral Music and Opera

*"Make a joyful noise to the Lord, all the earth;
break forth into joyous song and sing praises."*

—PSALM 98

KEY POINTS   ⓢ **StudySpace** online at www.wwnorton.com/enjoy

- The **Mass, Requiem Mass**, and the **oratorio** were the dominant choral forms of the Classical era.
- Haydn wrote two oratorios, including *The Creation*, which is based on the book of Genesis and on John Milton's *Paradise Lost*.
- Like Handel's *Messiah, The Creation* consists of solo arias, recitatives, ensembles, and choruses.
- In the Classical era, two types of Italian opera prevailed: *opera buffa* (comic opera) and *opera seria* (serious opera).

- *The Marriage of Figaro* is one of Mozart's most popular comic operas; it is based on a controversial play by Beaumarchais.
- In *The Marriage of Figaro*, the aristocracy is satirized, and the servants outsmart the nobility.
- In opera, each *aria* allows for emotional expression, while the *recitative* moves the action forward.

Mass, Requiem, and Oratorio

The late eighteenth century inherited a rich tradition of choral music from the Baroque. Among the principal genres were the Mass and Requiem. A **Mass,** you will recall, is a musical setting of the most solemn service of the Roman Catholic Church, and a **Requiem** is a musical setting of the Mass for the Dead. Both types were originally intended to be performed in church, but by the nineteenth century, they had

found a much larger audience in the concert hall. The blending of many voices in a
large space such as a church or cathedral
could not fail to be an uplifting experience.
For this reason, both the Catholic and
Protestant churches were patrons of
choral music throughout the ages. Haydn
and Mozart made significant contributions
to the Mass repertory; in particular,
Mozart's Requiem, his last composition, is
viewed as a masterpiece of the Classical
Viennese School.

The oratorio was another important
genre, made popular by Handel in such
works as *Messiah*. Haydn wrote two
oratorios—*The Creation* and *The Seasons*—
which attained enormous popularity and are often performed today.

A Turkish scene from an
opera performance at Eszterháza. The musician at the
harpsichord (far left, bottom)
is thought to be Haydn.
Anonymous 18th-century
watercolor.

Opera Types

Opera had become the branch of musical entertainment that reached the widest
public, and the opera house was now a center of experimentation. The opera of the
early eighteenth century accurately reflected the society from which it sprang. The
prevalent form was *opera seria*, "serious," or tragic, Italian opera, a highly formal-
ized genre inherited from the Baroque consisting mainly of recitatives and arias
specifically designed to display the virtuosity of star singers to the aristocracy. Its
rigid conventions were shaped largely by the poet Pietro Metastasio (1698–1782),
whose librettos, featuring stories of kings and heroes drawn from the legends of
antiquity, were set again and again throughout the century.

Opera seria

Increasingly, however, the need was felt for simplicity and naturalness, for a style
that reflected human emotions more realistically. One impulse toward reform came
from the operas of Christoph Willibald Gluck, whose achievements were described
earlier (see p. 164). Another reform gave rise to the popular comic opera that flourished in every country of Europe. Known in England as *ballad*, or *dialogue, opera*,
in Germany as *Singspiel*, in France as *opéra comique*, and in Italy as *opera buffa*,
this lighter genre was the rising middle class's response to the aristocratic form that
was inevitably supplanted.

Comic opera

Comic opera differed from opera seria in several basic ways. It was sung in the
language of the audience (the *vernacular*) rather than in Italian, which was the
standard language of international opera. It presented lively, down-to-earth plots
rather than the remote concerns of gods and mythological heroes. It featured an
exciting ensemble at the end of each act in which all the characters participated,
instead of the succession of solo arias heard in the older style. And it abounded in
farcical situations, humorous dialogue, popular tunes, and the impertinent
remarks of the *buffo*, the traditional character derived from the theater of buffoons, who spoke to the audience in a bass voice, with a wink and a nod. This was
a new sound in theaters previously dominated by the artificial soprano voice of the
castrato.

Buffo

As the Age of Revolution approached, comic opera became an important social
force whose lively wit delighted even the aristocrats it satirized. Classical opera buffa

IN HIS OWN WORDS

In an opera the poetry must be altogether the obedient daughter. . . . An opera is sure of success when the plot is well worked out, and when the words are written solely for the music, not shoved in here and there to suit some miserable rhyme. . . . The best of all is when a good composer, who understands the stage and is talented enough to make sound suggestions, meets a true phoenix, an able poet.

spread quickly, steadily expanding its scope until it culminated in the works of Mozart, the greatest dramatist of the eighteenth century.

MOZART'S COMIC OPERA *THE MARRIAGE OF FIGARO*

Mozart found his ideal librettist in Lorenzo da Ponte (1749–1838), an Italian-Jewish adventurer and poet whose dramatic vitality matched the composer's own. Their collaboration produced three great operas: *The Marriage of Figaro, Don Giovanni,* and *Così fan tutte* (*Women Are Like That*).

Da Ponte adapted his libretto for *The Marriage of Figaro* from a play by Pierre-Augustin Caron de Beaumarchais (1732–1799), a truly revolutionary work in that it satirized the upper classes and allowed a servant—Figaro, the clever and cocky valet of Count Almaviva—to outwit his master. Vienna was even more conservative than Paris: the play was forbidden there. But what could not be spoken could be sung. Mozart's opera was produced at Vienna's Imperial Court Theater in May 1786, and brought him his greatest success.

With *The Marriage of Figaro*, Mozart lifted comic opera to another dimension. In place of the stereotyped characters of opera buffa, he created real human beings who come alive through his music. The Count is a flirtateous ladies' man; the Countess is noble in her suffering. Her maid, Susanna, is pert and endlessly resourceful in resisting the advances of her master. Figaro is equally resourceful in foiling the schemes of the Count. And the Countess's page, Cherubino, is irresistible in his boyish innocence and ardor.

Act I

Cherubino's aria

The action weaves a complex story: the Count has designs on Figaro's bride, Susanna; the housekeeper is interested in Figaro; and Cherubino is smitten with the Countess. We first hear Cherubino's aria from Act I, "Non so più," which establishes his character as a young man in love with love. "I no longer know who I am or what I'm doing," he sings. "Every woman I see makes me blush and tremble." In Classical opera, the part of a young man was often sung by a soprano or alto (this is sometimes called a **trouser role**). In Mozart's opera, the mezzo-soprano voice is ideally suited to Cherubino's romantic idealism. (For the Italian and English text and an analysis of the aria, see Listening Guide 24.)

Vienna, Burgtheater, where *The Marriage of Figaro* was first performed.

Cherubino's aria is followed by recitative, the rapid-fire, talky kind of singing whose main function is to advance the plot. Eighteenth-century audiences accepted this change of texture and orchestration just as today we accept, in a Broadway musical, the change from song to spoken dialogue.

The action moves rapidly, with overtones of farce. Cherubino has sung his love song to the Countess in Susanna's room. When the Count arrives to ask Susanna to meet him that night in the garden, Cherubino hides behind a huge armchair. At this point, the music master Basilio, a gossip if ever there was one, arrives looking for the Count, who also tries to hide behind the chair. Susanna cleverly places herself between the Count and Cherubino, so that the page is able to slip in front of the chair and curl up in it, where she covers him with

"The Count discovers the Page." Detail of an illustration from the first Paris edition of Beaumarchais's comedy *Le Mariage de Figaro*, engraved by **Jean-Baptiste Liénard**, 1785.

a throw. With both the front and back of the armchair occupied, Susanna scolds Basilio as a busybody. At this point, the Count reveals his presence.

Susanna is aghast that the Count has been discovered in her room. The Count, having overheard Basilio say that Cherubino adores the Countess, is angry with the young man (see above). And Basilio thoroughly enjoys the rumpus he has stirred up. The action stops as Susanna, the Count, and Basilio join in a trio in which each character expresses individual emotions, with quick exchanges between the three voices and much repetition of text. No one has ever equaled Mozart's ability to match the demands of a dramatic situation with absolute musical forms, and this trio ("Cosa sento! Tosto andate"), which is set in a sonata form, is a good example.

The trio

When the Count finally pulls the cloth from the chair and discovers Cherubino, he vows to banish him from the estate. At this point, Figaro arrives with a group of peasants. He has told them that the Count has decided to abolish the "right of the first night," the hated feudal privilege that gave the lord of the manor the right to deflower every young woman in his domain. In their gratitude, the peasants have come to serenade their master, singing "His great kindness preserves the purity of a bride for the one she loves." Figaro, delighted to have forced the Count's hand, announces his impending marriage to Susanna, and the Count plays along by accepting the tributes of the crowd.

Figaro then intercedes for Cherubino with the Count, who relents and appoints the page to a captain's post in his regiment, and leaves with Basilio. The complications in the next three acts (and there are many) lead to a happy ending: the Count is reconciled with his wife, and Figaro wins his beloved Susanna.

Two centuries have passed since Mozart's characters first strutted across the stage. They live on today in every major opera house in the world, lifted above time and fashion by the genius of their creator.

Listening Guide 24

eLG 2 (49–56)
4 (65–72)

Mozart: *The Marriage of Figaro (Le nozze di Figaro)*, Act I, Scenes 6 and 7

(10:41)

DATE OF WORK:	1786
GENRE:	Opera buffa (Italian comic opera)
LIBRETTIST:	Lorenzo da Ponte
BASIS:	Play by Beaumarchais
PRINCIPAL CHARACTERS:	Figaro, servant to Count Almaviva (bass)
	Susanna, maid to Countess Almaviva (soprano)
	Cherubino, page (trouser role, sung by mezzo-soprano)
	Count Almaviva (baritone)
	Countess Almaviva (soprano)
	Basilio, music master (tenor)
	Doctor Bartolo (bass)
	Marcellina, his housekeeper (soprano)

Act I, Scenes 6 and 7
Scene 6: Aria, Cherubino.
(2:51)

WHAT TO LISTEN FOR: Breathless and quick opening of love song, reflecting the character's emotional state.
Return of opening (**A**) unifies the 4-part structure (**A-B-A-C**).

Form: **A-B-A-C**, followed by recitative
A—quick rhythms (in E flat):

Non so   più co·sa son, co·sa   fac·cio,

B—more lyrical (in B flat):

So   lo ai   no·mi d'a·mor di di·let·to,

A—return (in E flat).
C—begins quietly, then builds in E flat, modulates:

Par·lo d'a·mor ve·glian·do.

CHERUBINO

49	0:00	**A**	Non so più cosa son, cosa faccio,	I don't know what I am, what I'm doing;
			or di foco, ora sono di ghiaccio,	first I seem to be burning, then freezing;
			ogni donna cangiar di colore,	every woman makes me change color,
			ogni donna mi fa palpitar.	every woman I see makes me shake.
50	0:17	**B**	Solo ai nomi d'amor, di diletto,	Just the words "love" and "pleasure"
			mi si turba, mi s'altera il petto,	bring confusion; my breast swells in terror,
			e a parlare mi sforza d'amore	yet I am compelled to speak of love
			un desio ch'io non posso spiegar.	by a force which I cannot explain.

51	0:44	A	Non so più cosa son, ...	
52	1:04	C	Parlo d'amor vegliando,	I speak of love while waking,

			parlo d'amor sognando,	I speak of love while dreaming,
			all'acqua, all'ombra, ai monti,	to the water, to shadows, to mountains,
			ai fiori, all'erbe, ai fonti,	to the flowers, the grass, and the fountains,
			all'eco, all'aria, ai venti,	to the echo, to the air, to the winds
			che il suon de'vani accenti,	which carry the idle words
			portano via con se.	away with them.
		C	Parlo d'amor ...	
			E se non ho chi m'oda,	And if there is no one to listen,
			parlo d'amor con me!	I'll speak of love to myself!

(Seeing the Count in the distance, Cherubino hides behind the chair.)

Recitative: Susanna, Count, Basilio   (3:43)

WHAT TO LISTEN FOR: Rapid, conversational style that moves action ahead.
Fortepiano playing accompaniment, with cello.

CHERUBINO

53	2:51	Ah! Son perduto!	I'm done for!

SUSANNA

Che timor ... il Conte! Misera me!	I'm afraid ... the Count! Poor me!

(tries to conceal Cherubino)

COUNT ALMAVIVA *(entering)*

Susanna, tu mi sembri agitata e confusa.	Susanna, you seem to be agitated and confused.

SUSANNA

Signor, io chiedo scusa,	My lord, I beg your pardon,
ma, se mai, qui sorpresa,	but ... indeed ... the surprise ...
par carità, partite.	I implore you, please go.

COUNT

(sits down on the chair and takes Susanna's hand; she draws it forcibly away)

Un momento, e ti lascio. Odi.	One moment, then I'll leave. Listen.

SUSANNA

Non odo nulla.	I don't want to hear anything.

COUNT

Due parole: tu sai che ambasciatore	Just a word; you know that the king
a Londra il Re mi dichiarò;	has named me ambassador to London;
di condur meco Figaro destinai.	I had intended to take Figaro with me.

SUSANNA

Signor, se osassi—	My lord, if I dare—

COUNT *(rising)*

Parla, parla, mia cara,	Speak, speak, my dear,
e con quel dritto ch'oggi prendi su me,	and with that right you have of me today,
finchè tu vivi chiedi, imponi, prescrivi.	as long as you live, you may ask, demand, prescribe.

Listening Guide continues

SUSANNA

Lasciatemi, signor,	Let go of me, my lord,
dritti non prendo,	I have no rights,
non ne vò, non ne intendo.	I do not want them, nor claim them.
Oh me infelice!	Oh, what misery!

COUNT

Ah no, Susanna, io ti vò far felice!	Ah no, Susanna, I want to make you happy!
Tu ben sai quanto io t'amo;	You well know how much I love you;
a te Basilio tutto già disse.	Basilio has told you that already.
Or senti, se per pochi momenti meco	Now listen, if you would meet me
in giardin, sull'imbrunir del giorno,	briefly in the garden at dusk,
ah, per questo favore io pagherei . . .	ah, for this favor I would pay . . .

BASILIO *(outside the door)*

E uscito poco fa.	He went out just now.

COUNT

Chi parla?	Whose voice is that?

SUSANNA

O Dei!	Oh, heavens!

COUNT

Esci, ed alcun non entri.	Go, and let no one come in.

SUSANNA

Ch'io vi lasci qui solo?	And leave you here alone?

BASILIO *(outside)*

Da madama sarà, vado a cercarlo.	He'll be with my lady, I'll go and find him.

COUNT

Qui dietro mi porrò.	I'll get behind here.

(points to the chair)

SUSANNA

Non vi celate.	No, don't hide.

COUNT

Taci, e cerca ch'ei parta.	Hush, and try to make him go.

SUSANNA

Ohimè! che fate?	Oh dear! What are you doing?

(The Count is about to hide behind the chair; Susanna steps between him and the page. The count pushes her gently away. She draws back; meanwhile the page slips round to the front of the chair and hops in with his feet drawn up. Susanna rearranges the dress to cover him.)

BASILIO

Susanna, il ciel vi salvi!	Heaven bless you, Susanna!
Avreste a caso veduto il Conte?	Have you seen his lordship by any chance?

SUSANNA

E cosa deve far meco il Conte?	And what should his lordship be doing here
Animo, uscite.	with me? Come now, be gone!

BASILIO

Aspettate, sentite, Figaro di lui cerca.

But listen, Figaro is looking for him.

SUSANNA (*aside*)

Oh cielo!
Ei cerca chi, dopo voi, più l'odia.

Oh dear! Then he's looking for the one
man who, after you, hates him most!

COUNT (*aside*)

Vediam come mi serve.

Now we'll see how he serves me.

BASILIO

Io non ho mai nella moral sentito
ch'uno ch'ama la moglie odi il marito,
per dir che il Conte v'ama.

I have never heard it preached that
one who loves the wife should hate the husband;
that's a way of saying the Count loves you.

SUSANNA

Sortite, vil ministro dell'altrui sfrenatezza:
io non ho d'uopo della vostra morale,
del Conte, del suo amor!

Get out, vile minister of others' lechery!
I have no need of your preaching
nor of the Count or his lovemaking!

BASILIO

Non c'è alcun male.
Ha ciascun i suoi gusti.
Io mi credea che preferir
doveste per amante,
come fan tutte quante,
un signor liberal, prudente, e saggio,
a un giovinastro, a un paggio.

No offense meant.
Everyone to their own taste.
I thought you would have preferred
as your lover,
as all other women would,
a lord who's liberal, prudent, and wise,
to a raw youth, a mere page.

SUSANNA

A Cherubino?

To Cherubino?

BASILIO

A Cherubino! Cherubin d'amore,
ch'oggi sul far del giorno
passeggiava qui intorno per entrar.

To Cherubino! Love's little cherub
who early today
was hanging about here waiting to come in.

SUSANNA

Uom maligno, un'impostura è questa.

You insinuating wretch, that's a lie.

BASILIO

E un maligno con voi
chi ha gli occhi in testa?
E quella canzonetta,
ditemi in confidenza,
io sono amico,
ed altrui nulla dico,
è per voi, per madama?

Do you call it an insinuation
to have eyes in one's head?
And that little ditty,
tell me confidentially
as a friend,
and I will tell no one else,
was it written for you or my lady?

SUSANNA (*aside*)

Chi diavol gliel'ha detto?

Who the devil told him about that?

Listening Guide continues

BASILIO

A proposito, figlia, istruitelo meglio.	By the way, my child, you must teach him
Egli la guarda a tavola sí spesso,	better. At table he gazes at her so often
e con tale immodestia,	and so wantonly,
che s'il Conte s'accorge—	that if the Count noticed it—
e sul tal punto sapete, egli è una bestia—	on that subject, as you know, he's quite wild—

SUSANNA

Scellerato! e perchè andate voi	You wretch! Why do you go around
tai menzogne spargendo?	spreading such lies?

BASILIO

Io! che ingiustizia!	I! How unfair!
Quel che compro io vendo,	That which I buy I sell,
a quel che tutti dicono,	and to what is common knowledge
io non ci aggiungo un pelo.	I add not a tittle.

COUNT *(emerging from his hiding place)*

Come! che dicon tutti?	Indeed! And what is common knowledge?

BASILIO *(aside)*

Oh bella!	How wonderful!

SUSANNA

Oh cielo!	Oh heavens!

Scene 7: Terzetto (Trio), Count, Basilio, Susanna (4:07)

WHAT TO LISTEN FOR: Lively exchanges between 3 characters, each with different emotional reaction to the situation.

Structure reminiscent of a 3-part sonata-allegro form (with development and recapitulation).

Form: Sonata-type structure, with development and recapitulation
Style: Quick exchange between voices; much text repetition; each character with own emotional commentary

The Count—angry:

Basilio and the Count—comforting Susanna, who has fainted:

COUNT

54	6:34	Cosa sento! Tosto andate,	I heard it all! Go at once,
		e scacciate il seduttor!	throw the seducer out!

BASILIO

| In mal punto son qui giunto; | I have come at an unfortunate moment; |
| perdonate, o mio signor. | forgive me, o my lord. |

SUSANNA

| Che ruina! me meschina! | What a catastrophe! I am ruined! |
| Son' oppressa dal dolor! | Terror grips my heart! |

COUNT

| Tosta andate, andate . . . | Go at once, go . . . |

BASILIO

| In mal punto . . . | I have come . . . |

SUSANNA

| Che ruina! | What a catastrophe! |

BASILIO

| . . . son qui giunto; | . . . at an unfortunate moment; |

COUNT

| . . . e scacciate il seduttor. | . . . and throw the seducer out. |

BASILIO

| . . . perdonate, o mio signor. | . . . forgive me, o my lord. |

SUSANNA

Me meschina!	I am ruined!
Me meschina!	I am ruined!
Son' oppressa dal dolor.	Terror grips my heart.

BASILIO, COUNT *(supporting Susanna)*

| Ah! già svien la poverina! | Ah! The poor girl's fainted! |
| Come, oh Dio! le batte il cor. | O God, how her heart is beating. |

BASILIO

| Pian, pianin, su questo seggio— | Gently, gently on to the chair— |
| *(taking her to the chair)* | |

SUSANNA *(coming to)*

| Dove sono? Cosa veggio? | Where am I? What's this I see? |
| Che insolenza! andate fuor. | What insolence! Leave this room. |

BASILIO, COUNT

| Siamo qui per aiutarvi, . . . | We're here to help you, . . . |

BASILIO

| . . . è sicuro il vostro onor. | . . . your virtue is safe. |

COUNT

| . . . non turbarti, o mio tesor. | . . . do not worry, sweetheart. |

BASILIO

| Ah, del paggio, quel che ho detto, | What I was saying about the page |
| era solo un mio sospetto. | was only my own suspicion. |

Listening Guide continues

SUSANNA

E un'insidia, una perfidia,
non credete all'impostor.

It was a nasty insinuation,
do not believe the liar.

COUNT

55 8:27 Parta, parta il damerino, . . .

The young fop must go, . . .

SUSANNA, BASILIO

Poverino!

Poor boy!

COUNT

. . . parta, parta il damerino.

. . . the young fop must go.

SUSANNA, BASILIO

Poverino!

Poor boy!

COUNT

Poverino! poverino!
ma da me sorpreso ancor!

Poor boy! Poor boy!
But I caught him yet again!

SUSANNA

Come?

How?

BASILIO

Che?

What?

SUSANNA

Che?

What?

BASILIO

Come?

How?

SUSANNA, BASILIO

Come? che?

How? What?

COUNT

Da tua cugina,
l'uscio jer trovai rinchiuso,
picchio, m'apre Barbarina
paurosa fuor dell'uso.
Io, dal muso insospettito,
guardo, cerco in ogni sito,
ed alzando pian, pianino,
il tappeto al tavolino,
vedo il paggio.

At your cousin's house
I found the door shut yesterday.
I knocked and Barbarina opened it
much more timidly than usual.
My suspicions aroused by her expression,
I had a good look around,
and very gently lifting
the cloth upon the table,
I found the page.

(imitating his own action with the dress over the chair, he reveals the page)

Ah, cosa veggio?

Ah, what do I see?

SUSANNA

Ah! crude stelle!

Ah! wicked fate!

BASILIO

Ah! meglio ancora!

Ah! better still!

COUNT

56   9:30   Onestissima signora, . . .   Most virtuous lady, . . .

SUSANNA

Accader non può di peggio.   Nothing worse could happen!

COUNT

. . . or capisco come va!   . . . now I see what's happening!

SUSANNA

Giusti Dei, che mai sarà!   Merciful heaven, whatever will happen?

BASILIO

Cosí fan tutte . . .   They're all the same . . .

SUSANNA

Giusti Dei! che mai sarà   Merciful heaven! Whatever will happen?
Accader non può di peggio,   Nothing worse could happen!
ah no! ah no!   ah no! ah no!

BASILIO

. . . le belle,   . . . the fair sex,
non c'è alcuna novità,   there's nothing new about it,
cosí fan tutte.   they're all the same.

COUNT

Or capisco come va,   Now I see what's happening,
onestissima signora!   most virtuous lady!
or capisco, ecc.   Now I see, *etc.*

BASILIO

Ah, del paggio, quel che ho detto,   What I was saying about the page
era solo un mio sospetto.   was only my own suspicion.

SUSANNA

Accader non può di peggio, ecc.   Nothing worse could happen, *etc.*

COUNT

Onestissima signora, ecc.   Most virtuous lady, *etc.*

BASILIO

Cosí fan tutte, ecc.   They're all the same, *etc.*

From Classicism to Romanticism

*"I am in the world only for the purpose of composing.
What I feel in my heart, I give to the world."*

—FRANZ SCHUBERT

- ○ Like Beethoven, Franz Schubert is a transitional figure between eighteenth-century Classicism and the new spirit of Romanticism.

- ○ Schubert's symphonies and chamber music follow in the Classical tradition of Haydn, Mozart, and Beethoven; his songs, however, reflect the Romantic spirit.

We have studied three great masters of the Viennese Classical School: Haydn, Mozart, and Beethoven. Certain characteristics of Beethoven's music—his striking dynamic contrasts, his explosive accents, his expansion of strict Classical forms, his hymnlike slow movements, and the overall dramatic intensity of his music—clearly foreshadow the Romantic style.

The music of another Viennese master, Franz Schubert (1797–1828), reveals him as an heir to the Classical tradition. In his chamber music and symphonies, Schubert followed in a direct line of development from Haydn, Mozart, and Beethoven. But Schubert's life coincided with the first upsurge of Romanticism, and in his songs we can hear many of the prime interests of this new era, especially a fascination with nature. A discussion of Schubert's life and works appears in Chapter 43.

One song that beautifully captures the imagery of the subject is *The Trout* (*Die Forelle*), with its folklike melody and bubbling accompaniment. Schubert based a movement of his Piano Quintet in A major on this song, building a theme and variations that reveals a happy marriage of Classical and Romantic elements.

A COMPARISON OF CLASSICAL AND ROMANTIC STYLES

	CLASSICAL (C. 1750–1825)	ROMANTIC (C. 1820–1900)
COMPOSERS	Haydn, Mozart, Beethoven, Schubert	Beethoven, Schubert, Fanny Mendelssohn Hensel, Felix Mendelssohn, Clara Schumann, Robert Schumann, Chopin, Gottschalk, Liszt, Berlioz, Brahms, Tchaikovsky, Verdi, Wagner
MELODY	Symmetrical melody in balanced phrases and cadences; tuneful; diatonic, with narrow leaps	Expansive, singing melodies; wide ranging; more varied, with chromatic inflections
RHYTHM	Clear rhythmically, with regularly recurring accents; dance rhythms favored	Rhythmic diversity and elasticity; tempo rubato
HARMONY	Diatonic harmony favored; tonic-dominant relationships expanded, became basis for large-scale forms	Increasing chromaticism; expanded concepts of tonality
TEXTURE	Homophonic textures; chordal-vertical perspective	Homophony, turning to increased polyphony in later years of era
INSTRUMENTAL GENRES	Symphony, solo concerto, solo sonata, string quartet, other chamber music genres	Same large genres, adding one-movement symphonic poem; solo piano works
VOCAL GENRES	Opera, Mass, oratorio	Same vocal forms, adding works for solo voice and piano/orchestra
FORM	Ternary form predominant; sonata-allegro form developed; absolute forms preferred	Expansion of forms and interest in continuous as well as miniature programmatic forms
AUDIENCE	Secular music predominant; aristocratic audience	Secular music predominant; middle-class audience
DYNAMICS	Continuously changing dynamics through *crescendo* and *decrescendo*	Widely ranging dynamics for expressive purposes
TIMBRE	Changing tone colors between sections of works	Continual change and blend of tone colors; experiments with new instruments and unusual ranges
PERFORMING FORCES	String orchestra with woodwinds and some brass; 30-to-40-member orchestra; rise of piano to prominence	Introduction of new instruments (tuba, English horn, valved brass, harp, piccolo); much larger orchestras; piano predominant as solo instrument
VIRTUOSITY	Improvisation largely limited to cadenzas in concertos	Increased virtuosity; composers specified more in scores
EXPRESSION	Emotional balance and restraint	Emotions, mood, atmosphere emphasized; interest in the bizarre and macabre

229

Joseph Mallord William Turner (1775–1851), *Banks of the Loire*.

PART SEVEN

The Nineteenth Century

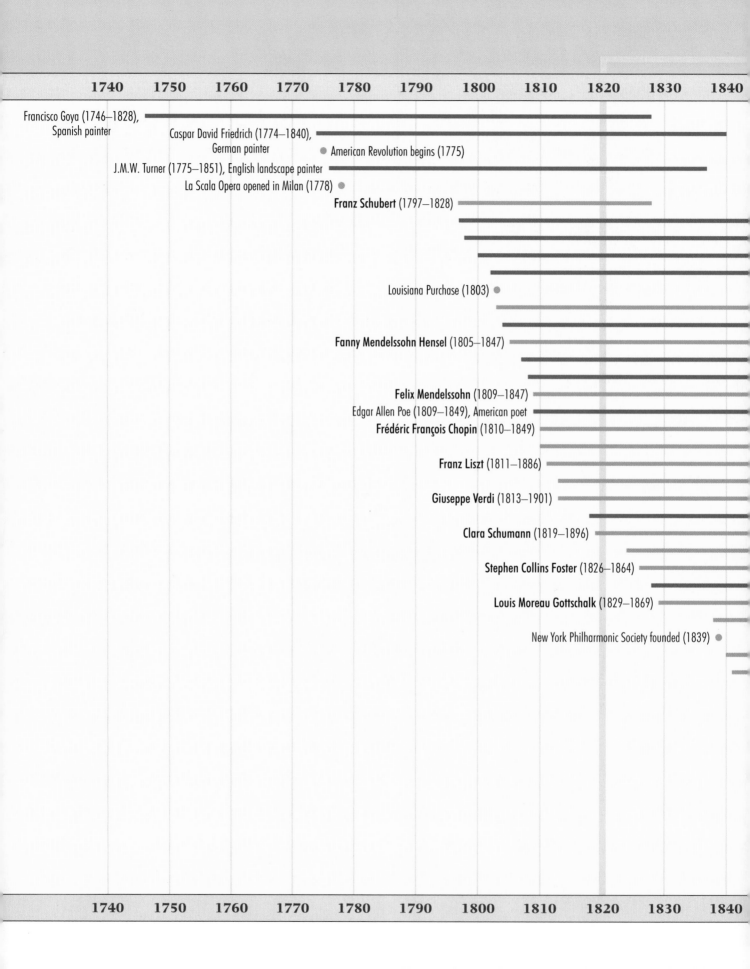

1740 1750 1760 1770 1780 1790 1800 1810 1820 1830 1840

Francisco Goya (1746–1828),
Spanish painter

Caspar David Friedrich (1774–1840),
German painter

American Revolution begins (1775)

J.M.W. Turner (1775–1851), English landscape painter

La Scala Opera opened in Milan (1778)

Franz Schubert (1797–1828)

Louisiana Purchase (1803)

Fanny Mendelssohn Hensel (1805–1847)

Felix Mendelssohn (1809–1847)
Edgar Allen Poe (1809–1849), American poet
Frédéric François Chopin (1810–1849)

Franz Liszt (1811–1886)

Giuseppe Verdi (1813–1901)

Clara Schumann (1819–1896)

Stephen Collins Foster (1826–1864)

Louis Moreau Gottschalk (1829–1869)

New York Philharmonic Society founded (1839)

1740 1750 1760 1770 1780 1790 1800 1810 1820 1830 1840

Romantic Era (1820–1900)

| 1850 | 1860 | 1870 | 1880 | 1890 | 1900 | 1910 | 1920 | 1930 | 1940 | 1950 |

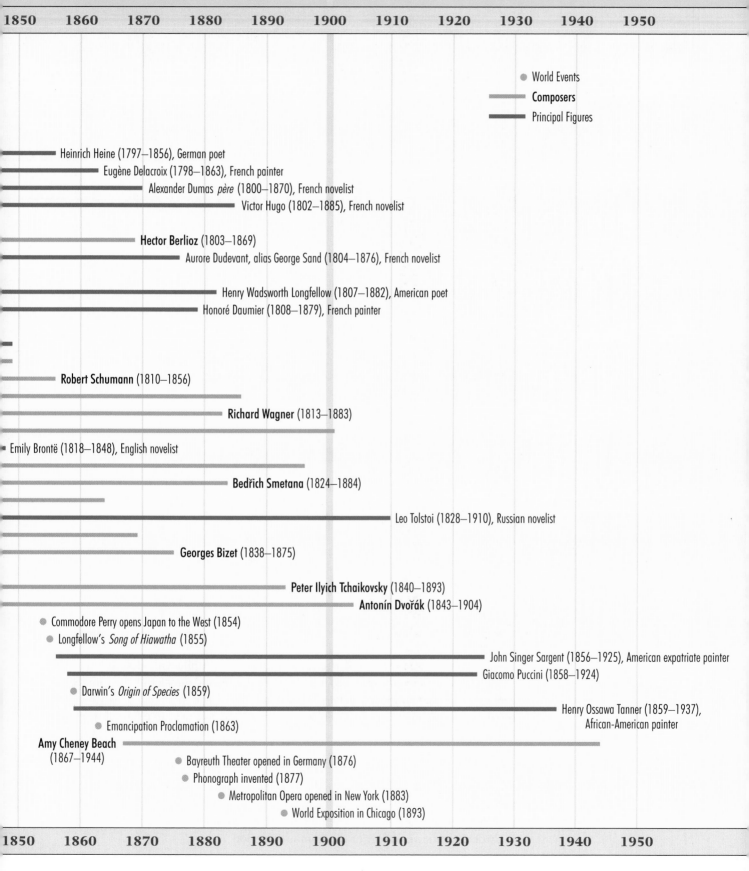

● World Events
Composers
Principal Figures

Heinrich Heine (1797–1856), German poet

Eugène Delacroix (1798–1863), French painter

Alexander Dumas *père* (1800–1870), French novelist

Victor Hugo (1802–1885), French novelist

Hector Berlioz (1803–1869)

Aurore Dudevant, alias George Sand (1804–1876), French novelist

Henry Wadsworth Longfellow (1807–1882), American poet

Honoré Daumier (1808–1879), French painter

Robert Schumann (1810–1856)

Richard Wagner (1813–1883)

Emily Brontë (1818–1848), English novelist

Bedřich Smetana (1824–1884)

Leo Tolstoi (1828–1910), Russian novelist

Georges Bizet (1838–1875)

Peter Ilyich Tchaikovsky (1840–1893)

Antonín Dvořák (1843–1904)

● Commodore Perry opens Japan to the West (1854)

● Longfellow's *Song of Hiawatha* (1855)

John Singer Sargent (1856–1925), American expatriate painter

Giacomo Puccini (1858–1924)

● Darwin's *Origin of Species* (1859)

Henry Ossawa Tanner (1859–1937), African-American painter

● Emancipation Proclamation (1863)

Amy Cheney Beach (1867–1944)

● Bayreuth Theater opened in Germany (1876)

● Phonograph invented (1877)

● Metropolitan Opera opened in New York (1883)

● World Exposition in Chicago (1893)

| 1850 | 1860 | 1870 | 1880 | 1890 | 1900 | 1910 | 1920 | 1930 | 1940 | 1950 |

The Romantic Movement

40

The Spirit of Romanticism

*"Music, of all the liberal arts, has the greatest
influence over the passions."*

—NAPOLEON BONAPARTE

KEY POINTS	**StudySpace** online at www.wwnorton.com/enjoy

○ The French Revolution resulted in the rise of a
middle-class, or bourgeois, society.

○ Romantic poets and artists abandoned traditional
subjects, turning instead to the passionate and the

fanciful; novels explored deep human conflicts and
exotic settings and subjects.

French Revolution

The Romantic era grew out of the social and political upheavals that followed the
French Revolution and came into full bloom in the second quarter of the nineteenth
century. The Revolution itself was a consequence of the inevitable clash between
momentous social forces and signaled the transfer of power from a hereditary land-
holding aristocracy to the middle class. This change was firmly rooted in urban commerce and industry, which emerged from the Industrial Revolution. The new society,
based on free enterprise, celebrated the individual as never before. The slogan of the
French Revolution—"Liberty, Equality, Fraternity"—inspired hopes and visions to
which artists responded with zeal. Sympathy for the oppressed, interest in simple folk
and in children, faith in humankind and its destiny, all formed part of the increasingly democratic character of the Romantic period.

The spirit of the French Revolution is captured in *Liberty Leading the People,* by **Eugène Delacroix** (1798–1863).

Romantic Writers

The Romantic poets rebelled against the conventional concerns of their Classical predecessors; these poets were drawn to the fanciful, the picturesque, and the passionate. One of the prime traits of all Romantic artists was their emphasis on intensely emotional expression. Another was a heightened awareness of themselves as individuals apart from all others. "I am different from all the men I have seen," proclaimed Jean Jacques Rousseau. "If I am not better, at least I am different." In Germany, a group of young writers created a new kind of lyric poetry that culminated in the art of Heinrich Heine, who became a favorite poet of Romantic composers. A similar movement in France was led by Victor Hugo, the country's greatest prose writer, and Alphonse de Lamartine, its greatest poet. In England, the revolt against the formalism of the Classical age produced an outpouring of emotional lyric poetry that reached its peak in the works of Byron, Shelley, and Keats.

Individualism

The newly won freedom of the artist proved to be a mixed blessing. Confronted by a world indifferent to artistic and cultural values, artists felt more and more cut off from society. A new type of artist emerged—the bohemian, a rejected dreamer who starved in an attic and who shocked the establishment through peculiarities of dress and behavior. Eternal longing, regret for the lost happiness of childhood, an indefinable discontent that gnawed at the soul—these were the

Sympathy for the oppressed underscored the democratic character of the Romantic movement. **Honoré Daumier** (1808–1879), *The Third-Class Carriage.*

In this Romanticized view inside a harem, the artist contrasts the petal-smooth skin of the figure against exotic Eastern textures and colors. *La Grande Odalisque* (1814), by **Jean-Auguste Dominique Ingres** (1780–1867).

ingredients of the Romantic mood. Yet the artist's pessimism was based in reality. It became apparent that the high hopes fostered by the Revolution were not to be realized overnight. Despite the brave slogans, all people were not yet equal or free. The new optimism gave way to doubt and disenchantment, a state of mind that was reflected in the arts and in literature.

Hugo dedicated *Les Misérables* "to the unhappy ones of the earth." The nineteenth-century novel found one of its great themes in the conflict between the individual and society. Among the memorable characters who exhibit the discontent of nineteenth-century society are Jean Valjean, the hero of Hugo's novel (well-known from the 1985 musical *Les Misérables*), Heathcliff in Emily Brontë's *Wuthering Heights*, and Tolstoy's Anna Karenina, in the novel of the same name.

Some writers sought escape by glamorizing the past, as Sir Walter Scott did in *Ivanhoe* and Alexandre Dumas *père* in *The Three Musketeers*. A longing for far-off lands inspired the exotic scenes that glow on the canvases of J. M. W. Turner and Eugène Delacroix. The Romantic world was one of "strangeness and wonder": the eerie landscape we meet in Samuel Taylor Coleridge's poem *Kubla Khan*, Nathaniel Hawthorne's novel *The Scarlet Letter*, and Edgar Allan Poe's poem *The Raven*.

Romanticism dominated the artistic output of the nineteenth century. It gave its name to a movement and an era and created a multitude of colorful works that still hold millions in thrall.

41

Romanticism in Music

"Music is the melody whose text is the world."
—ARTHUR SCHOPENHAUER

KEY POINTS StudySpace online at www.wwnorton.com/enjoy

o The Industrial Revolution spurred many technical advances in musical instruments, making them more affordable.

o Educational opportunities broadened as music conservatories were established across Europe and the Americas.

o The orchestra grew in size and sound when new and improved instruments were introduced; in response, composers demanded new levels of expression.

o Romantic composers used nationalistic folklore and exotic subjects.

o Romantic music is characterized by memorable melodies, richly expressive harmony, and broad, expanded forms.

o The Romantic era saw the rise of the virtuoso soloist and of amateur music-making.

o Women musicians achieved an elevated status in society as performers, teachers, composers, and music patrons.

Art mirrors the great social forces of its time. Thus Romantic music reflected the profound changes that were taking place in the nineteenth century at every level of human existence.

The Industrial Revolution brought with it the means to create more affordable and responsive musical instruments, as well as the technical improvements that strongly influenced the sound of Romantic music. For example, the addition of valves to brass instruments made them much more maneuverable so that composers like Wagner and Tchaikovsky could write melodies for the horns and trumpets that would have been unplayable in earlier eras. Several new wind instruments were developed as well, including the tuba and the saxophone. Improved manufacturing techniques provided the piano with a cast-iron frame and thicker strings, giving it a deeper and more brilliant tone. We will hear that a piano work by Chopin or Gottschalk sounds different from one by Mozart, not only because the Romantic era demanded a different kind of expression but also because composers were writing for a piano capable of effects that were never before possible.

The gradual democratization of an industrialized society broadened educational opportunities. The chief cities of Europe established new conservatories to train more and better musicians, and as a result nineteenth-century composers could count on performers whose skill was considerably more advanced.

As music moved from palace and church to the public concert hall, orchestras increased in size, giving composers a more varied and colorful means of expression. Naturally, this directly influenced the sound. New instruments such as the piccolo, English horn, and contrabassoon added varied timbres and extended the extreme high and low ranges of the orchestra (see Table on p. 237). The dynamic range also

Improved musical instruments

The bass saxhorn, a precursor to the modern tuba, was one of many new instruments designed by Adolphe Sax, inventor of the saxophone.

expanded. It was far greater than in the eighteenth-century ensemble—sweeping contrasts of loud (*fff*) and soft (*ppp*) now lent new drama to the music of the Romantics. And as orchestral music developed, so did the technique of writing for instruments—individually and together. ***Orchestration*** became an art in itself. Composers now had a palette as broad as those of painters, and they used it to create mood and atmosphere and to evoke profound emotional responses. With all these developments, it was no longer feasible to direct an orchestra from the keyboard or the first violin desk, as had been the tradition in the eighteenth century, and thus a central figure—the conductor—was needed to guide the performance.

Orchestration

In order to communicate their intentions as precisely as possible, composers developed a vocabulary of highly expressive terms. Among the directions frequently encountered in nineteenth-century musical scores are *dolce* (sweetly), *cantabile* (songful), *dolente* (weeping), *mesto* (sad), *maestoso* (majestic), *gioioso* (joyous), and *con amore* (with love, tenderly). These and similar terms suggest not only the character of the music but also the frame of mind of the composers.

Use of folklore

The interest in folklore and the rising tide of nationalism inspired Romantic composers to make increased use of the folk songs and dances from their native lands (see CP 11). As a result, a number of national idioms—Hungarian, Polish, Russian, Bohemian, Scandinavian, and eventually American—flourished, greatly enriching the melodic, harmonic, and rhythmic language of music. We will consider the diversity of these nationalistic expressions in the piano music of Polish-born Frédéric Chopin and New Orleans composer Louis Gottschalk, as well as in the orchestral music of the Eastern European musician Bedřich Smetana.

Exoticism

Nineteenth-century exoticism appeared first in the northern nations' longing for the warmth and color of the south, and then in the West's interest in the fairy-tale splendors of Asia and the Far East. The first impulse found expression in the works of German, French, and Russian composers who turned for inspiration to Italy and Spain; these include Mendelssohn's *Italian* Symphony and Bizet's opera *Carmen*.

The glamour of the East was brought to international attention by the Russian national school, whose music is pervaded by the fairy-tale background of Asia. Rimsky-Korsakov's orchestrally resplendent *Sheherazade*, Borodin's colorful opera *Prince Igor*, and even several dances from Tchaikovsky's famous *Nutcracker* ballet (see p. 325) are among the many Eastern-inspired works that found favor with Western audiences. A number of French and Italian opera composers also drew on exotic themes: Saint-Saëns in the biblical story of *Samson and Delilah;* Verdi in *Aida*, set in Egypt; and Puccini in his Japanese-inspired opera *Madame Butterfly* (see p. 319), which we will study.

Romantic Style Traits

The nineteenth century above all was the period when musicians tried to make their instruments "sing." Since Romantic melody was marked by a lyricism that gave it an immediate appeal, tunes by composers such as Chopin, Verdi, and Tchaikovsky have enjoyed an enduring popularity among the general public.

Nineteenth-century music strove for a harmony that was emotionally charged and highly expressive. Composers such as Richard Wagner employed combinations of pitches that were more chromatic and dissonant than those of their predecessors. Romantic composers expanded the instrumental forms they had inherited

Chromaticism and dissonance

from the Classical masters to give their ideas more time to play out. A symphony by Haydn or Mozart takes about twenty minutes to perform; one by Tchaikovsky, Brahms, or Dvořák lasts at least twice that long. As public concert life developed, the symphony became the most important genre of orchestral music, comparable to the novel in Romantic literature. New orchestral forms emerged as well, including the one-movement symphonic poem, the choral symphony, and works for solo voice with orchestra.

The Royal Pavilion at Brighton, England (1815–1818), with its Islamic domes, minarets, and screens, reflects the 19th-century fascination with Eastern culture. Designed by **John Nash** (1752–1835).

Music in the nineteenth century drew steadily closer to literature and painting. The connection with Romantic poetry and drama is most obvious in the case of music with words. However, even in their purely orchestral music, the Romantic composers responded to the mood of the time and captured with remarkable vividness the emotional atmosphere that surrounded nineteenth-century poetry and painting.

Nineteenth-century music was linked to dreams and passions—to profound meditations on life and death, human destiny, God and nature, pride in one's country, desire for freedom, the political struggles of the age, as well as to the ultimate triumph of good over evil. These intellectual and emotional associations, nurtured by the Romantic movement, brought music into a commanding position as a link between the artist's most personal thoughts and the realities of the outside world.

The Musician in Society

The emergence of a democratic society liberated the lives of composers and performers. Musical life reached the general populace, since performances were now in the public concert hall as well as in the salons of the aristocracy. Where eighteenth-century musicians had relied on aristocratic patronage and the favor of royal courts, nineteenth-century musicians were supported by the new middle-class

An orchestral Sunday concert in The Hague, The Netherlands. Sepia print, ca. 1820.

IN HIS OWN WORDS

When [Liszt] sits at the piano and, having repeatedly pushed his hair back over his brow, begins to improvise, then he often rages all too madly upon the ivory keys and lets loose a deluge of heaven-storming ideas, . . . One feels both blessedness and anxiety, but rather more anxiety. . . .

—HEINRICH HEINE

audience and could make a living in their profession. Indeed, as solo performers began to dominate the concert hall, whether as pianists, violinists, or conductors, they became "stars" who were idolized by the public.

With this expansion of musical life, composers and performing artists were called on to assume new roles as educators. Felix Mendelssohn, active as composer, pianist, and conductor, founded the Leipzig Conservatory, whose curriculum became a model for music schools all over Europe and America. Composer and conductor Robert Schumann became a widely read music critic. Franz Liszt, considered to be the greatest pianist of his time, taught extensively and trained a generation of great concert pianists. And opera composer Richard Wagner directed his own theater at Bayreuth, thus helping the newly interested public understand his music dramas.

WOMEN IN MUSIC

We have already observed a handful of women who were recognized in their day as virtuoso performers. Nineteenth-century society saw women make great strides in establishing careers as professional musicians. This path was now possible through the broadening of educational opportunities: in public conservatories, women could receive training as singers, instrumentalists, and even composers. Likewise, the rise of the piano as the favored chamber instrument—both solo and with voice or other instruments—provided women of the middle and upper classes with a performance outlet that was socially acceptable.

Although composition remained largely a man's province, some women broke away from tradition and overcame social stereotypes to become successful composers. Among them were Fanny Mendelssohn Hensel, known for her songs, piano music, and chamber works; Clara Schumann, a talented performer and composer of piano, vocal, and chamber music; and the American Amy Cheney Beach, one of the first female composers to be recognized in the field of orchestral music. (The issues and attitudes surrounding nineteenth-century women composers are discussed further in CP 13, on p. 288.)

Women also exerted a significant influence as patrons of music or through their friendships with composers. Novelist George Sand played an important role in Chopin's career, as did Princess Carolyne Sayn-Wittgenstein in that of Liszt's. Nadezhda von Meck is remembered as the mysterious woman who supported Tchaikovsky in the early years of his career and made it financially possible for him to compose. Several women of the upper class presided over musical salons where composers could gather to perform and discuss their music. One such musical center was the home of the Mendelssohn family, where Fanny Mendelssohn organized concerts that featured works by her more famous brother, Felix.

All in all, women musicians made steady strides toward professional equality throughout the nineteenth century and thereby laid the foundation for even greater achievements in the twentieth.

A salon concert hosted by the Berlin composer Bettina von Arnim, who is seated in the black dress. Watercolor by **Johann Carl Arnold**, c. 1855.

The Romantic Orchestra

BERLIOZ'S ORCHESTRA (*Symphonie fantastique*, 1830)	BRAHMS'S ORCHESTRA (Symphony No. 3, 1883)	TCHAIKOVSKY'S ORCHESTRA (*The Nutcracker*, 1892)
STRINGS	**STRINGS**	**STRINGS**
Violins 1	Violins 1	Violins 1
Violins 2	Violins 2	Violins 2
Violas	Violas	Violas
Cellos	Cellos	Cellos
Double basses	Double basses	Double basses
2 Harps		2 Harps
WOODWINDS	**WOODWINDS**	**WOODWINDS**
2 Flutes (1 on Piccolo)	2 Flutes	2 Flutes and Piccolo
2 Oboes	2 Oboes	2 Oboes, 1 English horn
2 Clarinets (1 on E-flat Clarinet)	2 Clarinets	2 Clarinets, Bass clarinet
English horn	2 Bassoons, Contrabassoon	2 Bassoons
4 Bassoons		
BRASS	**BRASS**	**BRASS**
4 French horns	4 French horns	4 French horns
2 Cornets, 2 Valved trumpets	2 Trumpets	2 Valved trumpets
3 Trombones (1 Bass trombone)	3 Trombones	2 Trombones, Bass trombone
2 Ophicleides		Tuba
PERCUSSION	**PERCUSSION**	**PERCUSSION**
Timpani	Timpani	Timpani
Cymbals		Cymbals, gong, triangle
Snare drum		Tambourine, castanets
Bass drum		Bass drum
Tubular bells (chimes)		Tubular bells (chimes)
		Other special effects (including toy instruments)
		Keyboard
		Celesta

Nineteenth-Century Art Song

42

The Romantic Song

"Out of my great sorrows I make my little songs."

—HEINRICH HEINE

| KEY POINTS | ⑤ **StudySpace** online at www.wwnorton.com/enjoy |

○ Typical Romantic song structures include *strophic* and *through-composed* forms; some songs fall between the two, into a *modified strophic* form.

○ The German art song, or *Lied*—for solo voice and piano—was a favored Romantic genre.

○ Composers wrote *song cycles* that unified a group of songs by poem or theme.

○ The poetry of the Lied used themes of love and nature; the favored poets were Goethe and Heine.

The art song met the nineteenth-century need for intimate personal expression. The form came into prominence in the early decades of the century and emerged as a favored example of the new lyricism.

Types of Song Structure

Strophic form

CD iMusic

Brahms: *Lullaby*

In the nineteenth century, two main song-structures prevailed. One already familiar is *strophic form*, in which the same melody is repeated with every stanza, or strophe, of the poem—hymns, carols, as well as most folk and popular songs are strophic. This form sets up a general atmosphere that accommodates all the stanzas of the text. The first may tell of a lover's expectancy, the second of his joy at seeing his beloved, the third of her father's harshness in separating them, and the fourth of her sad death, all sung to the same tune.

The other song type, what the Germans call *durchkomponiert*, or **through-composed**, proceeds from beginning to end, without repetitions of whole sections. Here the music follows the story line, changing according to the text. This makes it possible for the composer to mirror every shade of meaning in the words.

There is also an intermediate type that combines features of the other two. The same melody may be repeated for two or three stanzas, with new material introduced when the poem requires it, generally at the climax. This is a **modified strophic form**.

The Lied

Though songs have existed throughout the ages, the art song as we know it today was a product of the Romantic era. The **Lied** (plural, **Lieder**), as the new genre was called, is a German-texted solo vocal song with piano accompaniment. Among the great Romantic masters of this form of art song are Franz Schubert, Robert Schumann, Johannes Brahms, and Hugo Wolf. Women composers who contributed significantly to the genre include Fanny Mendelssohn Hensel, Clara Schumann, and Amy Cheney Beach. Some composers wrote groups of Lieder that were unified by a narrative thread or descriptive theme. Such a group is known as a **song cycle**; an example is Robert Schumann's *A Poet's Love*, which we will study in Chapter 44.

The rise of the Lied was fueled by the outpouring of lyric poetry that marked German Romanticism. Johann Wolfgang von Goethe (1749–1832) and Heinrich Heine (1797–1856) were the two leading figures among a group of poets who, like Wordsworth, Byron, Shelley, and Keats in English literature, favored short, personal, lyric poems. The texts of the Lied range from tender sentiment to dramatic balladry; its universal themes are love, longing, and the beauty of nature.

Another circumstance that popularized the Romantic art song was the emergence of the piano as the preferred household instrument of the nineteenth century. The piano accompaniment to a song translated its poetic images into music. Voice and piano together infused the short lyric form with feeling and made it suitable for amateurs and artists alike, in both the home and the concert hall.

Through-composed form

> *When I compose a song, my concern is not to make music but, first and foremost, to do justice to the poet's intention. I have tried to let the poem reveal itself, and indeed to raise it to a higher power.*
>
> —EDVARD GRIEG

IN HIS OWN WORDS

Song cycle

CD iMusic

"In the lovely month of May"

The immense popularity of the Romantic art song was due in part to the emergence of the piano as the universal household instrument. A lithograph by **Achille Devéria** (1800–1857), *In the Salon*.

43

Schubert and the Lied

"When I wished to sing of love, it turned to sorrow. And when I wished to sing of sorrow, it was transformed for me into love."

KEY POINTS | **StudySpace** online at www.wwnorton.com/enjoy

- ○ The Viennese composer Franz Schubert was a gifted song writer who created more than six hundred Lieder and several famous song cycles.
- ○ *Erlking*—a through-composed Lied based on a Ger-

man legend set in a dramatic poem by Goethe—is one of his most famous songs.
- ○ Schubert died young and impoverished, in part because of his bohemian lifestyle.

Franz Schubert's life has become a romantic symbol of the artist's fate. He was not properly appreciated during his lifetime, and he died very young, leaving the world a musical legacy of some nine hundred works.

His Life

 Franz Schubert

Franz Schubert (1797–1828) was born in a suburb of Vienna, the son of a schoolmaster. As a boy, he learned the violin from his father and piano from an elder brother; his beautiful soprano voice gained him admittance to the imperial chapel and school where the court singers were trained (he was one of the Vienna Choir Boys). His teachers were astonished at the musicality of the shy, dreamy lad. One of them remarked that Franz "had learned everything from God."

When his schooldays were over, the young Schubert tried to follow in his father's footsteps, but he was not cut out for the routine of the classroom. He found escape by immersing himself in the lyric poetry of the budding German Romanticism. As one of his friends said, "Everything he touched turned to song." Music came to him with miraculous spontaneity. *Erlking*, set to a poem by Goethe, was written when Schubert was still a teenager. The song, one of his greatest, won him immediate public recognition yet, incredibly, he had difficulty finding a publisher.

Schubert was not as well known as some composers of his era (the virtuoso violinist Paganini, for example, received much more critical attention), but he was appreciated by the Viennese public and his reputation grew steadily. Still, his musical world was centered in the home, in salon concerts amid a select circle of friends and acquaintances.

Later years   Schubert suffered deeply during his later years, largely owing to a progressive debilitation believed to be from the advanced stages of syphilis. He was often pressed for money, and sold his music for much less than it was worth. As his youthful exuberance gave way to the maturity of a deeply emotional Romantic artist, he perceived that he had lost the struggle with life. "It seems to me at times that I no longer belong to this world," he wrote. This emotional climate also pervades his magnificent song cycle *Winter's Journey*, in which the composer introduced a somber lyri-

In his unfinished oil sketch of a "Schubertiad," Romantic artist **Moritz von Schwind** (1804–1871) shows Schubert seated at the piano, next to singer Johann Michael Vogl, who premiered many of Schubert's songs.

cism new to music. Overcoming his discouragement, he embarked on his last efforts. To the earlier masterpieces he added, in the final year of his life, a group of profound works that includes the Mass in E flat, the String Quintet in C, three piano sonatas (published posthumously), and thirteen of his finest songs.

When he was already terminally ill, he managed to correct the proofs of the final part of *Winter's Journey*. His dying wish was to be buried near the master he worshipped above all others—Beethoven. Schubert was thirty-one years old when he died in 1828. His wish was granted.

> IN HIS OWN WORDS
>
> *No one understands another's grief, no one understands another's joy. . . . My music is the product of my talent and my misery. And that which I have written in my greatest distress is what the world seems to like best.*

His Music

Schubert's music marks the confluence of the Classical and Romantic eras. His symphonies are Classical in their clear form; in his Lieder and piano pieces, however, he was wholly the Romantic. The melodies have a tender and longing quality that matches the tone of the poetry they set.

In his chamber music, Schubert was a direct descendant of Haydn and Mozart. His string quartets, piano trios, and the familiar *Trout* Quintet, all masterworks, end the line of Viennese Classicism.

Chamber music

In his impromptus and other short piano pieces, the piano sings with a new lyricism. Finally, there are the songs, more than six hundred of them. Many were written down at breakneck speed, sometimes five, six, seven in a single morning. The accompaniments are especially descriptive: a measure or two can conjure up images of a rustling brook (in *The Trout*) or a horse riding through the night (in *Erlking*). The two superb song cycles, *The Lovely Maid of the Mill* and *Winter's Journey*, both on poems by Wilhelm Müller, convey impassioned feelings of love and despair.

Piano works and songs

ERLKING

This masterpiece of Schubert's youth captures the Romantic "strangeness and wonder" of Goethe's celebrated ballad. *Erlking* is based on a legend that whoever is touched by the king of the elves must die.

The eerie atmosphere of the poem is immediately established by the piano. Galloping triplets are heard against a rumbling figure in the bass. This motive pervades the song, helping to unify it. The poem's four characters—the narrator, the father, the

The Legend of *The Erlking* (c. 1860), as portrayed by **Moritz von Schwind** (1804–1871).

child, and the seductive elf—are all presented by one soloist but vividly differentiated through changes in the melody, register, harmony, rhythm, and accompaniment. The child's terror is suggested by clashing dissonance and a high vocal range. The father calms his son's fears with a more rounded vocal line, sung in a low register. And the Erlking cajoles the child in suavely melodious phrases set in a major key.

The song is through-composed; the music follows the action of the story with a steady rise in tension—and pitch—that builds almost to the end. The obsessive triplet rhythm slows down as the horse and rider reach home, then drops out altogether on the last line: "In his arms the child"—a dramatic pause precedes the two final words—"was dead." The work of an eighteen-year-old, *Erlking* was a milestone in the history of Romanticism (see Listening Guide 25).

Listening Guide 25

eLG 2 (57–64)
5 (1–8)

Schubert: *Erlking (Erlkönig)* (4:00)

DATE OF WORK:	1815
FORM:	Through-composed Lied
TEXT:	Narrative poem by Johann Wolfgang von Goethe
MEDIUM:	Solo voice and piano
TEMPO:	Schnell (fast)
CHARACTERS	(performed by one vocalist): Narrator: middle register, minor mode Father: low register, minor mode; reassuring Son: high register, minor mode; frightened Erlking: medium range, major mode; coaxing, then insistent

WHAT TO LISTEN FOR: Piano accompaniment establishes mood of urgency and drama for the Lied; piano's triplet rhythm continues until very last text line.
Narrative text with 4 characters (narrator, father, son, Erlking), each expressed through differing vocal registers.
Shifts from minor to major mode (for Erlking) and dissonance to project the boy's terror (each cry is a step higher).

57 0:00 Piano introduction—minor key and rapid repeated octaves in triplets set mood, simulating horse's hooves:

TEXT	TRANSLATION

NARRATOR (*minor mode, middle range*)

0:23

Wer reitet so spät durch Nacht und Wind?
Es ist der Vater mit seinem Kind;
er hat den Knaben wohl in dem Arm,
er fasst ihn sicher, er hält ihn warm.

Who rides so late through night and wind?
It is a father with his child;
he has the boy close in his arm,
he holds him tight, he keeps him warm.

FATHER (*low range*)

"Mein Sohn, was birgst du so bang
dein Gesicht?"

"My son, why do you hide your face
in fear?"

SON (*high range*)

"Siehst, Vater, du den Erlkönig nicht?
Den Erlenkönig mit Kron' und Schweif?"

"Father, don't you see the Erlking?
The Erlking with his crown and train?"

FATHER (*low range*)

"Mein Sohn, es ist ein Nebelstreif."

"My son, it is a streak of mist."

ERLKING (*major mode, melodic*)

58 1:29

"Du liebes Kind, komm, geh mit mir!
Gar schöne Spiele spiel' ich mit dir;
manch' bunte Blumen sind an dem Strand;
meine Mutter hat manch' gülden Gewand."

"You dear child, come with me!
I'll play very lovely games with you.
There are lots of colorful flowers by the shore;
my mother has some golden robes."

SON (*high range, frightened*)

59 1:51

"Mein Vater, mein Vater, und hörest du nicht,
was Erlenkönig mir leise verspricht?"

"My father, my father, don't you hear
the Erlking whispering promises to me?"

FATHER (*low range, calming*)

"Sei ruhig, bleibe ruhig, mein Kind;
in dürren Blättern säuselt der Wind."

"Be still, stay calm, my child;
it's the wind rustling in the dry leaves."

ERLKING (*major mode, cajoling*)

60 2:13

"Willst, feiner Knabe, du mit mir geh'n?
Meine Töchter sollen dich warten schön;
meine Töchter führen den nächtlichen Reih'n
und wiegen und tanzen und singen dich ein."

"My fine lad, do you want to come with me?
My daughters will take care of you;
my daughters lead the nightly dance,
and they'll rock and dance and sing you to sleep."

SON (*high range, dissonant outcry*)

61 2:31

"Mein Vater, mein Vater, und siehst du
nicht dort,
Erlkönigs Töchter am düstern Ort?"

"My father, my father,
don't you see
the Erlking's daughters over there in the shadows?"

FATHER (*low range, reassuring*)

"Mein Sohn, mein Sohn, ich seh' es genau,
es scheinen die alten Weiden so grau."

"My son, my son, I see it clearly,
it's the gray sheen of the old willows."

ERLKING (*loving, then insistent*)

62 3:00

"Ich liebe dich, mich reizt deine schöne Gestalt,
und bist du nicht willig, so brauch' ich Gewalt."

"I love you, your beautiful form delights me!
And if you're not willing, then I'll use force."

SON (*high range, terrified*)

63 3:12

"Mein Vater, mein Vater, jetzt fasst er mich an!
Erlkönig hat mir ein Leids gethan!"

"My father, my father, now he's grasping me!
The Erlking has hurt me!"

Listening Guide continues

NARRATOR (*middle register, speechlike*)

64 3:26

Dem Vater grauset's, er reitet geschwind,	The father shudders, he rides swiftly,
er hält in Armen das ächzende Kind,	he holds the moaning child in his arms;
erreicht den Hof mit Müh und Noth:	with effort and urgency he reaches the courtyard:
in seinen Armen das Kind war todt.	in his arms the child was dead.

Melody of son's dissonant outcry on "My father, my father":

Mein   Va - ter,   mein   Va - ter,

44

Robert Schumann and the Song Cycle

"Music is to me the perfect expression of the soul."

KEY POINTS

Ⓢ **StudySpace** online at www.wwnorton.com/enjoy

○ The German composer Robert Schumann is known for his symphonies, piano music, chamber music, and Lieder; he also established an important literary magazine for music criticism.

○ Many of Schumann's Lieder were written during his engagement to the pianist and composer Clara Wieck. These include *A Poet's Love*, a song cycle set to the poetry of Heinrich Heine.

The turbulence of German Romanticism, its fantasy and subjective emotion, found its voice in Robert Schumann. His music is German to the core yet transcends national styles.

Ⓢ **Robert Schumann**

His Life

Robert Schumann (1810–1856) was born in Zwickau, a town in southeastern Germany, the son of a bookseller whose love of literature was passed on to the boy. At his mother's insistence, he studied law, first at the University of Leipzig, then at Heidelberg. More and more he surrendered to his passion for music; it was his ambition to become a pianist. At last he won his mother's consent and returned to Leipzig to study with Friedrich Wieck, one of the foremost teachers of the day.

The young man practiced intensively to make up for his late start. Unfortunately, physical difficulties with the fingers of his right hand ended his hopes as a pianist. He then turned his interest to composing, and in a burst of creative energy produced, while still in his twenties, his most important works for piano. At the same time, Schumann's literary talent found expression in an important publication he established, *Neue Zeitschrift für Musik* (The New Journal for Music); under his direction, this became one of the leading journals of music criticism in Europe.

The hectic quality of the 1830s, rife with political uprisings across Europe, was intensified by Schumann's courtship of the gifted pianist and composer Clara Wieck (see Chapter 47), daughter of his teacher Friedrich. When Schumann first came to study with her father, Clara was an eleven-year-old prodigy. Five years later, Robert realized he loved her, but her father opposed their marriage with a vehemence that bordered on the psychopathic. At length, the couple ultimately appealed to the courts. The marriage took place in 1840, when Clara was twenty-one and Robert thirty. This was his "year of song," when he produced over a hundred of the Lieder that represent his lyric gift at its purest.

Marriage to Clara

The two musicians settled in Leipzig, pursuing their careers side by side. Clara became the foremost interpreter of Robert's piano works and, in the ensuing decade, contributed substantially to the spread of his fame. Yet her devotion could not ward off Robert's increasing withdrawal from the world. His moodiness and nervous exhaustion culminated, in 1844, in a severe breakdown. The couple moved to Dresden, where Robert seemed to recover, but then the periods of depression returned even more frequently. In 1850, Schumann was appointed music director at Düsseldorf, but he was ill-suited for public life and was forced to relinquish the post.

Schumann continued to experience auditory hallucinations. One story tells of him rising in the middle of the night to write down a theme that he imagined had been brought him by the spirits of Schubert and Mendelssohn. It was his last melody. A week later, in a fit of depression, he threw himself into the Rhine River. He was rescued by fishermen, and Clara had no choice but to place him in a private asylum near Bonn. His psychotic behavior gave way to advanced dementia, brought on by syphilis, from which he died two years later at the age of forty-six.

Clara Schumann at age 31, with Robert. Anonymous lithograph (1850).

His Music

Schumann's music reveals him as a true Romantic. His piano pieces overflow with impassioned melody, novel changes of harmony, and driving rhythms. The titles are characteristic: *Fantasiestücke* (*Fantasy Pieces*), *Romances*, *Scenes from Childhood*. He often attached literary meanings to his music and was especially fond of cycles of short pieces connected by a literary theme or musical motto.

Piano pieces

Schumann's four symphonies are thoroughly Romantic in feeling. These works, especially the first and fourth, communicate a lyric freshness that has preserved their appeal.

Symphonies

Lieder

As a composer of Lieder, Schumann ranks second only to Schubert. A common theme in his songs is love, particularly from a woman's point of view. His favored poet was Heine, for whom he had an affinity like Schubert's for Goethe. Especially notable are his several song cycles, the best known of which are *A Poet's Love*, on poems by Heine, and *A Woman's Love and Life*, on poems by Chamisso.

A POET'S LOVE

Schumann wrote his great song cycle *A Poet's Love* (*Dichterliebe*) in 1840, his "year of song," at lightning-fast speed. For the texts, he chose sixteen poems from the *Lyriches Intermezzo* by Heinrich Heine, who wrote some of the Romantic era's most poignant works. The songs tell no real story; rather, they follow a psychological progression that spirals downward from the freshness of love through a growing disappointment to complete despair.

We will consider the first song in the cycle, "In the lovely month of May." The piano's introduction to the first strophe sets a wistful rather than joyous mood. Schumann's setting evokes the fragility of a new love through its harmonic meandering between two key centers and by its lack of a final resolution—we are left suspended, knowing there is more to this story in the song that follows. The two text strophes are framed by the piano's introduction, interlude and postlude, which provide a circular shape to the song. We might wonder if this Lied is really about a new relationship, or rather the longing and desire of a lost or unrequited love. Clearly, Schumann was able to achieve the desired unity of expression in this perfect fusion of dramatic and lyric elements (see Listening Guide 26).

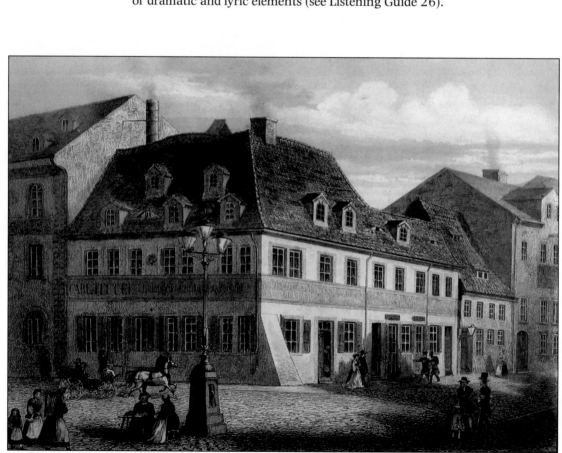

A 19th-century rendering of the house where Robert Schumann was born, in 1810, in Zwickau, Germany.

Listening Guide 26

eLG   2 (65–66)
5 (19–20)

Robert Schumann: "In the lovely month of May,"
from *A Poet's Love* (*Dichterliebe*), No. 1   (1:38)

DATE OF WORK:	1840
GENRE:	Lied, from a song cycle
FORM:	Strophic (2 strophes)
TEXT:	Lyric poem by Heinrich Heine
MEDIUM:	Solo voice and piano

WHAT TO LISTEN FOR: Melancholy mood of song.
Strophic form: 2 strophes treated identically.
Expressive piano part frames the strophes.
Harmonic meandering and lack of resolution of cadences.

		TEXT	TRANSLATION
65	0:00	Piano introduction.	
		Strophe 1	
	0:13	Im wunderschönen Monat Mai	In the lovely month of May,
		als alle Knospen sprangen,	as all the buds were blossoming,
		da ist in meinem Herzen	then in my heart
		die Liebe aufgegangen.	did love rise up.
66	0:39	Piano interlude.	
		Strophe 2	
	0:52	Im wunderschönen Monat Mai	In the lovely month of May,
		als alle Vögel sangen,	as all the birds were singing,
		da hab ich ihr gestanden	then did I confess to her
		mein Sehnen und Verlangen.	my longing and desire.
	1:18	Piano postlude.	

Opening of vocal line, suggesting minor key (F sharp):

Im wun - der-schö-nen Mo - nat   Mai,

Piano postlude, ending on dissonance with no final resolution of harmony:

The Nineteenth-Century Piano Piece

45

The Piano and Its Literature

*"I have called my piano pieces after the names of my favorite haunts
. . . they will form a delightful souvenir, a kind of second diary."*

—FANNY MENDELSSOHN HENSEL

KEY POINTS	Ⓢ **StudySpace** online at www.wwnorton.com/enjoy

○ In the Romantic era, the piano was both a popular instrument for home use and for virtuosos such as Liszt, Chopin, and the American pianist Louis Moreau Gottschalk.

○ Technical improvements to the nineteenth-century piano led to the development of the modern concert grand piano.

○ The short lyric piano piece, often with a fanciful title, was a favorite Romantic genre.

The rise in popularity of the piano helped shape the musical culture of the Romantic era. All over Europe and America, the instrument became a mainstay of music in the home (see CP10). It proved especially attractive to amateurs because, unlike the string and wind instruments, melody and harmony could be performed on one instrument together. Also popular was *four-hand piano music*, a chamber music form for two performers at one piano or occasionally at two; many works were arranged for this genre, which allowed for home and salon performances of orchestral and other large-ensemble music. The piano thus played a crucial role in the taste and experience of the new mass public.

Hardly less important was the rise of the virtuoso pianist. At first the performer was also the composer; Mozart and Beethoven introduced their own piano concertos to the public. With the developing concert industry, however, a class of virtuoso performers arose whose only function was to dazzle audiences by playing music composed by others.

The nineteenth century saw a series of crucial technical improvements that led to the development of the modern concert grand piano. Romantic composers' quest for greater power and dynamic range mandated increased string diameter and tension, which in turn required more bracing within the wooden piano case. Piano manufacturing eventually moved from the craft shop to the factory, allowing a huge increase in production at a significantly reduced cost. A standardized instrument was developed that had a metal frame supporting the increased string tension, as well as an improved mechanical action and extended range of notes—from five octaves to seven or more. At the Paris Exhibition of 1867, two American manufacturers took the top awards, among them Steinway, maker of some of today's finest pianos. By the early twentieth century, the piano had become a universal fixture in the homes of many middle-class and upper-class families.

This beautiful, ornate grand piano was made by Erard, c. 1840, for the Baroness of Kidderminster.

The Short Lyric Piano Piece

With its ability to project melodious and dramatic moods within a compact form, the short lyric piano piece was the equivalent to the song. Composers adopted new and sometimes fanciful terms for such works. Some titles—"Prelude," "Intermezzo" (interlude), "Impromptu" (on the spur of the moment), and "Nocturne" (a night piece), for example—suggest free, almost improvisational forms. Many composers turned to dance music and produced keyboard versions of the Polish mazurka and polonaise, the Viennese waltz, and the lively scherzo. Composers sometimes chose more descriptive titles, such as *Wild Hunt, The Little Bell,* and *Forest Murmurs* (all by Franz Liszt), and *The Banjo* by American composer Gottschalk (see p. 261).

The nineteenth-century masters of the short piano piece—Schubert, Chopin, Liszt, Felix Mendelssohn. Fanny Mendelssohn Hensel, Robert and Clara Schumann, and Brahms—showed inexhaustible ingenuity in exploring the technical resources of the instrument and its potential for expression.

CD iMusic

Mendelssohn: *Spring Song,* Op. 62, No. 6

German artist **Ludwig Richter** (1802–1884) portrays a typical family music-making scene in his woodcut *Hausmusik* (1851).

46

Chopin and Piano Music

"My life [is] an episode without a beginning and with a sad end."

- Frédéric Chopin dedicated his entire compositional output to the piano; he is said to have originated the modern piano style.
- Chopin lived and worked in Paris among the leading intellectuals and artists of France.

- His output includes études—highly virtuosic and technical study pieces—meditative nocturnes, preludes, and dances (including Polish mazurkas and polonaises), as well as sonatas and concertos for piano.

(S) **Frédéric Chopin**

Frédéric François Chopin (1810–1849) has been called the "poet of the piano." His music, rooted in the heart of Romanticism, made this era the piano's golden age.

His Life

Chopin, considered the national composer of Poland, was half French. His father emigrated to Warsaw, where he married a lady-in-waiting to a countess and taught French to the sons of the nobility. Frédéric, who proved to be musically gifted as a child, was educated at the newly founded Conservatory of Warsaw. At the age of twenty-one, he left for Paris, where he spent the rest of his career. Paris in the 1830s was the center of the new Romanticism. The circle in which Chopin moved included musicians such as Liszt and Berlioz, and literary figures such as Victor Hugo, George Sand, and Alexandre Dumas *père*. The poet Heinrich Heine became his friend as did the painter Eugène Delacroix (see p. 231). A man ruled by his emotions, Chopin was profoundly influenced by these leading intellectuals of France.

Through the virtuoso pianist Liszt, Chopin met Aurore Dudevant, "the lady with the somber eye," known to the world as the novelist George Sand. She was thirty-four, he twenty-eight when their famous friendship began. Madame Sand was brilliant and domineering; her need to dominate found its counterpart in Chopin's need to be ruled. She left a memorable account of the composer at work:

George Sand (Aurore Dudevant)

> His creative power was spontaneous, miraculous. It came to him without effort or warning. . . . But then began the most heartrending labor I have ever witnessed. It was a series of attempts, of fits of irresolution and impatience to recover certain details. He would shut himself in his room for days, pacing up and down, breaking his pens, repeating and modifying one bar a hundred times.

For the next eight years, Chopin spent his summers at Sand's estate at Nohant, where she entertained many of France's prominent artists and writers. These were productive years for the composer, although his health grew progressively worse and his relationship with Sand ran its course from love to conflict, jealousy, and hostility. They finally parted in bitterness.

Chopin died of tuberculosis in Paris at the age of thirty-nine. Thousands joined together at his funeral to pay him homage. The artistic world bid its farewell to the strains of the composer's own funeral march, from his Piano Sonata in B-flat minor.

His Music

Chopin was one of the most original artists of the nineteenth century. His style was entirely his own; there is no mistaking it for any other. He was the only master of the first rank whose entire creative life revolved around the piano, and he is credited with originating the modern piano style.

Modern piano style

Chopin's works are central to the pianist's standard repertory. The nocturnes—night songs, as the name implies—are melancholic and meditative. The preludes are visionary fragments; some are only a page in length, several consist of two or three lines. In the études, which crown the literature of the study piece, Chopin's piano technique is transformed into poetry. The impromptus are fanciful and capricious, and the waltzes capture the brilliance and coquetry of the salon. The mazurkas, derived from a Polish peasant dance, evoke the idealized landscape of his youth, and the polonaises revive the stately processional dance in which Poland's nobles hailed their kings.

Small-scale works

Among his larger forms are the four ballades, epic works of spacious proportions. The Sonatas in B minor and in B-flat minor are thoroughly Romantic in spirit, as are the two piano concertos.

Chopin giving a piano lesson to the opera singer Pauline Viardot. A caricature (1844) by **Maurice Sand.**

POLONAISE IN A MAJOR, OP. 40, NO. 1 (*MILITARY*)

One of Chopin's most heroic works is the *Military* Polonaise in A major; its insistent triple-meter rhythm derives from the traditional dance as does its sectional form, which resembles minuet-and-trio structure (see Listening Guide 27, p. 254). Liszt recognized the military splendor of the polonaise, claiming, "this dance is designed above all to draw attention to the men and to gain admiration for their beauty, their fine arts, their martial and courteous appearance." Bold rhythmic chords and widely displaced octaves played in both hands eventually give way to a more lyrical trio theme, under which the unrelenting rhythm continues and builds to a *fortissimo* climax, leading to a return of the opening stately march. This brilliant piano writing demands a high level of technique and a spirited, gutsy performance.

Chopin's music also depends on **tempo rubato**—the "robbed time," or "borrowed time," that is so characteristic of Romantic style. This performance style allows certain liberties be taken with the rhythm without upsetting the basic beat. The way Chopin taught it, the accompaniment—usually the left hand—was played in strict time, while above it the right-hand melody might hesitate a little here or hurry forward there. In either case, the borrowing had to be repaid before the end of the phrase. Rubato remains an essential ingredient of Chopin's style.

IN HIS OWN WORDS

When asked "what is rubato," Chopin replied: "My left hand, it is the master of the choir; my right, the singer."

Chopin and the Salon: From Paris to the Pacific

Although Chopin's music is central to the modern concert pianist's repertory—and thus a mainstay of today's concert hall performance—he composed for the more intimate atmosphere of the salon, or drawing room (the word derives from the French *salle*, or room). The salon was conceived in Paris during the first half of the nineteenth century as a gathering of musicians, artists, and intellectuals who shared similar interests and tastes, and was hosted by a wealthy aristocrat, often a woman.

It was also a place where professional performers and artists could mingle freely with amateurs. But Chopin, who arrived in Paris with "but one ducat in my pocket," found that although the wealthy clientele were eager to be entertained by him—and receive lessons from him as well—they were less inclined to accept him as an equal. He soon won over the hearts and purses of cosmopolitan Parisian circles with his music. It was at one of these events—a party hosted by the Countess d'Agoult, the mistress of the composer Franz Liszt—that Chopin met his future mistress, the author George Sand (whose real name was Baroness Aurore Dudevant; see p. 250).

As in the European salon, the piano became a focal point in gatherings of friends and families in nineteenth-century America. An English writer noted that "in cities and villages, from one extremity of the union to the other, wherever there is a good house . . . the ringing of pianos is almost as universal a sound as the domestic hum of life within." He swore that there

A Parisian salon concert depicted by **James Tissot** (1836–1902).

were "ten pianofortes for every American town or village to one in England."

In imitation of the great salons of Europe, American socialites opened their homes to musical and artistic gatherings. In Boston alone, there were five famous salons—all hosted by prominent women. These included the poet Amy Lowell; the painter Sara Choate Sears; two composers—Clara Kathleen Rogers and Amy Beach (see p. 290); and the patroness Isabella Stewart Gardiner. This last salon can be set apart from the others because it was not just a place where people chatted to background music but also a venue with near-perfect acoustics for performances. Gardiner sponsored some of the most renowned visiting artists in her salon. "I felt last night as though I were in a Hans [Christian] Anderson fairy tale," one visitor mused, "ready to go on a flying carpet at any moment."

Chopin's fame spread quickly in the Americas; women's music clubs arose in towns and cities across the United States as the principal venue for concert life, and especially piano performances, and his music soon reached Latin America as well. The first documented performance of Chopin's works was in Mexico City in 1854, and his music was published a few years later in Brazil (1859). With the publication of a biography of Chopin in 1895 by a Mexican writer, his place in the concert repertory of that country was secured.

The culture of the drawing-room piano even reached as far as Australia and New Zealand. One book, colorfully entitled *In the Land of Kangaroos and Gold Mines*, published in 1890, claimed that some 700,000 pianos had made their way into city and country houses in Australia, and even into simple huts.

Holly Hunter and Anna Paquin in the film *The Piano*, set in New Zealand in the 19th century.

This description evokes images of Jane Campion's art film *The Piano* (1993), in which a Victorian woman of Scottish heritage traveled, with her daughter and beloved piano, to New Zealand to join in an arranged marriage. In this haunting film, the protagonist, who has not spoken since the age of six, uses the piano as her means of expression, and among her favorite works are Chopin's exquisite preludes.

Terms to Note

salon
patroness

Chopin: Suggested Listening

Polonaise, Op. 40, No. 1 (*Military*)
Prelude in E minor, Op. 28, No. 4
Revolutionary Etude, Op. 10, No. 12
Waltz in D-flat major, Op. 64, No. 1 (*Minute*)

Listening Guide 27

eLG 2 (67–71) 5 (23–27)

Chopin: Polonaise in A major, Op. 40, No. 1 (*Military*) (5:29)

DATE OF WORK:	1838
FORM:	Ternary dance form (**A-B-A′**), with internal repeats: **A (a-a b-a b-a)–B** trio (**c-c′-c-c′ d-c-c′ d-c-c′)–A′ (a-b-a)**
MEDIUM:	Solo piano
TEMPO:	Allegro con brio

WHAT TO LISTEN FOR: 3-part dance form, with short repeated sections and variations (**c′**).
Use of traditional polonaise rhythm
Brilliant pianistic writing in martial style.
Widely displaced voicing of chords between hands.
More lyrical trio (**B**), played with rubato.

A section, key of A major.

67 0:00 Dotted-rhythm, martial theme, with triplet passagework (8 measures = **a**):

0:17 Repeated 8 measures (**a**).

68 0:33 Alternation of short dotted motive and triplet figure (8 measures = **b**),
followed by repeat of opening (**a** = 8 measures).

1:09 Repetition of small sections **b** + **a**.

B section (trio), key of D major

69 1:44 Disjunct, descending right-hand melody, accompanied by polonaise rhythm (**c + c′**):

2:17 Repeated opening section of trio (**c + c′**).

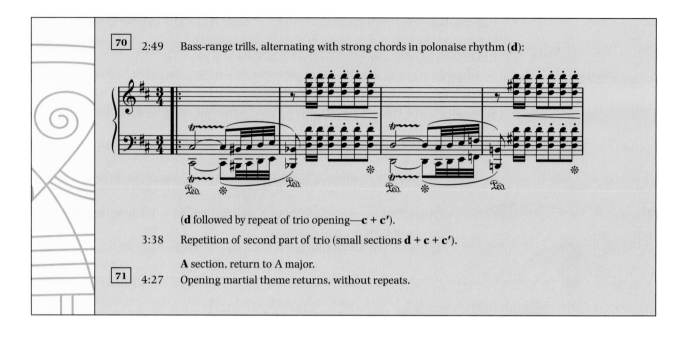

70   2:49   Bass-range trills, alternating with strong chords in polonaise rhythm (**d**):

(**d** followed by repeat of trio opening—**c** + **c′**).

3:38   Repetition of second part of trio (small sections **d** + **c** + **c′**).

A section, return to A major.
71   4:27   Opening martial theme returns, without repeats.

47

Clara Schumann: Pianist and Composer

"The practice of [music] is . . . a great part of my inner self.
To me, it is the very air I breathe."

○ Clara Wieck Schumann was a virtuoso pianist, composer, and leading interpreter of the music of Brahms, Chopin, and Robert Schumann, her husband.

○ She is known for her songs, piano music, and chamber music.

○ Her works are technically difficult and also deeply introspective.

Clara Schumann (1819–1896) is universally regarded as one of the most distinguished musicians of the nineteenth century. She was admired throughout Europe as a leading pianist of the era, but the world in which she lived was not prepared to acknowledge that a woman could be an outstanding composer. Hence, her considerable creative gifts were not recognized or encouraged during her lifetime.

Her Life

Clara Schumann's close association with two great composers—her husband, Robert Schumann (see Chapter 44), and her lifelong friend, Johannes Brahms

(see Chapter 53)—put her at the center of musical life. She studied piano from age five, made her first public appearance as a concert artist in Leipzig at age nine, and undertook her first extended concert tour several years later.

Marriage to Robert

A great crisis in her life came with the violent opposition of Friedrich Wieck, her father and teacher, to her marrying Robert Schumann, but she had the courage to defy him. She then faced the problems of a woman torn between the demands of an exacting career and her responsibilities as a wife and mother. She and Robert had seven children (an eighth died in infancy), yet she managed throughout those years to maintain her position as one of the outstanding concert artists of Europe. Liszt admired her playing for its "complete technical mastery, depth, and sincerity of feeling." She gave first performances of all Robert's important works, and became well known as a leading interpreter of both Brahms and Chopin.

Although Clara enjoyed a loving relationship with her husband, life became increasingly difficult. Robert suffered from shifting moods and frequent depressions that eventually led to a complete breakdown. After his death, she concertized in order to support herself and her children. Now she in turn was sustained by Brahms's devotion.

Clara had the talent, training, and background that many composers would envy, but from the beginning of her career she accepted the nineteenth-century attitude toward women composers. At twenty, she confided to her diary, "I once believed that I possessed creative talent, but I have given up this idea; a woman must not desire to compose—there has never yet been one able to do it. Should I expect to be the one? To believe this would be arrogant, something that my father once, in former days, induced me to do." (See CP 13, on women and music.)

Robert was sympathetic to her creativity, but he also accepted the prevailing attitudes. "Clara has composed a series of small pieces," he wrote in their joint diary, "which show a musical and tender ingenuity such as she never attained before. But to have children, and a husband who is always living in the realm of imagination, does not go together with composing. She cannot work at it regularly, and I am often disturbed to think how many profound ideas are lost because she cannot work them out."

Clara Schumann gave her last public concert at the age of seventy-two and succumbed to a stroke five years later, in 1896. Her dying wish was to hear her husband's music once more.

 **Clara Wieck Schumann**, at age 16, one year before she wrote her collection *Music for an Evening Entertainment*, Op. 6.

Her Music

Clara's output includes many small, intimate works such as songs and piano pieces. There are also two large-scale works, a piano concerto, and a trio for piano and strings; a number of virtuoso piano pieces; and, as a gesture of homage to her husband, a set of *Variations on a Theme by Robert Schumann*. While her early works leaned toward technical display, which showed off her phenomenal talent, the later ones were more serious and introspective, typical of the era in which she lived.

NOCTURNE, FROM *MUSIC FOR AN EVENING ENTERTAINMENT*

In 1836, Clara published a collection of six character pieces entitled *Music for an Evening Entertainment* (*Soirées musicales*, Op. 6), works that she had already performed with great success for Parisian audiences, and for the master Chopin. Robert Schumann, already smitten with the young woman, reviewed this collection; he claimed the works drew on "a wealth of unconventional resources" and had "an ability to entangle the secret more deeply twisting threads and then to unravel them." These remarks aptly describe the Nocturne from the set, which, rather than following the simple lyrical model established by Irish composer John Field, is rich in its harmonic invention and use of dissonance, in its innovative form, and in its complex rhythmic treatment. From the start, a meditative mood is unsettling by the unpredictability of melodic movement and the instability of the underlying harmonies. A contrasting middle section in D minor features an arched, dotted-rhythm melody set against lilting block chords; this inclusion of a distinctly different **B** section follows Chopin's innovation to the genre. The return of the opening melody is even more rapturous than the opening in its wide-ranging lines and rich harmonies (see Listening Guide 28).

Robert paid musical homage to his beloved Clara by making reference to the opening of her Nocturne in one of his own piano works, and he professed his admiration in a letter, describing this exquisite miniature as her "most precious" work.

> ### IN HER OWN WORDS
>
> *Composing gives me great pleasure . . . there is nothing that surpasses the joy of creation, if only because through it one wins hours of self-forgetfulness, when one lives in a world of sound.*

Listening Guide 28

eLG 3 (1–4)
5 (38–41)

Clara Wieck Schumann: Nocturne, from *Music for an Evening Entertainment (Soirées musicales)*, Op. 6

(4:39)

DATE OF WORK:	1835–36
COLLECTION:	6 miniature character pieces (toccatina, nocturne, polonaise, ballade, and 2 mazurkas)
FORM:	Ternary (**A-B-A'** + coda)
MEDIUM:	Solo piano
TEMPO:	Andante con moto
KEY:	F major

WHAT TO LISTEN FOR:
Right-hand melody throughout, featuring various ornamental notes, against left-hand accompaniment.
Expressive rhythmic devices, including rubato.
Rhythmic complexities, featuring note groupings of 3, 8, 9, and 11 in melody set against meter of 6/8.
Overall 3-part structure with coda.
Many chromatic pitches in melody and in harmonic accompaniment.
Middle section more "square," with block-chord accompaniment against dotted melody.

Listening Guide continues

A section

1 0:00 Left hand sets up broken-chord accompaniment.

0:06 Dreamy, expressive melody, featuring embellishments and use of rubato.

0:53 Return to opening melodic idea, with faster moving line; rhythmic and chromatic elaborations, in expanded range; slows to closing.

Elaborated melody from **A** section:

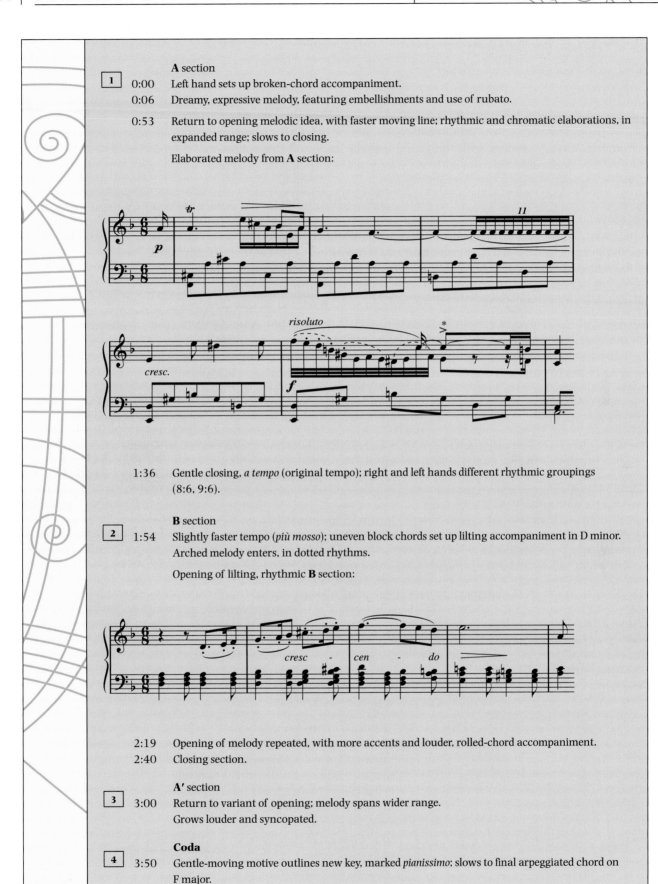

1:36 Gentle closing, *a tempo* (original tempo); right and left hands different rhythmic groupings (8:6, 9:6).

B section

2 1:54 Slightly faster tempo (*più mosso*); uneven block chords set up lilting accompaniment in D minor. Arched melody enters, in dotted rhythms.

Opening of lilting, rhythmic **B** section:

2:19 Opening of melody repeated, with more accents and louder, rolled-chord accompaniment.

2:40 Closing section.

A' section

3 3:00 Return to variant of opening; melody spans wider range.

Grows louder and syncopated.

Coda

4 3:50 Gentle-moving motive outlines new key, marked *pianissimo*; slows to final arpeggiated chord on F major.

48

Louis Gottschalk and Piano Music in America

"Syncopation is in the soul of every true American."
—IRVING BERLIN

○ The pianist Louis Moreau Gottschalk was the first internationally acclaimed American composer of classical music.

○ Gottschalk's music draws inspiration from African-American, Creole, and Latin American folk songs

and rhythms, and often quotes familiar tunes, particularly from Stephen Foster songs.

○ His piano work *The Banjo* evokes authentic banjo-playing styles the young Gottschalk heard in New Orleans' Congo Square.

One of the most original American spirits was the virtuoso pianist and composer Louis Moreau Gottschalk (1829–1869). A native of New Orleans who traveled widely, he became a master at assimilating traditional music into his virtuoso piano compositions, thereby blurring the lines between popular and classical music. He was the first American to achieve international fame as a classical composer.

⑤ **Louis Moreau Gottschalk**

His Life

The son of an English-born Jewish father and a French-Creole mother (her family escaped Haiti during the 1790s rebellion), Gottschalk grew up hearing the ethnically diverse music that filled the streets of New Orleans. He had an affinity for the Afro-Caribbean folk music that was part of his own heritage, and as a young child he listened fervently to the West Indian and African-American dances and songs performed at Congo Square.

Gottschalk was a child prodigy on the piano, able to recall French opera tunes he had heard and to create variations on them. By the time he was seven, he was skilled enough to take over his teacher's duties on organ at Mass, and at age eleven, he made his formal debut on piano. His father sent him, against his mother's wishes, to study in Paris, where he charmed the likes of Chopin and Berlioz with his pianistic talents and highly original compositions. Although his initial application for an audition at the Paris Conservatory was denied (the director believed that all Americans were "barbarians"), Gottschalk was soon hailed as the spokesperson for the music of the New World—some fifty years in advance of a challenge issued by Antonín Dvořák to find an authentic American voice (see p. 280).

Concert tours

Gottschalk drew rave reviews for his recitals in Europe—Berlioz claimed that "the boldness, the brilliancy, and the originality of his playing at once dazzles and astonishes." Despite his success abroad, Gottschalk returned to the United States in 1853 and concertized extensively, bringing classical music to the heartlands.

Gottshalk conducting a "monster concert." Lithograph (1862).

At one of my concerts [my friend] was seated in front of two ladies who consoled themselves for the total absence of "tunes" by seeing that, in the third part, I must play Home, Sweet Home *with variations. They waited patiently. The concert went on,* Home, Sweet Home *was encored, which did not prevent the ladies from saying: "But when is he going to play* Home, Sweet Home?"

He turned his interest to American tastes in music and, writing in a new "Western" idiom, produced his well-known *Tournament Galop*. In 1857, he sailed for Cuba, where he wrote operas and conducted an operatic theater in Havana. He also traveled to Puerto Rico and other Caribbean islands, absorbing their music and rhythms and producing some of his finest piano works. Gottschalk's diary describes his itinerant spirit: "I have wandered at random, yielding myself up indolently to the caprice of Fortune, giving a concert where I happened to find a piano."

With the onset of the Civil War in 1862, Gottschalk—a staunch Unionist—returned to the United States to perform in support of the Northern army, at which time he wrote *Union*, an extended paraphrase on various national tunes (including *The Star-Spangled Banner, Yankee Doodle*, and *Hail, Columbia!*). Over the next three years, he traveled thousands of miles, promoting both classical and popular music as well as education. When he reached California in 1865, he estimated he had given 1,100 recitals in America alone. While in northern California, he was embroiled in a scandal surrounding a female seminary student; he escaped aboard a steamer bound for Panama, never to return to the United States. Gottschalk spent his last four years in South America, where he promoted classical music and the public education system in general. One letter he sent home noted: "My fantasy on the national anthem of Brazil . . . pleased the emperor and tickled the national pride of my public. Every time I appear I must play it." While organizing "monster" concerts in Rio de Janeiro

Solo piano pieces   that involved some 650 musicians, Gottschalk contracted malaria and died in Brazil in December 1869, from an overdose of quinine used to treat the disease.

His Music

Although Gottschalk wrote a handful of operas, songs, and symphonic works, he is remembered today almost exclusively for his solo piano music. His early colorful works include *La Bamboula* (a Negro dance popular before the Civil War), *Creole*

Eyes, and *The Banjo* (see below). He exploited all manner of dance forms, including polkas, galops, and mazurkas, as well as various song forms from South America and the Caribbean. His highly syncopated music has been said to anticipate ragtime, an African-American piano style that peaked in popularity around 1900 (see p. 379). Several of his most popular compositions were in a melancholy vein; audiences demanded he repeat *The Last Hope* at every concert, and *The Dying Poet* became a cliché in the silent movie theater of the early twentieth century.

Gottschalk's music has enjoyed a recent surge in popularity since pianists and audiences have rediscovered his lively, folk-rooted melodies and rhythms. His first symphony, entitled *A Night in the Tropics*, is forward looking in its use of improvised Afro-Cuban percussion. His music is all the more accessible by his frequent quotations of familiar tunes, especially those of Stephen Foster. His very patriotic *Union* presents national airs simultaneously, forecasting the collage techniques used by another American pioneer, Charles Ives.

The Banjo Player (1856) by American painter **William Sydney Mount** underscores the role of this instrument in 19th-century minstrelsy.

THE BANJO

This jaunty piano work features highly syncopated rhythms and jagged melodic lines that simulate banjo strumming and picking techniques. The banjo was the most popular African-American instrument at the time, and Gottschalk certainly heard it played in his native New Orleans. *The Banjo*, subtitled *Grotesque Fantasy: An American Sketch*, freely presents two varied sections, the first largely rhythmic, set in the low range of the piano, and the second a high-range, banjo-style tune. The coda sounds the familiar strains of Stephen Foster's *Camptown Races* and evokes the spiritual *Roll, Jordan, Roll* as well. One of his most popular compositions, this brilliant, virtuosic work illustrates Gottschalk's innovative techniques and ideas as well as his dazzling originality (see Listening Guide 29).

Listening Guide 29	eLG	3 (5–11) 5 (42–48)

Gottschalk: *The Banjo* (*Le banjo: Fantasie grotesque*)	(3:11)
DATE OF WORK: 1854–55	
GENRE: Fantasy	
FORM: Five-part form (**A-B-A-B-A**) and coda	
MEDIUM: Solo piano	

Listening Guide continues

WHAT TO LISTEN FOR: Highly syncopated rhythms; regular 4-measure phrases.
Imitation of banjo strumming and picking.
Bass-line melodies, alternating with high-range, embellished tunes.
Alternation of two sections (**A + B**), plus coda.
Suggestion of *Camptown Races* tune in coda.

5 0:00 Brief, syncopated introduction, in octaves in both hands (8 measures).

A section
6 0:07 Rhythmic idea, in bass range of piano; repeated in 4-measure phrases; decorated with flourishes:

0:30 Simple, rocking-bass melody heard, and repeated.

B section
7 0:44 Fast-paced, high-range melody, marked brilliant; syncopated against regular bass:

4-note descending pattern repeated, then glissando.

A section
8 1:07 Return to **A** section.
1:27 Slow, rocking-bass melody.

B section
9 1:40 Fast, high-range melody returns.
4-note descending idea, followed by glissando.

A section
10 2:03 Opening rhythmic idea.
2:14 Rocking-bass melody.

Coda
11 2:24 *Camptown Races* tune heard, in simplified rhythm.
2:38 Tune heard an octave higher and faster.
Speed increases to closing high flourish, then final *fortissimo* chord.

Comparison of tune heard in coda with *Camptown Races* by Stephen Foster: **CD iMusic**

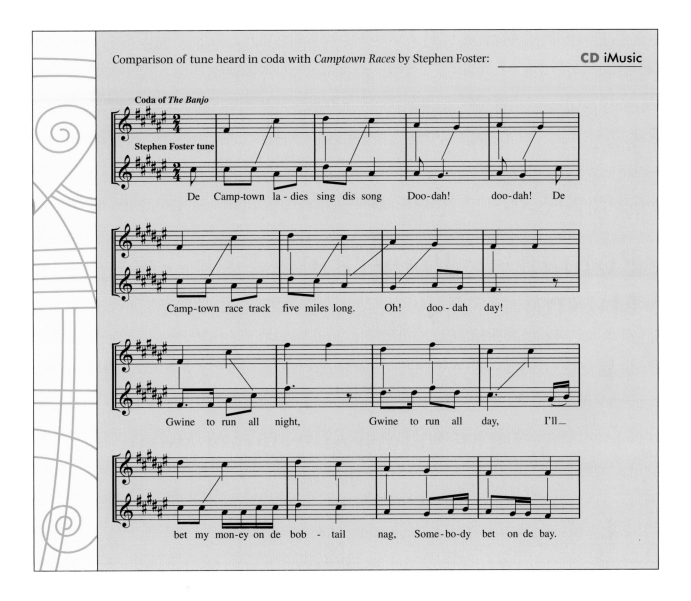

Coda of *The Banjo*

Stephen Foster tune

De Camp-town la - dies sing dis song Doo-dah! doo-dah! De

Camp-town race track five miles long. Oh! doo - dah day!

Gwine to run all night, Gwine to run all day, I'll—

bet my mon-ey on de bob - tail nag, Some-bo-dy bet on de bay.

Romantic Program Music

49

The Nature of Program Music

*"The painter turns a poem into a painting;
the musician sets a picture to music."*

—ROBERT SCHUMANN

○ Romantic composers cultivated *program music*—
instrumental music with a literary or pictorial
association supplied by the composer—over
absolute music.

○ The four main types of program music include the
concert overture, *incidental music* to a play, the
program symphony (a multimovement work), and
the *symphonic poem* (a one-movement work).

IN HIS OWN WORDS

*I have grown accustomed to
composing in our garden . . .
today or tomorrow I am
going to dream there the*
Midsummer Night's
Dream.

—*FELIX MENDELSSOHN*

Music often evokes specific visual images or ideas. When these associations are
provided by the composer, they are known as *program music*, or instrumental
music that has literary or pictorial associations. A title such as *King Lear* (by
Berlioz), for example, suggests specific characters and events, while the title *Pièces
fugitives* (*Fleeting Pieces*, by Clara Schumann) merely labels the mood or character
of the work. Program music, we saw earlier, is distinguished from *absolute*, or
pure, music, which consists of musical patterns that have no literary or pictorial
meanings.

Program music was especially important during the nineteenth century, when
musicians became sharply conscious of the connection between their art and the
world around them. Adding a programmatic title brought music closer to poetry and
painting, and helped composers relate their own work to the moral and political
issues of their time.

Varieties of Program Music

One type of program music came out of the opera house, where the overture was a rousing orchestral piece in one movement designed to serve as an introduction to an opera (or a play). Many operatic overtures became popular as separate concert pieces which, in turn, pointed the way to a new type of overture not associated with an opera: a single-movement concert piece for orchestra based on a literary idea, such as Tchaikovsky's *Romeo and Juliet*. This ***concert overture*** might evoke a land- or seascape or embody a literary or patriotic idea.

The concert overture

Another type of program music, ***incidental music***, usually consists of an overture and a series of pieces performed between the acts of a play and during important scenes. The most successful pieces of incidental music were arranged into suites (such as Mendelssohn's music for Shakespeare's *A Midsummer Night's Dream*). Incidental music is still important today, in the form of film music and background music for television.

Incidental music

The passion for program music was so strong that it invaded the symphony, usually a form of absolute music. Thus the ***program symphony***, a multimovement orchestral work came into being. Important examples are the program symphonies of Berlioz—including *Symphonie fantastique*, which we will study—and Liszt's *Faust* and *Dante* Symphonies.

Program symphony

Eventually, composers felt the need for a large form of orchestral music that would serve the Romantic era as the symphony had served the Classical. Franz Liszt created the symphonic poem (he first used the term in 1848), the nineteenth century's most original contribution to large forms.

Symphonic poem

A ***symphonic poem*** is program music for orchestra, in one movement, with contrasting sections to develop a poetic idea, suggest a scene, or create a mood. It differs from the concert overture, which usually retains one of the traditional Classical

Shakespeare's play *A Midsummer Night's Dream* inspired Felix Mendelssohn's incidental music as well as this fanciful canvas by **Henry Fuseli**, *Titania and Bottom* (c. 1790).

Like Liszt's *Faust* Symphony and Berlioz's *Damnation of Faust*, this painting of *Mephistopheles in Faust's Study* by **Eugène Delacroix** (1798–1863) draws on Goethe's retelling of the Faust legend.

forms, by having a much freer structure. The symphonic poem (also called *tone poem*) gave composers the flexibility they needed for a big single-movement form. It became the most widely used type of orchestral program music through the second half of the century. We will study two examples: *The Moldau* by the Bohemian composer Bedřich Smetana, and *Prelude to "The Afternoon of a Faun"* by Claude Debussy.

Program music is one of the most striking manifestations of nineteenth-century Romanticism. This new, descriptive genre impelled composers to express specific feelings; it proclaimed the direct relationship between music and life.

50

Berlioz and the Program Symphony

"To render my works properly requires a combination of extreme precision and irresistible verve, a regulated vehemence, a dreamy tenderness, and an almost morbid melancholy."

KEY POINTS

🅢 **StudySpace** online at www.wwnorton.com/enjoy

○ French composer and conductor Hector Berlioz wrote *Symphonie fantastique*, a five-movement program symphony, while living in Italy.

○ The program for the work drew on his personal life and on his infatuation and courtship with the actress Harriet Smithson.

○ Berlioz was an innovative writer for orchestra, introducing new colors and instrumental techniques to the ensemble.

○ The five movements of *Symphonie fantastique* are unified by a recurring theme (*idée fixe*) representing his beloved.

The flamboyance of Victor Hugo's poetry and the dramatic intensity of Eugène Delacroix's painting (see above) found their musical counterpart in the works of Hector Berlioz, whose music is intense, bold, and passionate. He was the first great proponent of musical Romanticism in France.

His Life

Hector Berlioz (1803–1869) was born in France in a small town near Grenoble. His father, a well-to-do physician, expected the boy to follow in his footsteps, and at eighteen Hector was sent away to attend medical school in Paris. The conservatory and the opera, however, intrigued Berlioz much more than the dissecting room. The following year, the youth made a decision that horrified his upper-middle-class family: he gave up medicine for music.

The Romantic revolution was brewing in Paris, and Berlioz, along with Hugo and Delacroix, found himself in the camp of "young France." Having been cut off by his parents, he gave music lessons and sang in a theater chorus to make ends meet. He became a huge fan of Beethoven and of Shakespeare, to whose plays he was introduced by a visiting English troupe. Berlioz fell madly in love with an actress in this troupe, whose portrayals of Ophelia and Juliet excited the admiration of the Parisians. In his *Memoirs*, which read like a Romantic novel, he describes his infatuation with Harriet Smithson: "I became obsessed by an intense, overpowering sense of sadness. I could not sleep, I could not work, and I spent my time wandering aimlessly about Paris and its environs."

Ⓢ **Hector Berlioz**

In 1830, Berlioz was awarded the coveted Prix de Rome, which gave him an opportunity to live and work in Italy. That same year he composed the *Symphonie fantastique*, his most celebrated work. After returning from Rome, he commenced a hectic courtship of Harriet Smithson. There were strenuous objections from both their families, and violent scenes, during one of which the excitable Hector attempted suicide. But he recovered, and the two were married.

Once the unattainable ideal had become a reality, Berlioz's passion cooled. It was Shakespeare he had loved rather than Harriet, and in time he sought the ideal elsewhere. All the same, the first years of his marriage were the most fruitful of his life. By age forty, he had produced most of his most famous works.

In the later part of his life, Berlioz conducted his music in nearly all the capitals of Europe. Paris, however, resisted him to the end. For his last major work, the opera *Béatrice et Bénédict*, he wrote his own libretto after Shakespeare's *Much Ado About Nothing* (see CP 14 on Shakespeare and music). Following this effort, the embittered composer ceased writing music and died seven years later, at the age of sixty-six.

Berlioz's *idée fixe* was inspired by the Shakespearean actress, Harriet Smithson.

His Music

Berlioz was one of the boldest innovators of the nineteenth century. His approach to music was wholly individual, his sense of sound unique. From the start, he had an affinity in his orchestral music for the vividly dramatic or pictorial program.

His works show the favorite literary influences of the Romantic period. *The Damnation of Faust*, for example, was inspired by Goethe; *Harold in Italy* (a program symphony with viola solo) and *The Corsair* (an overture) are based on works by the English poet Lord Byron. Shakespeare is the source for his overture *King Lear*, for his opera *Béatrice et Bénédict* (see above), and for his dramatic symphony *Romeo and Juliet*.

Berlioz's most important opera, *The Trojans*, on his own libretto after the ancient Roman poet Virgil, has been successfully revived in recent years. His sacred vocal works, including the Requiem and the *Te Deum*, are conceived on a similarly grandiose scale.

Orchestration

It was in the domain of orchestration that Berlioz's genius asserted itself most fully. His daring originality in handling the instruments opened up a new world of Romantic sound. His scores, calling for the largest orchestra that had ever been used (see Table on p. 237), abound in novel effects and discoveries (for example, dividing the strings into eight parts and bowing with the wood of the bow) that would serve as models for all who came after him. Indeed, the conductor Felix Weingartner called Berlioz "the creator of the modern orchestra."

SYMPHONIE FANTASTIQUE

Berlioz wrote his best-known program symphony when he was twenty-seven years old, drawing its story from his personal life. His score describes "a young musician of morbid sensibility and ardent imagination, in . . . lovesick despair, [who] has poisoned himself with opium. The drug, too weak to kill, plunges him into a heavy sleep accompanied by strange visions. . . . The beloved one herself becomes for him a melody, a recurrent theme that haunts him everywhere."

Idée fixe

The symphony's recurrent theme, called an **idée fixe** (fixed idea), symbolizes the beloved; it becomes a musical thread unifying the five diverse movements, though its appearances are varied in harmony, rhythm, meter, tempo, dynamics, register, and instrumental color. (See Listening Guide 30 for theme and analysis.) These transformations take on literary as well as musical significance, as the following description by Berlioz shows.

The program

I. *Reveries, Passions.* "[The musician] remembers the weariness of soul, the indefinable yearning he knew before meeting his beloved. Then, the volcanic love with which she at once inspired him, his delirious suffering . . . his religious consolation." The Allegro section introduces a soaring melody—the fixed idea.

II. *A Ball.* "Amid the tumult and excitement of a brilliant ball he glimpses the loved one again." This dance movement is in ternary, or three-part, form. In the middle section, the fixed idea reappears in waltz time.

III. *Scene in the Fields.* "On a summer evening in the country he hears two shepherds piping. The pastoral duet, the quiet surroundings . . . all unite to fill his heart with a long absent calm. But she appears again. His heart contracts. Painful forebodings fill his soul." The composer said that his aim in this pastoral movement was to establish a mood "of sorrowful loneliness."

IV. *March to the Scaffold.* "He dreams that he has killed his beloved, that he has been condemned to die and is being led to the scaffold. . . . At the very end the fixed idea reappears for an instant, like a last thought of love interrupted by the fall of the blade."

V. *Dream of a Witches' Sabbath.* "He sees himself at a witches' sabbath surrounded by a host of fearsome spirits who have gathered for his funeral. Unearthly sounds, groans, shrieks of laughter. The melody of his beloved is heard, but it has lost its noble and reserved character. It has become a vulgar tune, trivial and grotesque. It is she who comes to the infernal orgy. A howl of joy greets her arrival. She joins the diabolical dance. Bells toll for the dead. A burlesque of the *Dies irae*. Dance of the witches. The dance and the *Dies irae* combined."

Fourth movement

The fourth movement, a diabolical march in minor, exemplifies the nineteenth-century love of the fantastic. The theme of the beloved appears at the very end, on the clarinet, and is cut off by a grim *fortissimo* chord. In this vivid portrayal of the story, we clearly hear the final blow of the blade, the head rolling, and the resound-

Francisco Goya (1746–1828) anticipated the passionate intensity of Berlioz's music in this painting of the *Witches' Sabbath*, c. 1819–23.

ing cheers of the crowd. In the final movement, Berlioz enters into a kind of infernal spirit that nourished a century of satanic operas, ballets, and symphonic poems. The mood is heightened with the introduction of the religious chant *Dies irae* (Day of Wrath) from the ancient music for the Dead.

    Berlioz's music has grandeur of line and gesture, and an abundance of vitality and invention. He is one of the major prophets of his era.

Fifth movement

Dies irae

Listening Guide 30

eLG 3 (12–17)
5 (49–54)

Berlioz: *Symphonie fantastique*, Fourth Movement   (4:37)

DATE OF WORK:	1830
GENRE:	Program symphony, 5 movements
PROGRAM:	A lovesick artist in an opium trance is haunted by a vision of his beloved, which becomes an *idée fixe* (fixed idea).

I. *Reveries, Passions*

Largo, Allegro agitato e appassionato assai (lively, agitated, and very impassioned); introduces the main theme, the fixed idea:

Allegro agitato e appassionato assai

II. *A Ball*

Valse, Allegro non troppo (Waltz, not too fast);
A-B-A form, triple-meter dance.

Listening Guide continues

III. Scene in the Fields

Adagio; **A-B-A** form, 6/8 meter.

IV. March to the Scaffold

Allegretto non troppo; duple-meter march in minor mode.

V. Dream of a Witches' Sabbath

Largo-Allegro; diabolic dance, with *Dies irae*.

IV. March to the Scaffold

WHAT TO LISTEN FOR: Diabolical march with 2 themes, played by large orchestra.
Recurring melody (*idée fixe*) heard at closing, in clarinet.
Vivid musical portrayal of the beheading.

12 0:00 Opening motive: muted horns, timpani, and pizzicato low strings, forecasts syncopated rhythm of march (theme **B**):

13 0:24 Theme **A**—an energetic, downward minor scale, played by low strings, then violins (with bassoon obbligato):

14 1:31 Theme **B**—diabolical march tune, played, by brass and woodwinds:

15 1:56 Developmental section:
Theme **B**—in brass, accompanied by strings and woodwinds:
Theme **A**—soft, with pizzicato strings.
Theme **B**—brass, with woodwinds added.
Theme **A**—soft, pizzicato strings, then loud in brass.

16 3:02 Theme **A**—full orchestra statement in original form, then inverted (now an ascending scale).

17 4:05 *Idée fixe* (fixed idea) melody in clarinet ("a last thought of love"), marked "dolce assai e appassionato" (as sweetly and passionately as possible), followed by loud chord that cuts off melody ("the fall of the blade"):

Loud forceful chords close movement.

51

Musical Nationalism

*"I grew up in a quiet spot and was saturated from earliest childhood
with the wonderful beauty of Russian popular song. I am therefore
passionately devoted to every expression of the Russian spirit. In
short, I am a Russian through and through!"*

—PETER ILYICH TCHAIKOVSKY

KEY POINTS

 StudySpace online at www.wwnorton.com/enjoy

- Political unrest throughout Europe stimulated nationalism, which in music took many forms (use of folklore, and works written to celebrate national heros, events, or places).

- Prominent national schools of composers appeared in Russia, Scandinavia, Spain, England, and Bohemia, among other locales.

- The Bohemian master Bedřich Smetana wrote nationalistic music about his homeland, including a set of six symphonic poems entitled *My Country.* The most famous of these is *The Moldau.*

In nineteenth-century Europe, political conditions encouraged the growth of nationalism to such a degree that it became a decisive force within the Romantic movement. The pride of conquering nations and the struggle for freedom of suppressed ones gave rise to strong emotions that inspired the works of many creative artists.

The Romantic composers expressed their nationalism in a number of ways. Some based their music on the songs and dances of their people: Chopin in his mazurkas and polonaises, Liszt in his *Hungarian Rhapsodies,* Dvořák in his *Slavonic Dances.* A number wrote dramatic works based on folklore or peasant life—for example, the Russian fairy-tale operas and ballets of Tchaikovsky and Rimsky-Korsakov (see CP 11). Others wrote symphonic poems and operas celebrating the exploits of a national hero, a historic event, or the scenic beauty of their country; Tchaikovsky's *1812 Overture* and Smetana's *The Moldau* exemplify this trend.

In associating music with the love of homeland, composers were able to give expression to the hopes and dreams of millions of people. The political implications of this musical nationalism were not lost on the authorities. Many of Verdi's operas, for example, had to be altered again and again to suit the Austrian censor (his plots often portrayed rulers as unjust or suggested "dangerous" ideas). Finnish composer Jean Sibelius's orchestral hymn *Finlandia,* written for a national pageant in 1899, was banned in 1917 because the hymn promoted national identity for Finland, which was then a part of the mighty Russian empire. During the Second World War, the Nazis outlawed the playing of Chopin's polonaises in Warsaw and Smetana's descriptive symphonic poems in Prague because of the powerful symbolism behind these two works. We will consider one of these inspiring works—Smetana's *The Moldau,* today one of the most beloved pieces in the entire orchestral repertory.

A Czech Nationalist: Bedřich Smetana

"My compositions do not belong to the realm of absolute music, where one can get along well enough with musical signs and a metronome."

Bedřich Smetana

Bedřich Smetana (1824–1884) was the first Bohemian composer to achieve international prominence. He was born in a small village in eastern Bohemia (now the Czech Republic), the son of a master brewer. In his teens, he was sent to school in Prague, where his love for music was kindled by the city's active cultural life. Smetana's career, like those of other nationalist composers, played out against a background of political agitation. Bohemia was caught up in a surge of nationalist fervor that culminated in a series of uprisings against Austrian rule in 1848. The young Smetana joined the patriotic cause. After the revolution was crushed, the atmosphere in Prague was oppressive for those suspected of sympathy with the nationalists, so in 1856, he accepted a conducting position in Sweden.

My Country

On his return to Prague several years later, Smetana resumed his musical career by writing operas for the National Theater, where performances were given in his native tongue. Of his eight operas, *The Bartered Bride* won him worldwide fame. Today he is best known for *My Country* (*Má vlast*), a vast cycle of six symphonic poems whose composition occupied his time from 1874 to 1879. These works were inspired by the beauty of Bohemia's countryside, the rhythm of its folk songs and dances, and the pomp and pageantry of its legends. While writing the cycle, Smetana's health declined as a result of advanced syphilis, and, like Beethoven, he grew deaf. His diary reveals his deep suffering: "If my illness is incurable," he wrote, "then I should prefer to be delivered from this miserable existence."

THE MOLDAU

The Moldau, the second of the programmatic poems from *My Country*, represents Smetana's finest achievement in the field of orchestral music. In this work, the Bohemian river Moldau (Vltava in Czech) becomes a poetic symbol of the beloved homeland. (For the text of Smetana's program, see Listening Guide 31.) The music suggests first the rippling streams that flow through the forest to form the mighty river. Smetana then evokes a hunting scene by using French horns and trumpets, followed by a peasant wedding in a lilting folk dance. The mood changes to

The Moldau River flows in majestic peace through the Czech capital city of Prague.

enchantment as nymphs emerge from their fairy-tale haunts to hold their nightly revels under the moonlight; here, the melody is heard in muted strings over a bubbling accompaniment. The portrayal of the St. John Rapids musters all the brass and percussion, which announce the broad river theme in major mode. Finally, as the Moldau approaches the capital city of Prague, it flows past castles and fortresses that remind the composer of his country's proud history. The river then flows out to sea, as the music fades to a *pianissimo*, closing a work that has captured the imagination of listeners for over a century.

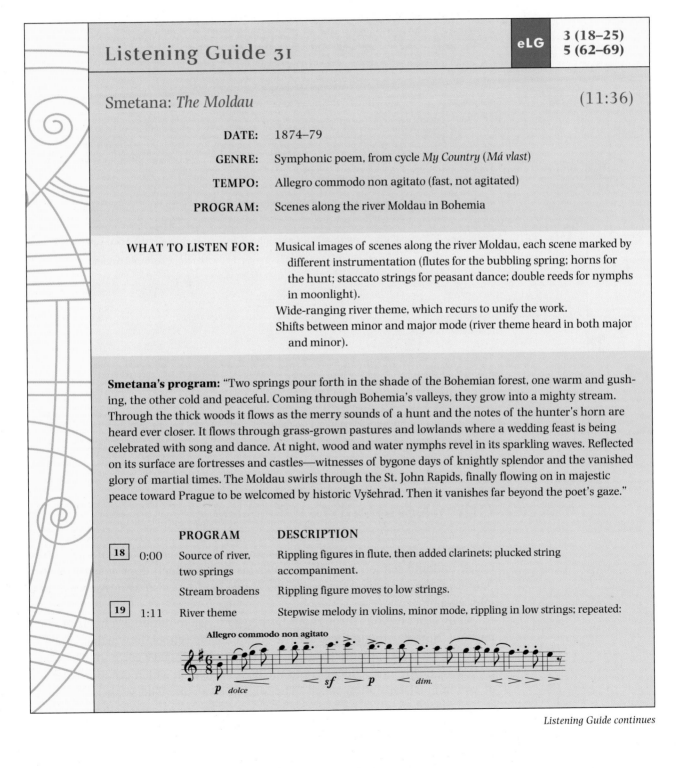

Listening Guide 31

eLG   **3 (18–25)**
       5 (62–69)

Smetana: *The Moldau*   (11:36)

DATE:	1874–79
GENRE:	Symphonic poem, from cycle *My Country* (*Má vlast*)
TEMPO:	Allegro commodo non agitato (fast, not agitated)
PROGRAM:	Scenes along the river Moldau in Bohemia

WHAT TO LISTEN FOR: Musical images of scenes along the river Moldau, each scene marked by different instrumentation (flutes for the bubbling spring; horns for the hunt; staccato strings for peasant dance; double reeds for nymphs in moonlight).
Wide-ranging river theme, which recurs to unify the work.
Shifts between minor and major mode (river theme heard in both major and minor).

Smetana's program: "Two springs pour forth in the shade of the Bohemian forest, one warm and gushing, the other cold and peaceful. Coming through Bohemia's valleys, they grow into a mighty stream. Through the thick woods it flows as the merry sounds of a hunt and the notes of the hunter's horn are heard ever closer. It flows through grass-grown pastures and lowlands where a wedding feast is being celebrated with song and dance. At night, wood and water nymphs revel in its sparkling waves. Reflected on its surface are fortresses and castles—witnesses of bygone days of knightly splendor and the vanished glory of martial times. The Moldau swirls through the St. John Rapids, finally flowing on in majestic peace toward Prague to be welcomed by historic Vyšehrad. Then it vanishes far beyond the poet's gaze."

		PROGRAM	**DESCRIPTION**
18	0:00	Source of river, two springs	Rippling figures in flute, then added clarinets; plucked string accompaniment.
		Stream broadens	Rippling figure moves to low strings.
19	1:11	River theme	Stepwise melody in violins, minor mode, rippling in low strings; repeated:

Allegro commodo non agitato

p dolce   *< sf > p*   *< dim.*   *< > > >*

Listening Guide continues

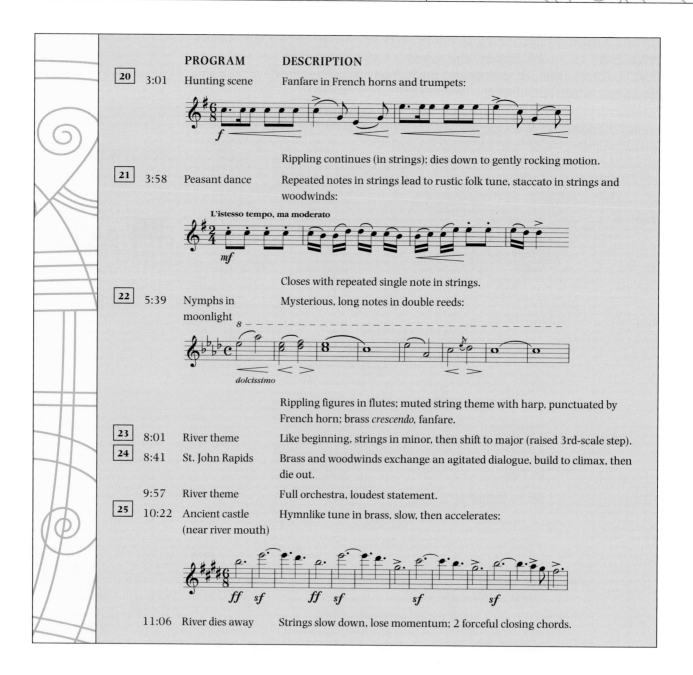

		PROGRAM	DESCRIPTION
20	3:01	Hunting scene	Fanfare in French horns and trumpets:

Rippling continues (in strings); dies down to gently rocking motion.

21	3:58	Peasant dance	Repeated notes in strings lead to rustic folk tune, staccato in strings and woodwinds:

Closes with repeated single note in strings.

22	5:39	Nymphs in moonlight	Mysterious, long notes in double reeds:

Rippling figures in flutes; muted string theme with harp, punctuated by French horn; brass *crescendo*, fanfare.

23	8:01	River theme	Like beginning, strings in minor, then shift to major (raised 3rd-scale step).
24	8:41	St. John Rapids	Brass and woodwinds exchange an agitated dialogue, build to climax, then die out.
	9:57	River theme	Full orchestra, loudest statement.
25	10:22	Ancient castle (near river mouth)	Hymnlike tune in brass, slow, then accelerates:

	11:06	River dies away	Strings slow down, lose momentum; 2 forceful closing chords.

Other Nationalists

Antonín Dvořák (1841–1904) stands alongside Smetana as a founder of the Czech national school. We will consider his music, which drew inspiration not only from the songs and dances of his native land but also from America, in a later chapter.

Many other regions throughout Europe gave rise to national schools of composition. Notable among these are the Scandinavian school, in which composers Edvard Grieg (Norway) and Jean Sibelius (Finland) both gave voice to their country's struggle for independence; and the Russian school, which produced a group of young musicians often called "The Mighty Five" (or "The Mighty Handful").

These composers, including Modest Musorgsky and Nikolai Rimsky-Korsakov, sought to free themselves from the German symphony, French ballet, and Italian opera and in doing so, expressed a true Russian spirit. England and Spain as well produced nationalistic composers whose music echoed the soul of their countries (see map below). We will consider American nationalism, which flowered relatively late, in another chapter.

A Polovetsian maiden and a Russian warrior. **Ivan Bilibin**'s (1876–1942) costume designs for Borodin's opera *Prince Igor*.

Schools of Musical Nationalism

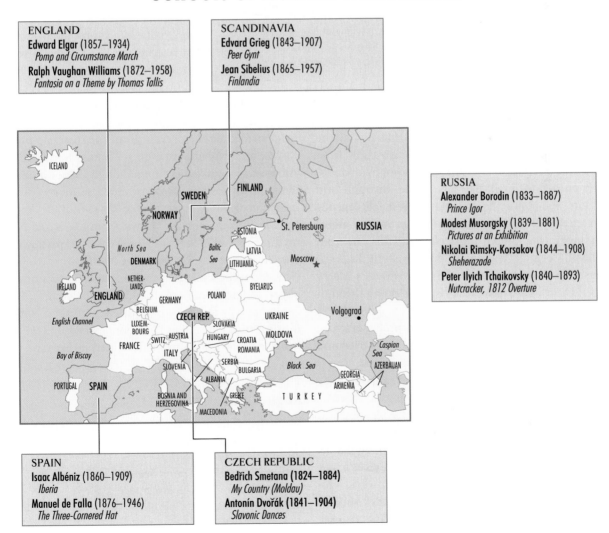

ENGLAND
Edward Elgar (1857–1934)
Pomp and Circumstance March
Ralph Vaughan Williams (1872–1958)
Fantasia on a Theme by Thomas Tallis

SCANDINAVIA
Edvard Grieg (1843–1907)
Peer Gynt
Jean Sibelius (1865–1957)
Finlandia

RUSSIA
Alexander Borodin (1833–1887)
Prince Igor
Modest Musorgsky (1839–1881)
Pictures at an Exhibition
Nikolai Rimsky-Korsakov (1844–1908)
Sheherazade
Peter Ilyich Tchaikovsky (1840–1893)
Nutcracker, 1812 Overture

SPAIN
Isaac Albéniz (1860–1909)
Iberia
Manuel de Falla (1876–1946)
The Three-Cornered Hat

CZECH REPUBLIC
Bedřich Smetana (1824–1884)
My Country (Moldau)
Antonín Dvořák (1841–1904)
Slavonic Dances

Music, Folklore, and Nationalism

Composers throughout the ages have looked to the folklore of their native lands for inspiration. We have seen that Bedřich Smetana was moved—in his case through deeply felt patriotism—to write a cycle of six symphonic poems entitled *My Country* that presents not only images of the scenery and history but also the folk legends of his beloved Bohemia. One work from the cycle, entitled *Sárka*, tells the Central European folktale about a warrior princess who, spurned by her lover, joins a group of other warrior-women to punish men. (Sárka may remind you of the modern TV warrior-princess Xena, who, with her band of outlaws, terrorized Greece until she reformed to fight evil.)

Prince Ivan with the magical firebird in a Russian folktale depicted by **Ivan Bilibin** (1876–1942).

Each culture has a value system that lies at the heart of its folklore: children often learn right from wrong and prepare for adulthood through folktales, which are transmitted, like folk music, through oral tradition. The characters we find in these folk legends are often rascals whose wrongdoings prove the moral of the story. One famous musical rogue, this one from medieval German legend, is portrayed in Richard Strauss's popular tone poem *Till Eulenspiegel's Merry Pranks* (1895). Till's adventures include riding through a marketplace and upsetting all the goods, disguising himself as a priest, mocking a group of professors, and finally paying the penalty for his pranks: he is tried and hanged, though his spirit cannot be suppressed.

Folk material inspired the Russian composer Igor Stravinsky in his ballet suite *The Firebird*, based on the tale of a mythical, glowing bird that was both a blessing and a curse to its captor. Magical birds abound in folklore and in music: perhaps the most famous is the phoenix, an Egyptian mythical bird that rises out of the ashes as a sign of hope and rebirth (you may remember Fawkes, who was Dumbledore's pet in the *Harry Potter* books). Musical compositions paying homage to this legendary creature range from traditional Chinese folk songs to Russian

ballets (*The Red Poppy* by Glière) and modern orchestral program music (*Phoenix Rising* by Thea Musgrave).

Folklore often transcends national boundaries. The French tales "Sleeping Beauty" and "Cinderella" (both from the 1697 collection by Charles Perrault) were set as Russian ballets (*The Sleeping Beauty* by Tchaikovsky in 1890 and *Cinderella* by Prokofiev in 1945); and a fanciful story by the German writer E. T. A. Hoffmann, in an expanded version by French writer Alexandre Dumas, served as the basis for Tchaikovsky's most famous ballet, *The Nutcracker* (1892), which we will study.

Today, favorite stories—Perrault's "Sleeping Beauty," the Grimms' "Beauty and the Beast," Hans Christian Andersen's "The Little Mermaid," the Arabian folktale of "Aladdin" from *The Thousand and One Nights*, and *Mulan*, based on a Chinese tale—are well known to several generations though Disney animated films. But some folk tales are much more recent. You undoubtedly know the stories of *The Lord of the Rings* by J. R. R. Tolkien (loosely drawn from the same Norse mythology that is the basis for Wagner's operatic cycle *The Ring*) and *The Chronicles of Narnia* by C. S. Lewis (which develops ideas from Greek and Roman mythology as well as from English and Irish fairy tales). These contemporary fantasies have already inspired classical music settings as well as film soundtracks, and are now firmly established in our modern literary heritage.

Suggested Listening

Prokofiev: *Peter and the Wolf* or *Cinderella* Ballet Suite
Smetana: *Sárka*, from *My Country*
Stravinsky: *The Firebird*
Tchaikovsky: *The Sleeping Beauty*
  CD iMusic *The Nutcracker* (see p. 325)
CD iMusic Wagner: *Ride of the Valkyries*, from *Die Walküre* (see p. 314)

Absolute Forms in the Nineteenth Century

52

The Romantic Symphony

"A great symphony is a man-made Mississippi down which we irresistibly flow from the instant of our leave-taking to a long foreseen destination."

—AARON COPLAND

KEY POINTS	(S) **StudySpace** online at www.wwnorton.com/enjoy

- The symphony continued as a favored Romantic genre alongside new programmatic forms (symphonic poem, program symphony).

- Many new instruments were added to the Romantic orchestra, which increased its size.

- The Romantic symphony was characterized by lyrical themes, colorful harmonies, and expanded proportions.

- The first movement of the Romantic symphony usually remained in sonata-allegro form, and the third movement was most often a spirited scherzo.

- The Bohemian composer Antonín Dvořák found inspiration in nationalist themes and traditional

music from his homeland and from the United States, where he lived for several years.

- While in the United States, Dvořák studied the traditional music of African Americans and incorporated elements of spirituals into his music (CP 12).

- The *New World* Symphony, Dvořák's most popular work today, is Classical in its structure but Romantic in its orchestral and harmonic color.

- The *New World* Symphony is loosely programmatic, inspired by Longfellow's poem *The Song of Hiawatha* and by the composer's impressions of the New World.

During the Classical period, the symphony became the most exalted form of absolute orchestral music. The three Viennese masters—Haydn, Mozart, and Beethoven—carried it to its highest level of formal beauty and status. They passed on to composers of the Romantic era a flexible art form that could be adapted to meet the emotional needs of the new age.

In the course of its development, the symphony gained weight and importance. Nineteenth-century composers found the symphony a suitable framework for their lyrical themes, harmonic experiments, and individual expressions. By the Romantic era, music had moved from palace to public concert hall, the orchestra had vastly increased in size (see Table on p. 237), and the symphonic structure was growing steadily longer and more expansive. As noted earlier, the nineteenth-century symphonists were not as prolific as their predecessors had been. Felix Mendelssohn, Robert Schumann, Brahms, and Tchaikovsky each wrote fewer than seven symphonies. These were in the domain of absolute music, while Liszt and Berlioz cultivated the program symphony.

IN HIS OWN WORDS

A symphony must be like the world; it must embrace everything.

—*GUSTAV MAHLER*

The Romantic Symphony Form

In the hands of Romantic composers, the standard four-movement Classical symphony took on new proportions. For example, the usual number and tempo scheme of the movements was not religiously followed; Tchaikovsky closed his *Pathétique* Symphony with a long, expressive slow movement, and Beethoven pushed the cycle to five movements in his *Pastoral* Symphony (No. 6).

First movement The first movement, the most dramatic of the Romantic symphony, generally retains the basic elements of sonata-allegro form. It might draw out the slow introduction, and it often features a long and expressive development section that ventures into distant keys and transforms themes into something the ear perceives as entirely new.

The 19th-century orchestra offered the composer new instruments and a larger ensemble. Engraving of an orchestral concert at the Covent Garden Theatre, London, 1846.

The second movement may retain its slow and lyrical nature but can also range in mood from whimsical and playful to tragic and passionate. This movement frequently takes a loose three-part form.

Second movement

Third in the cycle is a strongly rhythmic and exciting scherzo, with overtones of humor, surprise, caprice, or folk dance. Its mood can be anything from elfin lightness to demonic energy. The tempo marking—usually Allegro, Allegro molto, or Vivace—indicates a lively pace. Scherzo form generally follows the **A-B-A** structure of the minuet and trio. In some symphonies, such as Beethoven's Ninth, the scherzo is second in the cycle. We will see that Brahms wrote a melancholy waltz for the third movement of his Symphony No. 3.

Third movement

The fourth and final movement of the Romantic symphony has a dimension and character designed to balance the first. Often, this movement is a spirited Allegro in sonata-allegro form and may close the symphony on a note of triumph or pathos. The chart below reviews the standard form of the symphony.

Fourth movement

A TYPICAL ROMANTIC SYMPHONY

FIRST MOVEMENT	Sonata-allegro form Home key	Allegro
	Slow Introduction Exposition —Theme 1 (home key) —Theme 2 (contrasting key) —Closing theme (same contrasting key)	Optional Rhythmic character Lyrical character
	Development (free modulation)	Fragmentation or expansion of themes; introduction of new material; distant keys
	Recapitulation —Theme 1 (home key) —Theme 2 (home key) —Closing theme (home key)	
SECOND MOVEMENT	Sonata-allegro form, A-B-A form, or theme and variations Different key	Slow, lyrical; varied moods

THIRD MOVEMENT	Scherzo and trio, A-B-A
	Home Key
	    Scherzo, 2 sections
	    Trio, 2 sections
	Scherzo returns
		Triple meter, fast paced
		
		Sections repeated

FOURTH MOVEMENT	Sonata-allegro form, rondo form, or some other form Home Key	Allegro or presto; shorter and lighter than first movement

Dvořák's Influence on African-American Art Music

African-American singer Marian Anderson broke with tradition by including Negro spirituals in her "classical" song recital in Salzburg, Austria (1935).

The Bohemian composer Antonín Dvořák was inspired by traditional music of America (as well as of his native Bohemia)—specifically, spirituals, Creole tunes and dances, and what he perceived as music of Native Americans. Indeed, the two middle movements of his *New World* Symphony can be linked with Longfellow's epic poem *The Song of Hiawatha.*

What, then, of Dvořák's professed interest in the traditional music of African Americans? We know that the composer came to love the spirituals sung to him by his student Henry T. Burleigh (1866–1949), and he supposedly had a particular fondness for *Swing Low, Sweet Chariot* (a variant of this spiritual is evoked—perhaps coincidentally—in the first movement of the symphony). The rhythmic syncopations and the particular scale formations used in the *New World* Symphony (the minor mode with a lowered, or flatted, seventh degree) have often been cited as evidence of borrowings from African-American musical styles.

But Dvořák gave much more to American music than he took from it. As a respected teacher, he issued a challenge to American composers to throw off the domination of European music and forge paths of their own, using the "beautiful and varied themes . . . the folk songs of America."

Florence Price (1888–1953), the first African-American woman to be recognized as a distinguished composer, is believed to have drawn inspiration for her Symphony in E minor (1932) directly from Dvořák's *New World* Symphony. Price's work parallels Dvořák's in a number of ways, including original themes that allude to characteristic African-American rhythms and melodies. Price's piano music also explores her cultural heritage. Her Sonata in E minor presents a spiritual-like theme in the second movement, treated with gentle syncopations, and her suite *Dances in the Canebrakes* is based on African-American dances, including the cakewalk.

The composer who best rose to Dvořák's challenge was William Grant Still (1895–1978), whose output exceeds one hundred concert works in a wide variety of genres—symphonies, symphonic poems, suites, operas, ballets, chamber music, choral music, and songs. A nationalist, Still drew musical inspiration from African-American work songs, spirituals, ragtime, blues, and jazz. His *Afro-American* Symphony (1930), his best-known work today, is firmly rooted in the music of his African-American heritage.

Today, the "validation" of a vernacular music by art music standards described by William Grant Still is no longer necessary, since all musics are coming to be accepted as valuable products of the culture and people who created them.

Suggested Listening

Dvořák : *New World* Symphony, Second Movement
Spirituals (*Swing Low, Sweet Chariot* [**CD** iMusic];
   Sometimes I Feel Like a Motherless Child)
Still: *Afro-American* Symphony, Second Movement

DVOŘÁK AS A SYMPHONIST

Antonín Dvořák (1841–1904) is one of numerous late-Romantic composers who found inspiration in the traditional music of their native land. He was born in Bohemia (now part of the Czech Republic) and grew up in a village near Prague, where his father kept an inn. For a time, poverty threatened to rule out a musical career. However, at sixteen he secured a position in Prague playing the viola in the Czech National Theater under the baton of Smetana. By the time he was forty, Dvořák was a professor of composition at the Conservatory of Prague, a post in which he was able to exert an important influence on the musical life of his country.

Dvořák was known throughout Europe and the United States. In 1891, Jeannette Thurber, who ran the National Conservatory of Music in New York City, invited him to become its director. His stay in the United States was eminently fruitful, resulting in what has remained his most successful symphony, *From the New World*, a number of chamber music works, including the *American* Quartet, and the highly lyrical Cello Concerto.

Dvořák's family shortly after their arrival in America in 1892.

As a nationalist composer, Dvořák tried to steer his American pupils toward their native heritage. The melodies Dvořák heard from his African-American students appealed to the folk poet in him, and strengthened his conviction that American composers would find their true path only when they had thrown off the influence of Europe and sought their inspiration in the Native American, African-American, and traditional folk songs of their own country. This doctrine helped prepare the way for the rich harvest of American works by composers of the next generations. The composer eventually returned to his beloved Bohemia, where he died at the age of sixty-three, revered as a national artist.

Dvořák had a great gift for melody, a love of native folk tunes, and a solid craftsmanship, which enabled him to shape musical ideas into large forms notable for their clarity. He wrote his Symphony No. 9, subtitled *From the New World*, during his stay in the United States, and it received its first performance in New York in 1893. The whole symphony may be seen as a descriptive landscape, evoking the openness of the American prairie as well as the composer's longing for his homeland. It is set in a standard four-movement framework, the middle movements of which can be directly linked to the influence of Longfellow's *Song of Hiawatha*. The deeply felt English-horn tune that opens the second movement, a Largo, was made famous when sung as a kind of spiritual, set to the words "Goin' Home."

IN HIS OWN WORDS

In the Negro melodies of America I discover all that is needed for a great and noble school of music. These beautiful and varied themes are the product of the soil. . . . They are the folk songs of America, and your composers must turn to them.

53

Brahms and the Late Romantic Symphony

"It is not hard to compose, but it is wonderfully hard to let the superfluous notes fall under the table."

○ The German composer Johannes Brahms continued the Classical traditions of the Viennese masters, especially Beethoven.

○ Brahms studied with Robert Schumann, and after Schumann's death, remained a close friend of his wife, Clara.

○ Brahms is known for his four symphonies, his solo piano and chamber music, and his Lieder, which follow in the tradition of Schubert and Schumann.

○ Brahms's Third Symphony is Classical in its structures and proportions but highly Romantic in its tone.

Johannes Brahms

Johannes Brahms created a Romantic art in the purest Classical style. His veneration for the past and his mastery of musical architecture brought him closer to the spirit of Beethoven than any of his contemporaries.

His Life

Johannes Brahms (1833–1897) was born in Hamburg, the son of a musician (his father played horn, violin, and double bass) and a seamstress. As a youth, Johannes studied piano, cello, and French horn, and gave his first performance on piano at the age of ten. He soon helped increase the family's income by giving piano lessons and playing popular music in dance halls.

Brahms's early compositions greatly impressed Joseph Joachim, the leading violinist of the day, who arranged for Brahms to visit Robert Schumann at Düsseldorf and study with him. Schumann recognized in the shy young composer a future leader of the circle dedicated to absolute music. Robert and Clara Schumann took the young musician into their home, and their friendship opened up new horizons for him. But then came the tragedy of Schumann's mental collapse. With tenderness and strength, Brahms supported Clara through the ordeal of Robert's illness. (On Robert Schumann as a composer, see Chapter 44.)

Fourteen years his senior and the mother of seven children, Clara Schumann, herself a fine pianist and composer, appeared to young Brahms as the ideal of womanly and artistic achievement. (On Clara Schumann, see Chapter 47.) What began as filial devotion ripened into romantic passion. "You have taught me," he wrote her, "to marvel at the nature of love, affection, and self-denial. I can do nothing but think of you." This conflict was resolved in 1856 by Robert's death, after which he and Clara rebuilt their relationship into a lifelong friendship.

The death of his mother in 1865 had a profound impact on the composer, who wrote his German Requiem to her memory (see p. 292). He ultimately settled in Vienna where he became enormously successful, the acknowledged heir of the Viennese masters.

In 1896, Clara Schumann's declining health gave rise to his *Four Serious Songs*. Her death deeply affected the composer, already ill with cancer. He died ten months later, at the age of sixty-four, and was buried in Vienna not far from Beethoven and Schubert.

His Music

Brahms was a traditionalist; his aim was to show that new and important things could still be said in the tradition of the Classical masters.

His four symphonies are unsurpassed in the late Romantic period for their breadth of conception and design, yet their forms draw upon those of earlier eras. Among his other orchestral works, the *Variations on a Theme by Haydn* and his two concert overtures are often heard today. In his two piano concertos and his violin concerto, the solo instrument is integrated into a full-scale symphonic structure.

Orchestral music

Brahms captured the intimacy that is the essence of chamber music style. He is an important figure in piano music as well. His two variation sets, on themes by Handel and Paganini, represent his top achievement in that field. The Romantic in Brahms also found expression in short lyric piano pieces: the rhapsodies, ballades, capriccios, and intermezzi are among the treasures of the literature.

Chamber and solo music

As a song writer, Brahms stands in the direct line of succession to Schubert and Robert Schumann. His output includes about two hundred solo songs and an almost equal number for two, three, or four voices. The favorite themes are love, nature, and death. His *German Requiem*, written to biblical texts that he selected himself, made him more famous during his lifetime than any of his other works (see Chapter 56).

Vocal music

CD iMusic

Lullaby

SYMPHONY NO. 3 IN F MAJOR

Brahms did not attempt to write a symphony until he was past forty. He was fond of saying that it was no laughing matter to compose a symphony after Beethoven. "You have no idea," he told a friend, "how the likes of us feel when we hear the tramp of a giant like him behind us."

The Third Symphony, written in 1883 when Brahms was fifty years old, is the shortest of his four symphonies and the most Romantic in tone. In form, however, the work looks back to the Classical structures of the eighteenth century. The first movement, a conventional sonata-allegro, opens with a dramatic figure: a three-note motive (F-A♭-F) that is often related to the composer's personal motto, "Frei aber froh" (Free but happy—a motto that may allude to his bachelorhood). This motive permeates the entire symphony. The slow movement, a haunting Andante in sonata-allegro form, evokes the peacefulness of nature with its simple, hymnlike theme in the woodwinds.

Rather than following with a scherzo, Brahms writes a melancholy waltz in C minor, set in ternary form (see Listening Guide 32). The opening theme, a yearning cello melody, is heard throughout this impassioned orchestral "song without words," accompanied by restless string figures. First the violins, then the woodwinds take up the poignant melody, whose arched rise and fall suggests a huge orchestral sigh. The middle section, now in a major key, presents two themes set against an expressive, chromatic accompaniment. The return of the opening theme is newly orchestrated, heard first in the French horns and oboes, then in an emotional statement by the violins and cellos playing in octaves. A short coda brings back the mood of the middle section, and then closes quietly, with two soft pizzicato chords.

The finale, a dramatic sonata-allegro, features concise themes and abrupt changes of mood that challenge the listener and affirm the technical command and the creative invention of a great Romantic master.

A famous caricature of Brahms in his later years; the composer was a familiar sight in Vienna as he made his way to The Red Hedgehog, his favorite tavern.

Brahms: Symphony No. 3 in F major, Third Movement (6:24)

DATE OF WORK:	1883
GENRE:	Symphony
MEDIUM:	Orchestra (strings, woodwinds, and horns only in this movement)
MOVEMENTS:	I. Allegro con brio; sonata-allegro, F major
	II. Andante; modified sonata form, C major
	III. Poco allegretto; **A-B-A′** form, C minor
	IV. Allegro; sonata-allegro; F major

WHAT TO LISTEN FOR: Melancholy minor-key waltz melody in cellos, then violins, woodwinds, and French horns.

Regular, symmetrical phrases set in moderate triple meter.

3-part structure with modal shifts (minor-major-minor).

Rhythmic complexity through "three-against-two" patterns; syncopated rhythms that lean over the barline.

Third movement: Poco allegretto; A-B-A′ form, 3/8 meter, C minor

26 0:00   **A** section—yearning cello melody, accompanied by rustling string figures; symmetrical phrasing:

0:27   Violins repeat the cello theme, extending the range and dynamics.

0:52   2nd theme, played by violins, "leans" over the barline over moving cello line; violins and cellos join in brief duet:

1:27   Return of opening theme in flutes and oboes, with broader accompaniment.

27 1:57   **B** section—connected 3-note figure in woodwinds, in A-flat major, accompanied by offbeat sixteenth notes in the cellos:

3:27   Woodwinds hint at return to main theme, accompanied by sustained strings.

28 3:46   **A′** section—French horns announce the opening theme in C minor, with richer orchestration.

4:14   Oboes take up the haunting melody as accompaniment builds.

4:41   Theme 2, now heard in the clarinets and bassoons.

5:17   Violins and cellos take up the main theme, played in octaves for greater intensity; generally thicker and more contrapuntal accompaniment.

5:44   Brief coda; reminiscent of **B** section; last chord is punctuated by pizzicato strings.

54

The Romantic Concerto

*"We are so made that we can derive
intense enjoyment only from a contrast."*

—SIGMUND FREUD

KEY POINTS   **StudySpace** online at www.wwnorton.com/enjoy

- The Romantic concerto preserves the Classical three-movement structure but uses standard forms (e.g., sonata-allegro and first-movement concerto form) more freely.
- The concerto was a vehicle for brilliant virtuosic display by the soloist.

- Many concertos were written for a specific soloist and tailored to the technical abilities of that musician.
- Felix Mendelssohn preserves many Classical elements in his compositions, including his Violin Concerto in E minor.

Virtuosity and the Concerto

The origins of the Romantic concerto reach back to the late eighteenth century. Mozart and Beethoven, both formidable pianists, performed their concertos in public, delighting and dazzling their audiences. This element of virtuosic display, combined with appealing melodies, helped make the concerto one of the most widely appreciated types of concert music. As the concert industry developed, technical brilliance became a more and more important element of concerto style. We have noted that nineteenth-century composer-performers such as Paganini and Liszt carried virtuosity to new heights. This development kept pace with the increase in the size and resources of the symphony orchestra. The Romantic concerto became one of the most favored genres of the age. Felix Mendelssohn, Chopin, Liszt, Robert and Clara Schumann, Brahms, Tchaikovsky, and Dvořák all contributed to its literature.

Composers of the concerto often write with particular artists in mind. We have already seen that Mozart wrote piano concertos not only for himself but for several women performers of his time, including one of his students. The Violin Concerto of Felix Mendelssohn (see p. 286) was written for the virtuoso Ferdinand David, concertmaster of the Leipzig Gewandhaus Orchestra, which the composer conducted. Brahms consulted Joseph Joachim, the leading violinist of the day, when he wrote his Violin Concerto.

> **IN HIS OWN WORDS**
>
> *The demonic is that which cannot be explained in a cerebral and a rational manner. . . . Paganini is imbued with it to a remarkable degree, and it is through this that he produces such a great effect.*
> —JOHANN WOLFGANG
> VON GOETHE

The Romantic Concerto Form

The Romantic concerto retains the Classical three-movement form, opening with a dramatic Allegro, usually in sonata form, which is followed by a lyrical slow movement and a brilliant finale. The first movement, though, is usually freer than its Classical counterpart: the solo instrument may not wait for an orchestral exposition to make its first statement, and the cadenza, normally played at the close of the recapitulation and before the coda, may occur earlier, as part of the development. The second movement continues to present songful melodies, often in a loosely structured three-part form. And the finale, which brings the dramatic tension between soloist and orchestra to a head, often features another cadenza, leading the work to an exciting close.

FELIX MENDELSSOHN AND THE CONCERTO

The music of Felix Mendelssohn (1809–1847) represents the classicist trend within the Romantic movement.

Mendelssohn excelled in a number of roles—as pianist, conductor, organizer of music festivals, and educator. At twenty-six, he was named conductor of the Gewandhaus Orchestra in Leipzig and went on to transform the orchestra into the finest in Europe. Later he founded the Conservatory of Leipzig, which raised the standards for the training of musicians. Mendelssohn's happy life was shattered in 1847 by the death of his sister Fanny, to whom he was deeply attached. (We will consider a work by Fanny Mendelssohn Hensel in Chapter 57.) This blow, along with his very demanding musical career, brought on a stroke, from which he died at age thirty-eight.

 **Felix Mendelssohn**

Violin Concerto in E minor

Mendelssohn was dedicated to preserving the tradition of the Classical forms in an age that was turning from them. The Violin Concerto in E minor (1844), written three years before the composer's death, was Mendelssohn's last orchestral work and is one of the most popular violin concertos of all time. This work reveals the composer's special gifts: clarity of form, subtlety of orchestration, and a reserved, sentimental expression. The concerto's three-movement structure conforms to the classical ideals, although new ideas of unity have been imposed. For example, the three movements are to be played without pause, and a reference back to the first

A TYPICAL ROMANTIC CONCERTO

FIRST MOVEMENT	Concerto form (double exposition) Home key	Allegro
	Orchestral exposition —Several themes Solo exposition —Same themes and others Development Recapitulation Cadenza (solo instrument alone) Coda, or closing	Solo instrument may play at opening Cadenza may occur earlier
SECOND MOVEMENT	A-B-A form Contrasting key	Slow, lyrical, songful
THIRD MOVEMENT	Rondo form or sonata-allegro form Home key	Allegro or Presto Possible cadenza

movement occurs in the second, hinting at cyclical form. Also, the first movement, an Allegro molto appassionato (Very fast and impassioned), does away with the customary orchestral introduction in concerto form; rather, the solo violin announces the main theme almost immediately in a dramatic and expansive melody that forms a broad arch with balanced, symmetrical phrases. The work gives the soloist plenty of opportunity for brilliant display and, with its appealing melodies and formal clarity, displays the tender sentiment and classical moderation that are so typical of Mendelssohn's music.

55

The Rise of Classical Composition in America

"I hear America singing, the varied carols I hear."

—WALT WHITMAN

| KEY POINTS | ⓢ StudySpace online at www.wwnorton.com/enjoy |

- ○ The European musical tradition dominated in the United States throughout the nineteenth century, and most American musicians studied in Europe.
- ○ The late-nineteenth-century Second New England School of composition, which included Amy Beach, made its original mark on musical styles in America.

- ○ Amy Beach was active as a pianist, composer, and music educator.
- ○ Her Symphony in E minor was inspired by Dvořák's *New World* Symphony; her Violin Sonata in A minor shows the influence of Brahms.
- ○ Women musicians of the Romantic era were discouraged from pursuing professional careers as composers (CP 13).

By 1850, a vibrant musical life had grown up in major U.S. and Canadian cities, dominated by European composers and musicians, as we saw in the case of pianist Louis Moreau Gottschalk (see Chapter 48). Young Americans who were attracted to careers as performers or composers went abroad to complete their studies. When they returned home, they brought the European traditions with them. Virtuosity was admired by American audiences, who thronged to hear the "Swedish nightingale" Jenny Lind on her extended concert tour.

Although a taste for European styles of music prevailed in the Americas for much of the nineteenth century, the German-born conductor Theodore Thomas devoted his energies to cultivating orchestral music in America by setting up a concert series across the continent and establishing, in 1864, New York City's second professional orchestra (the Philharmonic Society had been formed in 1842). As a result, other orchestras—now venerable institutions—arose: these include the Boston Symphony Orchestra (founded in 1881), the Chicago Symphony (1891), and the Philadelphia Orchestra (1900).

IN HIS OWN WORDS

The way to write American music is simple. All you have to do is be an American and then write any kind of music you wish.

—*VIRGIL THOMSON*

Women and Music: A Feminist Perspective

Have you wondered why we study so few works by women composers? We have seen that in earlier eras, upper-class women frequently studied music, especially keyboard playing and singing—indeed, such study was a near necessity in proper society. Some, like the medieval abbess Hildegard of Bingen, were inspired to compose music but exclusively for the needs of the church; others, like Barbara Strozzi, performed and composed within the elite world of the Italian intellectual academies.

Although the gender barrier began to break down in the later nineteenth century, many still held the view that women lacked creativity in the arts. This attitude drove some women to pursue literary careers under male pseudonyms: George Eliot (alias Mary Ann Evans), George Sand (alias Baronne Aurore Dudevant), and Daniel Stern (alias Comtesse Marie d'Agoult), to name just three. Despite the social attitudes of the era, Clara Schumann and Fanny Mendelssohn Hensel, among others, saw their compositions published and critically acclaimed. But the odds were against them in this endeavor. George Upton, writing in 1880, claimed, "Not only are women too emotional and lacking in stamina to write music, but a woman's mind simply cannot grasp the scientific logic of music making," and even Clara Schumann herself remarked that "women always betray themselves in their compositions." Still, women made their musical mark, especially in songs, piano music, and chamber works.

Repression of women became an important social issue at the beginning of the twentieth century. A women's movement arose to bring about social reform: some worked against societal problems such as alcoholism, some fought for improved education, and many rallied for suffrage, or the right to vote. (It was not until 1920, with the passage of the Twentieth Amendment to the Constitution, that women won legal equality in the political arena.) By the turn of the century, some female musicians had adopted militant feminist perspectives.

One such activist was the English composer Ethel Smyth, a prominent suffragist who fought against sexual discrimination in music. Her *March of the Women* became the anthem of a feminist organization called the Women's Social and Political Union.

Not all women composers followed her courageous path. The American composer Amy Beach was more conservative, choosing to be known professionally as Mrs. H. H. A. Beach in deference to her married status; however, in later life, she headed several important educational organizations that reached out to both sexes.

Feminists today have posed some interesting questions regarding women composers. For example, do women and men speak differently through music? Is there a woman's "voice" in music, and if so, what characterizes it? More scientifically, does biology play a role in the creative process? Reviewers, mostly male, have criticized musical works by nineteenth-century women that

Boston had long been a major American center for classical music. In the eighteenth century, the city had generated the First New England School of composers, most of whom wrote sacred church music and arrangements of traditional hymn tunes. The strong church music tradition continued in the generations that followed, particularly with Lowell Mason (1792–1872), a composer of more than 1,200 original hymns and a dedicated music teacher. Mason is credited with getting music admitted into the public-school curriculum of Boston, which led to its general acceptance in public-school programs across the country.

With the Boston schools spearheading musical training for the general public, it is not surprising that this city also produced the first important composers to write music comparable in quality to that of European musicians. The earliest important failed to conform to traditional structural procedures (such as the symphony cycle or sonata-allegro form). Did women base their choice of forms on their concert settings (which were mostly salons instead of public halls), on the makeup of their audiences, or on their musical training, which usually occurred at home? Or did they avoid the common procedures of composition because of the "masculine" implications of the forms—which were, after all, designed and defined exclusively by men? Critics have not always applied the same standards to compositions by both sexes: while a woman might be criticized for writing music that was too "feminine," a man who writes music considered "feminine" (Chopin, for example) is credited with having a full range of emotional expression.

Popular music has opened up to a new woman's voice and to improved perceptions of women. While many contemporary songs have made demeaning references to women and expressed violent attitudes toward them, modern artists such as Salt 'N Pepa (the first successful female rap group), hip-hop artists Queen Latifah and

Pink, Mya, Lil' Kim and Christina Aguilera at the 2002 MTV awards singing "Lady Marmalade," a song from the film *Moulin Rouge*.

Missy Elliot, and the all-female cast of the Lilith Fair tours, organized by Sarah MacLaughlin, have sounded a strong voice against female bashing through their own artistic creations. The phrase "girl power"—popularized in the mid-1990s by the Spice Girls ("God help the mister who comes between me and my sisters," from *Love Thing*)—is now so commonplace that it is defined in the *Oxford English Dictionary*. Artists such as Tori Amos (*Little Earthquakes*, 1992), Gwen Stefani (*Just a Girl*, 1995), and Christina Aguilera (*Can't Hold Us Down*, 2002) movingly extol the power of women in contemporary music.

Suggested Listening

Works by Hildegard, Clara Schumann, Fanny Mendelssohn Hensel, Ethel Smyth, Meredith Monk, Libby Larsen, Salt 'N Pepa, Björk, Queen Latifah (*All Hail the Queen*), Alanis Morissette *(Under Rug Swept)*, Christina Aguilera *(Can't Hold Us Down)*

---

composer of this Second New England School was John Knowles Paine (1839–1906), whose Mass in D, modeled on Beethoven's *Missa solemnis,* was the first large-scale classical work by an American to be performed in Europe. From 1876 until his death thirty years later, Paine held the country's first professorship in music, at Harvard University.

One of Paine's students at Harvard was Arthur Foote (1853–1937), a Boston-based composer remembered today for his orchestral and chamber music, conceived in the Brahmsian tradition. Foote held a teaching position for some years at the New England Conservatory of Music, where he worked with another well-known composer, George Whitefield Chadwick (1854–1931). Born into a musical New England family, Chadwick was influential in giving an American flavor to music based on

The Second New England School

Amy Cheney Beach

European models. His symphonic works, most of which were premiered by the Boston Symphony Orchestra, and his five string quartets were well received. Chadwick left his mark on students both as a teacher and as director of the New England Conservatory in Boston.

A third composer who made important strides in turning the national path away from the Germanic style was Edward MacDowell (1860–1908), a New Yorker who studied piano and composition in Europe. His very popular *Woodland Sketches*, for piano, and his Second Orchestral Suite both incorporate Native American tunes. In 1896, MacDowell became the first professor of music at Columbia University.

Amy Cheney Beach, a contemporary of all these influential musicians, was widely recognized in her lifetime as the leading American woman composer. Renewed interest in her work has shown her to be in the forefront of the New England School of composition.

Amy Cheney Beach and Music in New England

Amy Cheney (1867–1944) was born in Henniker, New Hampshire, the only child of a wealthy industrialist and a gifted amateur singer and pianist. A child prodigy, Amy had a keen ear for music. She studied piano with her mother and later piano and composition in Boston. She published her first composition, a song set to a Longfellow poem, in 1883.

Amy concertized regularly and in 1885 performed Chopin's F-minor Piano Concerto in the first of several concerts she played with the Boston Symphony Orchestra. In the same year, she married Henry Harris Aubrey Beach, a forty-three-year-old physician and amateur singer.

Between 1885 and 1910, Amy Cheney Beach (or Mrs. H. H. A. Beach, as she chose to be known) produced a number of her major works. These include the Mass in E flat, the concert aria *Racing Clouds*, the *Gaelic* Symphony, and the Piano Concerto in C-sharp minor—all performed by prestigious musical groups such as the Boston Symphony Orchestra, the Symphony Society of New York, and the Handel and Haydn Society of Boston. Her *Festival Jubilate*, commissioned for the dedication of the Women's Building of the Chicago World Exposition of 1893, provided her with the international venue she needed to gain wide visibility and recognition as a composer.

In her later years, Beach helped shape the careers of many young musicians. She held leadership positions in the Music Educators National Conference and the Music Teachers National Association; she also served as co-founder and first president of the Society of American Women Composers. At her death in 1944, she left her royalties to the MacDowell Colony, a retreat for artists, writers, and composers in Peterborough, New Hampshire, where she spent a portion of each summer from 1921 on.

Beach's Symphony in E minor (the *Gaelic*), the first known symphony composed by an American woman, is a masterpiece that is thought to have been inspired by Dvořák's *New World* Symphony, also in E minor. Aware of Dvořák's suggestion that American composers look to their own folk music for inspiration (see CP 12), Beach noted that New Englanders were likely to be of Irish, Scottish, or English ancestry, and thus drew on these musical traditions in her *Gaelic* Symphony. In the realm of chamber music, Beach contributed many works, including the Violin Sonata in A minor. This well-constructed, appealing work, along with the *Gaelic* Symphony, signaled the final strains of American Romanticism. It also marks Beach's significant contribution to classical composition in North America.

IN HER OWN WORDS

The women composers of today have advanced in technique, resourcefulness, and force, and even the younger composers have achieved some effects which the great masters themselves would never have dared to attempt. The present composers are getting away more and more from the idea that they must cater to the popular taste, and in expressing their individual ideas, are giving us music of real worth and beauty.

Musical influences

Choral and Dramatic Music in the Nineteenth Century

56

Romantic Choral Music

*"I speak through my music. The only thing is that a
poor musician such as myself would like to believe
that he was better than his music."*

—JOHANNES BRAHMS

KEY POINTS	**StudySpace** online at www.wwnorton.com/enjoy

○ Choral music grew in popularity during the Romantic era and was an artistic outlet for the middle classes.

○ Favored genres in the nineteenth century include *part songs* (unaccompanied secular songs in three or four parts), the oratorio, the Mass, and the Requiem Mass.

○ Brahms's *German Requiem,* set to biblical texts chosen by the composer, is one of the masterworks of the romantic choral repertory.

The nineteenth century witnessed a spreading of the democratic ideal and an enormous expansion of the audience for music. This climate was uniquely favorable to choral singing, a group activity enjoyed by increasing numbers of amateur music lovers that played an important role in the musical life of the Romantic era.

Since singing in a chorus required different skills than playing in an orchestra, group singing attracted many people who had never learned to play an instrument or who could not afford to buy one. With a modest amount of rehearsal (and modest vocal quality), they could take part in the performance of great choral works. The members

Amateur choral groups

291

In the 19th century, enormous choral and orchestral forces were a common sight, as in this engraving of the opening concert at St. Martin's Hall, London, 1850.

IN HIS OWN WORDS

The oldest, truest, most beautiful organ of music, the origin to which our music owes its being, is the human voice.

—RICHARD WAGNER

of the chorus not only enjoyed a pleasant social evening once or twice a week but also, if their group was good enough, became a source of pride to their community.

Choral music offered the masses an ideal outlet for their artistic energies. The repertory centered on the great choral heritage of the past. Nevertheless, if choral music was to remain a vital force, its literature had to be enriched by new works that would reflect the spirit of the time. The list of composers active in this area includes some of the most important names of the nineteenth century: Schubert, Berlioz, Felix and Fanny Mendelssohn, Clara and Robert Schumann, Liszt, Verdi, Brahms, and Dvořák. These composers produced a body of choral music that represents some of the best creative efforts of the Romantic period.

Part songs

A vast literature of secular choral pieces appeared. These works, settings for chorus of lyric poems in a variety of moods and styles, were known as ***part songs***—that is, songs with three or four voice parts. Most of them were short melodious works, easy enough for amateurs. They gave pleasure both to the singers and to their listeners, and played an important role in developing the new audience of the nineteenth century.

The part songs of Fanny Mendelssohn Hensel (1805–1847) are fine examples of this newly emerging choral repertory. Although her talents as a composer have been overshadowed by those of her more famous brother Felix, she was a first-rate musician in her own right (see Chapter 57).

Sacred choral forms

Among the large-scale genres of choral music in the nineteenth century were the Mass, the Requiem Mass, and the oratorio. We have seen that all three were originally intended to be performed in church, but by the nineteenth century they had found a wider audience in the concert hall. This is certainly the case with Brahms's *German Requiem*, which is far removed from the traditions of the Catholic Church that gave birth to the genre.

BRAHMS'S *A GERMAN REQUIEM*

A German Requiem was rooted in the Protestant tradition into which Johannes Brahms was born. Its aim was to console the living and lead them to a serene acceptance of death as an inevitable part of life, hence its gentle lyricism. Brahms chose his text from the Old and New Testaments: from the Psalms, Proverbs, Isaiah, and Ecclesiastes as well as from Paul, Matthew, Peter, John, and Revelation. Brahms was not religious in the conventional sense, nor was he affiliated with any particular church. He was moved to compose his Requiem by the deaths first of his teacher and friend Robert Schumann, then of his mother, whom he idolized; but the piece transcends personal emotions and endures as a song of mourning for all humanity.

Written for soloists, four-part chorus, and orchestra, *A German Requiem* is in seven movements arranged in a formation resembling an arch. There are connections between the first and last movements, between the second and sixth, and between the third and fifth; that leaves the fourth movement, the widely sung chorus *How Lovely Is Thy Dwelling Place*, as the centerpiece.

This movement is based on a verse from Psalm 84 (see Listening Guide 33). The first two lines of the psalm are heard three times, separated by two contrasting sections that present the other lines. The form, therefore, is **A-B-A′-C-A′**. The first two sections for the most part move in quarter notes, but the third section (**C**) moves more quickly in a vigorous rhythm, better suiting the line "die loben dich immerdar" (that praise Thee evermore), with much expansion on *immerdar* (evermore). With the final reappearance of the **A** section, the slower tempo returns. Marked *piano* and *dolce* (soft and sweet), this passage serves as a coda that brings the piece to its gentle and serene close.

Fourth movement

Listening Guide 33

| | eLG | 3 (29–33) 6 (19–23) |

Brahms: *A German Requiem*, Fourth Movement (5:46)

DATE OF WORK:	1868
GENRE:	Protestant Requiem
MEDIUM:	4-part chorus, soloists, and orchestra
MOVEMENTS:	7

WHAT TO LISTEN FOR:	Lyrical choral melody unifies 5-part rondo structure.
	Changes in mode (major-minor) and texture (homorhythmic/ polyphonic).
	Use of word painting—quicker in **C** section, and drawn out at end.
	Emotional expressions of loss and acceptance of death.

Fourth Movement: Mässig bewegt (moderately agitated)

Text: Psalm 84
Form: Rondo (**A-B-A′-C-A′**)
Character: Lilting triple meter, marked *dolce* (sweetly)

Listening Guide continues

Opening melody—clarinets and flutes invert first phrase in chorus:

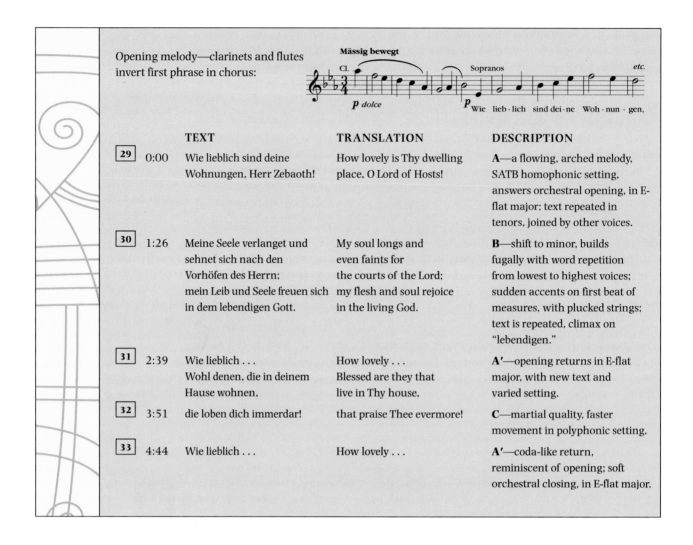

		TEXT	TRANSLATION	DESCRIPTION
29	0:00	Wie lieblich sind deine Wohnungen, Herr Zebaoth!	How lovely is Thy dwelling place, O Lord of Hosts!	**A**—a flowing, arched melody, SATB homophonic setting, answers orchestral opening, in E-flat major; text repeated in tenors, joined by other voices.
30	1:26	Meine Seele verlanget und sehnet sich nach den Vorhöfen des Herrn; mein Leib und Seele freuen sich in dem lebendigen Gott.	My soul longs and even faints for the courts of the Lord; my flesh and soul rejoice in the living God.	**B**—shift to minor, builds fugally with word repetition from lowest to highest voices; sudden accents on first beat of measures, with plucked strings; text is repeated, climax on "lebendigen."
31	2:39	Wie lieblich . . . Wohl denen, die in deinem Hause wohnen,	How lovely . . . Blessed are they that live in Thy house,	**A'**—opening returns in E-flat major, with new text and varied setting.
32	3:51	die loben dich immerdar!	that praise Thee evermore!	**C**—martial quality, faster movement in polyphonic setting.
33	4:44	Wie lieblich . . .	How lovely . . .	**A'**—coda-like return, reminiscent of opening; soft orchestral closing, in E-flat major.

57

Fanny Mendelssohn Hensel and the Romantic Part Song

"I want to admit how terribly uppity I've been and announce that six 4-part Lieder . . . are coming out next . . . My choir has enjoyed singing them . . . and I've made every effort to make them as good as possible."

KEY POINTS	StudySpace online at www.wwnorton.com/enjoy

○ Fanny Mendelssohn Hensel, sister of Felix Mendelssohn, was a talented composer and pianist. She is remembered today for Lieder, piano music, and choral works.

○ The *a cappella* part song *Under the Greenwood Tree*, set to a text from a Shakespeare play, was appropriate for amateur as well as professional choirs.

Fanny Mendelssohn Hensel: Her Life

Fanny Mendelssohn, the eldest of four children, was born into a highly cultured family (her grandfather, Moses Mendelssohn, was a leading Jewish scholar/philosopher). An important element of her background was the close relationship she maintained throughout her life with her younger brother Felix (see Chapter 55).

Raised in Berlin, Fanny received her earliest piano instruction from her mother, Lea, who claimed that the young girl was born with "Bach's fingers." She later studied theory and composition with the well-known composer and conductor Carl Friedrich Zelter. Her first surviving work is a Lied, written in 1819 for her father's birthday. The following year, she enrolled in the Berlin Singakademie.

Because of her gender, however, Fanny was actively discouraged from pursuing music as a career. Her father cautioned her to focus on "the only calling for a young woman—that of a housewife," and her brother Felix echoed the sentiment, claiming that "Fanny possesses neither the inclination nor the calling for authorship. She is too much a woman for that, as is proper, and looks after her house and thinks neither about the public nor the musical world unless that primary occupation is accomplished." Still, her creative talents were recognized by some: the poet Goethe wrote to Felix in 1825, asking that he "give my regards to your equally talented sister," and Felix even published several of her songs among his collections.

In 1829, Fanny Mendelssohn married the court artist Wilhelm Hensel, with whom she had a son, Sebastian. She remained active during the following years as a composer, pianist, and participant in the regular salon concerts held each Sunday at the Mendelssohn residence. With the death of her mother in 1842, Fanny took over the organization of the famous Sunday concerts.

Fanny died suddenly of an apoplectic stroke on May 13, 1847, while preparing to conduct a cantata written by her brother. Felix, having lost his dearest companion, died just six months later after a series of strokes.

Fanny Mendelssohn Hensel

IN HER OWN WORDS

I'm beginning to publish.... I hope I shall not disgrace you all, for I am no femme libre ... If it [my publication] succeeds ... and I receive further offers, I know it will be a great stimulus to me.... If not, I shall be at the same point where I have always been.

Her Music

Although her output is dominated by Lieder, choral part songs, and piano music, Fanny Mendelssohn Hensel also wrote some large-scale works. Important among these are her Piano Trio, Op. 11, a string quartet, several cantatas, and an oratorio. Although she was intelligent, witty, and confident in daily life, as a composer she lacked self-esteem. It was not until 1846 that she found the courage to publish her first set of songs, Opus 1, as well as a set of choral works.

Large-scale works

Fanny Mendelssohn Hensel's keyboard music is well crafted, reflecting her strong interest in Bach's contrapuntal procedures. Here and in her vocal music, her highly lyrical style displays a wide range of tonal, harmonic, and formal variety. Her complex piano accompaniments and her choice of German Romantic poets place her in the mainstream of the Lieder tradition. Throughout her creative life, she set texts by Goethe, her favorite poet and a family friend. She was influenced as well by the Romantic era's love of nature and was thus drawn to texts on this theme.

Keyboard music

Lieder

In 1846, the year before her death, Fanny wrote some two dozen part songs for choir. These were undoubtedly for performance at the Sunday concerts she hosted

Part songs

Music and Shakespeare

William Shakespeare's plays were the Renaissance equivalent of today's blockbuster movies, providing remarkable glimpses into the popular culture of the times. Nobility and common people alike flocked to see his latest productions. One of Shakespeare's particularly effective methods for social commentary was his plays' ballads, or popular English street songs. All range of characters—from clowns and rogues to spurned lovers—sang of poisonous concoctions, mesmerizing rituals, political wrongdoings, and broken hearts. Songs told of the cunning witches in *Macbeth* or Puck's love potions gone awry in *A Midsummer Night's Dream.* Some tunes were already well known to Shakespeare's audiences, such as in *The Merry Wives of Windsor* when Falstaff proclaims: "Let the sky rain potatoes! Let it thunder to the tune of *Greensleeves!*"

It comes as no surprise, then, that the master's words themselves would have inspired others to compose songs, operas, musicals, and even instrumental music based on his works. We will see that Fanny Mendelssohn read Shakespeare and set a choral song to *Under the Greenwood Tree* (*Unter des Laubdachs Hut,* a traditional tune sung in the play *As You Like It*). Berlioz wrote incidental music to *King Lear,* a symphony (with voices) on *Romeo and Juliet,* and an opera drawn from *Much Ado About Nothing.* Remember too that Berlioz was bewitched by a Shakespearean actress when he wrote his *Symphonie fantastique* (see p. 268).

Shakespeare's works have also fared well on the musical stage. *Romeo and Juliet,* for example, inspired many compositions, including an orchestral tone poem by Tchaikovsky and the Broadway musical *West Side Story,* by Leonard Bernstein (see p. 395). The well-

Audiences were entranced by the film *Shakespeare in Love* (1998), featuring Gwyneth Paltrow and Joseph Fiennes.

known Italian composer Verdi should be credited with setting more of Shakespeare's works than any other composer. These include his operas *Macbeth, Otello,* and *Falstaff* (which took its inspiration from both *The Merry Wives of Windsor* and *King Henry IV, Parts I and II*).

Shakespeare's writings remain as popular as ever today. His plays are celebrated at festivals around the globe, in the movies (*Hamlet,* 1996; *A Midsummer Night's Dream,* 1999, and *Shakespeare in Love,* 1998), and even with rock and hip-hop interpretations, including an updated Shakespeare's *Comedy of Errors* (titled *The Bomb-itty of Errors*) in an "add-rap-tation" that found success in both the United States and England. These combinations of pop culture and classic literature have helped keep younger generations tuned in to the classics.

Terms to Note

ballad
bard
Broadway musical

Suggested Listening

CD iMusic Bernstein's *West Side Story*
CD iMusic *Greensleeves*
Mendelssohn's *A Midsummer Night's Dream*

and at which she regularly conducted a choir of sixteen to twenty-four singers. In the same year, she published her six choral *Garden Songs*, Op. 3. Felix gave his nod of approval, writing "May you know only the pleasure of being a composer and none of the miseries; may the public only send you roses and never sand; may the printer's ink never seem black and oppressive to you."

UNDER THE GREENWOOD TREE

We will consider her four-voice part song *Under the Greenwood Tree*, an *a cappella* work with immediate lyrical appeal. The text comes from Shakespeare's pastoral comedy *As You Like It* (Act II, Scene 5), in which one of the lords who has been banished to the forest strikes up a ballad (see CP 14). Fanny had a great love for Shakespeare; her letters tell of reading his works to her husband, attending performances of his plays, and even sending Felix an alabaster bust of the playwright. This enchanting song is strophic, constructed of two verses, each followed by the chorus "Come hither." Interest is focused on changing textures (see Listening Guide 34): the choir sings together, then divides into imitative statements that set low-range voices (tenors and basses) against the upper ones (altos and sopranos), repeating lines and phrases to establish the high spirited mood as well as mirroring the meaning of Shakespeare's text.

Pre-Raphaelite artist **Dante Gabriel Rossetti** (1828–1882) looks back to music-making in Shakespeare's day in *Morning Music*.

The music of Fanny Mendelssohn Hensel has been unduly neglected over the years. The recent revival of her works, both in the concert hall and on recordings, has revealed her genuine talents and greatly enriched our modern-day understanding of the challenges faced by women musicians in the Romantic era.

Listening Guide 34	eLG	3 (34-37) 6 (24–27)

Fanny Mendelssohn Hensel: *Under the Greenwood Tree*
(Unter des Laubdachs Hut)   (1:53)

DATE OF WORK:	1846
GENRE:	Part song for 4-voice choir (SATB)
FORM:	Strophic, 2 verses with chorus
TEXT:	Song from Shakespeare's comedy *As You Like It*

WHAT TO LISTEN FOR: Buoyant, lilting 6/8 meter.
Alternation of homorhythmic setting with divided voices in imitative
  dialogue.
Strophic form (2 verses alternating with chorus); repeated text in chorus.

Listening Guide continues

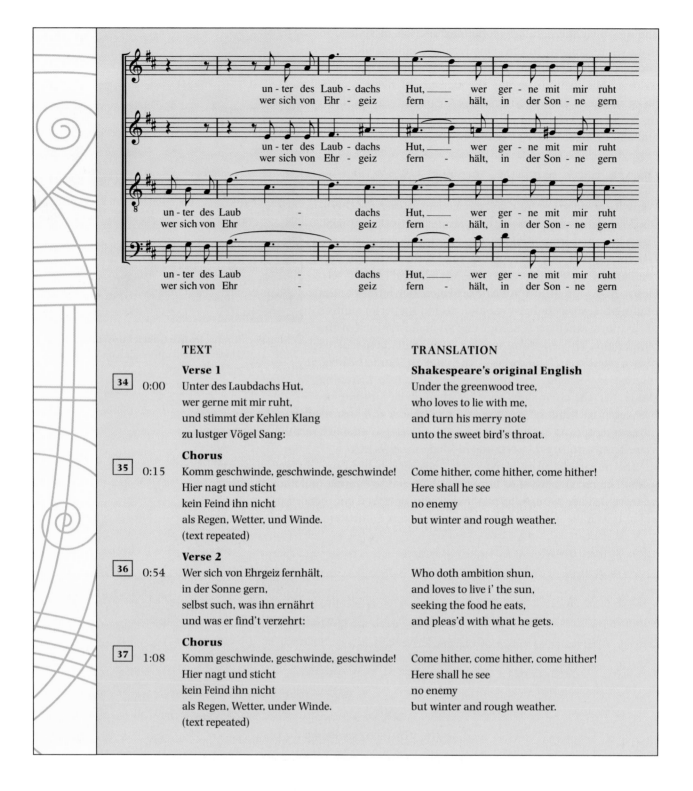

		TEXT	TRANSLATION
		Verse 1	**Shakespeare's original English**
34	0:00	Unter des Laubdachs Hut,	Under the greenwood tree,
		wer gerne mit mir ruht,	who loves to lie with me,
		und stimmt der Kehlen Klang	and turn his merry note
		zu lustger Vögel Sang:	unto the sweet bird's throat.
		Chorus	
35	0:15	Komm geschwinde, geschwinde, geschwinde!	Come hither, come hither, come hither!
		Hier nagt und sticht	Here shall he see
		kein Feind ihn nicht	no enemy
		als Regen, Wetter, und Winde.	but winter and rough weather.
		(text repeated)	
		Verse 2	
36	0:54	Wer sich von Ehrgeiz fernhält,	Who doth ambition shun,
		in der Sonne gern,	and loves to live i' the sun,
		selbst such, was ihn ernährt	seeking the food he eats,
		und was er find't verzehrt:	and pleas'd with what he gets.
		Chorus	
37	1:08	Komm geschwinde, geschwinde, geschwinde!	Come hither, come hither, come hither!
		Hier nagt und sticht	Here shall he see
		kein Feind ihn nicht	no enemy
		als Regen, Wetter, under Winde.	but winter and rough weather.
		(text repeated)	

58

Romantic Opera

"Opera is free from any servile imitation of nature. By the power of music it attunes the soul to a beautiful receptiveness."

—FRIEDRICH VON SCHILLER

○ Romantic opera developed distinct national styles in France, Germany, and Italy.

○ In France, *lyric opera* represented a merger between *grand opera* (serious historical dramas with spectacular effects) and *opéra comique* (comic opera with spoken dialogue).

○ In Germany, the genre of *Singspiel* (light, comic drama with spoken dialogue) gave way to more

serious works, including Richard Wagner's *music drama*, which integrated all elements of opera.

○ Both *opera seria* (serious opera) and *opera buffa* (comic opera) were favored in Italy; they marked the peak of the *bel canto* (beautiful singing) style.

○ Many Romantic composers turned to exotic plots for their operas, looking to faraway lands or cultures for inspiration.

For some four hundred years, opera has been one of the most alluring forms of musical entertainment. A special glamour is attached to everything connected with it—its superstar performers, extravagant scenic designs, even the glitter and excitement of opening nights.

At first glance, opera seems to demand that the spectator believe the unbelievable. It presents us with human beings caught up in dramatic situations, who sing to each other instead of speaking, even after they've been strangled or stabbed or shot. The reasonable question is: how can an art form based on so unnatural a procedure be convincing?

True enough, people in real life do not sing to each other. Neither do they converse in blank verse, as Shakespeare's characters do, nor live in rooms of which one wall is conveniently missing so that the audience may look in. All the arts employ conventions that are accepted by both the artist and the audience. Opera uses the human voice to project basic emotions—love, hate, jealousy, joy, grief—with an elemental force. The logic of reality gives way on the operatic stage to the power of music and the imagination.

> IN HIS OWN WORDS
>
> *I have never encountered anything more false and foolish than the effort to get truth into opera. In opera everything is based upon the untrue.*
> —PETER ILYICH TCHAIKOVSKY

The Development of National Styles

As one of the most important and best-loved theatrical genres of the nineteenth century, opera fostered different national styles in three European countries known for their music—France, Germany, and Italy.

FRANCE

In Paris, the opera center of Europe in the late eighteenth and early nineteenth centuries, *grand opera* was all the rage. This new genre, which focused on serious historical themes and was nourished by the propagandist purposes of France's new

Grand opera

leaders, suited the bourgeoisie's taste for the big and the spectacular very well. Complete with huge choruses, crowd scenes, ornate costumes and scenery, and elaborate dance episodes, grand opera was as much a spectacle as it was a musical event. Giacomo Meyerbeer (1791–1864), a German composer who studied in Italy, was largely responsible for bringing grand opera to Paris. His best-known work is *Les Huguenots* (1836)—a blend of social statement, history, and spectacle, with memorable melodies and rich orchestration.

Opéra comique   Less pretentious than French grand opera was ***opéra comique***, which required smaller performance forces, featured a simpler compositional style, and included spoken dialogue rather than recitatives. One of the lighter works that enchanted Parisian audiences was Jacques Offenbach's (1819–1880) *Orphée aux enfers* (*Orpheus in the Underworld,* 1858), which blended wit and satire into the popular model.

GERMANY

Nineteenth-century Germany had no long-established opera tradition, as France and Italy did. The immediate predecessor of German Romantic opera was the
Singspiel   ***Singspiel***, a light or comic drama with spoken dialogue. Mozart's *Die Zauberflöte* (*The Magic Flute*) is an early example of this style. The first composer to express the German Romantic spirit in opera was Carl Maria von Weber (1786–1826), whose best-known work is *Der Freischütz* (*The Freeshooter,* 1821). In this opera, supernatural beings and mysterious forces of nature intertwine with heroes and heroines to produce drama featuring simple and direct melodies that are almost folklike, accompanied by expressive timbres and harmonies. The greatest figure in German opera—and one of the most significant in the history of the Romantic era—was
Music drama   Richard Wagner, who created the ***music drama***, a genre that integrated theater and music completely (see Chapter 60).

ITALY

Italy in the early nineteenth century still recognized the opposing genres of ***opera seria*** (serious opera) and ***opera buffa*** (the Italian version of comic opera), legacies of an earlier period. Important composers of these styles include Gioachino Rossini

Margrave's Opera House in Bayreuth, 1879. A painting by **Gustav Bauernfeind** (1848–1904).

(1792–1868), whose masterpieces are *Il barbiere di Siviglia* (*The Barber of Seville*, 1816) and *Guillaume Tell* (*William Tell*, 1829); Gaetano Donizetti (1797–1848), composer of some seventy operas, including *Lucia di Lammermoor* (*Lucy of Lammermore*, 1835); and Vincenzo Bellini (1801–1835), whose *Norma* (1831) is preeminent for its lovely melodies. These operas marked the high point of a **bel canto** (beautiful singing) style, characterized by florid melodic lines delivered by voices of great agility and purity of tone. The consummate master of nineteenth-century Italian opera was Giuseppe Verdi, who sought to develop a uniquely national style (see Chapter 59).

CD iMusic

William Tell Overture

Bel canto style

Exoticism in Opera

We have seen that a yearning for far-off lands was an important component of the Romantic imagination. This urge found a perfect outlet in opera, which could be set anywhere in the world. Composers of opera were not terribly interested in authenticity; their primary concern was to create a picturesque atmosphere that would appeal to audiences. In other words, an exotic setting reflected the imagination of the composer rather than first-hand knowledge of a culture. If the action took place in Asia or Africa, the work was still in the musical language of the West, but that language was flavored with melodies, harmonies, and rhythms suggestive of the faraway locale.

A prime example is Verdi's *Aida*, which manages within the traditional idiom of Italian opera to evoke ancient Egypt under the pharaohs. The French composer Camille Saint-Saëns (1835–1921) turned to the Bible for the story of *Samson and Delilah.* Another biblical story inspired the German composer Richard Strauss to write *Salome*; although the opera is set in ancient Judea, Salome's *Dance of the Seven Veils* employs a tune reminiscent of a langorous Viennese waltz. The turn-of-the-century Italian master Giacomo Puccini (1858–1924) produced two well-known operas with Asian settings: *Turandot*, based on a legend of ancient China, and *Madame Butterfly*, a romantic drama set in late-nineteenth-century Japan, which we will study.

French composers have always been fascinated by Spain. Thus a number of French orchestral classics describe the colorful peninsula, as Bizet does in his alluring opera *Carmen.*

Italian singer Gabriella Besanzoni as a colorful Carmen.

CD iMusic

Toreador Song, from *Carmen*

Women in Opera

Opera was one medium that allowed women musicians a good deal of visibility. Only a few tried their hand at composing full-scale operas, but those who did were able to see a number of their works produced. The French composer Louise Bertin (1805–1877) had several operas produced at the exclusive Opéra-Comique in Paris, including *La Esmeralda* (1836), on a libretto based on Victor Hugo's well-known novel about the hunchback of Notre Dame.

Louise Bertin

Women opera singers were among the most prominent performers of their day, idolized and in demand throughout Europe and the Americas. One such international star was Jenny Lind (1820–1887), known as the "Swedish nightingale" and famous for her roles in operas by Meyerbeer, Donizetti, Weber, and Bellini. A concert artist as well, Lind made her American debut in 1850 in a tour managed with immense hoopla by circus impresario P. T. Barnum.

Jenny Lind

The famous singer Jenny Lind during a recital at Exeter Hall, London, 1855.

Maria Malibran

Pauline Viardot

Professional singing was often a family tradition: the offspring of the celebrated Spanish tenor Manuel García provide a case in point. A brilliant teacher, García coached two of his daughters to stardom. His eldest, Maria Malibran (1808–1836), became renowned as an interpreter of Rossini, whose works she sang in London, Paris, Milan, Naples, and New York. A riding accident brought her very successful career to a tragic close. Her youngest sister, Pauline Viardot (1821–1910; see p. 251), was highly acclaimed for her great musical and dramatic gifts. Viardot did much to further the careers of several French composers of operas and songs, and sang the premieres of vocal works by Brahms, Robert Schumann, and Berlioz. A composer herself, Viardot's intellectual approach to her art did much to raise the status of women singers.

59

Verdi and Italian Opera

"Success is impossible for me if I cannot write as my heart dictates!"

| KEY POINTS | ⑤ **StudySpace** online at www.wwnorton.com/enjoy |

○ The Italian nationalist composer Giuseppe Verdi is best known for his twenty-eight operas; they embody the spirit of Romantic drama and passion.

○ Many of Verdi's operas draw on well-known literary sources, including several from Shakespeare

plays (*Macbeth*, *Otello*, and *Falstaff* from *Merry Wives of Windsor*).

○ *Rigoletto*, Verdi's opera based on a play by Victor Hugo, is one of the most performed works in the repertory today.

In the case of Giuseppe Verdi, the most widely loved of operatic composers, time, place, and personality were happily merged. He inherited a rich musical tradition, his capacity for growth was matched by extraordinary energy and will, and he was granted a long life in which to engage fully his creative gift.

His Life

Born in a small town in northern Italy where his father kept an inn, Giuseppe Verdi (1813–1901) grew up amid the poverty of village life. His talent attracted the attention of a prosperous merchant and music lover who made it possible for the youth to pursue his studies. After two years in Milan, Verdi returned home to take a position as an organist. When he fell in love with his benefactor's daughter, the merchant in wholly untraditional fashion accepted the penniless young musician as his son-in-law. Verdi was twenty-three, Margherita sixteen.

Ⓖ **Giuseppe Verdi**

Three years later, Verdi returned to Milan with the manuscript of an opera, which was produced at the opera house of La Scala in 1839. The work brought him a commission to write three others. At this time, Verdi faced a string of crises in his life. His first child, a daughter, had died before he left for Milan. The second, a baby boy, was carried off by fever in 1839, a catastrophe followed several months later by the death of his young wife. "In a sudden moment of despondency I despaired of finding any comfort in my art and resolved to give up composing," he wrote.

As the months passed, the distraught young composer held to his decision. Then one night he happened to meet the director of La Scala (see p. 320), who insisted that he take home a libretto about Nebuchadnezzar, king of Babylon. Verdi returned to work, and the resulting opera, *Nabucco*, presented at La Scala in 1842, was a triumph that launched him on a spectacular career.

Italy at the time was liberating itself from Austrian Hapsburg rule. Verdi identified himself with the national cause from the beginning: "I am first of all an Italian!" he declared. In this charged atmosphere, his works took on special meaning for his compatriots. The chorus of exiled Jews from *Nabucco* became an Italian patriotic song that is still sung today.

Although he became a world-renowned figure, Verdi retained a simplicity that was at the core of both the artist and the man. He returned to his hometown, where he settled with his second wife, the singer Giuseppina Strepponi. She was his devoted companion for half a century. After Italy won independence, Verdi was urged to run for a seat in parliament because of the prestige his name would bring the new state. Although the task conformed to neither his talents nor his inclinations, he accepted and sat in the Chamber of Deputies for some years.

During his time in public life, he was somehow able to produce one masterpiece after another. He was fifty-seven when he wrote *Aida*. At seventy-three, he completed *Otello*, his greatest lyric tragedy. And in 1893, on the threshold of eighty, he astonished the world with *Falstaff.* In all, he wrote twenty-eight operas.

Verdi's death at eighty-seven was mourned throughout the world. He left the bulk of his fortune to a home for aged musicians that he had founded in Milan (still in operation today). Italy accorded him the rites reserved for a national hero. From the voices of thousands who marched in his funeral procession there arose the haunting melody of "Va pensiero sull' ali dorate" (Go, thought, on gilded wings), the chorus from *Nabucco*, with which he had inspired his fellow Italians sixty years earlier.

The singer Giuseppina Strepponi, Verdi's second wife, with a score of his opera *Nabucco* (1842).

His Music

Verdi's music stands as the epitome of Romantic drama and passion. Endowed with an imagination that saw all emotion in terms of action and conflict, Verdi was able to communicate a dramatic situation with shattering expressiveness. True Italian that he was, he prized melody above all; to him this was the most immediate expression of human feeling.

Early works   Of his fifteen early operas, the most important is *Macbeth*, his first work based on Shakespeare. Following in close succession came *Rigoletto* (which we will study), on a play by Victor Hugo; *Il trovatore* (*The Troubador*), derived from a fanciful Spanish play; and *La traviata*, based on *La dame aux camélias* (*The Lady of the Camellias*) by the younger Alexandre Dumas. In these works, the mature musical dramatist was revealed.

Middle and late periods   The operas of the middle period show Verdi writing on a more ambitious scale and incorporating elements of the French grand opera. The three most important are *A Masked Ball*, *The Force of Destiny*, and *Don Carlos*. These aims were carried even further in *Aida*, the work that ushers in his final period (1870–93). *Aida* was commissioned in 1870 by the ruler of Egypt to mark the opening of the Suez Canal. (You may know *Aida* as the recent Broadway show by Elton John and Tim Rice, which is based on Verdi's masterpiece.)

Last operas   For his last two operas, Verdi found an ideal librettist in Arrigo Boito (1842–1918), who brilliantly adapted two plays by Shakespeare. *Otello*, their first collaboration, is the high point of three hundred years of Italian lyric tragedy. After its opening night, the seventy-four-year-old composer declared, "I feel as if I had fired my last cartridge. Music needs youthfulness of the senses, impetuous blood, fullness of life." But he disproved his words when, six years later (1893), he completed *Falstaff*, based on Shakespeare's *Merry Wives of Windsor*. This luminous work ranks with the greatest comic operas.

RIGOLETTO

The writer Victor Hugo, an acknowledged leader of French Romanticism, was Verdi's source of inspiration for *Rigoletto*. Hugo's play *Le roi s'amuse* (*The King Is Amused*, 1832) was banned in France but achieved universal popularity through its adaptation in Verdi's opera. The plot, featuring lechery, deformity, irony, and assas-

Famous Welch baritone Bryn Terfel plays Falstaff in a Los Angeles Opera production (2005–6).

sination, revolves around a hunchbacked jester, Rigoletto, who is a fascinating study in opposites. (You will remember that Hugo wrote of another hunchback, in his historical novel *The Hunchback of Notre Dame*; the intriguing bell-ringer Quasimodo has inspired several well-known movies, including the Disney animated musical.) With a libretto by Francesco Piave, *Rigoletto* was Verdi's first great success.

The story is set in the Renaissance era at the ducal court of Mantua, a small city in northern Italy (Monteverdi wrote his early operas there). The first scene takes place in a great hall of the ducal palace, where a ball is in progress. The Duke, a notorious womanizer, woos the wife of one of his courtiers, the Count of Ceprano. The court jester, Rigoletto, mocks the unlucky husband to all who will listen, and then suggests to the Duke that the Count of Ceprano be disposed of. Meanwhile, gossiping courtiers spread a rumor that the hunchbacked jester has a mistress. An elderly nobleman, Monterone, interrupts the scene and accuses the Duke of having seduced his daughter. The Duke promptly has the aging father arrested; Rigoletto taunts Monterone, who returns his gibes with a curse.

In a dark alley, Rigoletto meets up with the assassin Sparafucile, who warns the jester that he has enemies and offers him his services. Arriving home, Rigoletto's spirits are raised when he sees his daughter, Gilda, whom he keeps in seclusion. He warns Gilda and her nurse to stay in the house and not admit anyone. As Rigoletto leaves, the Duke enters the garden, realizing then that the beautiful young woman he had noticed in church is the jester's daughter; she, however, did not tell her father of the attractive young man who had caught her eye. The Duke, claiming to be a poor student, professes his love to Gilda. As courtiers approach the house, he escapes. Believing that Gilda is the deformed jester's mistress, the courtiers plan to abduct her in retribution for Rigoletto's cruel taunting. When the father returns, he is tricked into being blindfolded, and Gilda is carried off as Rigoletto recalls Monterone's curse.

In Act II, the Duke realizes that his new love has vanished, and Rigoletto bemoans his own loss while striving to convince everyone that Gilda is indeed his daughter. Gilda is brought out and throws herself in her father's arms, ashamed of her behavior with the Duke. Rigoletto vows vengeance on the abductors.

The final act takes place on a stormy night at a tavern near the river. Sparafucile's sister, Maddalena, has lured the Duke to the lonely tavern, and Rigoletto forces Gilda to watch through a window as the Duke pursues Maddalena. Planning to send her away, Rigoletto then instructs his daughter to dress as a man for her escape. Meanwhile, it has been arranged that Sparafucile will kill the Duke and return his body to Rigoletto in a bag to be thrown in the river. However, Maddalena succumbs to the Duke's charms and begs her brother to spare the handsome nobleman. Sparafucile agrees, only if a substitute shows up at the tavern. Gilda, now in male attire, overhears the plan, and enters the tavern to sacrifice herself for the unworthy man she loves. Sparafucile returns the sack to Rigoletto, as arranged, but just as the hunchback is about to dispose of the body, he hears the Duke singing from an upstairs window. Horrified, he opens the sack to find a dying Gilda, who begs forgiveness for herself and the Duke. Rigoletto recalls the curse one last time, as Gilda dies in his arms.

The quartet scene from Verdi's *Rigoletto* in the London premiere (1853) at Covent Garden. Rigoletto and his daughter, Gilda (on the right), are watching the Duke and Maddalena inside the tavern.

IN HIS OWN WORDS

It seems to me that the best material I have yet put to music is Rigoletto. It has the most powerful situations, it has variety, vitality, pathos; all the dramatic developments result from the frivolous, licentious character of the Duke. Hence Rigoletto's fears, Gilda's passion, etc., which give rise to many dramatic situations, including the scene of the quartet.

Costumes for the first production of Verdi's *Rigoletto* at Teatro la Fenice, Venice, March 11, 1851.

Two of the most popular operatic moments of all time occur in Act III. The Duke sings the best-known of Verdi's tunes, "La donna è mobile" (Woman is fickle), a simple but rousing song accompanied by a guitarlike orchestral strumming. The orchestra previews the catchy melody, which is heard numerous times as a ritornello in a strophic setting that brings back the opening text as a refrain.

The quartet that follows shortly is a masterpiece of operatic ensemble writing. Each of the four characters presents a different point of view: the Duke woos Maddalena in a lovely bel canto–style melody, calling her "beautiful daughter of love"; Maddalena answers with a laughing line in short notes, "Ha! Ha! I laugh heartily"; Gilda, watching from outside, is heartbroken as she laments her lost love; and Rigoletto hushes her, swearing vengeance for such treatment of his beloved daughter. Although the text becomes increasingly more difficult to follow as the characters sing together, the emotions of each soar through clearly (see Listening Guide 35 for text and form).

These two show-stopping numbers ensured the immediate success of *Rigoletto*. It remains one of the most frequently performed operas of the international repertory.

Listening Guide 35

eLG 3 (38–43)
6 (28–33)

Verdi: *Rigoletto*, Act III, excerpts (8:13)

FIRST PERFORMANCE:	1851, Venice
LIBRETTIST:	Francesco Maria Piave
BASIS:	Play, *Le roi s'amuse,* by Victor Hugo
MAJOR CHARACTERS:	The Duke of Mantua (tenor)
	Rigoletto, the Duke's jester, a hunchback (baritone)
	Gilda, Rigoletto's daughter (soprano)
	Sparafucile, an assassin (bass)
	Maddalena, Sparafucile's sister (contralto)

WHAT TO LISTEN FOR:	Opening orchestral ritornello that returns to unify the aria.
	Memorable aria in a lilting triple meter, with 2 verses sung strophically.
	Quartet reflects the emotions and points of view of each character:
	the Duke, Maddalena, Gilda, and Rigoletto.

Aria: "La donna è mobile" (Duke)

Form: Strophic, with refrain

38 0:00 Orchestral ritornello previews the Duke's solo; opening melody of aria:

La don - na è mo - bi - le   qual pium - a al ven - to,   mut - a d'ac - cen - to

The Duke, in a simple cavalry officer's uniform, sings in the inn;
Sparafucile, Gilda, and Rigoletto listen outside.

DUKE

0:12	La donna è mobile	Woman is fickle
	qual piuma al vento,	like a feather in the wind,
	muta d'accento,	she changes her words
	e di pensiero.	and her thoughts.
	sempre un amabile	Always lovable,
	leggiadro viso,	and a lovely face,
	in pianto o in riso,	weeping or laughing,
	è menzognero.	is lying.
	La donna è mobile, etc.	Woman is fickle, etc.

39 1:10   Orchestral ritornello

1:21	È sempre misero	The man's always wretched
	chi a le s'affida,	who believes in her,
	chi lei confida	who recklessly entrusts
	mal cauto il core!	his heart to her!
	pur mai non sentesi	And yet one who never
	felice appieno	drinks love on that breast
	chi su quel seno	never feels
	non liba amore!	entirely happy!
	La donna è mobile, etc.	Woman is fickle, etc.

Sparafucile comes back in with a bottle of wine and two glasses, which he sets on the table; then
he strikes the ceiling twice with the hilt of his long sword. At this signal, a laughing young
woman in gypsy dress leaps down the stairs: the Duke runs to embrace her, but she escapes him.
Meanwhile Sparafucile has gone into the street, where he speaks softly to Rigoletto.

SPARAFUCILE

È là il vostr'uomo . . .	Your man is there . . .
Viver dee o morire?	Must he live or die?

RIGOLETTO

Più tardi tornerò l'opra a compire.	I'll return later to complete the deed.

Sparafucile goes off behind the house toward the river. Gilda and Rigoletto remain in the
street, the Duke and Maddalena on the ground floor.

Quartet: "Un dì" (Duke, Maddalena, Gilda, Rigoletto)

DUKE

40 2:44	Un dì, se ben rammentomi,	One day, if I remember right,
	o bella, t'incontrai . . .	I met you, O beauty . . .
	Mi piacque di te chiedere,	I was pleased to ask about you,
	e intesi che qui stai.	and I learned that you live here.
	Or sappi, che d'allora	Know then, that since that time
	sol te quest'alma adora!	my soul adores only you!

GILDA

Iniquo!	Villain!

Listening Guide continues

MADDALENA

Ah, ah! . . . e vent'altre appresso
le scorda forse adesso?
Ha un'aria il signorino
da vero libertino . . .

Ha, ha! . . . And perhaps now
twenty others are forgotten?
The young gentleman looks like
a true libertine . . .

DUKE *(starting to embrace her)*

Sí . . . un mostro son . . .

Yes . . . I'm a monster . . .

GILDA

Ah padre mio!

Ah, Father!

MADDALENA

Lasciatemi, stordito.

Let me go, foolish man!

DUKE

Ih che fracasso!

Ah, what a fuss!

MADDALENA

Stia saggio.

Be good.

DUKE

E tu sii docile,
non fare tanto chiasso.
Ogni saggezza chiudesi
nel gaudio e nell'amore.

And you, be yielding,
don't make so much noise.
All wisdom concludes
in pleasure and in love.

(He takes her hand.)

La bella mano candida!

What a lovely, white hand!

MADDALENA

Scherzate voi, signore.

You're joking, sir.

DUKE

No, no.

No, no.

MADDALENA

Son brutta.

I'm ugly.

DUKE

Abbracciami.

Embrace me.

GILDA

Iniquo!

Villain!

MADDALENA

Ebro!

You're drunk!

DUKE

D'amor ardente.

With ardent love.

MADDALENA

Signor l'indifferente,
vi piace canzonar?

My indifferent sir,
would you like to sing?

DUKE

No, no, ti vo' sposar.   No, no, I want to marry you.

MADDALENA

Ne voglio la parola.   I want your word.

DUKE *(ironic)*

Amabile fìgliuola!   Lovable maiden!

RIGOLETTO *(to Gilda, who has seen and heard all)*

È non ti basta ancor?   Isn't that enough for you yet?

GILDA

Iniquo traditor!   Villainous betrayer!

MADDALENA

Ne voglio la parola.   I want your word.

DUKE

Amabile figliuola!   Lovable maiden!

RIGOLETTO

È non ti basta ancor?   Isn't that enough for you yet?

Quartet (2nd part): "Bella fìglia" (Duke, Maddalena, Gilda, Rigoletto)

Overall form: **A-B-A′-C**

Diagram showing how characters interact in the ensemble and how they fit into the musical structure:

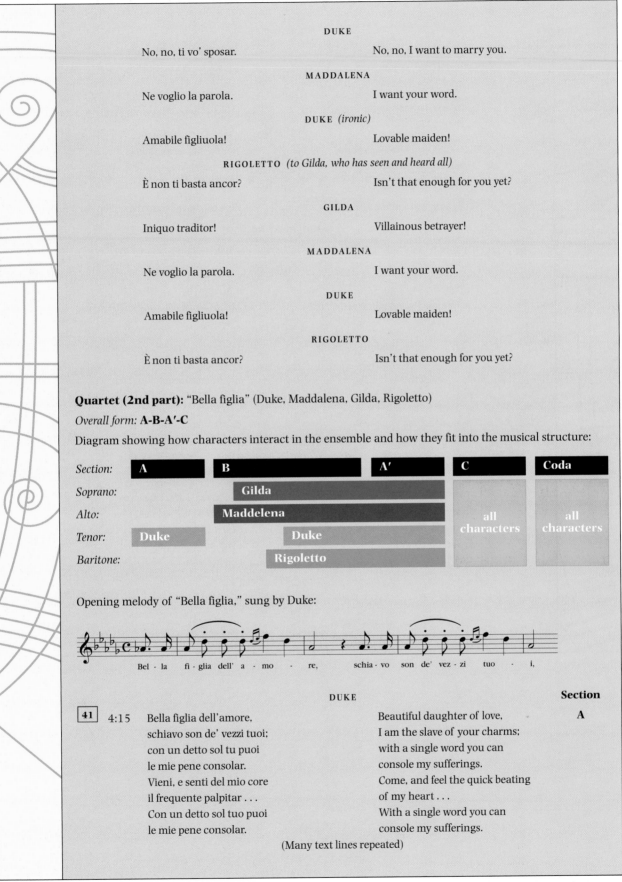

Opening melody of "Bella figlia," sung by Duke:

41	4:15	**DUKE**		Section
		Bella figlia dell'amore,	Beautiful daughter of love,	**A**
		schiavo son de' vezzi tuoi;	I am the slave of your charms;	
		con un detto sol tu puoi	with a single word you can	
		le mie pene consolar.	console my sufferings.	
		Vieni, e senti del mio core	Come, and feel the quick beating	
		il frequente palpitar . . .	of my heart . . .	
		Con un detto sol tuo puoi	With a single word you can	
		le mie pene consolar.	console my sufferings.	

(Many text lines repeated)

Listening Guide continues

42 5:19

MADDALENA

Ah! ah! rido ben di core,
chè tai baie costan poco.

Ha! Ha! I laugh heartily,
for such tales cost little.

B

GILDA

Ah! cosí parlar d'amore . . .

Ah! To speak thus of love . . .

MADDALENA

Quanto valga il vostro gioco,
mel credete, sò apprezzar.

Believe me, I can judge
how much your game is worth.

GILDA

. . . a me pur l'infame ho udito!

. . . I too have heard the villain so!

RIGOLETTO (to Gilda)

Taci, il piangere non vale.

Hush, weeping is of no avail.

GILDA

Infelice cor tradito,
per angoscia non scoppiar. No, no!

Unhappy, betrayed heart,
do not burst with anguish. Ah, no!

MADDALENA

Son avvezza, bel signore,
ad un simile scherzare.
Mio bel signor!

I'm accustomed, handsome sir,
to similar joking.
My handsome sir!

DUKE

43 6:01

Bella figlia dell'amore, etc.
Vieni!

Beautiful daughter of love, etc.
Come!

A'

RIGOLETTO

Ch'ei mentiva sei sicura.
Taci, e mia sarà la cura
la vendetta d'affrettar.
sì, pronta fia, sarà fatale,
io saprollo fulminar.
taci, taci . . .

You are sure that he was lying.
Hush, and I will take care
to hasten vengeance.
Yes, it will be swift and fatal,
I will know how to strike him down.
Hush, hush . . .

ALL CHARACTERS

7:27   Repeated text from above.

C

8:25   Coda, featuring all characters.

Coda

60

Wagner and the Music Drama

*"How strange! Only when I compose do I fully understand the
essential meaning of my works. Everywhere I discover secrets
which hitherto had remained hidden to my eyes."*

KEY POINTS	Ⓢ **StudySpace** online at www.wwnorton.com/enjoy

- ○ The German composer Richard Wagner revolutionized opera with his idea of the ***Gesamtkunstwerk***—a total work of art unifying all elements.
- ○ Wagner's operas—called ***music dramas***—are not sectional (in arias, ensembles, and the like) but are continuous; they are unifed by ***leitmotifs***, or

- recurring themes, that represent a person, place, or idea.
- ○ The emotional quality of Wagner's music is heightened by his extensive use of chromatic dissonance.
- ○ Wagner's most famous work is his four-opera cycle, *The Ring of the Nibelung.*

Richard Wagner looms as the single most important phenomenon in the artistic life
of the later nineteenth century. Historians often divide the period into "before" and
"after Wagner." The course of post-Romantic music is unimaginable without the
impact of this complex and fascinating figure.

His Life

Richard Wagner (1813–1883) was born in Leipzig, the son of a minor police official
who died when Richard was still an infant. The future composer was almost entirely
self-taught; he received in all about six months of instruction in music theory. At
twenty, he abandoned his academic studies at the University of Leipzig and obtained
a position as chorus master in a small opera house. Over the next six years, he gained
practical experience conducting in provincial theaters. He married the actress
Minna Planer when he was twenty-three and produced his first operas at this time.
He wrote the librettos himself, as he did for all his later works. In this way, he was
able to unify music and drama more than anyone had before.

Wagner was thirty when his grand opera *Rienzi* won a huge success in Dresden. With his next three works, *The Flying Dutchman, Tannhäuser,* and *Lohengrin,*
Wagner took an important step by shifting his focus from the drama of historical
intrigue to the idealized folk legend. He chose subjects derived from medieval German epics, displayed a profound feeling for nature, employed the supernatural as
an element of the drama, and glorified the German land and people. But the Dresden public was not prepared for *Tannhäuser.* They had come to see another *Rienzi*
and were disappointed.

A revolution broke out in Dresden in 1849. Wagner not only sympathized openly
with the revolutionaries but took part in their activities. When the revolt failed, he
fled to Weimar, where his friend Liszt helped him cross the border into Switzerland.
In Zurich, he commenced the most productive period of his career, including the creation of his important literary works, *Art and Revolution, The Art Work of the Future,*

Ⓢ **Richard Wagner**

**Wagner the
revolutionary**

Literary works

Music drama

and the two-volume *Opera and Drama*, which sets forth his theories of the **music drama**, the name he gave his concept of opera that integrated theater and music completely. He next proceeded to put theory into practice in the cycle of four music dramas called *The Ring of the Nibelung*. But when he reached the second act of *Siegfried* (the third opera in the cycle), he grew tired "of heaping one silent score upon the other" and laid aside the gigantic task. He turned to writing two of his finest works—*Tristan and Isolde* and *Die Meistersinger von Nürnberg*. (In English-speaking countries, many operas are commonly known by their original rather than translated titles.)

The years following the completion of *Tristan* were the darkest of his life. The musical scores accumulated in his drawer without hope of performance; Europe contained neither singers nor a theater capable of presenting them. At this point, a miraculous turn of events intervened. In 1864, an eighteen-year-old boy who was a passionate admirer of Wagner's music ascended the throne of Bavaria as Ludwig II. In one of his most artistically important acts, the young monarch summoned the composer to Munich, where *Tristan* and *Die Meistersinger* were performed at last. The king then commissioned him to complete the *Ring*, and Wagner took up where he had left off a number of years earlier.

Bayreuth

A theater was planned specifically for the presentation of Wagner's music dramas, which ultimately became the Festival Theater at Bayreuth (see illustration on p. 300). And to crown his happiness, the composer found a woman he considered his equal in will and courage—Cosima, the daughter of his old friend Liszt. She left her husband and children in order to join Wagner; they were married some years later, after Minna's death.

The Wagnerian gospel spread across Europe as a new art-religion. Wagner societies throughout the world gathered funds to raise the theater at Bayreuth. The *Ring* cycle was completed in 1874, and the four dramas were presented to worshipful audiences at the first Bayreuth Festival two years later.

Richard Wagner at Home in Bayreuth: a painting by **W. Beckmann**, 1882. To Wagner's right is his wife, Cosima; to his left, Franz Liszt and Hans von Wolzogen.

Wagner finished his last opera, *Parsifal* (1877–82)—a "consecrational festival drama" based on the legend of the Holy Grail—as he reached seventy. He died shortly thereafter and was buried at Bayreuth.

His Music

Wagner did away with the concept of separate arias, duets, ensembles, choruses, and ballets. His aim was to create a continuous fabric of melody that would never allow the emotions to cool. He therefore developed an "endless melody" that was molded to the natural inflections of the German language, more melodious than the traditional recitative, but more flexible and free than the traditional aria. Wagner's concept of opera, or **music drama** as his later works were known, was that of a total artwork (in German, ***Gesamtkunstwerk***), in which all the arts—music, poetry, drama, visual spectacle—were fused.

Endless melody

Music drama

The orchestra is the focal point and unifying element in Wagnerian music drama. It floods the characters and the audience in a rush of sound that embodies the sensuous ideal of the Romantic era. The orchestral tissue is fashioned out of concise themes, the ***leitmotifs***, or "leading motives"—Wagner called them basic themes—that recur throughout a work, undergoing variation and development as do the themes and motives of a symphony. The leitmotifs carry specific meanings, like the "fixed idea" of Berlioz's *Symphonie fantastique.* They have an uncanny power to suggest in a few notes a person, an emotion, an idea, an object (the gold, the ring, the sword) or a landscape (the Rhine, Valhalla, the lonely shore of Tristan's home). Through a process of continual transformation, the leitmotifs trace the course of the drama, the changes in the characters, their experiences and memories, and their thoughts and hidden desires.

Role of orchestra

Leitmotifs

Wagner based his musical language on chromatic harmony, which he pushed to its then farthermost limits. Chromatic dissonance gives Wagner's music its restless, intensely emotional quality. Never before had unstable pitch combinations been used so eloquently to portray states of soul.

Chromatic harmony

DIE WALKÜRE

The story of *The Ring of the Nibelung* centers on the treasure of gold that lies hidden in the depths of the Rhine River and is guarded by three Rhine Maidens. From this treasure is fashioned a ring that brings unlimited power to its owner. But there is a terrible curse on the ring; it will destroy the peace of mind of all who gain possession of it and bring them misfortune and death.

Thus begins the cycle of four dramas that ends only when the curse-bearing ring is returned to the Rhine Maidens. Gods and heroes, mortals and Nibelungs, intermingle freely in this tale of betrayed love, broken promises, magic spells, and general corruption brought on by the lust for power. Wagner freely adapted the story from the myths of the Norse sagas and the legends associated with a medieval German epic poem, the *Nibelungenlied.* (Norse mythology and Wagner's *Ring of the Nibelung* were also the inspiration for J. R. R. Tolkien's epic *Lord of the Rings* Trilogy and for the three popular movies of that literary work.)

Wagner wrote the four librettos in reverse order. First came his poem on the death of the hero Siegfried. This became the final opera, *Götterdämmerung,* in the course of which Siegfried, now possessor of the ring, betrays Brünnhilde, to whom he has

IN HIS OWN WORDS

True drama can be conceived only as resulting from the collective impulse of all the arts to communicate in the most immediate way with a collective public. . . . Thus the art of tone . . . will realize in the collective artwork its richest potential. . . . For in its isolation music has formed itself an organ capable of the most immeasurable expression— the orchestra.

Ride of the Valkyries, from Wagner's opera *Die Walküre*, in a design by **Carl Emil Doepler** (c. 1876).

sworn his love and is in turn betrayed by her. Wagner then realized that the events in Siegfried's life resulted from what had happened to him in his youth; the poem of *Siegfried* explains the forces that shaped the young hero. Aware that these in turn were determined by events set in motion before the hero was born, Wagner next wrote the poem about Siegfried's parents, Siegmund and Sieglinde, that became *Die Walküre*. Finally, this trilogy was prefaced by *Das Rheingold*, the drama that unleashes the workings of fate and the curse of gold out of which the entire action stems.

First performed in Munich in 1870, *Die Walküre* revolves around the twin brother and sister who are the offspring of Wotan by a mortal. (In Norse as in Greek and Roman mythology, kings and heroes were the children of gods.) The ill-fated love of the twins Siegmund and Sieglinde is not only incestuous but also adulterous, for she has been forced into a loveless marriage with the grim chieftain Hunding, who challenges Siegmund to battle.

The second act opens with a scene between Wotan and Brünnhilde. She is one of the Valkyries, the nine daughters of Wotan, whose perpetual task is to circle the battlefield on their winged horses and swoop down to gather up the fallen heroes, whom they bear away to Valhalla, where they will sit forever feasting with the gods. Wotan first tells Brünnhilde, his favorite daughter, that in the ensuing combat between Siegmund and Hunding, she must see to it that Siegmund is the victor. But Wotan's wife, Fricka, the goddess of marriage, insists that Siegmund has violated the holiest law of the universe, and that he must die. Although he argues with her, Wotan sadly realizes that even he must obey the law. When Brünnhilde comes to Siegmund to tell him of his fate, she yields to pity and decides to disobey her father. The two heroes fight, and Brünnhilde tries to shield Siegmund. At the decisive moment, Wotan appears and holds out his spear, upon which Siegmund's sword is shattered. Hunding then buries his own spear in Siegmund's breast. Wotan, overcome by his son's death, turns a ferocious look upon Hunding, who falls dead. Then the god rouses himself and hurries off in pursuit of the daughter who dared to defy his command.

Ride of the Valkyries

Act III opens with the famous Ride of the Valkyries, a vivid orchestral picture of these nine warrior maidens who are on their way from the battlefield back to Valhalla, carrying fallen heroes slung across the saddles of their winged horses. They meet on a summit, calling to one another with the fearsome cry, "Hojotoho! Heiaha!"

This prelude features some of Wagner's most brilliant scoring. The rustling strings and woodwinds give way to the memorable "Ride" theme (familiar from many movie

CD iMusic

Ride of the Valkyries

sound tracks and even from the *What's Opera, Doc?* Warner Brothers cartoon), which is sounded repeatedly by a huge and varied brass section through a dense orchestral texture that builds to several climaxes beneath the warriors' voices (see Listening Guide 36). The Valkyries (each given a descriptive name by Wagner, such as Helmwige, meaning warrior with helmet) gather on a rocky peak to await Brünnhilde; she is the last to arrive, carrying Sieglinde and several fragments of Siegmund's sword. Sieglinde wants to die, but Brünnhilde tells her she must live to bear his son, who will become the world's mightiest hero. Sieglinde takes refuge in the forest, while Brünnhilde remains to face her father's wrath. Her punishment is severe. She is to be deprived of her godhood, Wotan tells her, to become a mortal woman. No more will she sit with the gods, nor will she carry heroes to Valhalla. He will put her to sleep on a rock, and she will fall prey to the first mortal who finds her. Brünnhilde defends herself. In trying to protect Siegmund, was she not carrying out her father's innermost desire? She begs him to soften her punishment: let him at least surround the rock with flames so that only a fearless hero will be able to penetrate the wall of fire. Wotan relents and grants her request. He kisses her on both eyes, which close at once.

Striking the rock three times, he invokes Loge, the god of fire. Flames spring up around the rock, and the "magic fire" leitmotif is heard, followed by the "magic sleep" and "slumber" motives. The orchestra announces the theme of Siegfried, the fearless hero who in the next music drama will force his way through the flames and awaken Brünnhilde with a kiss. The curtain falls on a version of the Sleeping Beauty legend as poetic as any artist ever created.

Famous leitmotifs

Listening Guide 36

eLG 3 (44–49) 6 (34–39)

Wagner: *Die Walküre* (The Valkyrie), Act III, opening (5:36)

DATE OF WORK:	1856; first performed 1870, Munich
GENRE:	Music drama: second in cycle of 4 (*The Ring of the Nibelung*)
CHARACTERS:	Wotan, father of the gods (bass-baritone) Valkyries, the 9 daughters of Wotan Brünnhilde, favorite daughter (soprano), Ortlinde (soprano) Gerhilde (soprano), Helmwige (soprano) Schwertleite (alto), Waltraute (alto), Siegrune (alto) Rossweisse (alto), Grimgerde (alto)
ORCHESTRA:	Huge orchestra including: Strings (32 violins, 12 violas, 12 cellos, 8 double basses, 6 harps) Woodwinds (2 piccolos, 3 flutes, 3 oboes, 1 English horn, 1 bass clarinet, 3 bassoons) Brass (8 French horns, 3 trumpets, 1 bass trumpet, 3 tenor trombones, 1 bass trombone, 1 contrabass trombone, 4 Wagner tubas, 1 contrabass tuba) Percussion (timpani, cymbals, triangle, tenor drum, glockenspiel, gong)
WHAT TO LISTEN FOR:	Orchestra sets excited mood and image of flying warriors. Dotted figure gives way to famous "Ride" theme, heard in minor and major throughout scene. Focus on huge brass sound; alternation of high and low instruments. Chilling battle cries from Valkyries. Continuous fabric of orchestral music and singing.

Act III, Scene 1: Ride of the Valkyries

44 0:00   Orchestral prelude, marked Lively (Lebhaft), in 9/8 meter.

Listening Guide continues

0:08   Rushing string figure alternates with fast wavering in woodwinds, then insistent dotted figure [in brackets] begins in horns and low strings:

Swirling string and woodwind lines, accompanied by dotted figure.

45   0:23   Famous "Ride" motive, heard first in minor key in horns:

0:35   "Ride" motive, now heard in major key in trumpets:

4-note dotted motive exchanged between low and high brass instruments, heard above swirling idea.

46   1:06   "Ride" motive heard *fortissimo*, as curtain opens.

(*Four Valkyries, in full armor, have settled on the highest peak above a cave.*)

TEXT	TRANSLATION

GERHILDE *(calling from the highest peak)*

47   1:20

Hojotoho! Hojotoho! Heiaha! Heiaha!	Hoyotoho! Hoyotoho! Heiaha! Heiaha!
Helmwige! Hier! Hieher mit dem Ross!	Helmwige, here! Bring your horse here!

Gerhilde's disjunct battle cry, which is echoed by her sisters:

HELMWIGE *(answering in the distance)*

Hojotoho! Hojotoho! Heiaha!	Hoyotoho! Hoyotoho! Heiaha!

1:45   "Ride" motive heard in low brass, first in minor, then major; ideas exchanged between brass instruments.
Climax with timpani and cymbals on following cry, then descrescendo.

GERHILDE, WALTRAUTE, SCHWERTLEITE
(*calling out to Brünnhilde, who approaches*)

Heiaha! Heiaha!	Heiaha! Heiaha!

ORTLINDE

48   2:23

Zu Ortlinde's Stute stell' deinen Hengst,	Put your stallion next to Ortlinde's mare:
Mit meiner Grauen gras't gern dein Brauner!	Your bay will like grazing with my grey.

WALTRAUTE

Wer hängt dir im Sattel? / Who hangs from your saddle?

HELMWIGE

Sintolt, der Hegeling! / Sintolt the Hegeling!

SCHWERTLEITE

Führ deinen Braunen fort von der Grauen: / Take your bay away from my grey.
Ortlindes Märes trägt Wittig, den Irming! / Ortlinde's mare carries Wittig the Irming.

GERHILDE

Als Feinde nur sah ich Sintolt und Wittig! / I only saw them as enemies, Sintolt and Wittig.

ORTLINDE

Heiaha! Die Stute stösst mir der Hengst! / Heiaha! The mare is being shoved by the stallion!

GERHILDE *(laughing)*

Ha ha ha ha ha ha ha ha! / Ha ha ha ha ha ha ha!
Der Recken Zwist entzweit noch die Rosse! / The warriors' dispute upsets even the steeds!

HELMWIGE

Ruhig, Brauner! Brich nicht den Frieden. / Be still, my bay! Do not disturb the peace!

WALTRAUTE

Hoioho! Hoioho! Siegrune, hier! / Hoyoho! Hoyoho! Siegrune, here!
Wo säumst du so lang? / Where were you dallying so long?

3:06   "Ride" motive heard as Siegrune arrives.

SIEGRUNE

Arbeit gab's! / There was work to be done!
Sind die and'ren schon da? / Are the others already here?

SCHWERTLEITE, WALTRAUTE

Hojotoho! Hojotoho! Heiaha! / Hoyotoho! Hoyotoho! Heiaha!

GERHILDE

Heiaha! / Heiaha!

GRIMGERDE, ROSSWEISSE *(appear illuminated by flash of lighting)*

Hojotoho! Hojotoho! Heiaha! / Hoyotoho! Hoyotoho! Heiha!

WALTRAUTE

Grimgerd' und Rossweisse! / Grimgerde and Rossweisse!

GERHILDE

Sie reiten zu zwei. / They are riding abreast.

49   3:43   Ride motive heard *fortissimo*, at change to major key, in full orchestra with cymbals and triangle.

HELMWIGE, ORTLINDE, SIEGRUNE

Gegrüsst, ihr Reisige! Rossweiss' / Greetings, riders! Rossweisse
und Grimgerde! / and Grimgerde!

ROSSWEISSE, GRIMGERD

Hojotoho! Hojotoho! Heiaha! / Hoyotoho! Hoyotoho! Heiha!

Listening Guide continues

	THE OTHER 6 VALKYRIES	
4:14	Hojotoho! Hojotoho! Heiaha! Heiaha!	Hoyotoho! Hoyotoho! Heiaha! Heiaha!
	Gradual decrescendo in orchestra.	

GERHILDE

4:54	In'Wald mit den Rossen zu Rast und Weid'!	Into the woods with the steeds to rest and graze.

ORTLINDE

Führet die Mähren fern von einander,	Place the mares far from each other,
Bis unsrer Helden Hass sich gelegt!	Until our heroes' hatred is abated!

VALKYRIES (laughing)

Ha ha ha ha ha ha ha ha!	Ha ha ha ha ha ha ha ha!

HELMWIGE

Der Helden Grimm büsste schon die Graue!	The heroes' anger made even the grey suffer!

VALKYRIES (laughing)

Ha ha ha ha ha ha ha ha!	Ha ha ha ha ha ha ha ha!

ROSSWEISSE, GRIMGERDE

Hojotoho! Hojotoho!	Hoyotoho! Hoyotoho!

THE OTHER 6 VALKYRIES

Wilkommen! Wilkommen!	Welcome! Welcome!

61

Puccini and Late Romantic Opera

"God touched me with His little finger and said, 'Write for the theater, only for the theater.' And I obeyed the supreme command."

KEY POINTS	**StudySpace** online at www.wwnorton.com/enjoy

- The post-Romantic composer Giacomo Puccini wrote some of the best-loved operas of all time, including *La bohème* and *Madame Butterfly*.
- In *Madame Butterfly*, Puccini combines ***verismo*** (realism) and ***exoticism*** (Japanese music and cul-

ture), both popular at the end of the nineteenth century.
- The libretto for *Madame Butterfly* reflects end-of-the-century European-American interest in ***geisha*** culture.

Verismo

The Italian operatic tradition was carried on in the post-Romantic era by a group of composers that included Pietro Mascagni (1863–1945), Ruggero Leoncavallo (1857–1919), and Giacomo Puccini. These Italians were associated with a movement known as ***verismo*** (realism), whose advocates tried to bring into the theater the naturalism of writers such as Émile Zola and Henrik Ibsen. Instead of choosing historical or mythological themes, they picked subjects from everyday life and treated them in down-to-earth fashion. The most famous operas in this tradition include *La bohème* (*Bohemian Life,* 1896) and *Tosca* (1900), both by Puccini; *Cavalleria rusticana* (Rustic Chivalry, 1890), by Mascagni; and *Pagliacci* (The Clowns, 1892) by Leoncavallo. Although it was a short-lived movement, verismo had counterparts in Germany and France and produced some of the best-loved works in the operatic repertory.

His Life and Music

Giacomo Puccini was born in 1858 in Lucca, Italy, the son of a church organist in whose footsteps he expected to follow. But Puccini found himself more attracted to the theater and especially opera. In 1880 he traveled to Milan, where he studied at the Conservatory. His opera *Manon Lescaut* (1893) established him as the most promising among the rising generation of Italian composers. For this work, he teamed up with librettists Luigi Illica and Giuseppe Giacosa, both of whom also collaborated with him on the three most successful operas of the early twentieth century: *La bohème* (1896), *Tosca* (1900), and *Madame Butterfly* (1904).

Prosperity gave way to misfortune after Puccini's early successes. His travels to oversee the international premieres of several of his works were demanding. In 1903, a serious car crash left him bedridden for six months, and in 1908 his wife accused him of having an affair with a live-in assistant, thus causing a public scandal. Handsome and magnetic, Puccini evidently gave his wife reason to doubt his fidelity: "I am always falling in love," he once declared. "When I no longer am, make my funeral." In 1910, his *The Girl of the Golden West* received its world premiere at the Metropolitan Opera House in New York; this was followed by a trio of three one-act works that included *Gianni Schicchi* (1918), one of his best-loved masterpieces.

Puccini's last opera, *Turandot,* exemplifies his far-reaching search for new material. After considering texts by many authors, he settled on *Turandot,* a Chinese fairy tale about a beautiful but cruel princess. Ill with cancer, Puccini pushed on to complete the project, but he died in 1924 from a heart attack, before finishing the final scene. His friend Franco Alfano completed the opera, using Puccini's sketches. The first performance occurred in 1926 at La Scala, and was conducted by Arturo Toscanini, Puccini's greatest interpreter. The opera ended as Puccini had requested, without the final scene—Toscanini laid down his baton during the lament over the body of Li, turned to the audience and said in a choking voice, "Here ends the master's work."

MADAME BUTTERFLY

Puccini's inspiration for the opera *Madame Butterfly* came in 1900 during a visit to London, where he attended a performance of David Belasco's play *Madame Butterfly,* a dramatization of a short story by John Luther Long, which was in turn taken from Pierre Loti's tale *Madame Chrysanthème.* The composer immediately applied for rights to Belasco's work, acquired Long's story for his librettists Illica and Giacosa, and set to work on the piece. The libretto was completed in 1902, but Puccini insisted on further revisions and thus did not complete *Madame Butterfly* until 1904.

Although the composer was well established in the opera world, his new work suffered a disastrous premiere—rivaled only by the famous riot at the first performance of Stravinsky's ballet *Rite of Spring* (discussed in Chapter 66). When the revised *Madame Butterfly* was performed in Brescia three months after its premiere, it became an instant success.

Giacomo Puccini

IN HIS OWN WORDS

I have had a visit today from Mme. Ohyama, wife of the Japanese ambassador. She told me a great many interesting things and sang some native songs to me. She has promised to send me native Japanese music. I sketched the story of the libretto for her, and she liked it, especially as just such a story as Butterfly's is known to her as having happened in real life.

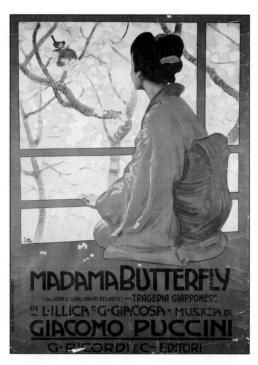

The geisha Cio-Cio-San on the cover of the earliest English vocal score of *Madame Butterfly*, published by Ricordi. Design by **Leopold Metlicovitz** (1868–1944).

Act I

CD iMusic

The Star-Spangled Banner

Like his other operas, *Madame Butterfly* tells the story of a tragic-heroic female protagonist—here, a young geisha named Cio-Cio-San (Madame Butterfly) from Nagasaki who renounces her profession and religion in order to marry an American naval officer named Pinkerton. (A *geisha* is most closely equivalent to a courtesan in Western culture.) The two, who have never met before, get married in a house promised to the couple by the marriage broker. Pinkerton departs soon thereafter. When he returns several years later—with his new American wife in tow—Pinkerton learns that Butterfly has given birth to their son and decides to take the child to America. Butterfly accepts his decision with dignity, but rather than return to her life as a geisha, she commits suicide (the samurai warrior's ritual known as *hara-kiri*). Despite its elements of **verismo** (or realism), Butterfly herself is not a believable character—yet it is her naivety and vulnerability that makes her a beloved heroine.

Madame Butterfly marks a turn-of-the-century interest in exoticism. The entire score is tinged with Japanese color: traditional Japanese melodies are juxtaposed with pentatonic and whole-tone passages, and instrument combinations evoking the timbres of a Japanese **gagaku** orchestra (harp, flute and piccolo, and bells) are heard. Simple moments in the score—a single, unaccompanied melody, for example—have their visual equivalents in the clear lines of Japanese prints. Here too Puccini captures the ritualistic aspect of Japanese life.

Act I opens with a brief reference to *The Star-Spangled Banner* (another exotic reference for Puccini), after which some of the main characters are introduced: Goro, the marriage broker; Sharpless, the American consul at Nagasaki; Suzuki, Butterfly's maid; and Pinkerton himself. All are busily preparing Butterfly's new house and awaiting her arrival. Meanwhile, Pinkerton sings about his carefree view on love, saying he welcomes pleasure wherever he can find it. All too quickly we learn that this marriage will not have a happy ending. Butterfly soon arrives with a group of friends, and she meets Pinkerton for the first time. The marriage festivities continue as more of Butterfly's family appears, only to be interrupted by her Uncle Bonze, a Buddhist priest, who announces that his niece has renounced her faith. Her shocked relatives quickly depart, and Pinkerton consoles his young wife.

Act II

Interior of Teatro alla Scala (La Scala), in Milan, Italy's most famous opera house.

Act II, Part 1, takes place three years after the marriage. Butterfly has heard nothing from her husband, which leads Suzuki to doubt that Pinkerton will ever return. She is quickly rebuked, however, in Butterfly's soaring aria, "Un bel dì" (One beautiful day), in which the young bride pictures their happy reunion and recalls Pinkerton's promise to return "when the robins build their nests" (see Listening Guide 37).

Sharpless then arrives with a letter from Pinkerton, who has asked him to seek out Butterfly. He starts to read the letter, but they are interrupted by a visit from the marriage broker and Prince Yamadori, who proposes to Butterfly. Sharpless urges her to accept—he knows that Pinkerton will be arriving soon but does not want to see her—but she refuses, stating that she is already married and that she would rather die by her own hand than return to her former life as a geisha. She also reveals to Sharpless that she has had Pinkerton's child.

The harbor cannon signals the arrival of a ship that Butterfly identifies immediately as Pinkerton's—the *Abraham Lincoln.* Butterfly dresses in her wedding gown in anticipation of their meeting. The scene closes with an orchestral interlude that leads to the final scene.

Dawn is breaking in Part 2 of Act II, and Butterfly struggles to stay awake after a sleepness night. Sharpless and Pinkerton arrive, along with Kate, Pinkerton's new wife; they are greeted by Suzuki, who informs them that Butterfly is resting. Pinkerton announces his intention to take the child to give him a good American upbringing, and then he and his new wife leave. When Butterfly awakens, she learns about Pinkerton and his American wife, and the fate of her young son. She accepts the situation with dignity but asks that Pinkerton return in half an hour for the boy. She says a final farewell to her son, and then stabs herself with her father's samurai dagger, which bears the inscription "He dies with honor who can no longer live with honor." In the distance, Pinkerton is heard desperately calling out her name.

A geisha committing suicide in the samurai *jigai* manner. Drawing by **Yoshitoshi Taiso** (1839–1892).

The aria "Un bel dì" is one of the most memorable in all opera literature. At first, Butterfly sings with a distant, ethereal quality, accompanied by solo violin, while she dreams of Pinkerton's return. The intensity rises when she envisons seeing his ship in the harbor. She relates the vision and her reaction in a speechlike melody that peaks on the word "morire" (die), as she explains how she will playfully hide from him at first in order not to die at their reunion. The emotional level builds—along with the dynamics—as Butterfly swears that "all this will happen." Her final soaring line climaxes on "l'aspetto" (I will wait for him), with the orchestra now playing the heartrending music at *fff.*

Listening Guide 37

eLG | 3 (50–51)
6 (52–53)

Puccini: "Un bel dì," from *Madame Butterfly*, Act II (4:35)

DATE OF WORK:	1904
LIBRETTISTS:	Giuseppe Giacosa and Luigi Ilica
BASIS:	Play by David Belasco, from short story by John Luther Long, derived from Pierre Loti's tale *Madame Chrysanthème*
SETTING:	Nagasaki, Japan, at the beginning of the 20th century
PRINCIPAL CHARACTERS:	Cio-Cio-San, or Madame Butterfly (soprano)
	Suzuki, her maid (mezzo-soprano)
	B. F. Pinkerton, lieutenant in the U.S. Navy (tenor)
	Sharpless, U.S. consul at Nagasaki (baritone)
	Goro, marriage broker (tenor)
	Prince Yamadori (tenor)
	Kate Pinkerton, American wife of Pinkerton (mezzo-soprano)
	Relatives and friends of Cio-Cio-San

Listening Guide continues

WHAT TO LISTEN FOR: Dreamlike quality of opening vocal line, with sparse, solo violin accompaniment.

Excited, speechlike singing as the emotional and dynamic levels rise.

Passionate, soaring climaxes on key words ("die," "await"), with rich, unison string writing.

Opening, ethereal vocal line:

Un_____ bel di, ve · dre · mo   le · var · si un fil di fu · mo

Final climactic moment on "l'aspetto" (I will wait for him):

Tien · ti   la tua   pa · u · ra, io con si · cu · ra   fe · de   l'a · spet · to.

		TEXT	TRANSLATION
50	0:00	Un bel dì, vedremo	One lovely day we'll see
		levarsi un fil di fumo	a thread of smoke rise
		sull'estremo confin del mare.	at the distant edge of the sea.
		E poi la nave appare—	And then the ship appears—
		poi la nave bianca entra nel porto,	then the white ship enters the harbor,
		romba il suo saluto.	thunders its salute.
		Vedi? E venuto!	You see? He's come!
		Io non gli scendo incontro. Io no.	I don't go down to meet him. Not I.
		Mi metto là sul cieglio del colle	I place myself at the brow of the hill
		e aspetto gran tempo e non mi pesa,	and wait a long time, but the long
		la lunga attesa.	wait doesn't oppress me.
		E uscito dalla folla cittadina	And coming out of the city's crowd
		un uomo, un picciol punto	a man, a tiny speck
		s'avvia per la collina.	starts toward the hill.
51	2:14	Chi sarà? Chi sarà?	Who will it be? Who?
		E come sarà giunto	And when he arrives
		che dirà? Che dirà?	what will he say? What?
		Chiamerà Butterfly dalla lontana.	He'll call Butterfly from the distance.
		Io senza dar risposta me ne starò nascosta	I'll stay hidden, partly to tease him
		un po' per celia	and partly not to die
		e un po' per non morire al primo incontro,	at our first meeting,
		ed egli alquanto in pena chiamerà:	and a little worried he'll call
		piccina mogliettina olezzo di verbena,	little wife, verbena blossom,
		i nomi che mi dava al suo venire	the names he gave me when he came here.
		tutto questo avverrà, te lo prometto.	All this will happen, I promise you.
		Tienti la tua paura,	Keep your fear to yourself,
		io con sicura fede l'aspetto.	with certain faith I am waiting for him.

62

Tchaikovsky and the Ballet

"Dance is the hidden language of the soul."

—MARTHA GRAHAM

○ Previously part of lavish entertainments, ballet was established as an independent art form in the eighteenth century, particularly in France and Russia.

○ The Russian choreographer Marius Petipa created

the *pas de deux* (dance for two), which became central to classical ballet.

○ The three ballets of Russian composer Peter Ilyich Tchaikovsky—*Swan Lake, Sleeping Beauty,* and *The Nutcracker*—remain favorites today.

Ballet—Past and Present

Dance is the most physical of the arts, depending as it does on the leaps and turns of the human body. Out of these movements it weaves an enchantment all its own. We watch with amazement as the ballerinas perform pirouettes and intricate footwork with the utmost grace, and their partners make leaps that seem to triumph over the laws of gravity. A special glamour attaches to the great dancers—Nureyev, Baryshnikov, and their peers—yet theirs is an art based on an inhumanly demanding discipline. Their bodies are their instruments, which they must keep in excellent shape in order to perform the gymnastics required of them. They create moments of elusive beauty, made possible only by total control of their muscles. It is this combination of physical and emotional factors that marks the distinctive power of ballet.

Ballet has been an adornment of European culture for centuries. Ever since the Renaissance it has been central to lavish festivals and theatrical entertainments presented at the courts of kings and dukes. Elaborate ballets were also featured in the French operas of Lully and Rameau and in the *divertissements* by French court composer Mouret (see p. 155).

The eighteenth century saw the rise of ballet as an independent art form. French ballet achieved preeminence in the early nineteenth century. Then Russian ballet came into its own, fostered by the patronage of the czar's court and helped along considerably by the arrival in 1847 of Marius Petipa, the great choreographer at St. Petersburg. Petipa created the dances for more than a hundred works, invented the structure of the classic *pas de deux* (dance for two; see p. 326), and brought the art of staging ballets to unprecedented heights.

The history of early-twentieth-century ballet is closely identified with the career of Serge Diaghilev (1872–1929), an impresario whose genius lay in his ability to recognize the genius of others. Diaghilev's dance company, the Ballets Russes, which he brought to Paris in the years before the First World War, opened up a new chapter in the cultural life of Europe. He surrounded his dancers—the greatest were Vaslav Nijinsky and Tamara Karsavina—with productions worthy

IN HIS OWN WORDS

O body swayed to music,
O brightening glance,
How can we know the
dancer from the dance?

—W. B. YEATS

Pas de deux

Serge Diaghilev

Tamara Karsavina (1885–1978) dances the role of the Firebird in a Ballets Russes production (1911).

of their talents. He invited artists such as Picasso and Braque to paint the scenery, and commissioned the three ballets—*The Firebird*, *Petrushka*, and *The Rite of Spring*—that catapulted the composer Igor Stravinsky to fame. (We will study Stravinsky's ballet *The Rite of Spring* in Chapter 66.) Diaghilev's ballets have served as models for the composers and choreographers who followed.

Peter Ilyich Tchaikovsky: His Life and Music

"Truly there would be reason to go mad were it not for music."

Few composers typify the end-of-the-century mood as does Peter Ilyich Tchaikovsky (1840–1893). He expressed above all the pessimism that engulfed the late Romantic movement.

Tchaikovsky was born at Votinsk in a distant province of Russia, the son of a government official. His family intended him for a career in the government; he graduated at nineteen from the aristocratic School of Jurisprudence in St. Petersburg and obtained a minor post in the Ministry of Justice. But at age twenty-three, he decided to resign his position and enter the newly founded Conservatory of St. Petersburg. He completed the music course there in three years and was immediately recommended by Anton Rubinstein, director of the school, for a teaching post in the new Moscow Conservatory. His twelve years in Moscow saw the production of some of his most successful works.

Extremely sensitive by nature, Tchaikovsky was subject to attacks of depression. The social issues associated with being a homosexual may have led him to marry a student of the conservatory, Antonina Milyukova, who was hopelessly in love with him but for whom he had no affection. His sympathy for her soon turned to revulsion, and, on the verge of a serious breakdown, he fled to his brothers in St. Petersburg within weeks of the marriage.

Good fortune followed when Nadezhda von Meck, the wealthy widow of an industrialist, launched him on the most productive period of his career. Her passion was music, especially Tchaikovsky's. Bound by the rigid conventions of her time and her class, she had to be certain that her enthusiasm was for the artist, not the man; hence she stipulated that she was never to meet the recipient of her patronage.

The following years saw the spread of Tchaikovsky's fame. He was the first Russian whose music appealed to Western tastes—his music was performed in Vienna, Berlin, and Paris—and in 1891 he was invited to participate in the ceremonies for the opening of Carnegie Hall in New York.

In 1893, immediately after finishing his Sixth Symphony, the *Pathétique*, he went to St. Petersburg to conduct it. The work met with a lukewarm reception, in part because Tchaikovsky, painfully shy in public, conducted his music without conviction. He died within several weeks, at the age of fifty-three. Although the cause of his death has never been established, its suddenness, and the tragic tone of his last

Peter Ilyich Tchaikovsky

Final year

work, led to rumors that he had committed suicide. Another theory, yet unproved, is that he contracted cholera from tainted water.

To Russians, Tchaikovsky is a national artist. He himself laid great weight on the national element in his music: "I am Russian through and through!" At the same time, Tchaikovsky was a cosmopolitan who came under the spell of Italian opera, French ballet, and German symphony and song. These he joined to the strain of folk melody that was his heritage as a Russian, imposing on this mixture his sharply defined personality.

THE NUTCRACKER

Tchaikovsky had a natural affinity for the ballet. Dances of all types are scattered throughout his works. His three ballets—*Swan Lake, The Sleeping Beauty,* and *The Nutcracker*—were not immediately popular with the dancers, who complained that the rhythms were too complicated. Within a few years, however, they had changed their view, and these three ballets established themselves as basic works of the Russian repertory.

The Nutcracker was based on a fanciful story by E. T. A. Hoffmann. An expanded version by Alexandre Dumas *père* served as the basis for choreographer Petipa's scenario, which was accepted by Tchaikovsky when he returned from his visit to the United States in 1891.

Act I takes place at a Christmas party during which two children, Clara and Fritz, help decorate the tree. Their godfather arrives with gifts, among them a nutcracker. The children go to bed but Clara returns to gaze at her gift, falls asleep, and begins to dream. (Russian nutcrackers are often shaped like a human head or a whole person, which makes it quite logical for Clara to dream, as she does, that this one was transformed into a handsome prince.) First, she is terrified to see mice scampering around the tree. Then the dolls she has received come alive and fight a battle with the mice, which reaches a climax in the combat between the Nutcracker and the Mouse King. Clara helps her beloved Nutcracker by throwing a slipper at

Act I

Mikhail Baryshnikov in an American Ballet Theater production of *The Nutcracker.*

The pas de deux from *The Nutcracker*, danced by Daria Klimentova and Dmitri Gruzdyev of the English National Ballet.

A traditional Russian nutcracker—a toy soldier who comes alive in Tchaikovsky's ballet.

CD iMusic

March, from *The Nutcracker*

the Mouse King, who is vanquished. The Nutcracker then becomes the Prince, who takes Clara away with him.

Act II takes place in Confiturembourg, the land of sweets, which is ruled by the Sugar Plum Fairy. The Prince presents Clara to his family, and a celebration follows, with a series of dances that reveal all the attractions of this magic realm.

The mood of the ballet is set by the Overture, whose light, airy effect Tchaikovsky achieved by omitting most of the brass instruments. The peppy *March* is played as the guests arrive for the party (see Listening Guide 38). "I have discovered a new instrument in Paris," Tchaikovsky wrote to his publisher, "something between a piano and a glockenspiel, with a divinely beautiful tone, and I want to introduce it into the ballet." The instrument was the ***celesta***, whose timbre perfectly suits the Sugar Plum Fairy and her veils. In the *Trepak* (Russian Dance, with the famous Cossack squat-kick), the orchestral sound is enlivened by a tambourine. The muted *Arab Dance* is followed by the *Chinese Dance*, in which bassoons set up an ostinato that bobs up and down against the shrill melody of flute and piccolo. *The Dance of the Toy Flutes* is extraordinarily graceful. Finally, the climax of the ballet comes with the *Waltz of the Flowers*, which has delighted audiences for more than a century. With its suggestion of swirling ballerinas, this finale conjures up everything we have come to associate with the Romantic ballet.

Listening Guide 38

eLG   3 (52–54)
6 (54–56)

Tchaikovsky: *The Nutcracker, March*   (2:13)

DATE OF WORK:	1892
GENRE:	Ballet (from which an orchestral suite was made)
BASIS:	E. T. A. Hoffmann story, expanded by Alexandre Dumas *père*
CHOREOGRAPHER:	Marius Petipa

SEQUENCE OF DANCES:

March   *Chinese Dance*
Dance of the Sugar Plum Fairy   *Dance of the Toy Flutes*
Trepak   *Waltz of the Flowers*
Arab Dance

March: **Tempo di marcia viva (lively march); A-B-A form, 4/4 meter, G major**

WHAT TO LISTEN FOR: Sprightly march tune in trumpets, answered by strings.
Shift from major to minor tonality in march.
Brief contrasting middle section, with staccato runs in woodwinds.

52 0:00   **A section**
Brass announce march theme:

0:06   Answered by strings in irregular
rhythms:

Alternation of 2 ideas.

53 0:59   **B section**
Short section, featuring staccato runs in woodwinds and strings.

54 1:11   **A section**
Brass march theme returns, answered by strings.

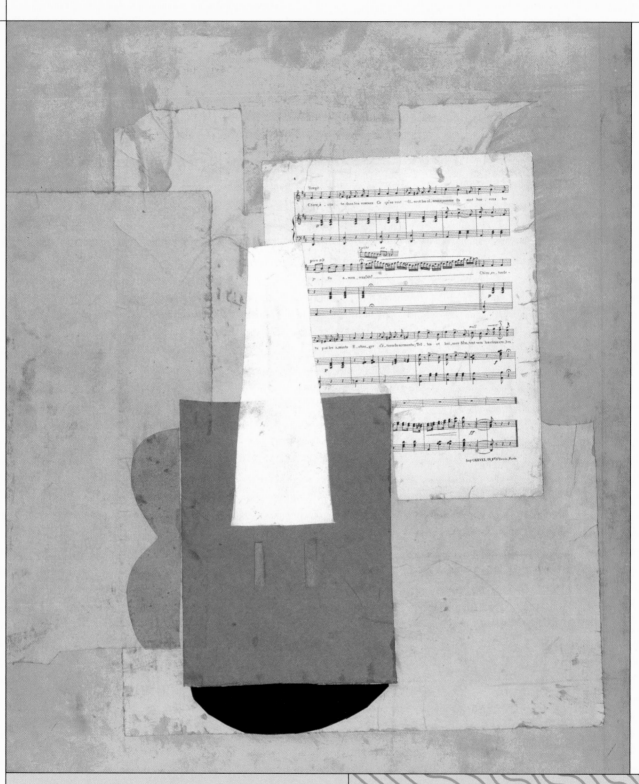

Pablo Picasso (1881–1973), *Violin and Sheet Music* (1912).

Impressionism in Music

This music scene is typical of the everyday activities captured by Impressionist artists. *Young Girls at the Piano* (1892), by **Pierre-Auguste Renoir** (1841–1919).

Impressionism surfaced in France at a crucial moment in the history of European music. Composers were beginning to feel that the possibilities of the major-minor system had been exhausted. Debussy and his followers were attracted to other scales, such as the church modes of the Middle Ages, which gave their music an archaic sound. They began to emphasize the primary intervals—octaves, fourths, fifths—and the parallel movement of chords in the manner of medieval organum. Impressionists responded especially to non-Western music: the Moorish strain in the songs and dances of Spain, and the Javanese and Chinese orchestras that performed in Paris during the World Exposition of 1889 (see CP 15). Here they found rhythms, scales, and colors that offered a bewitching contrast to the traditional sounds of Western music.

While Classical harmony looked upon dissonance as a momentary disturbance that found its resolution in consonance, composers now began to use dissonance for itself, freeing it from the need to resolve. They taught their contemporaries to accept tone combinations that had formerly been regarded as inadmissible, just like the Impressionist painters taught people to see colors in sky, grass, and water that had never been seen there before.

Impressionist composers made use of the entire spectrum of pitches in the ***chromatic scale***, and also explored the whole-tone scale, derived from various non-Western musics. A whole-tone scale is built entirely of whole-tone intervals: for example, C-D-E-F♯-G♯-A♯-C. The result is a fluid sequence of pitches that lacks the pull toward a tonic.

Chord structures

Impressionist composers also explored the use of parallel, or "gliding," chords, in which a chord built of intervals above one tone is duplicated immediately on a higher or lower tone. Such parallel motion, prohibited in the Classical system of harmony, was truly groundbreaking. Free from a strong tonal center and rigid harmonic guidelines, composers experimented with free treatment of dissonance, leading to daring new tone combinations. One such combination was the ninth chord, a set of five notes in which the interval between the lowest and highest tones was a ninth. The effect was one of hovering between tonalities, creating elusive effects that might be compared to the misty outlines of Impressionist painting.

Orchestral color

These floating harmonies demanded the most subtle colors. The lush, full sonority of the Romantic orchestra was replaced by a veiled blending of timbres: flutes and clarinets in their dark lower registers, violins in their lustrous upper range, trumpets and horns discreetly muted; and over the whole, a shimmering gossamer of harp, celesta, triangle, glockenspiel, muffled drum, and cymbal brushed with a drumstick. One instrumental color flows into another close by, as from oboe to clarinet to flute, in the same way that Impressionist painting moves from one color to another in the spectrum, as from yellow to green to blue.

Rhythm

Impressionist rhythm too shows the influence of non-Western music. The metrical patterns of the Classical-Romantic era, marked by a recurrent accent on the first beat of the measure, gave way to a new dreamlike style, where the music glides

The Impressionists took painting out of the studio and into the open air; their subject was light. **Claude Monet** (1840–1926), *Impression: Sun Rising.*

long, "Impressionism" had become a term of derision to describe the hazy, luminous paintings of Monet and his followers. A distinctly Parisian style, Impressionism counted among its exponents Edgar Degas (1834–1917) and Auguste Renoir (1841–1919). These artists wanted to capture on canvas the freshness of their first impressions. What fascinated them was the continuous change in the appearance of things. They ventured out of the studio into the open air to paint water lilies, a haystack, or a cathedral again and again at different hours of the day. Instead of mixing their pigments on the palette, they juxtaposed brush strokes of pure color on the canvas, leaving it to the eye of the viewer to do the mixing. An iridescent sheen bathes each painting as outlines shimmer and melt in a luminous haze.

The Impressionists abandoned the grandiose subjects of Romanticism. Their focus shifted to light and to "unimportant" material: still lifes, dancing girls, nudes; everyday scenes of middle-class life, picnics, boating and café scenes; nature in all its beauty, Paris in all its moods.

The Symbolist Poets

A parallel revolt against tradition took place in poetry with the Symbolists, who sought to suggest rather than describe, to present the symbol rather than state the thing. Symbolism as a literary movement gained prominence in the work of French writers Stéphane Mallarmé (1842–1898) and Paul Verlaine (1844–1896), both of whom were strongly influenced by the American poet Edgar Allan Poe (1809–1849). They were sensitive to the sound of a word as well as its meaning, and tried to evoke poetic images that affected all the senses. Through their experiments in free verse forms, the Symbolists were able to achieve in language an abstract quality that had once belonged to music alone.

IN HIS OWN WORDS

Symbolism . . . The secret of this movement is nothing other than this. . . . We were nourished on music, and our literary minds only dreamt of extracting from language virtually the same effects that music caused on our nervous system.

—PAUL VALÉRY

The Impressionist and Post-Impressionist Eras

63

Debussy and Impressionism

"For we desire above all—nuance,
Not color but half-shades!
Ah! nuance alone unites
Dream with dream and flute with horn."

—PAUL VERLAINE

| KEY POINTS | ⑤ **StudySpace** online at www.wwnorton.com/enjoy |

○ **Impressionism** was a French movement developed by painters who tried to capture their "first impression" of a subject through varied treatments of light and color.

○ The literary response to Impressionism was **Symbolism**, in which writings are suggestive of images and ideas rather than literally descriptive.

○ Impressionism in music is characterized by exotic scales (**chromatic, whole tone**), unresolved dissonances, parallel chords, rich orchestral color, and free rhythm, all generally cast in small-scale programmatic forms.

○ The most important French Impressionist composer was Claude Debussy. His orchestral work, *Prelude to "The Afternoon of a Faun,"* was inspired by a Symbolist poem.

○ Debussy, along with other late Romantic composers, was highly influenced by new sounds of non-Western and traditional music styles heard at the Paris World Exhibition of 1889.

The Impressionist Painters

In 1867, the artist Claude Monet (1840–1926), rebuffed by the academic salons, nevertheless found a place to exhibit his painting *Impression: Sun Rising.* Before

The Viennese symphonic tradition extended into the twentieth century through the works of Gustav Mahler (1860–1911), following in the illustrious line from Haydn, Mozart, Beethoven, and Schubert. His nine symphonies abound with lyricism, with long, flowing melodies and richly expressive harmonies. (The Tenth Symphony, complete in a draft at his death, has now been edited and made available for performance.) Mahler never abandoned the principle of tonality; he needed the key as a framework for his vast designs.

The spirit of song permeates Mahler's art. He followed Schubert and Robert Schumann in cultivating the song cycle. Among this best efforts is *The Song of the Earth* (*Das Lied von der Erde*, 1908), six songs with orchestra that mark the peak of his achievement in this genre. Mahler's text for *The Song of the Earth* was drawn from Hans Bethge's *Chinese Flute*, a translation—more accurately, stylization—of poems, including some by the great Chinese poet Li T'ai-po.

The Song of the Earth

These masters felt strongly the influence of Wagner. Alongside them, however, was a new generation that reacted vigorously against the extremes of Romantic harmony. And with this group of composers emerged the movement that more than any other ushered in the twentieth century—Impressionism.

The Kiss (1907–08), by **Gustav Klimt** (1862–1918), reflects how turn-of-the-century artists responded to the vogue for Eastern effects.

The Post-Romantic Era

"I came into a very young world in a very old time."

—ERIK SATIE

- Two important movements surfaced at the turn of the twentieth century: Post-Romanticism, in Germany and Austria; and Impressionism, in France.

- Viennese composer Gustav Mahler is remembered for his symphonies and song cycles with orchestral accompaniment.

- The arts in Vienna felt the influence of Far Eastern culture; Mahler's *The Song of the Earth* exemplifies this trend.

It became apparent toward the end of the nineteenth century that the Romantic impulse had run its course. Some composers of this period, from about 1890 to 1910, continued on the traditional path; others struck out in new directions; and still others tried to steer a middle course between the old and the new. But all were influenced in one way or another by Wagner's chromatic language.

Two important movements ushered in the twentieth century: Impressionism, heralded by the French composers Claude Debussy and Maurice Ravel, and post-Romanticism, exemplified in Italy by Giacomo Puccini (whose opera *Madame Butterfly* we studied) and in Germany and Austria by Richard Strauss and Gustav Mahler.

Germanic Post-Romanticism

The German composer Richard Strauss (1864–1949) was a beacon of post-Romanticism. Well-known for his vividly programmatic symphonic poems (*Don Juan* and *Till Eulenspiegel's Merry Pranks*, among others), Strauss conquered the operatic stage in the early years of the twentieth century with *Salome* (1905, from Oscar Wilde's play), *Elektra* (1909, from a version of the Greek tragedy), and *Der Rosenkavalier* (*The Cavalier of the Rose*, 1911). The last work is notable for its sensuous lyricism and entrancing waltzes.

Post-Romanticism, Impressionism, and Early Twentieth Century

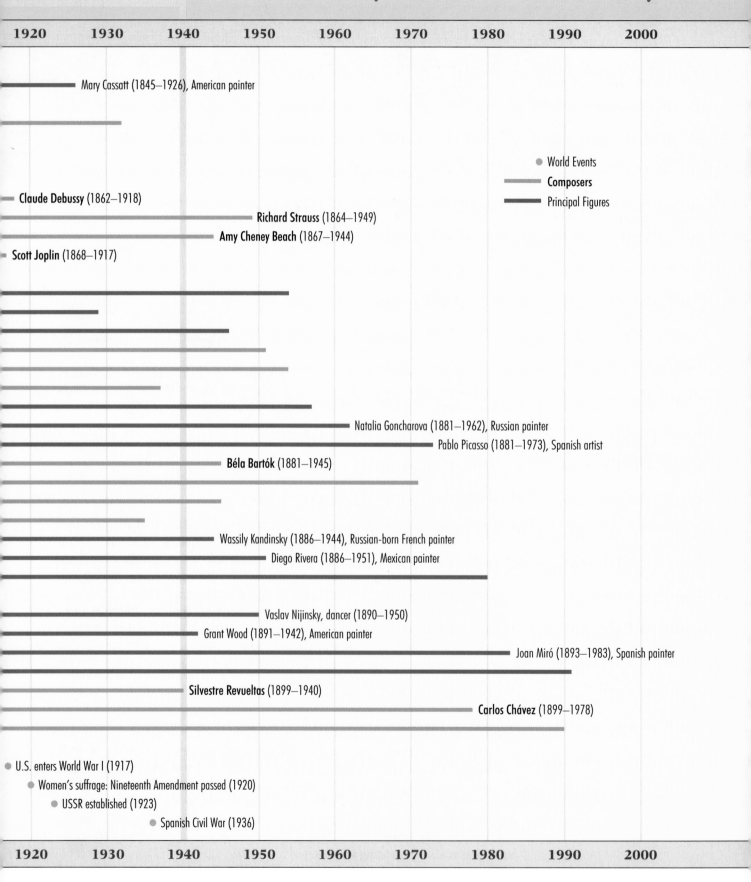

1920　1930　1940　1950　1960　1970　1980　1990　2000

Mary Cassatt (1845–1926), American painter

Claude Debussy (1862–1918)

Richard Strauss (1864–1949)

Amy Cheney Beach (1867–1944)

Scott Joplin (1868–1917)

Natalia Goncharova (1881–1962), Russian painter

Pablo Picasso (1881–1973), Spanish artist

Béla Bartók (1881–1945)

Wassily Kandinsky (1886–1944), Russian-born French painter

Diego Rivera (1886–1951), Mexican painter

Vaslav Nijinsky, dancer (1890–1950)

Grant Wood (1891–1942), American painter

Joan Miró (1893–1983), Spanish painter

Silvestre Revueltas (1899–1940)

Carlos Chávez (1899–1978)

- World Events
- **Composers**
- **Principal Figures**

- U.S. enters World War I (1917)
- Women's suffrage: Nineteenth Amendment passed (1920)
- USSR established (1923)
- Spanish Civil War (1936)

1920　1930　1940　1950　1960　1970　1980　1990　2000

Post-Romanticism, Impressionism, and Early Twentieth Century (1890–1940)

1830
1840
1850
1860
1870
1880
1890
1900
1910
Henri Rousseau (1844–1910), French primitive painter
Paul Gauguin (1848–1903), French painter
John Philip Sousa (1854–1932)
Georges Seurat (1859–1891), French painter
Gustav Mahler (1860–1911)
Frederic Remington (1861–1909), American sculptor
Suez Canal completed (1869)
Henri Matisse (1869–1954), French painter
Serge Diaghilev (1871–1929), Russian impressario
Piet Mondrian (1872–1946), Dutch painter
Arnold Schoenberg (1874–1951)
Charles Ives (1874–1954)
Maurice Ravel (1875–1937)
Constantine Brancusi (1876–1957), Romanian sculptor
Igor Stravinsky (1882–1971)
Anton Webern (1883–1945)
Alban Berg (1885–1935)
Oskar Kokoschka (1886–1980), German Expressionist painter
Paris World Exhibition (1889)
Martha Graham (1894–1991), American choreographer
Aaron Copland (1900–1990)
China becomes Republic (1912)
1830
1840
1850
1860
1870
1880
1890
1900
1910

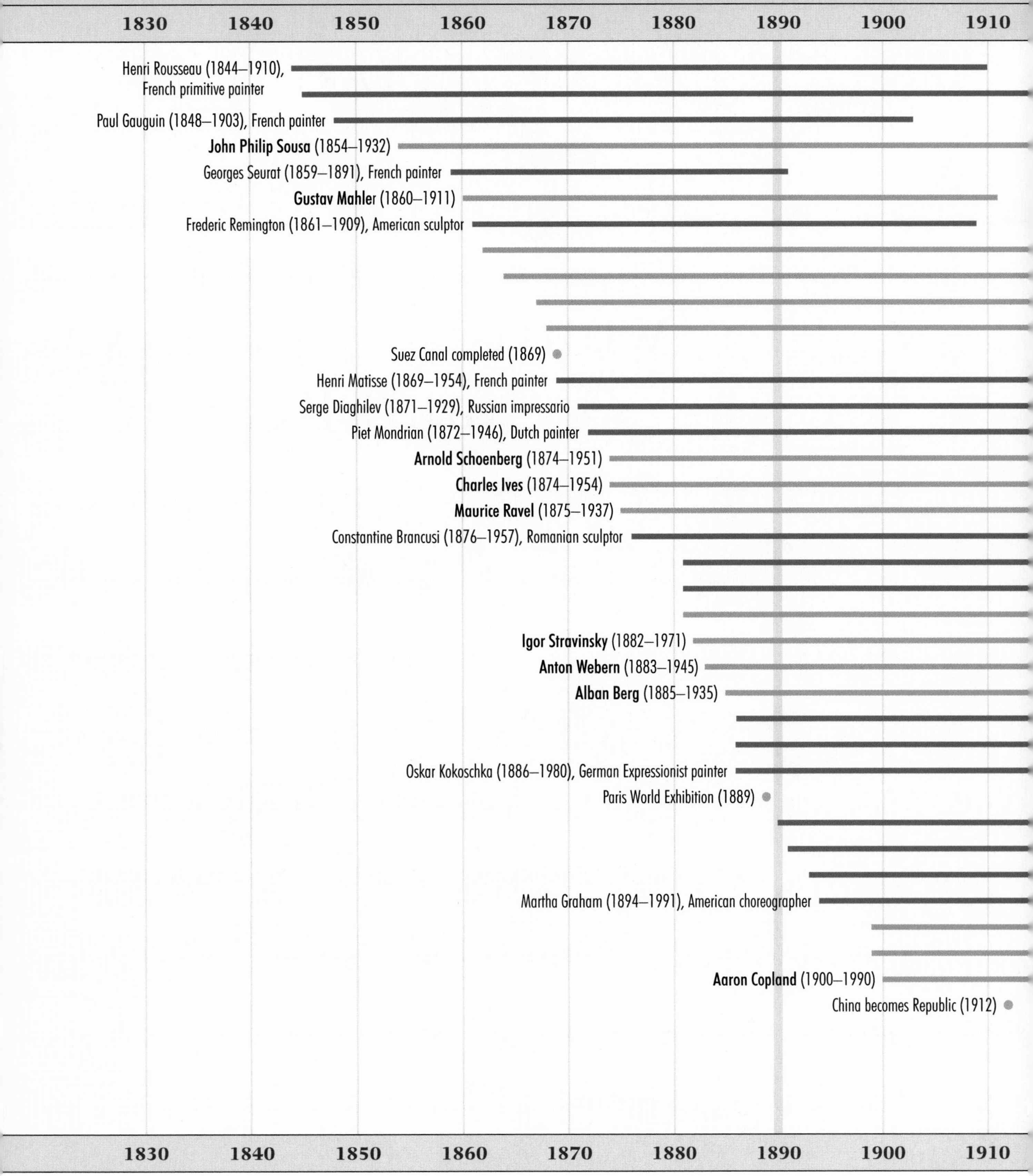

PART EIGHT

The Twentieth Century
and Beyond

In *The Boating Party*, by American painter **Mary Cassatt** (1845–1926), the eye is drawn toward the relaxed mother and child figures. Inspired by a Monet painting, this work features the strong lines and dramatic colors typical of second-generation Impressionists.

across the bar line from one measure to the next in a floating rhythm that discreetly obscures the pulse.

The Impressionists turned away from the large forms of the Austro-German tradition, such as symphonies and concertos. They preferred short lyric forms—preludes, nocturnes, arabesques—whose titles suggested intimate lyricism or painting, such as Debussy's *Clair de lune (Moonlight)*, *Nuages (Clouds)*, and *Jardins sous la pluie (Gardens in the Rain)*. In effect, the Impressionists substituted a thoroughly French conception of Romanticism for the Austro-German variety.

Small forms

Claude Debussy: His Life and Music

"I love music passionately. And because I love it, I try to free it from barren traditions that stifle it. It is a free art gushing forth, an open-air art boundless as the elements, the wind, the sky, the sea. It must never be shut in and become an academic art."

The most important French composer of the early twentieth century, Claude Debussy (1862–1918) was born near Paris in the town of St. Germain-en-Laye, where his parents kept a china shop. He entered the Paris Conservatory when he was eleven. Within a few years, he shocked his professors with bizarre harmonies that defied the rules.

Debussy was only twenty-two when his cantata *The Prodigal Son* won the coveted Prix de Rome. The 1890s, the most productive decade of his career, culminated in the opera *Pelléas and Mélisande*, based on the symbolist drama by the Belgian poet Maurice Maeterlinck. *Pelléas* was attacked for lacking in melody, form, and substance. Nevertheless, its quiet intensity and subtlety of nuance had a profound impact on the musical public, and it became an international success.

Claude Debussy

Pelléas and Mélisande

This opera made Debussy famous. He appeared in the capitals of Europe to conduct his works and wrote articles that established his reputation as one of the wittiest critics of his time. In the first years of the new century, he exhausted the Impressionist style and found his way to a new and tightly controlled idiom, a kind of distillation of Impressionism.

His energies sapped by the ravages of cancer, Debussy worked on with remarkable fortitude. But the outbreak of war in 1914 robbed him of all interest in music. France, he felt, "can neither laugh nor weep while so many of our men heroically face death." After a year of silence, he realized that he had to contribute to the struggle in the only way he could, "by creating to the best of my ability a little of the beauty that the enemy is attacking with such fury." Debussy died in March 1918 during the bombardment of Paris. The funeral procession made its way through deserted streets while the shells of the German guns ripped into his beloved city just eight months before victory was celebrated in France. French culture has ever since celebrated Debussy as one of its most distinguished celebrities.

Like the artist Monet and the writer Verlaine, Debussy considered art to be a sensuous experience. The grandiose themes of Romanticism offended his temperament as both a man and an artist. "French music," he declared, "is clearness, elegance, simple and natural declamation. French music aims first of all to give pleasure."

Rejection of traditional forms

Debussy turned against sonata-allegro form, regarding exposition-development-recapitulation as an outmoded formula. (At a concert once, he whispered to a friend, "Let's go—he's beginning to develop!") From the Romantic grandeur that left nothing unsaid, Debussy turned to an art of subtlety, expressed in short, flexible forms. These mood pieces evoke the favorite images of Impressionist painting: gardens in the rain, sunlight through the leaves, clouds, moonlight, sea, and mist.

Orchestral works

Because Debussy worked slowly, his fame rests on a comparatively small output; *Pelléas and Mélisande* is viewed by many as his greatest achievement. Among his orchestral compositions, the *Prelude to "The Afternoon of a Faun"* became a favorite with the public early on, as did the three nocturnes (*Clouds, Festivals, Sirens*) and *La mer (The Sea)*. His handling of the orchestra is thoroughly French, allowing individ-

Debussy chose this Japanese print, *The Hollow of the Wave off Kanagawa*, by **Katsushika Hokusai** (1760–1849), for the front cover of his orchestral work *La mer (The Sea)*.

ual instruments to stand out against the ensemble. In his scores, the melodic lines are widely spaced, the texture light and airy.

Debussy created a distinctive new style of writing for the piano and composed works that form an essential part of the modern repertory. Among his best-known works are *Clair de lune* (*Moonlight*, the most popular piece he ever wrote), *Evening in Granada, Reflections in the Water,* and *The Sunken Cathedral.* Many of his piano pieces demonstrate an interest in non-Western scales and instruments, which he first heard at the Paris Exhibition in 1889.

Debussy helped establish the French song as a national art form. In chamber music, he achieved an unqualified success with his String Quartet in G minor. The three sonatas of his last years—for cello and piano; violin and piano; and flute, viola, and harp—reveal him moving toward a more abstract and concentrated style.

PRELUDE TO "THE AFTERNOON OF A FAUN"

Debussy's best-known orchestral work was inspired by a pastoral poem by Symbolist writer Stéphane Mallarmé that evokes a landscape of antiquity. The text describes the faun, a mythological creature of the forest that is half man, half goat. This "simple sensuous passionate being" awakes in the woods and tries to remember: was he visited by three lovely nymphs, or was this but a dream? He will never know. The sun is warm, the earth fragrant. He curls himself up and falls into a wine-drugged sleep.

The work follows the familiar pattern of statement-departure-return (**A-B-A′**), yet the movement is fluid and rhapsodic, with almost every fragment of melody repeated immediately. The relaxed rhythm flows across the bar line in a continuous stream. By weakening the accent, Debussy achieved that dreamlike fluidity that is a prime trait of Impressionist music.

We first hear a flute solo in the velvety lower register. The melody glides along the chromatic scale, narrow in range and languorous. (See Listening Guide 39, pp. 338–39 for themes and an excerpt from the poem.) Glissandos on the harp usher in a brief dialogue in the horns. Such a mixture of colors had never been heard before.

Next, a more decisive motive emerges, marked *en animant* (growing lively). This is followed by a third theme, marked *même movement et très soutenu* (same tempo and very sustained)—an impassioned melody that carries the composition to an emotional climax. The first theme then returns in an altered guise. At the close, antique cymbals play *pianissimo.* (*Antique cymbals* are small disks of brass; the rims are struck together gently and allowed to vibrate.) "Blue" chords (with lowered thirds and sevenths) are heard on the muted horns and violins, sounding infinitely remote. The work finally dissolves into silence, leaving us, and the faun, in a dreamlike state.

The great Russian dancer Vaslav Nijinsky as the Faun in the 1912 ballet version of *L'après-midi d'un faune.* Design by **Léon Bakst** (1866–1924).

CULTURAL PERSPECTIVE 15

The Paris World Exhibition of 1889: A Cultural Awakening

How did people from distant regions of the world interact before the era of jet travel and electronic communications? One kind of event that has long brought people from various cultures together is a world exposition.

In 1889, France hosted an exposition marking the centenary of the French Revolution. The Eiffel Tower was the French showcase for this world's fair. Musicians from around the world performed for a receptive European public. One of the most popular exhibits, from the Indonesian island of Java, featured dancers and gamelan. (A gamelan is an ensemble of mainly percussion instruments—including gongs, chimes, and drums.) Many classical composers, including Claude Debussy and Maurice Ravel, heard this gamelan for the first time. Debussy wrote of its unique sound

to a friend: "Do you not remember the Javanese music able to express every nuance of meaning, even unmentionable shades, and which makes our tonic and dominant seem like empty phantoms for the use of unwise infants?" He attempted to capture something of this sound—its pentatonic scale, unusual timbre, and texture—in a number of his compositions, including the famous symphonic poem *La mer* (*The Sea*, 1905), the piano work *Pagodas* (from *Estampes*, 1903), and several piano preludes. Twentieth-century composers continued to explore the unique timbre of the gamelan, including the bold innovator John Cage, whom we will study in Chapter 77.

Other events sparked the imagination of visitors to the Paris Exhibition. Evening festivities included a parade of musicians representing the African nations of Algeria, Senegal, and the Congo, as well as Java, Anam (now Vietnam), and New Caledonia (a Pacific island off the Australian coast). Performances included belly dancers and whirling dervishes from the Middle East (see p. 215); African-American cakewalk dancers from the southern United States (a cakewalk was a nineteenth-century dance that featured rhythmic strutting and prancing arm-in-arm in a parody of white plantation owners' behavior); and dancing women from Cambodia.

Folk and popular musics traversed cultural boundaries at the Paris Exhibition. It was there that Debussy was introduced to traditional Russian songs in settings by Rimsky-Korsakov as well as the music of Hungarian and Spanish Gypsies. Like Bizet, Debussy attempted to capture the rhythms of the habanera and the strumming style of flamenco guitars in several of his piano works (*The Interrupted Serenade* and *Evening in Granada*).

The French composer Maurice Ravel was even more profoundly influenced by this new world of music. Born in the Basque region of France (where the Pyrénées separate France from Spain), Ravel imbued his *Spanish Rhapsody* with rich Iberian color, his violin work *Tzi-*

A Javanese gamelan orchestra plays various metallophones as accompaniment for a dance. In front, two dancers hold bow and arrow as part of the work they are performing.

gane (*Gypsy*, 1924) with showy, exotic effects, and his song cycle *Don Quixote to Dulcinea* (1933, based on the writings of Miguel de Cervantes) with authentic Spanish dance rhythms. Likewise, his most famous work, the hypnotic *Boléro* for orchestra, is accompanied by the insistent rhythm of a popular Spanish dance form. Nor did the mysteries of Asia escape Ravel: his orchestral song cycle *Sheherazade* (1903) was inspired by the Arabian folktales of *The Thousand and One Nights* (sometimes called *Arabian Nights* and the source for the stories of Aladdin and Ali Baba) and includes what he

believed was a Persian melody. A movement from the charming *Mother Goose Suite* (originally for piano), called *Empress of the Pagodas*, is based on a fairy tale about an empress who is serenaded during her bath by whimsical creatures playing fantastic instruments.

Ravel's broad-ranging interests drew him to folk songs from around the world (he arranged Greek, Hebrew, Italian, and French tunes, among others), to the newly popular African-American styles of ragtime, blues, and jazz (the second movement of his Violin Sonata is entitled *Blues*), and to the music of Madagascar (an African island and the subject of his intense song cycle *Songs of Madagascar*, 1925–26).

Today, we do not have to wait for a world exposition to experience music from around the world. We have only to tune in a PBS (Public Broadcasting System) special on Mexican mariachi bands, rent a library video of Japanese Noh drama, or locate a Web site on Irish step dancing to stimulate our eyes, ears, and imagination.

This watercolor of a *Cambodian Dancer* (1906), by **Auguste Rodin** (1840–1917), reflects the artistic interest in exotic subjects.

Terms to Note

gamelan
cakewalk

Suggested Listening

Debussy: *La mer, Pagodas* (from *Estampes*), or *Evening in Grenada*
CD iMusic Indonesian music (gamelan orchestra), *Tabu Kenilu Sawik*
Ravel: *Songs of Madagascar, Boléro, Tzigane, Sheherazade, Blues* (from Violin Sonata), *Don Quixote to Dulcinea*

Listening Guide 39

eLG   3 (55–59)
7 (1–5)

Debussy: *Prelude to "The Afternoon of a Faun"*
(Prélude à "L'après-midi d'un faune")   (9:45)

DATE OF WORK: 1894

GENRE: Symphonic poem

ORCHESTRA: Strings (with 2 harps), flute, oboes, English horn, clarinets, French
horns, and antique cymbals

BASIS: Symbolist poem by Stéphane Mallarmé

FORM: Free ternary (**A-B-A′**)

WHAT TO LISTEN FOR: Lyrical, sinuous melodies (opening is chromatic) that repeat.
Rich instrumental color, with individual timbres that stand out against
the orchestra; free-flowing rhythm gives a sense of floating.
Loose 3-part (ternary, or **A-B-A′**) structure.
Evocative mood that expresses the poem's sensuality.
Emotional climax in middle section that peaks in range, dynamics, and
textural density.

Opening of poem:

TEXT	TRANSLATION
Ces nymphes, je les veux perpétuer.	These nymphs I would perpetuate.
Si clair	So light
Leur incarnat léger, qu'il voltige dans l'air	their gossamer embodiment, floating on the air
Assoupi de sommeils touffus.	inert with heavy slumber.
Amais-je un rêve?	Was it a dream I loved?
Mon doute, amas de nuit ancienne, s'achève	My doubting harvest of the bygone night ends
En maint rameau subtil, qui, de meuré les vrais	in countless tiny branches; together remaining
Bois mêmes, prouve, hélas! que bien seul je m'offrais	a whole forest, they prove, alas, that since I am alone,
Pour triomphe la faute idéale de roses.	my fancied triumph was but the ideal imperfection of roses.
Réfléchissons . . . ou si les femmes dont tu gloses	Let us reflect . . . or suppose those women that you idolize
Figurent un souhait de tes sens fabuleux!	were but imaginings of your fantastic lust!

A Section

55   0:00   Opening chromatic melody in flute; passes from one instrument to another, accompanied
by muted strings and vague beat:

Très modéré   *etc.*

p doux et expressif

B Section

56   2:48   Clarinet introduces more animated idea, answered by rhythmic figure in cellos.

57   3:16   New theme, more animated rhythmically in solo oboe, builds in *crescendo:*

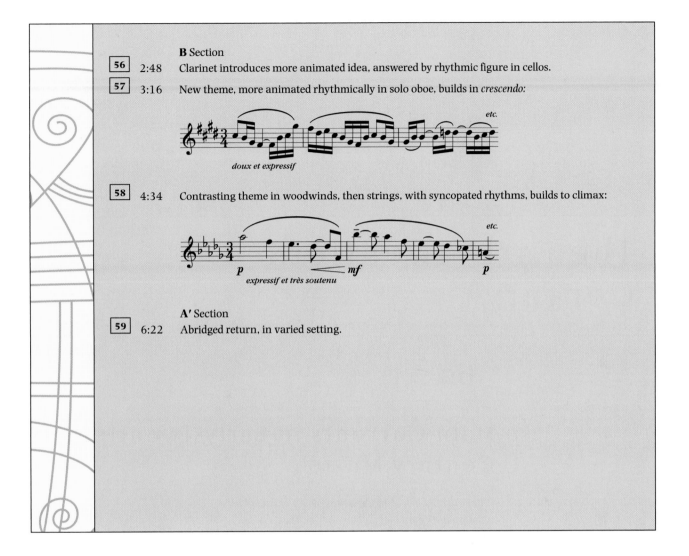

doux et expressif

58   4:34   Contrasting theme in woodwinds, then strings, with syncopated rhythms, builds to climax:

expressif et très soutenu

A′ Section

59   6:22   Abridged return, in varied setting.

The Early Twentieth Century

64

Main Currents in Early-Twentieth-Century Music

*"The entire history of modern music may be said to be
a history of the gradual pull-away from the German
musical tradition of the past century."*

—AARON COPLAND

- The diverse artistic trends of the early twentieth century were a reaction against Romanticism.
- Early-twentieth-century artistic trends explored simplicity and abstraction (interest in non-Western arts, Dadaism, Cubism) and the world of dreams and the inner soul (Surrealism, Expressionism).

- Expressionism was the German response to French Impressionism; in music, composers such as Schoenberg and Webern explored new harmonic systems and the extreme registers of instruments.
- The Neoclassical movement sought to revive balance and objectivity in the arts by returning to formal structures of the past.

The Reaction against Romanticism

Early-twentieth-century composers turned away from the Romantic past and suppressed Romanticism in their music. These new attitudes took hold just before the outbreak of the First World War (1914–1918). European arts sought to break away from overrefinement and tried to capture the spontaneity and the freedom from inhibition that was associated with primitive life. Artists were inspired by the abstraction of African sculpture, and Paul Gauguin and Henri Rousseau created exotic paintings of monumental simplicity (see below). Some composers turned to the vigorous energy of non-Western rhythm, seeking fresh concepts in the musics of Africa, Asia, and eastern Europe.

New Trends in the Arts

In the years immediately preceding the First World War, two influential arts movements arose: Futurism, whose manifesto of 1909 declared its alienation from established institutions and its focus on the dynamism of twentieth-century life; and Dadaism, founded in Switzerland after 1918. The Dadaists, principally writers and artists who reacted to the horrors of the war's bloodbath that had engulfed Europe, rejected the concept of art as something to be reverently admired. To make their point, they produced works of absolute absurdity. They also reacted against the excessive complexity of Western art by trying to recapture the simplicity of a child's worldview.

The Dada group, which included artists Hans Arp and Marcel Duchamp, merged into the school of Surrealism, which included Salvador Dali and Joan Miró (see p. 342), both of whom explored the world of dreams. Other styles of modern art included Cubism, the Paris-based style of painting embodied in the works of Pablo Picasso (see opposite Part Opener), which encouraged the painter to construct a visual world in terms of geometric patterns; and Expressionism, which we will see had a significant impact on music of the early twentieth century.

The powerful abstraction of African sculpture strongly influenced European art.

Surrealism and Cubism

Parisian painter **Paul Gauguin** (1848–1903) was drawn to the simplicity of Tahitian life and the emotional directness of his native subjects. *Nave, Nave Moe* (*Miraculous Source*, 1894)

Spanish artist **Joan Miró** (1893–1983) explores the surrealist world of dreams through the distortion of shapes. *Dutch Interior I.*

Expressionism

Expressionism was the German answer to French Impressionism. While the French explored radiant impressions of the outer world, the Germanic temperament preferred digging down to the depths of the soul. As with Impressionism, the impulse for the Expressionist movement came from painting. Wassily Kandinsky (1866–1944), Oskar Kokoschka (1886–1980), and Edvard Munch (1863–1944)—famous for *The Scream*—influenced the composer Arnold Schoenberg (see p. 353) and his followers just as the Impressionist painters influenced Debussy. Expressionism is reflected also in the writings of Franz Kafka (1883–1924). Expressionism in music reached its full tide in the dramatic works of the *Second Viennese School* (a term referring to Arnold Schoenberg and his disciples Alban Berg and Anton Webern).

The musical language of Expressionism favored a hyper-expressive harmonic language marked by extraordinarily wide leaps in the melody and by the use of instruments in their extreme registers. Expressionist music soon reached the boundaries of what was possible within the major-minor system. Inevitably, it had to push beyond.

Neoclassicism

One way of rejecting the nineteenth century was to return to earlier eras. Instead of revering Beethoven and Wagner, as the Romantics had done, composers began to emulate the great musicians of the early eighteenth century—Bach, Handel, Vivaldi, and Pergolesi—and the detached, objective style that is often associated with their music.

Neoclassicism tried to rid music of the story-and-picture meanings favored in the nineteenth century. Neoclassical composers turned away from the symphonic poem and the Romantic attempt to bring music closer to poetry and painting. They preferred absolute to program music, and they focused attention on craftsmanship and balance, a positive affirmation of the Classical virtues of objectivity and control.

Absolute music

The German Expressionist painter **Oskar Kokoschka** (1886–1980) reveals his terror of war in *Knight Errant* (1915).

65

New Elements of Musical Style

"To study music, we must learn the rules.
To create music, we must break them."

—NADIA BOULANGER

- Early-twentieth-century composers revitalized rhythm by increasing its complexity—using, for example, *polyrhythm, polymeter, changing meters,* or *irregular meters.*
- Melody was no longer the focus of a composition; the style was often more "instrumental" in character.
- New concepts of harmony (*polychords, polytonality, atonality*) pressed music beyond the traditional systems of tonality.
- The *twelve-tone method* (or *serialism*) devised by

Arnold Schoenberg was an important and influential compositional technique.

- Linear movement replaced vertical, chordal conceptions, and extreme dissonance became part of the sound palette.
- The early-twentieth-century orchestra grew smaller and focused on winds, percussion, and piano rather than on strings.
- Composers absorbed influences from ragtime, jazz, and other popular styles, which invigorated their works.

The New Rhythmic Complexity

Twentieth-century music discarded the standard rhythmic patterns of duple, triple, and quadruple meter. Now, composers explored the possibilities of nonsymmetrical patterns based on odd numbers: five, seven, eleven, or thirteen beats to the measure. In nineteenth-century music, a single meter customarily prevailed through an entire movement or section. Now the metrical flow shifted constantly (*changing meter*), sometimes with each measure. Formerly, one rhythmic pattern was used at a time. Now composers turned to *polyrhythm*—the simultaneous use of several rhythmic patterns. As a result of these innovations, Western music achieved something of the complexity and suppleness of Asian and African rhythms.

Changing meter

Polyrhythm

The new generation of composers preferred freer rhythms of the highest flexibility that gave their works an almost physical power and drive. This revitalization of rhythm is one of the major achievements of early-twentieth-century music.

Composers also enlivened their music with materials drawn from popular styles. Ragtime, with its elaborate syncopations, traveled across the Atlantic to Europe. The rhythmic freedom of jazz captured the ears of many composers, who strove to achieve something of the spontaneity that distinguished popular style.

The New Melody

Rhythm was not the only element in which symmetrical structure was abandoned; melody was affected, too. Twentieth-century composers rejected the neatly balanced phrase repetitions of earlier music. Their ideal was a direct, forward-driving melody from which all nonessentials had been cut away.

Instrumental melody

Nineteenth-century melody is fundamentally vocal in character; composers tried to make the instruments "sing." In contrast, early-twentieth-century melody is not conceived in relation to the voice. It abounds in wide leaps and dissonant intervals. Melody is often not even a primary element. Twentieth-century composers have greatly expanded our notion of what a melody is, creating tunes and patterns that would have been inconceivable a century ago.

The New Harmony

No single factor sets off early-twentieth-century music from that of the past more decisively than the new conceptions of harmony. The triads and four-note chords of traditional harmony gave way (in music of the Impressionists) to five-note combinations known as ninth chords (1-3-5-7-9). Twentieth-century composers added more "stories" to such chords, forming highly dissonant *polychords* of six and seven notes. The emergence of these complex "skyscraper" chords brought increased tension and dissonance to music and allowed the composer to play two or more streams of harmony against each other, creating *polyharmony*.

Polychords and polyharmony

NEW CONCEPTIONS OF TONALITY

The new sounds of twentieth-century music burst the confines of traditional tonality and called for new means of organization, extending or replacing the major-minor system. These approaches, in general, followed four principal paths—expanded tonality, polytonality, atonality, and twelve-tone music.

Atonality

The widespread use of chromatic harmony in the late nineteenth century led, in the early twentieth, to the free use of all twelve tones around a center. Although this approach retained the basic principle of traditional tonality—gravitation to the tonic—it wiped out the distinction between diatonic and chromatic and between major and minor modes. A further step followed logically: heightening the contrast of two keys by presenting them simultaneously, which resulted in *polytonality*. Confronting the ear with two keys at the same time meant a radical departure from the basic principle of traditional harmony: centering on a single key. Polytonality came into prominence with the music of Stravinsky, in such works as *The Rite of Spring* (see p. 347).

The idea of abandoning tonality altogether is associated with the composer Arnold Schoenberg, who advocated doing away with the tonic by giving the twelve tones of the chromatic scale equal importance—thus creating *atonal* music. (We will study an example of atonality in Schoenberg's song cycle *Pierrot lunaire*.) Atonality entirely rejected the framework of key. Consonance, according to Schoenberg, was no longer capable of making an impression; atonal music moved from one level of dissonance to another, functioning always at maximum tension, without areas of relaxation.

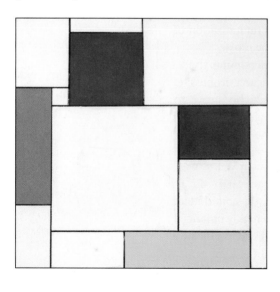

In *Composition Decentralisee* (1924), Dutch artist **Theo van Doesburg** (1883–1931) shows the influence of Cubism in his move toward a geometrically rational art.

THE TWELVE-TONE METHOD

Having accepted the necessity of moving beyond the existing tonal system, Schoenberg sought a unifying principle that would take its place. He found this in a strict technique, worked out by the early 1920s, that he called "the method of composing with twelve tones"—that is, with twelve equal tones. Each composition that uses Schoenberg's method, also known as *serialism*, is based on a particular arrangement of the twelve chromatic tones called a *tone row*. (The term *dodecaphonic*, the Greek equivalent of *twelve-tone*, is sometimes also used for Schoenberg's method.) This row is the unifying idea for that composition and serves as the source of all the musical events that take place in it.

Once established, a tone row is the basis from which a composer builds themes, harmonies, and musical patterns. Schoenberg provided flexibility and variety in this seemingly confining system through alternative forms of the tone row. A *transposed row* begins on a different note. In *inversion*, the movement of the notes is in the opposite direction, up instead of down and vice versa, so that the row appears upside down. *Retrograde* is an arrangement of the pitches in reverse order, so that the row comes out backward, and *retrograde inversion* turns the row upside down and backward. (You will remember that the same techniques were used in the Baroque fugue; see diagram on p. 160.)

Serialism
Tone row

Forms of the tone row

THE EMANCIPATION OF DISSONANCE

As we have discovered, the history of music has been the history of a steadily increasing tolerance on the part of listeners. Throughout this long evolution, one factor remained constant: a clear distinction was drawn between dissonance, the element of tension, and consonance, the element of rest. Consonance was the norm, dissonance the temporary disturbance. In many twentieth-century works, however, tension became the norm. Therefore, a dissonance can serve even as a final cadence, provided it is less dissonant than the chord that came before; in relation to the greater dissonance, it is judged to be consonant. Twentieth-century composers emancipated dissonance by freeing it from the obligation to resolve to consonance. Their music taught listeners to accept tone combinations whose like had never been heard before.

> IN HIS OWN WORDS
>
> *Every dissonance doesn't have to resolve if it doesn't happen to feel like it, any more than every horse should have its tail bobbed just because it's the prevailing fashion.*
> —GEORGE IVES,
> TO HIS SON CHARLES

Orchestration

The rich sonorities of nineteenth-century orchestration gave way to a leaner sound, one that was hard and bright, played by a smaller orchestra. The decisive factor in the handling of the orchestra was the change to a linear texture. Color came to be used in the new music not so much for atmosphere as for bringing out the lines of counterpoint and of form. The string section lost its traditional role as the heart of the orchestra; its tone was felt to be too warm. Attention was focused on the more penetrating winds. Composers favored darker instruments—viola, bassoon, trombone. The emphasis on rhythm brought the percussion group into greater prominence than ever before, and the piano, which in the Romantic era was preeminently a solo instrument, found a place in the orchestral ensemble.

Formalism

New Conceptions of Form

The first quarter of the century saw the final expansion of traditional forms in the gigantic symphonies and symphonic poems of Mahler and Strauss. What had been a concise, twenty-five-minute structure in the hands of Haydn and Mozart now could take over an hour and a half to play. As music could hardly go further in this direction, composers returned to the Classical ideals of tight organization and succinctness. In addition, they revived a number of older forms such as toccata, fugue, concerto grosso, and suite, while retaining the traditional symphony, sonata, and concerto. They valued the formal above the expressive, a principle known as *formalism*. The New Classicism, like the old, strove for purity of line and proportion.

Romanian sculptor **Constantin Brancusi** (1876–1957) revolutionized the movement to abstraction and reductive formalism in *The Kiss* (1908).

66

Stravinsky and the Revitalization of Rhythm

"I hold that it was a mistake to consider me a revolutionary. If one only need break habit in order to be labeled a revolutionary, then every artist who has something to say and who in order to say it steps outside the bounds of established convention could be considered revolutionary."

KEY POINTS

StudySpace online at www.wwnorton.com/enjoy

○ Russian composer Igor Stravinsky experimented boldly with rhythm and new instrumental combinations.

○ Stravinsky's musical language also explores the percussive use of dissonance, as well as polyrhythms and polytonality.

○ Stravinsky's early works, including his ballets *The Firebird, Petrushka,* and *The Rite of Spring,* are strongly nationalistic; the last of these re-creates rites of ancient Russia.

○ Stravinsky's style evolved throughout his life; he explored Neoclassical and serial (twelve-tone) techniques.

Igor Stravinsky

Certain artists embody the most significant impulses of their time and affect the cultural life in a most powerful fashion. One such artist was Igor Stravinsky, the Russian composer who for half a century reflected the main currents in twentieth-century music.

His Life

Igor Stravinsky (1882–1971) was born in Oranienbaum, a summer resort not far from St. Petersburg, where his parents lived. He grew up in a musical environment: his father was the leading bass singer at the Imperial Opera. Although he played the piano, his musical education was kept on the amateur level because his parents wanted him to study law. Still, while enrolled at the University of St. Petersburg, he continued his musical studies. At twenty, he submitted his compositions to the Russian master Nicolai Rimsky-Korsakov, with whom he subsequently worked for three years.

Serge Diaghilev

Success came early to Stravinsky. His music attracted the notice of Serge Diaghilev, the legendary impresario of the Paris-based Russian Ballet, who commissioned Stravinsky to write a score for *The Firebird,* which was produced in 1910. *The Firebird* was followed a year later by the ballet *Petrushka.* With dancers Vaslav Nijinsky and Tamara Karsavina in the leading roles, the production secured Stravinsky's position in the forefront of the modern movement. The spring of 1913 saw the staging of the third and most spectacular of the ballets Stravinsky wrote for Diaghilev,

The Rite of Spring

The Rite of Spring. On opening night, one of the most scandalous in modern music history, the revolutionary score touched off a near riot. People hooted and screamed, convinced that what they were hearing "constituted a blasphemous attempt to destroy music as an art." However, when the work was presented a year later at a symphony concert under conductor Pierre Monteux, it was received with enthusiasm and established itself as a masterpiece.

The outbreak of war in 1914 ended the way of life that had nurtured Diaghilev's sumptuous dance spectacles. Stravinsky and his family took refuge in Switzerland, their home for the next six years. In 1920, the Russian Revolution having severed Stravinsky's ties with his homeland, he settled in France and remained there until 1939. During these years, Stravinsky concertized extensively throughout Europe, performing his own music as pianist and conductor. In 1939, he was invited to deliver a lecture series at Harvard University. When the Second World War broke out, he decided to settle in California, outside Los Angeles; in 1945, he became an American citizen. Stravinsky's later concert tours around the world made him the most celebrated figure in twentieth-century music. He died in New York on April 6, 1971, at the age of eighty-nine.

American years

His Music

Stravinsky's style evolved continuously throughout his career, from the post-Impressionism of *The Firebird* and the primitivism of *The Rite of Spring* to the controlled classicism of his mature style and, finally, to the serialism of his late works.

Stravinsky was a leader in the revitalization of rhythm in European art music. His first success came as a composer of ballet, where rhythm is allied with body movement and expressive gesture. His rhythms were unparalleled in their dynamic power, furious yet controlled. Stravinsky reacted against the restless chromaticism of the Romantic period, but no matter how daring his harmony, he retained a sense of key. He is considered one of the great orchestrators, his music's sonority marked by a polished brightness and a texture so clear that, as Diaghilev remarked, "one can see through it with one's ears."

Early works

Nationalism predominates in such early works as *The Firebird*, *Petrushka*, and *The Rite of Spring*, the last of which re-creates sacrificial rites of ancient Russia. In the decade of the First World War, the composer turned to a more economic style; his *Soldier's Tale*, a dance-drama for four characters, is an intimate theater work accompanied by a seven-piece band. The most important work of the years that followed is *The Wedding*, a stylization of a Russian peasant wedding.

Stravinsky's Neoclassical period culminated in several major compositions. *Oedipus Rex* is an "opera-oratorio" whose text derives from a Greek tragedy by Sophocles. The *Symphony of Psalms*, for chorus and orchestra, regarded by many as the chief work of Stravinsky's maturity, was written, according to the composer, "for the glory of God." Equally admired is *The Rake's Progress*, an opera on a libretto by W. H. Auden and Chester Kallman, after Hogarth's celebrated series of engravings. Written as the composer was approaching seventy, this radiantly melodious score, which uses the set forms of Mozartean opera, stands as the essence of Neoclassicism. In the works written after he was seventy, which included the ballet *Agon* and the choral work *Threni: Lamentations of the Prophet Jeremiah* (both written in the 1950s), he showed an increasing receptiveness to the serial procedures of the twelve-tone style.

Neoclassical period

THE RITE OF SPRING

The Rite of Spring, subtitled *Scenes of Pagan Russia*, not only embodies the cult of primitivism that so startled its first-night audience, but also sets forth a new musical

IN HIS OWN WORDS

Mild protests against the music could be heard from the very beginning of the performance [of Rite of Spring*]. Then, when the curtain opened on the group of knock-kneed and long-braided Lolitas jumping up and down (Danse des adolescents), the storm broke. Cries of "Ta gueule" [Shut up] came from behind me. I heard Florent Schmitt shout "Taisez-vous garces du seizième" [Be quiet, you bitches of the sixteenth]; the "garces" of the 16th arrondissement were, of course, the most elegant ladies in Paris. The uproar continued, however, and a few minutes later I left the hall in a rage. . . . I have never again been that angry. The music was so familiar to me; I loved it, and I could not understand why people who had not yet heard it wanted to protest in advance.*

language characterized by the percussive use of dissonance, as well as polyrhythms and polytonality.

Stravinsky described how he "had a fleeting vision," which came to him as a "complete surprise. . . . I saw in my imagination a solemn pagan rite: sage elders, seated in a circle, watching a young girl dance herself to death. They were sacrificing her to propitiate the God of Spring." In Part I of the ballet, celebrations for the arrival of spring include a lustful abduction of women, a rivalry between two tribes, and a round dance. At the climax of these activities, the oldest and wisest man of the village is brought out for the ritual kissing of the earth, and the tribes respond joyfully and energetically.

Part II is more solemn. The women of the tribe, conducting a mysterious game, select a young maiden whom they will sacrifice in order to save the fertility of the earth. The Chosen One begins her fatal dance in front of the elders, and her limp body is eventually carried off to the Sun God Yarilo. The plot is vague, the anthropology is dubious, but the visions are effectively theatrical.

As a ballet, *The Rite of Spring* had a brief life, but the music survived independently as a concert piece. Today, it stands as one of the landmarks in twentieth-century symphonic literature. The size of the orchestra is monumental, even by the standards of late Romanticism. Stravinsky expands the ensemble to include eight French horns, five trumpets, five from each of the woodwind groups, and an extraordinary battery of percussion instruments. He often uses the full force of the brass and percussion to create a barbaric, primeval sound. Stravinsky ignores the natural lyric qualities of the string instruments, giving them percussive material such as pizzicato and successive down-bow strokes. The overall impact of the orchestration is harsh and loud, with constantly changing colors.

Stravinsky's melodies are modeled after Russian folk-songs—in fact, a number of authentic tunes are quoted—and the remaining melodic material, often presented in short fragments, use limited ranges and extended repetition in a folk-song-like manner. The harmonies are derived from an eclectic language, including whole-tone and octatonic (eight-tone) scales, polytonality, and dissonance.

Rhythm and meter

The energetic interaction between rhythm and meter is the most innovative and influential element of *The Rite of Spring*. In some scenes, a steady pulse is set up, only to serve as a backdrop for unpredictable accents or melodic entrances. In other passages, the concept of a regular metric pulse is totally abandoned as downbeats occur seemingly at random. With *The Rite of Spring*, Stravinsky freed Western music from the traditional constraints of metric regularity.

Part I

In the Introduction to Part I, *Adoration of the Earth*, a writhing bassoon melody set in its uppermost range depicts the awakening of the Earth in spring. At the conclusion of the Introduction, the melody, which is based on a Lithuanian folk tune, appears once again in the bassoon. Quietly, the strings follow with a four-note motive played pizzicato. This motive signals the end of the Introduction and establishes the duple pulse necessary for the ensuing rhythmic conflict.

The Dance of the Youths and Maidens erupts with a series of violent chords played percussively by the strings. The reiterated chords sound on unpredictable accents reinforced by the power of eight French horns, creating an intense conflict with the established meter. The harsh dissonance is fashioned from the combination of two traditional harmonies, resulting in a dissonant eight-note chord.

This opening section forms a block of sound that alternates with other blocks during *The Dance of the Youths and Maidens*. In the contrasting sections, new ideas are introduced. Most notable are three folklike melodies, the first of which (from Section D) is derived from an authentic folk tune. Unifying these diverse passages are the unchanging harmonies and a constant eighth-note motion that maintains the duple pulse. The newly introduced ideas begin to recur, often in a manner resembling an ostinato, as the level of activity increases. The dense texture and loud dynamics build to a climax at the end of the section (see Listening Guide 40).

The opening of *Game of Abduction* provides a brief respite from the dense activities. Another folk melody is introduced, which is subjected to a similar ostinato-like treatment. The level of activity quickly rises again, complete with brash horn calls. Adding to the frenzy are loud accents that sound randomly. Unlike the conflict in *The Dance of the Youths and Maidens*, there is no established pulse in this section. The overall effect is primitive and lusty. In Part II, Stravinsky continues with his primitive rhythmic treatment, eerie orchestration, and bitingly dissonant tonalities. The work culminates in the *Sacrificial Dance*, during which the young girl dances herself to death in a frenzied climax to the ballet.

The rhythmic arrangement of line and color in *The Dance* (1909–10), by **Henri Matisse** (1869–1954), is suggestive of the *Dance of the Youths and Maidens*, from Stravinsky's *Rite of Spring*.

Listening Guide 40

eLG 4 (1–7) 7 (12–18)

Stravinsky: *The Rite of Spring (Le sacre du printemps)*, Part I, excerpts   (4:32)

DATE OF WORK:	1913
GENRE:	Ballet (often performed as a concert piece for orchestra)
BASIS:	Scenes of pagan Russia
SCENARIO:	Nikolai Roerich and Igor Stravinsky
CHOREOGRAPHY:	Vaslav Nijinsky

SECTIONS:

Part I: *Adoration of the Earth*
Introduction
*Dance of the Youths and Maidens
*Game of Abduction
Spring Rounds
Games of the Rival Tribes
Procession of the Sage
Dance of the Earth

Part II: *The Sacrifice*
Introduction
Mystic Circle of the Adolescents
Glorification of the Chosen One
Evocation of the Ancestors
Ritual Action of the Ancestors
Sacrificial Dance

WHAT TO LISTEN FOR: Huge orchestral forces, with constantly changing timbral colors.
Violent rhythmic conflicts (changing meters, shifting accents).
Stagnant harmony built on eight-note chord.
Melodies derived from folk tunes.
Blocks of sound that alternate and merge together.

Listening Guide continues

Introduction, closing measures

Principal Instruments: bassoon, clarinets, pizzicato violins
Tempo: Lento (slow)

1   0:00   Folk tune played by the bassoon, from opening:

0:12   Pizzicato rhythmic figure in violins:

0:19   Clarinet flourish, followed by sustained string chord.
0:22   Violin figure returns to establish meter for next section.

Dance of the Youths and Maidens

Principal Instruments: strings, woodwinds, and brass
Tempo: *Tempo giusto* (twice as fast as the Introduction)
Form: Sectional (**A-B-A'-C-A-D-E-F-G-A"-F'**)

2   0:30   Strings play harsh, percussive chords (**A**), reinforced by 8 horns, with unpredictable accents:

0:37   English horn (**B**) plays the pizzicato motive from *Introduction*.
0:42   Brief return of opening accented chords (**A'**).
0:45   Motives combine with new ideas (**C**). Strings continue chords; English horn repeats its 4-note motive; loud brass interruptions and a descending melodic fragment.
1:02   Return of opening accented chords (**A**).

3   1:10   Bassoon plays syncopated folk melody (**D**), over accented string chords:

1:38   Steady eighth-note pulse (**E**); 4-note motive alternates between the English horn and trumpet; scurrying motives in the winds and strings, and sustained trills.
1:50   4-note motive (English horn, then violins) and sustained trills; low strings hit strings with the wood of their bows (*col legno*).

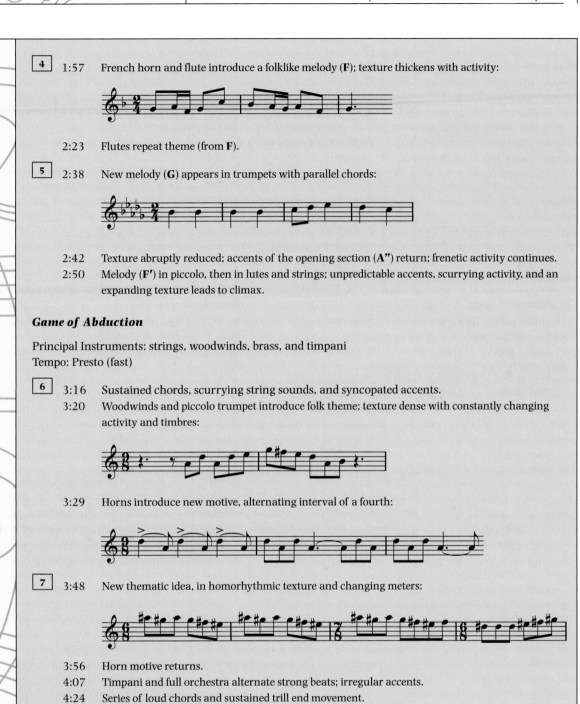

4 1:57   French horn and flute introduce a folklike melody (**F**); texture thickens with activity:

2:23   Flutes repeat theme (from **F**).

5 2:38   New melody (**G**) appears in trumpets with parallel chords:

2:42   Texture abruptly reduced; accents of the opening section (**A"**) return; frenetic activity continues.

2:50   Melody (**F′**) in piccolo, then in lutes and strings; unpredictable accents, scurrying activity, and an expanding texture leads to climax.

Game of Abduction

Principal Instruments: strings, woodwinds, brass, and timpani
Tempo: Presto (fast)

6 3:16   Sustained chords, scurrying string sounds, and syncopated accents.

3:20   Woodwinds and piccolo trumpet introduce folk theme; texture dense with constantly changing activity and timbres:

3:29   Horns introduce new motive, alternating interval of a fourth:

7 3:48   New thematic idea, in homorhythmic texture and changing meters:

3:56   Horn motive returns.

4:07   Timpani and full orchestra alternate strong beats; irregular accents.

4:24   Series of loud chords and sustained trill end movement.

67

Schoenberg and the Second Viennese School

"I personally hate to be called a revolutionist, which I am not. What I did was neither revolution nor anarchy."

KEY POINTS

StudySpace online at www.wwnorton.com/enjoy

- ○ Arnold Schoenberg, along with his students Alban Berg and Anton Webern, comprise the *Second Viennese School*.
- ○ Schoenberg was highly influenced by German *Expressionism* and was himself an Expressionist painter and playwright.
- ○ Schoenberg experimented with abandoning the tonal system; his *twelve-tone*, or *serial*, method revolutionized twentieth-century composition.

- ○ His song cycle, *Pierrot lunaire*, represents his atonal-Expressionist period, which preceded his twelve-tone period.
- ○ In *Pierrot lunaire*, Schoenberg joins the text and music through the vocal technique of *Sprechstimme* (spoken voice), accompanied by highly disjunct instrumental lines (*Klangfarbenmelodie*).

The German Expressionist movement manifested itself in the music of Arnold Schoenberg and his followers. Schoenberg's pioneering efforts in the breakdown of the traditional tonal system and his development of the twelve-tone method, described earlier, revolutionized musical composition. His innovations were taken further by his most gifted students, Alban Berg and Anton Webern (see p. 354). These three composers are often referred to as the *Second Viennese School* (the first being Haydn, Mozart, and Beethoven).

Second Viennese School

His Life

Arnold Schoenberg (1874–1951) was born in Vienna. He began to study the violin at the age of eight, and soon afterward made his initial attempts at composing. Having decided to devote his life to music, he left school while in his teens. For a time, he earned his living working in a bank, composing in his free hours. Soon he became acquainted with a young musician, Alexander von Zemlinsky, who for a few months gave him lessons in counterpoint. This was the only musical instruction he ever had.

Through Zemlinsky, young Schoenberg was introduced to the advanced musical circles of Vienna, which at that time were under the spell of Wagner's operas. In 1899, when he was twenty-five, Schoenberg wrote the string sextet *Transfigured Night*. The following year, several of his songs were performed in Vienna and created a scene. "And ever since that day," he once remarked with a smile, "the scandal has not ceased."

Schoenberg became active as a teacher and soon gathered about him a band of students that included Alban Berg and Anton Webern. With each new work, Schoenberg moved closer to taking as bold a step as any composer has ever taken—the rejection of tonality.

Arnold Schoenberg

The First World War interrupted Schoenberg's creative activity. Although he was past forty, he was called up for military duty in the Vienna garrison. His military service was followed by a compositional silence of eight years (1915–23), during which he evolved a set of structural procedures to replace tonality. His "method of composing with twelve tones" caused much bewilderment in the musical world. All the same, he was now firmly established as a leader of contemporary musical thought.

With the coming to power of Hitler in 1933, Schoenberg emigrated to America. Like many Austrian-Jewish intellectuals of his generation, he had grown away from his Jewish origins. Schoenberg converted to Lutheranism, but after leaving Germany, he returned to his Hebrew faith. He arrived in the United States in the fall of 1933; shortly afterward, he joined the faculty of the University of Southern California, and was later appointed professor of composition at the University of California in Los Angeles. He became an American citizen in 1940, taught until his retirement at the age of seventy, and continued his musical activities until his death seven years later.

Arnold Schoenberg completed this Expressionist painting, *The Red Gaze* (1910), just two years before he wrote *Pierrot lunaire*. It is highly reminiscent of Edvard Munch's *The Scream*.

His Music

Schoenberg's early works exemplify post-Wagnerian Romanticism; they still used key signatures and remained within the boundaries of tonality. The best-known composition of this era is *Transfigured Night*. In Schoenberg's second period, the atonal-Expressionist, he abolished the distinction between consonance and dissonance and any sense of a home key. The high point of this period is *Pierrot lunaire*. During this era, Schoenberg's interest in Expressionism was manifested not only in his music, but in his work as an artist (see above) and writer.

Schoenberg's third style period, exploiting the twelve-tone method, reached its climax in the Variations for Orchestra, Opus 31, one of his most powerful works. In the fourth and last part of his career—the American phase—he carried the twelve-tone technique to further stages of refinement. Several of the late works present the twelve-tone style in a manner markedly more accessible than earlier pieces, often with tonal implications. Among these are the cantata *A Survivor from Warsaw*.

PIERROT LUNAIRE

For his song cycle *Pierrot lunaire*, Schoenberg drew on the stock characters of the Italian *commedia dell'arte* (comedy of the arts), a comic theatrical entertainment that originated in the mid-sixteenth century. One of the most parodied characters is the clown Pierrot (Pagliaccio in Italian; Petrushka in Russian), who has been the model for pantomime for centuries.

Schoenberg chose the texts for his song cycle from a collection of poems by the Belgian writer Albert Giraud, a disciple of the Symbolists. Giraud's Pierrot was the poet-rascal-clown whose chalk-white face, passing abruptly from laughter to tears, enlivened every puppet show and pantomime in Europe. The poems were liberally spiced with elements of the macabre and the bizarre that suited the end-of-century taste for decadence; with their abrupt changes of mood from guilt and depression to atonement and playfulness, they fired Schoenberg's imagination. He picked

IN HIS OWN WORDS

Whether one calls oneself conservative or revolutionary, whether one composes in a conventional or progressive manner, whether one tries to imitate old styles or is destined to express new ideas . . . one must be convinced of the infallibility of one's own fantasy and one must believe in one's own inspiration.

twenty-one texts (in German translation), arranged them in three groups of seven, and set them for a female reciter and a chamber music ensemble of five players using eight instruments: piano, flute/piccolo, clarinet/bass clarinet, violin/viola, and cello.

Sprechstimme

One of Schoenberg's goals was to bring spoken word and music as close together as possible; he achieved this aim through *Sprechstimme* (spoken voice), a new style in which the vocal melody is spoken rather than sung on exact pitches and in strict rhythm. As Schoenberg explained it, the reciter sounds the written note at first but abandons it by immediately rising or falling in pitch—"the melody in the speaker's part is *not* meant to be sung." The result is a weird but strangely effective vocal line.

Tone-color melody

Schoenberg also experimented with what he called *Klangfarbenmelodie* (tone-color melody), in which each note of a melody is played by a different instrument, creating a shifting effect that evokes the moonbeams mentioned in the poems. Each text is a *rondeau*, a fifteenth-century verse form in which the opening lines return as a refrain in the middle of the poem and at its end (see p. 80).

We will focus on No. 18, *The Moonfleck* (*Der Mondfleck;* see Listening Guide 41 for the text), Pierrot, out to have fun, is disturbed by a white spot—a patch of moonlight—on the collar of his jet-black jacket. He rubs and rubs but cannot get rid of it. His predicament inspired Schoenberg to contrapuntal complexities of a spectacular kind. The piano introduces a three-voice fugue, while the other instruments unfold devices such as strict canons in diminution (smaller note values) and retrograde (backward). It is, according to composer George Perle, "a work that one never 'gets used to.'"

SCHOENBERG'S STUDENTS: BERG AND WEBERN

Following in his teacher's footsteps, Alban Berg (1885–1935) wrote music that emanated from the world of German romanticism. His most widely known composition is *Wozzeck* (1922), an opera based on a play by Georg Buchner and set in an atonal-Expressionist musical idiom. Here, Berg anticipated certain twelve-tone procedures, but also looked back to the tonal tradition and the leitmotif technique of Wagner. *Wozzeck* envelops the listener in a world of hallucinations, unveiled through Berg's great lyric imagination.

Anton Webern (1883–1945), on the other hand, carried the philosophy of brevity of statement to an extreme. He assigned each tone a specific function in the overall scheme using the device of Klangfarbenmelodie, or tone-color melody, described above. Webern often used instruments in their extreme registers as well. He employed Schoenberg's twelve-tone method with unprecedented strictness, moving toward complete control, or total serialism, thus establishing this compositional system as a major influence in twentieth-century music.

French Expressionist artist
Georges Rouault
(1871–1956) painted many images of the Pierrot character. *Blue Pierrots,* c. 1943.

Listening Guide 41

Schoenberg: *Pierrot lunaire,* No. 18   (0:51)

DATE OF WORK:	1912
GENRE:	Song cycle
MEDIUM:	Solo voice (mezzo-soprano) and 5 instrumentalists (violin/viola, cello, flute/piccolo, clarinet/bass clarinet, piano)
TEXT:	21 poems from Albert Giraud's *Pierrot lunaire,* all in rondeau form; cycle organized in 3 parts

Part I   Pierrot, sad clown figure, is obsessed with the moon, having drunk moonwine; his loves, fantasies, and frenzies are exposed.

1. *Moondrunk*
2. *Columbine*
3. *The Dandy*
4. *Pale Washerwoman*
5. *Valse de Chopin*
6. *Madonna*
7. *The Sick Moon*

Part II: Pierrot becomes ridden with guilt and wants to make atonement.

8. *Night*
9. *Prayer to Pierrot*
10. *Theft*
11. *Red Mass*
12. *Gallows Ditty*
13. *Beheading*
14. *The Crosses*

Part III: Pierrot climbs from the depths of depression to a more playful mood, but with fleeting thoughts of guilt; then he becomes sober.

15. *Homesickness*
16. *Vulgar Horseplay*
17. *Parody*
18. *The Moonfleck*
19. *Serenade*
20. *Homeward Journey*
21. *O Scent of Fabled Yesteryear*

18. *The Moonfleck (Der Mondfleck)*

Medium: Voice, piccolo, clarinet in B♭, violin, cello, piano
Tempo: Sehr rasche (very quickly)

WHAT TO LISTEN FOR: Use of Sprechstimme against fast, dissonant accompaniment.
Complex contrapuntal texture, with canonic treatment.
Musical and poetical refrain (on italic words "Einen weissen Fleck").
Flickering effects created by instruments, playing independently from vocal part.

Listening Guide continues

TEXT	TRANSLATION
8 0:00 *Einen weissen Fleck des hellen Mondes*	*With a fleck of white—from*
Auf dem Rücken seines schwarzen Rockes.	*the bright moon—on the back of his black jacket.*
So spaziert Pierrot im lauen Abend,	Pierrot strolls about in the
Aufzusuchen Glück und Abenteuer.	mild evening seeking his fortune and adventure.
Plötzlich stört ihn was an seinem Anzug,	Suddenly something strikes
Er beschaut sich rings und findet richtig—	him as wrong, he checks his
	clothes and sure enough finds
9 0:23 *Einen weissen Fleck des hellen Mondes*	*a fleck of white—from the*
Auf dem Rücken seines schwarzen Rockes.	*bright moon—on the back of his black jacket.*
Warte! denkt er: das ist so ein Gipsfleck!	Damn! he thinks: that's a
Wischt und wischt, doch—bringt ihn	spot of plaster! Wipes and
nicht herunter!	wipes, but—he can't get it
Und so geht er, giftgeschwollen, weiter,	off. And so goes on his way,
Reibt und reibt bis an den frühen Morgen—	his pleasure poisoned, rubs
Einen weissen Fleck des hellen Mondes.	and rubs till the early morning—
	a fleck of white—from the bright moon.

Opening, for voice and instruments:

Twentieth-Century Nationalism

68

Béla Bartók and the European Tradition

"The art of music above all other arts is the expression of the soul of a nation. The composer must love the tunes of his country and they must become an integral part of him."

—RALPH VAUGHAN WILLIAMS

| KEY POINTS | StudySpace online at www.wwnorton.com/enjoy |

- o Twentieth-century composers used more authentic folk and traditional elements in their nationalistic music than nineteenth-century composers.
- o National "schools" of composition developed across Europe in France, Russia, England, Germany, Spain, Scandinavia, and in various Eastern European countries.
- o Hungarian composer Béla Bartók collected traditional songs and dances from his native land, and

incorporated many of these elements into his compositions.

- o Bartók's music displays new scales and rhythmic ideas and a modern, polytonal harmonic language, all set in Classical forms.
- o His *Concerto for Orchestra* is a programmatic work that uses the whole ensemble as the "soloist."

Twentieth-century nationalism differed from its nineteenth-century counterpart in one important respect. Composers approached traditional music with a scientific spirit, prizing the ancient tunes precisely because they departed from the conventional mold. By this time, the phonograph had been invented. The new students of folklore took recording equipment into the field in order to preserve the songs exactly

Inspired by the German bombing of the Basque town of Guernica on April 28, 1937, this nationalistic painting was produced by **Pablo Picasso** for the Spanish Pavilion at the 1937 International Exhibition in Paris. *Guernica.*

as the village folk sang them, and the composers who used those songs in their works tried to retain the traditional flavor of the originals.

National Schools

French composers in the generation after Debussy and Ravel tried to capture the wit and spirit that are part of their national heritage. One group in particular, called *Les Six* (The Six), developed a style that combined objectivity and understatement with the Neoclassicism and the new concepts of harmony. Of this group, Darius Milhaud (1892–1974) is remembered today for his ballet *The Creation of the World* (1923) and for being a leader in the development of polytonality, Francis Poulenc (1899–1963) has emerged as the most significant figure of *Les Six.* One of the outstanding art song composers of his day, he also wrote several operas that are performed frequently, including *Dialogue of the Carmelites* (1957).

Les Six

In the post-Romantic period, the Russian school produced Sergei Rachmaninoff (1873–1943), whose piano works are enormously popular with the concertgoing public, especially his Second Piano Concerto and his *Variations on a Theme of Paganini.* In the next generation, two important figures emerged: Sergei Prokofiev (1891–1953) and Dmitri Shostakovich (1906–1975), the first Russian composer of international repute who was wholly a product of the musical culture during the period of the Soviet Union (1917–91).

Russian school

Two figures were of prime importance in establishing the modern English school—Ralph Vaughan Williams (1872–1958) and Benjamin Britten (1913–1976). Britten's works for the stage have established his reputation as one of the foremost opera composers of the era. Among his operas are *Peter Grimes* (1945, based on George Crabbe's poem *The Borough),* about an English fishing village, and *Billy Budd* (1951), after Herman Melville's story. You will recall that Britten's *Variations and Fugue on a Theme of Purcell (The Young Person's Guide to the Orchestra)* was discussed earlier (see Chapter 9).

English school

Among the composers who came into prominence in Germany in the years after the First World War, Paul Hindemith (1895–1963) was the most significant. He left Germany when Hitler came to power—his music was banned from the Third Reich as "cultural Bolshevism"—and spent two decades in the United States, during which he taught at Yale University. Carl Orff (1895–1982) took his point of departure from

German school

the clear-cut melodies and vigorous rhythms of Bavarian folk song. He is best known in North America for his stirring cantata *Carmina Burana* (1937), set to racy medieval lyrics. Kurt Weill (1900–1950) was one of the most arresting figures to emerge from Germany in the 1920s. For the international public, his name is indissolubly linked with *The Threepenny Opera* (1928), which he and the poet Bertolt Brecht adapted from *The Beggar's Opera* by John Gay.

Hungarian nationalism found its major representative in Béla Bartók, whom we will study. He collected and analyzed traditional songs, and made the folk element prominent in his music. The major figure of the modern Spanish school was Manuel de Falla (1876–1946), best-known for his ballet *The Three-Cornered Hat*, and works by Finland's Jean Sibelius (1865–1957)—especially his symphonies, Violin Concerto, and tone poem *Finlandia*—are currently enjoying a revival.

Béla Bartók: His Life and Music

"What is the best way for a composer to reap the full benefits of his studies in peasant music? It is to assimilate the idiom of peasant music so completely that he is able to forget all about it and use it as his musical mother tongue."

Béla Bartók (1881–1945) reconciled the traditional songs of his native Hungary with the main currents of European music, thus creating an entirely personal language.

Bartók was born in a small Hungarian town and studied at the Royal Academy in Budapest, where he came in contact with the nationalist movement that sought to escape the domination of German musical culture. His interest in folklore led him to realize that what passed for Hungarian in the eyes of the world was really the music of Roma, or Gypsies. The true Hungarian idiom, he decided, was found only among the peasants. He therefore toured the remote villages of the country, determined to collect the native songs before they died out forever (see illustration on p. 361).

Béla Bartók

The fall of the Hapsburg monarchy in 1918 released a surge of national sentiment that created a favorable climate for his music. In the following decade, Bartók became a leading figure in his country's musical life.

Troubled by the alliance between the Hungarian government and Nazi Germany on the eve of the Second World War, Bartók protested the performances of his music on the Berlin radio and at every opportunity took an anti-Fascist stand. To go into exile meant surrendering the position he enjoyed in Hungary, but he would not compromise. Bartók came to the United States in 1940 and settled in New York City.

Emigration to America

His American years were not happy ones. Sensitive and retiring, he felt uprooted, isolated in his new surroundings. In his final years, Bartók suffered from leukemia and was no longer able to appear in public. A series of commissions from various sources spurred him to compose his last works, which rank among his finest. "The trouble is," he remarked to his doctor shortly before the end, "that I have to go with so much still to say." He died in New York City at the age of sixty-four.

Final years

Bartók found that Eastern European traditional music was based on ancient modes, unfamiliar scales, and nonsymmetrical rhythms. These features freed him in his composing from what he called "the tyrannical rule of the major and minor keys" and brought him to new concepts of melody, harmony, and rhythm. Bartók's harmony can be bitingly dissonant. Polytonality abounds in his work; but despite an occasional leaning toward atonality, he never wholly abandoned the principle of key.

Melody and harmony

Rhythm

Bartók is one of the great rhythmic innovators of modern times. His pounding, stabbing rhythms constitute the primitive aspect of his art. Like Stravinsky, Bartók sometimes changed the meter at almost every bar and frequently used syncopations and repeated patterns (ostinatos). He, along with Stravinsky, played a major role in the revitalization of European rhythm, infusing it with earthy vitality and tension.

Form

The composer was more traditional in his choices of form—his model was the Beethoven sonata, but more tightly structured. In his middle years, he came under the influence of Baroque music and turned increasingly from thinking harmonically to thinking linearly. The resulting complex texture is a masterly example of modern dissonant counterpoint.

Orchestration

Bartók rejected the late Romantic orchestral sound for a palette of colors all his own. His orchestration ranges from brilliant mixtures to threads of pure color that bring out the intertwining melody lines. He is best known to the public for the three major works of his last period: the *Music for Strings, Percussion, and Celesta*, regarded by many as his masterpiece; the *Concerto for Orchestra*, a favorite with American audiences (and the work we will study); and his final effort, the Third Piano Concerto, an impassioned and broadly conceived work.

CONCERTO FOR ORCHESTRA

In the summer of 1943, two years before his death from leukemia, Bartók received a $1000 commission from Serge Koussevitzky, conductor of the Boston Symphony Orchestra, for a new work. The terminally ill composer rallied his strength and set to work on the *Concerto for Orchestra*, which he completed in October of the same year. He wrote that "the mood of the work represents, apart from the jesting second movement, a gradual transition from the sternness of the first movement and the lugubrious death-song of the third to the life-assertion of the last." The work, set in five movements, is called a concerto because of its tendency, as Bartók explained, "to treat the single orchestral instruments in a concertante or soloistic manner." Here, the virtuoso is the entire orchestra.

The first movement, a spacious Introduction, is in sonata-allegro form and makes use of a folklike pentatonic scale; the second is a joking "game of pairs" with short sections, each of which features a different pair of wind instruments; the third, called *Elegia*, is a contemplative and rhapsodic nocturne, or "night music"; the

Fourth movement

fourth (see Listening Guide 42, p. 362) is a songful Intermezzo that separates the two serious movements surrounding it; and the fifth is a rhythmic and primitive-sounding folk dance set in sonata-allegro structure.

The fourth movement, titled *Interrupted Intermezzo*, opens with a plaintive tune in the oboe and flute whose pentatonic structure evokes a Hungarian folk song. The nonsymmetrical rhythm, alternating between 2/4 and 5/8 meter, gives the movement an unpredictable charm. A memorable broad theme is then heard in the strings, highly reminiscent of the song *You Are Lovely, You Are Beautiful, Hungary*. The mood is interrupted by a harsh clarinet melody borrowed from the Russian composer Dmitri Shostakovich's Symphony No. 7, a musical portrayal of the Nazi invasion of Russia in 1942. Bartók made an autobiographical statement in this movement: "The artist declares his love for his native land in a serenade, which is suddenly interrupted in a crude and violent manner; he is seized by rough, booted men who even break his instrument." The two opening themes eventually return in a sentimental declaration of the composer's love for his homeland.

Bartók—A Folk-Song Collector

What kinds of music did the Hungarian composer Béla Bartók hear in the Eastern European villages he visited? He searched out and wrote down folk songs in an attempt to identify the national musics of various Eastern European cultures. Bartók took on this project not as a composer but as a folklorist who wanted to study traditional music scientifically. (Today, we would call him an ethnomusicologist, focusing on the cultural context of performance.) The many thousands of songs he collected reflect the very essence of these peoples—their social rituals (weddings, matchmaking, and dancing) and their religious ceremonies.

Béla Bartók in 1907, recording Slovakian folk songs on an acoustic cylinder machine in the Hungarian village of Zobordarázs.

Bartók drew extensively in his compositions from the melodies, rhythms, and poetic structures of this rich body of traditional music. He was partial to modal scales, especially those typical of Slovak and Romanian melodies. But rhythm was the primary attraction of this body of folk music and dance. Bartók tried at times to imitate the vocal style of Hungarian music, which is based on free speech-rhythms and follows the natural inflection of the language. At other times, he used the irregular folk dance rhythms typical of Bulgarian music. These propelling rhythms were driven by additive meters built from unit groups of 2, 3, or 4. Thus instead of dividing a 9/8 meter into regular divisions of 3, he might build it from irregular groups of 2 and 3 (2 + 3 + 2 + 2, for example; see the discussion of additive meters on p. 18). From this folk legacy Bartók fashioned a unique musical style.

One of the most important and well-documented groups is the Hungarian Romanies, or Gypsies, who were especially famous for their dance music, played by violinists and bagpipers. Bartók soon understood that theirs was not the traditional music he sought to collect but rather an urban, commercial style cultivated by professional performers. Beginning in the late eighteenth century, Roma bands were usually made up of two violins, a cimbalom (a zither-like instrument whose strings were struck), and a double bass. The Hungarian composer Franz Liszt, who also drew inspiration and themes from this music, publicly recognized the skill and musicianship of these performers in his book *The Gypsy in Music*. Roma ensembles remain popular in modern-day Hungary; they consist of professionally trained musicians playing all styles of music—art, traditional, and popular.

Terms to Note

ethnomusicology
fieldwork
additive meter

Suggested Listening

Bartók: *Music for Strings, Percussion, and Celesta*, Fourth Movement
Folk songs collected by Bartók
Gypsy (Roma) music
Liszt: *Hungarian Rhapsody* No. 2

Listening Guide 42

eLG 4 (10–16)
7 (35–41)

Bartók: *Interrupted Intermezzo*, from *Concerto for Orchestra* (4:20)

DATE OF WORK:	1943
GENRE:	Orchestral concerto
MOVEMENTS:	1. Introduction, Allegro non troppo/Allegro vivace; sonata-allegro form
	2. *Game of Pairs*, Allegretto scherzando; **A-B-A'** form
	3. *Elegia*, Andante non troppo; in 3 episodes
	4. *Interrupted Intermezzo*, Allegretto; rondo-like form
	5. Pesante/Presto; sonata-allegro form

Fourth Movement: *Interrupted Intermezzo*, Allegretto; rondo-like form, shifting meter (2/4, 5/8, 3/4, 5/8)

WHAT TO LISTEN FOR:	3 contrasting themes (1st is folklike and pentatonic; 2nd is broad and lyrical; 3rd interrupts with portrayal of a Nazi invasion that erupts in violence).
	Shifting meters and irregular rhythms.
	Polytonal and atonal harmonies.
	Rondo-like form, with recurrences of opening folk tune (**A-B-A'-C-B'-A"**).
	Sentimental mood representing composer's love for his homeland.

10 0:00 Dramatic 4-note introduction, unison in strings.

0:05 **A** section—plaintive, folklike tune, played by oboe in changing meter with asymmetrical rhythms:

Allegretto

Theme heard in flute and clarinets: dialogue continues in woodwinds and French horn.

11 1:00 **B** section—sweeping lyrical melody in violas, in shifting meter:

Calmo

Violins take up lyrical theme an octave higher, with countermelody in violas; marked "calmo" (calm).

12 1:44 **A'** section—dissonant woodwinds lead to varied statement of opening theme; more chromatic.

13 2:04 **C** section—tempo picks up; clarinet introduces new theme (from Shostakovich symphony):

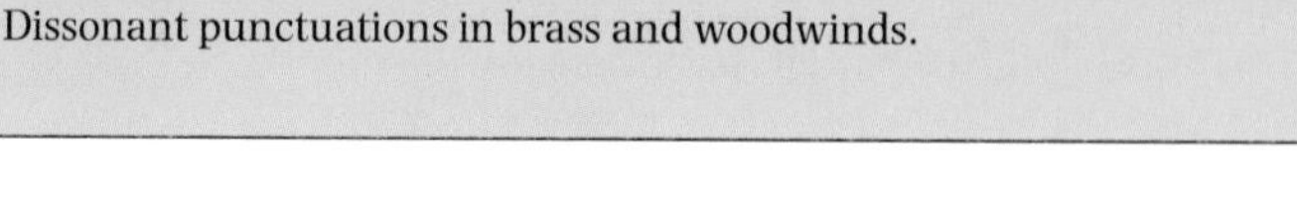

2:17 Dissonant punctuations in brass and woodwinds.

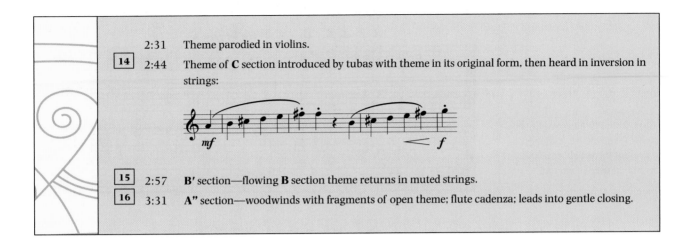

2:31   Theme parodied in violins.

14   2:44   Theme of **C** section introduced by tubas with theme in its original form, then heard in inversion in strings:

15   2:57   **B′** section—flowing **B** section theme returns in muted strings.

16   3:31   **A″** section—woodwinds with fragments of open theme; flute cadenza; leads into gentle closing.

69

American Musical Traditions

"Armies of men . . . have turned to a better life by first hearing the sounds of a Salvation Army band. The next time you hear a Salvation Army band, no matter how humble, take off your hat."

—JOHN PHILIP SOUSA

KEY POINTS

StudySpace online at www.wwnorton.com/enjoy

- Music publications in early America were largely devotional; some were written in a *shape-note* system designed for easy reading.

- The parlor and minstrel songs of nineteenth-century composer Stephen Foster were very popular during his lifetime and remain so today.

- The great bandmaster and composer John Philip Sousa fostered the American wind band tradition, an outgrowth of the British military band.

- Charles Ives drew on the music of his New England childhood—hymns, patriotic songs, brass band marches, and dance tunes—which he set in a very modern style, using polytonality and polyrhythms.

- African-American composer William Grant Still broke numerous racial barriers, earning a number of firsts for blacks in classical music. His *Afro-American Symphony* was the first work by an African-American to be performed by a major symphony orchestra.

Unlike the composers from the New England region (see p. 289), who derived much of their inspiration and techniques from European models, early-twentieth-century American masters often based their works on popular and traditional music of their native land.

A shape-note hymn entitled *Mear*, from *The Easy Instructor* (1801). The different shapes represent the syllables *fa, sol, la,* and *mi* used in singing.

Popular Music in Late-Nineteenth-Century America

We have noted already the rise of devotional music—notably spirituals and gospel hymns—among African Americans and whites in the nineteenth century (see CP 6). Publishers reached out to the public by issuing books of folk hymns and so-called white spirituals with music printed in **shape-note** notation, a new, easy system designed for people lacking music literacy. The melodies of the shape-note hymns, which resemble those of the ballads and fiddle tunes of the era, are set in simple four-part harmonizations. Publications such as *The Easy Instructor* (see above) and *The Sacred Harp* disseminated this repertory from New England to rural and urban audiences in the South and Midwest, where the hymns were used in singing schools, churches, and social gatherings. As a result, a body of hymns and anthems has been preserved not only in devotional music books, but through a continued oral tradition; some of these works remain popular even today in gospel and contemporary Christian music arrangements.

The title page to Stephen Foster's song *Jeanie with the Light Brown Hair* (1854).

Although the composers and lyricists of nineteenth-century gospel hymns are mostly forgotten today, one prophet of indigenous American song remains a household name: Stephen Foster (1826–1864), known for his lyrical parlor ballads, minstrel show tunes, and poignant plantation songs. Born on the Fourth of July, on the fiftieth anniversary of the signing of the Declaration of Independence, Foster strove to write a simpler music that could be understood by all. In this effort, he was successful. Among his most popular songs are *Oh, Susannah!* (1848) and *Camptown Races* (1850), both minstrel-show songs that remain in the common tradition; the well-known and highly nostalgic plantation songs *Old Folks at Home* (1851; the official state song of Florida) and *My Old Kentucky Home* (1853; the state song of Kentucky); and the timeless ballads *Jeanie with the Light Brown Hair* (1854) and *Beautiful Dreamer* (1864), the first a lament on the lost happiness in his marriage and the second, his last song, written in the style of an Italian air. There is no evidence that Foster took a political stand on the abolition of slavery, yet his songs gradually moved from the stereotypical depiction of African Americans in stock minstrel-show tradition to a more realistic image of a people experiencing pain, joy, and sorrow. *Angelina Baker* (1850), for example, is a slave's lament for a lover sent away, and *Oh! Boys, Carry Me 'Long* (1851) makes a request commonly heard in spirituals, for deliverance from pain

CD iMusic

Oh, Susannah!

Camptown Races

through death. Stephen Foster, America's most beloved songwriter, died an alcoholic in 1864, alone and in poverty.

America's vernacular tradition also included instrumental music, particularly performances by brass bands. An outgrowth of the British military band, wind groups thrived throughout the United States. First serving as regimental bands for colonial militia during the War of Independence, some of these groups continued after the war, and new ones were founded as well. One, the U.S. Marine Band (now called The President's Own), formed in 1798, initially consisted of two oboes, two clarinets, two French horns, bassoon, and drums. The refinement of rotary-valved brass instruments by various makers, including the Belgian Adolphe Sax (inventor of the saxophone),

The United States Marine Band marches in parade, with its director, John Philip Sousa (1854–1932), playing cornet (in right front).

revolutionized the makeup, however, of civic bands. Thus, by the Civil War era (1861–65), both Northern and Southern regiments marched to the sounds of brass groups. After the war, many bands reorganized as concert and dance ensembles; such was the case with the Union Army group under the direction of the virtuoso cornet player and band master Patrick S. Gilmore. Union bands first played the rousing *When Johnny Comes Marching Home*, to welcome back soldiers from North and South alike.

John Philip Sousa

America's greatest bandmaster was undoubtedly John Philip Sousa (1854–1932), who conducted the U.S. Marine Band from 1880 to 1892 and later formed the incomparable Sousa's Band. Known as "the march king," Sousa wrote over 130 marches for band, as well as dance music and operettas. He toured North America and Europe extensively with his group, delighting audiences with his *Semper Fidelis* (1888), *The Washington Post* (1889), the ever-popular *Stars and Stripes Forever* (1897), and band arrangements of ragtime, the newest rage (see p. 379). Almost single-handedly, Sousa created a national music for America that continues to resonate in its concert halls, on its streets, in its sports stadiums, and in the hearts of its people.

CD iMusic

Stars and Stripes Forever

One New England musician born into this rich environment of inspirational hymns, patriotic songs, and especially brass bands—his father was a Civil War bandmaster—was Charles Ives, who never forgot his nineteenth-century vernacular heritage even while nurturing very modern tendencies. One of Ives's most nostalgic songs, *The Things Our Fathers Loved*, reminisces on the music of bygone days in a medley of familiar tunes—some patriotic, some religious, some from the popular tradition—tinged with his own bittersweet harmonies. Like the familiar melodies he cites in his music, Ives has become an American classic.

Charles Ives

Another original voice was sounded by the African-American composer William Grant Still (1895–1978), the most important musical representative of the early-twentieth-century movement known as the Harlem (or "New Negro") Renaissance. Still sought "to elevate Negro musical idioms to a position of dignity and effectiveness in the fields of symphonic and operatic music." His *Afro-American Symphony* (1930)—loosely based on dialect poems by Paul Laurence Dunbar and evocative of blues and spirituals—was the first work by an African American to be performed by a major symphony orchestra and truly a landmark in black history.

William Grant Still

Music and the Patriotic Spirit

Music often fuels the emotions, inciting acts of heroism and patriotism that are remembered for generations through song. Many tunes well-known to most of us had their origins in wartime as well. The colonial troops of the American Revolution marched to the fife-and-drum strains of *Yankee Doodle*. *Dixie*, which became a rallying cry of the Civil War's Confederacy sounded against the North's *Battle Hymn of the Republic*.

Songwriter Irving Berlin joined with singer Kate Smith in a 1938 radio broadcast on Armistice Day (now Veterans Day) to build patriotic support in the United States as the Second World War was looming. The song that captured the hearts of millions then was *God Bless America*, now considered by many the country's "second national anthem." A new tide of patriotism has swept across the United States in response to the unthinkable events of September 11, 2001—the terrorist bombings of the World Trade Center and the Pentagon. And once again, the lyrics of *God Bless America* have resonated deeply in the hearts of all Americans.

The national anthems of many countries were the direct result of wartime emotions. The lyrics of *The Star-Spangled Banner* were written in 1814 by an attorney named Francis Scott Key during the English bombardment of Fort McHenry (a famous battle during the War of 1812). Key was aboard a small ship in the Baltimore Harbor, nervously watching the American flag over the fort and knowing that if it went down, so too would his beloved Baltimore. Thus the flag-inspired lyrics, which he adapted to the disjunct tune of an English drinking song that nearly everyone finds difficult to sing. France's *La Marseillaise* is another example of a revolutionary hymn ("Allons, enfants de la patrie! Le jour de gloire est arrivé," or "Arise, children of the homeland! The day of glory has arrived"). It was written in 1792, during the French Revolution, and in 1795 was adapted as the national anthem. Mexico's *Mexicanos, al grito de guerra* (Mexicans, to the War Cry), is another spirited song of independence.

Happily, the patriotic spirit is alive in peacetime as well. It has produced such notable anthems as Britain's *God Save the Queen* (or *King*)—the same tune to which we sing *America* ("My country, 'tis of thee") and the stately *Emperor's Hymn* by Haydn. The latter serves today as the national song of recently unified Germany, with the text "Einigkeit und Recht und Freiheit," or "Unity and right and liberty." Canada also adopted an anthem that draws together its multiethnic population—*O Canada*, written in 1880 by the French-Canadian Calixa Lavallée, was named the country's national hymn (in French and English) in 1980. The universality of music is illustrated in Israel's national anthem, *Hatikvah (The Hope)*, a moving poem of the Jewish people returning to their ancient homeland in the late nineteenth century, set to the melody of a haunting Bohemian folk song. In times of national crisis or pride, whether responding to a war or an Olympic victory, these memorable songs resound deep in the soul of a people.

Suggested Listening

America   **CD** iMusic

Battle Hymn of the Republic

Haydn, *Emperor* Quartet, Op. 76, No. 3, II

National anthems (United States, France, Canada)

A still from the film *Glory* (1989), documenting the first black army regiment during the Civil War.

70

Nationalism in the Americas: Aaron Copland and Silvestre Revueltas

"A nation creates music—the composer only arranges it."
—MIKHAIL GLINKA

KEY POINTS    **StudySpace** online at www.wwnorton.com/enjoy

- American composer Aaron Copland was inspired by songs of the Old West, and by Mexican dance music; his orchestral works and ballets (*Billy the Kid*) established his popularity.

- The music of Mexican composer Silvestre Revueltas is expressively nationalistic, with colorful, folkloric rhythms and melodies set in a modern, dissonant idiom.

- Revueltas' orchestral work *Homenaje a Federico García Lorca* pays homage to a Spanish writer who was executed in 1936 during the Spanish Civil War.

- The **mariachi ensemble** originated in the Mexican state of Jalisco as a theatrical orchestra of violins, harps, and guitars; the group played and sang **son**, the popular dance songs of the day.

In this chapter we will consider two unique voices of nationalism in the Americas. Aaron Copland (1900–1990), one of the most prolific and gifted composers of the twentieth century, was able to capture the spirit of the American experience—especially the Western frontiers—in his engaging, accessible works. Silvestre Revueltas, a Mexican composer of international acclaim, drew his inspiration from the popular culture of his homeland.

Aaron Copland: His Life and Music

"I no longer feel the need of seeking out conscious Americanism. Because we live here and work here, we can be certain that when our music is mature it will also be American in quality."

Aaron Copland

Copland was born "on a street in Brooklyn that can only be described as drab. . . . Music was the last thing anyone would have connected with it." During his early twenties, he studied in Paris with the famous teacher Nadia Boulanger; he was her first full-time American pupil.

In his growth as a composer, Copland mirrored the dominant trends of his time. After his return from Paris, he turned to the jazz idiom, a phase that culminated in his brilliant Piano Concerto. Then followed a period during which Copland the Neoclassicist experimented with the abstract and produced the Piano Variations, *Short Symphony*, and *Statements for Orchestra*.

He realized that a new public for contemporary music was being created by the radio, phonograph, and film scores. "It made no sense to ignore them [the audience] and to continue writing as if they did not exist." In this fashion, Copland was led to

Neoclassical period

what became a most significant development after the 1930s: his attempt to simplify the new music so that it would communicate to a large public.

The 1930s and 1940s saw the creation of works that established Copland's popularity. *El Salón México* (1936) is an orchestral piece based on Mexican melodies and rhythms. The three ballets, *Billy the Kid*, *Rodeo*, and *Appalachian Spring*, continue to delight international audiences. Among his film scores are *The City*, *Of Mice and Men*, *Our Town*, *The Red Pony*, and *The Heiress*, the last of which brought him an Academy Award. He wrote two important works during wartime: *A Lincoln Portrait*, for speaker and chorus, with texts drawn from Lincoln's own speeches, and the Third Symphony. In the 1960s, Copland demonstrated that he could handle twelve-tone techniques when he wrote his powerful *Connotations for Orchestra*.

BILLY THE KID

For the ballet based on the saga of Billy the Kid, Copland produced one of his freshest scores. Several classic cowboy tunes are used in this work as points of departure for his own creations; they flavor his music but are assimilated into his personal style rather than quoted literally.

Billy the Kid—the Brooklyn-born William Bonney—had a brief but intense career as a desperado and soon became one of the legends of the Wild West. The ballet touches on the chief episodes of his life. We see him first as a boy of twelve; when his mother is killed by a stray bullet in a street brawl, he stabs the man responsible for her death. Later, during a card game, he is accused of cheating and kills the accuser. Captured after a gun battle, he is put in jail, but he murders his jailer and gets away. A romantic interlude ensues when Billy joins his Mexican sweetheart in the desert. But he is tracked down and killed by his childhood friend Sheriff Pat Garrett. At the close, we hear a lament on the death of the notorious outlaw.

The concert suite Copland put together for *Billy the Kid* opens with *The Open Prairie*, which evokes a remote and spacious landscape, a poetic symbol of all that is vast and unchanging. In the first scene, *Street in a Frontier Town*, Copland uses tunes of the Wild West such as *Goodbye, Old Paint*; *The Old Chisholm Trail*; *Git Along, Little Dogies*; *The Streets of Laredo*; and *Great Grand-Dad*. (See Listening Guide 43.) But the composer decked them out with polyrhythms, polytonal harmonies, and dissonances made more striking because they fall on accented beats. The result is a music of powerful rhythmic thrust and vigorous physical activity, bursting with energy and excitement as it mounts to a *fortissimo* climax.

Music has a glorious way of leaping over barriers of race, religion, and nationality. And so it was the son of Russian-Jewish immigrants growing up on the streets of Brooklyn who created a musical image of the American West, the prairie, and the cowboy that is heard and recognized worldwide.

Listening Guide 43

eLG 4 (17–21)
7 (57–61)

Copland: *Billy the Kid*, Scene 1, *Street in a Frontier Town* (6:24)

DATE OF WORK:	1938 (ballet first performed); 1939 (orchestral suite)
GENRE:	Orchestral suite from ballet
BASIS:	Actual story of outlaw William Bonney (called Billy the Kid)

SECTIONS OF
ORCHESTRAL SUITE: | *The Open Prairie* | *Gun Battle* |
| *Street in a Frontier Town* | *Celebration* (after Billy's capture) |
| *Prairie Night (Card Game at Night)* | *Billy's Death* |

Copland's notes on the ballet: *The ballet begins and ends on the open prairie. The first scene is a street in a frontier town. Cowboys saunter into town, some on horseback, others on foot with their lassos; some Mexican women do a jarabe, which is interrupted by a fight between two drunks. Attracted by the gathering crowd, Billy is seen for the first time, a boy of twelve, with his mother. The brawl turns ugly, guns are drawn, and in some unaccountable way, Billy's mother is killed. Without an instant's hesitation, in cold fury, Billy draws a knife from a cowhand's sheath and stabs his mother's slayers. His short but famous career has begun. In swift succession we see episodes in Billy's later life—at night, under the stars, in a quiet card game with his outlaw friends, hunted by a posse led by his former friend Pat Garrett, in a gun battle. A drunken celebration takes place when he is captured. Billy makes one of his legendary escapes from prison. Tired and worn out in the desert, Billy rests with his girl. Finally the posse catches up with him.*

WHAT TO LISTEN FOR: Melodic paraphrases of a number of classic cowboy songs.
Shifting meters, including a dance in 5/8, and much syncopation.
Accented dissonance and polytonal harmonies.
Extensive use of percussion.
Dramatic and dissonant climax at end (death of Billy's mother).

Street in a Frontier Town; Moderato

| 17 | 0:00 | Piccolo solo, with tune *Great Grand-Dad:* Other woodwinds join in dialogue. |  |

| | 0:21 | New tune (paraphrased from *Git Along, Little Dogies*) in oboe and trumpet, almost in unison, with dissonance on strong beat (x): |  |

0:45   *Great Grand-Dad* heard in piccolo, while strings enter with dissonant tune from above.

0:57   Alternation of 2 tunes—the first in woodwinds and strings, second in trombones.

| 18 | 1:10 | Trumpet, with new, shifting-meter tune (4 + 3 + 4 + 3), and accompaniment in opposite meter (3 + 4 + 3 + 4): |  |

1:15   Strings take up shifting-meter tune; brass and strings return to dissonant tune, which dies out.

1:48   Large chords played *fortissimo* in full orchestra, punctuated by bass drum; disjunct tune based on *The Old Chisholm Trail*.

| 19 | 1:58 | Quick dance tune in strings in 4/4 (loosely based on *The Old Chisholm Trail*), accompanied by syncopated woodblock: |  |

Listening Guide continues

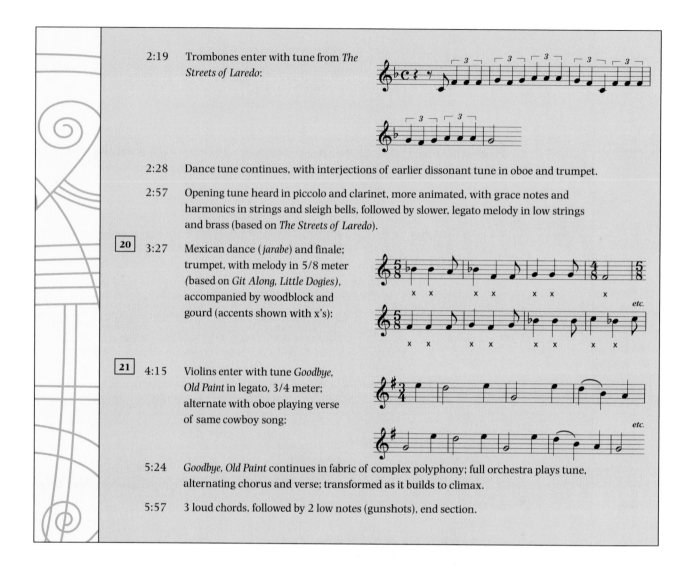

2:19   Trombones enter with tune from *The Streets of Laredo*:

2:28   Dance tune continues, with interjections of earlier dissonant tune in oboe and trumpet.

2:57   Opening tune heard in piccolo and clarinet, more animated, with grace notes and harmonics in strings and sleigh bells, followed by slower, legato melody in low strings and brass (based on *The Streets of Laredo*).

20   3:27   Mexican dance (*jarabe*) and finale; trumpet, with melody in 5/8 meter (based on *Git Along, Little Dogies*), accompanied by woodblock and gourd (accents shown with x's):

21   4:15   Violins enter with tune *Goodbye, Old Paint* in legato, 3/4 meter; alternate with oboe playing verse of same cowboy song:

5:24   *Goodbye, Old Paint* continues in fabric of complex polyphony; full orchestra plays tune, alternating chorus and verse; transformed as it builds to climax.

5:57   3 loud chords, followed by 2 low notes (gunshots), end section.

The murals of the Mexican painter **Diego Rivera** (1886–1937) glorify his native culture and people in an elegant social and historical narrative. *Flower Festival* (1925).

Silvestre Revueltas and Art Music Traditions in Mexico

"From an early age I learned to love [the music of] Bach and Beethoven. . . . I can tolerate some of the classics and even some of my own works, but I prefer the music of my people that is heard in the provinces."

The modern musical traditions of Mexico are rich and varied, drawing from the indigenous Amerindian cultures as well as from the country's Hispanic culture. Mexico's ties to Spain began in 1519, when Spanish soldiers colonized the country, and continued until 1821, when Mexico achieved its independence.

By the late nineteenth century, nationalistic stirrings lured musicians and artists alike to Amerindian and Mestizo cultures. (*Mestizos* are people of mixed Spanish and Amerindian ancestry; today they are the majority in Latin-American countries.)

Preserving the Musical Traditions of Mexico

The American composer Aaron Copland was intrigued by the freshness and color of Latin American music, and he tried to capture these elements in several of his works, including *Billy the Kid*. His relationship to Latin American music stretches back to his friendship with Mexican composer/conductor Carlos Chávez during the 1920s, when Chávez was in New York. The two musicians immediately bonded over their desire to break away from Eurocentric domination.

Copland accepted Chávez's invitation to visit Mexico City in the fall of 1932. During his four-month visit, the two frequented a popular dance hall. "When Chávez took me to an unusual night spot called El Salón México," Copland reminisced, "the atmosphere of the dance hall impressed me, and I came away with the germ of a musical idea." This idea manifested itself later in Copland's delightful orchestral work *El Salón México*, named after the dance hall.

While in Mexico, Copland sought out indigenous music and in particular was drawn to mariachi ensembles—colorful groups that included vocalists accompanied by violins, guitars, and sometimes trumpet and harp (see p. 373). He found their music vital, claiming that "Mexico offers something fresh and pure and wholesome."

Chávez, along with Silvestre and Revueltas, are at the core of the modernist school of Mexican art music. At first, both held their cultural roots close—Chávez wished to project "what is deepest in the Mexican soul." But he came to understand that cultural integration—a unification of the diverse groups that were part of Mexican history—was necessary to produce great art.

Chávez and Revueltas, like Copland, expressed their nationalism through the distinctly European genre of ballet. Daniel Catán (b. 1949), the pre-eminent Mexican composer today, continues this cultural integration by writing stage works that celebrate his Latin American roots. His ballet *Ausencia de flores* honors the centennial of the Mexican muralist José Clemente Orozco (1883–1949), and his operas, while acknowledging a debt to the European masters before him, represent not a "rejection of our tradition, . . . but rather the profound

Muralist **José Clemente Orozco** (1883–1949), a leader in the Mexican revolutionary movement, captures the spirit of the time in *Zapatistas* (1931).

assimilation of it." The literary sources for his operas include two Nobel Prize–winning Latin American writers: Mexican author Octavio Paz, on whose poem Catán's *Rappaccini's Daughter* (1994) is based; and Colombian novelist Gabriel García Márquez, whose famous novel *Love in the Time of Cholera* loosely inspired Catán's *Florencia en el Amazonas*, commissioned by the Houston Grand Opera and premiered in 1996. In this opera—the first Spanish-language work commissioned by an American opera company—Catán looked deeply into his own culture: "I'm going back to a Latin American story. I'm taking characters out of my own literature and my own mind."

Suggested Listening

CD iMusic Catán operas, including *Rappaccini's Daughter*
Copland: *Street in a Frontier Town*, from *Billy the Kid*
Orchestral works and ballets (Carlos Chávez)
Revueltas: *Homenaje a Federico García Lorca*
CD iMusic Traditional Mexican music (mariachi ensembles), *El Cihualteco*

The Mexican Revolution of 1910 further changed the artistic life of the country, conjuring strong feelings of patriotism. In the post–Revolutionary period composers did not wish to recreate the traditional music but only to evoke, or suggest, the character of this native music. Among those composers who have had a decisive influence on Mexican musical culture are Carlos Chávez (1899–1978) whose works are rich in Amerindian flavor, and Silvestre Revueltas (1899–1940), a Mexican composer of international acclaim. Revueltas is considered a representative of "mestizo realism," a movement that drew on elements of the traditional culture of contemporary Mexico.

His Life and Music

Early years

Born in the mountain state of Durango, Silvestre Revueltas was a child prodigy on violin and later studied composition at the Conservatorio Nacional de Música in Mexico City. He continued his studies in the United States, where he took his first post as conductor of a theater orchestra in Texas. In 1929, Revueltas was called home by his friend Carlos Chávez to serve as assistant conductor of the Orquesta Sinfónica de Mexico.

The 1930s were a high point in the development of music and art in Mexico, and it was in this environment that Revueltas produced some of his finest masterworks. His first orchestral piece, *Cuauhnahuac* (1930; the old name of the town of Cuernavaca), was Romantic in inspiration but modern in its dissonant harmonies and chromaticism. This work displays the colorful orchestration and vigorous rhythmic energy that became Revueltas's trademark.

After a falling out with Chávez in 1935, Revueltas formed a rival, but shortlived, orchestra. That same year, he collaborated with Paul Strand on the powerful film *Redes* (Nets), which focused on the struggles of the lower classes—in this case, fishermen seeking equal rights. Like Copland and Prokofiev (whom we will study later), Revueltas is recognized for his contributions to music in films.

Silvestre Revueltas

With the onset of the Spanish Civil War in the late 1930s, the intensely political Revueltas went to Spain, where he participated in the cultural activities of the Loyalist government. One of the early tragedies of the Civil War was the execution in 1936 of the poet Federico García Lorca by a Fascist firing squad. The openly homosexual García Lorca had made anti-Fascist statements and had provoked Franco with his politically controversial plays. (In Chapter 76, we will study a piece by American composer George Crumb that sets texts by García Lorca.) Revueltas's response to this event, his moving composition *Homenaje a Federico García Lorca* (*Homage to Federico García Lorca*), premiered in Madrid in 1937 during a Fascist bombing of the city. The review in the *Heraldo de Madrid* accorded Revueltas's music a "revolutionary status."

Late works

Upon his return home in late 1937, Revueltas's life began to fall apart. Like his idol, the artist Vincent Van Gogh, the composer shifted between the highs of his creative powers and the lows of self-destruction. Despite his acute alcoholism, for which he was institutionalized on several occasions, Revueltas continued to produce masterworks, including his best-known orchestral piece, *Sensemayá* (1938). This work was inspired by the verses of Afro-Cuban poet Nicolás Guillén—another anti-Fascist—which imitate onomatopoetically the sounds and rhythm of Afro-Cuban music and speak against colonial imperialism. His last work, left unfinished at his death but now completed and orchestrated, was a ballet entitled *La Coronela* about a female colonel attempting to overthrow a dictatorship. The composer died at age

forty of alcohol-induced pneumonia, a death his sister Rosaura called "senseless, incomprehensible, tragic."

Revueltas instills his music with colorful, folkloric elements while never quoting actual traditional songs; rather, he recreates native melodies and uses strikingly dancelike rhythms. His love for Mexican provincial music is immediately obvious, voiced through lyrical, direct melodies that are driven by complex rhythms utilizing techniques such as polyrhythms and ostinatos. Despite a very modern harmonic language rich in dissonance and chromaticism, Revueltas's music is deeply emotional and Romantic in its inspiration. His skillful handling of the orchestral palette—often with unusual instrumental combinations—evokes the picturesque *orquestas típicas*—the traditional orchestras—of Mexico.

Folkloric elements

HOMENAJE A FEDERICO GARCÍA LORCA

Written in Spain in 1937, *Homenaje a Federico García Lorca* erases the boundaries between popular and classical music. The work is for a chamber ensemble that is heavily balanced toward winds—the string section has only two violins and one bass—and includes piano. The first movement, *Baile* (Dance), develops into a quick-paced, duple-meter dance with a bitingly dissonant tune. The second movement, *Duelo* (Sorrow), makes use of an ostinato heard against a soulful melody.

The title of the last movement, *Son*, refers to a type of traditional Mexican dance. *Sones* (plural of *son*) are characterized by shifting meter, frequently moving between simple triple (3/4) and compound duple (6/8) meter. (We heard how Copland used shifting meter as well for the Mexican jarabe in *Billy the Kid.*) Revueltas's writing here is highly evocative of a Mexican **mariachi ensemble**, one of the most common groups that performs *sones.* The typical mariachi consists of several trumpets, violins, and guitars. Revueltas maintains the distinctive mariachi sound of paired trumpets and violins, while enriching the highest and lowest registers with high woodwinds and low brass and bass, and replacing the guitars with piano.

This movement, in a rondo-like form, begins explosively, tossing about fragmentary ideas with unrestrained energy. The strings and piano then establish a steady 6/8 pulse, over which the muted trumpet sounds a narrow-ranged theme built from whole tones (see Listening Guide 44, p. 374). Rhythmic confusion and percussive accents lead to the principal theme—a syncopated Mexican dance tune (the *son*) in the trumpets and violins, played in parallel thirds typical of mariachi style. The mariachi tune eventually returns in a full orchestral statement, set in a new key, followed by a final frenetic coda.

This carefree movement may seem like a strange homage to the slain poet. But the traditional Mexican view of life (and death) is to experience each day to the fullest—as Revueltas did. The poet Rafael Alberti praised *Homenaje a Federico García Lorca*, noting that "what Manuel de Falla did with . . . Spanish music . . . Silvestre Revueltas achieves with the accent of his own country—and in magisterial style."

> ### IN HIS OWN WORDS
>
> *There is in me a particular interpretation of nature. Everything is rhythm. . . . Everybody understands or feels it. . . . My rhythms are dynamic, sensual, vital; I think in images that meet in melodic lines, always moving dynamically.*

Music from the Mariachi Tradition

One strong voice of growing Mexican nationalism in the early 1900s was the traditional mariachi ensemble. The group originated in the mid-nineteenth century near Guadalajara, in the Jalisco region of western Mexico, as a string orchestra with both bowed and plucked instruments: violins, guitars (including a large acoustic bass guitar known as the **guitarrón**), and **vihuelas** (rounded-back folk guitars). In the

Guitarrón and vihuelas

Listening Guide 44

eLG 4 (22–29)
7 (62–69)

Revueltas: *Homenaje a Federico García Lorca*, Third Movement, *Son*   (2:55)

DATE OF WORK: 1937

MEDIUM: Chamber orchestra (piccolo, E-flat clarinet, 2 trumpets, trombone, tuba, piano, percussion, 2 violins, and bass)

FORM: Sectional, rondo-like (**A-B-A-C-A-C-B-A-C-Coda**)

OVERVIEW: I. *Baile* (Dance)
  II. *Duelo* (Sorrow)
  III. *Son*

WHAT TO LISTEN FOR: Unusual instrumentation, focused on winds along with 2 violins, piano, and bass.

Colorful, folklike character, with themes reminiscent of mariachi ensembles.

Strongly rhythmic and syncopated, with percussive accents; use of ostinatos.

Return of 3 thematic ideas in a rondo-like structure.

22   0:00   **A** section—rhythmic and highly syncopated, in shifting meter; 7-note melodic turns in piano and violins, with glissandos in violins (Violin I shown):

23   0:15   **B** section—piano and string ostinato introduces chromatic solo trumpet melody (accompanied by trombone):

0:29   **A** section—rhythmic punctuations, as in introduction.

24   0:35   **C** section—Mexican dance theme *(son)* in alternating meter (6/8 and 2/4 = sesquialtera); muted trumpets playing in parallel thirds:

Trumpets answered by violins and woodwinds.

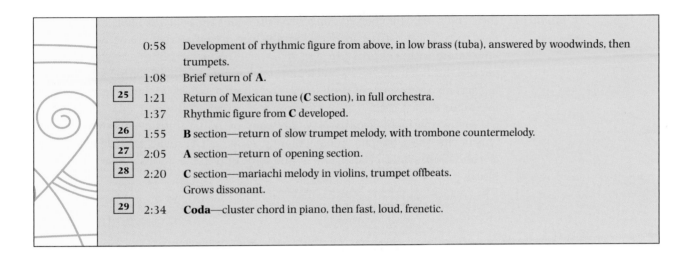

	0:58	Development of rhythmic figure from above, in low brass (tuba), answered by woodwinds, then trumpets.
	1:08	Brief return of **A**.
25	1:21	Return of Mexican tune (**C** section), in full orchestra.
	1:37	Rhythmic figure from **C** developed.
26	1:55	**B** section—return of slow trumpet melody, with trombone countermelody.
27	2:05	**A** section—return of opening section.
28	2:20	**C** section—mariachi melody in violins, trumpet offbeats. Grows dissonant.
29	2:34	**Coda**—cluster chord in piano, then fast, loud, frenetic.

1930s, the mariachi ensemble took on a distinctly urban sound, adding trumpets and other instruments. The mariachi tradition spread quickly, aided by the group Vargas de Tecalitán, who relocated to Mexico City and became involved in the political scene there. Radio broadcasts, movies (Mariachi Vargas de Tecalitán made over 200), and eventually television contributed to the growing popularity of this music.

The mariachi ensembles heard today were standardized during the 1950s. Modern players often wear the costumes of the *charros*—Mexican cowboys with wide-brimmed sombreros—or other, more regional dress. Typical instrumentation consists of a melody group, with violins and trumpets; and a rhythm section of vihuelas, guitar, guitarrón, and occasionally harp. Their repertory is largely traditional dances, many set in triple meter but with shifting accents and strong syncopations, a metric style known as **sesquialtera**. One of the most famous dance pieces is *Jarabe tapatío*, known in the United States as the *Mexican Hat Dance*.

The **son,** a mixture of native, Spanish, and African traditions, is a standard form of the mariachi. In fact, the *son jalisciense* (from the Jalisco region) stands at the heart of the original mariachi repertory. Our example is *El Cihualteco* (*The Man from Cihuatlán*), a *son jalisciense* that has been recorded by many ensembles. The traditional dance associated with this type of *son* is the *zapateado*, a Spanish flamenco-style dance featuring strongly syncopated rhythms against which the dancers drive

Modern ensembles

Sesquialtera

Son

The Mariachi Regio Internacional (violins, trumpets, guitar and guitarrón) performing in Plaza Garibaldi, home to many of Mexico City's mariachi bands.

El Cihualteco their boots into the floor. *El Cihualteco* (*The Man from Cihuatlán*) falls into the standard verse/chorus structure, with four-line verses (*coplas*) that are witty and sexual, alternating with a chorus (*Ay sí sí, ay no no*). The melodic lines are often played in parallel thirds (by the violins and trumpets), making the sound consonant. The shifting accents give a sense of restlessness and unpredictability to the triple meter of the lively dance.

Today, mariachi groups play all types of dance music—mambo, danzón, chachacha, salsa, cumbia, and popular music as well. Festivals are held in the western and southwestern United States, and some universities sponsor mariachi ensembles as part of their music programs.

Listening Guide 45

eLG **3 (60–64)**
8 (71–75)

Son jalisciense: *El Cihualteco (The Man from Cihuatlán)* (2:45)

GENRE:	*Son jalisciense* (dance song from Jalisco region)
MEDIUM:	Mariachi ensemble (violins, trumpets, guitars, guitarrón)
METER:	3/4 (with shifting accents)
FORM:	Strophic (verse, chorus)

WHAT TO LISTEN FOR: Syncopated melodic line and accompaniment.
Alternation of voice with instruments.
Violins and trumpets in parallel 3rds.
Shifting accents in 3/4 meter (groups of 2 vs. 3) = sesquialtera.

---

60 0:00 Introduction, with trumpets in thirds.

0:04 Bass guitar enters with syncopated line.

0:09 Violins with motive.

TEXT	TRANSLATION
61 0:13 **Verse 1**	
Arriba de Cihuatlán	Above Cihuatlán,
le nombran "la água escondida"	they call it "hidden waters,"
donde se van a bañar	where the dear Cihualtecan girls
Cihualtecas de mi vida.	go to bathe.

0:21 **Verse 1** repeated, with trumpet countermelody.

62 0:29 **Chorus**, with violins

Ay, sí, sí; ay, no, no.	Ay, yes, yes; ay, no, no.
Ay, sí, sí; ay, no, no.	Ay, yes, yes; ay, no, no.
Ay, sí; ay, no	Ay, yes; ay, no.
Ay, sí; ay, no.	Ay, yes; ay, no.

Three violins, accompanying chorus (*Ay, sí*), playing in triads; rhythm line shows alternation of duple and triple patterns; guitarrón plays syncopated pattern, sounding one octave lower than written:

0:44	De veras sí, de veras no.	Surely yes, surely no.
	Lo que te dije se te olvidó	You forgot what I told you
	y al cabo sí, y al cabo no.	and finally yes, and finally no.

0:51   Interlude featuring trumpets, with vocal interjections.

Trumpets in interlude, with passage in thirds:

63   1:07   **Verse 2**

	Cihualteco de mi vida,	Dear Cihualteco,
	dime quién te bautizó.	tell me who baptized you.
	¿Quien te puso "Cihualteco"	Who named "El Cihualteco"
	para que te cante yo?	so that I can sing to you?

1:14   **Verse 2** repeated, with trumpet obligato

1:22   **Chorus**

	Ay, sí, sí; ay, no, no.	Ay, yes, yes; ay, no, no.
	Ay, sí, sí; ay, no, no.	Ay, yes, yes; ay, no, no.
	Ay, sí; ay, no.	Ay, yes; ay, no.
	Ay, sí; ay, no.	Ay, yes; ay, no.

1:38	De veras si, de veras no.	Surely yes, surely no.
	Cuando ellas quieren, no quiero yo.	When they want to, they don't.
	Y al cabo sí, y al cabo no.	And finally yes, and finally no.

1:45   Interlude, with trumpet and vocal interjections and whistling.

64   1:57   Instrumental verse and chorus, with vocal interjections.

Popular Styles

71

Ragtime, Blues, and Early Jazz

All riddles are blues,
And all blues are sad,
And I'm only mentioning
Some blues I've had.

—MAYA ANGELOU

| KEY POINTS | Listen Online ⓢ **StudySpace** online at www.wwnorton.com/enjoy |

- *Jazz* arose in the early twentieth century and drew elements from African traditions and from Western popular and art music.

- Its roots are in West African music (including call-and-response singing) and in nineteenth-century African-American ceremonial and work songs (CP 19).

- *Ragtime* developed from an African-American piano style characterized by syncopated rhythms and sectional forms.

- Scott Joplin, often considered the "king of ragtime," is the first African-American composer to win international fame; he is remembered for his piano rags, especially *Maple Leaf Rag*.

- Louis Armstrong is one of the great early jazz performers (on trumpet); he also introduced *scat singing* (singing on syllables without meaning).

- Armstrong was first associated with **New Orleans–style jazz**, which is characterized by a small ensemble of players improvising simultaneously.

- *Blues* is an American genre of folk music based on a simple, repetitive, poetic-musical form with three-line strophes set to a repeating harmonic pattern of twelve bars.

- Billie Holiday was one of the leading female jazz singers, and was a composer as well.

Ragtime, blues, and jazz are rooted in the music of African Americans. These musical styles are part of the great American identity, and have captured the imagination of the world.

Jazz refers to a music created mainly by African Americans around the turn of the twentieth century as they blended elements drawn from African musics with the popular and art traditions of the West. One of the most influential precursors of jazz was ragtime, which gained popularity in instrumental ensemble arrangements by Scott Joplin.

Scott Joplin and Ragtime

Known as "the king of ragtime," Scott Joplin (1868–1917) was one of the first black Americans to gain importance as a composer. He was born in Texarkana, Texas, to a musical family. Joplin began his musical instruction on the guitar and bugle but soon showed such a gift for improvisation that he was given free piano lessons. He left home when he was only fourteen, after the death of his mother, and traveled throughout the Mississippi Valley playing in honky-tonks and piano bars, absorbing the current styles of folk and popular music. In 1885, he arrived in St. Louis, then the center of a growing ragtime movement.

Ragtime (or "ragged rhythm") was originally an African-American piano style marked by highly syncopated melodies. It first gained public notice as a form of instrumental ensemble music when Joplin and his small orchestra performed at the 1893 World Exposition in Chicago. Around this time, Joplin sought more formal musical training at the George R. Smith College in Sedalia, Missouri, where he studied music theory and composition. It was at a club in Sedalia that Joplin, surrounded by a circle of black entertainers, introduced his *Maple Leaf Rag*. Fame came to the composer in 1899 when the sheet music of the piece sold a million copies. In 1906, Joplin moved from St. Louis to Chicago and ultimately to New York, where he was active as a teacher, composer, and performer.

Joplin strove to elevate ragtime from a purely improvised style to a more serious art form that could stand on a level with European art music. Realizing that he must lead the way in this endeavor, he began work on his opera *Treemonisha*, which he finished in 1911. But the opera, produced in a scaled-down performance, was not well received, and Joplin fell into a severe depression from which he never fully recovered; he died in New York City on April 1, 1917. *Treemonisha* remained virtually unknown until its extremely successful revival in 1972 by the Houston Grand Opera. In 1976, nearly sixty years after his death, Joplin was awarded a Pulitzer Prize for his masterpiece.

Scott Joplin is best remembered today for his piano rags, which reflect his preoccupation with classical forms. These works exhibit balanced phrasing and key structures, combined with catchy, imaginative melodies. Like earlier dance forms, they are built in clear-cut sections, their patterns of repetition reminiscent of those heard in the marches of John Philip Sousa, whose own band frequently played arrangements of Joplin rags.

The *Maple Leaf Rag*, perhaps the best-known rag ever composed, is typical in its regular, sectional form. Quite simply, the dance presents a series of sixteen-measure phrases, called *strains*, in a moderate duple meter; each strain is repeated before the

Ⓢ **Scott Joplin**

CD iMusic

Pine Apple Rag

Title page of *Maple Leaf Rag* (1899), by Scott Joplin.

Maple Leaf Rag

Strains

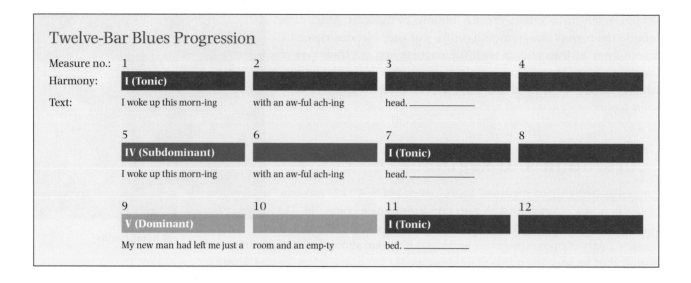

Twelve-Bar Blues Progression

Measure no.:	1	2	3	4
Harmony:	**I (Tonic)**			
Text:	I woke up this morn-ing	with an aw-ful ach-ing	head, _____	

	5	6	7	8
	IV (Subdominant)		**I (Tonic)**	
	I woke up this morn-ing	with an aw-ful ach-ing	head, _____	

	9	10	11	12
	V (Dominant)		**I (Tonic)**	
	My new man had left me just a	room and an emp-ty	bed. _____	

next one begins (see Listening Guide 46). As in most rags, the listener's interest is focused throughout on the syncopated rhythms of the melodies, played by the right hand, which are supported by an easy, steady duple-rhythm accompaniment in the left hand.

Joplin's sophisticated piano rags brought him worldwide recognition. Their continued popularity nearly a century later confirms that they are the work of a master.

Listening Guide 46

eLG 4 (30–34)
7 (70–74)

Joplin: *Maple Leaf Rag* (3:21)

DATE OF WORK:	Published 1899
GENRE:	Piano rag
PERFORMANCE:	Piano roll of Joplin performing on a 1910 Steinway player piano
FORM:	Sectional dance form; 4 sections, or strains (each of 16 measures), with repeats (**A-A-B-B-A-C-C-D-D**)
TEMPO:	Tempo di marcia; 2/4 meter

WHAT TO LISTEN FOR: Catchy, syncopated melodies (in right hand) accompanied by a steady, duple-meter rhythm (in left hand).
Sectional form, with four 16-measure phrases, each repeated (**A-A-B-B-A-C-C-D-D**).
Rolled, or arpeggiated, chords as decorative embellishments.
Change of key (to IV, or subdominant) in the trio (**C** section).

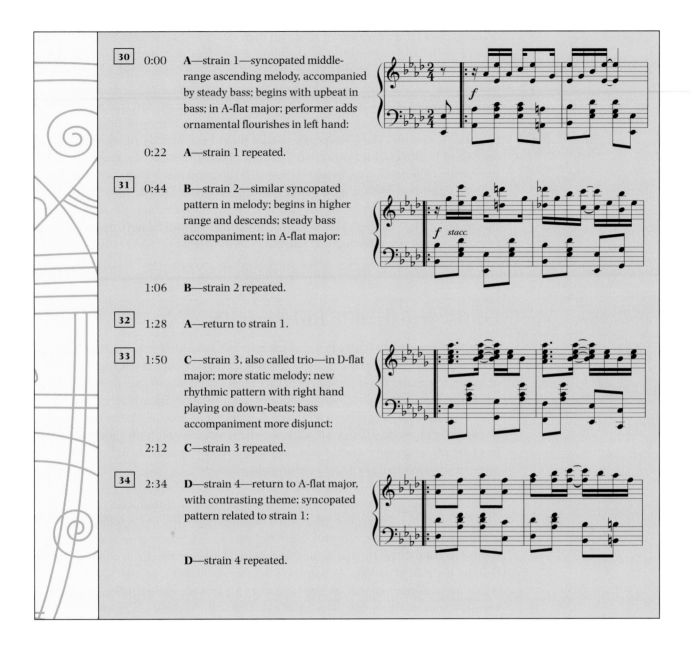

30   0:00   **A**—strain 1—syncopated middle-range ascending melody, accompanied by steady bass; begins with upbeat in bass; in A-flat major; performer adds ornamental flourishes in left hand:

0:22   **A**—strain 1 repeated.

31   0:44   **B**—strain 2—similar syncopated pattern in melody; begins in higher range and descends; steady bass accompaniment; in A-flat major:

1:06   **B**—strain 2 repeated.

32   1:28   **A**—return to strain 1.

33   1:50   **C**—strain 3, also called trio—in D-flat major; more static melody; new rhythmic pattern with right hand playing on down-beats; bass accompaniment more disjunct:

2:12   **C**—strain 3 repeated.

34   2:34   **D**—strain 4—return to A-flat major, with contrasting theme; syncopated pattern related to strain 1:

D—strain 4 repeated.

Blues and New Orleans Jazz

Blues is an American form of folk music based on a simple, repetitive, poetic-musical structure. The term refers to a mood as well as a harmonic progression, which is usually twelve (or occasionally sixteen) bars in length. Characteristic is the ***blue note***, a slight drop in pitch on the third, fifth, or seventh tone of the scale. A blues text typically consists of a three-line stanza of which the first two lines are identical. Its vocal style was derived from the work songs of Southern blacks.

    Blues is a fundamental form in jazz. The music we call jazz was born in New Orleans through the fusion of African-American elements such as ragtime and blues with other traditional styles—spirituals, work songs, and shouts. (For more on the roots of jazz, see CP 19.) In all of these styles, the art of improvisation was

Blues

Blue note

crucially important. Performers made up their parts as they went along, often with several musicians improvising at the same time. This seemingly chaotic practice worked because all the players knew the basic rules—the tempo, the form, the harmonic progression, and the order in which instruments were to be featured. A twelve-bar blues progression follows a standard harmonic pattern (see p. 380).

New Orleans jazz depended on the players' multiple improvisation to create a polyphonic texture. The trumpet or cornet played the melody or an embellished version of it; the clarinet was often featured in a countermelody above the main tune; the trombone improvised below the trumpet and signaled the chord changes; and the rhythm section—consisting of string bass or tuba, guitar and banjo, or piano and drums—provided rhythmic and harmonic support. Among the greats of New Orleans jazz were Joseph "King" Oliver (cornet), Sidney Bechet (soprano saxophone), Ferdinand "Jelly Roll" Morton (piano), and Louis "Satchmo" Armstrong (trumpet).

CD iMusic

When the Saints Go Marching In

Louis Armstrong and Early Jazz

IN HIS OWN WORDS

There's only two ways to sum up music: either it's good or it's bad. If it's good, you don't mess with it; you just enjoy it.

Louis Armstrong (1901–1971) was unquestionably the most important single force in the development of early jazz styles. He was a great improviser who used a variety of mutes to expand the capacities of his trumpet in range and tone color. To distinguish his unique melodic-rhythmic style of performance, his admirers coined the term "swing," which became a standard description of jazz. His 1926 recording of *Heebie Jeebies* introduced **scat singing**, in which syllables without meaning (*vocables*) are set to an improvised vocal line. Singer Ella Fitzgerald (1918–1996) later brought this technique to a truly virtuosic level.

Scat singing

Chorus

In jazz, a *chorus* is a single statement of melodic-harmonic pattern, like a twelve-bar blues progression. Armstrong's style of jazz introduced a number of new features, including solo rather than ensemble choruses. In his solos, only hints of the original tune are recognizable. Through such innovations, jazz was transformed into a solo art that presented improvised fantasias on chord changes rather than on a repeated melody. Armstrong's instrumental-like approach to singing, his distinctive inflections, and his improvisatory style were highly influential to jazz vocalists, paramount among them Billie Holiday, one of the leading female singers in jazz history.

THE JAZZ SINGER BILLIE HOLIDAY

"I can't stand to sing the same song the same way two nights in succession, let alone two years or ten years. If you can, then it ain't music; it's close-order drill or exercise or yodeling or something, not music."

Billie Holiday

Billie Holiday (1915–1959), known as Lady Day, was born in 1915 as Eleanora Fagan, daughter of a guitar player with the Fletcher Henderson Band. Abandoned by her father, Billie was raised by relatives who mistreated her. In 1928, with barely any formal education behind her, she went to join her mother in New York, where she probably worked as a prostitute. Around 1930, Billie began singing at clubs in Brooklyn and Harlem and was discovered in 1933 by a talent scout who arranged for her to record with the clarinetist Benny Goodman. This first break earned her thirty-five dollars.

The Roots of Jazz

Jazz has been viewed by many as a truly American art form, but in reality it draws together traditions from West Africa, Europe, and the Americas. The African origins of jazz evoke an earlier episode of American history: the slave trade from Africa. Many of the slaves brought to America came from the west coast of Africa. Their singing styles (call-and-response patterns and various vocal inflections) and storytelling techniques stem from African culture and remained alive for several centuries in both regions through oral tradition.

Black music in nineteenth-century America included dancing for ritual and ceremonial purposes and the singing of work songs (communal songs that synchronized the rhythm of group tasks; see CP 2, p. 60) and spirituals (a kind of religious folk song, often with a refrain). West African religious traditions mingled freely with the Protestant Christianity adopted by some slaves. The art of storytelling through music, typical of many West African tribes, and praise singing (glorifying deities or royalty) were other traditions retained by slaves that would contribute to spirituals and blues. Although both men and women took part in praise singing, the musical storyteller, called the griot, was traditionally a male who preserved and transmitted the history, stories, and poetry of the people.

The city of New Orleans fueled the early sounds of jazz. There, in Congo Square, slaves met in the pre–Civil War era to dance to the accompaniment of all sorts of instruments, including drums, gourds, mouth harps, and banjos. Their music featured a strong underlying pulse over which syncopations and polyrhythmic elaborations took place. Melodies incorporated African-derived techniques such as rhythmic interjections, vocal glides, and percussive sounds made with the tongue and throat and were often set in a musical scale with blue notes (lowered scale degrees on the third, fifth, or seventh of a major scale).

In the years after the Civil War and the Emancipation Proclamation (1863), a new style of music arose in the South, especially in the Mississippi Delta—country, or rural, blues, performed by a raspy-voiced male singer. This music voiced the difficulties of everyday life in a continuation of the storyteller, or griot, tradition. The vocal lines featured melodic pitch bending, or blue notes, sung over repeated bass patterns. Among the greatest blues singers were Charlie Patton (1891–1934) and the legendary B. B. King.

Dance music also flourished among Southern blacks, and one type in particular, ragtime, strongly influenced early jazz. Ragtime was the first African-American music to experience widespread popularity. This catchy style was soon heard across the country and in Europe, both as accompanied song and as solo piano music. The rhythmic vitality of ragtime fascinated European and American composers alike, including George Gershwin and Leonard Bernstein.

The Bamboula, danced in Congo Square, New Orleans, to the accompaniment of drums and singing, according to artist **E. V. Kemble** in 1885.

Terms to Note

spiritual	blue note	griot
call-and-response	ragtime	

Suggested Listening

CD iMusic African-American spirituals (*Swing Low, Sweet Chariot*)

CD iMusic New Orleans jazz, *When the Saints Go Marching In*, by the Kings of Harmony

CD iMusic Ragtime (*Pineapple Rag*, by Scott Joplin)
Rural blues (Charlie Patton)

By 1935, Billie was recording with some of the best jazz musicians of her day. As her popularity increased, she was featured with Count Basie's band, and in 1938, with Artie Shaw's group—making her one of the first black singers to break the color barrier and sing in public with a white orchestra. (At this time, there was a restriction barring whites and blacks from performing together on stage.)

By the 1940s, Billie's life had deteriorated, the result of alcohol and drug abuse and of ill-chosen relationships with abusive men. Her health—and her voice—suffered greatly because of her addictions, although she still made a number of memorable recordings. In May 1959, she was diagnosed with cirrhosis of the liver and died several months later, at the age of forty-four.

Billie Holiday had a unique talent that was immediately recognized by other musicians. Although her voice was untrained and her range small, she had a remarkable sense of pitch and an unfaulting delivery—a style she learned from listening to her two idols, Bessie Smith and Louis Armstrong.

We will hear a blues that Billie wrote and recorded in 1936, with Artie Shaw (clarinet) and Bunny Berigan (trumpet), and which she performed regularly throughout her career. It is a twelve-bar blues, with a short introduction and six choruses, some of which are instrumental (see Listening Guide 47). The first text-verse is a typical three-line strophe (as shown in the chart on p. 380), but as the work progresses, the form becomes freer. In the vocal verses, Billie demonstrates her masterful rhythmic flexibility and talent for jazz embellishments (scoops and dips on notes). In this performance, we also hear Artie Shaw's creative clarinet improvisations and Bunny Berigan's earthy, "gutbucket" trumpet playing (this refers to an unrestrained, raspy quality of tone). Shaw remembered this 1936 recording session some years later, saying that Billie was "already beginning to develop that distinctive style of hers which has been copied and imitated by so many singers of popular music that the average listener of today cannot realize how original she actually is."

IN HER OWN WORDS

I don't think I'm singing. I feel like I'm playing a horn. I try to improvise like . . . Louis Armstrong . . . what comes out is what I feel. I hate straight singing. I have to change a tune to my own way of doing it.

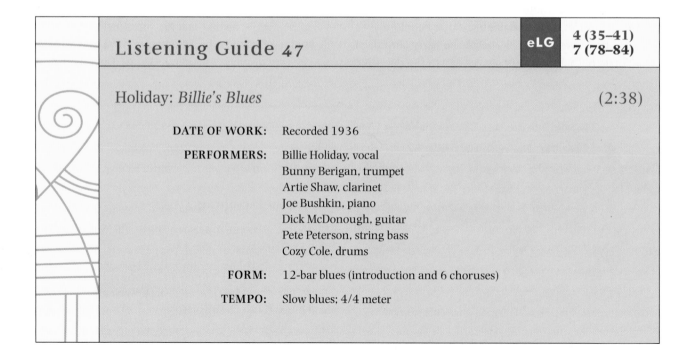

Listening Guide 47

eLG | **4 (35–41)**
7 (78–84)

Holiday: *Billie's Blues* (2:38)

DATE OF WORK:	Recorded 1936
PERFORMERS:	Billie Holiday, vocal
	Bunny Berigan, trumpet
	Artie Shaw, clarinet
	Joe Bushkin, piano
	Dick McDonough, guitar
	Pete Peterson, string bass
	Cozy Cole, drums
FORM:	12-bar blues (introduction and 6 choruses)
TEMPO:	Slow blues; 4/4 meter

WHAT TO LISTEN FOR: Repeated harmonic progression (12 bars), heard 6 times (after introduction).

Steady rhythm section keeps the beat under improvisations; slow, languid tempo with syncopated rhythms.

First vocal chorus (2) has typical blues text; others are more free.

Differing improvisational styles of 3 featured soloists: Holiday (voice), Shaw (clarinet), and Berigan (trumpet).

Pitch inflections (bent notes, blue notes, and scoops) typical of blues.

35 0:00 Introduction (4 bars)—bass and piano.

36 0:07 **Chorus 1**—ensemble (12 bars).

37 0:32 **Chorus 2**—vocal (12 bars):

> Lord, I love my man, tell the world I do,
> I love my man, tell th' world I do,
> But when he mistreats me, makes me feel so blue.

Opening of first vocal chorus, showing syncopated line, with slide at the end:

38 0:56 **Chorus 3**—vocal (12 bars):

> My man wouldn' gimme no breakfast,
> Wouldn' gimme no dinner,
> Squawked about my supper 'n put me outdoors,
> Had the nerve to lay a matchbox on my clothes;
> I didn't have so many but I had a long, long ways to go.

39 1:21 **Chorus 4**—solo clarinet improvisation (12 bars):

40 1:45 **Chorus 5**—solo trumpet improvisation (12 bars).

41 2:11 **Chorus 6**—vocal (12 bars):

> Some men like me 'cause I'm happy,
> Some 'cause I'm snappy,
> Some call me honey, others think I've got money,
> Some tell me, "Baby you're built for speed,"
> Now if you put that all together,
> Makes me ev'rything a good man needs.

72

The Swing Era and Beyond

"What's swinging in words? If a guy makes you pat your foot and if you feel it down your back, you don't have to ask anybody if that's good music or not. You can always feel it."

—MILES DAVIS

| KEY POINTS | Listen Online Ⓢ **StudySpace** online at www.wwnorton.com/enjoy |

- The 1930s saw the advent of the **swing era** (or **big band era**) and the brilliantly composed jazz of Duke Ellington.
- In the late 1940s, big band jazz gave way to smaller group styles, including **bebop, cool jazz**, and **West Coast jazz**.
- Charlie Parker (alto saxophone) and Dizzy Gillespie (trumpet) led the bebop movement, and Miles Davis (trumpet) established the lyrical cool jazz style.
- **Third stream jazz**, developed in the 1950s, combines elements of art music (instruments, forms, and tonal devices) and jazz to produce a new style.

- Recent trends include **fusion, Neoclassical style, free jazz**, and **new-age jazz**. Interactive technology (including MIDI) has been influential in modern jazz performance as well.
- Many art and popular music composers have been influenced by ragtime, blues, and jazz, including Stravinsky, Ravel, Copland, and George Gershwin.
- Known for his Tin Pan Alley songs and musical theater productions, Gershwin also sought to unite jazz and classical music in his instrumental works, including *Rhapsody in Blue* and his *Three Piano Preludes*.

Duke Ellington and the Big Band Era

"Somehow I suspect that if Shakespeare were alive today, he might be a jazz fan himself."

In the 1930s and '40s, the highly creative era of early jazz gave way to the swing, or big band, era. By this time, jazz had evolved into a musical style and aesthetic in its own right and was, without a doubt, America's voice in popular music. This was also the time of the Great Depression, the most severe economic slowdown in American history, which cost many musicians their livelihood but also provided an opening for new performers to gain a footing in the entertainment world. Jazz in particular provided new opportunities for black musicians. Among those who ascended to stardom in this era was Edward Kennedy "Duke" Ellington (1899–1974), whose group first went on the road in 1932 and remained popular until his death. His unique big-band style of jazz won over a wide audience—both black and white—who danced away its cares in clubs and hotel ballrooms across the country.

   "Duke" Ellington was born in Washington, DC, in 1899 and was playing in New York jazz clubs by the 1920s. He became famous as a composer in the following decade. The advent of the big bands brought a greater need for arranged, or written-down, music, and Ellington played a major role in this development. A fine pianist himself, he was an even better orchestrator. As one of his collaborators remarked, "He plays piano, but his real instrument is the orchestra."

Ellington's orchestral palette was much richer than that of the New Orleans band. It included two trumpets, one cornet, three trombones, four saxophones (some of the players doubling on clarinet), two string basses, guitar, drums, vibraphone, and piano. One of the theme songs for Ellington's orchestra was *Take the A Train*, written by composer/arranger Billy Strayhorn (1915–1967) and first recorded in 1941.

Ellington's multifaceted contribution influenced the world of jazz profoundly. As a composer, he brought his art to new heights and a newfound legitimacy; as an arranger, he left a rich legacy of works for a wide range of jazz groups; as a band leader, he has served as teacher and model to several generations of jazz musicians. America's cultural heritage would have been far poorer without him.

Duke Ellington (piano) and his band in a movie still from the Metro Goldwin Mayer musical *Cabin in the Sky* (1943).

Bebop and Later Jazz Styles

"It's taken me all my life to learn what not to play."

—DIZZY GILLESPIE

By the end of the 1940s, musicians had become disenchanted with big band jazz. Their rebellion resulted in the new styles known as bebop and cool jazz. *Bebop* (also known as *bop*) was an invented word mimicking the two-note phrase that is the trademark of this style. Trumpeter Dizzy Gillespie, saxophonist Charlie Parker, and pianists Bud Powell and Thelonious Monk were among the leaders of the bebop movement in the 1940s. Over the next two decades, the term "bebop" came to include a number of substyles like *cool jazz* (the "cool" suggesting a restrained, unemotional manner) and West Coast jazz. Trumpeter Miles Davis was the principal exponent of cool jazz, a laid-back style characterized by lush harmonies, lowered levels of volume, moderate tempos, and a new lyricism. *West Coast jazz* is a small-group, cool-jazz style featuring mixed timbres (one instrument for each color, without piano) and contrapuntal improvisations.

Latin American music has been highly influential in the development of jazz, chiefly its dance rhythms and percussion instruments (conga drum, bongos, and cowbells). In the 1930s and 1940s, Latin bandleaders such as Xavier Cugat brought Latin dance music—especially the rumba—into the mainstream. Latin elements were integral to the bebop style of the late 1940s as we will hear in *A Night in Tunisia*, by Dizzy Gillespie. The next decades saw a strong Brazilian, as well as Cuban, influence on jazz (see CP 20).

Let's consider a famous bebop work written by Dizzy Gillespie: the Latin-tinged *A Night in Tunisia*, which features two jazz legends—Charlie Parker (known as Bird) on alto saxophone, and a very young Miles Davis on trumpet. It is performed by a six-person ensemble in the unique musical language of bebop, a somewhat frenetic style that Ellington likened to "playing Scrabble with all the vowels missing." Because bebop is so reliant on improvisation, the standard performance usually presents the

Bebop

Cool jazz

West Coast jazz

Latin influence

Night in Tunisia

Charlie Parker was one of the most influential saxophonists of the 1940s.

entire tune first—here a thirty-two-bar song form (**A-A-B-A**, or chorus 1)—followed by several improvised choruses over the same chord pattern, or changes (see Listening Guide 48). A nervous, syncopated ostinato is established in the introduction, after which the disjunct tune is played on muted trumpet by Miles Davis, with a brief alto saxophone solo (in the **B** section). After a unison saxophone interlude, Charlie Parker plays a highly virtuosic, and now famous, *break* (a solo passage that interrupts the accompaniment—in this case, a flurry of sixteenth notes that moves all over the horn's range) that leads into the second chorus, split between Parker's and Davis's creative improvisations. Parker is known for his alternation of short rifflike passages (a *riff* is a short melodic ostinato heard in jazz) with more flowing lines. The last chorus features solos by the tenor saxophone, guitar, and finally, the trumpet; the work closes as it began, with the bass ostinato fading out. Gillespie's *A Night in Tunisia* has been recorded many times since, and is an

Break and riff   established jazz classic.

Listening Guide 48

eLG | 4 (42–47)
8 (6–11)

Gillespie/Parker: *A Night in Tunisia*   (3:01)

DATE:	Recorded 1946
PERFORMERS:	Charlie Parker Septet
	Charlie Parker, alto saxophone
	Miles Davis, trumpet
	Lucky Thompson, tenor saxophone
	Dodo Mamarosa, piano
	Arv Garrison, guitar
	Vic McMillan, bass
	Roy Porter, drums
FORM:	32-bar song form (**A-A-B-A**), in 3 choruses
TEMPO:	Moderate 4/4
KEY:	D minor

WHAT TO LISTEN FOR: Short motivic ideas (riffs) that are repeated; underlying bass ostinato.
Soloistic style (often featuring a single player).
Statement of tune, played by muted trumpet (Miles Davis) and alto saxophone (Charlie Parker).
Frenetic improvisational style of Charlie Parker in chorus 2.
Choruses 2 and 3: solo improvisations on trumpet, tenor saxophone, and guitar, with short melodic ideas alternating between lyrical lines.
Recap of tune, and final ostinato.

In a 1957 lecture, composer and jazz historian Gunther Schuller coined the term *third stream*, holding that the first stream was classical music, the second jazz, and the third a combination of the other two. Although the designation referred mainly to the instruments used, it was soon extended to include other elements as well, such as jazz performers' adoption of classical forms and tonal idioms.

Third stream jazz

Schuller's idea was picked up by a number of jazz musicians, among them pianist John Lewis (b. 1920), who formed the Modern Jazz Quartet. The ensemble played concerts that "swung" but also featured serious, composed works. More recently, trumpeter Wynton Marsalis demonstrated his mastery of both jazz and classical styles in his Pulitzer Prize–winning jazz oratorio *Blood on the Fields* (1996) and his Stravinsky-inspired *A Fiddler's Tale* (1998).

By the 1960s, new experiments were in the making. A free-style *avant-garde jazz* emerged, with tenor saxophonist John Coltrane as its leading exponent. At the same time, a hybrid style known as *fusion* arose that combined jazz improvisation with amplified instruments and the rhythmic pulse of rock. Trumpeter Miles Davis was an important catalyst in the advent of this style, and performers such as guitarist Jerry Garcia (1942–1995, of the Grateful Dead) and vibraphone player Gary Burton became proponents of the fusion sound.

Avant-garde jazz

Fusion

In the last several decades, jazz styles have taken conflicting turns. Modern bebop arose as a contemporary *Neoclassical style* of the 1980s, characterized by

Neoclassical style

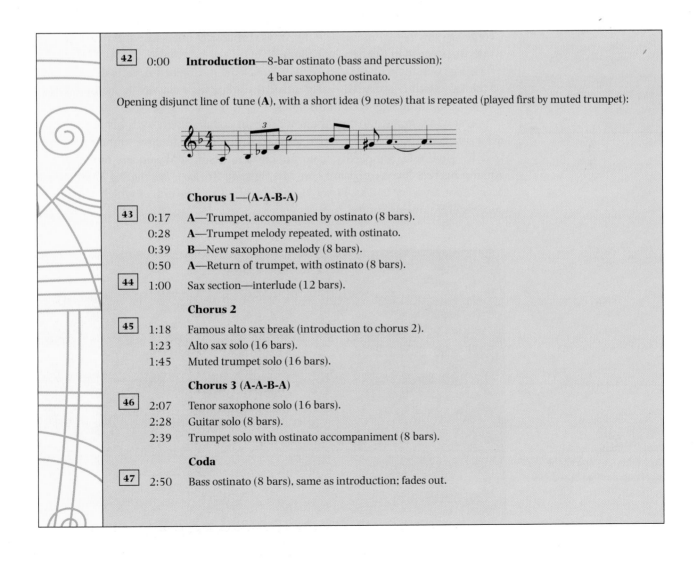

expanded tonalities, modal improvisation, and new forms merged with bebop's disjunct lines. Wynton Marsalis is one of the new voices of this Neoclassicism. ***Free jazz***, founded by saxophonist Ornette Coleman in the 1960s, has developed alongside the more mellow, contemplative strains of ***new-age jazz***, the latter best exemplified by saxophonist Paul Winter. New technologies, including MIDI (see Chapter 79) and interactive performance between musicians and computers, have opened a world of creative possibilities and sounds; meanwhile, other performers are looking back to the fundamentals of jazz, reinventing it for today's listeners.

Free jazz

New-age jazz

George Gershwin and the Merger of Classical and Jazz Styles

"Jazz has contributed an enduring value to America
in the sense that it has expressed ourselves."

We have noted a number of composers—European and American alike—who were drawn to the vernacular genres of ragtime, blues, and jazz, and who sought to integrate elements of these popular styles into their music. Ragtime fascinated Claude Debussy, who captured its spirit in *Golliwog's Cakewalk* (1906–08), and Igor Stravinsky, in *Ragtime for Eleven Instruments* (1918), *Piano-Rag Music* (1919), and a dance from *The Soldier's Tale* (1918). One American musician who mastered this fusion was George Gershwin—whose appealing songs, Broadway musicals, and instrumental works are steeped in the new jazz idiom.

George Gershwin (1898–1937) was one of the most gifted American musicians of the twentieth century. His early musical studies were classically focused, but it was jazz that ultimately caught his fancy.

Gershwin's songs, most of them written in collaboration with his brother Ira, drew on elements of ragtime, blues, and jazz to create a distinctive sound characterized by rhythmic complexity, colorful chromaticism, and sudden modulations. Among his best-loved songs are *Love Me, Oh Lady Be Good, Fascinating Rhythm, The Man I Love, Someone to Watch Over Me*, and *'S Wonderful*, several of which came from successful Broadway shows.

IN HIS OWN WORDS

The best music being written today . . . comes from folk sources. Jazz, ragtime, Negro spirituals and blues, Southern mountain songs, country fiddling, and cowboy songs can all be employed in the creation of American art-music, and are actually used by many composers now.

Paul Whiteman and His Orchestra was one of the most popular jazz ensembles in the 1920s.

It is in Gershwin's instrumental works, however, that he was able to merge the rhythmic vitality and harmonic language of jazz with classical forms. His first "classical" piece was *Rhapsody in Blue*, scored for piano and orchestra and premiered in 1924 with the Paul Whiteman ensemble (with Gershwin on piano) in a concert billed as "An Experiment in Modern Music." The critical response was very positive, and the work catapulted Gershwin to fame. He followed *Rhapsody* with his *Concerto in F* (1925), for piano and orchestra, performed at New York's Carnegie Hall, and his tone poem *An American in Paris* (1928), with Gershwin himself conducting the New York Philharmonic Orchestra in an open-air concert for an audience of 15,000. With these works, he successfully brought jazz into the concert hall and into the hearts of classical-music lovers.

Rhapsody in Blue

73

Musical Theater

"The hills are alive with the sound of music."
—OSCAR HAMMERSTEIN II

KEY POINTS   Listen Online **StudySpace** online at www.wwnorton.com/enjoy

- O American musical theater has roots in European *operetta*, which was brought to America by emigré composers.
- O Musicals feature romantic plots (some taken from novels), comic moments, appealing melodies, and large ensembles and dance numbers.
- O The great composer/lyricist teams include Rodgers and Hart (*Babes in Arms*), Rodgers and Hammerstein (*The Sound of Music*), Lerner and Lowe (*My Fair Lady*); other well-known composers of musicals are Stephen Sondheim (*Into the Woods*),

Andrew Lloyd Webber (*Phantom of the Opera*), and Claude-Michel Schonberg (*Les Misérables*).

- O Leonard Bernstein is remembered today as a conductor and composer of symphonic and choral music, film music, and musical theater works. His *West Side Story*, set in New York City amid turf wars of rival street gangs, updates the Romeo and Juliet legend.
- O Dance music from Latin America and the Caribbean has enjoyed continued popularity and has influenced many musical genres, including Bernstein's *West Side Story* (CP 20).

The Development of American Musical Theater

The American musical theater of today developed from the comic opera, or *operetta*, tradition of Johann Strauss Jr., Jacques Offenbach, and the British team of Gilbert and Sullivan. The genre was revamped to the American taste by composers such as Victor Herbert (1850–1924), whose works include charming shows like *Babes in Toyland* (1903) and *Naughty Marietta* (1910). The Broadway musical (or musical comedy) gradually evolved in the 1920s, with works like Sigmund Romberg's *Student Prince* (1924), set in a glamorized Old Heidelberg, and Jerome Kern's landmark *Show Boat* (1927), a tale of Mississippi River life that introduced the classic songs

Early musicals

Curly and Laurie in the "Dream Sequence" from the Rogers and Hammerstein hit musical *Oklahoma!* (1943).

Ol' Man River and *Can't Help Lovin' Dat Man of Mine*. In the ensuing decades, the musical established itself as America's unique contribution to world theater.

Traditional musical theater depended on romantic plots in picturesque settings enlivened by comedy, appealing melodies, choruses, and dances. Within the framework of a thoroughly commercial theater, a group of talented composers and writers created works that not only enchanted audiences but also generations to come. Among these were Burton Lane's *Finian's Rainbow* (1947), Cole Porter's *Kiss Me, Kate* (1948), Frank Loesser's *Guys and Dolls* (1950), Harold Rome's *Fanny* (1954), and Alan Jay Lerner and Frederick Loewe's *My Fair Lady* (1956).

Originally, the plots of musicals were contrived and silly, functioning mainly as scaffolding for the songs and dances. The emphasis gradually changed when composers began turning to sophisticated literary sources for their plots, which demanded more convincing treatment of characters and situations. *Show Boat* was based on an Edna Ferber novel, *Kiss Me, Kate* on Shakespeare's *The Taming of the Shrew*, *Guys and Dolls* on the stories of Damon Runyon, *Fanny* on a trilogy by Marcel Pagnol, and *My Fair Lady* on George Bernard Shaw's play *Pygmalion*. As the musicals' approach grew more serious, the genre outgrew its original limitations.

George Gershwin's masterpiece *Porgy and Bess* was so far ahead of its time that, despite its focus on African-American folk idioms, it did not become a success until a revival toured Europe in the 1950s. The work paved the way for musicals such as Leonard Bernstein's *West Side Story* (1957), one of the first musical theater pieces to end tragically, and Jerry Bock's *Fiddler on the Roof* (1964), based on stories by the great Yiddish writer Sholem Aleichem. Both works earned worldwide success, and both would have been unthinkable twenty years earlier because of the serious elements in their plots.

Rodgers and Hammerstein

The composer Richard Rodgers collaborated with two talented lyricists during his long career to produce some of the best-loved musicals of the twentieth century. Along with Lorenz Hart, he created a string of successful Broadway shows, including *Babes in Arms* (1937), which featured the now-classic ballad *My Funny Valentine* and the catchy tune *The Lady Is a Tramp*. After the death of Hart in 1943, Rodgers teamed up with Oscar Hammerstein II to write unforgettable musicals such as *Oklahoma!* (1943), *Carousel* (1945), *South Pacific* (1949), *The King and I* (1951), and *The Sound of Music* (1959). Here too the literary sources were of a high order. *Carousel* was based on Ferenc Molnár's *Liliom*, *Oklahoma!* on Lynn Riggs's *Green Grow the Lilacs*, *South Pacific* on the stories of James Michener, *The King and I* on *Anna and the King of Siam* by Margaret Landon, and *The Sound of Music* on the moving memoir of Baroness Maria von Trapp.

Stephen Sondheim

In the 1970s and 1980s, Stephen Sondheim brought the genre to new levels of sophistication in a series of works that included *A Little Night Music* (1973), *Sweeney Todd* (1979), *Sunday in the Park with George* (1983), and *Into the Woods* (1988). His shows of the 1990s continued his original musical voice and dramatic expression. *Assassins* (1991) was an off-Broadway production that abandoned narrative and offered a rather critical view of American vernacular music; in *Passion* (1994), he dropped the typical numbered musical tunes of most shows and wrote a symphonic score. Sondheim challenges his audiences with a dramatic style that is far more serious than those of his Broadway successors and peers. He uses complex musical language that shows an affinity for the classical masters Ravel and Copland.

A new era dawned with the advent of rock musicals such as Galt MacDermot's *Hair* (1968), The Who's *Tommy* (1969; music and lyrics by Peter Townshend), and Andrew Lloyd Webber's *Jesus Christ Superstar* (1971). Suddenly, the romantic show tunes to which millions of young Americans had learned to dance and flirt went completely out of fashion. After a while, however, lyricism returned. The British Lloyd Webber conquered the international stage with *Evita* (1978), *Cats* (1981), *Starlight Express* (1984), *The Phantom of the Opera* (1986), and *Sunset Boulevard* (1993)— works in which song and dance were combined with dazzling scenic effects, as in the court operas of the Baroque. Together with Frenchman Claude-Michel Schonberg's *Les Misérables* (1987) and *Miss Saigon* (1988)—the latter in collaboration with Alain Boublil—these musicals represented a new phenomenon. What had been almost exclusively an American product was now taken over by Europeans.

Andrew Lloyd Webber

Many "classic" musicals have enjoyed recent successful revivals on Broadway; among these are *Chicago* (revived again in the 2002 movie version); *The Sound of Music*; *Annie Get Your Gun*; *The Music Man*; *Kiss Me, Kate*; *Cabaret*; *Into the Woods*; *42nd Street*, *Assassins*, and *The Pajama Game*. A new category of musicals based on films has swept the Broadway stage, including the Disney studio's *Beauty and the Beast* (1994), *The Lion King* (1997), and *Tarzan* (2006), all based on the animated films. These works have reversed the standard order of a hit musical generating a film and opened up a new world of source material. Other recent shows have gone in this direction: Mel Brooks's award-winning comedy *The Producers* (2001), based on his 1967 film; *The Full Monty* (2001, with music and lyrics by David Yazbek), an Americanization of the risqué 1997 British film; *Thoroughly Modern Millie* (2002 Tony Award-winner), adopted from the 1967 film of the same name; *Spamalot* (2005 Tony Award-winner), based on the 1975 film *Monty Python and the Holy Grail*; and *Billy Elliot* (2006), based on the movie. The recent Broadway hit *Wicked* (2004), about the witches of Oz (see below), derives both from the classic L. Frank Baum book *The Wizard of Oz* (1901) and the well-known movie (1937, featuring Judy Garland).

Film-based musicals

Some musicals find their sources in older classics: Jonathan Larsen's hit show *Rent* (1996), a modern rock opera inspired by Puccini's opera *La bohème*, premiered

Recent musicals

Glinda, the "good" witch (Kristen Chenoweth, left) and Elphaba, the "bad" witch (Idina Menzel, right) from the musical *Wicked* (2004).

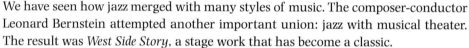

on the hundredth anniversary of the Italian masterwork; Stephen Flaherty's *Ragtime* (1996, with lyrics by Lynn Ahrens), a musical setting of the novel *Ragtime* (1975), by E. L. Doctorow, derives from the syncopated rhythmic style popular at the turn-of-the-century; and Elton John and Tim Rice's *Aida*, a Disney production, is based on Verdi's masterpiece of the same name about love and power in ancient Egypt. Dance has inspired a new type of musical in which choreography takes precedence over story line, as in *Bring in 'da Noise, Bring in 'da Funk* (1995), featuring tap star Savion Glover, and *Riverdance* (1994), with the sensational Irish step dancer Michael Flatley. The hit show *Contact* (2000) tells three stories entirely through dance, about people in pursuit of love. This trend has diversified into staged shows featuring rhythmic percussion and dancing, as in *Stomp* (1994), and brilliant visuals and pageantry like *Blast!* (2000). Many "jukebox" musicals, featuring songs by a popular artist or group, have opened in recent years, but none have achieved the success of *Mamma Mia* (1999), based on songs by the Swedish pop group ABBA.

Leonard Bernstein and the Broadway Musical

"Any composer's writing is the sum of himself, of all his roots and influences."

Ⓢ **Leonard Bernstein**

We have seen how jazz merged with many styles of music. The composer-conductor Leonard Bernstein attempted another important union: jazz with musical theater. The result was *West Side Story*, a stage work that has become a classic.

As a composer, conductor, educator, pianist, and television personality, Bernstein (1918–1990) enjoyed a spectacular career. He was born in Lawrence, Massachusetts, the son of Russian-Jewish immigrants. At thirteen, he was playing piano with a jazz band. He entered Harvard at seventeen (where he studied composition with Walter Piston), attended the prestigious Curtis Institute in Philadelphia, and then became a disciple of the conductor Serge Koussevitzky. In 1943, when he was twenty-five, Bernstein was appointed assistant to Artur Rodzinski, conductor of the New York Philharmonic. A few weeks later, a guest conductor, Bruno Walter, was suddenly taken ill, and Rodzinski was out of town. With only a few hours' notice, Bernstein took over the Sunday afternoon concert, which was being broadcast coast to coast, and led a stunning performance. Overnight he became famous. Fifteen years later, he was himself named director of the New York Philharmonic, the first American-born conductor (and the youngest conductor ever at age forty) to occupy the post.

Composer As a composer, Bernstein straddled the worlds of serious and popular music. He was thus able to bring to the Broadway musical a compositional technique and knowledge of music that few of its earlier practitioners had possessed. He had a genuine flair for orchestration—in his music the balance and spacing of sonorities, the use of the brass in the high register, and the idiomatic writing that shows off each instrument to its best advantage all bespeak a master. His harmonic idiom is spicily dissonant, his jazzy rhythms have great vitality, and his melodies soar.

Theater music Bernstein's feeling for the urban scene—specifically that of New York City—is vividly projected in his theater music. In *On the Town* (a full-length version of his ballet *Fancy Free)*, *Wonderful Town*, and *West Side Story*, he created a sophisticated kind of musical theater that explodes with movement, energy, and sentiment. His death in October 1990 aroused universal mourning in the music world and beyond.

WEST SIDE STORY

In *West Side Story*, Bernstein realized a dream: to create a musical based on the Romeo and Juliet story. This updated tale, with a book by playwright Arthur Laurents and lyrics by Stephen Sondheim (his first job as a lyricist), sets the saga amid turf wars of two rival street gangs in New York City. The hostility between the Jets (led by Riff) and their Puerto Rican rivals, the Sharks (led by Bernardo), is a modern-day counterpart of the feud between the Capulets and the Montagues in Shakespeare's play. In Bernstein's tragic tale, Tony, a former Jet, and Maria, Bernardo's sister, meet at a dance and

Richard Beymer and Natalie Wood in the "balcony scene" from the film *West Side Story*, directed by Robert Wise and Jerome Robbins.

immediately fall in love. Riff and Bernardo bring their two gangs together for a fight. When Tony tries to stop them, Riff is stabbed by Bernardo, and Tony in turn kills Bernardo. Tony begs Maria for forgiveness, but the gang warfare mounts to a final rumble in which Tony is killed. This story of star-crossed lovers unfolds in scenes of great tenderness, with memorable songs such as *Maria*, *Tonight*, and *Somewhere* alternating with electrifying dance sequences choreographed by Jerome Robbins.

We will hear first the *Mambo*, a part of the dance scene where Tony meets Maria. When the lively Latin beat starts, the Jets and Sharks are on opposite sides of the hall. At the climax of the dance, Tony and Maria catch a glimpse of each other across the room. A *mambo* is an Afro-Cuban dance with a fast and highly syncopated beat; in Bernstein's score, the bongos and cowbells keep the frenetic pulse under the shouts of the gang members and the jazzy riffs of the woodwinds and brass. The music dies away as Maria and Tony walk toward each other on the dance floor.

Mambo

The *Tonight* Ensemble is set later the same evening, after a fire-escape version of Shakespeare's famous balcony scene, where Tony and Maria first sing their love duet. As darkness falls, the two gangs anxiously await the expected fight, each vowing to cut the other down to size. Underneath the gang music, an ominous three-note ostinato is heard throughout. Tony's thoughts are only of Maria as he sings the lyrical ballad *Tonight* (an **A-A'-B-A"** form we have seen in jazz compositions; see Listening Guide 49) over an animated Latin rhythmic accompaniment. The gang music returns briefly, after which Maria and later Tony repeat their love song, their voices soaring above the complex dialogue in an exciting climax to the first act.

***Tonight* Ensemble**

CD iMusic

Tonight, from *West Side Story*

West Side Story remains, fifty years after its production, a timeless masterpiece of musical theater; its dramatic content, stirring melodies, colorful orchestration, and vivacious dance scenes continue to delight audiences of today.

Latin American Dance Music

A steel-drum player from the republic of Trinidad and Tobago.

The energetic rhythms of Leonard Bernstein's *West Side Story* do not sound particularly foreign to us, because they derive from a variety of Latin American musical styles. By the nineteenth century, a Cuban dance song known as the habanera—whose name derives from its native Havana—was popular in Europe.

Many types of dance music can be described as Afro-Cuban (we use the collective term "salsa" for various contemporary styles that mix rock and jazz with Caribbean musics). The Afro-Cuban conga is a favorite Latin-American Carnival dance whose name is also applied to the tall, single-headed drum used in much Latin American popular music (and heard in Bernstein's *West Side Story*).

The Carnival celebration in Trinidad and Tobago (an archipelago republic made up of various islands) is legendary, beginning just after New Year's and culminating on Mardi Gras ("Fat Tuesday," the day before Lent). Dance music and competitions abound during this time for calypso singers and steel drum players. Steel drums are percussion instruments fashioned from oil drums and made in various sizes to play in ensembles. The drums are cut to size and the ends made concave and hammered into segments, each of which is carefully tuned to a particular pitch. Pan bands are extremely popular today, playing all types of repertory (classical and popular); now heard worldwide, this ensemble's mellow sound and complex, syncopated rhythms are highly evocative of Caribbean musical culture.

Rock styles have been strongly influenced by urban dance music from the Caribbean. In the 1960s, ska, characterized by quick, off-the-beat rhythms and jazz instruments, resulted when Jamaican musicians imitated early rhythm-and-blues musician Fats Domino. This style led the way for reggae, a Jamaican style of music that slows down the quick beat of ska and emphasizes the role of the bass, placing it in a complex rhythmic relationship with the other parts. Bob Marley, one of the most important world music artists, remains the model for reggae musicians. Marley, along with fellow Jamaican artists Peter Tosh and Bunny Wailer, wrote music supporting the Afrocentric Rastafari movement. Today, Bob Marley's sons—all five of them—carry on this musical voice: in particular, youngest son Damian Marley's recent albums (especially *Welcome to Jamrock*, 2005) have won coveted Grammy awards and have been recognized for their explicit social commentary.

Reggae artist Damian Marley carries on the musical traditions begun by his father, Bob Marley.

Terms to Note

habanera	archipelago	pan band
Rastafari movement	Carnival	ska
salsa	steel drum	reggae
conga		

Suggested Listening

CD iMusic *Dougla Dance* (steel drum band)
Habanera, from Bizet's *Carmen*
Reggae (Bob Marley and the Wailers; Damian Marley)
Ska (Skatalites, Millie Small)

Listening Guide 49

eLG 4 (48–56) 8 (12–20)

Bernstein: *West Side Story*, excerpts (5:26)

DATE OF WORK:	1957
GENRE:	Musical theater
CHARACTERS:	Maria, a Puerto Rican girl, sister of Bernardo
	Tony, former member of the Jets
	Anita, Puerto Rican girlfriend of Bernardo
	Riff, leader of the Jets
	Bernardo, leader of the Sharks

Act I: The Dance at the Gym, *Mambo*   (1:48)

WHAT TO LISTEN FOR: Frenetic Afro-Cuban dance, with highly syncopated rhythms.
Rich orchestration featuring brass with Latin American rhythm
   instruments (bongo drums, cowbells).
Vocal interjections ("mambo") and rhythmic hand-clapping.

48 0:00   Percussion introduction, 8 bars, with bongos and cowbells; very fast and syncopated.

0:07   Brass, with accented chords; Sharks shout, "Mambo!"; followed by quieter string line,
accompanied by snare drum rolls; accented brass chords return; Sharks shout, "Mambo!" again.

0:28   High dissonant woodwinds in dialogue with rhythmic brass.

0:33   Trumpets play riff over *fff* chords:

Woodwinds and brass alternate in
highly polyphonic texture.

1:00   Rocking 2-note woodwind line above
syncopated low brass:

49 1:13   Solo trumpet enters in high range
above complex rhythmic
accompaniment:

Complex *fortissimo* polyphony until climax; rhythm slows as music dies away at close.

Act I: *Tonight* Ensemble   (3:38)

WHAT TO LISTEN FOR: Lively gang music in unison, with 3-note ostinato figure.
Soaring love song, with Tony and Maria.
Complex musical texture combines gang music with ballad (*Tonight*).
Fast and rhythmic tempo.

Setting: The neighborhood, 6:00–9:00 p.m. Riff and the Jets, Bernardo and
the Sharks, Anita, Maria, and Tony all wait expectantly for the coming of night.

Listening Guide continues

50   0:00   Short, rhythmic orchestral introduction featuring brass and percussion; based on 3-note ostinato:

TEXT	DESCRIPTION
RIFF AND THE JETS	Gangs sing in alternation:
The Jets are gonna have their day	
Tonight.	

BERNARDO AND THE SHARKS
The Sharks are gonna have
    their way
Tonight.

RIFF AND THE JETS
The Puerto Ricans grumble,
"Fair fight."
But if they start a rumble,
We'll rumble 'em right.

SHARKS
We're gonna hand 'em a surprise
Tonight.

JETS
We're gonna cut them down to size
Tonight.

SHARKS
We said, "OK, no rumpus,
No tricks."
But just in case they jump us,
We're ready to mix

51   0:42   Tonight!

BOTH
We're gonna rock it tonight,
We're gonna jazz it up and have us a ball!
They're gonna get it tonight;
The more they turn it on, the harder
    they fall!

Unison chorus, more emphatic and accented; with accented brass interjections.

JETS
Well, they began it!

Antiphonal exchange between gangs, punctuated by sharp chords in orchestra.

SHARKS
Well, they began it—

BOTH
And we're the ones to stop 'em once
    and for all,
Tonight.

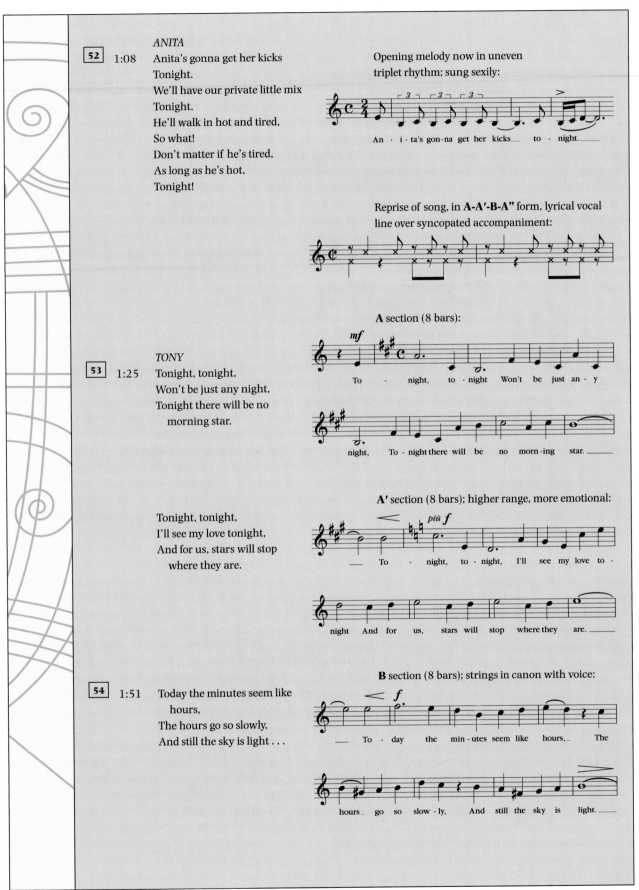

52 1:08 *ANITA*

Anita's gonna get her kicks
Tonight.
We'll have our private little mix
Tonight.
He'll walk in hot and tired,
So what!
Don't matter if he's tired,
As long as he's hot,
Tonight!

Opening melody now in uneven triplet rhythm; sung sexily:

An‧i‧ta's gon‧na get her kicks___ to‧night.

Reprise of song, in **A-A'-B-A"** form, lyrical vocal line over syncopated accompaniment:

A section (8 bars):

53 1:25 *TONY*

Tonight, tonight,
Won't be just any night,
Tonight there will be no
    morning star.

To‧night, to‧night Won't be just an‧y
night, To‧night there will be no morn‧ing star.___

A' section (8 bars); higher range, more emotional:

Tonight, tonight,
I'll see my love tonight,
And for us, stars will stop
    where they are.

To‧night, to‧night, I'll see my love to‧
night And for us, stars will stop where they are.___

B section (8 bars); strings in canon with voice:

54 1:51 Today the minutes seem like
    hours,
The hours go so slowly,
And still the sky is light . . .

To‧day the min‧utes seem like hours,___ The
hours___ go so slow‧ly, And still the sky is light.___

Listening Guide continues

Oh moon, grow bright,
And make this endless day
endless night!

A" section (8 bars); reaches climax, then cuts off:

2:14

Instrumental interlude.

RIFF (to Tony)
I'm counting on you to be there
Tonight!
When Diesel wins it fair and square
Tonight!
That Puerto Rican punk'll go down
And when he's hollered Uncle,
We'll tear up the town!

Return to opening idea, sung more vehemently.

Ensemble finale: Maria sings *Tonight* in high range, against simultaneous dialogue and interjections over the same syncopated dance rhythm that accompanied Tony's solo; dramatic climax on last ensemble statement of "Tonight!"

55 2:39	*MARIA (warmly)* [A] Tonight, tonight	*RIFF AND THE JETS* So I can count on you boy?
		TONY (abstractedly) All right.
		RIFF AND THE JETS We're gonna have us a ball.
	Won't be just any night,	*TONY* All right.
		RIFF Womb to tomb!
	Tonight there will be no morning star.	*TONY* Sperm to worm!
		RIFF I'll see you there about eight.
		TONY Tonight.
		JETS We're gonna rock it tonight!
	[A'] Tonight, tonight,	*SHARKS* We're gonna jazz it tonight!
	I'll see my love tonight,	*ANITA* Tonight, tonight, Late tonight. We're gonna mix it tonight.
	And for us, stars will stop where they are.	

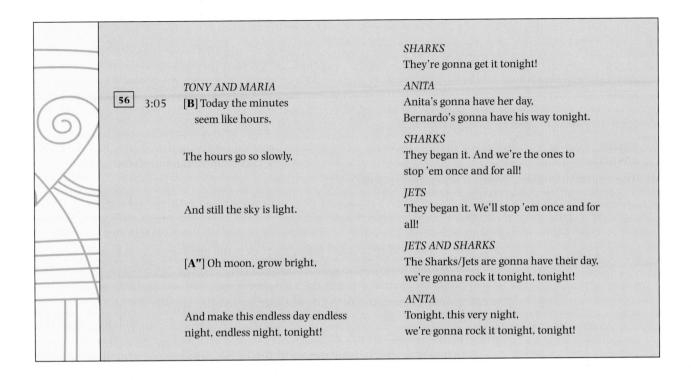

		TONY AND MARIA		SHARKS
				They're gonna get it tonight!
56	3:05	[B] Today the minutes seem like hours,		*ANITA*
				Anita's gonna have her day,
				Bernardo's gonna have his way tonight.
		The hours go so slowly,		*SHARKS*
				They began it. And we're the ones to stop 'em once and for all!
		And still the sky is light.		*JETS*
				They began it. We'll stop 'em once and for all!
		[A"] Oh moon, grow bright,		*JETS AND SHARKS*
				The Sharks/Jets are gonna have their day, we're gonna rock it tonight, tonight!
		And make this endless day endless night, endless night, tonight!		*ANITA*
				Tonight, this very night, we're gonna rock it tonight, tonight!

74

Rock and the Global Scene

"You know my temperature's risin',
The juke box's blowin' a fuse,
My heart's beatin' rhythm,
My soul keeps singin' the blues—
Roll over, Beethoven,
Tell Tchaikovsky the news."

—CHUCK BERRY

KEY POINTS   Listen Online (S) **StudySpace** online at www.wwnorton.com/enjoy

- o The rise of **rock and roll** in the 1950s is one of the most significant phenomena in twentieth-century music history.

- o Rock had its origins in rhythm and blues, country-western, pop music and gospel; early rock crossed racial lines, featuring both white and black performers.

- o The Beatles, first heard live in the United States in 1964, were highly influential because of their expressive experiments in various musical styles (including non-Western ones).

- o California groups also contributed to the expressiveness of rock, particularly to the emergence of **folk rock**.

- o The 1960s and 1970s saw the rise of many eclectic musical styles, including **acid rock, art rock, Latin rock, punk rock, disco, reggae,** and **new wave**.

- o Music videos and MTV were important media for the dissemination of rock in the 1980s; other developments led the way for the emergence of rap.

- ○ *Rap*, or *hip hop*, is one of the most popular forms of African-American music; like earlier rock styles, it has crossed racial lines and been adopted by white performers.
- ○ In the 1990s and beyond, *grunge rock, alternative rock,* and *global pop* have captured the listening audience, along with numerous revivals by well-known artists and groups.
- ○ The origins of *country-western music* derive from Appalachian folk songs; through the Grand Ol'

Opry and the Nashville recording industry, this style has developed commercially into one of the most widespread genres of popular music.

- ○ The range of *global pop* styles and performers continues to grow, as music from all corners of the world is made available—some in "authentic" recordings and performances, others in a blend of contemporary and traditional styles.

The rise of rock and roll and its offspring rock is the most important music phenomenon of the past half-century. Economically, rock music has become a multibillion-dollar industry; socially, it has had a far-reaching impact on fashion, language, politics, and religion; musically, it has dominated the popular scene for some fifty years and influenced virtually every other style of music—classical, jazz, country-western, and contemporary global pop.

Rhythm and blues

Rock and roll, which first emerged in the 1950s, was born of a union of African-American rhythm and blues with country-western. *Rhythm and blues*, a genre of dance music with roots in swing jazz, was popular from the late 1940s through the early 1960s. It is a predominantly vocal genre, featuring a solo singer accompanied by a small group including piano, guitar (acoustic or electric), acoustic bass, drums, and tenor saxophone. Its harmonies and structure are clearly drawn from twelve-bar blues and thirty-two-bar pop song form (we heard these in Chapters 71–72). As the name implies, the style is characterized by a strong, driving rhythm, usually in a quadruple meter, with an emphasis on the second and fourth beats of the measure, known as

Backbeat

backbeat. Of the great early rhythm and blues performers, almost all were African-Americans—for example, Louis Jordan, Ruth Brown, Bo Diddley, and "Big" Joe Turner.

In the mid-1950s, the term "rock and roll" was coined to describe a form of rhythm and blues that crossed racial lines. White singers like Bill Haley (*Rock Around the Clock*, with the Comets, 1954), Elvis Presley (*Heartbreak Hotel* and *Hound Dog*, from 1956), and Jerry Lee Lewis (*Great Balls of Fire*, 1957) combined "hillbilly" country

Rockabilly

music with the sounds of rhythm and blues. This style became known as *rockabilly*, which featured twelve-bar blues progressions and boogie rhythms (in triplet pat-

The irrepressible Chuck Berry, seen in three typical positions.

terns). At the same time, African-Americans like Chuck Berry (*Roll Over, Beethoven*, 1956), Fats Domino (*Blueberry Hill*, 1956), and Little Richard (*Tutti Frutti*, 1955–56) caught the attention of a white audience. The style of Little Richard clearly derived from gospel music, while Chuck Berry and Elvis Presley borrowed songs from the country-western repertory and played them with a rhythm-and-blues intensity. The new sounds of rock and roll, and the outrageous look and behavior that accompanied them, revolutionized the music industry's concept of markets, appealing to audiences across racial lines.

By the end of the 1950s many of the stars of rock and roll left the scene, and a new generation of ***teen idols*** emerged with a gentler, more lyrical style, drawing as much from Frank Sinatra as from Elvis Presley. The medium of radio furthered the crooning styles of white singers like Bobby Darin (*Splish, Splash*, 1958) and Paul Anka (*Puppy Love*, 1960). Meanwhile, black America was listening to the sound of ***soul***, a blend of gospel, pop, and rhythm and blues. Ray Charles (*I've Got a Woman*, 1954) is often considered to be the "father" of soul. Many of the top soul artists—Sam Cooke (*You Send Me*, 1958), James Brown (*Papa's Got a Brand New Bag*, 1965), and Aretha Franklin (*Respect*, 1967)—came from the American South. ***Motown*** (from Motortown, or Detroit), one of the first and most successful black-owned record labels, represented the soul sound of the industrial North. The label's many hit acts included Diana Ross and the Supremes (*Where Did Our Love Go*, 1964), Martha Reeves and the Vandellas (*Dancing in the Street*, 1964), and Smokey Robinson and the Miracles (*The Tracks of My Tears*, 1965).

In the mid-1960s, rock and roll was revitalized with the emergence of new groups, notably the Beach Boys in the United States, the Beatles, and the Rolling Stones in Britain. It was the Beatles, inspired by Motown and rock and roll, who provided direction amid a variety of styles. In 1964, this group from Liverpool, England, took America by storm, performing on television's highly popular *Ed Sullivan Show*. That year the Beatles also starred in a hit movie (*A Hard Day's Night*) and held the top five spots on the *Billboard* chart with *Can't Buy Me Love, Twist and Shout, She Loves You, I Want to Hold Your Hand*, and *Please Please Me*. This foursome—Paul McCartney on electric bass, George Harrison on lead guitar, John Lennon on rhythm guitar and harmonica, and Ringo Starr on drums—had a tight ensemble sound, featuring a strong backbeat and jangling guitars. John, Paul, and George had a distinctive vocal sound as well, singing unison and two- and three-part vocals in a high range, occasionally falsetto.

The Beatles' success was largely due to their creative experiments with other types of music. With Paul McCartney's lyrical ballad *Yesterday* (1965), the Beatles combined pop songwriting with a string quartet; and their albums *Rubber Soul* (1965) and *Revolver* (1966) introduced a new style, with poetic lyrics, complex harmonies, and sophisticated recording techniques. George Harrison took up the Indian sitar for the 1965 song *Norwegian Wood*, helping to spark a surge of interest in non-Western music in the pop marketplace. With these new sounds, the old rock and roll was gone, and the more complex style known as ***rock*** emerged.

In 1966, the Beatles retired from live performance and dedicated themselves to mastering the recording studio. The albums *Sgt. Pepper's Lonely Hearts Club Band* (1967) and *Abbey Road* (1969) were both stunning musical achievements that showcased their various songwriting abilities. Notable among the selections on these albums are John Lennon's *A Day in the Life*, Paul McCartney's *When I'm Sixty-Four*, and George Harrison's *Here Comes the Sun*. In 1970, the group broke up, its members

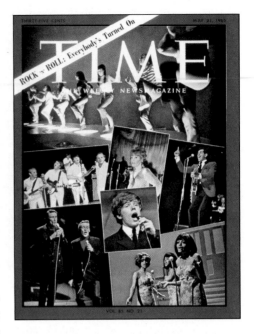

Cover of *Time* magazine (May 21, 1965), featuring rock and roll stars (top) the Shindig Dancers; (middle row) the Beach Boys, Petula Clark, Trini Lopez; (bottom row) the Righteous Brothers, Herman of Herman's Hermits, and the Supremes, with Diana Ross.

The Beatles

Rock

The Beatles (Paul, Ringo, John, George) on stage in November 1963.

going on to establish successful solo careers. John Lennon was shot and killed in 1980, and George Harrison died of cancer in 2001, cutting short their creative lives.

Meanwhile, the success of the Beatles in America had sparked a British invasion of rock groups—Herman's Hermits (*Mrs. Brown, You've Got a Lovely Daughter*, 1964), the Animals (*The House of the Rising Sun*, 1964), and especially the Rolling Stones (*Satisfaction*, 1965). Drawing from the American blues style of Muddy Waters, the Stones became the "bad boys" of rock: their lyrics, most by Mick Jagger, and their public behavior condoned sexual freedom, drugs, and violence. Sexual innuendo (*Let's Spend the Night Together*) and tales of violence (*Gimme Shelter*) are subjects typical of their songs. Despite the negative image they acquired, the Rolling Stones opened the path for styles that would emerge in the 1970s and 1980s, such as punk rock and heavy metal.

The Beach Boys

America's answer to this British invasion was to be found in a new generation of California bands. The Beach Boys (*God Only Knows* and *Good Vibrations*, both 1966), led by Brian Wilson, introduced new harmonic and melodic possibilities to rock songwriting and raised the standard for studio production. Another important California group was the Byrds, whose music combined the folk style of protest singers Bob Dylan and Joan Baez with the new sounds of rock, thereby creating *folk rock*. Their first release was their biggest hit: *Mr. Tambourine Man* (1965), a rock setting of words and music by Bob Dylan. Inspired by the success of this folk-rock hybrid, Bob Dylan introduced his own electric rock group at the 1965 Newport (Rhode Island) Folk Festival to the boos and catcalls of folk music purists. The fusion of folk protest songs with rock music proved to be a potent element in a growing political movement concerned with free speech, civil rights, and America's involvement in the Vietnam War (1957–75).

Acid rock

American rock maintained its rebellious image with *acid rock* (or *psychedelic rock*)—a style that focused on drugs, instrumental improvisations, and new sound technologies. The music represented a counter-cultural movement, with Utopian ideals, based in the Haight-Asbury district of San Francisco. The Jefferson Airplane (*White Rabbit*, 1967), featuring female lead singer Grace Slick, made no pretense about their politically and socially radical lyrics, and the Grateful Dead, with lead guitarist Jerry Garcia, performed lengthy improvisational "jams" enhanced by elaborate lighting and sound effects.

The culminating event for rock music of the 1960s was the Woodstock Festival, held in upstate New York in August 1969, where over 300,000 music fans gathered for four days of "peace, love, and brotherhood." Important performances were given by The Who (*My Generation*), Sly and the Family Stone (*I Want to Take*

The Grateful Dead, with guitarist and pop culture idol Jerry Garcia, at RFK Stadium, in Washington, DC, in a 1993 concert.

You Higher), Crosby, Stills, Nash and Young (*Suite: Judy Blue Eyes*), Jimi Hendrix (debuting his psychedelic rendition of *The Star-Spangled Banner*), Richie Havens (singing the spiritual *Motherless Child*), and a young group called Santana *(Soul Sacrifice)*. Other performers included the North Indian sitarist Ravi Shankar, raspy-voiced blues singer Janis Joplin (*Piece of My Heart*), and folk singers Joan Baez (*We Shall Overcome*) and Arlo Guthrie (*Comin' into Los Angeles*).

Woodstock

In 1970–71, the music world was shaken by the alcohol- and drug-related deaths of three superstars: the brilliantly innovative guitarist Jimi Hendrix, the soulful Janis Joplin, and the brooding lead singer of the Doors, Jim Morrison. Each was only twenty-seven years old. Acid rock seemed destined to become a short-lived style, but the Grateful Dead remained one of the world's top-grossing concert acts until the death of Garcia in 1995. The British group Pink Floyd has also exhibited great longevity: their 1973 album *Dark Side of the Moon*, with its ageless themes of madness and death, remained on the Top-200 charts for a record 751 weeks. Their operatic, two-album concept-piece, *The Wall* (1980), ensured them a place in the annals of rock. Both Pink Floyd and the Grateful Dead helped to spawn a new generation of improvisational **jam bands** and psychedelic **trance music** in the 1990s.

The legendary guitarist/ singer Jimi Hendrix at the Woodstock Festival (1969), flashing a peace sign to the audience.

Jam bands and trance music

The Eclecticism of the 1970s

Eclectic styles of rock were developing in the early 1970s that furthered the artistic ambitions found in acid rock. **Art rock** (sometimes called **progressive rock**), which used large forms, complex harmonies, and occasional quotations from classical music, was largely a British style, pioneered by the Moody Blues with their 1968 album *Days of Future Passed*, recorded with the London Symphony Orchestra. The Who experimented with rock's narrative possibilities, and the result was the first rock opera, *Tommy*, written by Peter Townshend and premiered in 1969. Three years later, keyboardist Keith Emerson, together with Greg Lake and Carl Palmer (the group became known as Emerson, Lake, and Palmer), produced an art rock piece based on the Russian composer Musorgsky's well-known suite—*Pictures at an Exhibition*. One American who experimented with art rock's large forms was Frank Zappa (1940–1993). Zappa, who counted the composers Bartók and Varèse among his influences, invited listeners to dissect his music: "These things are so carefully constructed that it breaks my heart when people don't dig into them and see all the levels that I put into them."

Art rock

Jazz was also an important influence on rock in the '70s. The Californian group Santana started out as an electric blues-rock band to which Carlos Santana, the son of a Mexican mariachi musician, fused the Latin jazz of artists like Tito Puente. The resulting style, called **Latin rock**, electrified the audience at Woodstock. Santana's unique sound came from their use of Latin and African percussion instruments— conga drums (of Afro-Cuban origin, played with bare hands), maracas (Latin-American rattles), and timbales (small kettledrums of Cuban origin)—their tight, Latin-style polyrhythms, and Carlos Santana's distinctive, and much-imitated, guitar tone. His band enjoyed international popularity in the early 1970s with hit songs such as *Evil Ways* (1969) and *Oyé Como Va* (1970). In 1999, with a new lineup of

Latin rock

> *When I'm onstage, I feel this incredible, almost spiritual experience . . . lost in a naturally induced high. Those great rock-'n'-roll experiences are getting harder and harder to come by, because they have to transcend a lot of drug-induced stupor. But when they occur, they are sacred.*
> —PETER TOWNSHEND

IN HIS OWN WORDS

band members, Santana capitalized on the resurgence in popularity of Latin rock; his album *Supernatural* won the Grammy for Record of the Year, Album of the Year, and Song of the Year (*Smooth*, with Rob Thomas).

The 1970s and 1980s saw the fragmentation of rock into many musical subgenres, and a continual procession of new groups. West Coast rock had a relaxed sound that evoked California, represented by groups like the Eagles (*Hotel California*, 1972) and the Doobie Brothers (*Listen to the Music*, 1972). The British invaded once again, **Heavy metal** this time with *heavy metal*, featuring exaggerated displays of virtuosity in the form of loud, distorted instrumental solos. Heavy metal, like art rock, was influenced by Western classical composers such as Mahler and Wagner but differed in its use of gothic, pagan, and satanic imagery. Led Zeppelin (*Stairway to Heaven*, 1971) and Black Sabbath (*Paranoid*, 1970) were among the most influential heavy metal bands **Glam rock** of the 1970s. *Glam rock* (also known as *glitter rock*) was a showy, theatrical style of performance, represented by Britain's outrageous David Bowie (*The Rise and Fall of Ziggy Stardust and the Spiders from Mars*, 1972), Lou Reed (*Walk on the Wild Side*, 1972), formerly of the New York band the Velvet Underground and the American band KISS, known for their trademark face paint (*Alive!* 1975). The outlandish costumes of glitter rock were quickly adopted by mainstream artists like the talented pianist Elton John (*Bennie and the Jets*, 1973; see illustration, p. 409).

Punk rock The ultimate rebellion came in the form of *punk rock*, a return to the basics of rock and roll—simple, repetitive, and loud—coupled with offensive lyrics and shocking behavior. The Ramones (*Blitzkrieg Bop*, 1976), a group from New York with a street-tough attitude and an arsenal of two-minute songs that were fast yet melodic, were the first punk group to make an impact. After touring England in 1976, they inspired many imitators, including the politically radical Sex Pistols (*Anarchy in the U.K.* and *God Save the Queen*, both from 1977), featuring lead singer Johnny Rotten. Other politically conscious groups soon followed, like the Clash, who focused their music on the central issues of the punk rebellion: unemployment (*Career Opportunities*), fascism (*Guns of Brixton*), racism (*White Riot*), and police brutality (*Police and Thieves*). The last work is a *cover* (a recording that remakes an earlier recording by another singer or group) of a reggae hit.

Other reactions to the difficult times of the 1970s included the commercial dance music known as *disco*, and *reggae*. Fostered in gay dance clubs, disco was characterized by repetitive lyrics, often sung in a high range, and a thumping, mechanical beat, exemplified by acts such as the Bee Gees (*Stayin' Alive*, 1977). Reggae is a Jamaican style with offbeat rhythms and chanted vocals that reflected the beliefs of a religious movement known as Rastafarianism (see CP 20). Representative reggae groups included Bob Marley and the Wailers (*Rastaman Vibrations*, 1977) and Black Uhuru. A new form of *soft rock*, yet another reaction to heavy metal and punk rock, was epitomized by artists such as the Carpenters (*We've Only Just Begun*, 1970) and Olivia Newton-John (*I Honestly Love You*, 1975), among others.

New wave *New wave*, a commercially accessible offshoot of punk rock, has been popular among British and American groups since the late 1970s. In Britain, the new wave scene was home to Elvis Costello (with the Attractions in *This Year's Model*, 1978) and the Police, with lead singer/bassist Sting (*Roxanne*, 1978; *Every Breath You Take*, 1986). The New York City scene developed around a number of clubs in lower Manhattan, most notably CBGB's (Country, Blue Grass, and Blues), where the group Blondie debuted in 1975. Featuring the attractive blond singer Deborah Harry, the group achieved commercial success with its album *Parallel Lines* (1978) and later turned to disco (*Heart of Glass*, 1980) and reggae styles (*The Tide Is High*, 1980). Arguably, America's most influential new wave group was the Talking Heads (*Psycho Killer*, 1977;

IN HIS OWN WORDS

I don't see any point in going on and playing dissonant music straight away because it will just turn people off. You can seduce an audience slowly . . . you just have to chip away at what their concept of music is.

—STING

Burning Down the House, 1983) who, like Blondie and the Ramones, played at CBGB's and whose lyrics (by singer-songwriter David Byrne) expressed the alienation and social consciousness of punk rock; their style embraced various world musics as well.

The 1980s and Beyond

"Music allowed me to eat. But it also allowed me to express myself. I played because I had to play. I rid myself of bad dreams and rotten memories."

—PRINCE

Madonna at Wembley Stadium, London, performing during her Blonde Ambition tour, 1990.

The single most important development in the 1980s was the music video. Now, instead of the radio, the visual medium (and especially MTV, or Music Television, which premiered in August 1981) was the principal means of presenting the latest music to the public. New and colorful performers came on the scene, and an image- and fashion-conscious aesthetic soon dominated rock. One giant in the video arena was Michael Jackson, who had gained early fame as lead singer of the Jackson Five (a group of brothers who had four number-one hits for Motown in 1969–70) and who then became a superstar in the 1980s. Jackson's album *Thriller* (1982–83) broke all previous sales figures; its hit songs included *The Girl Is Mine* (sung with Paul McCartney), *Billie Jean*, and *Beat It* (Jackson's version of the rumble scene from Bernstein's *West Side Story*). Jackson's trend-setting dance style, together with his talent as a ballad singer, helped to make him a worldwide celebrity. Other superstars of the 1980s include Bruce Springsteen (*Born in the USA*, 1984), Prince (*Purple Rain*, 1984), and Madonna, who launched her first big hit with *Like a Virgin* (1984), which she followed with the eclectic album *True Blue* (1986). She has achieved great success based not only on her carefully developed image as a sex object, but also her versatile sound and her ability to anticipate and set trends.

Music video

Michael Jackson

The 1980s saw many stars contributing their energies to social causes. The Irish group U2 sounded a unified voice of political activism and personal spirituality in their collection *The Unforgettable Fire* (1984). Following a series of concerts for Live Aid and Amnesty International, the group achieved stardom with the 1987 Grammy-winning album *The Joshua Tree*, which included two major hits: *With or Without You* and *I Still Haven't Found What I'm Looking For*. U2 continues to represent the social conscience of rock, with lead singer Bono actively working with international politicians on global causes such as debt relief and AIDS.

Rap and hip hop

The technological developments of the late 1970s and early 1980s paved the way for **rap**. This highly rhythmic style of musical patter emerged in New York during the 1970s as part of a cultural movement known as **hip hop**. The typical rap group consists of a DJ (disc jockey), who uses turntables to mix prerecorded sounds and beats, and MCs (master of ceremonies), who rhythmically rhyme over the DJs musical backdrop. The group Run DMC (*Raising Hell*, 1986) was largely responsible for the commercialization of rap; their collaboration with Aerosmith, covering the 1974 hit song *Walk This Way*, introduced the style to mainstream white audiences. Public Enemy, a politically oriented group from Long Island, New York, produced several highly influential rap albums (*It Takes a Nation of Millions to Hold Us Back*, 1988), and female rapper Queen Latifah made a strong case against the genre's frequent female bashing in *All Hail the Queen* (1989; see CP 13).

IN HIS OWN WORDS

If you're really a rapper, you can't stop rapping. . . . The album [The Return of the Real, 1996] is based around the words, not as much the music . . . it's based on the contexts and theories of life. . . . If you never get into the life, you wouldn't understand what I'm rapping about.

—ICE-T.

From left: Prakazrel "Pras" Michel, Wyclef Jean, and Lauryn Hill, members of U.S. hip-hop band The Fugees, perform on stage during a concert at the Hallenstadion in Zurich, Switzerland (2005).

Rap in its diversified forms has continued as one of the most popular types of African-American music and has been successfully adapted by white performers such as the Beastie Boys and Eminem. *Gangsta rap* of the 1990s has further disseminated the style through graphic descriptions of inner-city realities. This style was pioneered by the Compton, California, group N.W.A. (Nigga3 with Attitude), whose 1991 album *Efil4zaggin* ("Niggaz 4 Life" spelled backward) hit the top of the charts. Former N.W.A. member Ice Cube and fellow Compton rappers Snoop Doggy Dogg (*Doggystyle*, 1993) and Ice-T (*O.G.–Original Gangster*, 1991) have all made a successful transition from gangsta rap to film and television acting.

Hip-hop culture has become the "alternative" lifestyle of choice for many young people, urban and suburban. The riveting rhythms of hip hop have transcended racial boundaries; its sounds, slang, and fashions are now commonly featured on prime-time television, in movies, and in advertising.

The more mellow sounds of soul and rhythm and blues have changed with the times but are still extremely popular. The 1990s saw the rise of "divas," like Whitney Houston (*I Will Always Love You*, from the movie *The Bodyguard*, 1992) and Mariah Carey (*Daydreams*, 1995), both of whom utilize a heavily melismatic singing style, which has come to represent the new R & B (rhythm and blues) sound. Today, collaboration and "crossover" between the stars of hip hop and R & B has become one of the most marketable pop styles.

Hip-hop culture

The late 1980s and early 1990s also witnessed the success of a Seattle-based hybrid of punk and 1970s metal known as *grunge rock* (so-called after the unkempt appearance of the groups). Popular groups to come out of the grunge scene were Soundgarden, Nirvana, and Pearl Jam. Pearl Jam's *Ten* and Nirvana's *Nevermind* (both from 1991) were huge hits, tapping into a young audience looking for passion and authenticity in a world of slick, theatrical acts. In 1994, when Nirvana was at the height of its popularity, guitarist-songwriter Kurt Cobain committed suicide; his untimely death at twenty-seven—the same age that signaled the end for Jimi Hendrix, Janis Joplin, and Jim Morrison—turned their last album, *Unplugged in New York* (1994), into a chart-topping requiem.

Kurt Cobain of Nirvana, performing at the Reading Festival (England), 1992.

The "alternative" rock of the late 1990s exhibits a surprising breadth of styles. Beck (*Odelay*, 1996) combined 1990s hip hop, 1960s soul, 1930s country music, and even a bit of Schubert's *Unfinished* Symphony to create a fresh and futuristic sound. The Icelandic singer Björk (*Post*, 1995) has also been extremely innovative, moving from punk to jazz to electronic dance music to an elaborately conceived and arranged album consisting entirely of vocals (*Medulla*, 2005). Her other accomplishments include Best Actress honors at the Cannes Film Festival in 2000 for her role in the musical film *Dancer in the Dark*, for which she also composed the soundtrack.

As we enter the twenty-first century, we find successful women in all genres of popular music. Confessional piano-playing singers-songwriters like Tori Amos (*Under the Pink*, 1994) and Fiona Apple (*When the Pawn . . .* 1999) have garnered much critical praise for their complex compositions and introspective lyrics.

Neo-folk singers like Ani DiFranco (*Up Up Up Up Up Up*, 1999) have helped to redefine the role of the female "folk" singer. Women have brought new ideas to punk, ranging from the catchy pop-punk of Avril Lavigne (top-ten singles *Complicated* and *Sk8er Boi*, 2002) to the powerful social commentary of Sleater-Kinney (*The Woods*, 2005). The country pop group the Dixie Chicks broke into the mainstream with their number-one album *Fly* (2000). Even in the male-dominated world of rap, female artists like Missy "Misdemeanor" Elliot and Li'l Kim have claimed their share of the pop audience.

Recent years have seen a number of significant revivals as well. The Eagles regrouped for their "first farewell tour" (and for their induction into the Rock and Roll Hall of Fame). The Rolling Stones also continue to make successful tours (including a performance during halftime of Superbowl XL, January 2006). England's Elton John has matured from his glitter rock days of the 1970s, writing memorable songs for Broadway and Hollywood. American songwriter Bob Dylan has made a comeback as well, as a Kennedy Center honoree in the arts and compiler of a best-selling album, *Time Out Of Mind* (1997).

Today, older musical styles are being updated for twenty-first-century audiences. At the forefront is a melodic style of pop punk, represented by the northern California band Green Day (*American Idiot*, 2004), and the ska-influenced southern California group No Doubt (*Return of Saturn*, 2000), with their charismatic lead singer Gwen Stefani. Other groups are mining even more venerable strains of American music. For example, the White Stripes (*Get Behind Me Satan*, 2005) is a drum and guitar duo that plays raw electric blues and country music evoking the 1930s and 1940s, and Alicia Keys (*Songs in A Minor*, 2001) is a Grammy-winning singer-keyboardist who reinterprets the 1960s soul style of Aretha Franklin.

This overview of rock has highlighted a mere handful of groups and individuals whose influence is difficult to challenge. Rock is unquestionably here to stay, but popularity in this genre is fleeting; only time will tell which current artists and styles will be remembered tomorrow.

(Left) Singer Tori Amos in London, at the Hammersmith Apollo (2003),

(Right) The outrageous Elton John, performing at the Universal Amphitheater in Los Angeles, 1986.

Country-Western Music

"When people hear that [country] music, they get a feeling that they belong to the music and the music belongs to them."

—COUSIN MINNIE PEARL

Hillbilly music

The music known today as ***country-western*** has its origins in the mountains of Appalachia. Although the songs of this region had been studied as folklore for some years, the recording industry did not discover this wellspring of traditional music until the 1920s. Labeled ***hillbilly music***, these recordings became the Anglo-American counterpart to the "race records" that introduced the world to African-American blues. Two of the most important early acts were the Carter Family, known for their close harmonies and distinctive guitar style, and Jimmie Rodgers, who helped popularize the "blue yodel" and the steel guitar in popular music. Hollywood picked up on this rural sound and began producing movies featuring singing cowboys like Gene Autry (*Tumblin' Tumbleweeds*, 1936). Meanwhile, radio station WSM in Nashville, Tennessee, began broadcasting a weekly music showcase called *The Grand Ol' Opry*, which introduced many new acts to a national audience. One of the styles that debuted on *The Grand Ol' Opry* was ***bluegrass***, featuring traditional folk melodies played at quick tempos with improvised instrumental solos and high vocal harmonies. Bluegrass was largely the invention of the Monroe brothers, followed by influential instrumentalists such as Lester Flatt (guitar) and Earl Scruggs (banjo). Typically, bluegrass is played by an acoustic string band consisting of violin, mandolin, guitar, five-string banjo, and double bass, with some players also performing vocals. The professionalism that radio performances brought to country music also resulted in a highly polished ***Nashville sound***, with top-notch studio musicians backing singers like Patsy Cline (*Walkin' after Midnight*, 1957).

Country music legends June and Johnny Cash onstage in 1987.

By the 1950s, this folk-derived music had been electrified, creating a sound called ***honkytonk***, exemplified by Hank Williams (*Lovesick Blues*, 1949) and closely allied to early rock and roll. In fact, country star Johnny Cash (*I Walk the Line*, 1956) recorded at Sun Studios in Memphis, the same studio that gave the world Elvis Presley and Jerry Lee Lewis. By the end of the 1950s, country music was an established genre in its own right.

Classic country

Mainstream country

Country rock

Over the next four decades, country music continued to grow and diversify. The 1960s and 1970s was a period of ***classic country*** music, with artists like Loretta Lynn (*Coal Miner's Daughter*, 1970) and Merle Haggard (*Mama Tried*, 1968) staying true to their roots in southern folk music. Other artists, like John Denver (*Country Roads*, 1971) and Glen Campbell (*Rhinestone Cowboy*, 1973), tried for a more ***mainstream country*** sound, and some, like the Allman Brothers (*Ramblin' Man*, 1971), experimented with the guitar-driven sounds of ***country rock***. During the 1980s, the audience for country music increased even more, attracted to performers such as Dolly Parton (*9 to 5*, 1980) and Willie Nelson (*On the Road Again*, 1980), both of whom combined a traditional country sound with pop songwriting. Their success helped pave the way for the country music boom in the 1990s, featuring the very popular Garth Brooks (*No Fences*, 1990) and Shania Twain (*The Woman in Me*, 1995), among others. This genre, which began as humble folk music in the rural American South, is now a huge entertainment industry that is as popular in urban centers as in rural areas.

Global Pop

Today's most eclectic musical movement brings a new global perspective to the listener. Not really a single style, this movement promotes popular music of the third world, ethnic and traditional music from all regions, and collaborations between Western and non-Western musicians. **Global pop** has been around for some time. In the 1950s, television fans heard Afro-Cuban music—including mambos and rhumbas—played by Desi Arnaz on the sitcom *I Love Lucy* and enjoyed Harry Belafonte's vocal calypsos, a mixture of Jamaican and American styles. In the 1960s, the Brazilian bossa nova found favor (*The Girl from Ipanema*), and Ravi Shankar, along with the Beatles, brought Indian sitar music to the West. One style of global pop now enjoying widespread popularity is Cajun music.

BEAUSOLEIL AND THE REVIVAL OF CAJUN MUSIC

"When I was growing up, the word Cajun was never used. People finally started to become a little more proud of their culture. Even if you weren't as educated as a Philadelphia lawyer, you had something to offer, to give—a way of life."

—MICHAEL DOUCET

The varied music culture of Southwestern Louisiana developed from two distinct groups—Creoles (people of mixed French, Spanish, and African or Afro-Caribbean descent) and Cajuns (French colonists from the Canadian province of Nova Scotia who were exiled by the British; the word "Cajun" derives from Acadia, the former name of the Canadian region). These peoples shared French as a common language, and their musics evolved side by side. Cajuns absorbed the music of southern whites and blacks into their sound, and the fiddle, which often accompanied itself with a drone, became a central feature in their music. The guitar (a Spanish influence), the triangle (a French influence), and the accordion (introduced by German Jewish exiles) also contributed to the unique sound. The first Cajun recording was made in 1928; a year later, two musicians—Cajun fiddler Dennis McGee and Creole accordionist Amédé Ardoin—recorded the first merger of Cajun and Creole styles. The accordion also became the core of the Creole **zydeco** band. (The word *zydeco* is a phonetic spelling of *les haricots*, French for green beans.) This style arose in mid-century as a blend of African-American, Caribbean, and Cajun styles; the typical zydeco ensemble uses voice, fiddle, accordion, electric guitar, and washboard. Although some purists have tried to keep the two styles—Cajun and Creole—distinct, new generations of musicians have bridged the gap.

Both Cajun and zydeco music enjoyed widespread popularity during the late twentieth century. The Cajun group BeauSoleil and its leader Michael Doucet have been a strong force in the revival of this traditional music. BeauSoleil's first performance outside of Louisiana was in 1976, at Wolf Trap Peforming Arts Center in northern Virginia, where they played to a sold-out crowd. In 1984, they recorded the landmark album *Parlez nous à boire (Let's Talk about Drinking)*, which launched them to international fame. Since then, the group has played at New York's Carnegie Hall, been highlighted on Garrison Keillor's popular radio show *A Prairie*

IN HIS OWN WORDS

I won't play a song until I know every note and every word. Yes sir! Like that you can defend yourself, you don't stumble. You don't sing off time, either. . . . Like reading, you can hit each word right on the drummer's timing. Each time he'll hit, your word will fall right in line. That's music!

—ROY FUSILIER

Fiddle player Michael Doucet in a performance with the Cajun band BeauSoleil.

Home Companion, been nominated for several Grammy awards, and been featured in the soundtrack for the film *The Big Easy* (1987).

Think of Me (Jongle à moi) is a traditional dance song first recorded in the 1930s by the Cajun fiddler Jean-Baptiste Fuselier. BeauSoleil's performance features violin, accordion, and vocals, accompanied by guitar, drums, bass, and washboard. The tune spins out in eight-bar phrases followed by a turn, or bridge, of another eight bars. The fiddle and accordion vie throughout for the tune. Listen for some of the typical Cajun **Fiddle techniques** fiddle techniques, including *drones* (playing a sustained tone on one string and the tune on another), *double-stops* (playing two strings at once to produce a chord), *slides* (moving from one pitch to another by sliding the finger on the string while bowing), and *trills* (creating an ornament by quickly alternating between the main note and one directly above or below it). This is a toe-tapping dance music, quick-paced and rhythmic, with a highly syncopated melody that immediately draws in the listener. The texture is at times heterophonic, with various instruments elaborating on the bouncy tune. The text, in Cajun French (based on the northern French dialect spoken by the original Canadian settlers), has interjections that cannot be translated into English (for example, *yé yaille*; see Listening Guide 50).

Listening Guide 50

eLG   **4 (96–99)**
8 (66–69)

Think of Me (Jongle à moi), by BeauSoleil   (3:14)

FORM:	Tune built on 8-bar phrases (verse and bridge); alternation of vocal and instrumental verse
METER:	4/4
TEXTURE:	Heterophonic
BASIS:	Traditional Cajun fiddle tune, recorded in 1930s, by J. B. Fuselier
INSTRUMENTS:	Fiddle, guitar, accordion, washboard, drums, bass, vocals

WHAT TO LISTEN FOR:
- Rousing dance tune, with syncopated rhythms and wide-ranging instrumental lines.
- Typical Cajun fiddle (violin) techniques (drones, double-stops, slides, and trills).
- Unique timbre of accordion, blending with fiddle and guitar.
- Instrumental and vocal embellishments of tune.
- Text sung in Cajun French, with interjections (*yé yaille*).
- Regular structure, with 8-measure phrases, repeated and varied; a bridge (or *turn*) alternates with main tune.

96   0:00   Fiddle, with lively tune (8 bars), then varied (8 bars), accompanied by ensemble (accordion, guitar, and rhythm); opening 4 bars shown, with repeated notes and syncopations:

0:20   Accordion with syncopated tune (8 bars, varied from violin), then repeated (8 bars), accompanied by fiddle and ensemble; opening 4 bars:

97 0:39   Verse 1 (8+8 bars), with rhythm accompaniment; opening verse:

O mais,   o   o   o   yé   yail - le,   Quoi   faire   t'es   comme   ça?____

TEXT	TRANSLATION
O mais, o, yé yaille,	Oh, but oh, yé yaille,
Quoi faire t'es comme ça?	Why are you like that?
Jongle á moi, catin, bébé,	Think of me, darling baby,
O, une fois par jour.	At least once a day.
Yé, yé, yé, bébé,	Yé, yé, yé, bébé,
Tu connais que moi je t'appelais	You know that I called for you
Tous les samedis soir, catin,	Every Saturday night, darling,
Jongle á moi pendant la journée.	Think of me during the day.

0:59   Fiddle, with double-stops in rhythmic idea; guitar playing running bass line (8+8 bars).

98 1:17   Break in music, then bridge (turn) played twice (8+8 bars); begins in high range in fiddle, then descends and becomes disjunct; second time accompanied by cymbals; opening of bridge:

1:37   Fiddle, with tune and variation (8+8 bars).

1:56   Break in music; fiddle, with bridge; repeated with slides between notes in fiddle.

99 2:15   Verse 2, slightly varied from verse 1; with rhythmic accompaniment; opening of verse 2:

O____ O   O,   yé   yail - le,_____   Quoi   faire   t'es   comme   ça?____

TEXT	TRANSLATION
O mais, o, yé yaille,	Oh, but oh yé yaille,
Quoi faire t'es comme ça?	Why are you like that?
Jongle á moi, catin, bébé,	Think of me, darling baby,
O, une fois par jour.	At least once a day.
Yé, yé, yé, bébé,	Yé, yé, yé, baby,
Tu connais que moi je t'aimais	You know that I love you
Jongle á moi, catin, bébé,	Think of me, darling baby,
Jongle á moi pendant la journées.	Every night and every day.

2:34   Fiddle, with bridge in double-stops, sliding between notes repeated in high range, with scoops into notes (8+8 bars).

2:53   Break filled-in by guitar, leading to fiddle, with bridge; played twice, with slides, scoops, and trills.

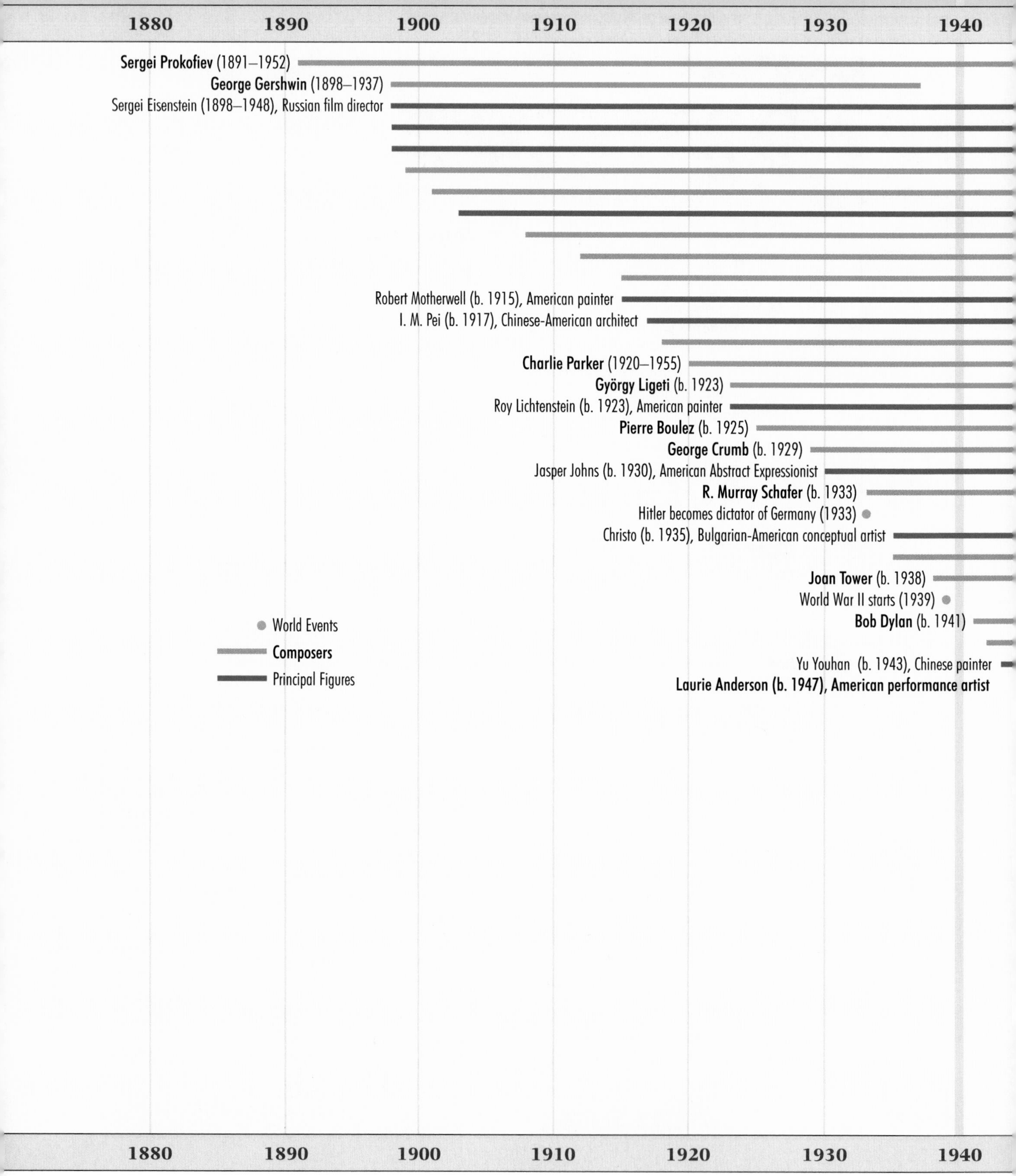
1880
1890
1900
1910
1920
1930
1940
Sergei Prokofiev (1891–1952)
George Gershwin (1898–1937)
Sergei Eisenstein (1898–1948), Russian film director
Robert Motherwell (b. 1915), American painter
I. M. Pei (b. 1917), Chinese-American architect
Charlie Parker (1920–1955)
György Ligeti (b. 1923)
Roy Lichtenstein (b. 1923), American painter
Pierre Boulez (b. 1925)
George Crumb (b. 1929)
Jasper Johns (b. 1930), American Abstract Expressionist
R. Murray Schafer (b. 1933)
Hitler becomes dictator of Germany (1933)
Christo (b. 1935), Bulgarian-American conceptual artist
Joan Tower (b. 1938)
World War II starts (1939)
Bob Dylan (b. 1941)
Yu Youhan (b. 1943), Chinese painter
Laurie Anderson (b. 1947), American performance artist
World Events
Composers
Principal Figures
1880
1890
1900
1910
1920
1930
1940

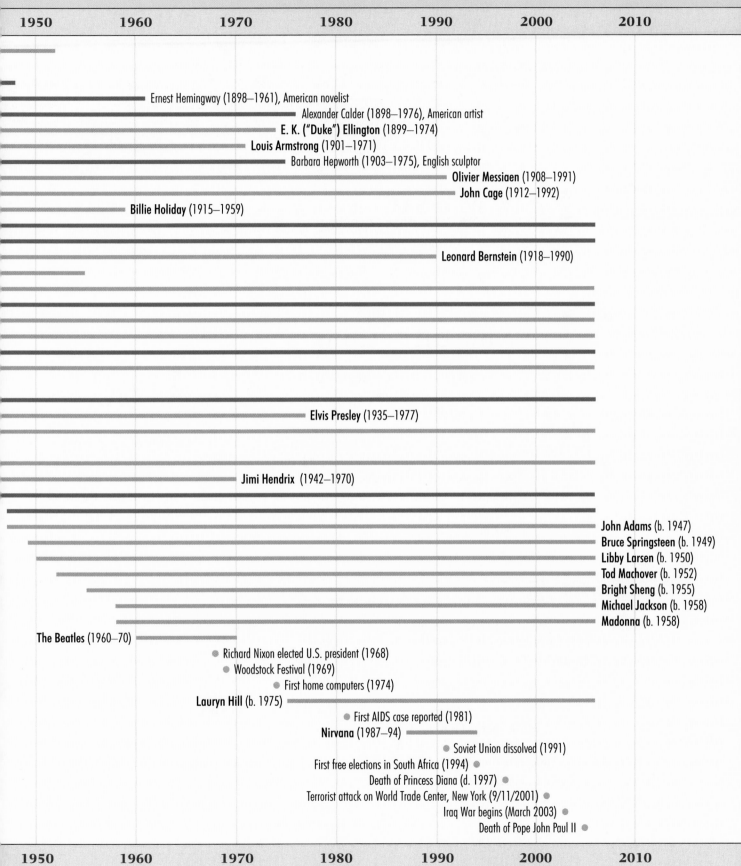

Later Twentieth Century and Beyond

| 1950 | 1960 | 1970 | 1980 | 1990 | 2000 | 2010 |

Ernest Hemingway (1898–1961), American novelist
Alexander Calder (1898–1976), American artist
E. K. ("Duke") Ellington (1899–1974)
Louis Armstrong (1901–1971)
Barbara Hepworth (1903–1975), English sculptor
Olivier Messiaen (1908–1991)
John Cage (1912–1992)
Billie Holiday (1915–1959)

Leonard Bernstein (1918–1990)

Elvis Presley (1935–1977)

Jimi Hendrix (1942–1970)

John Adams (b. 1947)
Bruce Springsteen (b. 1949)
Libby Larsen (b. 1950)
Tod Machover (b. 1952)
Bright Sheng (b. 1955)
Michael Jackson (b. 1958)
Madonna (b. 1958)

The Beatles (1960–70)
Richard Nixon elected U.S. president (1968)
Woodstock Festival (1969)
First home computers (1974)
Lauryn Hill (b. 1975)
First AIDS case reported (1981)
Nirvana (1987–94)
Soviet Union dissolved (1991)
First free elections in South Africa (1994)
Death of Princess Diana (d. 1997)
Terrorist attack on World Trade Center, New York (9/11/2001)
Iraq War begins (March 2003)
Death of Pope John Paul II

| 1950 | 1960 | 1970 | 1980 | 1990 | 2000 | 2010 |

The New Music

75

New Directions

"From Schoenberg I learned that tradition is a home we must love and forgo."

—LUKAS FOSS

The term "new music" has been used throughout history. Nearly every generation of creative musicians produced sounds and styles that had never been heard before. All the same, the innovations of the last half of the twentieth century have outstripped the most far-reaching changes of earlier times, truly justifying the label "new music." In effect, we have witnessed nothing less than the birth of a new world of sound.

| KEY POINTS | StudySpace online at www.wwnorton.com/enjoy |

- Musical trends in the later twentieth century mirrored movements in the other arts, including *abstract expressionism*, *pop art*, and *postmodernism*.

- Feminist as well as ethnic art and literature flourished.

- Modern theater and music merged into *performance art*, a multimedia genre explored by John Cage and Laurie Anderson, among others.

- Some composers moved in the direction of *total serialism*, imposing a more structured organizational system on their works, while others moved toward freer constructions (*aleatoric music*, *open form*).

- European and American composers alike responded to societal changes that occurred after World War II to produce experimental, or avant-garde, music in widely varied styles and genres.

- Canada has followed the lead of European countries—and France in particular—in establishing significant government-sponsored programs in the arts, with a goal of preserving the country's cultural heritage and promoting and disseminating the artistic products of its composers and performers (see CP 21).

The Arts since the Mid-Twentieth Century

The increasing social turmoil since the Second World War has been reflected in the arts, which passed through a period of violent experimentation with new media, new materials, and new techniques. Artists have freed themselves from every vestige of the past in order to explore new areas of thought and feeling.

A trend away from objective painting led to abstract expressionism in the United States during the 1950s and 1960s. In the canvases of painters such as Robert Motherwell and Jackson Pollock, space, mass, and color were freed from the need to imitate objects in the real world. The urge toward abstraction was felt equally in sculpture, as is evident in the work of artists such as Henry Moore and Barbara Hepworth.

At the same time, a new kind of realism appeared in the art of Jasper Johns, Robert Rauschenberg, and their colleagues, who owed some of their inspiration to the Dadaists of four decades earlier. Rauschenberg's aim, as he put it, was to work "in the gap between life and art." This trend culminated in pop art, which drew its themes and techniques from modern urban life: machines, advertisements, comic strips, movies, commercial photography, and familiar objects connected with everyday living. A similar aim motivated Andy Warhol's *Four Campbell's Soup Cans* and the comic strip art of Roy Lichtenstein (see p. 418).

Today, the term "postmodernism"—suggesting a movement away from formalism—is applied to a variety of styles, including conceptual art, minimalism, and environmental art. A familiar Neoclassical structure of the postmodern era is I. M. Pei's *Grand Louvre Pyramid*, in Paris (see p. 420), which has received much visibility in the book and movie of *The Da Vinci Code* (2006). Environmental art, sometimes called earthworks, is one manifestation of the minimalist movement, which advocates a bareness and simplicity (we will read about minimalism in music in Chapter 80). Bulgarian artist Christo, in collaboration with his wife

Three Standing Forms (1964), by English sculptor **Barbara Hepworth** (1903–1975), is an abstraction representing the relationship between nature and humankind.

Postmodernism

In abstract expressionism, space and mass become independent values, liberated from the need to express reality. *Elegy to the Spanish Republic No. 18,* by **Robert Motherwell** (1915–1991).

The German Reichstag (Parliament Building) in Berlin was wrapped in a silvery fabric by conceptual artist **Christo** (b. 1935) and **Jeanne-Claude** (b. 1935). The project, focused on the German symbol of democracy, took twenty-four years to accomplish.

Jeanne-Claude (both use their first names only), exploit installation art as a new way to view old landscapes and to draw attention to form through concealment. In 1995, they completed the wrapping of the German Parliament building (Reichstag; see above), a project for which the artists used over a million feet of fabric covered in aluminum and some 50,000 feet of blue cord to cover the structure.

Feminist and ethnic art

The feminist movement has affected mainstream developments in the art world since the late 1960s by focusing attention on issues of gender. Collaborative projects led by Judy Chicago have contributed much to this movement: an example is the celebrated artwork *The Dinner Party* (1979), a triangular table with thirty-nine place settings, which pays homage to important women throughout history. Serious attention has also been paid to global crosscurrents in the arts as well as to the artistic achievements of America's diverse ethnic communities, especially the African-American, Latino, and Native American communities. Faith Ringgold, one of the leading African-American artists today, is known for her "story quilts" that feature narrative paintings with quilted borders. Her recent *Jazz Series* depicts black musicians and life in the 1920s and '30s (see p. 417).

A national art of *perestroika* (openness) has arisen in countries of the former Soviet Union, and a nationalist style has developed in China as well; the canvases of Yu Youhan, for example, combine elements of pop art and the ancient Chinese art of block printing. In *Mao and Blonde Girl Analyzed* (1992; p. 418), the blonde girl, symbolic of involuntary Westernization, is juxtaposed with a portrait of the Chinese leader.

In the field of literature, poetry has lent itself to the most widespread experimentation. Many poets face the contemporary world with a profound sense

Feminist artist **Judy Chicago**'s *Holocaust Project Logo: From Darkness into Light* (stained glass, 1992).

African-American artist **Faith Ringgold** (b. 1930) celebrates the music of Charlie Parker and Dizzy Gillespie in *Groovin High* (1986), portraying couples dancing at the Savoy Ballroom in Harlem. Acrylic on canvas, tied-dyed, with fabric border.

of alienation. Modern American verse ranges from complex intellectualism to the Whitmanesque exuberance of the "beat generation," all using a great variety of forms. The poetry and literature of various cultural groups has received widespread attention. Among these, African-American poet Maya Angelou, West Indian Derek Walcott, Chinese dissident playwright Gao Xingjian, and Trinidad-born British writer V. S. Naipaul have received Nobel Prizes in literature.

Since drama and the novel are by their very natures based on an imitation of life, they have not remained indifferent to the new trends. The theater moved away from the social and psychological concerns that permeated the plays of Arthur Miller (such as *The Crucible*, 1953) and Tennessee Williams (*Cat on a Hot Tin Roof*, 1955) in the 1950s, turning instead to the "theater of the absurd," whose leading European proponents—Samuel Beckett (*Waiting for Godot*, 1956) and Eugene Ionesco (*Rhinoceros*, 1960)—viewed the world with a vast disillusionment. The spirit of the absurd also penetrated the novel; witness such works as *Catch 22* (1961), by Joseph Heller, and *Slaughterhouse Five* (1969), by Kurt Vonnegut, to name only two that caught the pulse of the 1960s.

Drama and the novel

More recent writers who have captured the attention of the literary world include British dramatists Tom Stoppard (*Rosencrantz and Guildenstern Are Dead*, 1967, based on two minor characters from Shakespeare's *Hamlet*) and Harold Pinter (*The French Lieutenant's Woman*, 1981), based on the novel by John Fowles; American playwright/screenwriter/actor Sam Shepard (*Buried Child*, 1978; *A Fool for Love*, 1983) and New York playwright Wendy Wasserstein (*The Heidi Chronicles*, 1989; *The Sisters Rosensweig*, 1993). Among the distinguished novelists of our time are Nobel laureates Saul Bellow (*Humboldt's Gift*, 1976) and Toni Morrison (*Beloved*, 1987) as well as Pulitzer Prize winners John Updike (*The Centaur*, 1963; the *Rabbit* tetralogy, 1960–91), Jane Smiley (*A Thousand Acres*, 1992), E. Annie Proulx (*The Shipping News*, 1994 and the short story *Brokeback Mountain*, 1997, which was recently released as a movie), and Richard Russo (*Empire Falls*, 2002). Several young novelists have recently achieved fame, including the British writer Zadie Smith, whose acclaimed *White Teeth* (2000) spawned a new literary genre called hysterical realism (featuring frenzied action, manic characters, and multiple secondary plot lines), and American writer Jonathan Franzen, whose novel *The Corrections* (2002) stirred a controversy

Recent writers

Roy Lichtenstein
(1923–1997) fully embraced popular mass culture in his comic-strip art. This work pays homage to the jazz standard *Stardust* by the American songwriter Hoagy Carmichael.

when the author questioned the value of its listing on Oprah Winfrey's Book Club list. Latin-American writers who have risen to prominence include Gabriel García Márquez, who has produced some of the great novels of our age (*One Hundred Years of Solitude*, 1967; *Love in the Time of Cholera*, 1985; and *Memoirs of My Melancholy Whores*, 2005). Some modern writers have received attention for their uncensored portrayals of society. Tom Wolfe, a leading figure in the 1960s in literary experiments that became known as New Journalism, has kept his finger on the pulse of America with *The Bonfire of the Vanities* (1984–85), and Salman Rushdie's novel *The Satanic Verses* (1988), condemned by the Muslim world, has been recognized for its blunt attack on religious bigotry. Recently, the delightful *Harry Potter* children's series, by J. K. Rowling, has caused controversy among conservative religious groups, who claim the fantasies endorse witchcraft and wizardry, and Dan Brown's widely read novel *The Da Vinci Code* (2003) has provoked much criticism for its blasphemous portrayal of the Catholic Church and the book's loose interpretation of history.

Linked to developments in modern theater is ***performance art***, which combines visual stimuli with theater and music. The term "happening" was coined in the 1960s to describe this semi-improvised multimedia event, which was often highly dependent on audience participation. The experimental composer John Cage was intrigued by this art form (see p. 428), as is Laurie Anderson, who uses a combination of popular music, storytelling, comic routines, and high-tech equipment to address social issues.

Film Finally, film—of all the arts the one most securely chained to popular storytelling—has also responded to the twin impulses of experimentation and abstraction. "New wave" directors include Jean-Luc Godard (*Breathless*, 1959), Federico Fellini (*La Strada*, 1959; *8½*, 1963), Michelangelo Antonioni (*Blowup*, 1966; *The Passenger*, 1975), and Louis Malle (*My Dinner with André*, 1981; *Au revoir, les enfants*, 1987). In

In *Mao and Blonde Girl Analyzed* (1992), **Yu Youhan** (b. 1943) combines elements of Chinese peasant paintings and pop art with socialist realism. Acrylic on canvas.

A hyperkinetic scene of urban life, from Godfrey Reggio's film *Koyaanisqatsi* (1983), for which Philip Glass wrote the minimalist musical score.

films like Alain Resnais's *Last Year at Marienbad* (1962) and Ingmar Bergman's *Persona* (1966), the abstract expressionist urge was realized on the screen.

A number of national cinemas have come into their own in the past several decades. In the 1970s, German filmmakers, among them Rainer Werner Fassbinder (*The Marriage of Maria Braun*, 1978), were world leaders in the genre. Japanese and Chinese films have also received critical attention, especially those of China's Zhang Yimou (*Raise the Red Lantern*, 1991; *The Story of Qiu Ju*, 1992), which depict tragedies suffered under the Communists, and director Ang Lee, who with *Crouching Tiger, Hidden Dragon* (2000) brought martial-arts films to a new, breathtaking artistic level. Composer Tan Dun wrote an exquisite score for this film and for Zhang Yimou's *Hero* (2003), which follows in a similar artistic tradition. Polish filmmaker Krzysztof Kieślowski has also presented poignant views of his native country throwing off Communist rule (*Three Colors* trilogy: *Blue*, 1993; *White*, 1994; *Red*, 1994). South African film directors Darrell James Roudt (*Yesterday*, 2004) and Gavin Hood (*Tsotsi*, 2005) have received international accolades. The genre of nonnarrative film is best exemplified by American Godfrey Reggio (*Koyaanisqatsi*, 1983; *Powaqqatsi*, 1988), whose visual collages soar against the minimalist music of Philip Glass (see illustration above). Such "art films" have given us profound insights into the lives of people all over the world. We will explore the long-term marriage of film and music in popular and art cultures in Chapter 78.

The artworks mentioned above are only a few landmarks in the second half of the twentieth century, but they are enough to indicate that all the arts have become increasingly intellectual, experimental, and abstract.

Toward Greater Organization in Music

While Schoenberg's twelve-tone method moved toward a much stricter organization of sound material, it remained for later generations to extend the tone-row principle to elements of music other than pitch—such as durations (time values), dynamic values (degrees of loudness), and timbres. Registers and densities, types of attack, and size of intervals might also be organized serially. By thus extending the serial principle in all possible directions, a composer could achieve a totally organized fabric. This move toward *total serialism* resulted in an extremely complex, ultrarational

Total serialism

IN HIS OWN WORDS

One of the things a cartoon does is to express violent emotion and passion in a completely mechanical and removed style. To express this thing in a painterly style would dilute it; . . . the ways of seeing and composing and unifying are different and have different ends.
—ROY LICHTENSTEIN

The *Grand Louvre Pyramid*, at the entrance to the Louvre, provides a Neoclassical skylight for viewing Paris's historic museum. It was designed by the Chinese-American architect **I. M. Pei** (b. 1917).

music. Composers like Karlheinz Stockhausen and Pierre Boulez pushed the experience of listening to music to unprecedented limits.

Toward Greater Freedom in Music

"My music liberates because I give people the chance to change their minds in the way I've changed mine."

—JOHN CAGE

The urge toward a totally controlled music had its counterpart in the desire for greater, even total, freedom from all predetermined forms and procedures. Composers may opt for a throw of dice to determine rhythm and melody, or perhaps build their pieces around a series of random numbers generated by a computer. They may let the performer choose the order in which the sections are to be played, or indicate the general range of pitches, durations, and registers but leave it up to the performer to fill in the details.

Such indeterminate music is known as *aleatoric* (from *alea*, the Latin word for "dice"). In aleatoric music, the overall form may be clearly indicated, but the details are left to choice or chance. On the other hand, a composer might indicate the details of a composition clearly enough but leave its overall shape to choice or chance; this type of flexible structure is known as *open form*, which has an increased reliance on improvisation—a technique common in Baroque music and in jazz.

Contemporary attitudes have liberated not only forms but also the restrictions of the chromatic scale. Electronic instruments make possible the use of sounds that lie "in the cracks of the piano keys"—the *microtonal* intervals, such as quarter tones, that are smaller than semitones—and very skilled instrumentalists and vocalists have now mastered these novel scales, borrowed from various world musics.

CD iMusic

Avaz of Bayate Esfahan

The Postwar Internationalism

The Second World War and the events leading up to it disrupted musical life in Europe much more than in North America, with the result that the United States

Jasper Johns' (b. 1930) collage *Three Flags* (1958) superimposes three canvasses on one another to play with how the viewer perceives a work, using images "the mind already knows."

forged ahead in certain areas. The first composer to apply serial organization to dimensions other than pitch was the American Milton Babbitt, and the experiments of John Cage anticipated and influenced similar attempts abroad. Once the war was over, however, the Europeans quickly made up for lost time. Intense experimentation went on in Italy, Germany, France, England, the Netherlands, and Scandinavia. Serial and electronic music also took root in Japan, while the music of the Far East has in turn influenced Western composers.

A number of Europeans have achieved international reputations. Italian composer Luciano Berio (1925–2003) founded the electronic studio in Milan, which became a center for avant-garde activity. His music explores a wide range of contemporary trends: serialism, electronic technologies, and indeterminacy. Greek composer Iannis Xenakis (1922–2001) used his training as an engineer and architect to explore mathematical concepts in music, while Krzysztof Penderecki (b. 1933), Poland's foremost composer, achieved a unique texture in his *Threnody for the Victims of Hiroshima* (1960) for fifty-two string instruments. In this dramatic work, the composer created a new graphic notation to show an instrument's role in producing novel sounds (such as striking the soundboard or playing behind the bridge) and dense clusters played in quarter-tones.

Some composers recast pre-existing music either through quoting work of another composer or in a collage, featuring multiple quotations. Berio incorporated parts of Gustav Mahler's Symphony No. 2 into his *Sinfonia* (1968–69), while German composer Karlheinz Stockhausen (b. 1928) created a collage in *Hymnen* (1967) from various national anthems, which he combined with electronic sounds, voices, and instruments. Russian composer Sofia Gubaidulina (b. 1931), a leader among modern women composers, parodies J. S. Bach's *Musical Offering* in her Violin Concerto entitled *Offertorium* (1980), setting the Baroque masterpiece in a modern, Webernesque style.

Performance artist Laurie Anderson on tour, singing and playing electric violin for her album *Life on a String* (2001).

Public Support for New Music

While many contemporary composers have needed to solicit support from private sponsors and especially from universities, some countries have had the foresight to keep their arts and culture alive through government sponsorship. This public support is common in Europe, and France in particular has been a leader in the propagation of new music. In 1969, French president George Pompidou created the Institut de Recherche et Coordination Acoustique/Musique (Institute for Music/Acoustic Research and Coordination), or IRCAM, a center he placed under the leadership of the composer/conductor Pierre Boulez. IRCAM became, and remains, the only center of its kind around the globe dedicated to contemporary musical research and production. IRCAM's facilities in Paris are a part of the exquisite Pompidou Center, famous for its postmodern architectural design.

Canada has followed the lead of European countries in government support for the arts. As early as 1944, the Canadian Music Council was formed to promote and provide information about music across Canada, and provincial governments throughout the country soon established arts programs (the first was in Saskatchewan in 1948). The city of Vancouver formed a municipal Arts Council in 1946, the first of its kind in North America.

Music was also a concern of the Canada Council, a government organization created in 1957 to preserve its national and multicultural identity. One manifestation of this goal was the Société de Musique Contemporaine du Québec (Quebec Society for Contemporary Music), founded in Montreal in 1966 and first headed by composer Jean Papineau-Couture (1916–2000), considered the father of contemporary Canadian music. This association is dedicated to the promotion and dissemination of contemporary music, both Canadian and international; its concert series and festivals across Canada often feature premieres of works by Canadian composers. In 1959, the Canadian Music Centre, a centralized library and information center, was established for the dissemination and promotion of Canadian concert, operatic, educational, and church music. This organization has been highly effective in providing composers and performers with much needed publicity and visibility worldwide.

This nationalistic pride was extended to popular music as well, when in 1970 the Canadian government passed a regulation requiring AM radio stations to

The Pompidou Center in Paris, France, constructed 1971–77, is a prime example of postmodern architecure.

A Native American legend is the theme of R. Murray Schafer's *Princess of the Stars,* performed at dawn at Two Jack Lake in the Canadian Rockies as part of the 1981 Banff Arts Festival.

devote a full 30 percent of their musical programming to Canadian content, and a year later the Juno Awards, sponsored by Canada's music industry, were held. Since then, many Canadian composers and performers have been launched to fame. Recent winners include rocker Neil Young, jazz vocalist Diana Krall, and the Tafelmusik Baroque Orchestra, whom we have heard on several recordings. Also among recent honorees is R. Murray Schafer (b. 1933), Canada's best-known living composer, who has helped keep his nation in the forefront of contemporary music.

The United States has a government-funded national arts agency as well—the National Endowment for the Arts (NEA), founded in 1965. The agency's support for artists and for arts education programs has been severely undermined in recent years by a dwindling budget—indeed, the current budget ($121 million) is a fraction of the cost of even one B-1 bomber. The NEA's goals are lofty and far-reaching: to preserve our cultural and artistic heritage and to bring the arts—including contemporary music—to all communities throughout the country.

Suggested Listening

Works by contemporary Canadian composers—Henry Brant, Alexina Louie, Jean Papineau-Couture, R. Murray Schafer, John Weinzweig

Suggested Web Topic

Canadian Music Centre (for featured composers and music)

76

The New Virtuosity of the Modern Age

- Contemporary music often calls for innovative and highly virtuosic instrumental or vocal effects that challenge performers to new expressive and technical levels.

- In his song cycle *Ancient Voices of Children*, which uses the voice as a virtuosic instrument, American composer George Crumb set texts by the Spanish poet Federico García Lorca.

Avant-garde techniques and effects

Avant-garde musical styles call for a new breed of instrumentalists and vocalists to cope with the music's technical demands. We have only to attend a concert of avant-garde music to realize how far the art of piano playing or singing has moved from the world of Chopin or Schubert. The piano keyboard may be slammed with fingers or fist; the player may reach inside to pluck the strings directly, or a piece may call for bits of metal, wood, or paper to be inserted into the strings to alter the timbre. A violinist may tap or even slap the instrument. Vocal music runs the gamut from whispering to shouting, including all manner of moaning and hissing. Wind players have learned to produce a variety of double-stops, extreme pitches (high and low), and microtones; and the percussion section has been enriched by an astonishing variety of instruments creating special effects. We will see how one extraordinary singer—Jan DeGaetani—developed a specialized technique that inspired modern composers to write for her. Singer and composer Cathy Berberian (see p. 425) was also influential in shaping contemporary compositions; she gained fame through her 1958 premiere of *Aria* by John Cage, a work in which she had to create her own melody from the composer's purposely vague indications, singing in five languages and changing between widely varying vocal styles and techniques. We will consider here the work of the American George Crumb, who has sounded an original voice in the diverse world of avant-garde music.

George Crumb and Avant-Garde Virtuosity

"Music [is] a system of proportions in the service of a spiritual impulse."

George Crumb (b. 1929), a professor of composition at the University of Pennsylvania until his retirement in 1999, has been recognized for the emotional character of his music, which comes from his highly developed sense of the dramatic. His use of contemporary techniques for expressive ends is extremely effective with audiences and in concert halls, and his compositions have won him numerous awards and honors, including a Pulitzer and a Grammy Award.

Crumb has shown a special affinity for the poetry of Federico García Lorca, the great poet who was killed by the Fascists during the Spanish Civil War and to whom the Mexican composer Silvestre Revueltas dedicated his work *Homenaje a Federico García Lorca* (see p. 373). Crumb's works based on García Lorca's poetry include

George Crumb

In this musical score by singer Cathy Berberian, drawings from comic strips challenge the performer to shape pictures, words, and sounds into a unified structure. *Stripsody,* for solo voice (1966).

Ancient Voices of Children; *Night Music I*; four books of madrigals; *Songs, Drones, and Refrains of Death*; and *Night of the Four Moons*.

ANCIENT VOICES OF CHILDREN

Ancient Voices of Children is a cycle of songs for soprano, boy soprano, oboe, mandolin, harp, electric piano, and percussion. Like many contemporary composers, Crumb uses the voice here like an instrument, in a vocal style he describes as ranging "from the virtuosic to the intimately lyrical."

Several contemporary singers have trained their voices to perform virtuosic modern techniques that require great vocal agility, precise pitch, and a crystal clear tone. These techniques include singing microtones; exploring extended registers, wide leaps, and awkward intervals; and singing without text (wordless melody, called **vocalise**). One of the most notable singers is the American mezzo-soprano Jan DeGaetani (1933–1989), who has collaborated with George Crumb and premiered his *Ancient Voices* song cycle in 1970 at the Library of Congress in Washington, DC.

Crumb's score abounds in unusual effects, many inspired by musics of distant cultures. The soprano opens with a fanciful vocalise that is reminiscent of a rhapsodic East Asian melody. She sings into an electrically amplified piano, arousing a shimmering cloud of sympathetic vibrations. The pitch is "bent" to produce microtones that typify some styles of Asian music. The score includes a toy piano, a harmonica, and a musical saw as well as a rich array of percussion instruments—many borrowed from other cultures—such as Tibetan prayer stones, Japanese temple bells, tuned tom-toms (high-pitched drums of African origin), as well as Latin-American claves (wooden clappers) and maracas (a kind of rattle). Also heard are marimba, vibraphone, sleigh bells, glockenspiel plates, tubular bells, and gong (tam-tam). The composer explained why he picked this unusual combination: "I was conscious of an urge to fuse . . . unrelated stylistic elements . . . a suggestion of Flamenco with a Baroque quotation . . . , or a reminiscence of Mahler with . . . the Orient."

The first song from this cycle, *The Little Boy Is Looking for His Voice* (*El niño busca su voz*; see Listening Guide 51), displays a free and fantastic character. The soprano part offers a virtuoso exhibition of what the voice can do in the way of cries, sighs, whispers, buzzings, trills, and percussive clicks. There are even passages marked "fluttertongue"—an effect generally associated with instruments. Throughout, Crumb captures the improvisational spirit of Spanish flamenco song. The passion is here, the sense of mystery and wonder—but in a thoroughly twentieth-century setting.

In *Ancient Voices*, Crumb accurately portrays the dark intimations of García Lorca's poetry. The work has justly established itself as a prime example of contemporary imagination and feeling.

IN HIS OWN WORDS

I have sought musical images that enhance and reinforce the powerful yet strangely haunting imagery of Lorca's poetry. I feel that the essential meaning of this poetry is concerned with the most primary things: Life, death, love, the smell of the earth, the sounds of the wind and the sea.

FEDERICO GARCÍA LORCA 1898 · 1936

ITALIA 650

This Italian stamp celebrates the centenary of the Spanish poet Federico García Lorca. The background depicts the Andalusion countryside with horsemen and Gypsy women.

Listening Guide 51

eLG 4 (67–69)
8 (34–36)

Crumb: *Ancient Voices of Children*, First Movement (4:30)

DATE OF WORK:	1970
GENRE:	Song cycle (5 songs and 2 instrumental interludes)
TEXT:	Poems by Federico García Lorca

WHAT TO LISTEN FOR: Opening *vocalise*, or wordless melody, with many virtuosic effects (flutter-tonguing, hissing, clicking, trills); voice used instrumentally.
Rhapsodic, improvisatory-like vocal line.
Voice singing into amplified piano, producing sympathetic vibrations.
Pure timbre of boy soprano (on second verse), singing offstage.

1. *The Little Boy Is Looking for His Voice (El niño busca su voz)*

Medium: Soprano, boy soprano, electric piano, harp, tam-tam (gong), other percussion

		TEXT	TRANSLATION	DESCRIPTION
67	0:00			Opens with an elaborate vocalise for soprano, including cries, trills, other vocal gymnastics; she sings into piano with pedal down for resonance.
68	2:48	El niño busca su voz. (La tenía el rey de los grillos.) En una gota de agua buscaba su voz el niño.	The little boy is looking for his voice. (The king of the crickets had it.) In a drop of water the little boy looked for his voice.	**Strophe 1**—sung by soprano alone with turns, trills, hisses; she continues with low-pitched recitation.
69	3:34	No la quiero para hablar; me haré con ella un anillo que llevará mi silencio en su dedo pequeñito.	I don't want it to speak with; I will make a ring of it so that he may wear my silence on his little finger.	**Strophe 2**—overlaps strophe 1; boy soprano sings offstage through cardboard tube; folk-like character to melody.

Virtuosic vocal line, at beginning of strophe 1:

77

Contemporary Composers Look to World Music

"I believe composers must forge forms out of the many influences that play upon them and never close their ears to any part of the world of sound."

—HENRY COWELL

KEY POINTS   (S) **StudySpace** online at www.wwnorton.com/enjoy

o Composer John Cage invented the ***prepared piano*** to simulate the sound of the Javanese *gamelan* orchestra.

o The ***gamelan*** is an ensemble of metallic percussion instruments played in Indonesia (on the islands of Java and Bali, in particular).

o The music of Chinese-American composer Bright Sheng merges Eastern and Western sound material and concepts.

o *The Moon Reflected on the Second Springs* is a traditional Chinese piece for the two-string fiddle (***erhu***).

o Improvisation, where the performer takes a role in the compositional process, is common not only in jazz but also in the solo genres of various Asian countries, including China, India, and Iran (CP 22).

Throughout the course of history, the West has felt the influence of other cultures. Twentieth-century composers, as we have seen, found inspiration in the strong rhythmic features of songs and dances from the borderlands of Western culture—southeastern Europe, Asiatic Russia, the Near East, and parts of Latin America (see the world map at the back of this book). We have also noted how American musicians combined the powerful rhythmic impulse of African styles with the major-minor tonality of Western art music to produce a rich literature of spirituals, work songs, and shouts—and ultimately ragtime, blues, jazz, swing, and rock.

A number of contemporary composers have also responded to the philosophy of the Far East, notably Zen Buddhism and Indian thought. Among them are three Californians whose work has attracted much notice: Henry Cowell, Harry Partch, and especially John Cage, whose name was associated with the avant-garde scene for nearly seventy years.

Important Experimenters

Henry Cowell (1897–1965) was drawn toward a variety of non-Western musics. His studies of the music of Japan, India, and Iran as well as rural Ireland and America led him to combine Asian instruments with traditional Western ensembles, as he did in his two koto concertos (1962 and 1965). (The *koto* is a Japanese zither with thirteen strings stretched over bridges and tuned to one of a variety of pentatonic scales.) Cowell also experimented with foreign scales, which he harmonized with Western chords. The piano provided a medium for several of his innovations; two

Composer Harry Partch plays one of his experimental instruments—a kind of marimba—assisted by conductor Jack Login.

Ⓢ **John Cage**

CD iMusic
─────────────
Tabuh Kenilu Sawik (Sumatra, Indonesia)

examples were *tone clusters* (groups of adjacent notes that are sounded with the fist, palm, or forearm) and the plucking of the piano strings directly with the fingers.

The piano also lent itself to experiments with new tuning systems. One of the first to attempt microtonal music for the piano was Charles Ives (see p. 365), who wrote for pianos tuned a quarter tone apart. But perhaps the most serious proponent of this technique was Harry Partch (1901–1974), who single-mindedly pursued the goal of a microtonal music. In the 1920s, he developed a scale of forty-three microtones to the octave and adapted Indian and African instruments to fit this tuning. Among his original idiophones are cloud-chamber bowls (made of glass), cone gongs (made of metal), the diamond marimba (made of wood), and tree gourds. Such instruments make melody and timbre, rather than harmony, the focus of his music. Partch's experiments helped shape the pioneering genius of John Cage.

The Music of John Cage

"I thought I could never compose socially important music. Only if I could invent something new, then would I be useful to society."

John Cage (1912–1992) represents the type of eternally questing artist who no sooner solves one problem than presses forward to another. Born in Los Angeles, Cage attended Pomona College, then left school to travel in Europe. He exhibited an early interest in non-Western scales, which he learned from his mentor, Henry Cowell. Cage was also a student of Arnold Schoenberg, and he explored compositions with fixed tone rows but eventually became persuaded that future advancement would occur through rhythm rather than pitch. This abiding interest in rhythm led him to explore the possibilities of percussion instruments. He soon realized that the traditional division between consonance and dissonance had given way to a new opposition between music and noise, as a result of which the boundaries of the one were extended to include more of the other. The composer prophesied in 1937 that "the use of noise to make music will continue and increase until we reach a music produced through the aid of electrical instruments, which will make available for musical purposes any and all sounds that can be heard."

In 1938, Cage invented what he called the "prepared piano," consisting of nails, bolts, nuts, screws, and bits of rubber, wood, or leather inserted at crucial points in the strings of an ordinary grand piano. From this instrument came a myriad of sounds whose overall effect resembled that of a Javanese *gamelan*. Cage wrote a number of works for the prepared piano, notably the set of *Sonatas and Interludes* (1946–48; we will consider Sonata V). The music reflects the composer's preoccupation with East Asian philosophy. "After reading the work of Ananda K. Coomaraswamy, I decided to attempt the expression in music of the 'permanent emotions' of Indian tradition: the heroic, the erotic, the wondrous, the mirthful, sorrow, fear, anger, the odious, and their common tendency toward tranquility." A quest for tranquility pervaded Cage's life and work.

Cage's interest in indeterminacy, or chance, led him to compose works in which performers make choices by throwing dice. He also relied on the *I Ching* (Book of Changes), an ancient Chinese method of throwing coins or marked sticks for chance numbers, from which he derived a system of charts and graphs governing the series of events that could happen within a piece. These experiments established Cage as a decisive influence in the artistic life of the mid- and later twentieth century.

Cage maintained an intense interest in exploring the role of silence. This led to his composition entitled *4'33"*, without any musical content at all, consisting of four minutes and thirty-three seconds of "silence." Audience members are expected to become aware of the sounds in the hall or outside it, the beating of their hearts, or the sounds floating around in their imagination. The piece was first performed by the pianist David Tudor in 1952. He came out onstage, placed a score on the piano rack, sat quietly for the duration of the piece, then closed the piano lid and walked off the stage. Some critics considered the piece a hoax or a not-so-clever trick. Yet Cage viewed it as one of the most radical statements he had made (and he made many) against the traditions of Western music, one that raised profound questions. What is music, and what is noise? And what does silence contribute to music? In any case, *4'33"*, which can be performed by anyone on any instrument, always makes us more aware of our surroundings.

John Cage's prepared piano works call for screws and nails to be inserted between the strings.

4'33"

CAGE'S SONATAS AND INTERLUDES

Sonatas and Interludes represents Cage's crowning achievement for the prepared piano. In this set of works, he approximates the subtle sounds of the Javanese gamelan and preserves the effect of music floating above time. The pieces are free from the accents and dynamism of the West, and they capture the meditative character of East Asian thought.

There are sixteen Sonatas in this set, ordered in four groups of four Sonatas, and separated by Interludes (see Listening Guide 52). Cage provides detailed instructions at the beginning of the score, indicating that forty-five of the piano's eighty-eight keys should be prepared by inserting various types of materials (described on p. 428) at distances carefully specified by the composer. He further explains that "mutes of various materials are placed between the strings of the keys used, thus effecting transformations of the piano sounds with respect to all of their characteristics." The effect is varied, depending upon the material inserted, its position, and whether the soft pedal is depressed. Some strings produce a nonpitched, percussive thump while others produce tones whose pitch and timbre are altered. This music is not concerned with the simultaneous sounding of pitches (harmony) but with the timbral effects and the rhythmic groupings of sounds.

Sonata V is short but highly structured; its overall shape is binary, with each section repeated (**A-A-B-B**). The sonority of the prepared piano is almost ethereal, remarkably like the gamelan orchestra of pitched and nonpitched instruments (see p. 431), and far removed from the timbre we associate with the piano. Cage's music for prepared piano is made of wholly original sounds that delight the ears and, according to the composer, "set the soul in operation."

IN HIS OWN WORDS

Once in Amsterdam, a Dutch musician said to me, "It must be very difficult for you in America to write music, for you are so far away from the centers of tradition." I had to say, "It must be very difficult for you in Europe to write music, for you are so close to the centers of tradition."

Listening Guide 52

eLG   4 (65–66)
8 (29–30)

Cage: Sonata V, from *Sonatas and Interludes*

(1:23)

DATE OF WORK:	1946 (first performed 1949)
OVERALL FORM:	16 Sonatas, in 4 groups of 4, each group separated by an Interlude
FORM OF MOVEMENT:	Binary (**A-A-B-B**)
MEDIUM:	Prepared piano

WHAT TO LISTEN FOR: Percussive effects, both pitched and unpitched.
Ethereal non-Western timbre sounding like gongs (gamelan).
Changing rhythmic flow, seemingly without a clear meter.

65 0:00   **A** section—18 measures, grouped in irregular phrases (4 + 5 + 4 + 5 = 18).

Opening of Sonata V, with regular rhythmic movement:

(una corda pedal)

2-voice texture at opening, with irregular sense of meter.

0:12   Upper line sustained over moving, lower line (in last 9 measures).

0:20   **A** section repeated.

66 0:38   **B** section— 22½ measures, in irregular phrases (4 + 5 + 4 + 5 + 4½ = 22½).
Rests break movement into sections.

0:46   Quicker tempo, lines more disjunct and accented.

Second half of **B** section, with more disjunct lines and accents:

0:55   Sustained dissonance at closing.

1:00   **B** section repeated.

The Javanese Gamelan

"Simply said, gamelan music is the most beautiful music in the world, and I for one see no reason to do any other kind of music ever again."

—LOU HARRISON

Indonesia, a highly populated country in Southeast Asia, has many diverse cultures and musical traditions. One of the most important traditions is the gamelan, an orchestra of metallic percussion played on the Indonesian islands of Java, Bali, and Sunda. A gamelan is composed of melodic-percussive instruments, each with its own function within the orchestra. The music is generally played from memory, passed as an oral tradition from master musician to apprentice. It is only in recent years that a notational method has been devised.

Tuning

Gamelan music is often heard in ritual ceremonies, including court performances (there are four courts in central Java alone) and **wayang**, or shadow-puppet theater. Two tunings are used: **sléndro**, a pentatonic tuning, and **pélog**, a heptatonic (or seven-note) tuning. While court music often combines gamelans with these divergent tunings, the use of *sléndro* tuning for the puppet theater is a centuries-old practice. The instruments used in the puppet theater include soft and loud metallophones (instruments with tuned metal bars that are struck with a mallet), gongs of various sizes, wooden xylophones, drums, and voice.

A traditional Javanese gamelan, with metallophones, playing for a meeting of OPEC (Organization of Petroleum Exporting Countries) in Jakarta.

Our selection is a kind of overture (called *Patalon*) to the shadow-puppet play (see Listening Guide 53). Like many Javanese dramas, the story comes from the great Hindu epic, the *Ramayana*. (Java is today predominately Islamic, although Hindu and Buddhist beliefs are also important to the culture.) The epic tells of the evil king Rahwana who kidnapped Sinta, wife of King Rama. This particular play depicts the *Ramayana* episode in which the evil king's brother Wibisana is cast out from the kingdom for suggesting that Rahwana return Sinta to her husband.

In Javanese music, the interaction of the melodic movement with the cyclical rhythmic structure (called **colotomic structure**) determines the form of the work. Here, the melodic framework (**balungan**) is based on the pentatonic scale (*sléndro*—a gapped scale that includes the notes 1, 2, 3, 5, and 6, or C, D, E, G, and A), as the work unfolds in a series of five sections. The first, including the introduction, is slow and stately—the melody can be heard in the highest-pitched metallophone, which sounds each note of the pattern twice. This is followed by a short, loud passage. The singer elaborates on the melody in quite a different way from the instruments, but both singer and instruments converge on accented notes. The drum marks the transition to the third section, which increases in tempo and excitement. The composition *Palaran Pucung* intervenes, played in a soft style using the quiet instruments so that the voice can be featured. At dramatic moments in the text, accents jolt the listener. The loud instruments assert themselves again in the fourth section, and the

Melodic and rhythmic structures

Javanese shadow-drama puppets of the King Rama, hero of the Hindu epic *Ramayama,* and his wife Sinta (left), who is kidnapped and later recovered.

singer drops out. A quiet interlude leads to the final, fast-paced section that signals the close of the overture and the entrance of the dances and puppet characters. On the approach to the final cadence, the tempo slackens considerably; the musicians prolong the resolution of the last chord, and then, led by the gong, each strikes the last note in his own time.

This exotic sound has fascinated Western musicians and listeners alike, from their first exposure. Remember that Debussy, after hearing Javanese music for the first time at the Paris World Exhibition of 1889 (see CP 15), said that the gamelan "contained every nuance of meaning, even unmentionable shades, and makes our tonic and dominant seem like empty phantoms for the use of unwise children."

Multicultural Influences in Contemporary Society

The impulse toward a world music sound has continued beyond John Cage with composers such as Philip Glass, Terry Riley, and Steve Reich (see p. 460). Also in this category are several com-

Listening Guide 53	eLG	3 (65–69) 8 (83–87)

Javanese Gamelan Music: *Patalon* (4:24)

REGION:	Central Java, Indonesia
FUNCTION:	Accompaniment for a wayang (traditional shadow-puppet drama)
GENRE:	*Patalon* (overture), from Act I of play
MEDIUM:	Gamelan orchestra, consisting of: Soft metallophones (*gender, slenthem*) Loud metallophones (*demung, saron, peking*) Various gongs (*kempul, bonang, kenong*) Drums (*kendang*) Wooden xylophone (*gambang*) Voice (*pesindèn*)
CHARACTERISTICS:	Pentatonic melodies in *sléndro* scale, played in *patet* (mode) *manyura*, colotomic (cyclical) structure, polyrhythmic
STRUCTURE:	5 distinct sections *Ayak-Ayakan* *Srepegan* *Palaran Pucung* *Srepegan Banyumasan* *Sampak sléndro manyura*

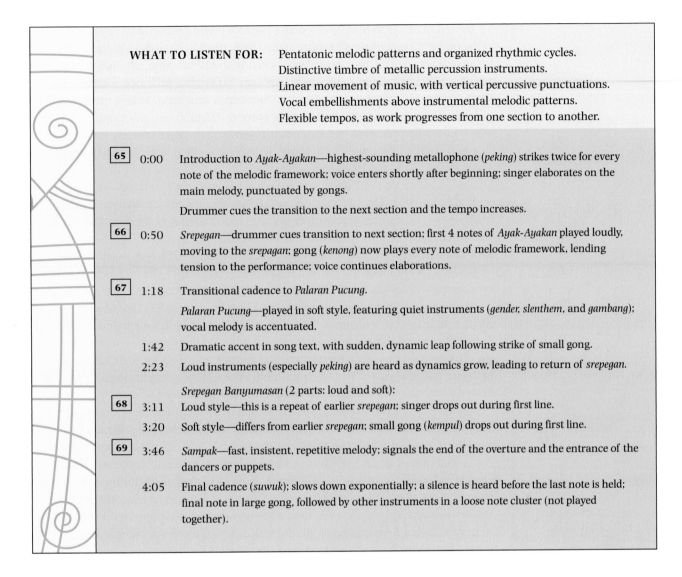

WHAT TO LISTEN FOR: Pentatonic melodic patterns and organized rhythmic cycles.
Distinctive timbre of metallic percussion instruments.
Linear movement of music, with vertical percussive punctuations.
Vocal embellishments above instrumental melodic patterns.
Flexible tempos, as work progresses from one section to another.

65 0:00   Introduction to *Ayak-Ayakan*—highest-sounding metallophone (*peking*) strikes twice for every note of the melodic framework; voice enters shortly after beginning; singer elaborates on the main melody, punctuated by gongs.

Drummer cues the transition to the next section and the tempo increases.

66 0:50   *Srepegan*—drummer cues transition to next section; first 4 notes of *Ayak-Ayakan* played loudly, moving to the *srepagan*; gong (*kenong*) now plays every note of melodic framework, lending tension to the performance; voice continues elaborations.

67 1:18   Transitional cadence to *Palaran Pucung*.

Palaran Pucung—played in soft style, featuring quiet instruments (*gender, slenthem,* and *gambang*); vocal melody is accentuated.

1:42   Dramatic accent in song text, with sudden, dynamic leap following strike of small gong.

2:23   Loud instruments (especially *peking*) are heard as dynamics grow, leading to return of *srepegan*.

Srepegan Banyumasan (2 parts: loud and soft):

68 3:11   Loud style—this is a repeat of earlier *srepegan*; singer drops out during first line.

3:20   Soft style—differs from earlier *srepegan*; small gong (*kempul*) drops out during first line.

69 3:46   *Sampak*—fast, insistent, repetitive melody; signals the end of the overture and the entrance of the dancers or puppets.

4:05   Final cadence (*suwuk*); slows down exponentially; a silence is heard before the last note is held; final note in large gong, followed by other instruments in a loose note cluster (not played together).

posers who drew on their Asian heritage as well as the traditions of the West; these include Tan Dun (b. 1957), known for his exquisite martial arts film scores (see p. 448), and the Chinese-American composer Bright Sheng, whose use of traditional instruments in Western contexts lends a distinctive sound to his work. To demonstrate these multicultural and rhythmic influences, we will explore Sheng's work, showing the interaction between unique timbres, set against traditional Chinese music.

Bright Sheng and the Meeting of Musical Cultures

"People acknowledge artistic license; I embrace cultural license."

Bright Sheng (b. 1955) is one of the most innovative composers on the contemporary scene. He blends two different musical cultures—Western and Asian—into a new soundscape that respects the essence of each. Even his name crosses cultures: his official Chinese name is Sheng Song-Liang (Liang means "bright lights"), so he uses Bright as his Anglicized first name.

Bright Sheng

Born and raised in Shanghai, Sheng began studying piano at the age of four. But at the onset of the Cultural Revolution in 1966, the Red Guards took away his piano because it was considered "bourgeois." During the Revolution, all high schools and colleges were shut down, and Sheng was sent to Qinghai province, formerly part of Tibet. There, his talents allowed him to work as a musician. When the Revolution ended in 1976, he was one of the first to enter the Shanghai Conservatory of Music, where he studied composition. He came to New York in 1982 to study at Queens College and then at Columbia University, where he worked with Leonard Bernstein, Mario Davidovsky, and Chou Wen-chung.

Since coming to the United States, Sheng has won many awards—including the coveted MacArthur Foundation "Genius" Fellowship for "exceptional originality and creativity"—and has received numerous commissions from orchestras and from solo performers. He currently holds the Leonard Bernstein Distinguished Professor Chair at the University of Michigan. In addition, as an adviser for the Silk Road Project—the musical interpretation of Far Eastern trade routes (see p. 83)—Sheng has been a strong force, along with cellist Yo-Yo Ma, in preserving these traditional musical cultures.

CD iMusic

In a Mountain Path

Much like the Hungarian composer Béla Bartók (see p. 359), Bright Sheng writes music that transcends national boundaries by integrating Western and Eastern elements. His compositional approach merges what he finds most important in Western music—its emphasis on harmony and counterpoint—with the Chinese affinity for linear sounds—a soloist or a traditional ensemble playing in unison. He blends elements of both styles while respecting the integrity of each.

Sheng's first important commission, which won him a Pulitzer nomination, was *H'un* (*Lacerations*): *In Memoriam 1966–75*, a dramatic orchestral portrait of the Cultural Revolution that tells the composer's story as a "victim, witness, and survivor." The work is full of anger and thus lacks melodies—"I realized" he wrote, "that even a tragic melody is too beautiful." Generally, however, his music is highly lyrical, often evoking elements of Chinese folk songs. Several of his concertos combine Chinese solo instruments (**pipa**, a kind of lute; and **sheng**, a mouth organ) with the Western orchestra. In his *Spring Dreams*, Sheng writes for solo cello accompanied by traditional Chinese orchestra, an ensemble comprised of bowed strings, in particular the **erhu**; plucked strings, including the *pipa*; a hammered dulcimer called the **yangqin**; winds, including a bamboo flute called **dizi**, the double-reeded **suona** and the *sheng*; and various gongs, bells, and drums. We will hear several of these instruments in a performance of traditional Chinese music (p. 436).

China Dreams

Sheng's symphonic suite *China Dreams*, composed between 1992 and 1995, is a nostalgic work—he admits being homesick for China when he wrote it. The suite, set in four movements, is scored for a large orchestra, in the Western tradition. We will hear the opening *Prelude*, which is highly evocative of Chinese folk music, particularly from the northwest region where Sheng lived for seven years. Hauntingly lyrical pentatonic melodies in the woodwinds and upper strings are punctuated by rough, dissonant figures in the brass and low strings. Sliding glissando figures suggest Asian melodic styles, as does the overall linear flow of the music (see Listening Guide 54). The agitated and percussive *Fanfare* that follows may allude to some of the horrors remembered by the composer. The third movement, entitled *The Stream Flows*, is scored for strings alone and draws on a well-known folk song from the Yunnan province in southern China. The suite closes with *The Last Three Gorges of the Long River* (referring to the Yangtze River, the longest in Asia). This movement, which the composer says came to him in a dream, brings back the nostalgic themes of the *Prelude*. In this and his other compositions, Sheng's merger of Eastern and Western ideas does much to enrich the listener's understanding of both cultures.

Listening Guide 54

eLG 4 (70–75) 8 (40–45)

Sheng: *China Dreams: Prelude* (5:09)

DATE OF WORK:	1995
MEDIUM:	Orchestra, with piano, celesta, and diverse percussion instruments
GENRE:	Symphonic suite
	Prelude *The Stream Flows*
	Fanfare *The Three Gorges of the Long River*
FORM:	3-part structure

WHAT TO LISTEN FOR: Asian folklike lines; linear textures evoked.
Lyrical pentatonic melodies in woodwinds and strings.
Melodies subtly syncopated over barlines; fluid meter.
Brilliant orchestration; instrument families juxtaposed.
Brass and harp used percussively; dissonant punctuations.
Sliding (glissando) effects in low brass, timpani, strings.

70   0:00   Oboe and English horn, with haunting pentatonic melody with grace notes, accompanied by viola line and plucked low strings:

0:29   Melody taken over by clarinets, interrupted by quick flourishes in double reeds and trumpets; punctuated by harp and percussion; very Asian sound:

1:08   Melody passed to bass clarinet, closes on held note (fermata).

71   1:23   Pace slackens (*meno mosso*); new version of melody in violas:

Sharp, percussive notes plucked in violins and harp; crescendos to *fortissimo*.

Listening Guide continues

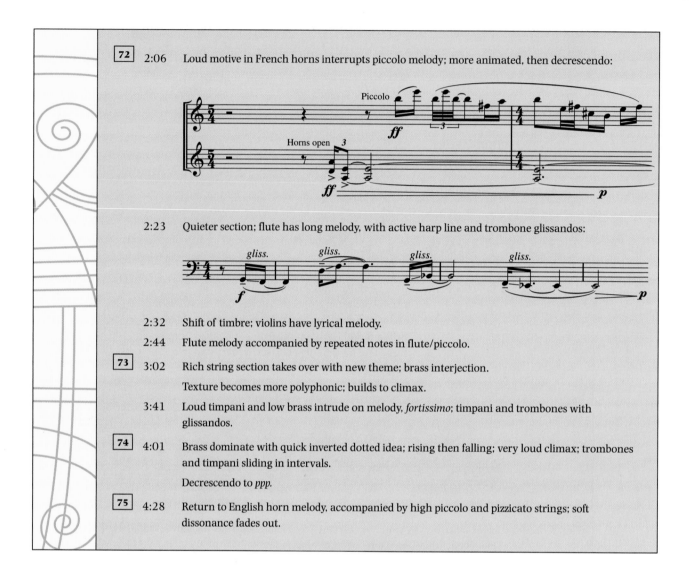

72 2:06 Loud motive in French horns interrupts piccolo melody; more animated, then decrescendo:

2:23 Quieter section; flute has long melody, with active harp line and trombone glissandos:

2:32 Shift of timbre; violins have lyrical melody.

2:44 Flute melody accompanied by repeated notes in flute/piccolo.

73 3:02 Rich string section takes over with new theme; brass interjection.

Texture becomes more polyphonic; builds to climax.

3:41 Loud timpani and low brass intrude on melody, *fortissimo*; timpani and trombones with glissandos.

74 4:01 Brass dominate with quick inverted dotted idea; rising then falling; very loud climax; trombones and timpani sliding in intervals.

Decrescendo to *ppp*.

75 4:28 Return to English horn melody, accompanied by high piccolo and pizzicato strings; soft dissonance fades out.

An Introduction to Chinese Traditional Music

Let us now consider a well-known Chinese piece, played on traditional instruments, and how it can be related to the scales and textures of Bright Sheng's orchestral work *China Dreams*.

The musician who composed and first performed this work is known as Abing (1883–1950). According to the official biography written by a Chinese music historian, Abing's original name was Hua Yanjun, and he was born in Wuxi, in the eastern province of Jiangsu (see world map in back of book). Both his parents died when Abing was young; he was adopted by a Daoist monk, who taught him music. (*Daoism* is one of China's major philosophies and religions, based on the teachings of sixth-century-B.C.E. philosopher Lao-tse.) As an apprentice Daoist, Abing played in the wind and percussion ensemble of the local temple. He was eventually expelled from the Daoist group for playing their music in secular settings, and became a wandering street musician. In his mid-thirties, he went blind—some say as a result of contracting syphilis.

Abing was able to make a meager living by singing and playing the two-stringed fiddle (*erhu*) and the lute (*pipa*). In his music, much of it improvised on the spot, he

Improvisation as Compositional Process

Some modern Western art compositions and especially jazz tunes allow performers the freedom to "compose" a work on the spot, through improvisation. This practice is also found in other cultures: the musician starts with something definable—be it a scale, a mode, a tune, or a set of rules—and then creates the music through a series of specific performance conventions unique to that musical style—a style that is understood by both practitioner and audience.

Bahram Osqueezadeh plays the Iranian santur.

The Chinese piece, *The Moon Reflected on the Second Springs* (*Er quan ying yue*; see p. 438), offers the performer some freedom of interpretation. Generally played on the erhu, the work is built on a pentatonic (five-note) scale. The song's phrases are first heard in a low range on the instrument. As the four skeletal phrases are repeated, the degree of elaboration grows, the range widens, and the tension level rises. Changes in rhythms, melodic shape, articulations (bowing and plucking), embellished notes, and inflections (pitch bending) are some of the ways that the performer puts an individual stamp on the work. Much like a jazz standard, however, the work retains its overall shape and familiarity.

In contrast, the classical music of India features the performer in the role of composer. The starting point is the *raga*, which provides a set of rules, not a prescribed tune, for how the melody moves up and down. A raga (from the Sanskrit word "to color") is much more than a scale; it sets the mood of a piece while providing material for endless variations. In addition, each raga has an overriding rhythmical structure determined by the *tala*, a complex cycle of beats and subbeats.

Every raga begins with an improvised prelude that is unmeasured and is followed by a fixed piece in the measured tala. The *tabla* (a set of hand drums) sets up the rhythm—played slowly at first, then accelerating—giving a sense of climax to the work. In *Bhimpalási*, a

North Indian (Hindustani) piece performed by the esteemed sitar player Ravi Shankar, the raga evokes a mood of tenderness a deeply felt longing. (A *sitar* is a plucked string instrument—a long-necked lute—with six main strings and many side and sympathetic strings; see illustration on p. 50.) Shankar first demonstrates the ascending (five-note) and descending (seven-note) form of the raga on the sitar (see p. 112 for the pitches), and counts out the fourteen-beat tala. Our example then jumps into the gat, where the sitar begins exploring and extending melodic ideas in various registers over the complex drumming of the tabla and the underlying drone of another string instrument, the *tambura*. We hear microtonal pitches when the strings are pulled sideways to inflect a note, making the sound dip lower.

A similar kind of melodic development occurs in the classical music of Iran. In this style, based on the ancient music of Persia, there is again no distinction between the performer and composer. Musicians think in terms of short melodic units that form a melody type and mode, which is introduced and then expanded through an organic process. In *Avaz of Bayate Esfahan*, performed on the santur—a hammer dulcimer popular in Iran today—a unique scale is presented in the rhapsodic introduction that employs pitches not heard in the well-tempered Western system. We might feel that these metronomical, lowered pitches evoke a melancholy or sadness in us, similar to our reaction when we hear a minor mode. This music features ornamental grace-notes as well as tremolos to extend and enhance the sound of the instrument.

In all these examples, the form of the composition is highly dependent on improvisation: it is the inventiveness of the performer that makes a work successful and comprehendible to the listener, regardless of the building materials and creative processes from which it is fashioned.

Terms to Note

microtone	tala	tambura	erhu
inflection	sitar	santur	yangquin
raga	tabla		

Suggested Listening

China: *The Moon Reflected on the Second Springs* (*Er quan ying yue*) (erhu and yangqin)

CD iMusic India: *Bhimpalási* (sitar, tambura, tabla)

CD iMusic Iran: *Avaz of Bayate Esfahan* (santur)

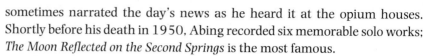

Man playing the erhu.

sometimes narrated the day's news as he heard it at the opium houses. Shortly before his death in 1950, Abing recorded six memorable solo works; *The Moon Reflected on the Second Springs* is the most famous.

Abing's pieces are viewed as traditional music because they were created through improvisation and thus took their shape gradually, and because they have been orally disseminated in differing versions, like folk music (in this case, they have also been written down for posterity). Today, Abing's music is highly revered; it forms part of the standard repertory at music conservatories for erhu and pipa players, further blurring the lines between art and traditional music.

This humble Chinese musician would have been surprised to read some of his biographies, written under the Communist regime (which came to power in 1949), that have romanticized his life and turned him into a revolutionary hero of the people. Questions have even arisen over the descriptive title of the work we will hear, which was probably given to the composition after a long period of performance and development. Although some have searched for political meaning behind the name, most scholars believe it refers to a scenic site outside the city of Wuxi, near the Second Springs pavilion.

The Moon Reflected on the Second Springs was originally conceived for solo *erhu*, a bowed, two-string fiddle played resting upright on the upper leg, with a snakeskin-covered sound box and with its bow hairs fixed between the two strings. Our modern recorded version adds the *yangqin*, a hammered dulcimer with a trapezoidal sound box strung with metal strings that are struck (or hammered) with strips of bamboo (see illustration at left). The work is based on a pentatonic scale (D-E-G-A-B) that uses only the intervals of major seconds and minor thirds (as shown in Listening Guide 55).

The melody is made up of four musical phrases, which are repeated and ornamented with many types of embellishments (trills, slides, glissandos, grace notes, bent notes, and tremolos, among others) in a process aptly described as "adding flowers" (*jia hua*). The haunting melody begins slowly, in a low range and rhythmically free, and then ascends very gradually and expressively. The yangqin adds depth to the linear movement, offering new melodic decoration and rhythmic pulses with its gently hammered tremolos.

Master yangqin player in performance.

The complete melodic outline of the work is repeated several times, with newly invented ornamentation at each appearance. In this performance, a poignant climax is reached in the third statement of the melody, with the erhu "singing" out beautifully in the instrument's highest range. Our excerpt stops before the final statement, which releases some of the tension. The version we hear today of *The Moon Reflected on the Second Springs* has, like most traditional pieces, been shaped over several generations since its modest beginnings, when it was performed by a blind, gifted Chinese musician.

Listening Guide 55

eLG 4 (93–95) 8 (63–65)

Abing: *The Moon Reflected on the Second Springs*
(Er quan ying yue), excerpt   (4:08)

DATE:	First recorded in 1950 by Abing
MEDIUM:	Erhu (2-string fiddle), with yangqin (hammered dulcimer)
GENRE:	Chinese traditional music, from Jiangsu region
SCALE:	Pentatonic (5-note), with pitches D-E-G-A-B
FORM:	4 musical phrases, repeated and elaborated
TEMPO:	Slow, with very gradual acceleration

WHAT TO LISTEN FOR: Lyrical melody with 4 phrases, derived from pentatonic scale. Entire melody played 3 times, each with new embellishments. Unique timbre of bowed erhu supported by hammered yangqin. Exploration of varied articulations and registers of solo erhu; reaches a climax in highest range.

93 0:00 Short, rhythmically free introduction by erhu is followed by lyrical melodic phrase 1, played in low range; accompanied by yangqin; ends on low G:

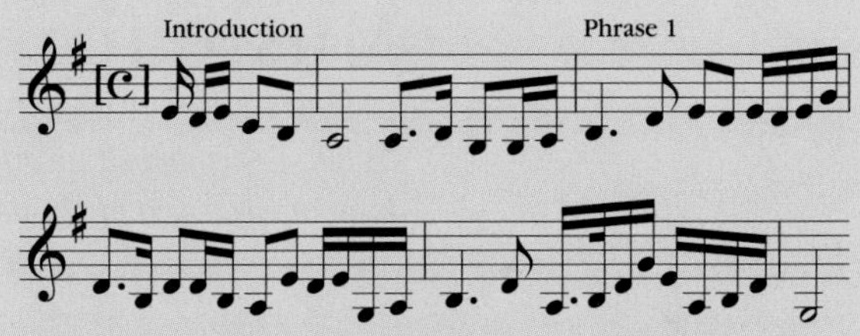

0:35 Melodic phrase 2—begins up an octave, in middle range and louder, with brief countermelody on yangqin; ends on sustained D:

0:48 Melodic phrase 3—higher range, begins with soft staccato note, ends on sustained pitch of G:

1:06 Melodic phrase 4—returns to middle range; serves as a short closing idea ending on D:

Listening Guide continues

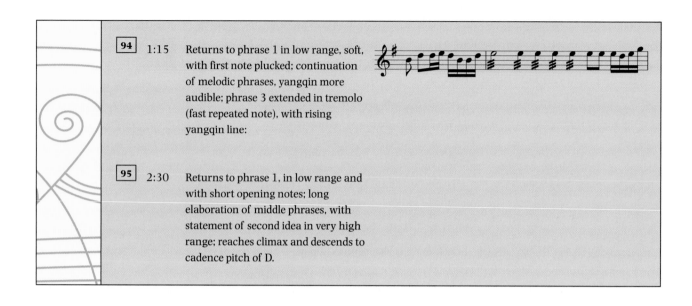

| 94 | 1:15 | Returns to phrase 1 in low range, soft, with first note plucked; continuation of melodic phrases, yangqin more audible; phrase 3 extended in tremolo (fast repeated note), with rising yangqin line: |
| 95 | 2:30 | Returns to phrase 1, in low range and with short opening notes; long elaboration of middle phrases, with statement of second idea in very high range; reaches climax and descends to cadence pitch of D. |

78

Music for Films

*"A film is a composition and the musical composition
is an integral part of the design."*

—H. G. WELLS

KEY POINTS   Listen Online Ⓢ **StudySpace** online at www.wwnorton.com/enjoy

- Music sets the mood, helps establish the characters, and creates a sense of place and time in a film.
- There are two principal types of music in a film—*underscoring* and *source music*.
- Silent films were generally accompanied by solo piano or organ.
- Film music may be newly composed or may borrow from Classical or popular repertory; rock, country/western, and jazz gained favor in film music after the late 1940s.
- The late 1930s is considered the Golden Age of films and film music.

- The Russian composer Sergei Prokofiev wrote scores for two epic films—*Alexander Nevsky* (1938) and *Ivan the Terrible* (1944–45)—both about Russian historical figures and both directed by Sergei Eisenstein.
- Post–World War II films used music sparingly, and composers explored more modern special effects.
- The film music of John Williams marks a return to full orchestral resources and the use of *leitmotifs* (recurring themes) associated with characters or situations.
- In the 1980s, the synthesizer had a significant influence on the film music industry.

Music has helped to create some of the most memorable moments in film history. The opening of *2001: A Space Odyssey*, the Paris montage from *Casablanca*, and the shower scene in *Psycho* are all accompanied by music that has become an integral part of American culture. Yet most film music functions in a less spectacular manner. With the viewer's attention focused on dialogue, visual images, and general sound effects, music often goes unnoticed. Indeed, many film composers take great pride in the unobtrusive qualities of their artistic contributions. Listening to music in film can be challenging, but the effort is rewarded with a better understanding of film as an art form.

The Role of Music in Film

The most important function of music in film is to set a mood. Choices of musical style, instrumentation, and emotional quality are critical in creating the director's vision. Even the absence of music in a scene or an entire movie (Hitchcock's *Lifeboat*, 1944) can contribute to the overall tone of a film.

Setting the mood

Most Hollywood films use music to reflect the emotions of a given scene. In *Gone With the Wind* (1939), Max Steiner's score deftly supports Scarlett O'Hara's shift from love to anger when she is rejected by Ashley at Twin Oaks. Likewise, John Williams guides the viewer's emotions at the end of *E.T.: The Extra-Terrestrial* (1982) from sorrow at the apparent death of E.T. through joy at his recovery, excitement at the chase scene, to sadness at his final farewell. Howard Shore's scores to *The Lord of the Rings* trilogy play a major role in creating the dark, brooding mood surrounding Frodo's quest, but it also brings out the contrasting moments of humor and tenderness. Many scenes in Hollywood movies would be unthinkable, if not laughable, without musical support.

But music does not necessarily need to mirror every emotion or action on the screen. In some films, the composer will establish a single dominant mood for the entire narrative, which is sustained no matter what happens on screen. This detached approach towards music, which is more prevalent in European films, is effectively used by John Williams in his score to *Schindler's List* (1993). The music for this horrific tale of the Holocaust creates a pervading mood of sadness throughout, always reminding the viewer of the inevitability of these historic events.

Elijah Wood as the heroic hobbit Frodo Baggins in *The Lord of the Rings* trilogy (2001–03).

Composers can sometimes create irony by supplying music that contradicts what is being shown on the screen. This technique is called *running counter to the action*. In James Horner's music to the final scene of *Glory* (1989), the triumphant music reflects the moral victory of black soldiers finally being allowed to fight in the Civil War and runs counter to the observed massacre of the black regiment. Perhaps the best-known musical/visual contradiction is the chilling climactic scene of *The Godfather* (1972). While the audience hears Bach organ music during a baptism, it sees the brutal and systematic murders of Michael Corleone's enemies. In one bold scene, we hear Michael become Godfather to an infant in Church and see Michael become Godfather to the mob family on the streets. A number of action films since the 1990s, including Quentin Tarantino's *Pulp Fiction* (1994) and *Kill Bill, Vol. 1* and *Vol. 2* (2003–2004), contain scenes of graphic violence accompanied by light-hearted rock music. This jarring contrast produces a sense of black comedy and raises questions about the superficial treatment of violence in today's media.

Running counter to the action

In addition to setting moods, music can play an important role in establishing character. The appearance of a dashing romantic hero might be accompanied by a passionate melody; the image of a soldier could be supported with a strong march; and

Establishing character

a worldly woman might be shown with a sultry saxophone melody heard in the background. In *Titanic* (1997), music helps delineate the social levels of the principal characters. A string quartet plays elegant chamber music to the upper-deck aristocrats while Irish dance music energizes the lower levels occupied by the common people.

Place and time
Music can also help create a sense of place and time. The sitar in *Gandhi* (1982), the bagpipes in *Braveheart* (1995), and the guitar in *Brokeback Mountain* (2005) all help transport the viewer to different locales. Similarly, the addition of a harpsichord may suggest an eighteenth-century tale; the singing of Gregorian chant conjures up images of the Middle Ages; and resounding trumpet fanfares typically accompany scenes of the mighty ancient Romans. The musical instruments do not have to be authentic but merely suggest a time period. Indeed, the combination of diverse folk instruments from China and Eastern Europe creates an antique quality that compliments the realism in *The Passion of the Christ* (2004).

Popular tunes can also help set a more precise date for events. Jazz music might accompany stories set in the 1920s or 1930s, while rock music from the 1960s or early 1970s might appear in a film about the Vietnam War. The soundtrack for *Forrest Gump* (1994) takes the listener on a brief history of rock and roll, as we watch Forrest grow from boyhood to manhood.

Underscoring

Source music
There are two principal types of music in a film. *Underscoring*, which is what most people think of as film music, occurs when music comes from an unseen source, often an invisible orchestra. But music can also function as part of the drama itself; this is referred to as *source music*. For example, someone may turn on a radio, a couple may enter a concert hall or a dance room, or a character may be inspired to sing. In each instance, the music stems from a logical source within the film and functions as part of the story itself. Source music can be a fascinating part of the drama. In *Rear Window* (1954), Hitchcock employs only source music, which emanates from the various apartments on the block. Source music can also tell us a great deal about a character. In *Boyz 'N the Hood* (1991), source music of classical jazz, Motown, and rap helps define the principal figures of the story.

In an attempt to create musical unity within the context of an ongoing dramatic flow, many film composers turned to models created by Liszt and Wagner and incorporated the techniques of leitmotifs (see p. 313) and thematic transformation. In *Jaws* (1975), John Williams creates a two-note oscillating leitmotif that warns the audience of the shark's presence. Perhaps inspired by Wagner's *Ring Cycle*, Williams also introduces a multitude of leitmotifs for the *Star Wars* trilogy. Each motif—the opening fanfare (which becomes the theme for Luke Skywalker), Yoda's gentle melody, and Darth Vader's intense march—supports the general nature of the character. Yet these musical motives can also be transformed to reflect totally different events. The theme for Luke Skywalker can sound sad or distorted when he is in trouble, triumphant when he is victorious. One of the finest musical moments of the trilogy occurs in *The Return of the Jedi* (1983). At the death of Darth Vader, his once terrifying theme is transformed into a gentle tune played by the woodwinds and harp (symbolizing the character's death).

IN HIS OWN WORDS

Nonsense. The idea [of film music] originated with Richard Wagner. Listen to the incidental scoring behind the recitatives in his operas. If Wagner had lived in this century, he would have been the Number One film composer.

—MAX STEINER
(RESPONDING TO THE IDEA THAT HE HAD INVENTED FILM MUSIC)

Music in the Silent Film Era

On December 28, 1895, Louis and Auguste Lumière showed a series of short films to a Parisian audience. This event is generally considered the birth of cinema. During this presentation, a pianist reportedly accompanied the films by improvising on popular tunes. From the beginning, then, film music was used to establish a mood, and throughout the so-called *silent film era*, it continued to function in this manner. As films moved from vaudeville houses to nickelodeons (small shops converted to movie theaters with the usual admission price of a nickel) to the movie palaces of the 1920s, musicians enhanced the visual experience of silent films. In the literally thousands of movie theaters that sprang up in the United States, the solo piano initially was the most common type of musical accompaniment for silent films. The organ was also suitable for film accompaniment, and soon special organs were built that were capable of producing a wide range of musical colors and effects, such as gunshots, animal noises, and traffic sounds.

Larger theaters featured ensembles with more musicians. The major movie palaces in cities like New York, Chicago, and Los Angeles would likely have had a full symphony orchestra numbering about fifty musicians. Special feature films were sometimes presented with over one hundred performers, including both instrumentalists and singers.

Three types of music were played during the showings of films: borrowings from Classical music, arrangements of well-known tunes (popular, patriotic, or religious), and newly composed music. Music directors of the theater generally created the music. Ideally, they would preview the film, taking notes on the moods of various scenes. After gathering enough suitable music, often with considerable borrowings from the classics, they would rehearse the musicians and be ready for the show.

Ride of the Klansmen (Ku Klux Klan), from the historic and explicitly racist silent film *Birth of a Nation* (1915), by D. W. Griffith.

The quality of these performances varied greatly from theater to theater. Hence filmmakers increasingly turned to composers to create original scores for their films. The French composer Camille Saint-Saëns is generally credited with writing the first original film score—for *L'Assassinat du Duc de Guise* (1908).

The most important American composer of film music during the silent era is Joseph Carl Breil, who wrote the score for D. W. Griffith's landmark and controversial film *The Birth of a Nation* (1915; see illustration above). Breil's score contains all three types of music mentioned above. Substantial quotes from Classical works (for example, Wagner's *Ride of the Valkyries* used for the ride of the Klansmen), numerous quotes of patriotic tunes for the Civil War scenes, and new music featuring a number of leitmotifs establish this work as the first great American film score.

Joseph Carl Breil

The Sound Era

In 1926, the Warner Bros. Studio unveiled the Vitaphone system, which synchronized music played on a phonograph with action shown on a reel of film. The first feature film using this technology, *Don Juan* (1926), was recorded with music performed by the New York Philharmonic. In the following year, Warner Bros. released *The Jazz Singer*, which employed synchronized underscoring, several songs recorded live by Al Jolson, and two brief passages of spoken words. The spoken words created an enormous public sensation, and talking pictures quickly displaced silent films.

In the transition to sound, difficulties in coordinating music and dialogue led to the temporary abandonment of music. But advancements in technology were rapid, and *King Kong* (1933), with a full symphonic score by Max Steiner, reestablished the prominent role of music in films.

During the 1930s, quality films were produced at an unprecedented rate, and Hollywood entered a Golden Age that fostered music as a central feature of film. In shaping the classical film score, Hollywood called upon the service of two composers from Vienna: Max Steiner and Erich Korngold.

Max Steiner, a child prodigy, came to Hollywood in 1929. After scoring *King Kong*, he composed a number of important works before starting his masterpiece, *Gone With the Wind* (1939). For this epic film of love and war, Steiner wrote an unprecedented three hours and forty-five minutes of music. The leitmotif for Scarlett's plantation (Tara's theme) became the first blockbuster film theme and remains one of the most popular and recognizable of all movie melodies. Steiner worked on over three hundred films, and his credits include numerous memorable works, among them *Casablanca* (1942).

The son of a major music critic in Vienna, Erich Korngold, like Steiner, was a child prodigy. Richard Strauss, Gustav Mahler, and Giacomo Puccini were among the many admirers of the young Korngold. A master of orchestral color and thematic development, Korngold provided a model for future film composers with only a handful of film scores, his most famous being *The Adventures of Robin Hood* (1938).

After World War I, filmmakers in Europe were unable to match the commercial accomplishments of the Hollywood industry. Instead, they tended to focus more on the artistic qualities of film. Germany had a brief flourishing of filmmaking prior to Hitler's rise to power. The expressionistic film *The Cabinet of Dr. Caligari* (1920) made a sensation both in Europe and in the United States. Because of the film's distorted visions—horizontal and vertical lines are avoided and the sets are deliberately artificial—this tale of insanity became one of the earliest works to incorporate modern music.

Movie poster from the classic adventure-fantasy *King Kong* (1933), featuring a film score by Max Steiner.

Dmitri Shostakovich

In France, film was embraced by a significant number of art music composers. Unlike their American counterparts, who seemingly held film music in disdain, Erik Satie, Jacques Ibert, Germaine Tailleferre, Darius Milhaud, and Arthur Honegger all eagerly adopted the new art form. Honegger provided music for perhaps the most remarkable French film of the 1920s, Abel Gance's *Napoleon* (1927).

Under the leadership of Lenin (1917–24), the Soviet Union also became a major force in filmmaking. As in France, the major composers of this country contributed greatly to the artistic success of their film industry. Dmitri Shostakovich composed his first film score in 1929, and completed fifteen more during the 1930s, including *The Great Citizen* (1937), which was largely created by Stalin himself. Sergei Prokofiev (1891–1953) worked on eight Soviet films, of which two were created for the Soviet Union's leading film director, Sergei Eisentein: *Alexander Nevsky* (1938) and *Ivan the Terrible* (1944–45).

The Postwar Years

Following World War II, film music underwent a number of significant changes. Due to financial constraints, the lush symphonic score of the Golden Age gradually declined, and many films used music sparingly. Composers also explored new musical styles, including the use of popular genres as well as contemporary art music.

Bernard Herrmann and Miklós Rózsa are two early pioneers from this period. In his first film score, for Orson Welles' classic *Citizen Kane* (1941), Herrmann creates a dark atmosphere by using low instrumental colors and tone clusters. He later continued to incorporate disturbing modernistic material in his scores for Hitchcock's *Vertigo* (1958) and *Psycho* (1960) and for Martin Scorsese's *Taxi Driver* (1976). Miklós Rózsa, who is best remembered for his scores to epics like *Ben-Hur* (1959), was the first to use an electronic instrument in film music. In Hitchcock's *Spellbound* (1945), he added the **Theremin** (the first fully electronic instrument) to create an eerie effect during the passages suggesting dementia.

As the film industry allowed for more daring musical sounds in films, several prominent American composers of art music turned their attention to the genre, most notably Aaron Copland and Leonard Bernstein. Copland (see p. 367) wrote music for five Hollywood feature films and received four Oscar nominations. He won the Award for Best Music, Original Score, in 1949 for *The Heiress*. Bernstein (see p. 394) composed an original film score for only one movie, Elia Kazan's masterpiece *On the Waterfront* (1954). His score supports this tale of corruption and redemption with a mixture of modern and jazz elements. The powerful ending is one of the finest moments in film music. In 1961, Bernstein's Broadway hit *West Side Story* was converted to film and won a near record-breaking ten Oscars.

From the late 1940s through the 1960s, popular music gradually moved from its restricted role as source music to underscoring. Dmitri Tiomkin created a landmark score in 1952 for *High Noon* when he incorporated a country/western ballad sung by Tex Ritter, both in the opening credits and during scenes showing the isolation of Sheriff Will Kane. The tune created a public sensation, and soon popular movie themes were in demand for every Hollywood film. One of the greatest composers of movie themes, Henry Mancini emerged in the 1960s to create a series of major hits in films such as *Breakfast at Tiffany's* ("Moon River," 1961), *The Days of Wine and Roses* (1962), and *The Pink Panther* (1964).

Rock music came of age with Hollywood movies. In 1955, the release of *The Blackboard Jungle*, featuring *Rock Around the Clock* by Bill Haley and the Comets, propelled the song to the top of the Billboard chart, marking the beginning of the Rock era. Hollywood quickly made a movie star of Elvis Presley, who made pictures at a rate of three a year for nearly a decade. Landmark films with rock music include *The Graduate* (1967) and *Easy Rider* (1969), which created rock albums rather than just singles; *Shaft* (1971), with an Oscar-winning, full-rock score by Isaac Hayes; and *Saturday Night Fever* (1977), whose soundtrack by the Bee Gees sold over thirty million copies, creating a model for the future use of rock music in films.

In the new environment of film music, composers needed to be versatile and be able to write in all musical styles, including modern and popular. Two of the finest craftsmen from this time were Elmer Bernstein and Jerry Goldsmith. Bernstein helped introduce jazz as underscoring in the disturbing portrayal of a drummer addicted to drugs (played by Frank Sinatra) in *The Man with the Golden Arm* (1955). He later composed such divergent scores as the energetic *The Magnificent Seven* (1960) and the thoughtful *To Kill a Mockingbird* (1962). He maintained a prolific output that includes *Ghostbusters* (1984) and *Wild Wild West* (1999). Goldsmith likewise had a lengthy and versatile career. His scores range from the expressionistic *Planet of the Apes* (1968) to the dark *Chinatown* (1974), the Rambo action movies, the sports tale *Hoosiers* (1986), and many of the *Star Trek* series, including *Star Trek: Nemesis* (2002).

Bernard Herrmann

Miklós Rózsa

Aaron Copland

Leonard Bernstein

Elmer Bernstein

Jerry Goldsmith

IN HIS OWN WORDS

I think that the composer, because of the success of the Williams scores, is in a somewhat better position now than he has been in for some time. The attitudes appear to be a little bit looser, less doctrinaire on the part of the producers. There was one time a feeling . . . that they wanted either a rock score or a commercial score.

—ELMER BERNSTEIN

In this *Star Wars* scene—featuring Han Solo (Harrison Ford), Obi-Wan Kenobi (Alec Guinness), Luke Skywalker (Mark Hamill), and Chewbacca (Peter Mayhew)—John Williams's score heightens the drama as the starship is drawn into the tractor beam of the Death Star.

Beyond *Star Wars*

Star Wars (1977) revolutionized the movie industry by inundating the audience with spectacular visual and aural effects. Critical to the phenomenal success of this film is the brilliant score by John Williams, which features a return to the colorful virtuoso symphony, the unabashed emotional underscoring, and the system of leitmotifs that were hallmarks of the film scores from the Golden Age.

John Williams began composing for television in the 1950s, working on shows such as *Gilligan's Island*. Shifting to the big screen in the 1960s, he wrote a series of scores for disaster films, which culminated in his exhilarating score for *Jaws* (1975). By the end of the 1970s, he had established himself as Hollywood's foremost composer and had three blockbusters: *Star Wars* (1977), *Close Encounters of the Third Kind* (1977), and *Superman* (1978). During the 1980s, Williams scored six of the top ten box-office hits in the decade: the two *Star Wars* sequels, the *Indiana Jones* trilogy, and *E.T.: The Extra-Terrestrial*. Williams has maintained a steady output of quality film scores up to the present time. Among his best-known works in recent years are *Schindler's* List (1993), *Jurassic Park* (1995), the trilogy of *Star Wars* prequels, the first three *Harry Potter* films, and *Munich* (2005).

WILLIAMS: *RAIDERS MARCH*, FROM *RAIDERS OF THE LOST ARK*

The *Raiders March*, first heard in its entirety during the closing credits of *Raiders of the Lost Ark* (1981), is fashioned from two leitmotifs in the film. The first, belonging to Indiana Jones, recalls Copland's American style with its disjunct theme and stuttering accompaniment. Featuring the brass and percussion, it projects a character that well suits our courageous and confident protagonist. The second represents Marion Ravenwood, and its lush setting suggests the love relationship that she has with Indiana.

The contrasting moods of the two melodies help delineate the **A-B-A′** march structure (see Listening Guide 56, p. 448). In the **A** section, the Indiana Jones theme is presented in the **a-b-a′** form; the principal melody is heard four times, each of which grows in intensity. Marion's theme, primarily heard in the strings, projects a passionate songlike character and functions as the trio section. Typical

John Williams

of many **A-B-A** structures by composers such as Tchaikovsky, the reprise of the **A** section is abbreviated to just **b-a'**. Adding to the playful quality of the work are several strong dissonances, including the final chord.

Another important figure in the revival of the symphonic score is James Horner. A product of the music schools of both University of Southern California (USC) and University of California at Los Angeles (UCLA), he received critical attention for his music to *Star Trek II: The Wrath of Khan* (1982) and *Star Trek III: The Search for Spock* (1984). Horner created an international sensation with his song and underscoring for *Titanic* (1997). Among his other well-known scores are *Field of Dreams* (1989), *Apollo 13* (1995), and *Braveheart* (1995).

James Horner

The synthesizer had a major impact on films during the 1980s (see p. 451) and has been an enormous aid to the composer, in part because of its ease in creating scores and parts. It also serves as a useful tool for the film director, who can now hear the general sound of the music before hiring a studio orchestra. The synthesizer's ability to reproduce the sounds of acoustic instruments has also led to its inclusion in the modern studio orchestra where it not only imitates the sound of individual instruments, such as a harp, piano, or drums, but also gives support to the general sound of the strings. In some films, a synthesizer has substituted for an entire orchestra, as in the Oscar-winning score to *Chariots of Fire* (1981).

Synthesizer

Because use of the synthesizer as a performing instrument was largely the domain of popular musicians, the newest generation of film composers features a significant number who lack traditional university training. Two prominent examples of the new breed are Danny Elfman and Hans Zimmer. Elfman, the founder of the rock group Oingo Boingo, began composing film scores with *Pee-Wee's Big Adventure* (1985). Continuing to work with director Tim Burton, Elfman expanded his technique in *Beetlejuice* (1988), *Batman* (1989), *Edward Scissorhands* (1990), *The Nightmare Before Christmas* (1993), and *Men in Black* (1997). Elfman's most recent works include the two *Spider-Man* films (2002 and 2004) and the delightful *Charlie and the Chocolate Factory* (2005). Hans Zimmer, like Elfman, comes from a popular-music and synthesizer background. Among his early films are two Academy Award winners for Best Picture, *Rain Man* (1988) and *Driving Miss Daisy* (1989). His other well-known scores include *The Lion King* (1994), *Gladiator* (2000), *Madagascar* (2005), *Batman Begins* (with James Newton Howard, 2005), and *Pirates of the Caribbean: Dead Man's Chest* (2006).

Danny Elfman

Hans Zimmer

The adventurer Indiana Jones (Harrison Ford) attempts to recover a sacred idol in the jungles of South America, in *Raiders of the Lost Ark* (1981). The music of John Williams accompanies all the movies in the series.

Toby Maguire as the title character in *Spider-Man* (2002), with a film score by Danny Elfman.

In recent years, women composers have started to gain prominence in film composition. Rachel Portman became the first woman to win an Academy Award for Best Music, Original Score, for *Emma* (1996) which was based on the Jane Austen novel of the same name. Born in England and trained at Oxford, Portman also composed music for the thoughtful *Joy Luck Club* (1993) and received an Oscar nomination for her score to *The Cider House Rules* (1999) and wrote scores for *Chocolat* (2000) and *The Manchurian Candidate* (2004). Songwriter Diane Warren has been prominent in Academy Award presentations as well, receiving five nominations since 1996. Most recently, she has contributed songs to a variety of popular films, including *Legally Blonde II* (2003), *Love Actually* (2003), and *The Princess Diaries II* (2004).

During the 1990s, several American composers of art music have turned to the medium of film. John Corigliano, a leading figure in the New Romanticism, received an Oscar for his haunting music to *The Red Violin* (1999), played by solo violinist Joshua Bell. The score is an overarching theme and variations that incorporates Baroque, Romantic, Chinese, and modern musical styles. Following in his footsteps, the Chinese-American composer Tan Dun won an Oscar for *Crouching Tiger, Hidden Dragon* (2000), and Brooklyn-born Elliot Goldenthal was honored with the same award for *Frida* (2002).

Minimalism found its way into films during the 1990s with popular scores such as *The Matrix* (1999), as well as *The Truman Show* (1998) and *The Hours* (2002) by Philip Glass (see p. 460), whose minimalistic style has had much popular appeal. Thomas Newman, the son of famed film composer Alfred Newman, has employed the style effectively in a number of films, including *Shawshank Redemption* (1994), *American Beauty* (1999), and *Finding Nemo* (2003).

The history of film music is now over a century old. During this time, the medium has attracted many of the world's best-known composers, including Camille Saint-Saëns, Arthur Honegger, Aaron Copland, George Gershwin, Leonard Bernstein, William Walton, Silvestre Revueltas, Sergei Prokofiev, Tan Dun, and Philip Glass. The Hollywood industry also supported a number of specialists, such as Max Steiner, Miklós Rózsa, Elmer Bernstein, and John Williams, who composed film music quickly, effectively, and almost exclusively. While each composer brought an individual approach to his art, three general tendencies can be observed: the incorporation of the principles established by Wagner's music dramas, the assimilation of the ever-changing trends in popular music, and the constant search for fresh, new sounds. After one hundred years, film music remains a strong, vibrant medium and an integral part of the art of filmmaking.

IN HIS OWN WORDS

Writing the melody is the easy part. . . . But then, it's what you do with it. That's the skill, that's the art, that's what makes a great film score.

—DANNY ELFMAN

Listening Guide 56	eLG	4 (57–64) 8 (21–28)

John Williams: *Raiders March*, from *Raiders of the Lost Ark*

DATE OF WORK:	1981
GENRE:	Film score
FORM:	Ternary (**A-B-A'** coda)

WHAT TO LISTEN FOR: Instrumentation (brass, percussion) and beat of a traditional march.
Principal melodies derived from leitmotifs in the film.
Overall **A-B-A′** form (March-Trio-March), with sectional divisions
   and repeats.
Disjunct opening theme set against stuttering ostinato accompaniment.
Lyric trio section, featuring strings.
Occasional dissonant harmony.

March: Section **A (a-b-a′)**

57 0:00   Introduction; stuttering rhythmic ostinato setup.

0:07   **a section**—Disjunct march tune played by trumpet:

0:21   March tune repeated, with fuller accompaniment; offbeats on cymbals.

58 0:36   **b section**—strings present a contrasting idea:

Closes in disjunct cadence figure:

0:52   **b section**—contrasting idea repeated in brass with extended cadential section:

59 1:17   **a′ section**—opening march returns with a more vigorous accompaniment.

1:36   Modulates up a half step; imitative answer in trombones.

1:52   Cadential figure (from **b**) brings the March section to a close.

Trio: Section **B (c-d-c′)**

60 2:08   **c section**—lyrical melody in low strings, with undulating accompaniment:

Trio theme repeated and developed.

61 2:41   **d section**—violins and cellos in dialogue with phrases of **c** section.

62 3:08   **c′ section**—soaring violins play trio theme; slows to cadence.

March Reprise: Section **A (b-a′)**

63 3:32   **b section**—accompaniment of opening returns; theme played by French horn, with extended
cadence in brass.

64 4:12   **a′ section**—accompaniment pattern intensifies with louder dynamics and fuller orchestration;
march theme stated, then repeated with answering phrases in the trombones.

4:47   Coda—reiterates rhythmic ideas from march tune, leading to a loud and dissonant closing.

79

Technology and Music

*"I have been waiting a long time for electronics to free music
from the tempered scale and the limitations of musical instruments.
Electronic instruments are the portentous first step toward the
liberation of music."*

—EDGARD VARÈSE

KEY POINTS   Ⓢ **StudySpace** online at www.wwnorton.com/enjoy

- *Musique concrète*, which began in the late 1940s, used natural sounds recorded on magnetic tape as a new medium for composition.

- In the early 1950s, the German school of *electronische Musik* created compositions using electronically generated sounds.

- By the late 1960s, smaller, cheaper synthesizers were available to many musicians and composers.

- Digital technology, beginning with the invention of FM synthesis in the 1970s, revolutionized the world of electronic music.

- Computers can generate sounds, create compositions, and interact with synthesizers via the *Musical Instrument Digital Interface (MIDI)*.

- One of the most innovative composers of interactive music is Tod Machover, who writes for electronically enhanced *hyperinstruments*.

- Modern composers are moving toward interactive performances involving a live audience, either directly or via the Internet.

The Technological Revolution

The most important development in art music during the last fifty years was the emergence of electronic music. New instruments such as the Theremin (see p. 445), and the Hammond organ—both of which produce sounds electronically—predicted a future that was quickly realized by the booming revolution of technology.

Musique concrète   Two trends emerged simultaneously in the late 1940s and early 1950s: *musique concrète* in France and *electronische Musik* in Germany. *Musique concrète* was based in Paris and headed by Pierre Schaeffer. It relied on sounds (made by any natural source, including musical instruments) that were recorded onto magnetic tape and then manipulated by various means—for example, by changing the speed of the playback, reversing the direction of the tape, or processing the sounds through external devices such as filters.

The manifestations of natural sounds gave way to artificially generated ones, and a wide variety of sound equipment came into use. Within a few years, studios

Tape music   for the production of *tape music* (an extension of *musique concrète*) sprang up in many of the chief musical centers of Europe and America. With the raw sound (either naturally or electronically produced) as a starting point, the composer could isolate its components, alter its pitch, volume, or other dimensions, play it backward, add reverberation (echo), filter out some of the overtones (the series of tones naturally produced by a resonating body that sound above the fundamental frequency), or add other components by splicing and overdubbing. Even though all these operations were laborious and time-consuming—it might take many hours to process only a minute or two of finished music—composers hastened to experiment with the new medium.

Electronische Musik occurred during the early 1950s, in Cologne, Germany, and by 1953, German composer Karlheinz Stockhausen had begun working in the studio there and had already produced two *Electronic Studies* (1953–54), followed by his electronic masterpiece *Song of the Youths* (*Gesang der Jünglinge*, 1956), a composition integrating the human voice with electronically generated sounds. The heart of this German system was the oscillator, which could generate several waveforms, each capable of a different timbre. This electronically generated waveform could be subjected to filters, reverberation, amplifiers, and other devices. Eventually, these many components would be packaged together in a single console with a piano keyboard interface to become our modern-day *synthesizer*.

The first to devise a completely integrated package of electronic components for sound generation was the RCA music synthesizer, completed in 1955. A second version of the RCA synthesizer was delivered to Columbia-Princeton's Electronic Music Center in 1959. Unfortunately, the size and cost of this device prohibited other institutions from purchasing synthesizers of their own, and very few composers had the luxury of being able to work at the Electronic Music Center. Composing on the RCA synthesizer also proved to be tedious and time consuming, and hours were spent programming the machine to produce just a few minutes of music.

By the 1960s, however, both Robert Moog and Donald Buchla had created more compact and affordable synthesizers suited for mass production. These newer synthesizers capitalized on the transistor technology developed in the late 1950s (the RCA synthesizer used bulky vacuum tubes, whereas transistors used only a fraction of that space) and the more efficient voltage-controlled oscillator as developed by Moog. Morton Subotnick's *Silver Apples of the Moon* (1967) was realized on one of these newer synthesizers and has the distinction of being the first electronic music composition commissioned by a record company. But it was a recording called *Switched-On Bach*, made in 1968 by Walter Carlos (who later became Wendy Carlos, through a sex change), that catapulted the synthesizer and the genre of electronic music to instant fame. The Moog synthesizer that Carlos used for the recording was quickly adopted by many musicians in the world of popular music. Carlos's synthesizer music can also be heard on the soundtracks of Stanley Kubrick's films *A Clockwork Orange* (1971) and *The Shining* (1980).

This initial wave of commercially available synthesizers, like those made by Moog, Buchla, ARP, Roland, and Oberheim, marked the era of *analog* synthesis. But by the late 1960s, a new wave of technology known as *digital frequency modulation synthesis* had already been developed by John Chowning at Stanford University. Synthesis by means of frequency modulation (FM) depends on a series of sine-wave generators interacting to produce new, more complex, waveforms. (These digital waveforms are represented by a string of discrete numbers as opposed to analog signals, such as electrical current, which are continuous in nature). In 1983, the Yamaha DX7, one of the best-selling synthesizers of all time, was unveiled and retailed for slightly under $2,000. During that same year, a standardized communications protocol known as the *Musical Instrument Digital Interface* (MIDI) was officially adopted and incorporated into all new music synthesizers. MIDI allows synthesizers to communicate not only with one another, but with other devices such as computers, signal processors,

Robert Moog, creator of the pioneering Moog synthesizer.

drum machines, and even mixing boards. Specially designed software allows composers to record MIDI data (such as pitch, duration, volume, etc.) on the computer for playback on one or more synthesizers. By the mid-1980s, digital sampling synthesizers, capable of digitizing short audio samples, became affordable to the average musician. Digital samplers allow performers and composers to recreate a realistic sounding grand piano, trumpet, violin, bird call, car crash, or any other sound that can be sampled. With the affordability of digital synthesizers and personal computers, and their ability to communicate with one another, the digital revolution took the world of electronic music by storm.

Computer music Computer music, however, did not wait for the invention of MIDI to become integrated with the world of electronic music. Research in this field had already begun with the pioneering work of Max Mathews at Bell Laboratories in the 1950s. While Mathews explored the idea of using a computer to synthesize sounds via his series of MUSIC software programs (eleven versions in all), other composers—notably Lejaren Hiller—used the computer to generate music compositions.

Important Figures in Electronic Music

Electronic music has two novel aspects. The most immediately obvious one, the possibility to create new sounds, has impelled many musicians to use the medium. Equally important, the composer of electronic music can work directly with the sounds and produce a finished work without the help of an intermediary performer.

Edgard Varèse One of the pioneers of electronic music was the French composer Edgard Varèse (1883–1965), who turned to this medium relatively late in his life. His composition *Poème électronique* (1956–58), commissioned for a sound-and-light show at Philips Pavilion at the 1958 Brussels World's Fair, consisted of both electronic and *concrète* sounds recorded onto multi-channel tape. Varèse combined natural sounds (for example, the human voice) with electronically generated sounds and subjected them to tape music techniques such as altering the tape speed, using filters, and adding reverberation. The result was recognizable sounds—voices, bells, a flying airplane—along with pulse-generated percussion sounds and synthetic tones.

Combining electronic sounds with live music has also proved fertile, especially since many composers had worked in both media. Works for soloist and recorded tape became common, even "concertos" for tape recorder (or live-performance synthesizer or computer) and orchestra. Two important composers who have worked in this mixed medium are Mario Davidovsky (b. 1934), formerly a professor of composition at Columbia University and director of the Columbia-Princeton Electronic Music Center in New York, and Milton Babbitt (b. 1916), whose early electronic works were composed at the Columbia-Princeton Electronic Music Center. Among Davidovsky's works for tape and live performer is a series known as *Synchronisms* (1963–88), dialogues for solo instrument and prerecorded tape. No. 1, for flute and tape, is particularly effective because of the flute's purity of tone, wide range of dynamics, and agility in pitch and articulation. "The attempt here," Davidovsky writes, "has been made to preserve the typical characteristics of

Edgar Varèse's *Poème électronique* was composed as part of a multimedia show for the Philips Pavilion, designed by **Le Corbusier**, at the 1958 Brussels World's Fair.

the conventional instruments and the electronic medium respectively—yet to achieve integration of both into a coherent musical texture."

Electronic music has permeated the commercial world of music-making in a big way. Much of the music we hear today as movie and TV soundtracks is electronically generated, although some effects resemble the sounds of conventional instruments so closely that we are not always aware of the new technology. Popular music groups have been "electrified" for some years, but now most of them regularly feature synthesizers and samplers that both simulate conventional rock band instruments and produce altogether new sounds.

Tod Machover and Musical Interactivity

"The technique we invented . . . is a fantastic way not only to extend virtuosic instruments but to break down boundaries and open doors to musical experiences for ordinary music lovers."

One of the most creative minds in the world of music technology today is Tod Machover (b. 1953). His explorations into interactivity—between performers and computers as well as the audience and at-home listeners—have made him a leader in the contemporary music scene.

Tod Machover

Tod Machover grew up in New York City and began his music studies as a cellist. His parents, a piano teacher and a computer-graphic specialist, nurtured his dual interests in music and technology. Like most teenagers, he was interested in rock and began experimenting in the mid-1960s by amplifying his cello and manipulating its sound. He studied composition at The Juilliard School under Elliott Carter and Roger Sessions and became increasingly interested in computers. Machover was fascinated, he writes, by "the idea of being able to go straight from the imagination to programming this machine to produce anything I wanted."

Machover spent five years in Paris as Director of Musical Research at Pierre Boulez's IRCAM, the French government center for contemporary music. There he explored the European musical avant-garde and, ironically, came to value American innovators like John Cage and Charles Ives. In developing his own voice, he revisited his interest in rock music because of its rhythmic vitality, texture, timbre, and accessibility. His goal, he says, is to "make people pay attention and listen carefully."

His opera *VALIS* (1986), based on a science fiction novel by Philip Dick, was commissioned by the Georges Pompidou Center (see illustration, p. 422). In this work, he combined images and sound to redefine opera—not only that, he built his own theater, invented electronic scenery, and created a new opera orchestra with live computer instrumentation—all with a goal of attracting a new audience to the genre. This experience led Machover to begin working with **hyperinstruments**, which he explains are interactive machines "designed to augment and expand performance virtuosity in real time, using intelligent, interactive machines."

Hyperinstruments

Today, Machover is a professor of music and media at the Massachusetts Institute of Technology (MIT). He recognizes that music is first and foremost a performance art and should retain its focus on human expressivity and communication. He therefore creates "smart" computers that can follow the gestures and intentions of virtuoso performers—even if the performers know little about electronics—and thereby allows the performers to remain in control. In his work *Toward the Center* (1988–89), four of the six instruments are amplified and transformed electronically, and the keyboard and percussion parts are performed on MIDI controllers.

Musical Interactivity

Computers, and all the technological resources that go along with them, have radically changed our musical lives. We interact with music on a daily basis, whether downloading favorite songs to our iPods or mp3 players, selecting or creating polyphonic ringtones for our cellphones, finding new music from independent bands and artists on MySpace and YouTube profiles, or casting our votes in real time on our cells for the most talented American Idol vocalist.

For over fifty years, composers and performers have sought ways to harness technology to the creative musical process. We have mentioned works from the 1960s and 1970s in which live performers were accompanied by a pre-recorded tape. But this integration of conventional instruments and electronic ones was static. Today's broadened possibilities for communication between computers and humans has opened up new interactive musical relationships among performers (who can be connected to each other in various ways), between performers and composers, and between performers and a computer. The digital world makes virtual instruments, performers, and even listeners a possibility. We will see how virtuosity and expressivity of performers can be interpreted and expanded through digital means.

Early "computer" music was designed to simulate human music-making. Max Mathews, often viewed as the father of computer music, created the first "singing

Astronaut Dr. Dave Bowman (Keir Dullea) dismantles the "brains" of the supercomputer HAL-9000 aboard Discovery One, in the sci-fi classic film *2001: A Space Odyssey* (1968).

computer" shown in the classic movie *2001: A Space Odyssey* (1968), when the computer *HAL* hummed *A Bicycle Built for Two* as it died. The invention of MIDI technology facilitated more innovations for composers. Mathews developed programs designed for live performance, including one called Radio Baton that allowed the user to conduct an orchestral performance of MIDI files, with control over dynamics, tempo, and balance between the instruments.

Composers first combined keyboard synthesizers with computers to create more flexible and expressive instruments. We mentioned one pioneer in this area, Morton Subotnick, who used a Buchla synthesizer capable of unique tone colors and pitch controls for his album *Silver Apples of the Moon* (1967). Another landmark work that utilized Max Mathews' applications was Pierre Boulez's *Repons* (1981–84), for large ensemble and interactive computer, in which the computers extended the musical vocabulary and structure of the work. Here, Boulez used spatial acoustics as well, with the audience seated between the orchestra and the soloists whose playing was altered by real-time electronics.

Several important centers for interactive music research exist in both Europe and America, including IRCAM, the French government center for contemporary music (see p. 422), and the MIT Media Center, directed by composer Tod Machover (see p. 453). One intriguing project, at MIT, has involved capturing the complex gestures of a conductor and turning them into musical controls. Tod Machover collaborated on a device known as the Dextrous Hand Master, a glove controller that measures the expressive hand gestures and even subtle finger movements of a conductor's left hand with great precision and speed. In Machover's *Bug-Mudra* (1990; for two guitars, percussion, and live computer electronics), the conductor sets the tempo with the right hand while the left hand controls balance among the instruments as well as color and articulation. (The "bug" in the title refers to a computer bug, and "Mudra" is a word for hand gestures in classical Indian dance.) This idea of a hyper-conductor has been extended to electronically enhanced instruments of all types, including the hypercello work by Machover discussed in this chapter (see p. 456).

Interactivity can draw the listener into the music-making process as well. In 1995, Carla Scaletti introduced her project *Public Organ: An Interactive Networked Sound Installation* at the International Computer Music Conference, held in Banff, Canada, and simultaneously on the Internet. She explained that her composition was "a sometimes-humorous-sometimes-serious commentary on the Internet [that] invites participants to experience linking, lurking, looping and collective thinking" and asked her audience to contribute graffiti and images of themselves that could be incorporated instantly into the installation. Tod Machover has also viewed the creative process as a collaboration with the audience—whether present physically or connected electronically—thus breaking down the boundary between listener and creator. His *Brain Opera*, which premiered in 1996 at New York's Lincoln Center, was also online. Audience members first played informally with his enhanced hyperinstruments, then the formal performance incorporated recordings from the audience and Web participants. This work has now been installed permanently in the House of Music in Vienna, a modern, interactive museum dedicated to sound and music.

In recent years, composers and performers have experimented with various innovative approaches to computer-supported collaborative music, including shared sonic environments, online improvisation, and interconnected performance networks. Moreover, there has been a concerted effort to apply technological resources to music pedagogy. One of IRCAM's educational programs, created in conjunction with the French ministry of education, encourages young musi-

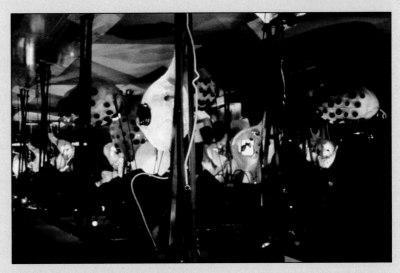

The audience participates in the compositional process in this installation from Tod Machover's *Brain Opera* (1996).

cians to interact in various ways with musical compositions, including deconstructing and reconstructing the musical structure and manipulating the sound or timbral effects. The overall goal of this program is to explore novel methods and tools that involve more people in the process of music-making and creation. You might want to investigate your own musical talents by experimenting with these new learning environments.

Terms to Note

MIDI
hyperinstrument

Suggested Listening

Machover: *Bug-Mudra* and *Begin Again Again . . .*
Soundtrack to *2001: A Space Odyssey*

Suggested Web Topics

IRCAM
Brain Opera

Cellist Yo-Yo Ma performing Tod Machover's *Begin Again Again . . . .*

Begin Again Again . . .

CD iMusic

J. S. Bach: Sarabande, from Cello Suite No. 2

The computer's role is to follow, complement, and underscore the musical development of the work, with an eye toward increasing the available sound-palette of traditional instruments. Machover's more recent compositions seek a seamless combination of acoustic instruments with electronics. His orchestral work *Sparkler* (2001) represents one such futuristic vision, which he has coupled in performance with his *Toy Symphony* (2003), created as a model for children to express themselves by interacting with high-tech music toys.

We will consider a work for solo hypercello, *Begin Again Again . . . ,* written for the virtuoso Yo-Yo Ma and premiered at the Tanglewood Festival in 1991 and recently revised. Machover conceived the piece as the first in a trilogy based on Dante's epic medieval poem the *Divine Comedy.* Exploring the possibility of renewal after suffering, *Begin Again Again . . .* represents the rolling inferno of Dante's poem, with the hypercello plunging musical depths. The hypercello line gravitates toward the middle D pitch on the instrument, trying to ascend from it but constantly being pulled lower.

Structurally, *Begin Again Again . . .* is in two large parts, each beginning with a theme followed by four variations in which the melodic contours, rhythms, and harmonies return in varying guises ranging from driving rock to intense lyricism. According to the composer, the music is "a whirlwind alternating between tormented questions ('Where am I? Where am I going? How am I going to get out of here?') and frenzied, disco-like assertions." The electronic accompaniment takes on various timbres throughout the work, but the cellist is in control of an array of devices for producing and transforming sound. In turn, the computer responds to the performer's nuances, including bow angle and pressure, as well as finger and wrist positions—thereby extending, but in no way controlling, the sound world of the soloist. The piece is so virtuosic that the composer asked Yo-Yo Ma, after a rehearsal for the premiere, "Is there any hair left on your bow?"

Machover's work was inspired by the stately Sarabande of Bach's solo Cello Suite No. 2, a work well known to all serious cellists. The Introduction (or the theme) of *Begin Again Again . . .* evokes Bach's work in contour, key center, and in various Baroque-like gestures, including tremolos (trills in the Bach) and arpeggiated chords (see Listening Guide 57). On our recording, we skip to Variation 3, "Emphatic," which angrily sets out a version of the theme in the cello's dark, low register, then repeats this melodic idea in a "warm and singing" line that grows disjunct and begins to bounce in staccato notes through the instrument's range. This builds to the next variation, entitled "Very Rapid and Precise," characterized by accented rhythms on insistently repeated notes from the theme, then slides (or glissandos) to other notes. At first, these are short slides, but as the work speeds to a feverish pace (marked "Almost Hysterical"), the pitches become less distinct as the player's bow races across the strings, closing in a long glissando to the highest note possible on the fingerboard. Here the cellist, now at the center of the piece, plays a songful soliloquy—"beginning again again"—to the accompaniment of various innovative electronic timbres and effects.

A cellist himself, Machover writes of his love affair with the instrument: "I wanted my instrument to be able to sing, expressing as much between the notes as on them." He notes the "human" qualities of the cello as well: it is the size of the human body, has the range of the male and female voice combined, and has vibrations that are felt throughout the performer's body, from head to toe. In *Begin Again Again . . . ,* Machover explores the full possibilities of this expressive instrument.

Listening Guide 57

Machover: *Hyperstring Trilogy: Begin Again Again . . .* , excerpts   (5:30)

DATE OF WORK:	1991; revised 2004
GENRE:	Theme and variations
MEDIUM:	Solo hypercello and live computer electronics

MOVEMENTS:

*Introduction (theme, part 1)	Timbre Dream (theme, part 2)
Delicate and Varied	Lyrical and Intimate
Energetic	Fluttering—Interior
*Emphatic—Warm and Singing	Growing—Majestic
*Very Rapid and Precise	Broad—Intense
	Coda: Powerful and Steady

WHAT TO LISTEN FOR: Rich, lyrical quality of cello; wide range possibilities.
Phrases and gestures drawn from Baroque style (Bach Sarabande).
Highly rhythmic and virtuosic character.
Electronic sounds provide varied accompaniment; different timbres,
     chords, and rhythmic support.
Work builds to a climactic close.

Introduction (theme, part 1)   1:28

76   0:00   Slow, expressive theme, rising a half step with tremolo, then outlining opening of Bach
Sarabande (see theme at end of listening guide):

0:25   Faster movement, wide-ranging, accented and staccato; accompanied by computer sounds.

0:32   Hint of opening returns; following by wide-ranging lines and many tremelos, accompanied by
computer-generated sounds.
Pace quickens (accelerando) on rising line, reaching repeated pitch D.

77   1:01   Opening theme heard in cello's high range, with "squeaky" electronic sounds:

Variation 3: Emphatic—Warm and Singing   2:42

78   0:00   Loud dissonant chord begins dramatic low-range variation of theme in changed rhythm;
intermittent dissonant chords punctuate cello line:

Listening Guide continues

0:15   Cello returns to low-range statement, marked Warm and Singing; line quickens and soars upward, accompanied by string-like electronic sounds; double stops (playing 2 notes simultaneously) used for emphasis.

0:40   Reminiscences of Bach heard while full range of cello is explored; tremolos and double stops heard throughout.

1:30   More rhythmic, accented line; disjunct and wide ranging, becoming frenetic.

79   1:55   *Fortissimo* low pitch, marked "con bravura" (with fierceness), begins slower restatement of opening thematic idea;

More chromatic with prominent computer accompaniment; explodes into next variation.

Variation 4: Very Rapid and Precise   1:20

80   0:00   High-pitched and rhythmic on repeated notes, then short glissandos and quick staccato movement:

0:27   Repeated pitch played *fortissimo* gives way to staccato notes a half step apart, then wider glissandos; rhythmic character continues as range widens.

81   0:54   Becomes feverish (marked Almost Hysterical) in pace and virtuosity; moves widely through instrument's range; simulated sounds moving in fast, repeated "chords":

More glissandos lead to closing upward sweep, with "windchime" effect dying out.

Opening of Sarabande from J. S. Bach, Cello Suite No. 2:

80

Some Current Trends

"Now that things are so simple, there's so much to do."
—MORTON FELDMAN

KEY POINTS   **StudySpace** online at www.wwnorton.com/enjoy

- The more recent compositional styles of *minimalism* and *New Romanticism* seek to appeal to audiences that have been alienated by highly intellectual and structural approaches to contemporary music.

- *Minimalist music* is based on repetitive melodic, rhythmic, or harmonic patterns with few or slowly changing variations. The music can sound hypnotic (as in new age music) or motor-driven and frenzied. The most important exponents are Steve Reich and Philip Glass.

- *Spiritual minimalism* is a recent trend characterized by a simple, nonpulsed music that springs from deep religious convictions. Estonian com-

poser Arvo Pärt's choral music (including *Cantate Domino canticum novum*) represents this style.

- American composer John Adams takes an eclectic approach that combines elements of minimalism with traits of New Romanticism (using a lush harmonic language), forging a *post-minimalist style*.

- *New Romanticism* favors the harmonic language of the late Romantic era; the music is often coupled with a highly virtuosic style and novel instrumental combinations. Libby Larsen's song cycle *Sonnets from the Portuguese*, set to the poetry of Elizabeth Barrett Browning, exemplifies this approach.

The emphasis on intellectual and constructivist tendencies in music—in short, serialism—has given way in recent years to two trends, both of which aspire to immediate audience appeal. One trend is *minimalism*, embraced by composers who strip their compositions down to the barest essentials in order to let the listener concentrate on a few basic details. The other is *New Romanticism*, which represents a look back to the lush harmonic language and the allure of Romantic and Post-Romantic composers. We will consider representatives from both of these eclectic movements.

Minimalism and Post-Minimalism

The urge toward a minimalist art first found expression in painting and sculpture and since the 1970s, has been a significant force in music. The salient feature of minimalism is the repetition of melodic, rhythmic, and harmonic patterns with very little variation. The music changes so slowly that it can have a hypnotic effect, and indeed the term "trance music" has attached itself to some of these works. In minimalist music, time moves at a different pace from what most of us are accustomed to.

By simplifying melody, rhythm, and harmony within an unwavering tonality, the minimalists have turned away from the complex, highly intellectual style of Schoenberg, Webern, and Boulez. Instead, they open themselves to modes of thought emanating from emerging countries—especially the contemplative art of India and the quasi-obsessive rhythms of some African cultures—and to jazz, pop,

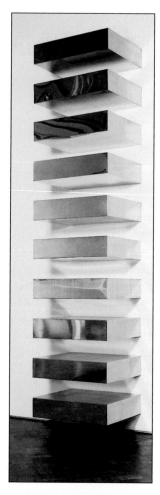

Sculptor **Donald Judd** uses space as a building material, along with polished copper, in this repetitive minimalist work. *Untitled* (1969).

and rock. Although influenced by the early ideas of John Cage, minimalists for the most part reject his interest in indeterminacy and chance. They prefer to control their sounds.

Two widely known minimalists are Steve Reich (b. 1936), whose music achieves a trancelike quality that derives from his study of non-Western—especially African—music, and Philip Glass (b. 1937) whose style draws on the musical traditions of India and Africa as well as the techniques of rock and progressive jazz. His most important works include *Glassworks* (1983); his operas *Einstein on the Beach* (1976), *Satyagraha* (1980), *Akhnaten* (1984); the chamber opera *La Belle et la Bête* (1994); and the filmscores for *The Hours* (2002) and *The Illusionist* (2006).

One branch of minimalism that has developed, mostly at the hands of European composers, is a nonpulsed music inspired by religious beliefs and expressed in deceptively simple—and seemingly endless—chains of lush modal or tonal progressions. The major representatives of this deeply meditative music, often referred to as ***spiritual minimalism***, are Arvo Pärt, an Estonian composer who combines the mysticism of Russian Orthodox rituals with elements of Eastern European folk music; and John Tavener (b. 1944), an English composer whose style combines elements of New Romanticism with a devout spiritualism. Tavener's powerful choral work *Song for Athene* was heard by millions at the close of the funeral service for Princess Diana on September 6, 1997; its text, "Alleluia. May flights of angels sing thee to thy rest," is drawn from Shakespeare's *Hamlet* and from the Orthodox Vigil Service.

Arvo Pärt and Spiritual Minimalism

"Arvo Pärt's music accepts silence and death, and thus reaffirms the basic truth of life, its frailty compassionately realised, its sacred beauty observed and celebrated."

—PAUL HILLIER

Arvo Pärt (b. 1935) was born and raised in Estonia, formerly a republic of the Soviet Union (USSR). As a youth, Pärt studied piano, but the instrument on which he practiced needed repairs to its middle register so badly that he explored the sounds of the extreme upper and lower registers. While a student, he worked as a recording engineer for the Estonian State Radio and supported himself by writing music for films and stage productions.

Medieval and Renaissance music

Ⓢ **Arvo Pärt**

In his early compositions, Pärt explored both Neoclassical and serial techniques. An interest in the music of J. S. Bach led him to use a tone row that incorporated the B-A-C-H motive (which, in German, translates as the pitches of B flat, A, C, B natural). These early works are set in a Baroque imitative style. One such composition is *Collage sur B-A-C-H* (1964), in which Pärt transcribes a Bach dance and then distorts it nearly beyond recognition.

There have been several notable periods of compositional silence from Pärt; in the early 1970s, he studied medieval and Renaissance music. When he returned to composition in 1976, there was a new-found spiritualism at the root of his music. He shunned serialism in favor of a style all his own—***tintinnabulation*** (after the Latin word for ringing of bells). "I created my tintinnabular style, and was declared mad . . . ." Three works from 1977 catapulted Pärt, and his tintinnabular sound, to international fame: *Fratres*, a chamber work that explores the interval of open fifths; *Cantus in memoriam Benjamin Britten*, for string orchestra and bells; and *Tabula Rasa*, a kind of Baroque concerto for two violins.

Pärt's religious convictions made life in the Soviet Union difficult (the state position was atheism), and in 1980 he and his family left, eventually settling in what was then West Berlin. Since 1980, Pärt has focused his creative efforts on Latin and Orthodox choral music, including a *Te Deum* that evokes—but does not use—Gregorian chant; a Magnificat; and *Kanon Pokajanen* (on Russian Orthodox texts).

Pärt's choral work on Psalm 95, *Cantate Domino canticum novum* (O sing to the Lord a new song), is a captivating example of his tintinnabular style (see Listening Guide 58). Here, the composer returns to the simplicity of medieval chant for his inspiration: lyrical, conjunct lines move freely, always following the Latin text. At the same time, the work seems to dance along lightly, interrupted by brief moments of silence. Pärt does not use traditional notation; instead, he provides only black noteheads to indicate pitch, adding dashes to lengthen a note at the end of a phrase (one dash approximately doubles the value; two dashes triple it—the same as doubling an eighth note to equal a quarter, or tripling it to equal a dotted quarter note). This notation is very similar to notating Gregorian chant today; you can see an example in Listening Guide 2, on page 73.

Each section of Pärt's work begins with a fluid, monophonic line to which is joined a second line, or countermelody, that moves with the first, but in contrary motion, or inversion. At key points in the psalm text, the texture expands to the four-part choir (the added voices doubling in octaves, thus retaining a two-line texture), still in strict homorhythmic movement. There are clear examples of word painting, as when the full choir (SATB) proclaims "his glory among all the nations," and,

Tintinnabulation

IN HIS OWN WORDS

Tintinnabulation is an area I sometimes wander into when I am searching for answers—in my life, my music, my work. . . . Here I am alone with silence. I have discovered that it is enough when a single note is beautifully played. This one note, or a silent beat, or a moment of silence, comforts me. I work with very few elements—with one voice, with two voices.

Listening Guide 58

eLG 4 (82–85) 8 (52–55)

Pärt: *Cantate Domino canticum novum (O sing to the Lord a new song)* (2:50)

DATE OF WORK:	1977 (rev. 1996)
MEDIUM:	SATB chorus and organ
TEXT:	Psalm 95 (Catholic Bible); Psalm 96 (Protestant Bible)

WHAT TO LISTEN FOR:
Chantlike melodies in repetitive patterns.
Free-flowing rhythms, following text, with pauses at text punctuation.
Contrasting, or mirror, motion between the voices.
Voices often paired SA and TB.
Changing textures: 1 voice, 2 voices, and 4 voices.
Tintinnabular, or bell-like, style.
Occasional harsh dissonances (intervals of 2nds).

	TEXT	TRANSLATION	VOICES (WITH ORGAN)
82 0:00	Cantate Domino canticum novum:	O sing to the Lord a new song:	Sopranos
	Cantate Domino omnis terra.	Sing to the Lord, all the earth.	
	Cantate Domino, et benedicite nomini ejus:	Sing to the Lord, bless his name;	Sopranos and Altos
	Annuntiate de die in diem salutare ejus.	Tell of his salvation from day to day.	

Listening Guide continues

Annuntiate inter gentes gloriam ejus,	Declare his glory among the nations.	SATB
In omnibus populis mirabilia ejus.	His marvelous works among all the peoples.	

83 0:35

Quoniam magnus Dominus, et laudabilis nimis:	For great is the Lord, and greatly to be praised.	Tenors
Terribilis est super omnes deos.	He is to be feared above all gods.	
Quoniam omnes dii gentium daemonia:	For all the gods of the people are idols;	Tenors and Basses
Dominus autem coelos fecit.	But the Lord made the heavens.	
Confessio et pulchritudo in conspectu ejus:	Honor and majesty are before him;	
Sanctimonia et magnifcentia in sanctificatione ejus.	Strength and beauty are his salvation.	

84 1:09

Afferte Domino patriae gentium,	Ascribe to the Lord, o families of the peoples.	Sopranos
Afferte Domino gloriam et honorem:	Ascribe to the Lord glory and strength;	
Afferte Domino gloriam nomini ejus.	Ascribe to the Lord the glory due his name.	
Tollite hostias, et introite in atria ejus:	Bring an offering, and come into his courts.	Sopranos and Altos
Adorate Dominum in atria sancto ejus.	Worship the Lord in holy array.	
Commoveatur a facie ejus universa terra:	Tremble before him, all the earth;	SATB
Dicite in gentibus quia Dominus regnavit.	Say among the nations, "The Lord reigns.	

85 1:52

Etenim corexit orbem terrae qui non commovebitur:	Yea, the world is established, it shall never be moved.	Tenors
Judicabit populus in aequitate.	He will judge the peoples with equity."	
Laetentur caeli, et exsultet terra:	Let the heavens be glad, and let the earth rejoice;	Tenors and Basses
Commoveatur mare, et plenitudo eius:	Let the sea roar, and all that fills it;	
Gaudebunt campi, et omnia quae in eis sunt.	Let the field exult, and every thing in it.	
Tunc exsultabunt omnia ligna silvarium	Then shall all the trees of the wood sing for joy	SATB
A facie Domini, quia venit:	Before the Lord, for he comes;	
Quoniam venit iudicare terram.	For he comes to judge the earth.	
Judicabit orbem terrae in aequitate,	He will judge the world with righteousness,	
Et populos in veritate sua.	And the peoples with his truth.	

Duet between sopranos and altos, moving in contrary motion, showing free rhythmic notation (arrows mark stressed dissonances of interval of 2nd):

near the end, announces that "all the trees of the wood sing for joy." The bell-like, or tintinnabular, style is achieved by weaving together two melodic lines that hover around a central pitch (B flat) and by triadic pitches in the organ that seem to ring throughout. Pärt's serenely religious music rejects the sounds of modernity, returning to a purity and simplicity that reopens communication with the listener. Conductor Paul Hillier praises Pärt's ability to create, with the simplest of means, "an intense, vibrant music that stands apart from the world and beckons us to an inner quietness and an inner exaltation."

John Adams and Post-Minimalism

*"Whenever serious art loses track of its roots in
the vernacular, then it begins to atrophy."*

A composer who would respond to the emotional impulses of the New Romantics by seeking to expand the expressive gamut of minimalist music was bound to appear. John Adams (b. 1947), the best known of the minimalist composers, answered this call. Adams was educated at Harvard University and thus was steeped in serialism. In his dorm room, he preferred to listen to rock: "I was much inspired by certain albums that appeared to me to have a fabulous unity to them, like *Disraeli Gears, Abbey Road, Dark Side of the Moon*, and Marvin Gaye's *What's Going On?*" In 1971, he drove his Volkswagen Beetle cross-country to San Francisco, where he still lives, and he began teaching at the San Francisco Conservatory of Music in 1972. Adams quickly became an advocate for contemporary music in the Bay Area, serving as an adviser to the San Francisco Symphony and establishing its New and Unusual Music Series.

John Adams

Strongly influenced by Steve Reich, Adams's music is marked by warm sonorities, a high energy level, and a more personal approach. He first gained notice with two hypnotic, minimalist works—*Phrygian Gates* (for piano, 1977) and *Shaker Loops* (for string septet, 1978)—and earned a national reputation with *Harmonium* (1980–81) and *Harmonielehre* (1984–85), both written for the San Francisco Symphony, the latter named after Arnold Schoenberg's treatise on tonal harmony.

Adams attracted much attention with his opera *Nixon in China* (1987), which was a collaboration with the imaginative director Peter Sellars and the poet/librettist Alice Goodman. The opera takes place in Beijing, China, during the historic visit of former President Nixon in November 1972. Adams's score is playful and full of irony, and the orchestral sonority is brightened by the addition of saxophone and synthesizers. The opera was enthusiastically received and played to sold-out houses.

Operas

The works that followed show Adams increasingly aware of the sumptuous orchestration and expressive harmonies of the New Romantics. His next opera, *The Death of Klinghoffer* (1991), touched a sensitive international nerve. Based on the 1985 hijacking of the cruise liner *Achille Lauro* by Palestinian terrorists and their murder of the Jewish-American passenger Leon Klinghoffer, this opera has been misunderstood and ill-received. Adams's recent stage works include *I Was Looking at the Ceiling and Then I Saw the Sky* (1995), a comic, satiric work set in Los Angeles at the time of the Northridge Earthquake (1994), and more recently, *El Niño* (2000), a Nativity oratorio modeled on Handel's *Messiah*.

Adams won a Pulitzer Prize for his recent composition *On the Transmigration of Souls* (2002), which was commissioned by the New York Philharmonic to mark the

The historic handshake between President Richard Nixon and Chinese Communist Party Chairman Mao Tse-tung in February 1972. The event was the inspiration for John Adams's 1987 opera *Nixon in China*.

first anniversary of the destruction of the World Trade Towers on September 11, 2001. This powerful work has a text based on missing-persons' signs posted after the disaster, and a reading of the victim's names.

Recently Adams has returned to opera to write *Dr. Atomic*, on the first test of a nuclear weapon, which premiered in 2005 by San Francisco Opera. "If opera is actually going to be part of our lives," he notes, "it has to deal with contemporary topics."

TROMBA LONTANA (DISTANT TRUMPET)

This short orchestral work is one of two fanfares Adams wrote in 1986, both as commissions by major symphony orchestras. The two complement each other: *Short Ride in a Fast Machine* is an exuberant and propulsive work, while *Tromba lontana* is a quiet, introspective piece, really an "anti-fanfare." The latter was commissioned by the Houston Symphony in celebration of the Texas Sesquicentennial. The title *Tromba lontana* refers to the two solo trumpets, placed at opposite sides of the stage, that play an antiphonal dialogue over a complicated, undulating orchestral background. The atmosphere is mysterious—even stratospheric—with shimmering oscillations and silvery sonorities that bespeak Adams's unique minimalist language. The opening bell-like timbre—produced by glockenspiel, vibraphone, and small cymbals called **crotales** as well as harmonics in the strings—is evocative of Far Eastern music. This gives way to murmuring strings over which the trumpets begin their distant call. Their motive grows in range and intensity as more instruments join in the active accompaniment. When the two trumpets overlap, their lines create close dissonances. Just as gradually as the work climaxes, it lessens in intensity and quietly dies out to nothing (marked *niente* in the score; see Listening Guide 59).

Admired by audiences and critics alike, *Tromba lontana* is one of Adams's most performed works. American conductor Leonard Slatkin found its understated emotional message appropriate as a last-minute replacement on the BBC Symphony Orchestra program he directed on September 14, 2001, just three days after the terrorist attacks on New York and the Pentagon.

The New Romanticism

Quotation music

Modern composers have tried various means to connect with their audiences. In addition to working with small, simpler ideas, as we saw with minimalism, musicians have explored eclecticism through the mixture of past styles with contemporary ones, in other words, in a postmodern idiom. This might take the form of **quotation music**, in which a recognizable work is cited, or simply use a more familiar and accessible musical vocabulary, such as those of the Romantic and post-Romantic masters. One of the precursors of the New Romanticism is American composer Samuel Barber (1910-1981), whose elegiac *Adagio for Strings* (1936) is suffused with the feeling and grand gestures of the nineteenth century. The New Romantic approach has been particularly popular among women composers as well, and Libby Larsen is one of the most successful proponents of this contemporary style.

Listening Guide 59

eLG   4 (86–90)
8 (56–60)

Adams: *Tromba lontana (Distant Trumpet)*   4:11

DATE OF WORK:	1986, fanfare commissioned by the Houston Symphony Orchestra
MEDIUM:	Orchestra with 2 solo trumpets (at opposite sides of stage)

WHAT TO LISTEN FOR: Mesmerizing, repetitive accompaniment.
Solo trumpet theme growing out of small idea.
Alternation and imitation between 2 trumpets.
Metallic, bell-like timbres in percussion.
Sustained strings playing harmonics and repeated notes in woodwinds.

86   0:00   Bell-like, high-pitched accompaniment in percussion, woodwinds, and strings; regular repeating.

0:07   Solo trumpet enters on sustained note, then oscillates between 2 pitches; syncopated
theme develops with wider, disjunct range:

87   1:01   Second trumpet enters, in imitation of first trumpet; active accompaniment continues and grows
more dissonant; French horns have sustained chords.

88   1:42   Trumpet 1 develops disjunct theme beginning with an interval of a third; accompaniment grows
more intense; high sustained pitches in violins:

2:19   2nd trumpet enters with rising disjunct theme; rising dynamic level; percussion (suspended
cymbal) prominent in accompaniment.

89   2:54   Two trumpets have quick, imitative exchanges in faster, staccato rhythm; overlapping parts:

90   3:10   Return to shorter trumpet idea from opening, in staccato notes;
accompaniment fades gradually in volume and intensity.

3:40   Final echolike exchanges between solo trumpets; accompaniment dies out on sustained D-major
chord; regular pulse in bells (glockenspiel) until closing.

Libby Larsen and the Musical Voice of Women

*"Music exists in an infinity of sound. I think of all music as existing
in the substance of the air itself. It is the composer's task to order
and make sense of sound, in time and space, to communicate
something about being alive through music."*

Ⓢ **Libby Larsen**

Born in Delaware and raised in Minneapolis, Libby Larsen (b. 1950) studied composition at the University of Minnesota with Dominick Argento. At age twenty-two, she co-founded the Minnesota Composers' Forum, now the American Composers' Forum. This group has become a strong advocate in this time of limited support for the arts in the United States (see CP 21). Larsen is also a passionate spokesperson for the music education of children and the general public.

She has held composer-in-residence positions with diverse institutions such as the Arnold Schoenberg Institute in Los Angeles, the Philadelphia School of the Arts, the Colorado Symphony, and the Minneapolis Orchestra, and has received commissions from the popular men's choral group The King's Singers and from renowned soprano Frederica von Stade.

Many of Larsen's operas and stage works are inspired by writings of women. Her best-known work is *Frankenstein, the Modern Prometheus,* an opera that takes a new perspective on Mary Shelley's famous novel. Her one-act opera *Eric Hermannson's Soul* is adapted from a short story by American writer Willa Cather, and her choral opera *Barnum's Bird* focuses on showman P. T. Barnum and his "Swedish nightingale," Jenny Lind.

Larsen is especially known for her songs set to texts by strong women, including the wives of England's Henry VIII (*Try Me, Good King*) and sharpshooter Calamity Jane (*Songs from Letters*); the nineteenth-century Swedish singer Jenny Lind (*A Word from Your Jenny*) and American Impressionist painter Mary Cassatt (*Mary Cassatt*); and modern women such as Jihan Sadat, widow of Egypt's slain leader (*Coming Forth into Day*). When asked about what inspires her choice of texts, Larsen replied: "The musicality of the text and a deep connection to those words. . . . I love poetry. I love prose. I read voraciously. I memorize the text and repeat it over and over, using different tempos until I find the natural flow of the words." We will consider her song cycle *Sonnets from the Portuguese* set to works by the Victorian poet Elizabeth Barrett Browning (1806–1861).

SONNETS FROM THE PORTUGUESE

Larsen worked closely with the singer Arleen Auger, who premiered this work (her 1994 recording won a Grammy). The two women shared an affinity for Elizabeth Barrett Browning, and particularly for her *Sonnets from the Portuguese,* love poems secretly written during her courtship with Robert Browning. These poems, and the compelling love story behind them, have fascinated readers since their publication in 1850. Each sonnet marks a point in the continuing relationship and expresses the depth and strength of a woman's love. Larsen and Auger saw, within the romanticized language, a highly creative woman grappling with the same issues that face women today, and chose six poems that spoke to both of them. Among those selected is Sonnet 43, "How do I love thee?" perhaps the most widely recognized opening line of poetry, and Sonnet 40, "Oh, yes! They love through all this world of ours."

We will consider the last two songs. Numbers 5 and 6. "Oh, yes!" sets Sonnet No. 40 (see Listening Guide 60 for text). This poem makes allusions that are difficult to decipher on first reading: the reference to Musselmans and Giaours

(Muslims and infidels, or Christians) is surely based on the poet's familiarity with the writings of Lord Byron (in particular, *The Giaour*, 1813; and *The Siege of Corinth*, 1816, a tale of the Turkish attack on this Greek city). Browning also draws on her classical knowledge of Homer's *Odyssey* and Ovid's *Metamorphoses* in referring to the one-eyed monster (Cyclops) Polyphemus. In this sonnet, Browning strikingly contrasts her beloved against these unfeeling figures.

The song is unsettling in its constantly shifting meter, between 4/4, 5/4, and 7/4. Two contrasting ideas are set up immediately with the voice's rising third on "Oh, yes!" answered by the instrumentalists' descending interval (a diminished fifth, also called a *tritone*). The music grows faster, louder, and more harshly dissonant and chromatic at the mention of Musselmans and Giaours. The song climaxes on the line "and not so much will turn the thing called love to hate," after which the voice moves more freely with a curvy melisma on "my Beloved." The closing recalls the opening exchanges, now more accented, on "Too late!"

The last song, "How do I love thee?" flows more freely in a slow 6/8 meter. The voice sings the well-known opening text line alone, after a gentle introduction. The tempo picks up, as the melody carefully paints the text, moving lower on "depth," then higher on "breadth," soaring on "height," and stretching upward on "my soul can reach." The text spins out with clarity and sensitivity; the engaging melodic contours make singing seem the most natural form of expression. At the end, we are left suspended, aware of the fragility of love and life itself. Larsen has been hailed in *USA Today* as "the only English-speaking composer since Benjamin Britten who matches great verse with fine music so intelligently and expressively."

Portrait of the poet Elizabeth Barrett Browning (1806–1861) painted in 1853 by **Thomas Buchanan Read** (1822–1872).

Listening Guide 60	eLG	4 (91–92) 8 (61–62)

Larsen: *Sonnets from the Portuguese*, Nos. 5 and 6   6:09

DATE OF WORK: 1993

GENRE: Song cycle (6 songs)

MEDIUM: Soprano with chamber ensemble (flute, oboe, 2 clarinets, bassoon, 2 horns, string quintet, harp, percussion)

BASIS: Sonnets by Elizabeth Barrett Browning

SONGS: 1. "I thought once how Theocritus had sung"
2. "My letters!"
3. "With the same heart, I said, I'll answer thee"
4. "If I leave all for thee,"
5. "Oh, yes!"
6. "How do I love thee?"

Listening Guide continues

Song No. 5: "Oh, yes!" (Sonnet 40)

2:34

WHAT TO LISTEN FOR: Disjunct lines and quick exchanges between solo voice and pointilistic woodwinds, which punctuate free vocal line.
Shifing meters and irregular phrasing.
Alternation of speechlike quality with lyrical lines.
Dissonance and chromaticism with reference to Musselmans and Giaours.

TEXT	DESCRIPTION
91 0:00 Oh, yes! They love through all this world of ours!	Disjunct exchanges, voice and instruments.
I will not gainsay love, called love forsooth.	Lyrical, strings and oboe; irregular phrases.
I have heard love talked in my early youth	Staccato cello line; voice slows.
And since, not so long back but that the flowers	
Then gathered, smell still. Musselmans and Giaours	In tempo; chromatic (Musselmans).
Throw kerchiefs at a smile, and have no ruth	
For any weeping. Polypheme's white tooth	Chromatic lines in voice and instruments.
Slips on the nut, if after frequent showers,	Crescendo builds,
The shell is over-smooth; and not so much	reaches dissonant climax,
Will turn the thing called love, aside to hate	
Or else to oblivion. But thou art not such	gently and freely.
A lover, my Beloved! Thou canst wait	winding melisma on "beloved."
Through sorrow and sickness, to bring souls to touch,	
And think it soon when others cry "Too late."	Return to opening disjunct idea.

Opening, with quick, disjunct exchanges between the voice and instruments:

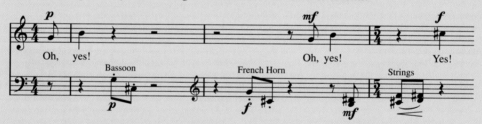

Fluid, chromatic lines for reference to Polypheme's tooth:

Solo, winding melisma on "beloved":

Song No. 6: "How do I love thee?" (Sonnet 43)   **3:35**

WHAT TO LISTEN FOR: Free-flowing, arched lines according to the text.

Lilting 6/8 meter.

Quick-moving, syllabic line openings on "I love thee."

Expressive use of instruments.

Subtle text-painting (rising line on "my soul can reach," octave leap on "sun").

TEXT	DESCRIPTION
92 0:00	Introduction, woodwinds and strings.
How do I love thee? Let me count the ways.	Sung freely, like a recitative.
I love thee to the depth and breadth and height	In tempo, with gently arched melody.
My soul can reach, when feeling out of sight	Rising line, with repeated text; slightly accelerating.
For the ends of Being and ideal Grace.	Closing cadence at end of first text quatrain.
I love thee to the level of everyday's	Returns to arched melodic idea; syllabic setting.
Most quiet need, by sun and candle-light.	Octave leap on "sun"; echoed by cello.
I love thee freely, as men strive for Right;	*Più mosso* (with more motion); phrases on high notes.
I love thee purely, as they turn from Praise.	
I love thee with the passion put to use	
In my old griefs, and with my childhood's faith. Ah!	Line crescendos; closes in vocalise, then
I love thee with a love I seemed to lose	instrumental interlude, slower, then gradually accelerates.
With my lost saints. I love thee with the breadth	Reaches climax.
Smiles, tears, of all my life!—and, if God choose,	Instruments in imitation on closing motive;
I shall but love thee better after death.	gentle closing chord with harp arpeggio.

Opening line, sung freely:

Word painting, with rising line to imply reaching soul:

Syllabic, recitation-like treatment of phrase "I love thee":

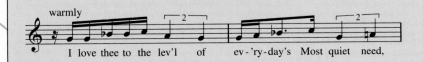

Coda

"Just listen with the vastness of the world in mind.
You can't fail to get the message."

—PIERRE BOULEZ

These pages have included a variety of facts—cultural, historical, biographical, and analytical—that have entered into the making of music and that we must consider if we seek to listen intelligently to music. Like all books, this one belongs to the domain of words, and words have no power over the domain of sound. They are helpful only insofar as they lead us to enjoy the music.

The enjoyment of music depends on perceptive listening, which (like perceptive anything) is achieved gradually, with practice and effort. By studying the circumstances out of which a musical work issued, we prepare ourselves for its multiple meanings; we open ourselves to that exercise of mind and heart, sensibility and imagination, that makes listening to music a unique experience. But in building up our musical perceptions—that is, our listening enjoyment—let us always remember that the ultimate wisdom rests neither in dates nor in facts. It is to be found in one place only: the sounds themselves.

Musical Notation

The Notation of Pitch

Musical notation presents a kind of graph of each sound's duration and pitch. These are indicated by symbols called **notes**, which are written on the **staff**, a series of five parallel lines separated by four spaces:

Staff

The positions of the notes on the staff indicate the pitches, each line and space representing a different degree of pitch.

A symbol known as a **clef** is placed at the left end of the staff to determine the relative pitch names. The **treble clef** (𝄞) is used for pitches within the range of the female singing voices, and the **bass clef** (𝄢) for a lower group of pitches, within the range of the male singing voices.

Clefs

Pitches are named after the first seven letters of the alphabet, from A to G. (From one note named A to the next is the interval of an **octave**.) The pitches on the treble staff are named as follows:

Pitch names

And those on the bass staff:

Octave

For pitches above and below these staffs, short extra lines called **ledger lines** can be added:

Middle C—the C that, on the piano, is situated approximately in the center of the keyboard—comes between the treble and bass staffs. It is represented by either the first ledger line above the bass staff or the first ledger line below the treble staff, as the following example makes clear. This combination of the two staffs is called the *great staff* or *grand staff*:

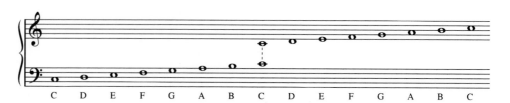

C D E F G A B C D E F G A B C

Accidentals   Signs known as *accidentals* are used to alter the pitch of a written note. A *sharp* (♯) before the note indicates the pitch a half step above; a *flat* (♭) indicates the pitch a half step below. A *natural* (♮) cancels a sharp or flat. Also used are the *double sharp* (×) and *double flat* (♭♭), which respectively raise and lower the pitch by two halftones—that is, a whole tone.

In many pieces of music, where certain sharped or flatted notes are used consistently throughout, these sharps or flats are written at the beginning of each line of **Key signature**   music, in the *key signature*, as seen in the following example of piano music. Notice that piano music is written on the great staff, with the right hand usually playing the notes written on the upper staff and the left hand usually playing the notes written on the lower:

CD iMusic

Beethoven: *Für Elise*

The Notation of Rhythm

The duration of each musical tone is indicated by the type of note placed on the staff. **Note values**   In the following table, each note represents a duration, or *value*, half as long as the preceding one:

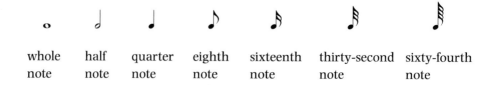

| whole | half | quarter | eighth | sixteenth | thirty-second | sixty-fourth |
| note | note | note | note | note | note | note |

In any particular piece of music, these note values are related to the beat of the music. If the quarter note represents one beat, then a half note lasts for two beats, a whole note for four; two eighth notes last one beat, as do four sixteenths. The following chart makes this clear:

Notes		Beats (in quadruple or 4/4 time)

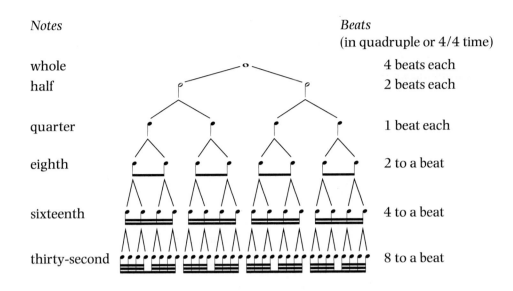

whole		4 beats each
half		2 beats each
quarter		1 beat each
eighth		2 to a beat
sixteenth		4 to a beat
thirty-second		8 to a beat

When a group of three notes is to be played in the time normally taken up by only two of the same kind, we have a *triplet*:

Triplet

If we combine successive notes of the same pitch, using a curved line known as a *tie*, the second note is not played, and the note values are combined:

Tie

beats: 4 + 4 = 8   2 + 4 = 6   1 + ½ = 1½

A *dot* after a note enlarges its value by half:

Dot

beats: 2 + 1 = 3   1 + ½ = 1½   ½ + ¼ = ¾

Time never stops in music, even when there is no sound. Silence is indicated by symbols known as *rests*, which correspond in time value to the notes:

Rests

whole rest	half rest	quarter rest	eighth rest	sixteenth rest	thirty-second rest	sixty-fourth rest

The metrical organization of a piece of music is indicated by the *time signature*, which specifies the meter: this appears as two numbers written as in a fraction. The upper numeral indicates the number of beats within the measure; the lower one shows which note value equals one beat. Thus, the time signature 3/4 means that there are three beats to a measure, with the quarter note equal to one beat. In 6/8 time, there are six beats in the measure, each eighth note receiving one beat. Following are the most frequently encountered time signatures:

Time signature

duple meter	2/2	2/4	
triple meter	3/2	3/4	3/8
quadruple meter		4/4	
sextuple meter		6/4	6/8

Measures and bar lines

The examples below demonstrate how the music notation system works. The notes are separated into measures, shown by a vertical line (called a ***bar line***).

Mozart: *Ah! vous dirai-je, maman (= Twinkle, Twinkle, Little Star and the Alphabet Song)*

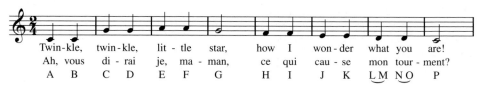

Clef: Treble
First pitch: C
Key signature: none (key of C major)
Meter: Duple (2/4)
CD iMusic: This is the original piano version of the tune, composed by Mozart. Notice how turns decorate the familiar melody.

Brahms: *Lullaby (Wiegenlied)*

Clef: Treble
First pitch: A
Key signature: 1 flat (B♭) = 5 key of F major
Meter: Triple (3/4)
Other features: Begins on an upbeat, after two rests
CD iMusic: This is the original vocal version by Brahms, sung in German. You probably know the English lyrics.

Battle Hymn of the Republic (Civil War song)

Clef: Treble
First pitch: G
Key signature: none = key of C major
Meter: Quadruple (4/4)
Other features: Many dotted rhythms
CD iMusic: This is a nineteenth-century brass band version of the tune from the Civil War era. They play only the familiar chorus.

Greensleeves (English traditional song)

Clef: Treble
First note: E
Key signature: 1 sharp (F♯) = key of E minor
Meter: Sextuple (6/8)
Other features: Pick-up note, dotted rhythms, added accidentals
CD iMusic: This Elizabethan-era song is played here on classical guitar.

Glossary

absolute music Music that has no literary, dramatic, or pictorial program. Also *pure music*.

a cappella Choral music performed without instrumental accompaniment.

accelerando Getting faster.

accent The emphasis on a *beat* resulting in its being louder or longer than another in a measure.

accompagnato Accompanied; also a *recitative* that is accompanied by orchestra.

accordion A musical instrument with a small keyboard and free-vibrating metal *reeds* that sound when air is generated by pleated *bellows*.

acid rock Genre of American *rock* that emerged in the late 1960s, often associated with psychedelic drugs. Its style featured heavy amplification, instrumental improvisation, new sound technologies, and light shows.

acoustic guitar A *guitar* designed for performance without electronic amplification.

acoustic music Music produced without electronics, especially amplifiers.

active chords In the *diatonic* system, chords which need to resolve to the *tonic chord*. These include the *dominant chord* and the *subdominant chord*.

adagio Quite slow.

additive meter Patterns of *beats* that subdivide into smaller, irregular groups (e.g., 2 + 3 + 2 + 3 = 10); common in certain Eastern European musics.

ad libitum Indication that gives the performer the liberty to omit a section or to improvise.

aerophone Instruments such as a *flute*, whistle, or *horn* that produce sound by using air as the primary vibrating means.

agitato Agitated or restless.

Agnus Dei A section of the *Mass*; the last musical *movement* of the *Ordinary*.

alap An umetered, improvised *prelude* in Indian music, introducing the *raga*, or *mode*, of the composition.

aleatory Indeterminate music in which certain elements of performance (such as *pitch*, *rhythm*, or *form*) are left to choice or chance.

alla breve See *cut time*.

allegro Fast, cheerful.

Alleluia An item from the *Proper* of the *Mass* sung just before the reading of the Gospel; *neumatic* in style with a long *melisma* on the last syllable of the word "Alleluia."

allemande German dance in moderate duple time, popular during the Renaissance and Baroque periods; often the first *movement* of a Baroque *suite*.

alternative rock A broad term denoting any of several subgenres of *rock and roll* that emerged since the late 1980s. These styles, such as *grunge rock* and *indie rock*, often incorporate elements of *punk rock*.

alto Lowest of the female voices. Also *contralto*.

amplitude see *volume*.

Analog Synthesis Synthesis of waveforms by way of analog circuits.

andante Moderately slow or walking pace.

answer Second entry of the *subject* in a *fugue*, usually pitched a fourth below or a fifth above the *subject*.

anthem A religious choral composition in English; performed liturgically, the Protestant equivalent of the *motet*.

antiphonal Performance style in which an ensemble is divided into two or more groups, performing in alternation and then together.

antique cymbals Small disks of brass, held by the player (one instrument in each hand), that are struck together gently and allowed to vibrate.

arabesque Decorative musical material or a composition based on florid *embellishment*.

aria Lyric song for solo voice with orchestral accompaniment, generally expressing intense emotion; found in *opera*, *cantata*, and *oratorio*.

arioso Short, *aria*-like passage.

arpeggio Broken chord in which the individual tones are sounded one after another instead of simultaneously.

Ars antiqua *Polyphonic* musical style, usually French, from the period c. 1160–1320.

Ars nova Fourteenth-century French *polyphonic* musical style whose themes moved increasingly from religious to secular.

art rock Genre of *rock* that uses larger forms and more complex harmonies than other popular styles; occasionally quotes examples from classical music. Also *progressive rock*.

a tempo Return to the previous *tempo*.

atonality Total abandonment of *tonality* (centering in a *key*). Atonal music moves from one level of *dissonance* to another, without areas of relaxation.

attacca "Attack," proceed without a pause between *movements*.

augmentation Statement of a *melody* in longer note values, often twice as slow as the original.

aulos *Double-reed* pipe; played for public and religious functions in ancient Greece.

avant-garde jazz A free-style *jazz* that developed in the 1960s; John Coltrane was a major proponent.

backbeat In *rock and roll* and related *genres*, the second and fourth *beats* of the measure.

bagpipe Wind instrument popular in Eastern and Western Europe that has several tubes, one of which plays the melody while the others sound the *drones*, or sustained notes; a windbag is filled by either a mouth pipe or a set of *bellows*. See also *uilleann pipes*.

balalaika *Guitar*-like instrument of Russia with a triangular body, fretted neck, and three strings; often used in traditional music and dance.

ballad A form of English street song, popular from the sixteenth through the eighteenth centuries. Ballads are characterized by narrative content and *strophic form*.

ballade French poetic form and *chanson* type of the Middle Ages and Renaissance with courtly love texts. Also a Romantic genre, especially a lyric piano piece.

ballad opera English comic opera, usually featuring spoken dialogue alternating with songs set to popular tunes; also called dialogue opera.

ballet A dance form featuring a staged presentation of group or solo dancing with music, costumes, and scenery.

ballet de cour Courtly French *ballet* of the sixteenth and seventeenth centuries.

balungan The melodic-structural framework in Javanese music.

banjo Plucked-string instrument with round body in the form of a single-headed drum and a long, fretted neck; brought to the Americas by African slaves.

baritone Male voice of moderately low range.

baritone horn See *euphonium*.

bas Medieval category of soft instruments, used principally for indoor occasions, as distinct from *haut*, or loud, instruments.

bass Male voice of low *range*.

bass clarinet Woodwind instrument, with the lowest range, of the *clarinet* family.

bass drum *Percussion instrument* played with a large, soft-headed stick; the largest orchestral drum.

basse danse Graceful court dance of the early Renaissance; an older version of the *pavane*.

basso continuo Italian for "continuous bass." See *figured bass*. Also refers to performance group with a bass, chordal instrument (*harpsichord*, *organ*), and one bass melody instrument (*cello*, *bassoon*).

bassoon *Double-reed* woodwind instrument with a low range.

bass viol See *double bass*.

baton A thin stick, usually painted white, used by *conductors*.

beat Regular pulsation; a basic unit of length in musical time.

bebop Complex *jazz* style developed in the 1940s. Also *bop*.

bel canto "Beautiful singing"; elegant Italian vocal style characterized by florid melodic lines delivered by voices of great agility, smoothness, and purity of tone.

bell tree Long stick with bells suspended from it, adopted from *Janissary music*.

bellows An apparatus for producing air currents in certain wind instruments (*accordion*, *bagpipe*).

bent pitch See *blue note*.

big band Large *jazz* ensemble popular in 1930s and 1940s, featuring sections of *trumpets*, *trombones*, *saxophones* (and other *woodwinds*), and rhythm instruments (*piano*, *double bass*, drums, and *guitar*).

big band era See *swing era*.

binary form Two-part (**A-B**) form with each section normally repeated. Also *two-part form*.

biwa A Japanese *lute*, similar to the Chinese *pipa*.

bluegrass *Country-western* music style characterized by quick *tempos*, improvised instrumental solos, and high-range vocal harmonies.

blue note A slight drop of pitch on the third, fifth, or seventh tone of the scale, common in *blues* and *jazz*. Also *bent pitch*.

blues African-American form of secular *folk music*, related to *jazz*, that is based on a simple, repetitive poetic-musical structure.

bodhran Hand-held frame drum with a single goatskin head; used in Irish traditional music.

bongo A pair of small drums of differing pitches; held between the legs and struck with both hands; of Afro-Cuban origin.

bop See *bebop*.

bossa nova Brazilian dance related to the *samba*, popular in the 1950s and 1960s.

bourrée Lively French Baroque dance type in *duple meter*.

bowed fiddle Any of a variety of medieval bowed string instruments.

branle Quick French group dance of the Renaissance, related to the *ronde*.

brass instrument Wind instrument with a cup-shaped mouthpiece, a tube that flares into a bell, and slides or valves to vary the pitch. Most often made of brass or silver.

brass quintet Standard chamber ensemble made up of two *trumpets*, *horn*, *trombone*, and *tuba*.

break *Jazz* term for a short improvised solo without accompaniment that "breaks" an ensemble passage or introduces an extended solo.

bridge Transitional passage connecting two sections of a composition; also *transition*. Also the part of a string instrument that holds the strings in place.

buffo In *opera*, a male singer of comic roles, usually a *bass*.

bugle *Brass instrument* that evolved from the earlier military, or field, *trumpet*.

cadence Resting place in a musical *phrase*; music punctuation.

cadenza Virtuosic solo passage in the manner of an improvisation, performed near the end of an *aria* or a *movement* of a *concerto*.

Cajun music Eclectic Louisiana traditional style that draws from French *folk music* as well as from music of Southern whites and blacks; *fiddle* is used as a solo instrument, sometimes accompanying itself with a *drone*.

cakewalk *Syncopated*, strutting dance of nineteenth-century origin; developed among Southern slaves in a parody of white plantation owners.

call-and-response Performance style with a singing leader who is imitated by a *chorus* of followers. Also *responsorial singing*.

calypso A style of music and dance developed in Trinidad, but also popular elsewhere in the Carribean. Calypso is strongly associated with *Carnival* celebrations.

canon Type of *polyphonic* composition in which one musical line strictly imitates another at a fixed distance throughout.

cantabile Songful, in a singing style.

cantata Vocal genre for solo singers, *chorus*, and instrumentalists based on a lyric or dramatic poetic narrative. It generally consists of several *movements*, including *recitatives*, *arias*, and ensemble numbers.

cantor Solo singer or singing leader in Jewish and Christian liturgical music.

cantus firmus "Fixed melody," usually of very long notes, often based on a fragment of *Gregorian chant* that served as the structural basis for a *polyphonic* composition, particularly in the Renaissance.

capriccio Short lyric piece of a free nature, often for piano.

Carnival The festive season just before Lent in the Christian calendar, which has historically been a vibrant time for music-making. Regions known for Carnival music are Venice, Brazil, the Caribbean Islands, and New Orleans.

carol English medieval *strophic* song with a *refrain* repeated after each stanza; now associated with Christmas.

cassation Classical instrumental genre related to the *serenade* or *divertimento* and often performed outdoors.

castanets *Percussion instruments* consisting of small wooden clappers that are struck together. They are widely used to accompany Spanish dancing.

castrato Male singer who was castrated during boyhood to preserve the soprano or alto vocal register, prominent in seventeenth- and early-eighteenth-century *opera*.

celesta *Percussion instrument* resembling a miniature upright *piano*, with tuned metal plates struck by hammers that are operated by a keyboard.

cello See *violoncello*.

celtic harp See *Irish harp*.

chachacha A Cuban dance developed in the 1950s, it derives its name from the characteristic rhythmic pattern.

chaconne Baroque form similar to the *passacaglia*, in which the *variations* are based on a repeated chord progression.

chamber choir Small group of up to about twenty-four singers, who usually perform *a cappella* or with piano accompaniment.

chamber music Ensemble music for up to about ten players, with one player to a part.

chamber sonata See *sonata da camera*.

chanson French *monophonic* or *polyphonic* song, especially of the Middle Ages and Renaissance, set to either courtly or popular poetry.

chart Colloquial or *jazz* term for a score or arrangement.

chimes *Percussion instrument* of definite pitch that consists of a set of tuned metal tubes of various lengths suspended from a frame and struck with a hammer. Also *tubular bells*.

Chinese block *Percussion instrument* made from a hollowed rectangular block of wood that is struck with a beater.

choir A group of singers who perform together, usually in parts, with several on each part; often associated with a church.

chorale Congregational hymn of the German Lutheran church.

chorale prelude Short Baroque *organ* piece in which a traditional *chorale* melody is embellished.

chorale variations Baroque *organ* piece in which a *chorale* is the basis for a set of *variations*.

chord Simultaneous combination of three or more *tones* that constitute a single block of *harmony*.

chordal *Texture* comprised of *chords* in which the *pitches* sound simultaneously; also *homorhythmic*.

chordophone Instrument that produces sound from a vibrating string stretched between two points; the string may be set in motion by bowing, striking, or plucking.

chorus Fairly large group of singers who perform together, usually with several on each part. Also a choral *movement* of a large-scale work. In *jazz*, a single statement of the melodic-harmonic pattern.

chromatic *Melody* or *harmony* built from many if not all twelve semitones of the *octave*. A *chromatic scale* consists of an ascending or descending sequence of *semitones*.

church sonata See *sonata da chiesa*.

cimbalom A type of Hungarian *dulcimer* with strings that are struck. Related to the *zither*.

clarinet *Single-reed* woodwind instrument with a wide range of sizes.

clavecin French word for *harpsichord.*

claves A Cuban clapper consisting of two solid hardwood sticks; widely used in Latin American music.

clavichord Stringed *keyboard instrument* popular in the Renaissance and Baroque that is capable of unique expressive devices not possible on the *harpsichord.*

clavier Generic word for *keyboard instruments,* including *harpsichord, clavichord, piano,* and *organ.*

climax The high point in a melodic line or piece of music, usually representing the peak of intensity, *range,* and *dynamics.*

closed ending Second of two endings in a secular medieval work, usually cadencing on the final.

coda The last part of a piece, usually added to a standard form to bring it to a close.

codetta In *sonata form,* the concluding section of the *exposition.* Also a brief *coda* concluding an inner section of a work.

collage A technique drawn from the visual arts whereby musical fragments from other compositions are juxtaposed or overlapped within a new work.

collegium musicum An association of amateur musicians, popular in the Baroque era. Also a modern university ensemble dedicated to the performance of early music.

col legno *String instrument* technique in which the strings are hit with the wood of the bow.

colotomic structure Cyclic, interlocking rhythmic structure in Javanese gamelan music.

comic opera See *opéra comique.*

commedia dell'arte Type of improvised drama popular in sixteenth- and seventeenth-century Italy; makes use of stereotyped characters.

common time See *quadruple meter.*

compound meter *Meter* in which each beat is subdivided into three rather than two.

computer music A type of electro-acoustic music in which computers assist in creating works through sound synthesis and manipulation.

con amore With love, tenderly.

concertante Style based on the principle of opposition between two dissimilar masses of sound; *concerto*-like.

concert band Instrumental ensemble ranging from forty to eighty members or more, consisting of wind and *percussion instruments.* Also *wind ensemble.*

concertina Small, free-reed, *bellows*-operated instrument similar to an *accordion;* hexagonal in shape, with button keys.

concertino Solo group of instruments in the Baroque *concerto grosso.*

concertmaster The first-chair violinist of a symphony *orchestra.*

concerto Instrumental genre in several *movements* for solo instrument (or instrumental group) and *orchestra.*

concerto form Structure commonly used in first *movements* of *concertos* that combines elements of Baroque *ritornello* procedure with *sonata-allegro form.* Also *first-movement concerto form.*

concerto grosso Baroque *concerto* type based on the opposition between a small group of solo instruments (the *concertino*) and *orchestra* (the *ripieno*).

concert overture Single-movement concert piece for *orchestra,* typically from the Romantic period and often based on a literary program.

conductor Person who, by means of gestures, leads performances of musical ensembles, especially *orchestra,* bands, or *choruses.*

con fuoco With fire.

conga Afro-Cuban dance performed at Latin American *Carnival* celebrations. Also a single-headed drum of Afro-Cuban origin, played with bare hands.

conjunct Smooth, connected *melody* that moves principally by small *intervals.*

con passione With passion.

consonance Concordant or harmonious combination of *tones* that provides a sense of relaxation and stability in music.

continuous bass See *basso continuo.*

continuous imitation Renaissance *polyphonic* style in which the *motives* move from line to line within the *texture,* often overlapping one another.

contour The overall shape of a melodic line. It can move upward, downward, or remain static.

contrabass See *double bass.*

contrabassoon *Double-reed* woodwind instrument with the lowest *range* in the woodwind family. Also *double bassoon.*

contralto See *alto.*

contrapunctus A composition using imitative *counterpoint.*

contrapuntal *Texture* employing *counterpoint,* or two or more melodic lines.

cool jazz A substyle of *bebop,* characterized by a restrained, unemotional performance with lush harmonies, moderate volume levels and tempos, and a new lyricism; often associated with Miles Davis.

cornet Valved *brass instrument* similar to the *trumpet* but more mellow in sound.

cornetto Early instrument of the brass family with woodwind-like finger holes. It developed from the cow horn but was made of wood.

Council of Trent A council of the Roman Catholic Church that convened in Trent, Italy, from 1543 to 1565 and dealt with Counter-Reformation issues, including the reform of liturgical music.

counterpoint The art of combining in a single *texture* two or more melodic lines.

countermelody An accompanying *melody* sounded against the principal *melody.*

countersubject In a fugue, a secondary theme heard against the *subject;* a countertheme.

country rock A hybrid of *country-western* and *rock* music, fusing the themes and sound of *country-western* with the driving rhythms and instrumentation of *rock.*

country-western Genre of American popular music derived from traditional music of Appalachia and the rural

South, usually vocal with an accompaniment of *banjos*, *fiddles*, and *guitar*.

courante French Baroque dance, a standard *movement* of the *suite*, in *triple meter* at a moderate *tempo*.

courtesan An educated, refined woman who entertained men intellectually and sexually.

cover Recording that remakes an earlier, often successful, recording with the goal of reaching a wider audience.

cowbell Rectangular metal bell that is struck with a drumstick; used widely in Latin American music.

Credo A section of the *Mass*; the third musical *movement* of the *Ordinary*.

crescendo Growing louder.

crossover Recording or artist that appeals primarily to one audience but becomes popular with another as well (e.g., a *rock* performer who makes *jazz* recordings).

crotales A pair of small pitched cymbals mounted on a frame; also made in *chromatic* sets.

crumhorn Early *woodwind instrument*, whose sound is produced by blowing into a capped *double reed* and whose lower body is curved.

cut time A type of *duple meter* interpreted as 2/2 and indicated as ¢; also called *alla breve*.

cyclical form Structure in which musical material, such as a *theme*, presented in one *movement* returns in a later *movement*.

cymbals *Percussion instruments* consisting of two large circular brass plates of equal size that are struck sidewise against each other.

da capo An indication to return to the beginning of a piece.

da capo aria Lyric song in *ternary*, or **A-B-A**, form, commonly found in *operas*, *cantatas*, and *oratorios*.

dastgāh The modal structure in Persian music. The dastgāh comprises not only a *diatonic* scale, but also melodic *motives* and an ascribed character.

decibel A unit of measurement of *amplitude* or *volume*.

decrescendo Growing softer.

development Structural reshaping of thematic material. Second section of *sonata-allegro form*; it moves through a series of foreign *keys* while *themes* from the *exposition* are manipulated.

dialogue opera See *ballad opera*.

diatonic *Melody* or *harmony* built from the seven tones of a *major* or *minor scale*. A diatonic scale encompasses patterns of seven *whole tones* and *semitones*.

Dies irae Chant from the *Requiem Mass* whose text concerns Judgment Day.

digital frequency modulation synthesis (FM) A form of audio synthesis whereby the *frequency* of the waveform is modulated, creating a more complex waveform and a different *timbre*.

diminuendo Growing softer.

diminution Statement of a melody in shorter note values, often twice as fast as the original.

disco Commercial dance music popular in the 1970s, characterized by strong percussion in a *quadruple meter*.

disjunct Disjointed or disconnected melody with many leaps.

dissonance Combination of tones that sounds discordant and unstable, in need of resolution.

divertimento Classical instrumental genre for chamber ensemble or soloist, often performed as light entertainment. Related to *serenade* and *cassation*.

divertissement Grand entertainment of the French Baroque, characterized by spectacle and grandeur, intended for light entertainment or diversion.

Divine Offices Cycle of daily services of the Roman Catholic Church, distinct from the *Mass*.

dizi Traditional Chinese *flute* made of bamboo.

doctrine of the affections Baroque doctrine of the union of text and music.

dodecaphonic Greek for "twelve-tone"; see *twelve-tone music*.

dolce Sweetly.

dolente Sad, weeping.

dominant The fifth scale step, *sol*.

dominant chord *Chord* built on the fifth scale step, the V chord.

double bass Largest and lowest-pitched member of the bowed string family. Also called *contrabass* or *bass viol*.

double bassoon See *contrabassoon*.

double exposition In the *concerto*, twofold statement of the themes, once by the *orchestra* and once by the soloist.

double reed A *reed* consisting of two pieces of cane that vibrate against each other.

double-stop Playing two notes simultaneously on a string instrument.

doubles *Variations* of a dance in a French keyboard suite.

downbeat First *beat* of the *measure*, the strongest in any *meter*.

drone Sustained sounding of one or several tones for harmonic support, a common feature of some *folk musics*.

drum chimes A set of drums tuned to a musical scale, common in Africa and South and Southeast Asia.

dulcimer Early folk instrument that resembles the *psaltery*; its strings are struck with hammers instead of being plucked.

duo An ensemble of two players.

duo sonata A chamber group comprised of a soloist with piano. Also, in the Baroque period, a *sonata* for a melody instrument and *basso continuo*.

duple meter Basic metrical pattern of two *beats* to a *measure*.

duplum Second voice of a *polyphonic* work, especially the medieval *motet*.

duration Length of time something lasts; e.g., the vibration of a musical sound.

dynamics Element of musical expression relating to the degree of loudness or softness, or volume, of a sound.

electric guitar A *guitar* designed for electronic amplification.

electronische Musik Electronic music developed in Germany in the 1950s that uses an oscillator to generate and alter waveforms.

embellishment Melodic decoration, either improvised or indicated through *ornamentation* signs in the music.

embouchure The placement of the lips, lower facial muscles, and jaws in playing a wind instrument.

Empfindsamkeit German "sensitive" style of the mid-eighteenth century, characterized by melodic directness and *homophonic* texture.

encore "Again"; an audience request that the performer(s) repeat a piece or perform another.

English horn *Double-reed* woodwind instrument, larger and lower in *range* than the *oboe*.

entenga Tuned drum from Uganda; the royal drum ensemble of the former ruler of Buganda.

episode Interlude or intermediate section in the Baroque *fugue* that serves as an area of relaxation between statements of the *subject*.

equal temperament Tuning system based on the division of the *octave* into twelve equal *half steps*; the system used today.

erhu Bowed, two-string fiddle from China, with its bow hairs fixed between the strings; rests on the leg while playing.

espressivo Expressively.

estampie A dance form prevalent in late medieval France, either with voice or purely instrumental.

ethnomusicology Comparative study of musics of the world, with a focus on the cultural context of music.

étude Study piece that focuses on a particular technical problem.

euphonium Tenor-range brass instrument resembling the *tuba*. Also *baritone horn*.

exoticism Musical style in which *rhythms*, *melodies*, or instruments evoke the color and atmosphere of far-off lands.

exposition Opening section. In the *fugue*, the first section in which the voices enter in turn with the *subject*. In *sonata-allegro form*, the first section in which the major thematic material is stated. Also *statement*.

Expressionism A style of visual art and literature in Germany and Austria in the early twentieth century. The term is sometimes also applied to music, especially composers of the *Second Viennese School*.

falsetto Vocal technique whereby men can sing above their normal *range*, producing a lighter sound.

fantasia Free instrumental piece of fairly large dimensions, in an improvisational style; in the Baroque, it often served as an introductory piece to a *fugue*.

fantasy See *fantasia*.

fiddle Colloquial term for *violin*; often used in traditional music. Also a bowed medieval string instrument.

fife A small wooden transverse *flute*, with fewer holes than a *piccolo*, traditionally associated with the military.

figured bass Baroque practice consisting of an independent bass line that often includes numerals indicating the harmony to be supplied by the performer. Also *thorough-bass*.

film music Music that serves either as background or foreground for a film.

first-movement concerto form See *concerto form*.

first-movement form See *sonata-allegro form*.

fixed forms Group of forms, especially in medieval France, in which the poetic structure determines musical repetitions. See also *ballade*, *rondeau*, *virelai*.

flat sign Musical symbol (♭) that indicates lowering a pitch by a *semitone*.

fluegelhorn Valved brass instrument resembling a bugle with a wide bell, used in *jazz* and commercial music.

flute Soprano-range woodwind instrument, usually made of metal and held horizontally.

flutter tonguing Wind instrument technique in which the tongue is fluttered or trilled against the roof of the mouth.

folk music. See *traditional music*.

folk rock Popular music style that combines *folk music* with amplified instruments of *rock*.

form Structure and design in music, based on repetition, contrast, and variation; the organizing principle of music.

formalism Tendency to elevate formal above expressive value in music, as in *Neoclassical* music.

forte (*f*) Loud.

fortissimo (*ff*) Very loud.

four-hand piano music Chamber music genre for two performers playing at one or occasionally two *pianos*, allowing home or *salon* performances of orchestral arrangements.

free jazz Modern *jazz* style developed in the 1960s by Ornette Coleman.

French horn See *horn*.

French overture Baroque instrumental introduction to an *opera*, ballet, or *suite*, in two sections: a slow opening followed by an *Allegro*, often with a brief reprise of the opening.

frequency Rate of vibration of a string or column of air, which determines *pitch*.

fugato A fugal passage in a nonfugal piece, such as in the *development* section of a *sonata-allegro form*.

fuging tune *Polyphonic*, imitative setting of a *hymn* or *psalm*, popular in Great Britain and the United States from the eighteenth century.

fugue *Polyphonic* form popular in the Baroque era in which one or more themes are developed by imitative *counterpoint*.

fusion Style that combines *jazz* improvisation with amplified instruments of *rock*.

gagaku Traditional court music of Japan.

galliard Lively, *triple meter* French court dance.

gamelan Musical ensemble of Java or Bali, made up of *gongs*, *chimes*, *metallophones*, and drums, among other instruments.

gangsta rap A particularly violent style of rap, with lyrics depicting gangs and street life.

gat A North Indian composition for melodic instruments, with a fixed rhythmic pattern, or *tala*, usually of sixteen beats.

gavotte *Duple meter* Baroque dance type of a pastoral character.

geisha In Japan, a woman professionally trained in conversation, dancing, and music in order to entertain men.

genre General term describing the standard category and overall character of a work.

Gesamtkunstwerk German for "total artwork"; a term coined by Richard Wagner to describe the synthesis of all the arts (music, poetry, drama, visual spectacle) in his late operas.

gigue Popular English Baroque dance type, a standard *movement* of the Baroque *suite*, in a lively *compound meter*.

gioioso Joyous.

glee club Specialized vocal ensemble that performs popular music, college songs, and more serious works.

glissando Rapid slide through *pitches* of a *scale*.

glitter rock Theatrical, flamboyant *rock* style popular in the 1970s.

global pop Collective term for popular third-world musics, ethnic and traditional musics, and eclectic combinations of Western and non-Western musics. Also world beat.

glockenspiel *Percussion instrument* with horizontal, tuned steel bars of various sizes that are struck with mallets and produce a bright metallic sound.

Gloria A section of the *Mass*; the second musical *movement* of the *Ordinary*.

Goliard song Medieval Latin-texted secular song, often with corrupt or lewd lyrics; associated with wandering scholars.

gong *Percussion instrument* consisting of a broad circular disk of metal, suspended in a frame and struck with a heavy drumstick. Also *tam-tam*.

gospel music Twentieth-century sacred music style associated with Protestant African Americans.

grace note Ornamental note, often printed in small type and not performed rhythmically.

Gradual Fourth item of the *Proper* of the *Mass*, sung in a *melismatic* style, and performed in a *responsorial* manner in which soloists alternate with a choir.

grand opera Style of Romantic *opera* developed in Paris, focusing on serious, historical plots with huge choruses, crowd scenes, elaborate dance episodes, ornate costumes, and spectacular scenery.

grave Solemn; very, very slow.

Gregorian chant *Monophonic* melody with a freely flowing, unmeasured vocal line; liturgical chant of the Roman Catholic Church. Also *plainchant* or *plainsong*.

griot West African poet or musician who is responsible for preserving and transmitting the history, stories, and poetry of the people.

ground bass A repeating *melody*, usually in the bass, throughout a vocal or instrumental composition.

grunge rock Seattle-based *rock* style characterized by harsh guitar chords; hybrid of *punk rock* and *heavy metal*.

guijira In music from the Basque region, the alternation between 3/4 and 6/8 meters.

güiro An idiophone of Latin American origin, comprised of a hollow gourd with notches, across which a stick is scraped.

guitar Plucked-string instrument originally made of wood with a hollow resonating body and a fretted fingerboard; types include *acoustic* and *electric*.

guitarra moresca A strummed string instrument introduced to Spain by the Moors.

guitarrón A large, six-stringed bass *guitar*, common in *mariachi* ensembles.

habanera Moderate *duple meter* dance of Cuban origin, popular in the nineteenth century; based on characteristic rhythmic figure.

half step Smallest *interval* used in the Western system; the *octave* divides into twelve such *intervals*; on the *piano*, the distance between any two adjacent keys, whether black or white. Also *semitone*.

Hammond organ An early type of electronic *organ*, developed by Laurens Hammond.

harmonica Mouth *organ*; a small metal box on which free reeds are mounted, played by moving back and forth across the mouth while breathing into it.

harmonics Individual pure sounds that are part of any musical tone; in string instruments, crystalline tones in the very high *register*, produced by lightly touching a vibrating string at a certain point.

harmonic variation The procedure in which the *chords* accompanying a *melody* are replaced by others. Often used in *theme and variations* form.

harmonium *Organ*-like instrument with free metal reeds set in vibration by a *bellows*; popular in late-nineteenth-century America.

harmony The simultaneous combination of notes and the ensuing relationships of *intervals* and *chords*.

harp Plucked-string instrument, triangular in shape with strings perpendicular to the soundboard.

harpsichord Early Baroque *keyboard instrument* in which the strings are plucked by quills instead of being struck with hammers like the *piano*. Also *clavecin*.

haut Medieval category of loud instruments, used mainly for outdoor occasions, as distinct from *bas*, or soft, instruments.

heavy metal *Rock* style that gained popularity in the 1970s, characterized by simple, repetitive ideas and loud, distorted instrumental solos.

heptatonic scale Seven-note *scale*; in non-Western musics, often fashioned from a different combination of *intervals* than *major* and *minor scales*.

Hertz (Hz.) In acoustics, a measurement of *frequency*.

heterophonic *Texture* in which two or more voices (or parts) elaborate the same melody simultaneously, often the result of *improvisation*.

hip hop Black urban art forms that emerged in New York City in the 1970s, encompassing *rap* music, break dancing, and graffiti art as well as the fashions adopted by the artists. The term comes from the strings of *vocables*, or nonsense syllables, used by rap artists.

homophonic *Texture* with principal *melody* and accompanying *harmony*, as distinct from *polyphony*.

homorhythmic *Texture* in which all *voices*, or lines, move together in the same *rhythm*.

honkytonk A genre of *country-western* music developed in the 1950s that was heavily influenced by *rock and roll*.

horn Medium-range valved brass instrument that can be played "stopped" with the hand as well as open; also French horn.

hornpipe Country dance of British Isles, often in a lively *triple meter*; optional dance movement of solo and orchestral Baroque suite; a type of *duple meter* hornpipe is still popular in Irish traditional dance music.

hymn Song in praise of God; often involves congregational participation.

hyperinstrument Interactive electronic instruments designed to expand the possibilities of human expressivity and virtuosity. Developed by Tod Machover at MIT.

idée fixe "Fixed idea"; term coined by Berlioz for a recurring musical idea that links different movements of a work.

idiophone Instrument that produces sound from the substance of the instrument itself by being struck, blown, shaken, scraped, or rubbed. Examples include bells, rattles, xylophones, and cymbals.

imitation Melodic idea presented in one *voice* and then restated in another, each part continuing as others enter.

Impressionism A French movement developed by visual artists who favored vague, blurry images intended to capture an "impression" of the subject. Impressionism in music is characterized by exotic *scales*, unresolved *dissonances*, parallel *chords*, rich orchestral *tone color*, and free *rhythm*.

improvisation Creation of a musical composition while it is being performed, seen in Baroque *ornamentation*, *cadenzas* of *concertos*, jazz, and some non-Western musics.

incidental music Music written to accompany dramatic works.

inflection Small alteration of the *pitch* by a microtonal *interval*. See also *blue note*.

instrument Mechanism that generates musical vibrations and transmits them into the air.

interlude Music played between sections of a musical or dramatic work.

intermedio In the Italian Renaissance, a work performed between the acts of a play.

intermezzo Short, lyric piece or *movement*, often for *piano*. Also a comic *interlude* performed between acts of an eighteenth-century *opera seria*.

Internet radio Radio stations that convert their signal into digital format and transmit it over the worldwide Web.

interval Distance and relationship between two *pitches*.

inversion Mirror or upside-down image of a *melody* or pattern, found in *fugues* and twelve-tone compositions.

Irish harp Plucked-string instrument with about thirty strings; used to accompany Irish songs and dance music (also *celtic harp*).

isicathamiya A distinctive South African singing style, blending European-based *harmony* and aesthetics with elements of the earlier *mbube* style. Traditional groups are all-male and *a cappella*.

isorhythmic motet Medieval and early Renaissance *motet* based on a repeating rhythmic pattern throughout one or more voices.

Italian overture Baroque *overture* consisting of three sections: fast-slow-fast.

jam band A group that focuses on live performance rather than commercial recordings. Jam bands, such as the Grateful Dead and Phish, combine many different musical traditions, most notably *folk*, jazz, rock, and *country-western*, in a highly improvisational and expressive style.

Janissary music Music of the military corps of the Turkish sultan, characterized by *percussion instruments* such as *triangle*, *cymbals*, *bell tree*, and *bass drum* as well as *trumpets* and *double-reed* instruments.

jarabe Traditional Mexican dance form with multiple sections in contrasting *meters* and *tempos*, often performed by *mariachi* ensembles.

jazz A musical style created mainly by African Americans in the early twentieth century that blended elements drawn from African musics with the popular and art traditions of the West.

jazz band Instrumental ensemble made up of reed (*saxophones* and *clarinets*), brass (*trumpets* and *trombones*), and rhythm sections (*percussion*, *piano*, *double bass*, and sometimes *guitar*).

jia hua Literally, "adding flowers"; an embellishment style in Chinese music using various ornamental figures.

jig A vigorous dance developed in the British Isles, usually in *compound meter*; became fashionable on the Continent as the *gigue*; still popular as an Irish traditional dance genre.

jongleurs Medieval wandering entertainers who played instruments, sang and danced, juggled, and performed plays.

jongleuresses Female *jongleurs*, or wandering entertainer/minstrels.

jota A type of Spanish dance song characterized by a quick *triple meter* and *guitar* and *castanet* accompaniment.

karaoke "Empty orchestra"; popular nightclub style from Japan where customers sing the melody to accompanying pre-recorded tracks.

kettledrums See *timpani*.

key Defines the relationship of *tones* with a common center or *tonic*. Also a lever on a keyboard or woodwind instrument.

keyboard instrument Instrument sounded by means of a keyboard (a series of keys played with the fingers).

keynote See *tonic*.

key signature Sharps or flats placed at the beginning of a piece to show the *key* of a work.

Klangfarbenmelodie Twentieth-century technique in which the notes of a melody are distributed among different instruments, giving a pointillistic *texture*.

koron In Persian music, a *pitch* in between the natural pitch and a flat, notated as a flat sign with a triangular head.

koto Japanese plucked-string instrument with a long rectangular body, thirteen strings, and movable bridges or frets.

kouta A short Japanese song traditionally sung by a *geisha* for private or theatrical entertainment.

Kyrie The first item of the *Ordinary* in the Roman Catholic *Mass*. Its construction is threefold, involving three repetitions of "Kyrie eleison" (Lord, have mercy), three of "Christe eleison" (Christ, have mercy), and again three of "Kyrie eleison."

lamellophone Plucked *idiophone* with thin metal strips; common throughout sub-Saharan Africa.

lamentoso Like a lament.

largo Broad; very slow.

Latin jazz A *jazz* style influenced by Latin American music, which includes various dance rhythms and traditional *percussion instruments*.

Latin rock Subgenre of *rock* featuring Latin and African *percussion instruments (maracas, conga drums, timbales)*.

legato Smooth and connected; opposite of *staccato*.

Leitmotif "Leading motive," or basic recurring *theme*, representing a person, object, or idea, commonly used in Wagner's operas.

libretto Text, or script, of an *opera*, prepared by a librettist.

Lied German for "song"; most commonly associated with the solo art song of the nineteenth century, usually accompanied by *piano*.

Lieder Plural of *Lied*.

lining out A *call-and-response* singing practice prevalent in early America and England; characterized by the alternation between a singer leader and a *chorus* singing heterophonically.

liturgy The set order of religious services and the structure of each service, within a particular denomination (e.g., Roman Catholic).

lute Plucked-string instrument of Middle Eastern origin, popular in western Europe from the late Middle Ages to the eighteenth century.

lyre Ancient plucked-string instrument of the *harp* family, used to accompany singing and poetry.

lyric opera Hybrid form combining elements of *grand opera* and *opéra comique* and featuring appealing melodies and romantic drama.

madrigal Renaissance secular work originating in Italy for voices, with or without instruments, set to a short, lyric love poem; also popular in England.

madrigal choir Small vocal ensemble that specializes in *a cappella* secular works.

maestoso Majestic.

Magnificat Biblical text on the words of the Virgin Mary, sung polyphonically in church from the Renaissance on.

major scale Scale consisting of seven different tones that comprise a specific pattern of *whole* and *half steps*. It differs from a *minor scale* primarily in that its third degree is raised half a step.

mambo Dance of Afro-Cuban origin with a characteristic highly syncopated *quadruple-meter* rhythmic pattern.

mandolin Plucked-string instrument with a rounded body and fingerboard; used in some *folk musics* and in *country-western* music.

maracas Latin-American rattles *(idiophones)* made from gourds or other materials.

march A style incorporating characteristics of military music, including strongly accented *duple meter* in simple, repetitive rhythmic patterns.

marching band Instrumental ensemble for entertainment at sports events and parades, consisting of wind and *percussion instruments*, drum majors/majorettes, and baton twirlers.

mariachi Traditional Mexican ensemble popular throughout the country, consisting of *trumpets*, *violins*, *guitar*, and bass *guitar*.

marimba *Percussion instrument* that is a mellower version of the *xylophone*; of African origin.

masque English genre of aristocratic entertainment that combined vocal and instrumental music with poetry and dance, developed during the sixteenth and seventeenth centuries.

Mass Central service of the Roman Catholic Church.

mazurka Type of Polish folk dance in *triple meter*.

mbube "Lion"; *a cappella* choral singing style of South African Zulus, featuring *call-and-response* patterns, close-knit harmonies, and *syncopation*.

measure Rhythmic group or metrical unit that contains a fixed number of *beats*, divided on the musical staff by bar lines.

medium Performing forces employed in a certain musical work.

Meistersinger A German "master singer," belonging to a professional guild. The Meistersingers flourished from the fourteenth through the sixteenth centuries.

melismatic Melodic style characterized by many notes sung to a single text syllable.

melodic variation The procedure in which a melody is altered while certain features are maintained. Often used in *theme and variations* form.

melody Succession of single *tones* or *pitches* perceived by the mind as a unity.

membranophone Any instrument that produces sound from tightly stretched membranes that can be struck, plucked, rubbed, or sung into (setting the skin in vibration).

meno Less.

mesto Sad.

metallophone *Percussion instrument* consisting of tuned metal bars, usually struck with a mallet.

meter Organization of rhythm in time; the grouping of *beats* into larger, regular patterns, notated as *measures*.

metronome Device used to indicate the *tempo* by sounding regular beats at adjustable speeds.

mezzo forte (*mf*) Moderately loud.

mezzo piano (*mp*) Moderately soft.

mezzo-soprano Female voice of middle range.

micropolyphony Twentieth-century technique encompassing the complex interweaving of all musical elements.

microtone Musical interval smaller than a *semitone*, prevalent in some non-Western musics and in some twentieth-century art music.

MIDI Acronym for Musical Instrument Digital Interface; technology standard that allows networking of computers with electronic musical instruments.

minimalism Contemporary musical style featuring the repetition of short melodic, rhythmic, and harmonic patterns with little variation. See also *post-minimalism* and *spiritual minimalism*.

Minnesingers Late medieval German poet-musicians.

minor scale *Scale* consisting of seven different *tones* that comprise a specific pattern of *whole* and *half steps*. It differs from the *major scale* primarily in that its third degree is lowered half a step.

minuet and trio An **A-B-A** form (**A**= minuet; **B** = trio) in a moderate *triple meter*; often the third *movement* of the Classical *multimovement cycle*.

misterioso Mysteriously.

modal Characterizes music that is based on *modes* other than major and minor, especially the early church *modes*.

mode *Scale* or sequence of notes used as the basis for a composition; major and minor are modes.

moderato Moderate.

modified sonata-allegro A statement (*exposition*) and restatement (*recapitulation*) of *themes* without the *development* section typical in *sonata-allegro form*.

modified strophic form Song structure that combines elements of *strophic* and through-composed forms; a variation of *strophic form* in which a section might have a new *key*, *rhythm*, or varied melodic pattern.

modulation The process of changing from one *key* to another.

molto Very.

monody Vocal style established in the Baroque, with a solo singer(s) and instrumental accompaniment.

monophonic Single-line *texture*, or *melody* without accompaniment.

monothematic Work or *movement* based on a single *theme*.

morality play Medieval drama, often with music, intended to teach proper values.

motet *Polyphonic* vocal *genre*, secular in the Middle Ages but sacred or devotional thereafter.

motive Short melodic or rhythmic idea; the smallest fragment of a *theme* that forms a melodic-harmonic-rhythmic unit.

Motown A record company, originally from Detroit, that moved to Los Angeles in 1971. Also the associated musical style—a fusion of *gospel*, *rock and roll*, and *rhythm and blues*.

movement Complete, self-contained part within a larger musical work.

mp3 A file-compression format applied to audio files; term is short for Moving Pictures Expert Group 1 Layer 3.

MTV Acronym for music television, a cable channel that initially presented nonstop *music videos*.

multimovement cycle A three- or four-*movement* structure used in Classical-era instrumental music—especially the *symphony*, *sonata*, *concerto*—and in *chamber music*; each *movement* is in a prescribed *tempo* and *form*; sometimes called *sonata cycle*.

multiphonic Two or more *pitches* sung or played simultaneously by the same voice or instrument.

muses Nine daughters of Zeus in ancient mythology; each presided over one of the arts.

musical Genre of twentieth-century musical theater, especially popular in the United States and Great Britain; characterized by spoken dialogue, dramatic plot interspersed with songs, ensemble numbers, and dancing.

Musical Instrument Digital Interface See *MIDI*.

musical saw A handsaw that is bowed on its smooth edge; *pitch* is varied by bending the saw.

musical sound See *tone*.

music drama Wagner's term for his operas.

music video Video tape or film that accompanies a recording, usually of a popular or *rock* song.

musique concrète Music made up of natural sounds and sound effects that are recorded and then manipulated electronically.

mute Mechanical device used to muffle the sound of an instrument.

nakers Medieval *percussion instruments* resembling small *kettledrums*, played in pairs; of Middle Eastern origin.

Nashville sound A style of *country-western* influenced by record producers centered in Nashville. These producers had a broad knowledge of music and the industry, and cultivated a more mainstream style.

Neoclassical jazz A modern *jazz* style characterized by expanded *tonalities*, modal improvisations, and new forms; Wynton Marsalis is a proponent of this style.

Neoclassicism A twentieth-century style that combined elements of Classical and Baroque music with modernist trends.

neumatic Melodic style with two to four notes set to each syllable.

neumes Early musical notation signs; square notes on a four-line staff.

new age Style of popular music of the 1980s and 1990s, characterized by soothing *timbres* and repetitive forms that are subjected to shifting variation techniques.

new-age jazz A mellow, reflective *jazz* style exemplified by Paul Winter and his ensemble.

New Orleans jazz Early *jazz* style characterized by multiple improvisations in an ensemble of *cornet* (or *trumpet*), clarinet (or *saxophone*), trombone, piano, double bass (or *tuba*), banjo (or *guitar*), and drums; repertory included *blues*, *ragtime*, and popular songs.

New Romanticism A contemporary style of music that employs the rich harmonic language and other elements of Romantic and post-Romantic composers.

new wave Subgenre of *rock* popular since the late 1970s, highly influenced by simple 1950s-style *rock and roll*; developed as a rejection of the complexities of *art rock* and *beauty metal.*

ninth chord Five-tone *chord* spanning a ninth between its lowest and highest *tones.*

nocturne "Night piece"; introspective work common in the nineteenth century, often for *piano.*

Noh drama A major form of Japanese theater since the late fourteenth century; based on philosophical concepts from Zen Buddhism.

noise Sounds without a distinct *pitch.*

nonmetric Music lacking a strong sense of *beat* or *meter*, common in certain non-Western cultures.

non troppo Not too much.

note A musical symbol denoting *pitch* and *duration.*

nuevo tango A form of tango, developed in the 1950s by Astor Piazzola, that incorporates *fugue*, chromaticism, *dissonance*, and elements of *jazz.*

oboe Soprano-range, *double-reed* woodwind instrument.

octave *Interval* between two tones seven diatonic pitches apart; the lower note vibrates half as fast as the upper and sounds an octave lower.

ode Secular composition written for a royal occasion, especially popular in England.

offbeat A weak *beat* or any pulse between the beats in a measured rhythmic pattern.

Office See *Divine Offices.*

open ending First ending in a medieval secular piece, often cadencing on a *pitch* other than the final, which was generally the most prominent note in an early church mode.

open form Indeterminate contemporary music in which some details of a composition are clearly indicated, but the overall structure is left to choice or chance.

opera Music drama that is generally sung throughout, combining the resources of vocal and instrumental music with poetry and drama, acting and pantomime, scenery and costumes.

opera buffa Italian comic *opera*, sung throughout.

opéra comique French comic *opera*, with some spoken dialogue.

opera seria Tragic Italian *opera.*

operetta A small-scale operatic work, generally light in tone, with spoken dialogue, song and dance.

ophicleide A nineteenth-century *brass instrument* (now obsolete) with *woodwind* fingering holes; used by Berlioz, among others; the parts are generally played today on *tuba.*

opus number (op.) A number, often part of the title of a piece, designating the work in chronological relationship to other works by the same composer.

oral tradition Music that is transmitted by example or imitation and performed from memory.

oral transmission Preservation of music without the aid of written notation.

oratorio Large-scale dramatic genre originating in the Baroque, based on a text of religious or serious character, performed by solo voices, *chorus*, and *orchestra*; similar to *opera* but without scenery, costumes, or action.

orchestra Performing group of diverse instruments in various cultures; in Western art music, an ensemble of multiple strings with various *woodwind*, *brass*, and *percussion instruments.*

orchestral bells See *chimes.*

orchestration The technique of setting instruments in various combinations.

Ordinary Sections of the Roman Catholic *Mass* that remain the same from day to day throughout the church year, as distinct from the *Proper*, which changes daily according to the liturgical occasion.

organ Wind instrument in which air is fed to the pipes by mechanical means; the pipes are controlled by two or more keyboards and a set of pedals.

organal style *Organum* in which the Tenor sings the melody (original chant) in very long notes while the upper voices move freely and rapidly above it.

organum Earliest kind of *polyphonic* music, which developed from the custom of adding voices above a *plainchant*; they first ran parallel to it at the interval of a fifth or fourth and later moved more freely.

ornamentation See *embellishment.*

ostinato A short melodic, rhythmic, or harmonic pattern that is repeated throughout a work or a section of one.

overture An introductory *movement*, as in an *opera* or *oratorio*, often presenting melodies from *arias* to come. Also an orchestral work for concert performance.

pan band An ensemble comprised of a variety of *steel drums* and a percussion section known as the "engine room."

panharmonicon An automatic instrument designed to simulate a whole *orchestra* using *organ* pipes and mechanical percussion-devices. Beethoven's *Battle Symphony*, also known as *Wellington's Victory*, was originally written for the panharmonicon.

panpipes Wind instrument consisting of a series of small vertical tubes or pipes of differing length; sound is produced by blowing across the top.

pantomime Theatrical *genre* in which an actor silently plays all the parts in a show while accompanied by singing; originated in ancient Rome.

part song Secular vocal composition, unaccompanied, in three, four, or more parts.

partita See *suite.*

pas de deux A dance for two that is an established feature of classical ballet.

paso doble Marchlike Spanish dance in *duple meter.*

passacaglia Baroque form (similar to the *chaconne*) in moderately slow *triple meter*, based on a short, repeated base-line melody that serves as the basis for continuous variation in the other voices.

passepied French Baroque court dance type; a faster version of the *minuet*.

Passion Musical setting of the Crucifixion story as told by one of the four Evangelists in the Gospels.

pastorale Pastoral, country-like.

patalon An overture from a Javanese shadow-puppet play; performed by *gamelan*.

patron (patroness) A person who supports music or musicians; a benefactor of the arts. See also *patronage*.

patronage Sponsorship of an artist or a musician, historically by a member of the wealthy or ruling classes.

pavane Stately Renaissance court dance in duple meter.

pedal point Sustained *tone* over which the *harmonies* change.

pélog Heptatonic (7-note) tuning used in Javanese *gamelan* music.

penny whistle See *tin whistle*.

pentatonic scale Five-note pattern used in some African, Far Eastern, and Native American musics; can also be found in Western music as an example of exoticism.

percussion instrument Instrument made of metal, wood, stretched skin, or other material that is made to sound by striking, shaking, scraping, or plucking.

perfect pitch The innate ability to reproduce any *pitch* without hearing it first.

performance art Multimedia art form involving visual as well as dramatic and musical elements.

period-instrument ensemble Group that performs on historical instruments or modern replicas built after historical models.

perpetuum mobile Type of piece characterized by continuous repetitions of a rhythmic pattern at a quick *tempo*; perpetual motion.

phasing A technique in which a musical pattern is repeated and manipulated so that it separates and overlaps itself, and then rejoins the original pattern; getting "out of phase" and back "in sync."

phrase Musical unit; often a component of a *melody*.

phrygian One of the church *modes* often associated with a somber mood; built on the pitch E using only white keys.

pianissimo (pp) Very soft.

piano (p) Soft.

piano Keyboard instrument whose strings are struck with hammers controlled by a keyboard mechanism; pedals control dampers in the strings that stop the sound when the finger releases the key.

pianoforte Original name for the *piano*.

piano quartet Standard chamber ensemble of *piano* with *violin*, *viola*, and *cello*.

piano quintet Standard chamber ensemble of *piano* with *string quartet* (two *violins*, *viola*, and *cello*).

piano trio Standard chamber ensemble of *piano* with *violin* and *cello*.

piccolo Smallest *woodwind instrument*, similar to the *flute* but sounding an *octave* higher.

pipa A Chinese *lute* with four silk strings; played as solo and ensemble instrument.

pipe A medieval *flute* with three holes that is blown at one end through a mouthpiece.

pitch Highness or lowness of a *tone*, depending on the *frequency*.

pizzicato Performance direction to pluck a string of a bowed instrument with the finger.

plainchant See *Gregorian chant*.

plainsong See *Gregorian chant*.

plectrum An implement made of wood, ivory or another material used to pluck a *chordophone*.

poco A little.

polka Lively Bohemian dance; also a short, lyric *piano* piece.

polonaise Stately Polish processional dance in *triple meter*.

polychoral Performance style developed in the late sixteenth century involving the use of two or more *choirs* that alternate with each other or sing together.

polychord A single *chord* comprised of several *chords*, common in twentieth-century music.

polyharmony Two or more streams of *harmony* played against each other, common in twentieth-century music.

polymeter The simultaneous use of several *meters*, common in twentieth-century music and certain African musics.

polyphonic Two or more melodic lines combined into a multivoiced *texture*, as distinct from *monophonic*.

polyrhythm The simultaneous use of several rhythmic patterns or *meters*, common in twentieth-century music and in certain African musics.

polytextual Two or more texts set simultaneously in a composition, common in the medieval *motet*.

polytonality The simultaneous use of two or more *keys*, common in twentieth-century music.

portative organ Medieval *organ* small enough to be carried or set on a table, usually with only one set of pipes.

positive organ Small single-manual *organ*, popular in the Renaissance and Baroque eras.

post-minimalism Contemporary style combining lush harmonies of New Romanticism with high-energy rhythms of minimalism; John Adams is a major exponent.

prelude Instrumental work preceding a larger work.

prepared piano *Piano* whose sound is altered by the insertion of various materials (metal, rubber, leather, and paper) between the strings; invented by John Cage.

presto Very fast.

program music Instrumental music endowed with literary or pictorial associations, especially popular in the nineteenth century.

program symphony Multimovement programmatic orchestral work, typically from the nineteenth century.

progressive rock See *art rock*.

Proper Sections of the Roman Catholic *Mass* that vary from day to day throughout the church year according to the particular liturgical occasion, as distinct from the *Ordinary*, in which they remain the same.

Psalms Book from the Old Testament of the Bible; the 150 psalm texts, used in Jewish and Christian worship, are often set to music.

psaltery Medieval plucked-string instrument similar to the modern *zither*, consisting of a sound box over which strings were stretched.

psychedelic rock See *acid rock*.

punk rock Subgenre of *rock*, popular since the mid-1970s; characterized by loud volume levels, driving rhythms, and simple forms typical of earlier *rock and roll*; often contains shocking lyrics and offensive behavior.

pure music See *absolute music*.

quadrivium Subdivision of the seven liberal arts; includes the mathematical subjects of music, arithmetic, geometry, and astronomy.

quadruple meter Basic metrical pattern of four beats to a measure. Also *common time*.

quadruple stop Playing four notes simultaneously on a string instrument.

quadruplum Fourth voice of a *polyphonic* work.

quartal harmony *Harmony* based on the *interval* of the fourth as opposed to a third; used in twentieth-century music.

quarter tone An *interval* halfway between a *half step*.

quotation music Music that parodies another work or works, presenting them in a new style or guise.

rabab Any of a variety of bowed string instruments from the Islamic world, most held upright. The medieval *rebec* was derived from these instruments.

raga Melodic pattern used in music of India; prescribes *pitches*, patterns, *ornamentation*, and extramusical associations such as time of performance and emotional character.

ragtime Late-nineteenth-century *piano* style created by African Americans, characterized by highly syncopated melodies; also played in ensemble arrangements. Contributed to early *jazz* styles.

range Distance between the lowest and highest *tones* of a *melody*, an instrument, or a voice.

rap Style of popular music in which rhymed lyrics are spoken over rhythm tracks; developed by African Americans in the 1970s and widely disseminated in the 1980s and 1990s; the style is part of the larger culture of *hip hop*.

rebec Medieval bowed-string instrument, often with a pear-shaped body.

recapitulation Third section of *sonata-allegro form*, in which the thematic material of the *exposition* is restated, generally in the *tonic*. Also *restatement*.

recitative Solo vocal declamation that follows the inflections of the text, often resulting in a disjunct vocal style; found in *opera*, *cantata*, and *oratorio*. Can be *secco* or *accompagnato*.

recorder End-blown *woodwind* instrument with a whistle mouthpiece, generally associated with early music.

reed Flexible strip of cane or metal set into a mouthpiece or the body of an instrument; set in vibration by a stream of air. See also *single reed* and *double reed*.

reel Moderately quick dance in *duple meter* danced throughout the British Isles; the most popular Irish traditional dance type.

refrain Text or music that is repeated within a larger form.

regal Small medieval reed *organ*.

reggae Jamaican popular music style characterized by offbeat rhythms and chanted vocals over a strong bass part; often associated with the religious movement Rastafarianism.

register Specific area in the range of an instrument or voice.

registration Selection or combination of stops in a work for *organ* or *harpsichord*.

relative key The major and minor key that share the same *key signature*; for example, D minor is the relative minor of F major, both having one flat.

repeat sign Musical symbol (𝄆 𝄇) that indicates repetition of a passage in a composition.

Requiem Mass Roman Catholic *Mass* for the Dead.

resolution Conclusion of a musical idea, as in the progression from an *active chord* to a rest chord.

response Short choral answer to a solo *verse*; an element of liturgical dialogue.

responsorial singing Singing, especially in *Gregorian chant*, in which a soloist or a group of soloists alternates with the choir. See also *call-and-response*.

restatement See *recapitulation*.

retrograde Backward statement of melody.

retrograde inversion Mirror image and backward statement of a *melody*.

rhythm The controlled movement of music in time.

rhythm and blues Popular African-American music style of the 1940s through 1960s featuring a solo singer accompanied by a small instrumental ensemble (*piano*, *guitar*, *double bass*, drums, tenor *saxophone*), driving rhythms, and *blues* and pop song forms.

rhythmic modes Fixed rhythmic patterns of long and short notes, popular in the thirteenth century.

rhythmic variation The procedure in which note lengths, *meter*, or *tempo* is altered. Often used in *theme and variations* form.

riff In *jazz*, a short melodic *ostinato* over changing harmonies.

ring shout Religious dance performed by African-American slaves, performed with hand clapping and a shuffle step to *spirituals*.

ripieno The larger of the two ensembles in the Baroque *concerto grosso*. Also *tutti*.

ritardando Holding back, getting slower.

ritornello Short, recurring instrumental passage found in both the *aria* and the Baroque *concerto*.

rock A style of popular music with roots in *rock and roll* but differing in lyric content, recording technique, song length and form, and range of sounds. The term was first used in the 1960s to distinguish groups like the Beatles and the Rolling Stones from earlier artists.

rockabilly An early style of *rock and roll*, fusing elements of *blues*, *rhythm and blues*, and *country-western* music.

rock and roll American popular music style first heard in the 1950s; derived from the union of African-American *rhythm and blues, country-western*, and pop music.

rock band Popular music ensemble that depends on amplified strings, percussion, and electronically generated sounds.

rocket theme Quickly ascending rhythmic melody used in Classical-era instrumental music; the technique is credited to composers in Mannheim, Germany.

Rococo A term from the visual arts that is frequently applied to eighteenth-century French music, characterized by simplicity, grace, and delicate *ornamentation*.

romance Originally a *ballad*; in the Romantic era, a lyric instrumental work.

ronde Lively Renaissance "round dance," associated with the outdoors, in which the participants danced in a circle or a line.

rondeau Medieval and Renaissance fixed poetic form and *chanson* type with courtly love texts.

rondo Muscial form in which the first section recurs, usually in the *tonic*. In the Classical *multimovement cycle*, it appears as the last *movement* in various forms, including **A-B-A-B-A, A-B-A-C-A**, and **A-B-A-C-A-B-A**.

rosin Substance made from hardened tree sap, rubbed on the hair of a bow to help it grip the strings.

round Perpetual *canon* at the *unison* in which each voice enters in succession with the same *melody* (for example, *Row, Row, Row Your Boat*).

rounded binary Compositional form with two sections, in which the second ends with a return to material from the first; each section is usually repeated.

rubato "Borrowed time," common in Romantic music, in which the performer hesitates here or hurries forward there, imparting flexibility to the written note values. Also *tempo rubato*.

rumba Latin American dance of Afro-Cuban origin, in *duple meter* with syncopated *rhythms*.

rural blues American popular singing style with raspy-voiced male singer accompanied by acoustic steel-string *guitar*; features melodic *blue notes* over repeated bass patterns.

sackbut Early *brass instrument*, ancestor of the *trombone*.

sacred music Religious or spiritual music, for church or devotional use.

salon A gathering of musicians, artists, and intellectuals who shared similar interests and tastes, hosted by a wealthy aristocrat.

salsa "Spicy"; collective term for Latin American dance music, especially forms of Afro-Cuban origin.

saltarello Italian "jumping dance," often characterized by triplets in a rapid 4/4 time.

samba Afro-Brazilian dance, characterized by *duple meter, responsorial* singing, and *polyrhythmic* accompaniments.

sampler Electronic device that digitizes, stores, and plays back sounds.

Santería A pantheistic Afro-Cuban religion combining elements of traditional Yoruban beliefs with Catholicism.

santur A Middle Eastern hammer dulcimer, with a trapezoidal sound box and 12 to 18 sets of metal strings.

Sanctus A section of the *Mass*; the fourth musical *movement* of the *Ordinary*.

sarabande Stately Spanish Baroque dance type in *triple meter*, a standard *movement* of the Baroque *suite*.

sarangi Bowed *chordophone* from north India with three main strings and a large number of metal strings that vibrate sympathetically.

saxophone Family of *single-reed* woodwind instruments commonly used in the concert and *jazz band*.

scale Series of tones in ascending or descending order; may present the notes of a *key*.

scat singing A *jazz* style that sets syllables without meaning *(vocables)* to an improvised vocal line.

scherzo Composition in **A-B-A** form, usually in *triple meter*; replaced the *minuet and trio* in the nineteenth century.

secco *Recitative* singing style that features a sparse accompaniment and moves with great freedom.

Second Viennese School Name given to composer Arnold Schoenberg and his pupils Alban Berg and Anton Webern; represents the first efforts in *twelve-tone* composition.

secular music Nonreligious music; when texted, usually in the vernacular.

semitone Also known as a *half step*, the smallest *interval* commonly used in the Western musical system.

sequence Restatement of an idea or *motive* at a different *pitch* level.

serenade Classical instrumental *genre* that combines elements of *chamber music* and *symphony*, often performed in the evening or at social functions. Related to *divertimento* and *cassation*.

serialism Method of composition in which various musical elements (*pitch, rhythm, dynamics, tone color*) may be ordered in a fixed series. See also *total serialism*.

sesquialtera In Spanish and Latin American music, an unequal *meter* based on the alternation of duple and triple time within groups of six beats.

seventh chord Four-note combination consisting of a *triad* with another third added on top; spans a seventh between its lowest and highest tones.

sextuple meter Compound metrical pattern of six *beats* to a *measure*.

sforzando (sf) Sudden stress or accent on a single *note* or *chord*.

shake A *jazz* technique in which brass players shake their lips to produce a wide vibrato.

shakuhachi A Japanese end-blown *flute*.

shamisen Long-necked Japanese *chordophone* with three strings.

shape-note Music notation system originating in nineteenth-century American church music in which the shape of the note heads determines the *pitch*; created to aid music reading.

sharp sign Musical symbol (♯) that indicates raising a pitch by a *semitone*.

shawm Medieval wind instrument, the ancestor of the *oboe*.

sheng A reed mouth *organ* from China.

side drum See *snare drum*.

simple meter Grouping of *rhythms* in which the *beat* is subdivided into two, as in duple, triple, and quadruple meters.

sinfonia Short instrumental work, found in Baroque *opera*, to facilitate scene changes.

single reed A *reed* consisting of one piece of cane vibrating against another part of the instrument, often a mouthpiece.

Singspiel Comic German drama with spoken dialogue; the immediate predecessor of Romantic German *opera*.

sitar Long-necked plucked *chordophone* of northern India, with movable frets and a rounded gourd body; used as solo instrument and with *tabla*.

ska Jamaican urban dance form popular in the 1960s, influential in *reggae*.

sléndro *Pentatonic* tuning used in Javanese *gamelan* music; a gapped *scale* using tones 1, 2, 3, 5, 6.

slide In bowed string instruments, moving from one *pitch* to another by sliding the finger on the string while bowing.

slide trumpet Medieval *brass instrument* of the *trumpet* family.

snare drum Small cylindrical drum with two heads stretched over a metal shell, the lower head having strings across it; played with two drumsticks. Also *side drum*.

soca A style of music and dance derived from *calypso*, mixing elements of *soul*, funk, *ska* and *calypso*.

soft rock Lyrical, gentle *rock* style that evolved around 1960 in response to hard-driving *rock and roll*.

son A genre of traditional Mexican dances that combine compound duple with triple meters.

sonata Instrumental genre in several *movements* for soloist or small ensemble.

sonata-allegro form The opening *movement* of the *multimovement cycle*, consisting of themes that are stated in the first section (*exposition*), developed in the second section (*development*), and restated in the third section (*recapitulation*). Also *sonata form* or *first-movement form*.

sonata cycle See *multimovement cycle*.

sonata da camera Baroque *chamber sonata*, usually a suite of stylized dances. Also *chamber sonata*.

sonata da chiesa Baroque instrumental work intended for performance in church; in four *movements*, frequently arranged slow-fast-slow-fast. Also *church sonata*.

sonata form See *sonata-allegro form*.

song cycle Group of songs, usually *Lieder*, that are unified musically or through their texts.

son jalisciense A *son* in the style that originated in the Mexican State of Jalisco.

soprano Highest-ranged voice, normally possessed by women or boys.

soul A black American style of popular music, incorporating elements of *rock and roll* and *gospel*.

source music A film technique in which music comes from a logical source within the film and functions as part of the story.

sound Vibrations perceived by the human ear; a musical sound is described by its *pitch* and its *duration*.

sousaphone *Brass instrument* adapted from the *tuba* with a forward bell that is coiled to rest over the player's shoulder for ease of carrying while marching.

spiritual Folklike devotional *genre* of the United States, sung by African Americans and whites.

spiritual minimalism Contemporary musical style related to *minimalism*, characterized by a weak pulse and long chains of lush progressions—either *tonal* or *modal*.

Sprechstimme A vocal style in which the melody is spoken at approximate *pitches* rather than sung on exact *pitches*; developed by Arnold Schoenberg.

staccato Short, detached *notes*, marked with a dot above them.

statement See *exposition*.

steamroller effect A drawn-out *crescendo* heard in Classical-era instrumental music; a technique credited to composers in Mannheim, Germany.

steel drum A *percussion instrument* made from an oil drum, developed in Trinidad during the 1930s and 1940s.

stile concitato Baroque style developed by Monteverdi, which introduced novel effects such as rapid repeated notes as symbols of passion.

stile rappresentativo A dramatic *recitative* style of the Baroque period in which melodies moved freely over a foundation of simple *chords*.

stopping On a string instrument, altering the string length by pressing it on the fingerboard. On a *horn*, playing with the bell closed by the hand or a *mute*.

strain A series of contrasting sections found in rags and marches; in *duple meter* with sixteen-measure themes or sections.

streaming audio Music that is played directly from the Web, in real time, and does not require downloading.

stretto In a *fugue*, when entries of the *subject* occur at faster intervals of time, so that they overlap forming dense, imitative *counterpoint*. Stretto usually occurs at the climactic moment near the end.

string instruments Bowed and plucked instruments whose sound is produced by the vibration of one or more strings. Also *chordophone*.

string quartet *Chamber music* ensemble consisting of two *violins*, *viola*, and *cello*. Also a multimovement composition for this ensemble.

string quintet Standard chamber ensemble made up of either two *violins*, two *violas*, and *cello* or two *violins*, *viola*, and two *cellos*.

string trio Standard chamber ensemble of two *violins* and *cello* or of *violin*, *viola*, and *cello*.

strophic form Song structure in which the same music is repeated with every stanza (strophe) of the poem.

Sturm und Drang "Storm and stress"; late-eighteenth-century movement in Germany toward more emotional expression in the arts.

style Characteristic manner of presentation of musical elements (*melody, rhythm, harmony, dynamics, form*, etc.).

subdominant Fourth scale step, *fa*.

subdominant chord *Chord* built on the fourth scale step, the IV chord.

subject Main idea or *theme* of a work, as in a *fugue*.

suite Multimovement work made up of a series of contrasting dance movements, generally all in the same *key*. Also *partita* and *ordre*.

suona Traditional Chinese instrument with a *double reed*, similar to the Western *oboe*.

swing *Jazz* term coined to described Louis Armstrong's style; more commonly refers to *big band* jazz.

Swing Era The mid-1930s to the mid-1940s, when *swing* was the most popular music in the United States. The most important musicians of the swing era were Duke Ellington, Louis Armstrong, and Benny Goodman.

syllabic Melodic style with one note to each syllable of text.

symphonic poem One-*movement* orchestral form that develops a poetic idea, suggests a scene, or creates a mood, generally associated with the Romantic era. Also *tone poem*.

symphony Large work for *orchestra*, generally in three or four *movements*.

syncopation Deliberate upsetting of the *meter* or pulse through a temporary shifting of the *accent* to a weak *beat* or an *offbeat*.

synthesizer Electronic instrument that produces a wide variety of sounds by combining sound generators and sound modifiers in one package with a unified control system.

Syrinx See *panpipes*.

tabla Pair of single-headed, tuned drums used in north Indian classical music.

tabor Cylindrical medieval drum.

tag *Jazz* term for a *coda*, or a short concluding section.

tala Fixed time cycle or *meter* in Indian music, built from uneven groupings of *beats*.

tambourine *Percussion instrument* consisting of a small round drum with metal plates inserted in its rim; played by striking or shaking.

tam-tam See *gong*.

tango A Latin American dance involving couples in tight embrace; characterized by abrupt movements and syncopated rhythms.

Te Deum Song of praise to God; a text from the Roman Catholic rite, often set *polyphonically*.

tempo Rate of speed or pace of music.

tempo rubato See *rubato*.

tenor Male voice of high *range*. Also a part, often structural, in *polyphony*.

tenor drum *Percussion instrument*, larger than the *snare drum*, with a wooden shell.

ternary form Three-part (**A-B-A**) form based on a statement (**A**), contrast or departure (**B**), and repetition (**A**). Also *three-part form*.

tertian harmony *Harmony* based on the *interval* of the third, particularly predominant from the Baroque through the nineteenth century.

texture The interweaving of melodic (horizontal) and harmonic (vertical) elements in the musical fabric.

thematic development Musical expansion of a *theme* by varying its melodic outline, *harmony*, or *rhythm*. Also *thematic transformation*.

thematic transformation See *thematic development*.

theme Melodic idea used as a basic building block in the construction of a composition. Also *subject*.

theme and variations Compositional procedure in which a *theme* is stated and then altered in successive statements; occurs as an independent piece or as a *movement* of a *multimovement cycle*.

theme group Several *themes* in the same *key* that function as a unit within a section of a form, particularly in *sonata-allegro form*.

Theremin An early electronic instrument from the 1920s, named after its inventor Leon Theremin.

third *Interval* between two *notes* that are two *diatonic* scale steps apart.

third stream *Jazz* style that synthesizes characteristics and techniques of classical music and *jazz*; term coined by Gunther Schuller.

thorough-bass See *figured bass*.

three-part form See *ternary form*.

throat singing A vocal technique in which more than one *tone* is produced simultaneously: a deep fundamental *pitch* with reinforced harmonics above the fundamental.

through-composed Song structure that is composed from beginning to end, without repetitions of large sections.

timbales Shallow, single-headed drums of Cuban origin, played in pairs; used in much Latin American popular music.

timbre The quality of a sound that distinguishes one voice or instrument from another. Also *tone color*.

timbrel Ancient *percussion instrument* related to the *tambourine*.

timpani *Percussion instrument* consisting of a hemispheric copper shell with a head of plastic or calfskin, held in place by a metal ring and played with soft or hard padded sticks. A pedal mechanism changes the tension of the head, and with it the *pitch*. Also *kettledrums*.

Tin Pan Alley Nickname for the popular music industry centered in New York from the nineteenth century through the 1950s. Also the style of popular song in the United States during that period.

tintinnabulation A bell-like style developed by Estonian composer Arvo Pärt, achieved by weaving conjunct lines that hover around a central *pitch*; from the Latin word for bell.

tin whistle Small metal end-blown *flute* commonly used in Irish traditional music.

toccata Virtuoso composition, generally for *organ* or *harpsichord*, in a free and rhapsodic style; in the Baroque, it often served as the introduction to a *fugue*.

tom-tom Cylindrical drum without snares.

tone A sound of definite *pitch*.

tonal Based on principles of major-minor *tonality*, as distinct from *modal*.

tonality Principle of organization around a *tonic*, or home, *pitch*, based on a major or minor *scale*.

tone cluster Highly dissonant combination of *pitches* sounded simultaneously.

tone color See *timbre*.

tone poem See *symphonic poem*.

tone row An arrangement of the twelve *chromatic* tones that serves as the basis of a *twelve-tone* composition.

tonic The first note of the *scale* or *key*, do. Also *keynote*.

tonic chord *Triad* built on the first scale *tone*, the I chord.

total serialism Extremely complex, totally controlled music in which the twelve-tone principle is extended to elements of music other than *pitch*.

traditional music Music that is learned by *oral transmission* and is easily sung or played by most people; may exist in variant forms. Also *folk music*.

tragédie lyrique French serious *opera* of the seventeenth and eighteenth centuries, with spectacular dance scenes and brilliant choruses on tales of courtly love or heroic adventures; associated with J.-B. Lully.

trance music A style of dance music fusing techno and house music. The name derives from the throbbing *beats* designed to put the listener in a trance-like state.

transition See *bridge*.

transposition Shifting a piece of music to a different pitch level.

tremolo Rapid repetition of a *tone*; can be achieved instrumentally or vocally.

triad Common *chord* type, consisting of three *pitches* built on alternate *tones* of the *scale* (e.g., steps 1-3-5, or *do-mi-sol*).

triangle *Percussion instrument* consisting of a slender rod of steel bent in the shape of a triangle, struck with a steel beater.

trill Ornament consisting of the rapid alternation between one *tone* and the next or sometimes the *tone* below.

trio An ensemble of three players.

trio sonata Baroque *chamber sonata* type written in three parts: two melody lines and the *basso continuo*; requires a total of four players to perform.

triple meter Basic metrical pattern of three beats to a *measure*.

triple-stop Playing three notes simultaneously on a string instrument.

triplet Group of three equal-valued notes played in the time of two; indicated by a bracket and the number 3.

triplum Third voice in early *polyphony*.

tritonic Three-note scale pattern, used in the music of some sub-Saharan African cultures.

trobairitz Female *troubadours*, composer-poets of southern France.

trombone Tenor-range brass instrument that changes *pitch* by means of a movable double slide; there is also a bass version.

troubadours Medieval poet-musicians in southern France.

trouser role In Classical *opera*, the part of a young man, written for a soprano or alto singer.

trouvères Medieval poet-musicians in northern France.

trumpet Highest-pitched *brass instrument* that changes *pitch* through valves.

tuba Bass-range *brass instrument* that changes *pitch* by means of valves.

tubular bells See *chimes*.

turn A *bridge*, or alternate phrase, in Cajun dance music.

tutti "All"; the opposite of solo. See also *ripieno*.

twelve-bar blues Musical structure based on a repeated harmonic-rhythmic pattern that is twelve *measures* in length (I-I-I-I-IV-IV-I-I-V-V-I-I).

twelve-tone music Compositional procedure of the twentieth century based on the use of all twelve chromatic tones (in a *tone row*) without a central tone, or *tonic*, according to prescribed rules.

two-part form See *binary form*.

uilleann pipes Type of *bellows*-blown *bagpipe* used in Irish traditional music; *bellows* are elbow-manipulated.

underscoring A technique used in films in which the music comes from an unseen source.

union pipes See *uilleann pipes*.

unison Interval between two *notes* of the same *pitch*; the simultaneous playing of the same *note*.

upbeat Last *beat* of a *measure*, a weak *beat*, which anticipates the *downbeat*.

vamp Short passage with simple *rhythm* and *harmony* that introduces a soloist in a *jazz* performance.

variation The compositional procedure of altering a pre-existing musical idea. See also *theme* and *variations*.

verismo Operatic "realism," a style popular in Italy in the 1890s, which tried to bring naturalism into the lyric theater.

vernacular The common language spoken by the people as distinguished from the literary language, or language of the educated elite.

verse In poetry, a group of lines constituting a unit. In liturgical music for the Catholic Church, a phrase from the Scriptures that alternates with the *response*.

Vespers One of the *Divine Offices* of the Roman Catholic Church, held at twilight.

vibraphone A *percussion instrument* with metal bars and electrically driven rotating propellers under each bar that produces a *vibrato* sound, much used in *jazz*.

vibrato Small fluctuation of *pitch* used as an expressive device to intensify a sound.

vielle Medieval bowed-string instrument; the ancestor of the *violin*.

Viennese School Title given to the three prominent composers of the Classical era: Haydn, Mozart, and Beethoven.

vihuela A type of Mexican *guitar* with a rounded back, common in *mariachi* ensembles.

villancico Spanish vernacular musical and poetic form consisting of several stanzas (coplas) and a *refrain* (estribillo) at the beginning and end. Can be *monophonic* or *polyphonic*; sacred or secular.

viola Bowed-string instrument of middle *range*; the second-highest member of the *violin* family.

viola da gamba Family of Renaissance bowed-string instruments that had six or more strings, was fretted like a *guitar*, and was held between the legs like a modern *cello*.

violin Soprano, or highest-ranged, member of the bowed-string instrument family.

violoncello Bowed-string instrument with a middle-to-low range and dark, rich sonority; lower than a *viola*. Also *cello*.

virelai Medieval and Renaissance fixed poetic form and *chanson* type with French courtly texts.

virtuoso Performer of extraordinary technical ability.

vivace Lively.

vocable Nonlexical syllables, lacking literal meaning.

vocalise A textless vocal melody, as in an exercise or concert piece.

voice In a *fugue*, a melodic line. Keyboard *fugues* of the late Baroque period, such as those by J. S. Bach, commonly have four distinct *voices* even though they are played by a single musician.

volume Degree of loudness or softness of a sound. See also *dynamics*.

waltz Ballroom dance type in *triple meter*; in the Romantic era, a short, stylized *piano* piece.

washboard A rhythm instrument used in certain styles of traditional music; an *idiophone* built from a laundry implement that is scraped with a metal rod or with the fingers.

Wayang Javanese shadow-puppet theater.

West Coast jazz *Jazz* style developed in the 1950s, featuring small groups of mixed *timbres* playing contrapuntal improvisations; similar to *cool jazz*.

whole step Interval consisting of two *half steps*, or *semitones*.

whole-tone scale Scale pattern built entirely of *whole-step* intervals, common in the music of the French Impressionists.

wind ensemble See *concert band*.

woodwind Instrumental family made of wood or metal whose tone is produced by a column of air vibrating within a pipe that has holes along its length.

woodwind quintet Standard chamber ensemble consisting of one each of the following: *flute, oboe, clarinet, bassoon*, and *horn* (not a *woodwind instrument*).

word painting Musical pictorialization of words from the text as an expressive device; a prominent feature of the Renaissance madrigal.

work song Communal song that synchronized group tasks.

xylophone *Percussion instrument* consisting of tuned blocks of wood suspended on a frame, laid out in the shape of a keyboard and struck with hard mallets.

yangqin A Chinese hammered *dulcimer* with a trapezoidal sound box and metal strings that are struck with bamboo sticks.

zither Family of string instruments with sound box over which strings are stretched; they may be plucked or bowed. Zithers appear in many shapes and are common in traditional music throughout Europe, Asia, and Africa.

zortziko Basque dance in *compound meter* with many dotted rhythms.

zurna A double-reeded instrument from the Middle East and other Islamic areas. The *shawm* was derived from this instrument.

zydeco A combination of traditional French Cajun music, *rhythm and blues*, rock and roll, Caribbean music and *country-western*. The typical ensemble consists of voice, *fiddle, accordion, electric guitar*, and *washboard*.

Credits

Every effort has been made to reach the rights holders for each image. Please contact W. W. Norton & Company with any updated information.

Opp. Part 1: (Marc Chagall, *La Musicienne*) Private Collection. Photo: Christie's Images/The Bridgeman Art Library © 2006 Artists Rights Society (ARS), New York/ADAGP, Paris; p. 2: Digital Vision/Getty Images; p. 3: Kevin Dodge/Corbis; p. 4: Photo: Matthew Imaging/Courtesy the Los Angeles Philharmonic; p. 5: Tony Arruza/Corbis; p. 8: Photonica/Getty Images; p. 9: Rufus F. Folkks/Corbis; p. 11: G. Anderhub/Lebrecht Music & Arts Photo Library; p. 12: Royalty-Free/Corbis; p. 14: Musée National d'Art Moderne, Centre Georges Pompidou, Paris, France. Photo: CNAC/MNAM/Réunion des Musées Nationaux/Art Resource, NY. © 2006 Estate of Alexander Calder/Artists Rights Society (ARS), New York; p. 16: Archivo Iconografico, S.A./Corbis; p. 17: Musée National d'Art Moderne, Centre Georges Pompidou, Paris, France. Photo: CNAC/MNAM/ Réunion des Musées Nationaux/Art Resource, NY; p. 20: Civico Museo Bibliografico Musicale, Bologna, Italy. Photo: Scala/Art Resource, NY; p. 21: AFP/Getty Images; p. 23: Musée National d'Art Moderne, Centre Georges Pompidou, Paris, France. © 2006 Artists Rights Society (ARS), New York/VG Bild-Kunst, Bonn; p. 28: Chip East/Reuters/Corbis; p. 30: The Israel Museum, Jerusalem, Israel. Photo: The Bridgeman Art Library; p. 32: Galleria d'Arte Moderna, Milan, Italy. Photo: Alinari/Art Resource, NY. © 2006 Artists Rights Society (ARS), New York/SIAE, Rome; p. 34: National Gallery Collection. By kind permission of the Trustees of the National Gallery, London/Corbis; p. 37: (left) Steve J. Sherman/AP Photos; p. 37: (right) Annie Griffiths Belt/Corbis; p. 38: (top left) Dave G. Houser/Post-Houserstock/Corbis; p. 38: (top right) Ludovic Maisant/Corbis; p. 38: (bottom) Bruno De Hogues/Getty Images; p. 41: (bottom left) Sigi Tischler/epa/Corbis; p. 41: (bottom right) Reuters/Corbis; p. 42: (top right) Mr. D. Owsley; p. 42: (bottom) Tim Mosenfelder/Corbis; p. 43: (top) Courtesy Greg Kessler Photography; p. 44: (top) Chris Stock/Lebrecht Music & Arts Photo Library; p. 44: (bottom left) Courtesy of Frank Salomon Associates; p. 44: (bottom right) Chris Stock/Lebrecht Music & Arts Photo Library; p. 45: (top) AFP/Getty; p. 45: (bottom left)

Fabrice Coffrini/epa/Corbis; p. 45: (bottom right) Royalty-Free/Corbis; p. 46: (bottom) Paul Sancya/AP Photos; p. 47: (top) Time Life Pictures/Getty Images; p. 48: Courtesy Herbert Barrett Management; p. 49: Photo of Elektra Women's Choir by David Cooper; p. 50: (top) Photo by David Lee/Courtesy Banff International String Quartet Competition; p. 50: (bottom) Jimin Lai/Getty Images; p. 52: (top) Cincinnati Symphony Orchestra, 2005, Paavo Järvi, Music Director. Photo credit: Mark Lyons. Courtesy Cincinnati Symphony Orchestra; p. 54: (top) Courtesy of Indiana University School of Music; p. 54: (bottom) Reuters/Corbis; p. 59: Morton Beebe, S.F./Corbis; p. 60: Earl & Nazima Kowall/Corbis; p. 61: Courtesy of www.americusbrassband.org; p. 62: (left) Private Collection. Photo: Erich Lessing/Art Resource, NY; p. 62: (right) Kunsthaus, Zurich, Switzerland. Photo: Erich Lessing/Art Resource, NY. © 2006 Estate of Pablo Picasso/Artists Rights Society (ARS), New York; Opp. Part 2 (Master of the St. Lucy Legend, *Mary Queen of Heaven*) National Gallery of Art, Washington, DC, Samuel H. Kress Collection. Image © 2005 Board of Trustees, National Gallery of Art, Washington, DC; p. 67: (top) Musée de l'Oeuvre de Notre Dame, Strasbourg, France. Photo: The Bridgeman Art Library; p. 67: (bottom) Palazzo Pubblico, Siena, Italy. Photo: Scala/Art Resource, NY; p. 68: Private Collection. Photo: The Bridgeman Art Library; p. 69: Bibliothèque Municipale, Laon, France. Photo: Erich Lessing/Art Resource, NY; p. 71: Photo: Erich Lessing/Art Resource, NY; p. 74: Royalty-Free/Corbis; p. 76: Courtesy of Heidelberg University Library; p. 77: Bibliothèque Nationale, Paris; p. 80: By permission of the British Library; p. 83: By permission of the British Library; p. 84: Galleria dell'Accademia, Florence. Photo by Erich Lessing/Art Resource, NY; p. 86: The Louvre, Paris, France. Photo: Bridgeman-Giraudon/Art Resource, NY; p. 87: Ric Ergenbright/Corbis; p. 88: Photo: Andrew Cowin; Travel Ink/Corbis; p. 89: The Louvre, Paris, France. Photo: Réunion des Musées Nationaux/Art Resource, NY; p. 90: Warder Collection; p. 98: (top) Musée Carnavalet, Paris; p. 101: (top) Musée de Berry, Bourges; p. 101: (bottom) Lebrecht Music & Arts Photo Library; p. 104: Niedersächsisches Landesmuseum, Hannover; p. 107: Accademia, Venice, Italy. Photo Scala/Art Resource, NY; Opp. Part 3 (Hans Hofmann, *Rising Moon*) Private Collection. Photo: Art Resource, NY. © 2006

Estate of Hans Hofmann/Artists Rights Society (ARS), New York; p. 114: The Museum of Modern Art, New York. The Riklis Collection of McCrory Corporation (1076.83). Photo: Digital Image © The Museum of Modern Art/Licensed by Scala/Art Resource, NY. © 2006 Artists Rights Society (ARS), New York/VG Bild-Kunst, Bonn; Opp. Part 4 (Jan Vermeer, *Lady Seated at a Virginal*) National Gallery, London. Photo: The Bridgeman Art Library; p. 117: (top) The Metropolitan Museum of Art, Purchase. Joseph Pulitzer Bequest, 1924. (24.197.2, recto) Photograph © The Metropolitan Museum of Art; p. 117: (bottom) National Museum of Women in the Arts. Gift of Wallace and Wilhelmina Holladay; p. 118: (top) Museo del Prado, Madrid, Spain. Photo Scala/Art Resource, NY; p. 118: (bottom) The Metropolitan Museum of Art, H. O. Havemeyer Collection. Bequest of Mrs. H. O. Havemeyer, 1929 (29.100.6) Photograph © 1992 The Metropolitan Museum of Art; p. 120: (top) Reuters/Corbis; p. 120: (bottom) Bettmann/Corbis; p. 122: Residenz, Wuerzburg, Germany. Photo by Erich Lessing/Art Resource, NY; p. 123: (top) Private Collection, London; p. 123: (bottom) The Louvre, Paris, France. Photo: Scala/Art Resource, NY; p. 126: Galleria Spada, Rome, Italy. Photo: Scala/Art Resource, NY; p. 127: Royal Academy of Music/Lebrecht Music & Arts Photo Library; p. 130: Gemaeldegalerie, Staatliche Kunstsammlungen, Dresden, Germany. Photo: Erich Lessing/Art Resource, NY; p. 134: (top) Lebrecht Music & Arts Photo Library; p. 136: (top) Nationalgalerie, Staatliche Museen zu Berlin, Berlin, Germany. Photo: Bildarchiv Preussischer Kulturbesitz/ Art Resource, NY; p. 140: By courtesy of the National Portrait Gallery, London; p. 145: Gregory Maldonado, Founder, Music Director, Los Angeles Baroque Orchestra; p. 146: (bottom) Printed by permission of the curator of the Russell Collection of Early Keyboard Instruments, University of Edinburgh; p. 148: Civico Museo Bibliografico Musicale Rosssini, Bologna, Italy. Photo: Scala/Art Resource, NY; p. 149: Alte Pinakothek, Munich, Germany. Photo by Erich Lessing/Art Resource, NY; p. 153: National Gallery, Prague, Czech Republic. Photo: Giraudon/Art Resource, NY; p. 155: Photo: Scala/Art Resource, NY; p. 158: Dave Bartruff/Corbis; p. 159: Offentliche Kunstsammlung, Basel, Junstsmuseum. Photo: Offentliche Kunstsammlung Basel, Martin Buhler. © 2006 The Josef and Anni Albers Foundation/Artists Rights Society (ARS), New York; p. 163: National Gallery Collection. By kind permission of the Trustees of the National Gallery, London; p. 164: Villa Widmann-Foscari, Veneto, Italy. Photo: Cameraphoto/Art Resource, NY; Opp. Part 5 (Wassily Kandinsky, *Contrasting Sounds*) Musée National d'Art Moderne, Centre Georges Pompidou, Paris, France. Photo: CNAC/MNAM/Réunion des Musées Nationaux/Art Resource, NY. © 2006 Artists Rights Society (ARS), New York/ADAGP, Paris; p. 167: Tate Gallery, London. Photo: Tate Gallery, London/Art Resource, NY. © 2006 Bridget Riley. All Rights Reserved; p. 170: Photo: Art Resource, NY. © 2006 The M. C. Escher Company-Holland. All Rights Reserved; Opp. Part 6 (Jacques-Louis David, Detail from *The Consecration of the Emperor Napoleon I and Coronation of the Empress Josephine in the Cathedral of Notre-Dame de Paris, 2*) The Louvre, Paris. Photo: Erich Lessing/Art Resource, NY; p. 177: (top) Charles O'Rear/Corbis; p. 177: (bottom) Joseph Sohm; ChromoSohm Inc./Corbis; p. 178: The Huntington Library, Art Collections, and Botanical Gardens, San Marino, California/SuperStock, Inc.; p. 181: (bottom) Musée de Picardie, Amiens, France.

Photo: Giraudon/Art Resource, NY; p. 183: Lebrecht Music & Arts Photo Library; p. 184: Ali Meyer/Corbis; p. 185: (top) Musée Conde, Chantilly, France. Photo: Erich Lessing, Art Resource, NY; p. 188: From a study by Dr. Gordon Shaw. Courtesy Dr. Mark Bodner, Mind Institute, Costa Mesa, CA; p. 190: Casa Goldoni, Venice, Italy/The Bridgeman Art Library; p. 192: Royal College of Music, London; p. 193: (bottom) Courtesy of the Ibusz-Hungarian Travel Company; p. 194: Esterhazy Castle, Eisenstadt, Austria. Photo: Erich Lessing/Art Resource, NY; p. 198: Beethoven-Haus, Bonn; p. 200: Beethoven-Haus, Bonn/ AKG Images; p. 201: Peter Turnley/Corbis; p. 207: International Stiftung, Mozarteum, Salzburg; p. 209: AKG Images; p. 210: (top) Österreichische Nationalbibliothek, Vienna; p. 210: (bottom) Bibliothèque Nationale, Paris; p. 211: (top) Beethoven-Haus, Bonn. H. C. Bodmer Collection. Photo: Beethoven-Haus/AKG Images; p. 211: (bottom) Historisches Museum der Stadt Wien, Vienna, Austria. Photo: Erich Lessing/Art Resource, NY; p. 214: Courtesy of the Topkapi Palace Museum; p. 215: Dave Bartruff/Corbis; p. 217: Deutsches Theatermuseum, Munich; p. 218: Historisches Museum der Stadt, Vienna, Austria/The Bridgeman Art Library; Opp. Part 7 (Joseph Mallord William Turner, *Banks of the Loire*) Worcester Art Museum, Massachusetts. Photo: Bridgeman Art Library; p. 231: (bottom) The Metropolitan Museum of Art, H. O. Havemeyer Collection, Bequest of Mrs. H. O. Havemeyer, 1929. (29.100.129) Photograph (c) 1984 The Metropolitan Museum of Art. Photo by Malcolm Varon; p. 231: (top) The Louvre, Paris, France. Photo: Bridgeman-Giraudon/Art Resource, NY; p. 232: The Louvre, Paris. Photo: Erich Lessing/Art Resource, NY; p. 233: Edinburgh University, Collection of Historic Musical Instruments (#3115). Photo by Antonia Reeve; p. 235: (top) Adam Woolfitt/ Corbis; p. 235: (bottom) From *Romantic Music*, Leon Plantinga, W. W. Norton, New York, 1984; p. 236: Freies Deutsches Hochstift-Goethemuseum, Frankfurt; p. 239: Germanische Nationalmuseum, Nuremberg; p. 240: Archivo Iconographico, S.A./Corbis; p. 241: Schubert-Museum, Vienna; p. 242: Schack-Galerie, Munich; p. 244: Lebrecht Music & Arts Photo Library; p. 245: Bettmann/Corbis; p. 246: Robert Schumann Haus; p. 249: (top) The Metropolitan Museum of Art, Gift of Mrs. Henry McSweeney, 1959. (59.76) Photograph by Sheldon Collins. Photograph © 1988 The Metropolitan Museum of Art; p. 249: (bottom) Staatliche Kunstsammlungen Dresden/ Deutsche Fotothek Dresden; p. 250: (top) Lebrecht Music & Arts Photo Library; p. 250: (bottom) Bettmann/Corbis; p. 252: Manchester Art Gallery, UK. Photo: Bridgeman Art Library; p. 253: Miramax/Photofest; p. 256: Lebrecht Music & Arts Photo Library/Colouriser AL; p. 259: Lebrecht Music & Arts Photo Library; p. 260: New York Public Library, Astor, Lenox, Tilden Foundations; p. 261: The Long Island Museum of American Art, History & Carriages. Gift of Mr. and Mrs. Ward Melville, 1955; p. 265: Photo: Tate Gallery, London, Great Britain/Art Resource, NY; p. 266: Wallace Collection, London, UK/ The Bridgeman Art Library; p. 267: (top) Lebrecht Music & Arts Photo Library; p. 267: (bottom) Lebrecht Music & Arts Photo Library; p. 269: Museo Nacional del Prado, Madrid; 272: (top) The Art Archive/Corbis; p. 272: (bottom) Wolfgang Kaehler/ Corbis; p. p. 275: (left) From *Ivan Bilibin*, Aurora Art Publishers, Leningrad; p. 275: (right) From *Ivan Bilibin*, Aurora Art Publishers, Leningrad; p. 276: Collection Archiv f. Kunst & Geschichte/AKG-Images; p. 278: Private Collection/Bridgeman

TRANSLATIONS

Index

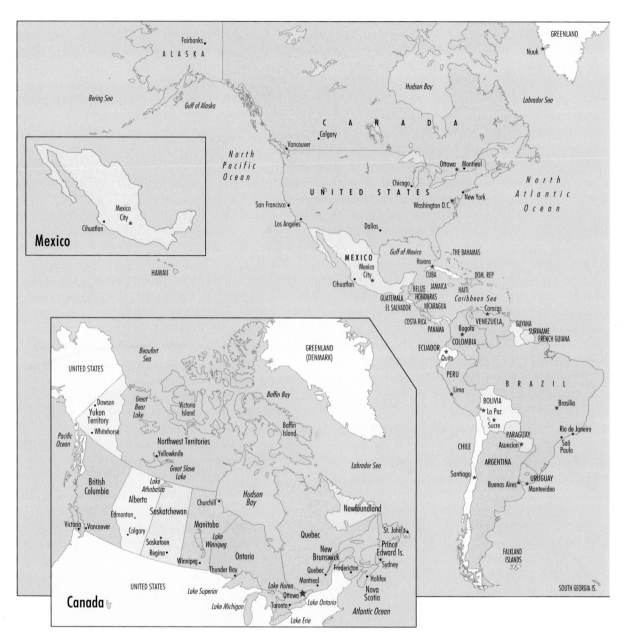

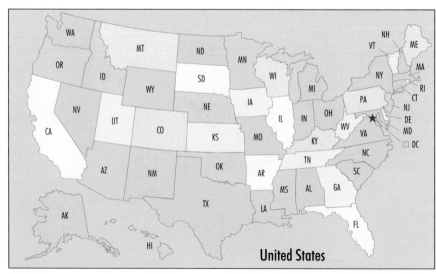

ICELAND

SWEDEN
NORWAY
FINLAND
St. Petersburg
North Sea   ESTONIA
DENMARK   Baltic   LATVIA
Sea
LITHUANIA
IRELAND U.K. NETH.   BYELARUS
BELGIU   GERMANY POLAND
English Channel LU
FRANCE   UKRAINE
Bay of Biscay
See detail
at bottom
of page
Black
Sea   GEORGIA AZERBAIJAN
PORTUGAL SPAIN   ARMENIA
ALBANIA   Caspian TURKMENISTAN
GREECE   TURKEY   Sea
TUNISIA CYPRUS SYRIA
MOROCCO   LEBANON   IRAQ   IRAN
ISRAEL
JORDAN
KUWAIT
ALGERIA   LIBYA   EGYPT   QATAR
SAUDI ARABIA U.A.E.
Red
WESTERN   Sea   OMAN
SAHARA
MAURITANIA   ERITREA YEMEN
MALI   NIGER   CHAD SUDAN   DJIBOUTI
SENEGAL BURKINA
GAMBIA   NIGERIA   SOMALIA
GUINEA   BENIN   ETHIOPIA
GUINEA   IVORY   CENTRAL AFRICAN
BISSAU   COAST   CAMEROON   REPUBLIC UGANDA
SIERRA GHANA TOGO   DEMOCRATIC REP. KENYA
LEONE   GABON   OF THE CONGO Kampala
LIBERIA   REP.   RWANDA
OF THE   BURUNDI
CONGO   TANZANIA
COMOROS
ANGOLA   ZAMBIA   MALAWA
South   NAMIBIA   ZIMBABWE   MADAGASCAR
Atlantic   BOTSWANA   MOZAMBIQUE
Ocean
SWAZILAND
SOUTH
AFRICA   LESOTHO

R   U   S   S   I   A
Sea of
Okhotsk
Moscow   Omsk Novosibirsk
Volgograd
KAZAKHSTAN
MONGOLIA   Vladivostok
NORTH KOREA
UZBEKISTAN   Beijing Sea of
KYRGYZSTAN   SOUTH KOREA Japan
TAJIKISTAN   C   H   I   N   A   East
China   JAPAN
AFGHANISTAN   Sea
Wuxi
PAKISTAN   NEPAL BHUTAN   TAIWAN
I   N   D   I   A
Arabian   BANGLADESH   South
Sea   MYANMAR LAOS   China   Philippine Sea
Bay of   THAILAND   Sea   PHILIPPINES
Bengal KAMPUCHEA VIETNAM   PALAU
BRUNEI   PAPUA
SRI LANKA   MALAYSIA   NEW
Indian   Ocean   SUMATRA I N D O N E S I A   GUINEA
Java Sea
JAVA   BALI   Timor Sea
AUSTRALIA

North Sea
SWEDEN   ESTONIA
DENMARK   Riga
Copenhagen   LITHUANIA LATVIA
Baltic Sea   Vilnius
IRELAND   Dublin   Gdansk   Minsk
U.K.   NETH. Berlin POLAND   BYELARUS
London   GERMANY   Warsaw
BELGIUM   Kraków   Kiev
LUX.   CZECH REP.   Lvov
Paris   SLOVAKIA   UKRAINE
Nantes   AUSTRIA HUNGARY   MOLDOVA
English Channel   SWITZ.   SLOVENIA   ROMANIA
FRANCE   ITALY   CROATIA   Bucharest
Bay of Biscay   Toulouse   BOSNIA &   Constanta
Bayonne   HERZEGOVINA SERBIA   BULGARIA   Black Sea
MONTENEGRO   F.Y.R.O.M.
PORTUGAL   Madrid   Rome   ALBANIA   Ankara
Barcelona   Naples   GREECE   TURKEY
Lisbon   SPAIN   Sevilla   Athens
Gibraltar   Europe